MAGILL'S
SURVEY
OF
SCIENCE

MAGILL'S SURVEY OF SCIENCE

SPACE EXPLORATION SERIES

Volume 4
1431-1916
Soyuz 9–Spaceplanes

Edited by

FRANK N. MAGILL

SALEM PRESS
Pasadena, California   Englewood Cliffs, New Jersey

4p

Library of Congress Cataloging-in-Publication Data
Magill's survey of science. Space exploration series/
edited by Frank N. Magill
    p. cm.
    Bibliography: p.
    Includes index
    1. Astronautics. 2. Outer space—Exploration. I.
Magill, Frank Northen, 1907-
TL790.M24   1989   88-38267
629.4—dc19   CIP
ISBN 0-89356-600-4 (set)
ISBN 0-89356-604-7 (volume 4)

06/12/92

CONTENTS

SPACE EXPLORATION

SOYUZ 9

Date: June 1 to June 19, 1970
Type of mission: Manned Earth-orbiting spaceflight
Country: The Soviet Union

The Soyuz 9 mission of cosmonauts Andrian Nikolayev and Vitali Sevastyanov established a long-duration record for manned spaceflight.

Principal personages
ANDRIAN NIKOLAYEV, the Soyuz 9 commander
VITALI SEVASTYANOV, the Soyuz 9 flight engineer
SERGEI KOROLEV, Chief Designer of the Soviet space program

Summary of the Mission

The Soyuz 9 mission of cosmonauts Andrian Nikolayev and Vitali Sevastyanov established a new space endurance record. Between June 1 and June 19, 1970, the two Soviet cosmonauts traveled almost 12 million kilometers and completed 286 orbits of Earth. The previous record of fourteen days in space had been established by the American astronauts Frank Borman and James Lovell aboard Gemini 7 in December, 1965. The previous Soviet record had been the six-day spaceflights by seven cosmonauts flying simultaneous Soyuz missions 6, 7, and 8 in October, 1969.

Extended stays in space by cosmonauts and astronauts were planned from the very beginning of manned spaceflight. Yet doctors who specialized in aerospace medicine did not know how humans would endure long exposure to weightlessness or whether pilots would still be able to function during extended stays in orbit.

The original Chief Designer of the Soviet space program, Sergei Pavlovich Korolev, would die before his dream of extended spaceflight became reality. His goal was to prove that cosmonauts would be able to perform a successful mission to the Moon. Technical and political problems in 1967 and 1968 forced the Soviets to abandon their manned lunar program, and they initiated the Salyut space station program in January, 1969. This shift in emphasis to longer missions made it even more necessary for the Soviets to acquire long-duration spaceflight experience.

Soyuz 9 was launched at 2200 Moscow time, the first manned spacecraft launched at night, from the Baikonur space center in Kazakhstan. The launch vehicle was the A-2 (Soyuz). The spacecraft itself had been specially modified to support a long mission; the rendezvous and docking mechanisms had been replaced by additional life-support equipment.

The cosmonaut crew was commanded by a veteran pilot, forty-year-old Colonel Andrian Nikolayev, who had spent four days in space on Vostok 4 in August, 1962. Nikolayev was a member of the original group of Soviet cosmonauts chosen in March, 1960, and was well-known among his colleagues for his ability to endure extremes of isolation, temperature, and stress. Making his first flight was Vitali Sevastyanov, who was thirty-five years old. Sevastyanov was a civilian aerospace engineer who had assisted in the development of the Soyuz spacecraft and served as an instructor to cosmonauts prior to joining the group in 1967.

Soyuz 9 was inserted into a near-circular orbit ranging from a perigee, or low point, of 207 kilometers to an apogee, or high point, of 220 kilometers. The inclination was 51.7 degrees, and the period of the orbit was 88.59 minutes. On the fifth orbit, the Soyuz engines were fired to raise the perigee to prevent decay of the orbit. The process was repeated on the seventeenth orbit, leaving Soyuz 9 in a 247-by-268-kilometer orbit. On June 15, the orbit was deliberately lowered so that the atmospheric drag would force the Soyuz to reenter if the engines failed to fire after their unprecedented exposure to raw space.

During the first two days of the mission, Sevastyanov and Nikolayev both suffered from what was later known as "space adaptation syndrome," the temporary disorientation caused by the body's adjustment to weightlessness. This syndrome is characterized by nausea and the feeling that one is toppling over backward. The cosmonauts had difficulty sleeping the first night but ultimately settled into a routine in which they would sleep eight hours a night, eat four meals a day, and exercise for two hours each day.

Unlike American astronauts Borman and Lovell, cosmonauts Nikolayev and Sevastyanov did not wear pressure suits during their mission and were not confined to their chairs: The internal space of the Soyuz command module and spherical orbital module was 9 cubic meters, sufficient to allow the men to float freely. They removed their woolen flight suits and slept in shorts and T-shirts. Cabin temperature was maintained at 22 degrees Celsius. The cosmonauts slept simultaneously—and so soundly at times that Soviet mission controllers had to waken them with a siren.

For the first time, Soviet cosmonauts were able to heat food by means of an electric coil, allowing them to add soup and coffee to their menu. Water was treated with silver ions rather than chlorine to preserve taste. The cosmonauts also carried an electric razor.

The men's personalities were complementary: Nikolayev was more taciturn and Sevastyanov more chatty. Nikolayev was later to remark, "If Vitali hadn't spoken to me during the flight, there'd have been silence."

Because of the northerly geographical location of the Soviet Union, Soviet manned spacecraft fly over their homeland for only eight hours each day. The length and nature of the Soyuz 9 mission required an unprecedented deployment of space tracking vessels around the world. Communications were maintained by the ships *Nevel, Kegostrov, Morzhovets, Dolinsk, Ristna, Bezhitsa*, and the new *Kosmonaut Vladimir Komarov*. The lead operator, or communicator with the crew, was Voskhod 2 veteran cosmonaut Alexei Leonov.

The Soviet news agency TASS had announced that Soyuz 9 would be devoted to "medico-biological research," but other activities took place as well: Nikolayev and Sevastyanov played a game of "Earth-space" chess with cosmonaut training chief

Nikolai Kamanin and fellow cosmonaut Viktor Gorbatko. (The game ended in a draw.) On June 8, they celebrated the sixth birthday of Nikolayev's daughter, Yelena, whose mother was cosmonaut Valentina Tereshkova. Mother and daughter visited the flight control center at Yevpatoriya in the Crimea and spoke directly to the cosmonauts. Scientific and engineering experiments included observations of Earth and tests of an electro-optic orientation device.

On June 14, at an altitude of 200 kilometers, the cosmonauts took part in a complex three-way experiment with a research vessel in the Indian Ocean and a Meteor satellite. The intent was to measure temperature and wind velocities in different layers of the atmosphere.

While the cosmonauts did have days of rest (on the ninth and seventeenth days), the rigors of the eighteen-day mission were severe. Following landing on June 19, 1970, in a field 75 kilometers west of the city of Karaganda, Nikolayev and Sevastyanov had to be carried from their Soyuz on stretchers. (For the first time, a videotape of this landing was shown on Soviet television.) The traditional cosmonaut welcome at a Moscow airport did not occur, as Nikolayev and Sevastyanov were moved directly to the hospital. They were not fully recovered until ten days after landing.

The Soyuz 9 mission lasted 17 days, 16 hours, and 59 minutes. This record stood for less than a year, when it was eclipsed by cosmonauts Georgi Dobrovolsky, Aleksandr Volkov, and Viktor Patsayev aboard the first Salyut space station. (These cosmonauts were to die upon reentry.)

Knowledge Gained

Some fifty experiments were conducted by Nikolayev and Sevastyanov during their 424 hours in space. Data resulting from meteorological, astronomical, and geophysical observations were considered useful to scientists, but medical data on the cosmonauts initially proved quite disappointing to Soviet space doctors. In spite of the program of exercise and controlled diet, both cosmonauts experienced a protracted and difficult readjustment to life on Earth. For more than a week after their return, the cosmonauts felt as if they were subjected to twice the force of gravity. Walking was difficult, and even lying in bed was uncomfortable.

Cosmonauts on previous, shorter missions had suffered from space adaptation syndrome during the early hours of their missions: Gherman Titov on Vostok 2; Valentina Tereshkova on Vostok 6; and Vladimir Komarov, Konstantin Feoktistov, and Boris Yegorov on Voskhod 1. Yet no cosmonauts had suffered such long-lasting effects. Since the entire Soviet manned space effort was by this time concentrated on operations in Earth orbit, it was essential to know how long cosmonauts could safely live and work in space. Soyuz 9 had not only failed to provide a definitive answer; indeed, it had only raised more questions.

Ten months later, cosmonauts Vladimir Shatalov, Alexei Yeliseyev, and Nikolai Rukavishnikov were launched aboard Soyuz 10 for a planned thirty-day mission aboard the first Salyut space station. Very little had been learned since Soyuz 9. It was later reported that, during the Soyuz 9 mission, the spacecraft had suffered a breakdown in its automatic orientation system, forcing the cosmonauts to put Soyuz into a manual, controlled roll (in order to keep the spacecraft evenly heated). The rolling reportedly increased the cosmonauts' sensitivity to vertigo and, doctors concluded, probably contributed to their difficulty in readjusting to Earth's gravitational pull.

Context

This conclusion—that the cosmonauts' experience with the manual roll increased their sense of vertigo—proved to be correct, though it would be five years before Soviet doctors could give medical evidence to support it. The Soyuz 10 crew failed to board the first Salyut and returned to Earth after only two days. The Soyuz 11 cosmonauts died in an accident unrelated to the length of their mission—though doctors in the recovery team who were the first to reach the cosmonauts had feared that the length of the mission had caused unknown medical problems.

The American doctors were the first to be concerned about the results of Soyuz 9. Three long-duration missions of thirty to sixty days were planned for the Skylab program in 1973. To ensure that the Skylab astronauts would not suffer from severe disorientation, doctors insisted that they adhere strictly to their exercise program. The Skylab 2 crew of Charles Conrad, Joseph Kerwin, and Paul Weitz did return to Earth in good condition, leading some doctors to conclude that the health of cosmonauts Nikolayev and Sevastyanov might also have been impeded by their confinement. Skylab's internal volume was more than 300 cubic meters, thirty times that of Soyuz 9—indeed, larger than that of the Salyut and Mir space stations. Skylab 4 astronauts Gerald Carr, Edward Gibson, and William Pogue, returning to Earth after setting a space endurance record of eighty-four days, also suffered far fewer ill effects than did Nikolayev and Sevastyanov.

Until the thirty-day Soyuz 17 mission of cosmonauts Alexei Gubarev and Georgi Grechko aboard Salyut 4 in early 1975, there was no Soviet manned flight whose data could be compared to that of Soyuz 9. Soyuz 17 paved the way for a sixty-three-day mission later in 1975, a mission flown by a cosmonaut crew consisting of Pyotr Klimuk and Soyuz 9 veteran Vitali Sevastyanov. In increments of approximately thirty days, the Soviet space endurance record crept upward. In 1988, cosmonauts Vladimir Titov and Musa Manarov, aboard the space station Mir, completed a mission lasting an entire year.

Bibliography

Baker, David. *The History of Manned Space Flight.* Rev. ed. New York: Crown Publishers, 1985. An extensive history of manned spaceflight in both the United States and the Soviet Union from World War II to the early 1980's. With special emphasis on the evolution of space technology.

Clark, Phillip. *The Soviet Manned Space Program.* New York: Crown Publishers, 1988. The first full-length post-*glasnost* study of the Soviet manned space program, containing new and interesting revelations about Chief Designer Korolev and the Soyuz spacecraft.

Lebedev, Lev Aleksandrovich, et al. *Sons of the Blue Planet*. Translated by Prema Pande. NASA TT F-728. New Delhi: Amerind Publishing Co., 1973. The translation of a 1971 volume commissioned by NASA, this book contains biographical sketches of cosmonauts Nikolayev and Sevastyanov as well as a brief account of the Soyuz 9 mission.

Oberg, James E. *Red Star in Orbit*. New York: Random House, 1981. This controversial and readable history of the Soviet manned space program discusses Soyuz 9 only briefly but provides a balanced view of Soviet space triumphs and failures.

Riabchikov, Evgeny. *Russians in Space*. Edited by Nikolai P. Kamanin. Translated by Guy Daniels. Garden City, N.Y.: Doubleday and Co., 1971. The translation of a memoir by a noted Soviet space journalist, this book provides personal glimpses into the lives of the early Soviet cosmonauts, including Nikolayev and Sevastyanov (as well as Chief Designer Sergei Korolev).

U.S. Congress. Senate. Committee on Aeronautical and Space Sciences. *Soviet Space Programs, 1971-1975*. Vol. 1. 94th Cong., 2d sess. Washington, D.C.: Government Printing Office, 1976. This readable and detailed study contains a lengthy chapter on Soviet space medicine.

Michael Cassutt

Cross-References

SOYUZ 10 and 11

Date: April 23 to June 30, 1971
Type of mission: Manned space station flights
Country: The Soviet Union

The Soviet Union hailed Salyut as the world's first space station and proclaimed it a more important and logical step in space exploration than lunar missions. The first crew sent to Salyut 1, on Soyuz 10, failed to occupy the station; the second crew, on Soyuz 11, died during reentry after a record stay in orbit inside the station.

> *Principal personages*
> VLADIMIR A. SHATALOV, the Soyuz 10 command pilot
> ALEXEI S. YELISEYEV, the Soyuz 10 flight engineer
> NIKOLAI RUKAVISHNIKOV, the Soyuz 10 test engineer
> GEORGI DOBROVOLSKY, the Soyuz 11 command pilot
> VLADISLAV VOLKOV, the Soyuz 11 flight engineer
> VIKTOR PATSAYEV, the Soyuz 11 test engineer

Summary of the Mission

The Salyut 1 space station was successfully launched into orbit by a D-1 launch vehicle with 10.7 million newtons of thrust on April 19, 1971, one week after the tenth anniversary of Yuri Gagarin's historic Vostok 1 flight. Soyuz 10 was designed to ferry cosmonauts Vladimir Shatalov, Alexei Yeliseyev, and Nikolai Rukavishnikov to Salyut 1 for an extended visit. Soyuz 10 was launched atop an A-2 booster rocket from the Baikonur cosmodrome on April 23, 1971, at 2:45 A.M. Moscow time. The early launch time was dictated by the need for a rendezvous with Salyut. Code-named "Granit," the 6,600-kilogram Soyuz 10 spacecraft achieved an orbit from which a rendezvous could be effected.

Shatalov was born December 8, 1927, in Petropavlovsk, Kazakhstan. In 1949 he was graduated from the Kachinsk Air Force College. He enrolled in the Moscow Air Force College in 1953. Ultimately, Shatalov achieved the rank of lieutenant general in the Soviet Air Force. Selected as a cosmonaut in 1963, he served as backup pilot for Soyuz 3 and flew as command pilot of Soyuz 4 and Soyuz 8. After his Soyuz mission, Shatalov became the Soviet cosmonaut corps' director of flight training.

Yeliseyev was born July 13, 1934, in Ahizdra. He attended the Bauman Higher Technical School in Moscow and earned a master of technical science degree in engineering. Yeliseyev was selected as a civilian cosmonaut in 1966. He flew as a technical scientist on the Soyuz 4 and 5 joint mission, performing an extravehicular transfer from Soyuz 5 to Soyuz 4, and also on Soyuz 8. Soyuz 10 was his third spaceflight with Shatalov. Yeliseyev also served as Soviet flight director for the joint Soviet-U.S. Apollo-Soyuz Test Project.

Rukavishnikov was born September 18, 1932, in the Siberian town of Tomsk. He was graduated in 1957 from the Moscow Engineering and Physics Institute, and he became a spacecraft designer. Expert in engineering physics, Rukavishnikov was selected as a civilian cosmonaut in 1967. After Soyuz 10, he flew as flight engineer on Soyuz 16, served as a backup Apollo-Soyuz Test Project cosmonaut, and was command pilot of Soyuz 33.

The 20-meter-long Salyut space station had been placed in a 200-by-220-kilometer orbit. During the time between Salyut's launch and the launch of Soyuz 10, all Salyut systems and scientific equipment were thoroughly checked to ensure that the station was ready for human occupation. Soyuz 10 performed a series of automatic orbital change maneuvers during its first day in space, bringing the cosmonauts to within visual range (14 kilometers) of Salyut early on their second day in orbit. Salyut had executed four automatic maneuvers in support of the rendezvous.

Shatalov assumed manual control at a distance of 180 meters for the final approach to docking. After ninety minutes of manually controlled formation flying, Soyuz 10 lined up with Salyut 1, docking with the space station at 4:47 A.M. Moscow time on April 24.

Soyuz 10 remained docked with Salyut 1 for five hours and thirty minutes, but no cosmonaut transfer into Salyut was reported. Shatalov backed Soyuz 10 away from the space station, and the Soyuz spacecraft remained in orbit for an additional sixteen hours, landing 118 kilometers northwest of Karaganda at 2:40 A.M. on April 25. Soyuz 10 had completed thirty-two orbits in 1 day, 23 hours, 45 minutes, and 54 seconds of flight.

Soyuz 11 was launched at 7:25 A.M. Moscow time on June 6, 1971, by an A-2 booster rocket from the Baikonur cosmodrome. Aboard were Georgi Dobrovolsky, Vladislav Volkov, and Viktor Patsayev. The cosmonauts used the call signs Yantar 1, 2, and 3.

Dobrovolsky was born June 1, 1928, in Odessa. He was graduated from the Chuguyev Air Force School and joined the cosmonaut corps in 1963. Dobrovolsky was a lieutenant colonel in the Soviet Air Force at the time of his death on Soyuz 11.

Volkov was born November 23, 1935, in Moscow. He entered the Moscow Aviation Institute in 1953 and then worked as an engineer before his selection as a civilian cosmonaut in 1966. Volkov flew as flight engineer on Soyuz 7 before losing his life on Soyuz 11. His autobiography, *We're Stepping into the Sky*, was posthumously published.

Patsayev was born June 19, 1933, in Aktybinsk, Kazakhstan. He was graduated from the Penzensk Industrial Institute in 1955, was selected as a civilian cosmonaut in 1967, and earned a master of science degree in 1971. Soyuz 11 was Patsayev's only spaceflight.

When Soyuz 11 entered its second orbit, Salyut 1 had a 4,000-kilometer lead. Because Salyut was in a higher orbit, however, the faster Soyuz craft gradually caught up over the course of the day. By 6:00 A.M. on June 7, Soyuz 11 was within 400 kilometers of the space station. Dobrovolsky initiated an altitude adjustment to bring Soyuz 11 into Salyut's orbit. By 7:26 A.M., Soyuz 11 was within 10 kilometers of the space station. A pair of omnidirectional antennae on Salyut transmitted signals to Soyuz 11, and the automatic approach phase began. Spacecraft thrusters fired to reduce the separation distance. Dobrovolsky took over manual control of Soyuz 11 when the spacecraft was only 100 meters away from the station. He oriented Soyuz 11 so that its docking apparatus entered the docking cone at the front of the space station.

A mechanical docking also mated the Soyuz and Salyut hydraulic and electrical systems. The cosmonauts performed a series of spacecraft checks, making sure pressure integrity was being maintained in all seals and in the Salyut access tunnel. After several hours, permission was granted for the cosmonauts to transfer to Salyut. Patsayev opened the connecting hatch and pulled himself through the docking tunnel. He was followed by flight engineer Volkov and then by commander Dobrovolsky. The three shared a customary hug in celebration of their success; they had accomplished what Soyuz 10 had failed to do in April. The cosmonauts immediately began an exhaustive check of the Salyut systems. They also arranged for the Soyuz spacecraft to draw electrical power directly from Salyut's solar batteries, thereby preserving Soyuz's power for reentry at the end of the long mission. All major Soyuz systems could now be monitored by telemetry through Salyut consoles.

One of the cosmonauts' first tasks was to transfer Salyut to a higher, more stable orbit. Mooring thrusters and attitude control thrusters were fired. The cosmonauts reported observing the flaring of thruster exhaust and luminous particles during these maneuvers. After a second thruster firing, Salyut was in an optimum orbit.

Although scientific investigations began on the first day of occupancy, many pieces of scientific equipment had to be unpacked, assembled or adjusted, and prepared for use. Almost three days were required to complete the preparatory work for extended operations. The cosmonauts set up various systems to make Salyut a reasonably comfortable place to live. One new item which made spaceflight more like life on Earth was the inclusion of a small table where the cosmonauts could sit down for meals.

On June 20, one day after Patsayev's thirty-eighth birthday, Salyut 1 completed its one thousandth orbit. Soyuz 11 had completed 206 orbits. There were nine days remaining in the flight.

During the flight, daily television reports from Salyut were transmitted to the Soviet people. The deployment of Salyut 1 was hailed as a more significant feat than the American lunar landings, and the Soyuz 11 crew members rapidly became national heroes. The Soviet people eagerly awaited the cosmonauts' return and a celebration of the historic flight that had restored national pride in the Soviet space program.

At noon on June 29, Soyuz 11 completed its 358th orbit. The cosmonauts received instructions to terminate their Salyut activities, prepare Salyut for autonomous operation, restore power to Soyuz 11, store all data and specimens to be returned to

Earth for analysis in the descent module, undock Soyuz 11 from the space station, and land the descent module in the Soviet Union. The cosmonauts donned woolen flightsuits and leather helmets rather than full pressure suits. The hatch between the Soyuz orbital module and the Salyut transfer compartment was closed. Soyuz 11 undocked from Salyut at 9:28 P.M., June 29. All spacecraft systems were normal, and the undocking was uneventful.

Early the next morning, at 1:35 A.M., Soyuz 11's attitude was corrected for reentry and its braking rockets were fired. After the burn was completed, Soyuz 11 moved out of communications range, and the cosmonauts prepared for separation of the orbital and equipment modules from the descent module. When slight gravity was registered, ten minutes after reentry initiation, the two modules were jettisoned. The rest of the descent appeared uneventful. Twenty minutes after the jettison, the descent module landed on target, about 800 kilometers southwest of Sverdlovsk. Recovery crews arrived quickly, but when they opened the spacecraft hatch, they discovered the cosmonauts seated in their contour couches, dead.

The Soviet people were shocked. They had eagerly awaited the return of the cosmonaut-heroes. Official celebrations had already been organized. Instead, state funerals would have to be held. The U.S. space program sent official condolences to Moscow over the deaths of the three cosmonauts, and astronaut Thomas P. Stafford attended the full state ceremony held in Moscow, serving as one of the pallbearers. The cosmonauts were cremated and their ashes interred in the Kremlin wall.

There was little the Soviets could do to hide the loss of life. An announcement was made shortly after the recovery, but the exact cause of the accident would not be known in the West until years later when the United States and Soviet Union began planning the Apollo-Soyuz Test Project. At first, there was concern that the long spaceflight had caused the deaths, that reentry had been too stressful for the cosmonauts' weakened bodies. In fact, the cosmonauts died because of a procedural mistake compounded by an unfortunate mechanical mishap. The explosive separation of the orbital module from the descent module had forced open a cabin exhaust valve, and air had rapidly escaped from the cabin as it depressurized. The rapid decompression was over in forty-five seconds. Soyuz 11 went out of proper reentry attitude, but the automatic control system quickly restored the spacecraft's alignment. By that time, however, the cosmonauts were already dead.

Knowledge Gained

Soyuz 11 was primarily a scientific mission, and a significant amount of valuable data was collected in a wide variety of disciplines. The cosmonauts grew a small garden aboard Salyut as part of a study of closed-loop environments. Called "Oasis," the garden contained a growing medium in which cabbage, onion, and flax seeds were placed. Flax was selected because of its particularly strong sensitivity to Earth's gravitational field. It was hoped that comparison of the spaceborne flax with control flax plants on Earth would shed light on the effects of gravity on plant growth. Onion was selected for its suitability for genetic experiments. Cabbage was selected for its potential nutritional value as a food source. Patsayev served as Salyut's gardener. Each day he administered twenty squeezes of water from a special water reservoir to the plants using a rubber bulb. Automatic cameras monitored plant growth throughout the flight. Hydroponic methods of cultivation were used. Other biological experiments involved the hatching of frog eggs and genetic studies of fruit fly populations.

A special astrophysical observatory, called "Orion," was installed on the exterior of Salyut. Long exposure to space before Soyuz 11 arrived had not significantly degraded the system's capabilities. Observations of selected celestial targets were made in the gamma-ray region of the electromagnetic spectrum. Dobrovolsky activated the gamma-ray telescope and monitored its operation while Volkov maintained the orbital complex's attitude and stability.

The cosmonauts studied the phenomenon of high-frequency electromagnetic resonance in Salyut's transmitting antennae using the "Era" multipurpose apparatus. They observed high-frequency resonance when the orbital complex passed through low-temperature plasma environments.

Earth observation and photography consumed a large portion of the cosmonauts' work schedule. Panoramic observations of large areas of Earth were made. Geologic studies provided information useful in determining the structure of Earth's core. Oceanographic studies observed water flow and water resources in the world's oceans. Data collected on fish school locations and plankton populations were useful to biologists and commercial fishermen alike. Meteorological observations made from Salyut were compared with weather data from Meteor satellites. Upper atmospheric processes were studied to determine effects of the world's overall climate and vegetation distribution. More specific studies were made over the Soviet Union: Cloud cover in the Volga region was photographed by the cosmonauts for comparison with a television survey of the same region by the Meteor satellite, and spectral surveys of areas such as the Caspian Sea collected data useful for agriculture, land reclamation, geodesy, forestry, and cartography.

Most significant to manned spaceflight were the medical and biological experiments. Because weightlessness leads to muscle atrophy, cardiovascular system deconditioning, and bone decalcification, the cosmonauts were provided with special coveralls, referred to as "Penguin suits," which simulated gravity's effects on the human osteomuscular system. It was hoped that these suits would eliminate or at least minimize bone decalcification. The cosmonauts approved of these suits, claiming that they were comfortable enough to wear continuously. Radiation dosage, light and contrast sensitivity of the eye, metabolic and cardiovascular functions, and excretory samples were periodically monitored.

Because of the difficulties cosmonauts Nikolayev and Sevastyanov experienced in readjusting to terrestrial conditions after Soyuz 9, Soviet doctors had been concerned that there might be a limit to human tolerance of weightlessness. The Soyuz 11 crew, however, surpassed the eighteen-day Soyuz 9 endurance record without noticeable disabilities.

Context

Soyuz 10 was a major disappointment to the Soviet space program. There had been far too much official publicity surrounding the Soyuz 10 mission for it to have been simply a short test flight including rendezvous and docking but no crew habitation of Salyut 1. After the Soyuz 10 landing, a number of contradictory official statements were released. Some called Soyuz 10 a totally successful test of joint Soyuz/Salyut systems; others described the flight as an important step in the space program. One report suggested that Rukavishnikov had experienced unpleasant physical symptoms. Exactly why Soyuz 10 was terminated early is known only to Soviet mission controllers and the cosmonauts themselves.

Shatalov required ninety minutes of manual flying to complete the docking of the spacecraft to Salyut. That seems excessive. Perhaps Soyuz 10 experienced control difficulties or the Salyut was not as stable as desired. If Rukavishnikov was experiencing severe spacesickness, that would have been reason enough to terminate the flight before docking; if Rukavishnikov was not ill, however, then a mechanical problem must have arisen. One possibility is that a hard docking impact damaged the transfer tunnel, leaving the cosmonauts unable to open the hatch separating the Soyuz orbital module and the Salyut space station.

Whatever the difficulty, Soyuz 10 came as an anticlimax to a string of successful Soyuz missions. Soyuz 4 and 5 demonstrated rendezvous and docking. The Soyuz 6, 7, and 8 group flight bolstered Soviet confidence in joint orbital maneuvers and demonstrated a growing maturity in mission direction and flight control. Soyuz 9 gained medical data necessary for planning long habitations on Salyut and qualified Soyuz for extended stays in orbit. All was ready for the first human occupation of a true space station. Unfortunately, Soyuz 10 failed, and habitation of Salyut 1 was left to the next mission, launched less than two months later. The short period between Soyuz 10 and Soyuz 11 suggests that there was no major design deficiency which prevented a Soyuz 10 crew transfer to Salyut 1.

Soyuz 11 set a new endurance record of 23 days, 18 hours, 21 minutes, and 43 seconds, but this feat was overshadowed by the tragic loss of life at the mission's end. Salyut 1 was never again inhabited, and after completing twenty-eight hundred Earth orbits, it was commanded to deorbit on October 11, 1971. Thus, Soyuz 11, an important step foward in long-duration spaceflight, ended with the deaths of three courageous cosmonauts and the destruction of the world's first space station. Two years would pass before cosmonauts again ventured into space. Meanwhile, American astronauts were compiling an amazing record of flight endurance and scientific experimentation aboard the Skylab orbital workshop.

After the Soyuz 11 tragedy, Soyuz once more became a two-man spaceship. Subsequent crew members would wear full pressure suits during ascent and reentry. Had the Soyuz 11 cosmonauts been wearing such suits, they would have survived. (Spacesuits had been eliminated earlier in the program to provide room for a third cosmonaut.) The spacecraft cabin pressure valve was redesigned. The Soyuz 11 valve had taken less than sixty seconds to bleed the cabin's atmosphere, but more than two minutes were needed to close the valve manually; the cosmonauts had lost consciousness while attempting to halt the depressurization. Nearly a year would pass before a redesigned Soyuz would be flight-tested, unmanned.

Bibliography

Dmitriyev, A. Yu., et al. *From Spaceships to Orbiting Stations*. 2d ed. NASA technical translation, NASA TT F-812. Washington, D.C.: Government Printing Office, 1973. A Soviet account of the progression of cosmonautics and manned spaceflight from Sputnik to Salyut 1. Includes data collected by unmanned lunar and interplanetary Soviet probes.

Furniss, Tim. *Manned Spaceflight Log*. Rev. ed. London: Jane's Publishing Co., 1986. Provides detailed accounts of all manned spaceflights. Entries are arranged chronologically rather than by nationality or program. The work's strong point is its coverage of Soviet manned spaceflights. An essential reference for serious spaceflight researchers. Clearly written.

Oberg, James E. *Red Star in Orbit*. New York: Random House, 1981. An excellent overview of Soviet operations in space. Stresses both internal and external political influences on program development. Particularly interesting is the discussion of Khrushchev's influence on early Soviet space efforts. Photographs document Soviet space disinformation policies. Suitable for all readers.

Riabchikov, Evgeny. *Russians in Space*. Edited by Nikolai P. Kamanin. Translated by Guy Daniels. Garden City, N.Y.: Doubleday and Co., 1971. Presents Soviet space activities from Sputnik 1 to Soyuz 11 from an official viewpoint. Contains numerous cosmonaut quotations, conversations, and anecdotes. An interesting source, but propagandistic in nature. There are remarkable differences between Oberg's and Riabchikov's interpretations of the same events.

U.S. Congress. House. Committee on Science and Technology. *Astronauts and Cosmonauts Biographical and Statistical Data*. Report prepared by Congressional Research Service, the Library of Congress. 99th Cong., 1st sess., rev. ed. 1985. Offers brief biographical sketches of American astronauts and Soviet cosmonauts. Includes photographs of every person listed. Both flight crew and backup crew assignments are covered.

U.S. Congress. Senate. Committee on Commerce, Science, and Transportation. *Soviet Space Programs: 1981-1987*. Report prepared by Congressional Research Service, the Library of Congress. 100th Cong., 1988. Committee Print. This text compiles an enormous array of data about Soviet manned spaceflight efforts. Despite a few glaring errors, accurate details are given about the Soviet space program's development toward Salyut space station and Mir space station operations. Historical context is provided along with an analysis of Soviet strengths and weaknesses. Suggested for serious spaceflight observers.

David G. Fisher

Cross-References

SOYUZ 12

Date: September 27 to September 29, 1973
Type of mission: Manned Earth-orbiting spaceflight
Country: The Soviet Union

Soyuz 12 was the first manned flight of the new Soyuz variant specifically designed to act as a ferry to Salyut orbital stations. It carried two cosmonauts on a test flight lasting for two days.

Principal personages
VASILI LAZAREV, the commander
OLEG MAKAROV, the flight engineer
ALEXEI GUBAREV, the backup commander
GEORGI GRECHKO, the backup flight engineer

Summary of the Mission

During 1973, the Soviet Union had launched and lost two Salyut orbital stations. On April 3, Salyut 2 was launched, but this station apparently suffered from attitude control problems after routine maneuvers in orbit and was abandoned before the first crew could be launched. Approximately one month later, on May 11, another Salyut was launched. This second station seemed to have failed either during the launch sequence or immediately after orbital injection. It was identified as Kosmos 557, its true identity hidden by the Soviet authorities.

Following these expensive losses, the Soviet Union was faced with an odd situation. The manned program had been grounded following the Soyuz 11 loss in 1971 (three cosmonauts were killed during the return from orbit), and a new Salyut station would not be ready until the middle of 1974. Because of the forthcoming Apollo-Soyuz Test Project, the pressure was on the Soviets to recommence manned flights. Without a station with which to dock, Soyuz 12 launched on a short "solo" mission.

As a result of the Soyuz 11 accident, the Soyuz descent module had been redesigned to allow the cosmonauts to wear pressure suits, which would protect them against a repeat of the Soyuz 11 depressurization (the previous model could carry up to three men, but without pressure suits). The spacecraft's power system had also been changed: Instead of carrying wings of solar cells to harness the Sun's heat, the spacecraft now carried chemical batteries, which could be recharged in orbit when the Soyuz docked with a Salyut. Even so, the chemical batteries carried sufficient power for only about two days. During 1972-1973, there were two unmanned Soyuz test flights (Kosmos 496 and Kosmos 573), and Soyuz 12 would match the mission durations of these two craft.

On September 27, 1973, at 1218 Greenwich mean time (GMT) the manned Soyuz 12 was launched into a low orbit with an inclination (the angle between the orbital plane and the equator) of 51.6 degrees and an orbit of 181 by 229 kilometers.

The mission commander was Vasili Lazarev, and his flight engineer was Oleg Makarov. Both cosmonauts were on their first space mission. In retrospect, the Salyut-related nature of the Soyuz 12 mission was demonstrated to Western observers in the choice of the backup crew, Alexei Gubarev and Georgi Grechko, who would later fly on Soyuz 17, the first visit to the Salyut 4 orbital space station.

The mission of the Soyuz 12 crew was comparatively simple. The cosmonauts would test the spacecraft's new design, perform orbital maneuvers, and return to Earth. A minimum of scientific work was scheduled for the flight. Within seven hours of launch, the Soyuz cosmonauts had maneuvered the spacecraft to a near-circular 327-by-344-kilometer orbit. This was the altitude which the "civilian" Kosmos 557 Salyut station should have attained, and it was the same altitude that the Salyut 4 would reach. Thus, the cosmonauts had simulated the maneuvers required to reach the altitude of an already-orbiting space station. During the first day of flight, the Soviet authorities announced that the mission would last for two days—thus precluding any rumors that the flight might have been curtailed early.

Apart from testing the Soyuz systems, apparently the only work undertaken by Lazarev and Makarov was the photographic observation of Earth. Makarov took Earth resources photographs using a handheld multispectral camera (that is, a camera that is sensitive to specific parts of the spectrum), while Lazarev simultaneously took photographs of the same areas with an ordinary camera. The film in Makarov's camera was sensitive from the visible to infrared wavelengths.

After completing the Soyuz 12 flight program, the cosmonauts reoriented the spacecraft. While passing over the southern part of the Atlantic Ocean, they fired the spacecraft's main engine to bring them out of orbit. The spacecraft split into its three component modules—orbital, descent (with the crew), and instrument. The orbital and instrument modules would be left to burn in the atmosphere, while, at an altitude of 7.5 kilometers, the descent module main parachute opened. The heatshield was discarded just before touchdown, allowing three solid-propellant rockets to fire, cushioning the final landfall for the cosmonauts. They returned to Earth on September 29, at 11:34 A.M. about 400 kilometers southwest of Karaganda in Kazakhstan.

Knowledge Gained

Soyuz 12 was not launched specifically with the aim of gaining new knowledge or undertaking any major experiments in orbit. It was simply a flight to "man-rate" the Soyuz spacecraft after its modifications. The sole scientific work identified with this mission is the photography of Earth in different spectral bands using handheld cameras. A few of these Earth resources photographs taken by the crew have been published in the Soviet Union.

Context

With the flight of Soyuz 12 successfully completed, the Soviet manned space program had returned to flight status after a hiatus of twenty-seven months. While the Salyut orbital station had proved troublesome during 1973, the interim Soyuz 12 mission had test-flown the redesigned space station ferry during a short mission, proving that it could, in theory, carry cosmonauts to and from orbital stations.

The flight of Soyuz 12 was also a boost for the parallel Soyuz program connected with the 1975 Apollo-Soyuz Test Project flight: Between the Soyuz 11 loss in 1971 and 1975, the United States would launch six manned missions (three Apollo lunar missions and three Apollo/Skylab missions), and there were worries in some quarters that in 1975 the Soyuz program would have accomplished only limited missions. In fact, following Soyuz 12 there would be two solo Soyuz flights and five space station crew visits launched (although only three of these visits would be successful).

Bibliography

Clark, Phillip S. "The Civilian Salyut Programme." In *The Soviet Manned Space Programme*. London: Salamander, 1988. Although this book focuses on the civilian Salyut space station program, the mission of Salyut Soyuz 12 is also discussed.

Ezell, Edward Clinton, and Linda Neuman Ezell. *The Partnership: A History of the Apollo-Soyuz Test Project*. NASA SP-4209. Washington, D.C.: Government Printing Office, 1978. Although its focus is the Apollo-Soyuz Test Project, this book reviews the entire Soyuz program—from inception to the flight of Soyuz 19. Includes useful appendices and illustrations.

Furniss, Tim. *Manned Spaceflight Log*. Rev. ed. New York: Jane's Publishing Co., 1986. Arranged chronologically, this source covers all Soviet spaceflight until 1986. Written in easily understood language. Contains rare photographs.

Johnson, Nicholas L. *Handbook of Soviet Manned Space Flight*. San Diego: Univelt, 1980. An authoritative description of the Soyuz 12 mission is included in this comprehensive review of Soviet manned spaceflight.

Oberg, James E. *Red Star in Orbit*. New York: Random House, 1981. An excellent summary of Soviet spaceflight, with emphasis on politics as they influence both program evolution and technological developments. Illustrated.

U.S. Congress. House. Committee on Science and Technology. *Astronauts and Cosmonauts Biographical and Statistical Data*. Report prepared by Congressional Research Service, Library of Congress. 99th Cong., 1st sess., rev. ed. 1985. Committee Print. Includes brief biographical sketches of American astronauts and Soviet cosmonauts. Photographs of each person are included.

Phillip S. Clark

Cross-References

The Apollo-Soyuz Test Project, 132; Soyuz 10 and 11, 1436; Soyuz 17, 1460; Soyuz 18A, 18B, and 20, 1464; The Soyuz Interkosmos Missions, 1489.

SOYUZ 13

Date: December 18 to December 26, 1973
Type of mission: Manned Earth-orbiting spaceflight
Country: The Soviet Union

The flight of Soyuz 13 marked the first time a Soviet manned space mission was dedicated entirely to scientific goals. The objective of Soyuz 13 was to continue orbital flight operations with space station-type experiments during a temporary suspension of manned space station activity caused by technical problems.

Principal personages
ANATOLI A. BLAGONRAVOV, Chairman of the Commission for the Exploration and Use of Outer Space, Soviet Academy of Sciences
VLADIMIR N. CHELOMEI, thought to be the "Chief Designer" of the Soviet space progam
GRIGOR GURZADYAN, the designer of the Orion-2 ultraviolet telescope
PYOTR KLIMUK, the command pilot
VALENTIN LEBEDEV, the civilian flight engineer
LEONID SEDOV, Academician and Chairman of the Interdepartmental Commission of Interplanetary Communications, Soviet Academy of Sciences
VLADIMIR A. SHATALOV, Commander of the Cosmonaut Corps
ALEXANDER VINOGRADOV, Vice President of the Soviet Academy of Sciences
L. A. VOSKRESENSKY, the designer of the Soyuz spacecraft

Summary of the Mission

The Soyuz 13 mission was an eight-day flight with no docking with a Salyut space station. The mission was conceived primarily as an orbiting astronomical observatory, but other activities were conducted in support of past and future space station experiments. Soyuz 13 was the first Soviet manned spaceflight totally dedicated to scientific experiments.

Launch of the Soyuz 13 spacecraft (code-named Kavkaz, meaning "Caucasus") from the Baikonur cosmodrome came at 14 hours, 55 minutes Moscow time, on December 18, 1973. An A-2 booster placed the spacecraft into an initial orbit of 188 by 246 kilometers, but after completion of orbital maneuvers on the fifth revolution, the orbit of Soyuz 13 was 225 by 272 kilometers, inclined 51.56 degrees to the equator, with an orbital period of 89.22 minutes. Soyuz 13 flew significantly higher than the standard orbit used by previous solo Soyuz missions. The actual orbit was very close to that planned for the future joint American/Soviet Apollo-Soyuz Test

Project flight, and was thought by some analysts to be a demonstration mission for that project.

The two-man crew of Soyuz 13 consisted of rookie cosmonauts Major Pyotr Klimuk, the commander, and civilian Valentin Lebedev, the flight engineer. The backup crewman for Klimuk is unknown; the backup for Lebedev was Vitali Sevastyanov. As with all Soviet manned space missions for many years after the fatal flight of Soyuz 11, the crew of Soyuz 13 was restricted to two cosmonauts instead of three: The fatal depressurization of the Soyuz 11 craft had made it necessary for the crew to wear full spacesuits during launch and recovery. In preparation for the astronomy experiments, Klimuk and Lebedev received extensive training in the use of the Orion-2 telescope.

The primary objectives of the Soyuz 13 mission were to conduct astrophysical experiments with the Orion-2 telescope assembly, and experiments in the production of protein mass with the Oasis-2 experiment. Both these experiments had predecessors which had flown aboard the Salyut 1 space station two years before. Other mission objectives included the study of blood flow to the brain with the Levka apparatus, experiments with higher plants, Earth observation, and navigational experiments.

Two major modifications performed to the Soyuz in preparation for its observatory mission converted the spacecraft into a small manned orbiting laboratory. The docking adapter, normally on the forward part of the orbital module, was not needed on this flight and was replaced with the Orion-2 telescope complex. The orbital module itself, normally used as a living area for the crew, was turned into a space laboratory. Another modification concerned the spacecraft's solar panels: Starting with the previous Soyuz flight, solar panels had been discontinued from the service module; because of the length of the Soyuz 13 mission, however, the solar panels were reinstated.

The Orion-2 telescope had been designed by Grigor Gurzadyan of Armenia. An ultraviolet telescope, it was capable of studying the electromagnetic emissions of celestial bodies in the ultraviolet range, between 2,000 and 3,000 angstroms—wavelengths inaccessible to ground-based telescopes because Earth's atmosphere blocks these wavelengths. The telescope was mounted entirely outside the spacecraft (unlike its Orion-1 predecessor, which had been mounted inside the Salyut 1 space station), on a three-axis platform which stabilized the apparatus within 2 or 3 seconds of arc point accuracy. Described by the Soviets as a wide field ultraviolet meniscus telescope, the instrument could cover a field of view 20 degrees square and viewed celestial objects through a special ultraviolet transparent window of crystalline quartz. A dome-shaped canopy shielded the telescope from temperature extremes as the spacecraft entered and exited Earth's shadow. A window opened in the canopy to allow exposures that lasted between one and twenty minutes.

The Orion-2 system was automatic, but it still took both cosmonauts to operate the apparatus. Lebedev worked the Orion-2 control panel from inside the orbital module, while Klimuk oriented the spacecraft from the command module to within a few degrees of the target area. The Orion-2 system then took over and pointed the instruments within three to five angular seconds of the target by referencing a widely separated star and using a system of 13 electric motors for control. Film cassettes for the Orion-2 system could be changed through the forward orbital module hatch, which normally opened into the docking adapter. Because of this system, an extravehicular activity (EVA) was not needed to service the telescope. On the second day of flight operations, the crew was said to be "degreasing" the Orion telescope system. The Soviets also stated that the telescope system was used for space navigation experiments and Earth resources studies. By the completion of the eight-day mission, the Orion system had been used for sixteen observation sessions.

An instrument for studying solar emissions in several portions of the X-ray band was also attached to the Orion-2 system and was operated during the sixty-fifth orbit. The X-ray instrument had a field of view of 70 degrees and simultaneously photographed Earth for comparison. Since the Orion-2 system was mounted on the orbital module, it was jettisoned in space at the completion of the mission. Only the exposed film was returned to Earth.

The orbital module contained the Oasis-2 "greenhouse" experiment. This was an experimental biological system for growing nutritive protein during a lengthy spaceflight. The experiment was a follow-up to a six-month ground study during which three persons had lived in a closed ecological system. The Oasis-2 consisted of two connected cylinders. One cylinder was used to grow water oxidizing bacteria grown with hydrogen generated by electrolysis. Oxygen produced by the electrolysis was passed to the second cylinder, which contained urobacteria (which break down urea). The bacteria absorbed the oxygen and released carbonic acid, which was passed back to the first cylinder and used for the synthesis of biomass. The control panel for the experiment contained a peristaltic pump (a pump with a wavelike action) which the cosmonauts periodically activated during the flight to circulate a nutrient solution to the bacteria in the cylinders. The pump ran for a total of 12 hours during the flight and used almost all the nutrient carried for the experiment.

To study blood flow to the brain during weightlessness, Klimuk and Lebedev used the Levka (lion's cub) experiment, which consisted of an exerciser that was stretched with a 15-kilogram force thirty times per minute. Electrodes attached to the cosmonauts recorded the response of cerebral blood vessels to the exercise by measuring bioelectrical potentials in the brain.

Soyuz 13 also performed navigation experiments to test the accuracy of control systems and test new instruments for attitude control using Earth and stars as references.

Earth resources were studied by Soyuz 13 using a special nine-lensed multispectral camera which used three separate film strips to photograph several areas of Earth simultaneously. Two of the films used were sensitive to visible light; the third was sensitive to the infrared region. Each lens had color filters; thus, many different spectra could be taken. In addition, an RSS-2 spectrograph photographed the day and twilight horizons and photographed reflected solar radiation from several natural formations on Earth.

According to cosmonaut General Vladimir Shatalov, the reentry of Soyuz 13 on

December 26, 1973, caused some anxious moments because of low clouds and a snowstorm in the landing area. Nevertheless, Klimuk and Lebedev landed safely at 11 hours, 50 minutes Moscow time. Touchdown was 200 kilometers southwest of Karaganda, Kazakhstan, and the crew was out and walking around several minutes after the landing. The mission had orbited Earth 128 times and had lasted for 188 hours and 55 minutes.

Knowledge Gained

The Soyuz 13 mission was dedicated primarily to astrophysical observations by the Orion-2 ultraviolet telescope complex. The resulting data returned from this instrument marked the first time that chromospheres were discovered around cold stars. The Orion-2 instrument also took the first ultraviolet spectra of planetary nebulae (expanding gas shells blown off dying stars).

During the operation of the Orion instrument, the Soyuz 13 cosmonauts made ten thousand ultraviolet spectrograms of three thousand stars in the constellations Taurus, Orion, Gemini, Auriga, and Perseus. The telescope obtained spectrograms of stars down to the tenth magnitude—and, in the case of one exposure near the star Capella in the constellation Auriga, down to the eleventh magnitude (approximately 50 times dimmer than the faintest star seen by the naked eye). Moreover, operating in the ultraviolet region, the Orion instrument recorded two thousand stars not previously cataloged.

The Oasis-2 "greenhouse" experiment had important implications for long-duration spaceflights, which require that large quantities of food, water, and air be regenerated to minimize the need to carry these supplies in large reserves. The density of the biomass protein grown in the experiment increased thirty-five times during the eight-day flight. A similar ground-based version of the experiment produced significantly less protein. The first protein produced by the Oasis was said to have been gathered only two days after launch.

Other biological experiments included studies of chlorella and duckweed in space. Chlorella absorbs carbon dioxide and returns oxygen to the air, making it an important space research item for the Russian space station effort. The duckweed was initially dormant at launch, being in its normal winter hibernation state: turions, or sprouts. Once in orbit, the cosmonauts placed the turions in a vial and added kinetin to revive them. Nutrients were then added to the duckweed, and its growth process in weightlessness was studied by introducing traceable substances.

Since blood tends to redistribute itself toward the upper body in a weightless state, the Soviets were especially interested in the circulation of blood to the brain during weightlessness. Soviet space medicine specialists theorized that the disorientation and "spacesickness" felt by most cosmonauts for the first few days of spaceflight was probably caused by an increase of blood in the brain. Studies were performed in orbit by the Soyuz 13 crew using the Levka apparatus to investigate this theory.

Some of the initial Soviet multispectral Earth resources observations were carried out by Soyuz 13 using a nine-lensed camera to photograph portions of the Earth in different wavelengths of light.

The Soyuz 13 experiments also returned spectra of Earth's horizon as seen from space to study the distribution of dust particles and pollution in the atmosphere.

Context

Soyuz 13 set a new direction for Soviet manned spaceflight, marking the first time that a Russian manned space mission was conducted entirely for scientific reasons. All previous Soviet manned launches had either political propaganda or military overtones as well.

The fact that the mission was heavily weighted toward science was a reflection on the then-grounded Soviet space station program. After the tragic death of the Salyut 1/Soyuz 11 crew in 1971, Soviet manned spaceflight activity had ground to a halt as the technical details of the disaster were studied and repairs were implemented. Additionally, shortly before the Soyuz 13 mission, both the Salyut 2 and the acknowledged third space station, Kosmos 557, had failed, suffering loss of control and disintegrating in orbit before a crew could be launched to board them. These ongoing technical difficulties in their space station program, coupled with the success of the American Skylab space station program, made a manned space mission necessary to carry out space station-type experiments that would further the work begun on Salyut 1 and bridge the gap until another space station could become operational.

Initially, there was Western speculation after the launch of Soyuz 13 that the flight would be an in-orbit inspection of Kosmos 613, launched November 30, 1973, and thought to be another failed Salyut space station. Later analysis, however, showed that Kosmos 613 was really a long-duration unmanned test of the Soyuz spacecraft in a powered-down state.

The flight of Soyuz 13 also marked the first time in the twelve years of manned spaceflight that Soviet cosmonauts and American astronauts were in orbit at the same time. When Klimuk and Lebedev were launched, the American Skylab 4 astronauts were in the thirty-second day of their eighty-four-day flight. Differing radio frequencies and orbits prevented the two crews from communicating or sighting each other while in space. They did, however, cooperate in other ways: As a prelude to the planned Apollo-Soyuz Test Project, George Low of the National Aeronautics and Space Administration (NASA) provided the Soviets with a special-sensitivity film for the Orion-2 ultraviolet telescope experiment.

Bibliography

Gatland, Kenneth. *Manned Spacecraft*. Rev. ed. New York: Macmillan, 1976. A chronology of worldwide events leading to the development of manned spaceflight by both the United States and the Soviet Union. Contains numerous illustrations detailing the design and functions of American and Soviet manned spacecraft. Descriptive narratives provide details of all manned spacecraft and their missions. Suitable for general audiences.

Johnson, Nicholas L. *Handbook of Soviet Manned Space Flight*. San Diego: Univelt, 1980. A technical chronology of Soviet manned spaceflight. Aimed at the advanced reader, this handbook emphasizes the technical details of the Soviet manned programs and summarizes the mission results. One of the most authoritative sources of information on Soviet manned space programs. Contains many drawings and illustrations detailing Soviet manned spaceflight hardware.

McDougall, Walter A. . . . *The Heavens and the Earth: A Political History of the Space Age*. New York: Basic Books, 1985. This well-researched and heavily footnoted historical text describes and analyzes the decisions by the leaders of both the United States and the Soviet Union and their effects on the respective space programs. Heavy emphasis on the key political and technological leaders of the time. Relates how the American and Soviet space programs became an integral part of Cold War politics. Suitable for general audiences.

Smolders, Peter. *Soviets in Space*. New York: Taplinger Publishing Co., 1974. A well-illustrated narrative on all aspects of the Soviet space program. Heavy emphasis is placed on manned activities. Suitable for general audiences, it concentrates on the successful aspects of Soviet space missions as they were reported by the Soviet Union. Contains numerous diagrams and photographs illustrating the technical details of Soviet spacecraft and their missions.

Turnill, Reginald. *The Observer's Spaceflight Directory*. London: Frederick Warne, 1978. A lavishly illustrated summary of spaceflight activities by all nations. Lists chronologies of major manned and unmanned space missions. Technical narrative describes worldwide space activities by nation and program, providing details on spacecraft, mission summaries, and program results. One-third of the directory is devoted to Soviet programs. Suitable for advanced readers at high school and college levels.

U.S. Congress. Office of Technology Assessment. *Salyut: Soviet Steps Toward Permanent Human Presence in Space—A Technical Memorandum*. OTA-TM-STI-14. Washington, D.C.: Government Printing Office, 1983. An overview of Soviet manned spaceflight with emphasis on the Soviet Salyut space station program. Illustrated with many excellent drawings of Soviet spacecraft and boosters by Charles Vick. Intermediate-level reading.

U.S. Congress. Senate. Committee on Commerce, Science, and Transportation. *Soviet Space Programs: 1976-1980*. Part 2, *Manned Space Programs and Space Life Sciences*. Report prepared by Congressional Research Service, the Library of Congress. 98th Cong., 2d sess., 1984. Committee Print. Contains comprehensive descriptions of all phases of Soviet manned spaceflight, as well as a detailed overview of the technical development of Soviet manned space activities, scientific investigations, space medicine research, and the political effects of Soviet space exploration. Suitable for a general audience.

Robert Reeves

Cross-References

The Apollo-Soyuz Test Project, 132; Biological Effects of Space Travel on Humans, 188; Comets, 245; U.S. and Soviet Cooperation in Space, 259; Cosmonauts and the Soviet Cosmonaut Program, 273; Earth Resources Mapped from Satellites, 306; Soviet Launch Vehicles, 742; The Salyut Space Station, 1233; Skylab 4, 1303; Solar and Stellar Flares, 1315; The Solar X-Ray Region, 1390; The Soyuz-Kosmos Program, 1396; Soyuz 10 and 11, 1436; Space Centers and Launch Sites in the Soviet Union, 1592; Air and Space Telescopes, 2014.

SOYUZ 14 and 15

Date: June 25, 1974, to January 24, 1975
Type of mission: Manned military space station flights
Country: The Soviet Union

Salyut 3, the first manned military space mission, conducted photoreconnaissance to assess the usefulness of the station for military activities; although the results of its mission were mixed, Salyut 3 was the start of the Soviets' rebuilding effort after several years of setbacks. Soyuz 14 and 15 carried the first two crews to the Salyut 3 space station.

Principal personages
VLADIMIR N. CHELOMEI, spacecraft designer
PAVEL R. POPOVICH, Soyuz 14 commander
YURI ARTYUKHIN, Soyuz 14 flight engineer
GENNADI SARAFANOV, Soyuz 15 commander
LEV DEMIN, Soyuz 15 flight engineer
BORIS VOLYNOV, backup commander, Soyuz 14/15
VITALI ZHOLOBOV, backup flight engineer, Soyuz 14/15

Summary of the Missions

The Salyut 3 space station was the first successful attempt to fly a manned military reconnaissance spacecraft. While the use of manned space stations for reconnaissance had been envisioned since the early 1920's, it was not until the military Salyut missions of the 1970's that its feasibility was actually tested in space. The Salyut space station program began in early 1969. It was to undertake both scientific and military missions using the same basic technology and hardware. Development was split between the bureau headed by Sergei Korolev (civilian Salyut) and the bureau headed by Vladimir N. Chelomei (military Salyut).

The military Salyut had two pressurized sections. The midsection was the crew's living area. There were two bunks (one of which folded into the wall to save space), a special sofa for medical tests, hot and cold water faucets, dining table, shower, toilet, storage for clothes and linens, and a small library. Behind the midsection was the work module. This had a corridor down its left side and was divided into several sections. The forward section had the instrument panels to control the station's operations. Behind this was the reconnaissance camera. It was mounted in a large cone-shaped casing, which extended nearly to the ceiling. The optical system was a 10-meter focal length telescope. From an orbital altitude of 240 kilometers, it could resolve objects as small as 30 to 46 centimeters.

The reconnaissance camera was on a par with that of the United States' Big Bird unmanned reconnaissance satellites. To achieve this resolution, the Salyut had to be held very steady. Any vibration of the camera from the crew moving around would blur the photographs. Stability was achieved by using two separate control systems.

The first was a number of small rocket thrusters. These controlled its basic attitude and stabilized the station. For fine attitude control during photoreconnaissance runs, an inertial sphere was used. This was a spherical gyroscope spun within a magnetic field. As the gyroscope spun, the station would move in the opposite direction. This provided the capability for fine attitude control of the station while conserving rocket fuel. The military Salyut also carried receivers for picking up Western radio and radar transmissions. Electrical power for the military Salyut was provided by two large solar panels attached to the station's sides. They could be rotated to follow the Sun even as the station was oriented toward Earth. Solar cells were mounted on both sides of the panels to take advantage of the light reflected from Earth (which had a strength of about 20 percent that of direct sunlight).

The manned Soyuz transport spacecraft docked at the rear of the work module. Around the outer rim were the maneuvering engines. These had to be fired periodically to raise the station's orbit. Because of its low orbit, the station was affected by atmospheric drag. The extremely thin atmosphere at its altitude gradually slowed the station, lowering its orbit and bringing it closer to Earth. If left uncorrected, the station would reenter the atmosphere and burn up. The low orbit was necessary, however, for maximum photographic resolution.

At the forward end of the military Salyut was the reentry capsule. This was used to return the film and tapes to Earth once the flight was completed. Its payload was about 500 kilograms. The crew had access to it through a hatch in the forward end of the midsection. Once it separated, the capsule oriented itself and fired an on-board retro-rocket, reentered, and parachuted to a landing in Soviet Central Asia. The complete military Salyut space station was 14.4 meters long and 4 meters wide. Its total weight was 18,900 kilograms. The launch vehicle was the D-1 Proton booster (also designed by Vladimir N. Chelomei's bureau).

The first military Salyut was Salyut 2, launched on April 3, 1973. After eleven days in orbit, it had suffered a malfunction which made it impossible to launch the planned manned mission. It took fourteen months for the Soviets to correct the problems. Salyut 3 was launched from Tyuratam at 2238 Greenwich mean time (GMT) on June 25, 1974. Its D-1 booster placed it into a 260-by-210-kilometer orbit, with an inclination of 51.57 degrees. Over the next nine days its orbit changed several times. Finally, on July 3, it was in a 270-by-247-kilometer orbit and was ready to receive its first crew.

Soyuz 14 lifted off from Tyuratam at 1851 GMT on July 3. Its two-man crew consisted of Colonel Pavel R. Popovich (commander) and Lieutenant Colonel Yuri Artyukhin (flight engineer). Soyuz 14 docked with the station twenty-four hours after launch. The crew was soon busy aboard its new home.

The crew worked a normal day—eight hours of experiments, eight hours of maintenance and housekeeping, and eight hours of sleep. Scientific experiments included measuring polarized light reflected from the atmosphere, culturing bacteria, and performing medical tests. Experiments concerning blood flow were important for determining the effects of prolonged weightlessness. The Soviets had established the goal of permanent habitation of space, so it was necessary to learn the physical limitations of humans in space. Hardware checkouts included measuring the flex of the solar panels caused by their vibration and testing a water recycling system. In all, four hundred scientific and technical experiments were performed.

Of particular importance was what the Soviets called Earth resources studies. These were apparently tests of the high resolution photoreconnaissance equipment. The equipment was set up on July 9 and runs were conducted from July 10 to July 16. It was subsequently reported that the crew used code words to conceal their activities. In addition, targets were laid out near the Tyuratam launch site for the crew to observe and photograph.

After two weeks in orbit, the crew began packing up for their return to Earth. On July 19, Popovich and Artyukhin entered the Soyuz 14 spacecraft, separated from the Salyut 3, and reentered the atmosphere. The capsule landed in Kazakhstan after a flight of 15 days, 17 hours, and 30 minutes. The crew was unharmed by the prolonged weightlessness and was able to leave the spacecraft without assistance.

Soyuz 15, the second mission to Salyut 3, was launched at 1958 GMT on August 26, 1974. The crew consisted of Lieutenant Colonel Gennadi Sarafanov (commander) and Colonel Lev Demin (flight engineer). At age forty-eight, Demin had become the oldest man and the first grandfather to go into space. The planned mission duration was about thirty days (double Soyuz 14's flight time). When the crew attempted to dock with Salyut 3 on their sixteenth orbit, the automatic rendezvous system malfunctioned. Soyuz 15 was approaching the station at too high a speed and docking had to be interrupted. Several more attempts were made, but each ended in failure. The crew now had to make an emergency return to Earth. Unlike the Salyut spacecraft, the Soyuz 15 did not have solar panels; all of its electrical power came from batteries. To conserve power, the crew shut off telemetry and voice transmissions. Sarafanov and Demin made a successful reentry and landed at 2010 GMT on August 29. The total time of the mission was 2 days, 12 minutes. The Soyuz 15 failure destroyed Soviet plans for back-to-back missions to Salyut 3. The next launch attempt could not be made until October at the earliest. This would be after the station's ninety-day lifetime had been exceeded; therefore it was considered too great a risk.

On September 23, the reentry capsule containing the exposed film and tape was separated and recovered. This brought Salyut 3's useful life to a close. It continued to orbit Earth for the next three months, undergoing engineering tests. Finally on January 24, 1975, after seven months in orbit, Salyut 3's engines fired. It was deorbited and burned up over the Pacific Ocean.

Knowledge Gained

The purpose of Salyut 3 was to test the feasibility of manned military reconnaissance. The secrecy about such activities, and the Soviets' refusal to acknowledge that they conducted any such activities, makes any judgments about its success difficult. The Soyuz 14 crew performed only about four days of photoreconnaissance runs. The amount of data, both in terms of intelligence and experience with manned reconnaissance, would seem to be limited. Yet this may not be entirely correct. The military Salyut was capable of both manned and unmanned operations. Unmanned operations would assess the military Salyut's usefulness but could provide no information on the advantages and limitations of a human crew undertaking military activities.

More encouraging were the scientific experiments. Soyuz 14/Salyut 3 was the first successful Soviet space station mission. Much of what the Soyuz 11/Salyut 1 mission accomplished was lost with the deaths of the crew. Soyuz 14/Salyut 3 not only was able to undertake a wide range of scientific experiments but also reaped the rewards. The research environment was much better than that which earlier Soviet crews had experienced. Instead of performing experiments in a cramped capsule, the crew enjoyed a relatively roomy space station.

Other important data were obtained in the biological sciences; experiments were conducted to measure how the crew's bodies adapted to weightlessness and how they readapted to Earth's gravity. The Soyuz 14 mission provided a baseline for subsequent Salyut missions.

It is clear that the failure of the Soyuz 15 crew to dock meant the loss of significant data (its thirty-day lifetime would have been twice that of Soyuz 14). Also, the Soyuz 14's crew spent considerable time with hardware tests of the new station's systems, which cut into the time available for data gathering. On balance, the research results of Salyut 3 were at best mixed.

Context

Salyut 3 provided the first hard, if limited, data on man's military usefulness in space. Before Salyut 3, only theoretical studies and laboratory tests had been conducted. Salyut 3 also underlined the largely military nature of the Soviet space program. The United States had, in the 1960's, been planning a dedicated manned military space project—the Manned Orbiting Laboratory. It was canceled in 1969, however, before any manned flights could take place. The Soviets were more persistent in this endeavor.

In the larger view, Salyut 3 was the start of a long recovery process for the Soviet space program. During the six years before the Salyut 3 mission, the Soviet space program had seen one setback after another—the death of the Soyuz 11 crew, the loss of Salyut 2, and the loss of Kosmos 557—while the Americans had triumphed with Apollo 8, Apollo 11, and Skylab. This greatly diminished the reputation for achievement in space that the Soviets had built up during the early and mid-1960's. In rebuilding their space program, the Soviets adapted the United States' pattern of step-by-step development, with each mission building on the previous one. The Soviets also generally avoided the headline-grabbing but ultimately self-defeating space spectacular. This rebuilding would take the next decade to complete. The Soyuz 15 docking failure was the first indication that the road back was not going to be an easy one.

Bibliography

Furniss, Tim. *Manned Spaceflight Log*. Rev. ed. London: Jane's Publishing Co., 1986. This book is made up of capsule summaries of the first 128 manned spaceflights. The vital statistics for each mission are listed—name, launch date, site, vehicle, flight type, flight time, spacecraft weight, and crew. The text describes the events of the mission. Suitable for general audiences.

Johnson, Nicholas L. *Handbook of Soviet Manned Space Flight*. San Diego: Univelt, 1980. Technical survey of the Soviet space program up to 1980. Organized by type of spacecraft, the text describes each spacecraft's design, test flights, and operational missions. Included is some material on the military Salyut. The book contains numerous photographs and drawings of Soviet spacecraft and hardware. Suitable for high school and college audiences.

Oberg, James E. *Red Star in Orbit*. New York: Random House, 1981. Popular account of the Soviet space program from its origins in the 1930's through the successes of the late 1950's and early 1960's, the setbacks of the early 1970's, and the long road back. The author, an aerospace engineer with the Space Transportation System program, includes several pages on the military Salyut program. Suitable for general audiences.

Peebles, Curtis. *Guardians: Strategic Reconnaissance Satellites*. Novato, Calif.: Presidio Press, 1987. Survey of the history, technology, and political background of reconnaissance satellites and their profound impact on international relations. Includes chapters on the Soviet military Salyut program and the United States' Manned Orbiting Laboratory. Heavily illustrated, with an appendix listing all military space launches and a nontechnical explanation of orbital mechanics. Suitable for high school and college audiences.

U.S. Congress. Office of Technology Assessment. *Salyut: Soviet Steps Toward Permanent Human Presence in Space—A Technical Memorandum*. OTA-TM-STI-14. Washington, D.C.: Government Printing Office, 1983. An overview of the Salyut program. It includes a brief history of an early Soviet program and the Salyut's technical features, characteristics, activities, and impact on foreign policy. Several drawings of the various Salyut versions are used. Recommended for general audiences.

U.S. Senate. Committee on Commerce, Science, and Transportation. *Soviet Space Programs, 1976-80: Manned Space Programs and Space Life Sciences, Part 2*. 98th Cong., 2d sess., 1984. Committee Print. One of a three-part series on Soviet space activities published periodically by the United States government. Part 2 covers the Soviet manned program. Descriptions of all manned or related missions are provided, experiments are listed, and tables provide statistical data. The book also contains numerous drawings of Soviet spacecraft, giving design details and interior layout. Recommended for high school and undergraduate students.

Curtis Peebles

Cross-References

SOYUZ 17

Date: December 26, 1974, to February 9, 1975
Type of mission: Manned space station flight
Country: The Soviet Union

Soyuz 17 was the first manned visit to the new Salyut 4 orbital laboratory. It carried two cosmonauts, who spent nearly thirty days on the station.

Principal personages
ALEXEI GUBAREV, the commander
GEORGI GRECHKO, the flight engineer
PYOTR KLIMUK, the backup commander
VITALI SEVASTYANOV, the backup flight engineer

Summary of the Mission

With the success of manned operations on the military Salyut 3 during the Soyuz 14 visit in 1974, it was time for the so-called civilian Salyut program to resume manned operations. On December 26, 1974, at about 0415 Greenwich mean time (GMT) a three-stage Proton booster was launched from the Tyuratam site. Within ten minutes, a new Soviet space station was in orbit. Named Salyut 4, it had a mass of about 18,900 kilograms. During the first four days in orbit, the station was maneuvered from an initial 215-by-252-kilometer orbit to a 338-by-351-kilometer orbit. Both orbits had an inclination (the angle between the orbital plane and the equator) of 51.6 degrees. The space station was ready to receive its first crew.

While little information had been released about the major experiments aboard Salyut 3, it was disclosed that Salyut 4 was packed with equipment which would allow the cosmonauts to pursue a rigid program of scientific research. The major research instrument was the orbital solar telescope, OST 1, designed to capture solar radiation within the 800-to-1,300-angstrom range. Having a mirror diameter of 2.5 meters, the telescope allowed both photographs and spectrographs of the Sun to be taken simultaneously with a resolution of 1 angstrom. It was possible to respray the telescope's mirror in orbit, allowing refurbishment after the instrument had been subjected to meteoric particles in space.

On January 10, 1975, at 2153 GMT, the 6,825-kilogram Soyuz 17 was launched with two cosmonauts, Alexei Gubarev and Georgi Grechko, on board. Both men were on their first spaceflight, although they had acted as backup cosmonauts for earlier missions. (They had been paired in 1972-1973 and had acted as a team to back up the Soyuz 12 cosmonauts.)

During their first day in orbit, the cosmonauts tested the Soyuz spacecraft systems and performed a series of orbital maneuvers. The actual docking with Salyut 4 was to occur on the second day of the flight. The first phase of the rendezvous was entirely automatic and delivered Soyuz to within 100 meters of Salyut. From that distance, the cosmonauts completed the docking of Soyuz with Salyut manually. The final docking was achieved on January 12 at 0125 GMT. After the docking, the cosmonauts checked that the seals between the spacecraft hatches were airtight, opened the hatches, and then entered their new home.

During the mission, almost daily progress reports were announced by the Soviets. Commenting on Salyut 4 on January 14, 1975, the former cosmonaut and then-current Salyut designer Konstantin Feoktistov said that the operating altitude of about 350 kilometers would ensure that the propellant consumption would be reduced to half the value required for low-orbit Salyuts.

The two cosmonauts began pursuing their program of scientific experimentation. Prior to this flight, the longest successful Soviet flight had lasted 17.7 days (Soyuz 9 in 1970). Although the Soviets had access to the public Skylab biomedical data, they wished to take advantage of this lengthy mission and obtain their own data relating to the human body's adaptation to weightlessness.

Gubarev and Grechko completed regular medical checks. The cosmonauts wore special suits which tended to make the body curl into a fetal position, requiring that the body's muscles be used to maintain a normal posture in orbit. Thus, muscles which would not normally be used in space were being exercised regularly. It was thought that since the legs in particular are not used for walking in space (because of the weightless environment) a serious weakening of the muscles and a dangerous loss of calcium might result. It was uncertain whether a "point of no return" would be reached, a point of physical deterioration after which the cosmonauts could not function on Earth.

The Chibis suit was also used for important medical work in orbit. In the weightlessness of space, there is a tendency for the blood to pool in the upper part of the body. The Chibis suit was designed to counter this effect. It fits over the lower part of the body; when worn, it forms a seal near the feet and around the torso: The pressure is then reduced in the leg area, forcing the blood to flow through the leg arteries and veins and making the heart pump more intensively. If the heart is not forced to pump, then its muscles deteriorate—causing serious problems when crew members are subjected to the gravitational force on Earth.

On January 16, the Salyut crew switched on the OTS 1 solar telescope for the first time and began to test it. The previous day they had used the teleprinter for the first time. (This instrument allowed the ground controllers to send messages to the cosmonauts without interrupting their work load.) On January 17, the Filin telescope system was used to observe the Crab nebula (the remains of a supernova, or exploding star, which erupted in 1054).

On January 19, it was revealed that Salyut was using ion sensors to control the station's orientation. Detectors would measure the direction of ion (charged atom) flow and then orient the station relative to that flow. It was claimed by the Soviets that this was the most efficient way of controlling the station's attitude.

An innovation came on February 3, when the cosmonauts were able to respray the mirror of the OTS 1 in orbit. The original mirror surface had become contaminated during the first few weeks in orbit, and the mirror was resprayed with aluminum by Grechko using a remote control system.

On February 7, it was announced that the cosmonauts were beginning to prepare for their return to Earth, as Salyut systems were being checked and experimental results were transferred to the Soyuz 17 descent module. After finally slowing down Salyut's systems, Soyuz 17—with Gubarev and Grechko on board—undocked from Salyut on February 9 at 0608 GMT. The Soyuz descent module landed at 1103 GMT, some 100 kilometers northeast of Tselinograd, Kazakhstan. The preliminary medical examinations showed that the cosmonauts had withstood their month in orbit with no permanent ill effects.

Knowledge Gained

The Soyuz 17 visit to the Salyut 4 orbital station was only the second successful manned mission to a Soviet orbital station. The mission was the longest to be flown by Soviet cosmonauts at that time, and it allowed the Soviets to begin accumulating data on the biomedical changes which the human organism undergoes during orbital flights of more than a week or two. Although full details of the observations undertaken by the cosmonauts are not known, Gubarev and Grechko had a large array of astronomical and other scientific equipment aboard Salyut 4 and were able to initiate a research program which would be continued by the next crew to board the station.

Context

Soyuz 17 was at its time the third longest manned space mission to be completed (the American Skylab 3 and Skylab 4 missions had been longer, at 59 days and 84 days respectively). During the Soyuz 17 mission, the cosmonauts devoted the most experimental time to biomedical research (about five days). Other experiments were conducted in the areas of solar observation, X-ray observation, infrared observation, atmospheric research, and Earth resources research.

The visit of Soyuz 17 to Salyut was considered to be a great success by the Soviet authorities. With the impending launch of two complex spacecraft toward Venus the following June and the Apollo-Soyuz mission in July, as well as the Salyut 4 program, the Soviet space program promised to be eventful in 1975.

Bibliography

Clark, Phillip S. "The Civilian Salyut Programme." In *The Soviet Manned Space Programme*. London: Salamander, 1988. The focus of this chapter is the civilian Salyut program, but all flights to the space station are discussed.

Furniss, Tim. *Manned Spaceflight Log*. Rev. ed. New York: Jane's Publishing Co., 1986. This resource includes capsule summaries of manned spaceflights. Each mission is listed with statistics such as launch times, vehicle type, and names and responsibilities of the crew members.

Hooper, Gordon R. "Missions to Salyut 4." *Spaceflight Magazine*, June, 1975: 219-225.

This article provides a detailed summary of the cosmonauts' activity on Salyut 4.

Johnson, Nicholas L. *Handbook of Soviet Manned Spaceflight*. San Diego: Univelt, 1980. A technical survey of Soviet spaceflight up to 1980. Organized by type of spacecraft, this book includes material on the Soyuz/Salyut missions. Illustrated with photographs and drawings.

Oberg, James E. *Red Star in Orbit*. New York: Random House, 1981. This popular account of the Soviet space program offers the beginning student of space exploration a review of Soviet successes and failures from the late 1950's until the early 1980's. Several pages are devoted to the Salyut program.

U.S. Congress. Office of Technology Assessment. *Salyut: Soviet Steps Toward Permanent Human Presence in Space—A Technical Memorandum*. OTA-TM-STI-14. Washington, D.C.: Government Printing Office, 1983. An overview of the Salyut program. Includes a brief history of an early Soviet program and the Salyut's technical features, activities, and crew. Illustrated.

Phillip S. Clark

Cross-References

The Apollo-Soyuz Test Project, 132; Soyuz 10 and 11, 1436; Soyuz 12, 1444; Soyuz 14 and 15, 1454; Soyuz 18A, 18B, and 20, 1464.

SOYUZ 18A, 18B, and 20

Date: April 5, 1975, to February 16, 1976
Type of mission: Manned and unmanned Earth-orbiting spaceflights
Country: The Soviet Union

The failure of the first Soyuz 18 mission, later dubbed Soyuz 18A, prompted the launch of a second Soyuz 18 so that Salyut 4 could be manned again before its useful life was over. Later, Soyuz 20 was flown unmanned to test the responses of various biological specimens to extended weightlessness and the response of the Soyuz spacecraft to extended orbital flight.

Principal personages

VASILI LAZAREV, the Soyuz 18A commander
OLEG MAKAROV, the Soyuz 18A flight engineer
PYOTR KLIMUK, the Soyuz 18B commander and the backup
    commander of Soyuz 18A
VITALI SEVASTYANOV, the Soyuz 18B flight engineer and the
    backup flight engineer of Soyuz 18A
VLADIMIR KOVALYONOK, the Soyuz 18B backup commander
YURI PONOMAREV, the Soyuz 18B backup flight engineer

Summary of the Missions

Following the visit of Soyuz 17 to Salyut 4, the orbit of the Salyut space station was allowed to decay—a natural reduction in altitude caused by the friction of Earth's upper atmosphere—until March 22. The altitude was then increased from 330 by 340 kilometers to 337 by 350 kilometers. Another slight adjustment to the orbit was made on April 1 when it was again increased from 337 by 349 kilometers to 339 by 351 kilometers. This suggested that the station was being readied for another manned visit.

On April 5 at 1102 Greenwich mean time (GMT), a three-stage booster carrying the intended Soyuz 18 spacecraft was launched for a rendezvous with Salyut 4. The four strap-on boosters of the launch vehicle separated about 120 seconds after launch. Some 40 seconds later, the tower of the payload shroud ignited to take away the shroud. The shutdown of the second-stage core booster occurred at about T plus 275 seconds. After the core engine stopped firing, explosive bolts should have fired to separate the core from the third-stage rocket for orbital insertion, but only half of the bolts fired. When the third-stage engine ignited, the core was still partially attached and the assembly was rapidly becoming unstable. A normal abort would have required the use of the payload shroud and the tower which had separated about two minutes earlier. Without the shroud and escape tower, the cosmonauts' only hope of escape was to fire the Soyuz instrument module engine to separate their spacecraft and take them away from the booster.

This done, the Soyuz spacecraft flew to a peak altitude of 192 kilometers. The spacecraft rotated through 180 degrees and split into its three separate modules. As the manned descent module returned to Earth, the cosmonauts were subjected to deceleration overloads of 14 to 15 times their normal weights (or 14 to 15 g). These are excessive gravitational overloads, but the cosmonauts' major concern was on which side of the Sino-Soviet border they would land. Landing occurred a mere 320 kilometers short of the Chinese border, and 1,574 kilometers from the launch site. The aborted flight had lasted 21 minutes and 27 seconds.

Calculations suggest that if the Soyuz (subsequently designated Soyuz 18A) had reached Salyut 4, a flight lasting until at least May 26 and probably until June 7 had been intended.

Following the launch failure of Soyuz 18A, the orbit of Salyut 4 went uncorrected until the middle of May, when a series of orbital maneuvers placed Salyut in the proper altitude to receive a crew. On May 24, at 1458 GMT, a second Soyuz 18 was launched carrying cosmonauts Pyotr Klimuk and Vitali Sevastyanov, who had acted as backup cosmonauts for the previous two manned launches. Because their flight was originally unscheduled, a new backup team was put together at short notice. The backup commander was Vladimir Kovalyonok, and the backup flight engineer Yuri Ponomarev, who, because of medical problems, was destined never to make a spaceflight.

Docking procedures of the 6,850-kilogram Soyuz 18B with Salyut 4 began on May 25. At 1811 GMT the two spacecraft had a relative velocity of 12 meters per second. At a distance of 1.5 kilometers, the Soyuz automatic docking system computer sensed that the relative velocity was excessive. A minor maneuver reduced the spacecraft's speed. At 1821 the two spacecraft were 800 meters apart and entering Earth's shadow. At a distance of 100 meters, the cosmonauts took manual control from aboard Soyuz 18B, with an approach velocity of 0.3 meter per second. The cosmonauts were out of touch with ground controllers when docking occurred at 1844. The event could not be confirmed on Earth until the spacecraft was again in direct communication with the ground. The cosmonauts transferred to Salyut 4 at midnight on May 25.

Once aboard Salyut, the crew's first task was to bring the station back from its "mothballed" condition. Although the life-support systems had been activated remotely before the crew arrived, all the scientific equipment had been packed away by the crew of Soyuz 17.

On May 27, the cosmonauts were busy checking the station's power supply and life-support systems, preparing the scientific apparatus, and loading the photographic equipment which they had brought with them. Once more, biological experiments were activated.

The life-support system was a major worry for the ground controllers during the Soyuz 18B mission. All manned operations aboard Salyut 4 had been scheduled to end in June (two months after the aborted launch in April). When the second Soyuz 18, scheduled to remain docked with Salyut until sometime in July, was launched, no one was certain how well the Salyut life-support system would endure the extra use. There had been reports that the crew of Soyuz 18B described mold growing around the walls of the station as the air regeneration system began to falter, and by late July, when the crew abandoned the station, it was apparently impossible to see through the windows because of contamination.

After three days on board Salyut 4, the cosmonauts reported that all of its systems were fully reactivated and that they were ready to begin their research program. Biomedical experimentation included a water recycling system and a "space garden." The crew also conducted research with astronomical equipment. In early June they observed X-ray sources in the constellations of Scorpio, Virgo, and Cygnus. Orienting the station for such work was apparently done in two stages: First, the cosmonauts pointed Salyut's instruments roughly at the area to be studied, and second, the station's automatic systems performed the precise pointing for the actual observations.

After two weeks in orbit, Klimuk and Sevastyanov had settled into the routine of a long space station residency. Medical observers on Earth were pleased with the cosmonauts' adaptation to weightlessness.

On June 8 and 9, the cosmonauts spent time taking photographs of Earth's surface—particularly the "black-soil zone of the European part of the Soviet Union," northern Kazakhstan, the republics of central Asia, and the Kuril Islands. They used cameras sensitive to different parts of the electromagnetic spectrum to obtain "false color" images of Earth which could be used on the ground for monitoring Earth's natural resources. After being in orbit for a month, on June 24, the cosmonauts performed maintenance on spacecraft systems, although exact details of the work were not disclosed.

On July 19, the cosmonauts began to prepare for their return to Earth. It was expected that the cosmonauts would be returning to Earth with about 600 spectrograms of the Sun's active regions and recordings of X rays from ten different sources. They had photographed approximately 8.5 million square kilometers of the Soviet Union for Earth resources studies.

On July 21, as Soyuz 19 was returning to Earth after its successful mission with Apollo 18, Klimuk and Sevastyanov were busy aboard Salyut 4 performing final experiments and preparing the station for automatic flight. During the working day, they spent about two hours on physical exercises, preparing their bodies for the impact of gravity when they returned to Earth.

On July 24, the Soyuz 18B propulsion system was ignited to raise the orbit of the Salyut/Soyuz complex from 335 by 344 kilometers to 335 by 360 kilometers. Another maneuver the following day raised the orbit to 342 by 361 kilometers.

On July 26, the cosmonauts transferred the results of their two months in orbit to the Soyuz descent module, and at 1056 GMT Soyuz 18 undocked from Salyut. After retrofire the cosmonauts landed 56 kilometers northeast of Arkalyk in Kazakhstan at 1418 GMT. They had landed 2 kilometers from the Soyuz 19 landing site.

The two cosmonauts were returned to the Tyuratam-Baikonur launch site for detailed medical examinations. Their blood pressures were normal, as were their pulse rates, but they had lost weight. Klimuk had lost 3.8 kilograms and Sevastyanov 1.9 kilograms. It took the two men about ten days to readapt completely to terrestrial conditions—the predicted period. During that time, the cosmonauts underwent complete postflight medical inspections which lasted up to eight hours each day.

One experiment which had long been expected for a Salyut crew and which did not take place was a spacewalk. There is no hint that one was planned for the Soyuz 17 visit to Salyut 4, so probably one was planned by the original Soyuz 18 mission, launched (and aborted) in April, 1975. Since the actual Soyuz 18B flight occurred as Salyut 4 was drawing close to the operational limits of its environmental system, a spacewalk would have been risky. There had not been a Soviet spacewalk since January, 1969—when the crew of Soyuz 4 was exchanged for Soyuz 5. Another spacewalk would not be performed until December, 1977, during the Soyuz 26 residency aboard Salyut 6.

After the two-month manned flight of Soyuz 18B, the orbit of Salyut 4 was allowed to decay until early November, 1975. The station's propulsion system was used to raise the orbit from 330 by 351 kilometers to 344 by 353 kilometers in preparation for Soyuz 20. On November 17 at 1437 GMT, the unmanned Soyuz 20 spacecraft was launched toward Salyut. Initially it was said that the purpose of the flight was to test the improved Soyuz systems. Two days later at 1920 GMT, Soyuz 20 completed a fully automatic docking with Salyut 4. It is probable that this was the first test of the software and hardware modifications which would later become crucial to operation of the unmanned Progress cargo freighters. The Soyuz 20 docking also opened the way for a crew rescue if a Soyuz ferry should fail in orbit; a disabled spacecraft could be cast off from the space station, and a new, unmanned Soyuz could be docked with the station to rescue the stranded crew.

Soyuz 20 carried a biological payload, including turtles and Drosophila flies. Some twenty species of plants—including cacti, gladiolus bulbs, and seeds of corn and legumes—were carried in special containers. The effects of weightlessness and cosmic radiation on these specimens would be studied when the Soyuz 20 descent module returned to Earth.

Few in-flight comments were made about Soyuz 20. On February 16, 1976, it was announced that Soyuz 20 had undocked from Salyut 4 and had been successfully recovered inside the Soviet Union. It was later revealed that the undocking had occurred on February 15 at 2304 GMT and that the landing had occurred at about 0224 GMT the following day.

After the return of Soyuz 20, the orbit of Salyut 4 continued to decay. After the November, 1975, maneuver, there were no more maneuvers until February 2, 1977, when the station was tracked in a 186-by-187-kilometer orbit. The station's propulsion system was switched on for a final time, bringing it out of orbit to reenter the atmosphere over the Pacific Ocean. Any large pieces of debris which survived the fiery journey through the atmosphere would fall harmlessly into the Pacific Ocean.

Knowledge Gained

The failure of the Soyuz launch vehicle during the first Soyuz 18 attempt meant that none of the scientific experiments which had been planned could be undertaken. Yet an unplanned abort mode of the launch vehicle was proved the hard way — in flight.

The successful flight of the second Soyuz 18 allowed the Soviets to match the duration of the United States' Skylab 4 mission, and it gave the Soviets more biomedical data on the adaptation of the human body to the weightless environment. Although the Soviet techniques for overcoming the effects of prolonged space missions would not be greatly improved until after the first residency aboard the Salyut 6 orbital station, the experience of Soyuz 18B was essential for Soviet biomedical research.

For the first time, a crew had been operating aboard a Soviet orbital station long enough to undertake a major program of astronomical and Earth observation research, and the experience gained from the Salyut 4 missions would form the basis of the work undertaken by later Soviet civilian orbital stations.

The mission of Soyuz 20 was mainly technological in nature, to determine if the spacecraft could endure three months in orbit, but the opportunity was taken to fly some biological specimens. This allowed the Soviets to acquire biomedical data about extended space missions (at that time the 84-day mission of the final Skylab crew was the only source of biomedical data for this duration of space mission).

Context

The launch failure of Soyuz 18A was particularly unfortunate, coming only three months before the Apollo-Soyuz joint mission. Although the same type of launch vehicle had been flown on routine missions before the joint flight, the failure raised questions about the wisdom of the joint flight. The Soviets wanted to complete manned Salyut 4 operations as soon as possible because the station was scheduled only to support crews for the first seven to eight months of its flight.

In mid-July, the work routine on Salyut 4 was overshadowed by the forthcoming joint flight of the Soviet Soyuz 19 and the American Apollo 18. The United States questioned the Soviets' capability to control the two missions simultaneously and was informed that the Soviets had two control centers: Salyut 4 would be controlled from the older site, and the Apollo-Soyuz Test Project would be controlled from the newer Kaliningrad center. On July 14, it was announced that Soyuz 18B would be returning to Earth in the last ten days of July. At any rate, the Salyut mission was operating at an altitude of about 350 kilometers and the Apollo-Soyuz mission at 225 kilometers, so there was no chance of one mission interfering with the other. The orbit of Salyut would allow it to pass over the Apollo-Soyuz craft every two days, but there were no plans for joint observations with the two Soviet crews.

July 15, the day the Apollo-Soyuz spacecraft were launched, was a routine day aboard Salyut 4, beginning with detailed medical checks and exercises in orbit. The Soyuz 18B crew would be returning to Earth with about 50 kilograms of scientific results. The next day it was noted that a conversation had taken place between the Salyut 4 crew and the Apollo-Soyuz cosmonauts during the twenty-first orbit of the new spacecraft. The Soyuz 19 commander, Alexei Leonov, congratulated the "old-timers" aboard the space laboratory and informed them that he and Kubasov had just completed some minor repair work on a faulty television camera.

The successful completion of the Soyuz 18B visit to Salyut 4 allowed the Soviets to match the biomedical data which the Americans had gained from the three Skylab residences from 1973 to 1974. The Soyuz 18B mission performed solar, X-ray, and Earth resources observations, as well as atmospheric and biomedical research and technical experimentation.

Soyuz 18B remained the longest-duration Soviet manned spaceflight for more than two years, until Salyut 6 was in orbit.

The Soyuz 20 mission had two purposes: The first was to return biological data after three months in orbit, and the second was to man-rate the spacecraft for a three-month space mission. One assumes that the biological work must have been successful, but the success of the three-month man-rating of the spacecraft is doubtful. Certainly none of the Soyuz spacecraft flown to support Salyut 5 or Salyut 6 matched the Soyuz 20 duration (Soyuz 32 flew for more than one hundred days following the Soyuz 33 failure, but it returned to Earth unmanned), therefore, one might speculate that there might have been some problems on Soyuz 20 which were not serious enough for an unmanned flight to be terminated but could have caused difficulty on a manned flight.

Bibliography

Ezell, Edward Clinton, and Linda Neuman Ezell. *The Partnership: A History of the Apollo-Soyuz Test Project*. NASA SP-4209. Washington, D.C.: Government Printing Office, 1978. This book focuses on the Apollo-Soyuz Test Project but provides an overview of the Soyuz program from its early days to the flight of Soyuz 19. Excellent background reading for the Soyuz 18A and 18B missions. Includes a long list of references, several appendices, and many photographs.

Johnson, Nicholas L. *Handbook of Soviet Manned Space Flight*. San Diego: Univelt, 1980. Authoritative descriptions of the Salyut 4 orbital laboratory, the Soyuz 18A abort, and the Soyuz 18 occupation of the space station are provided. Suitable for high school and above.

Oberg, James E. *Red Star in Orbit*. New York: Random House, 1981. Gives a gripping account of Soviet spaceflight operations, stressing the impact of both internal and international politics on program evolution. Also discusses technological achievements. Photographs are included. Recommended for anyone interested in the Soviet space program.

_____ . *Uncovering Soviet Disasters: Exploring the Limits of Glasnost*. New York: Random House, 1988. Written by one of the foremost Western authorities on Soviet technology, this books examines the causes, effects, and politics of a wide range of Soviet disasters. Includes an account of the Chernobyl nuclear accident of 1986, as well as of the Soyuz 18A launch abort. Appendices provide disaster locations and a chronology.

U.S. Congress. Office of Technology Assessment. *Salyut: Soviet Steps Toward Permanent Human Presence in Space—A Technical Memorandum*. OTA-TM-STI-14. Washington, D.C.: Government Printing Office, 1983. This short text provides an overview of the Salyut space station program. It includes some history and details the Salyut's technical features and characteristics. Artists' renditions of the spacecraft are provided.

Phillip S. Clark

Cross-References

The Apollo-Soyuz Test Project, 132; The Salyut Space Station, 1233; The Soyuz-Kosmos Program, 1396; Soyuz 10 and 11, 1436; Soyuz 12, 1444; Soyuz 14 and 15, 1454; Soyuz 17, 1460; Soyuz 25, 26, and 27, 1482.

SOYUZ 21, 23, and 24

Date: June 22, 1976, to August 8, 1977
Type of mission: Manned military space station flights
Country: The Soviet Union

The second and last military Salyut to be manned successfully, Salyut 5 had three Soyuz spacecraft launched to it during its lifetime. Although it was only a marginal success, Salyut 5 was the culmination of the Soviet recovery effort.

Principal personages

BORIS V. VOLYNOV, the Soyuz 21 commander
VITALI ZHOLOBOV, the Soyuz 21 flight engineer
VYACHESLAV ZUDOV, the Soyuz 21 backup commander and Soyuz 23 commander
VALERI ROZHDESTVENSKY, the Soyuz 21 backup flight engineer and Soyuz 23 flight commander
VIKTOR GORBATKO, the Soyuz 23 backup commander and Soyuz 24 commander
YURI GLAZKOV, the Soyuz 23 backup flight engineer and Soyuz 24 flight engineer

Summary of the Missions

It was a year and a half after Salyut 3 was de-orbited that the next launch of a military Salyut was made. The time in between these Salyut missions was spent analyzing the intelligence, engineering, and scientific data that the Salyut 3 mission produced. It also gave the Soviets a chance to process the results and experiences of the civilian Salyut 4 mission.

Salyut 5 was launched from Tyuratam at 1804 Greenwich mean time (GMT) on June 22, 1976. The D-1 booster placed it into a 260-by-219-kilometer orbit, with an inclination of 51.6 degrees. Over the next thirteen days, it changed its orbit several times. Finally, on July 5, it reached a 274-kilometer circular orbit. Western space observers quickly identified it as a military Salyut. Its orbit was lower (250 kilometers versus 350 kilometers for a civilian Salyut), and it transmitted on a radio frequency previously used for Soviet reconnaissance satellites.

The first manned mission to Salyut 5 was launched on July 6. Soyuz 21 lifted off at 1209 GMT. The crew consisted of Boris V. Volynov (commander) and Vitali Zholobov (flight engineer). As with the Soyuz 3 crews, both members were military officers. (Conversely, on the civilian Salyuts, the flight engineer was always a civilian.) The next day, on its eighteenth orbit, Soyuz 21 docked with Salyut 5.

After the crew members boarded, they spent several days checking out the station's systems and preparing the scientific experiments. It was believed by Western observers that the flight was to be a long one—approximately ninety days. To study the effects of a weightless environment on the human body, the crew underwent a series of medical experiments while in space. These included measurements of blood pressure, temperature, circulation, respiration rate, electrical heart activity, and brain activity. To measure the crew's weight loss, a special scale was used. The crew had a regular exercise program, using a treadmill and special clothing which put stresses on the body which simulated those of gravity. Other biological experiments included studies of guppy and danio fish and their eggs to see how they adapted to weightlessness. The crew also grew seeds and made studies of the effects of radiation.

Another major area of research was materials processing. The crew studied the growth of crystals in a weightless environment. Another experiment looked at the forming of alloys in space. In a weightless environment, materials which do not mix on Earth can form alloys. The materials used included dibenzyl and toluene and a mixture of bismuth, lead, tin, and cadmium. The crew also soldered small-diameter stainless steel tubes and tested a pump which used no moving parts.

Other scientific work centered on studies of Earth's atmosphere. A hand-held spectrograph was used for these measurements. This broke the light into a spectrum, and the light and dark areas showed smoke, dust, and other particles in the atmosphere. An infrared scanner was used to measure the amount of water vapor in the upper atmosphere. Much of the crew's time was taken up by Earth resources studies—mineral deposits, fault areas, mud slides, proposed rail lines, and dam locations were photographed.

As with Salyut 3, the main emphasis was on military photoreconnaissance. During the early part of the flight, the crew could have observed a large military exercise—Operation Sevier. This involved air and naval exercises east of Siberia. Photography of targets in the United States and China was also possible. One indication of the flight's military goals was the lack of Soviet press coverage. Sometimes two or more days would go by without any mention of the flight. The coverage also gave few details. In contrast, during the Salyut 4 flight there had been extensive and detailed coverage of the crew's activities. One further indication of the military nature of the flight was the scrambling of voice transmissions to prevent eavesdropping.

As the crew began their eighth week in space, it appeared that the flight would continue for some time. On August 20, the Soviets reported that solar radiation was favorable for prolonged flight. There was, however, one disquieting development. On August 18, it was reported that ground controllers were transmitting music up to the crew to counteract the effects of isolation and so-called sensory deprivation, the lack of normal sights, sounds, smells, and other stimulants. At its worst, sensory deprivation can result in hallucination. Still, as of the morning of August 24, it appeared that the flight would continue. At noon, Moscow time, the Soviets suddenly announced that Soyuz 21 would come down that night. Volynov and Zholobov quickly packed experiment results and logs into the Soyuz 21. The crew set the Salyut 5's systems for unmanned operations, boarded the Soyuz 21, and separated from Salyut 5. Two orbits later, Soyuz 21 fired its retro-rockets and reentered the atmosphere. The capsule touched down at 1834 GMT, after 49 days, 6 hours, and 25 minutes in space.

The sudden announcement and the night landing were clear indications that the mission had been called down early. (It would have been three more weeks before a normal afternoon landing could be made.) The reason for the premature landing was not clear, but speculation centered on medical problems. A year later, the Soviets released data which indicated that the crew's condition had deteriorated in the last ten days of the mission. Another report stated that an acrid odor had started to emanate from the life support system. The crew was unable to fix the problem. The odor became intolerable, forcing the crew to leave.

Whatever the problem, the Soviets apparently believed that it could be corrected, and preparations went ahead for the launch of a second mission to Salyut 5. Soyuz 23 was launched from Tyuratam at 1740 GMT on October 14, 1976. The crew for this mission included Vyacheslav Zudov and Valeri Rozhdestvensky. Unlike the Soyuz 21 mission, the Soyuz 23 flight was to be a relatively brief one. The intended duration was only fourteen days. The Soyuz 23 maneuvered and closed on the Salyut 5. On its eighteenth orbit, the automatic rendezvous system was activated. Soon after there was a failure of the electronics, and the docking was canceled. (Zudov, many years later, referred to engine trouble as the cause of the failure.) Once more an emergency night landing had to be made before electrical power was exhausted. The crew shut down unnecessary systems and began radio silence. Retro-fire came on the thirty-third orbit and was normal. The weather in the recovery zone was appalling, with wind, snowstorm, and temperatures as low as −17 degrees Celsius. As the capsule descended under its parachute, it drifted toward Lake Tengiz. Soyuz 23 splashed down about 1.6 kilometers from shore after 2 days and 7 minutes in space. As the capsule bobbed in the freezing water, the crew tried to keep warm. Zudov curled up to conserve heat and tried to imagine that he was at the Soviet Black Sea resort of Sochi (known for its warm weather). Outside, divers struggled to put a line on the capsule. The first attempt failed. Amphibious vehicles could not reach it. Finally, a line was attached to the capsule, but a helicopter was unable to lift it out of the water. With the crew still on board, the capsule was dragged through the water and across a frozen swamp before reaching ground firm enough for the helicopter to land. According to one account, it took six hours for the recovery to be made. Zudov later said that the recovery took ten and a half hours.

The failure of Soyuz 23 cast doubt on the future of Salyut 5. When Soyuz 15 had failed to dock with Salyut 3, there was no attempt to fly another manned mission to the station. Salyut 3 had separated its film return capsule, had undergone engineering tests, and had been de-orbited. With Salyut 5, the Soviets were willing to take bolder measures. Four months after the Soyuz 23 docking abort, Soyuz 24 was launched on February 7, 1977, at 1612 GMT. The crew, consisting of Viktor Gorbatko (commander) and Yuri Glazkov (flight engineer), was able to dock successfully with Salyut 5. Departing from normal procedure, the crew members did not immediately board the station. Rather, they spent the first night aboard the Soyuz 24. This implied that there was some type of life-support problem. In any event, the crew boarded Salyut 5 the next day and began experiments. These were a continuation of the earlier work of the Soyuz 21 crew—medical tests, biological experiments, zero-gravity metal crystallization, Earth resources studies, and military reconnaissance. The mission (like that planned for Soyuz 23) was to be a relatively brief one.

On February 16, the Soviets announced that the mission had reached the halfway point. On February 25, the Soyuz 24 separated and landed. The crew had been in space 17 days, 17 hours, and 26 minutes. The next day, the recovery capsule was de-orbited. Salyut 5 continued to orbit until August 8, 1977, when it was de-orbited and allowed to burn up on reentry. This brought the military Salyut program to a close.

Knowledge Gained

Despite medical and hardware problems, the Salyut 5 provided considerable information on man's military usefulness in space. Judging by the Soviets' subsequent actions, one would conclude that the observation of Earth over a wide area of land and ocean was the most successful aspect of the mission. After the military Salyut program ended, the Soviets continued to undertake military activities on civilian Salyut stations. These included participation in Soviet air, land, and sea military exercises and the observation of the spread of smoke or gas over wide areas (apparently to determine what areas needed additional coverage). The Salyut crews have also worked with Soviet naval units for ocean surveillance and to establish an orbiting command post. Cosmonauts have also monitored the launch of Soviet intercontinental ballistic missiles and interception to warheads by antiballistic missiles. Ironically, one conclusion drawn from the military Salyut flights was that photoreconnaissance was better handled by unmanned spacecraft.

In the areas of science and technology, Salyut 5 made several contributions. The Soyuz 21 mission added more data to Soviet knowledge on the human reaction to prolonged weightlessness. The medical and hardware problems showed what to avoid. Salyut 5 was also the Soviets' first chance to perform materials processing experiments in space. For the short term, this allowed testing of the equipment and a first indication of the most promising research areas. For the long term, the Salyut 5 experiments opened the way to new alloys and medicines which were difficult or impossible to produce in the gravity of Earth.

Another experiment with great importance for the future was the test of the weightless fuel pump. Presumably meant for the Progress resupply spacecraft, this pump meant that a space station was no longer limited to the fuel supply that it carried at launch.

Context

If the mission of Salyut 3 marked the start of the Soviet space program's recovery, then Salyut 5 marked the end of its first phase. It was a long road with several failures and marginal missions. Yet through these problems, the Soviet space program gained experience and maturity. This growth can best be seen by contrasting Salyuts 3 and 5. When Soyuz 15 failed to dock, Salyut 3's usefulness was at an end. On Salyut 5, the Soyuz 21 flight was cut short, but the Soviets regrouped and launched Soyuz 23. When it failed to dock, the Soviets were still able to overcome this setback and launch Soyuz 24. The Soviet space program was able to salvage the activities which had been planned for the Soyuz 23 mission. Thus, even with the premature landing of the Soyuz 21 flight, the Salyut 5 was successful overall. The knowledge and experience gained set the stage for the triumph of Salyut 6 and, a decade later, for the permanent habitation of space.

In contrast to the resurgent Soviet space program, the United States' effort was starting a slow decline. This was not apparent at the time. Indeed, only a few days after Salyut 5 reentered, the prototype space shuttle, *Enterprise*, made its first glide flight. Yet even at this point, the technical problems, public and governmental apathy, budget shortages, and decay of management skills in the U.S. space program were present.

Bibliography

Furniss, Tim. *Manned Spaceflight Log*. Rev. ed. New York: Jane's Publishing Co., 1986. The book, updated annually, is made up of capsule summaries of the first 128 manned spaceflights. The vital statistics for each mission are listed—name, launch date, site, vehicle, flight type, flight time, spacecraft weight, and crew. The text describes the events of the mission.

Johnson, Nicholas L. *Handbook of Soviet Manned Space Flight*. San Diego: Univelt, 1980. A technical survey of the Soviet space program up to 1980, organized by type of spacecraft. Each spacecraft's design, test flights, and operational missions are described. Includes some material on the military Salyut, as well as numerous photographs and drawings of Soviet spacecraft and hardware.

Oberg, James E. *Red Star in Orbit*. New York: Random House, 1981. Popular account of the Soviet space program from its origins in the 1930's through the successes of the late 1950's and early 1960's, the setbacks of the early 1970's, and the long road back. Oberg is an aerospace engineer with the U.S. space shuttle program. Includes several pages on the military Salyut program.

Peebles, Curtis. *Guardians: Strategic Reconnaissance Satellites*. Novato, Calif.: Presidio Press, 1987. Survey of the history, technology, and political background of reconnaissance satellites and the profound impact they have on international relations. Includes chapters on the Soviet military Salyut program and the United States' Manned Orbiting Laboratory. Heavily illustrated. Includes an appendix listing all military space launches and nontechnical explanation of orbital mechanics.

U.S. Congress. Office of Technology Assessment. *Salyut: Soviet Steps Toward Permanent Human Presence in Space—A Technical Memorandum*. OTA-TM-STI-14.

Washington, D.C.: Government Printing Office, 1983. An overview of the Salyut program. This booklet includes a brief history of an early Soviet program and the Salyut's technical features, characteristics, activities, and impact on foreign policy. Contains several drawings of the various Salyut versions.

U.S. Congress. Senate. Committee on Commerce, Science, and Transportation. *Soviet Space Programs: 1976-1980*. Part 2, *Manned Space Programs and Space Life Sciences*. 98th Cong., 2d sess., 1984. Committee Print. One of a three-part series on Soviet space activities published periodically by the United States government. This particular booklet covers the Soviet manned program. Descriptions of all manned or related missions are provided, experiments are listed, and tables present statistical data. Also contains numerous drawings of Soviet spacecraft, giving design details and interior layout. Recommended for high school and undergraduate students.

Curtis Peebles

Cross-References

Biological Effects of Space Travel on Humans, 188; Cosmonauts and the Soviet Cosmonaut Program, 273; Electronic Intelligence Satellites, 361; Soviet Launch Vehicles, 742; Ocean Surveillance Satellites, 1085; The Salyut Space Station, 1233; The Soyuz-Kosmos Program, 1396; Soyuz T-15, 1562; Space Shuttle Missions 15 and 21: *Discovery* and *Atlantis*, 1751; Spy Satellites, 1937.

SOYUZ 22

Date: September 15 to September 23, 1976
Type of mission: Manned Earth-orbiting spaceflight
Country: The Soviet Union

The main purpose of Soyuz 22 was to test a newly acquired multispectral camera. Soyuz 22 was the first Soviet mission to use equipment not manufactured in the Soviet Union. It was also the last Soyuz flight before those spacecraft became dedicated support vehicles to the Salyut space stations.

Principal personages
VALERI F. BYKOVSKY, the commander
VLADIMIR AKSYONOV, the flight engineer
VLADIMIR A. SHATALOV, Chief of Cosmonaut Training
YURI V. MALYSHEV and
GENNADI STREKALOV, members of the backup crew
LEONID POPOV, a member of the support crew
ANATOLI FILIPCHENKO, the chief capsule communicator

Summary of the Mission

The flight of Soyuz 22 (*Yastreb*) was launched on September 15, 1976, just after the Apollo/Soyuz linking and just before the Soyuz missions became dedicated to the support of the Salyut space stations. The spacecraft's name, "Yastreb" (hawk), was taken from the call sign of Valeri Bykovsky, the commander, as was customary.

Bykovsky was one of the first cosmonauts ever selected. (Yuri Gagarin had also been a member of this very elite group.) Of the twenty chosen, only twelve ever went into space. Bykovsky had flown jet fighter aircraft and had been a parachute instructor in the Soviet Air Force. He was known to be an excellent pilot, able to make calm, split-second decisions in complex situations while still retaining a bold approach to flight.

In 1960, Bykovsky had volunteered to test the original space-training devices, including the isolation chamber and the gravity chamber. His first flight had been on Vostok 5, launched on June 14, 1963. Bykovsky and Valentina Tereshkova, the first woman in space, together set a new duration record which stood for two years. In 1968 Bykovsky was graduated from the Zhukovsky Military Air Academy and became Training Manager of the Yuri Gagarin Cosmonaut Training Center. Bykovsky later flew on Soyuz 31, which docked with Salyut 6.

Bykovsky was characterized by his fellow cosmonauts as possessing a fiery temperament. Yet he was also known to be a shy, pensive man, who was at times unsociable and self-centered. He was the fifth Soviet cosmonaut, and accumulated 20 days, 17 hours, and 47 minutes in space during his career.

Vladimir Aksyonov, the Soyuz 22 flight engineer, was graduated from the Mytishchi Engineering Technical School near Moscow in 1953. He was later graduated from the Chuguyev Air Force Officers' School. After spending four years as a jet pilot, Aksyonov became the head of the test flying department of Sergei Korolev's design bureau. In 1973, he was selected to be a cosmonaut. The Soviets tended to make cosmonaut selections by career groupings; the cosmonauts chosen in 1973 had all been engineers. Aksyonov was the thirty-sixth Soviet cosmonaut, amassing 11 days, 20 hours, and 11 minutes in space.

Soyuz 22 was a two-man mission which lasted 7 days, 21 hours, and 52 minutes. The spacecraft measured 7.5 meters in length, 2.72 meters in diameter, and weighed 6,800 kilograms; it was the backup spacecraft for the Apollo-Soyuz Test Project (ASTP), which had flown on July 17, 1975. Soyuz 22 had a total payload weight of 6,500 kilograms. Its instrumentation weighed 2,600 kilograms, the orbital module 900 kilograms, the descent module 2,750 kilograms, and the camera module 250 kilograms. The primary purpose of Soyuz 22, according to official accounts, was the testing of the prototype multispectral MKF-6 camera. This prototype was the very first non-Soviet equipment flown in space by the Soviet Union. It was made by Karl Zeiss Jena of East Germany. The camera's code name was Raduga, or "rainbow," and it had a tile-covered exterior. It was mounted where the docking equipment on the ASTP spacecraft had been.

The camera took photographs in six different spectra: 8,400 angstroms (infrared), 7,200 angstroms (infrared), 6,600 angstroms (red), 6,000 angstroms (orange), 5,400 angstroms (green), and 4,800 angstroms (blue). The camera used 70-millimeter film; each film cassette weighed 13 kilograms and contained 1,200 frames. The camera's resolution was purported to be no better than 20 meters, a degree of accuracy common to peaceful, Earth resources cameras. Military surveillance, on the other hand, generally requires resolution in centimeters. (Furthermore, Soviet military flights are usually identified as Kosmos flights.) It is possible, however, that the camera was capable of resolving much smaller images, perhaps as small as 10 meters, because of the spacecraft's low altitude. Indeed, it was reported by a member of an East German astronautical society that small cottages were visible in photographs taken 250 kilometers from Earth.

The orbit of Soyuz 22 (280 by 250 kilometers, with an inclination of 64.75 degrees) was calculated to take the capsule over East Germany, the camera's origin. On the fourth revolution, the inclination angle widened to 65 degrees, an excellent position from which to monitor North Atlantic Treaty Organization maneuvers in Sweden. This fired suspicions of espionage by Western nations. There were other possible military uses of the multispectral camera. It could have photographed the movement of bioluminescence from plankton, which could be studied to discover submarine maneuvers. Also, ship movements could have been monitored to assist in tracking methodology.

The MKF-6 prototype camera was designed to operate for only two weeks and was comparatively fragile. It required the use of both hands, which is difficult in a weightless environment. There were East German technicians in ground control to assist Bykovsky and Aksyonov with the camera testing.

In its function as an Earth resources camera, the camera was extremely useful. The results were studied by geologists, cartographers, soil improvement specialists, and agronomists. The camera was used to identify experimental croplands and to assist in the control of natural areas. The salinization, or swamping, of irrigated land was checked. Geobotanic mapping was performed, and the development of natural and anthropogenic processes was documented. Tilled land was studied to compare actual acreage with land management records. Monitoring of grazing lands and crop forecasting were also aided by the photographs. Cartographers would normally require one and a half years to acquire all the mapping information that the multispectral camera acquired in four or five minutes. Both aerial and ground photographs were taken at the same time as the Soyuz 22 mission for comparison studies and to assist with data interpretation.

The only other experimentation performed on Soyuz 22 was the Biokat work with seeds and fish, continued from the ASTP mission. ("Biokat" refers to the thermostatically controlled environmental capsules in which the experiments took place.)

Soyuz landed 150 kilometers northwest of Tselinograd on September 23, 1976.

Knowledge Gained

In the light of the normally conservative pace of the Soviet space program's development, the Salyut 6 space station, actually a modified Soyuz craft, included many innovative design changes. The twenty-two mission tests are thought to have been the catalysts for many of these changes. For example, a new minicomputer which constantly plotted the spacecraft's orbit was installed, and a communications uplink was established through a teletypelike printer, providing twenty-four-hour monitoring from Earth. Before Salyut 6, cosmonauts had to endure abnormal sleep patterns to maintain communications. This uplink was a major step forward for the Soviets in improving the biological functioning of the cosmonauts. Another system which may have been tested on Soyuz 22 was a unified fuel system; in this system, both the high-thrust maneuvering engines and the low-thrust altitude engines could use the same fuel, allowing for refueling at the same time.

Other innovations were a new type of heat radiator, a shower, an air processing unit, and medical monitoring devices. Also added were a "lower body negative pressure suit," to improve circulation, and a treadmill and bicycle for exercise. Clearly, much effort was made to maintain the health of cosmonauts during longer duration flights.

Testing of the multispectral camera resulted in several modifications, such as the strengthening of its components and structure to withstand the stress of lift-offs and dockings. It was also reworked to allow for handling with one hand, enabling the cosmonaut operator to maneuver himself in zero gravity.

Context

The Soyuz 22 flight occurred during the dearth of American manned spaceflight following the ASTP mission, Apollo's last flight. In the United States, the Skylab program had ended and the shuttle program would take six years to develop. In general, the American space program operated on a "giant leap" basis—a period of ground-based scientific development resulted in a tremendous advance in space science. The Soviet program continually launched spacecraft with relatively small innovations in each flight. Yet Soyuz 22 appeared to be a troubleshooting mission.

According to one source, the Soyuz 22 flightplan may have included problem simulations to judge reaction times and the ability to devise solutions quickly. Aksyonov and Bykovsky may have simulated problems for the ground crew or vice versa. Aksyonov once stated, "A test pilot should not conceal anything. He must report everything to the earth. He is obliged to do so." This attitude, coupled with his background in engineering and testing new spacecraft, marks Aksyonov as an excellent test cosmonaut. For his part, Bykovsky bragged about his self-control and, in fact, reacted well in several difficult situations as a test pilot.

Following the ASTP mission, it was noted that the Soyuz instrument panel took on the appearance of the Apollo panel. It is possible that further innovations, resulting from knowledge gained during the ASTP mission, were tested on Soyuz 22.

Soyuz 22 was used as a test flight to verify the multispectral camera and to perform further experimentation with Biokat. Immediately following Soyuz 22, however, the many innovations introduced into Salyut 6 indicate that more than the camera had been tested. The unusual timing (the last free-flying mission in the midst of many Salyut docking flights) also indicates the experimental nature of the flight.

Bibliography

Chernushov, Mikhail. *Space World* O-9-178 (October, 1978): 31. Special correspondent Mikhail Chernushov reports from the Soviet mission control center on the new multispectral camera used in Salyut and the advances in photography it makes possible.

Froehlich, Walter. *Apollo-Soyuz*. NASA EP-109. Washington, D.C.: Government Printing Office, 1976. This small book gives the background history and effects of the Apollo-Soyuz linking. It explains the experiments carried on the flight, some of which were continued on Soyuz 22. Suitable for the lay reader.

Hart, Douglas. *The Encyclopedia of Soviet Spacecraft*. New York: Bison Books, 1987. A large, well-illustrated presentation of all Soviet spacecraft, manned and unmanned. It discusses each mission in a thorough yet succinct manner.

Hooper, Gordon R. *The Soviet Cosmonaut Team*. Woodbridge, England: GRH Publications, 1986. A comprehensive biographical study of the cosmonauts. The book attempts to piece together the history of early Soviet spaceflight, in the absence of detailed records. Interesting reading for a general audience.

Khabarov, Stanislaw. "Russian Report." *Space World* O-2-170 (February, 1978): 40. Discusses the Soviet mission control center and its interaction with Soyuz 22.

_____ . "Russian Report." *Space World* O-3-171 (March, 1978): 30. Discusses the two cosmonauts of Soyuz 22 and their capabilities and attitudes with respect to flight testing.

Makarov, Oleg. "Salyut: An International Spaceport." *Space World* P-4-184 (April, 1979): 15-17. The entire issue is devoted to Salyut 6, which followed the Soyuz 22 mission. The technical sophistication of the new generation of space station is emphasized.

U.S. Congress. Senate. Committee on Commerce, Science, and Transportation. *Soviet Space Programs: 1976-1980*. Part 2, *Manned Space Programs and Space Life Sciences*. Report prepared by Congressional Research Service, the Library of Congress. 98th Cong., 2d sess., 1984. Committee Print. A readable narrative and commentary, with an overview of manned space activities in the first chapter. One of the few sources available for complete, factual information on the Soviet space program.

Ellen F. Mitchum

Cross-References

SOYUZ 25, 26, and 27

Date: September 29, 1977, to March 16, 1978
Type of mission: Manned Earth-orbiting spaceflight
Country: The Soviet Union

The Salyut 6 space station provided a new spectrum of opportunities for manned operations in space: Long-duration missions by cosmonauts became feasible and productive, principally because the station could accommodate both manned visits and unmanned resupply missions during the primary crew's extended stay. After a disappointing beginning, the crews of Soyuz 25, 26, and 27 successfully demonstrated the value of these important new capabilities.

Principal personages
VLADIMIR KOVALYONOK, the Soyuz 25 commander
VALERI RYUMIN, the Soyuz 25 flight engineer
YURI ROMANENKO, the Soyuz 26 commander
GEORGI GRECHKO, the Soyuz 26 flight engineer
VLADIMIR DZHANIBEKOV, the Soyuz 27 commander
OLEG MAKAROV, the Soyuz 27 flight engineer

Summary of the Missions

A new era in the human efforts to live and work in space began with the launch of the first of the second-generation Soviet space stations on September 29, 1977. Salyut 6 (*salyut* is the Russian word for "salute") was designed for an eighteen-month life, with significant enhancements over preceding members of the Salyut family. The principal improvement was the addition of a second docking facility. Previous stations had only one such facility, located at the forward end. The presence of a second port, added to the aft end, would allow for both manned and unmanned transport craft to visit while the long-duration crew kept its ferry craft docked at the other port. This innovation made possible the resupply of the craft as well as visits by other cosmonauts to relieve the primary crew.

By October 9, Salyut 6 had reached its operational orbital altitude of about 350 kilometers. Two days later, at 0240 Greenwich mean time (GMT), Vladimir Kovalyonok and Valeri Ryumin were launched into space aboard Soyuz 25. (*Soyuz* is the Russian word for "union.") Their goal was to rendezvous with the orbiting station, board it, and begin their duties—conducting experiments on the effects of reduced gravity on themselves as well as on certain materials, photographing and observing Earth, and evaluating the performance of the new space station. A very smooth flight led to the rendezvous of Soyuz 25 with Salyut 6 on October 10, but the crew members were unable to dock with the space station despite several attempts. With fuel running low, and the Soyuz batteries capable of providing power for only about two days without receiving help from the Salyut systems, the cosmonauts were forced to abandon their efforts. At 0326 GMT, they were back on Earth.

The failure of Soyuz 25 to dock was a hindrance to the development of orbital operations for the Soviet Union. If the new craft could not be manned, it would be a major defeat. It was unclear if the fault was with the docking mechanism on Salyut 6 or on Soyuz 25 (since that part of the Soyuz spacecraft had to be jettisoned before the return to Earth). Soyuz 25 did not have enough fuel to try to dock with the aft port after failing to do so at the forward port.

On December 10, at 0119 GMT, Yuri Romanenko and Georgi Grechko lifted off from the launch facility in Tyuratam aboard Soyuz 26. Grechko was a specialist in the docking system, and space planners believed that his expertise might help in understanding the problem. Grechko and Romanenko successfully docked at the aft port at 0302 GMT on December 11 and were inside their new home within three hours. Before investigating the suspect forward docking port, the new tenants spent a week preparing Salyut 6 for occupancy.

On December 19, the crew conducted the first Soviet extravehicular activity (EVA, or spacewalk) in nearly nine years—and only the third in the Soviet space program's history. Using a new spacesuit with completely self-contained life-support equipment, Grechko inspected the docking unit. He was relieved to find that everything was in perfect condition, so the failure must have been with Soyuz 25's equipment. With the prospect for continuing operations with the new Salyut space station now very good, Grechko took the opportunity to inspect the outside of the craft. On the outside, he affixed the Medusa experiment, designed to study the effects of radiation in space on amino acids and other biologically important compounds. The samples would remain there, exposed to space, until Soyuz 29 crewmen recovered them in July, 1978.

The crew members settled into their new lives in space with tasks ranging from Earth observations to astronomical measurements to studies of their own adaptation to spaceflight. The interior of Salyut 6 was similar to earlier Salyuts, but some additions had been made to make the cosmonauts' stay more pleasant. The walls had been covered with bright, soft cloth, sound insulation was 50 percent greater than on earlier stations, and a shower had been provided. Twenty portholes were available for observation, providing the crew with ample opportunities to view their home planet. An exercise bicycle was mounted on the ceiling to help keep the crew members in good physical condition, and books, recorded music, and videotapes were available for their enjoyment. The cosmonauts also tried to cultivate a small garden, and they enjoyed watching tadpoles, aboard as part of a biology experiment on the effects of weightlessness on growth.

Unlike previous Salyut crews, Romanenko and Grechko lived according to a twenty-four-hour schedule. Earlier, crew schedules had been shifted to accommodate convenient communication opportunities with ground stations. This practice, inconvenient for the cosmonauts, was not continued on Salyut 6 because the strategic placement of tracking ships in the oceans provided increased communication coverage, and onboard recorders were available to store data until a ground-based receiver was within communication range.

The cosmonauts' stay in orbit would be limited, however, because the Soyuz (used for the return to Earth) could not be reactivated safely after more than ninety days in space. Also, supplies would eventually be depleted. With the confidence that the forward docking port was functional, Vladimir Dzhanibekov and Oleg Makarov were launched in Soyuz 27 at 1226 GMT on January 10, 1978. They docked at that port at 1406 GMT the next day, while Romanenko and Grechko waited safely in their own Soyuz in case of problems. The visitors delivered letters, newspapers, books, and research equipment to Romanenko and Grechko and spent five days on board conducting experiments with their hosts.

The Soyuz 26/Salyut 6/Soyuz 27 complex was 29 meters long, and it weighed more than 32 metric tons. In order to test the stability and dynamics of this orbital assembly, the crew engaged in the "resonance" experiment. While they jumped on their exercise treadmill, sensors throughout the complex measured its vibrations.

Before leaving, Dzhanibekov and Makarov transferred their custom-contoured couches from Soyuz 27 to Soyuz 26. They landed on Earth in the older craft on January 16 at 1119 GMT, leaving the fresher Soyuz 27 for the crew still in space.

Another very important event came a few days later. On January 20 at 0823 GMT, Progress 1 was launched. For two days it pursued Salyut 6. The modified, unmanned Soyuz docked at the aft port (vacated when Soyuz 26 was returned to Earth) on January 22 at 1012 GMT. The first of a family of resupply craft, Progress 1 carried 907.2 kilograms of propellant for Salyut 6 and 1,179.36 kilograms of cargo. Since a cosmonaut uses up to 30 kilograms of expendables per day, the value of having the resupply capability is evident. The crew spent nine days unloading the mail, newspapers, air and water filters, food (including fresh fruit—a welcome change from dehydrated and canned food), water, clothing, and scientific equipment. Progress also replaced some of the air lost during the EVA and during routine use of the onboard air lock for trash disposal.

The new propulsion system design in Salyut 6 allowed for in-orbit refueling. On February 2 and 3, Progress pumped its supply of propellants into Salyut's storage tanks. This first-ever orbital refueling ensured that Salyut 6 could continue its mission. In still another valuable service, the engines on Progress 1 were used to raise the orbit of the docked assembly on February 5. Before undocking the Progress, Romanenko and Grechko filled it with trash and old equipment. It was commanded to leave at 0553 GMT on February 6 and burned up over the Pacific Ocean two days later.

On March 3, Soyuz 28 docked with Salyut 6. The crew members, Alexei Gubarev and Czechoslovakian "guest cosmonaut" Vladimir Remek, spent a week with the experienced inhabitants of the station conducting experiments and celebrating the political aspects of this first Interkosmos flight with a cosmonaut from another Soviet Bloc nation. In another example of the value of visiting crews, Soyuz 28 brought some photographs of Earth that Romanenko and Grechko had taken earlier.

The Soyuz 27 crew had returned the film to Earth; after it had been developed, samples were returned to the photographers in orbit so they could complete their coverage of ground targets. The visitors departed on March 10, carrying with them data from experiments and photographic observations conducted by the crew.

In preparation for their own return from this long-duration mission, Romanenko and Grechko began several days of intensive exercise and medical examinations. Having surpassed the Skylab endurance record of eighty-four days on March 4, the condition of the crew upon returning was of great interest and great concern. The cosmonauts spent several days "mothballing" Salyut 6 and undocked Soyuz 27 at 0800 GMT on March 16, after having lived there for about ninety-five days. They landed on Earth at 1119 GMT, establishing a new space endurance record of 96 days and 10 hours.

Knowledge Gained

While on board Salyut 6, the crews conducted many experiments to learn more about living and working in space. The benefits of conducting research from space orbit were recognized immediately. Photographs of Earth taken with a large camera supplied by East Germany allowed for detailed studies of Earth in different wavelengths of light. Each photograph covered an area 225 kilometers by 155 kilometers, and overlapping coverage allowed the production of stereo images. These pictures, with a resolution of about 20 meters, are very useful for mapping, studying new geological features, and locating valuable mineral deposits. Their worth becomes apparent when one realizes, as one Soviet official noted, that 1 million square kilometers can be photographed from orbit in about ten minutes. To perform the same job with aerial photography would require several years.

There had been some uncertainties about the docking of visiting craft to the Salyut/Soyuz complex prior to this mission. Engineers were concerned that the joining of a third spacecraft to the others might lead to large stresses in the vehicles and cause structural damage. Although the resonance experiment did reveal that the large system bent and swayed under some conditions, the motion was not significant enough to cause important problems.

One of the instruments delivered by Progress 1 was the 23-kilogram Splav furnace. Connected to an air lock so that its excess heat would radiate into space, it was used to test welding and soldering techniques in the absence of gravity and to study the melting and crystallizing of a variety of metals. The cosmonauts were able to produce samples of mercury cadmium telluride superior to what can be achieved on Earth. This material is important in the manufacturing of infrared receivers for medical applications, geological prospecting, and military sensing.

The largest instrument on Salyut 6 was a 650-kilogram telescope with a 1.5-meter-diameter aperture. With twelve-power magnification, it was used principally to view Earth's atmosphere to learn more about ozone and other constituents. One surprising finding was the discovery of previously unknown emissions of long-wavelength radiation in the area of thunderstorm formations. The telescope also was directed toward planets, stars, galaxies, the material between stars, and even the Moon during an eclipse. Viewing these sources in several wavelength ranges added pieces to the puzzles about these objects.

The cosmonauts themselves were the subjects of a variety of investigations, and their extended stay in space was an important test of the human species' adaptability to that unfamiliar environment. Late in the mission, the two men suffered headaches and unpleasant sensations near their hearts. Both problems were determined later to be caused by excessive fatigue. Nevertheless, unlike some later crews, they never quarreled during their long stay in the confined quarters. After they spent more than ninety-six days without the pull of gravity, that force felt uncomfortably strong to Romanenko and Grechko on Earth. They had exercised only about one-third as much as they were supposed to while in space, a fact that may explain their difficult adjustment. By March 31, they were completely readapted to the Earth environment; they had reattained their preflight physical conditions.

Context

Salyut 6 was the first space station with a means of being resupplied. Crew visits to Skylab and the earlier Salyut stations were limited in duration, both by the fuel supply for the station and by stored expendables such as air, water, food, and the components of the scientific equipment (film for cameras, for example). The new capability to deliver more of these essentials to orbiting workers made extended stays in space feasible. In later years, the Soviet Union would send repair equipment to orbiting crews, sometimes even including videotapes of procedures worked out by cosmonauts in simulations on the ground. Much equipment could be used on the orbiting station, since it was no longer necessary to launch all experiments with the space station. As equipment ceased to function or became outdated, replacements could be provided. Even small satellites could be included in a delivery, with the crew launching them through an air lock in the station. The long stays in the small stations would be made more bearable by the delivery of gifts from home and visits from fellow cosmonauts. In fact, as the duration of stays in space continued to increase, Yuri Romanenko himself would temporarily regain the record for space endurance by spending more than 326 days in orbit in 1987.

From these early long-duration missions, the importance of exercising regularly while in space became clear. The difficulty the Soyuz 26 cosmonauts had in re-adapting to gravity was attributed to their failure to adhere to an exercise regimen. The muscles normally used to resist the pull of gravity weakened when the cosmonauts spent long periods in space. Later, crews appreciated this important lesson, and strenuous exercise regimens on subsequent flights helped mitigate some of the effects of weightlessness.

Salyut 6, designed for eighteen months of use in space, went on to exceed all expectations. Cosmonauts would eventually spend more than 676 days on board the station, and its service spanned more than four years. It was commanded into a destructive reentry into the atmosphere on July 29, 1982, but shortly before that, on

April 19, Salyut 7 was launched. Salyut 7 and its successor, Mir (the Russian word for "peace"), incorporated changes and improvements based upon the lessons of the Salyut 6 work. Using many of the techniques first demonstrated on the early missions to Salyut 6, the cosmonauts on missions to Salyut 7 and the Mir spacecraft continued to pave the way toward humans' eventual permanent presence in space.

Bibliography

Furniss, Tim. *Manned Spaceflight Log*. Rev. ed. New York: Jane's Publishing Co., 1986. With a description of every manned mission into space through Soyuz T-15 in March, 1986, this book is entertainingly written and should be enjoyed by general audiences. It provides the essential facts from each flight and allows the reader to understand any flight in the context of mankind's efforts to explore and work in space.

Hooper, Gordon R. "Mission to Salyut 6." *Spaceflight Magazine* 20 (March-December, 1978). This series in a popular magazine provides an almost day-to-day account of the activities on Soyuz 25 through Soyuz 28. The chronological presentation is dry but complete. Suitable for the general reader.

Johnson, Nicholas L. *Handbook of Soviet Manned Space Flight*. San Diego: Univelt, 1980. This book provides a detailed description of the history of Soviet manned spaceflight through the third long-duration mission on Salyut 6. Suitable for college-level readers, it includes many technical descriptions and drawings of the spacecraft and their systems. The book also contains many references and an extensive bibliography.

Oberg, James E. *Red Star in Orbit*. New York: Random House, 1981. The author presents a history of the Soviet Union's manned exploration of space from the first flight to midway through the Salyut 6 program. Accessible to all audiences, the book includes accounts of spaceflights and some interesting descriptions of Soviet cover-ups in their space program.

U.S. Congress. Senate. Committee on Commerce, Science, and Transportation. *Soviet Space Programs: 1976-1980*. Part 2, *Manned Space Programs and Space Life Sciences*. 98th Cong., 2d sess., 1984. Committee Print. This authoritative source is part of an ongoing series on the history of Soviet space activities. Readers will find a wealth of detail on design and performance of the spacecraft and associated experiments. Many references are included.

Marc D. Rayman

Cross-References

Biological Effects of Space Travel on Humans, 188; Cosmonauts and the Soviet Cosmonaut Program, 273; Food and Diet for Space Travel, 454; Soviet Launch Vehicles, 742; Materials Processing in Space, 933; The Mir Space Station, 1025; The New Astronomy and the Study of Electromagnetic Radiation, 1066; The Salyut Space Station, 1233; The Skylab Program, 1285; Skylab 4, 1303; Soyuz 10 and 11,

THE SOYUZ INTERKOSMOS MISSIONS

Date: March 2, 1978, to May 22, 1981
Type of mission: Manned space station flights
Countries: The Communist Bloc nations

The age of international manned space travel was opened in March, 1978, when Czechoslovakian pilot Vladimir Remek became the first person from a nation other than the Soviet Union or the United States to travel into space. Over the next three years, citizens of nine other nations, all of them members of the Interkosmos consortium, made flights to the Salyut 6 space station.

Principal personages
ALEXEI S. YELISEYEV, the Salyut 6 flight director
KONSTANTIN P. FEOKTISTOV, the Salyut 6 chief designer
VLADIMIR A. SHATALOV, the chief cosmonaut trainer
VASILI LAZAREV, the chief Interkosmos trainer

Summary of the Missions

On March 2, 1978, at 6:28 P.M. Moscow time, the spacecraft Soyuz 28 was launched from the Baikonur cosmodrome in Soviet Kazakhstan for a scheduled docking with the Salyut 6 space station. The Soviet news agency Telegrafnoye Agentstvo Sovetskogo Soyuza (TASS) announced that the two crew members were commander Alexei Gubarev, a veteran Soviet cosmonaut making his second spaceflight, and cosmonaut-researcher Vladimir Remek, a Czechoslovakian pilot who became the first citizen of a nation other than the Soviet Union or the United States to venture into space.

In the seventeen years that followed the flight of Yuri Gagarin, thirty-three Soviet citizens and forty-one Americans had flown in space. Between March, 1978, and May, 1981, nine Interkosmos researchers would join the list, opening the age of international manned space travel.

Interkosmos was a consortium originally formed in 1966 by the Soviet Union to assist eight of its allies in the exploitation of space. The other eight members were Czechoslovakia, Poland, East Germany, Bulgaria, Hungary, Cuba, Mongolia, and Romania. At the time of Soyuz 28 in March, 1978, Interkosmos had launched seventeen unmanned satellites and space probes.

Plans for a series of manned Interkosmos Soyuz missions were announced in September, 1976, and pairs of pilots from Czechoslovakia, Poland, and East Germany arrived at the Gagarin Cosmonaut Training Center (located in Star City, about thirty kilometers from Moscow) in December of that year to begin training under the supervision of veteran cosmonaut Vasili Lazarev. Ten more pilots joined them in April, 1978, and two pilots from the Republic of Vietnam were added to the group in June, 1979, shortly after their nation joined Interkosmos.

On March 3, 1978, at 8:10 P.M., Remek and Gubarev docked Soyuz 28 with the orbiting Salyut 6 space station and joined cosmonauts Yuri Romanenko and Georgi Grechko, who had been aboard since December, 1977. The next day, March 4, Gubarev and Remek joined Romanenko and Grechko in a toast of cherry juice, celebrating a new space endurance record. (The previous record—eighty-four days in space—had been set by U.S. Skylab 4 astronauts in 1973-1974.) Remek spent the next six days supervising the operation of scientific, medical, and technical experiments developed by Czech scientists and doctors, primarily a materials processing (crystal growth) experiment called Morava. The cosmonauts also tested Extinktsiya, a system designed to collect data on the change in stars' brightnesses when they set behind Earth's night horizon, and Oxymeter, an experiment developed to study oxygen in human tissue in the conditions of weightlessness. Results of these experiments were returned to Earth by Remek and Gubarev on March 10, 1978, when they touched down at 4:25 P.M., 310 kilometers west of Tselinograd in Kazakhstan.

The next two Soyuz missions involved the expedition crew of cosmonauts Vladimir Kovalyonok and Alexander Ivanchenkov, who boarded Salyut 6 on June 15, 1978. Twelve days later, at 6:27 P.M. on June 27, Soyuz 30 was launched carrying Soviet commander Pyotr Klimuk and Polish cosmonaut-researcher Miroslaw Hermaszewski. Following a linkup with the Salyut 6/Soyuz 29 complex the next day, Hermaszewski and Klimuk went to work on a series of five Polish experiments and six others developed jointly by Soviet, Czech, and East German specialists. Perhaps the most notable of the experiments was Sirena, a forty-six-hour-long materials processing experiment designed to produce semiconductors. Hermaszewski and Klimuk returned to Earth at 4:31 P.M. on July 5, 1978.

The next Soyuz Interkosmos mission, Soyuz 31, was launched on August 26, 1978, at 5:51 P.M. The crew consisted of Soviet commander Valeri Bykovsky and East German cosmonaut-researcher Sigmund Jähn. In addition to overseeing more experiments in materials processing and Earth resources photography, Jähn and Bykovsky exchanged spacecraft with the main Salyut crew. Leaving Soyuz 31 attached to the station, the Interkosmos team boarded Soyuz 29, which had been in orbit for more than one hundred days, returning to Earth at 2:40 P.M. on September 3. This procedure was necessary to allow cosmonauts to remain aboard Salyut for missions lasting more than three to four months, since that was thought to be the safe operating lifetime of a Soyuz spacecraft. The exchange was not, however, performed on all Interkosmos missions.

The next Soyuz Interkosmos mission proved problematic. One day after launch from Baikonur at 8:24 P.M. on April 10, 1979, Soyuz 33—with commander Nikolai Rukavishnikov and Bulgarian researcher Georgi Ivanov on board—was in the final stages of approach to Salyut 6 when a malfunction occurred. Valeri Ryumin and Vladimir Lyakhov, the cosmonauts on Salyut, could only watch with frustration as the main maneuvering engine on Soyuz 33 suddenly failed. Ryumin would later write that he saw the exhaust flame from Soyuz 33 change colors. Soyuz 33 slid past

Salyut 6, its docking attempt ended, while mission controllers frantically tried to identify the problem.

Finally, Rukavishnikov and Ivanov were told to reenter at the next opportunity, using a smaller backup engine to maneuver out of orbit. This emergency procedure meant that the angle of the Soyuz 33 reentry would be steeper and the gravitational force on the cosmonauts greater. Complicating matters was the need for a return at night. Cosmonaut chief Vladimir Shatalov reassured the cosmonauts, and the reentry and landing at 7:35 P.M. on April 12, 1979, were successful.

The Soyuz 33 failure caused the postponement of the flight by Hungarian researcher Bertalan Farkas, which had been scheduled for Soyuz 34 in July, 1979. Soyuz 34 was flown unmanned to Salyut 6 instead.

Later Soyuz Interkosmos missions to Salyut 6 were free of incident. Soyuz 36, manned by Farkas and Soviet commander Valeri Kubasov, was finally launched at 9:21 P.M. on May 26, 1980. Joining cosmonauts Ryumin (on his second consecutive six-month mission) and Leonid Popov aboard Salyut 6 on May 27, Farkas supervised a slate of ten Hungarian experiments. One of these experiments was intended to produce the drug interferon. After successfully exhanging Soyuz vehicles, Farkas and Kubasov returned to Earth in Soyuz 35 at 6:07 P.M. on June 3, 1980.

Soyuz 37, manned by Soviet commander Viktor Gorbatko and Vietnamese researcher Pham Tuan, was launched at 9:33 P.M. on July 23, 1980, during the time of the 1980 Moscow Olympics. Pham Tuan, a veteran of the Vietnam War, was the first Asian to travel into space. There was some controversy concerning the publicity surrounding his mission: The Soviet news agency TASS claimed that Pham Tuan had shot down an American B-52 bomber in 1972, a claim which was quickly denied by the U.S. Department of Defense.

Pham Tuan and Viktor Gorbatko's technical experiments focused on Earth resources and the environment. The two men photographed flooding and erosion associated with the Mekong River in Vietnam, for example. The cosmonauts performed another vehicle exchange, returning to Earth in Soyuz 36 at 6:15 P.M. on July 31, 1980.

Cuban air force pilot Arnaldo Tamayo Méndez became the first black in space aboard Soyuz 38, which was launched at 10:11 P.M. on September 18, 1980. Méndez and Soviet commander Yuri Romanenko docked with Salyut 6 on September 19 and spent the next seven days operating some thirty experiments, many of them devised by Cuban scientists. Mendez suffered from spacesickness throughout much of the mission. The cosmonauts returned to Earth on September 26, 1980, landing at 6:54 P.M. in Kazakhstan.

Two Interkosmos missions remained to be flown, but by the end of October, 1980, Salyut 6 had been operating for three years, more than one year longer than its estimated lifetime. This situation caused some problems for Soviet space officials. A newer model of the Soyuz, called Soyuz T, had been tested in 1980 and was ready for manned operations. Only two of the older Soyuz vehicles remained, and they were configured for the remaining Interkosmos missions to Salyut 6. Abandoning the vehicles would be prohibitively expensive, and retraining the crews to fly on Soyuz T would cause a delay of one year or longer.

Therefore, during the summer of 1980, plans were made to launch a repair and refurbishment crew (Soyuz T-3) to Salyut 6 in November, 1980; if the cosmonauts judged that Salyut 6 could continue to operate for another set of visits, a new expedition team (Soyuz T-4) would be launched to serve as hosts for Soyuz 39 and Soyuz 40.

Soyuz T-3—with cosmonauts Leonid Kizim, Oleg Makarov, and Gennadi Strekalov—was the first three-man Soviet cosmonaut team since the ill-fated Soyuz 11 mission nine years earlier, during which a rapid depressurization had caused the deaths of all cosmonauts aboard. Soyuz T-3 was launched on November 27, 1980, at 5:18 P.M., and it docked with Salyut 6 on November 28. During the next two weeks, the cosmonauts repaired Salyut's temperature control system, the air-to-ground telemetry system, and the automatic refueling system. They also worked on the Splav furnace and the station's greenhouse. The cosmonauts returned to Earth on December 10, 1980, at 12:26 P.M., clearing the way for renewed operations.

On March 12, 1981, at 10:00 P.M., Soyuz T-4 was launched from Baikonur. The spacecraft carried cosmonauts Vladimir Kovalyonok (veteran of an earlier stay aboard Salyut 6) and Viktor Savinykh, a new cosmonaut who had been one of Salyut 6's designers and flight controllers.

Interkosmos missions resumed on March 22, 1981, at 5:59 P.M., when Soyuz 39 was launched. Jugderdemidiyn Gurragcha of the Mongolian People's Army, the son of a shepherd, was the cosmonaut-researcher, and Salyut veteran Vladimir Dzhanibekov was the commander. Gurragcha, an aerospace engineer, had been educated in the Soviet Union and was fluent in Russian, which allowed program managers to develop a more ambitious set of experiments for him to supervise. The experiments related to studies of Mongolia's natural resources and required the use of cameras already aboard Salyut 6, in addition to the new visual polarizational analyzer. Gurragcha and Dzhanibekov also tested a holographic television communications system before reboarding Soyuz 39, separating from the Salyut 6/Soyuz T-4 complex, and landing in Kazakhstan on March 30, 1981.

The final Interkosmos mission to Salyut 6 began at 8:17 P.M. on May 15, 1981. Dumitru Prunariu, twenty-eight years old and a senior lieutenant in the Romanian air force, was the cosmonaut-researcher. The commander was Salyut 6 veteran Leonid Popov. Several of the instruments Prunariu and Popov installed on Salyut 6—for example, instruments which would measure dynamic disturbances to scientific apparatus caused by the operation of other equipment aboard the station—were designed for automatic use, since it was clear that manned visits to Salyut 6 would soon be ending. Other experiments included Minidoza (a test of the influence of Earth's radiation belts on general background radiation), Kapillyar (a materials processor that could be used to manufacture superthin solar power cells), and Informatsiya (a series of tests designed to measure changes in the cosmonauts' mental functions before and after launch).

Prunariu and Popov undocked their Soyuz 40 spacecraft from the station at 1:37 P.M. on May 22; at 4:58 P.M. they had landed in the prime recovery zone in Kazakhstan.

Knowledge Gained

Several published reports have indicated that scientists of the Interkosmos member nations were disappointed in the results of their Salyut 6 experiments, but some disillusionment is inescapable: Delicate scientific experiments and manned spaceflight are often incompatible, as the American experience with shuttle-Spacelab missions has shown.

The Soyuz Interkosmos missions did, however, make it possible for smaller nations such as Cuba and Czechoslovakia to collect data from experiments designed by their own specialists and tailored to their own specific needs. These data were especially useful in the area of Earth resources; in fact, some space experts believe that Earth resources data can be valuable enough to justify the cost of an entire space program. Perhaps more important, these smaller nations began to build the scientific and technical infrastructure necessary for developing their own manned and unmanned space research programs.

Context

For a variety of reasons, the central one being the enormous costs associated with manned spaceflight, it has often been assumed that manned missions would ultimately become international. For example, early space planners envisioned manned missions to the Moon and Mars directed by the United Nations. Yet, from 1961 to 1978, all space travelers were citizens of the United States or the Soviet Union.

International tensions, cultural and technical differences, and even language barriers prevented such missions for many years. The nine manned Soyuz Interkosmos missions, however, proved that they were possible. During that time, a score of foreign pilots and engineers were welcomed into the community of the cosmonaut training center near Moscow. Some of these men had studied in the Soviet Union, but not all of them had. Some represented nations, such as Romania, that had had significant political disagreements with the Soviet Union.

The missions took place and succeeded in proving that citizens of different nations could, indeed, forget their disagreements when challenged by a common goal.

Bibliography

Bond, Peter. *Heroes in Space: From Gagarin to Challenger*. New York: Basil Blackwell, 1987. A well-researched book on the Soviet space program, this source emphasizes the activities of the various crews, resulting in a more personal account of the mission goals.

Cassutt, Michael. *Who's Who in Space: The First Twenty-five Years*. Boston: G. K. Hall and Co., 1987. Contains complete biographical entries on all the Interkosmos cosmonauts and their Soviet mission commanders.

Hart, Douglas. *The Encyclopedia of Soviet Spacecraft*. New York: Bison, 1987. A large volume describing all Soviet spacecraft known to exist in 1987. The mission activities are thoroughly covered. Appropriate for a general readership.

Oberg, James E. *Red Star in Orbit*. New York: Random House, 1981. This controversial and readable history of the Soviet manned space program discusses the Interkosmos missions, with emphasis on the training of guest cosmonauts and their flights to Salyut 6.

Turnill, Reginald, ed. *Jane's Spaceflight Directory*. London: Jane's Publishing Co., 1987. Updated annually, this text is an invaluable reference. It discusses the highlights of each of the nine Interkosmos missions to Salyut 6.

U.S. Congress. Office of Technology Assessment. *Salyut: Soviet Steps Toward Permanent Human Presence in Space—A Technical Memorandum*. OTA-TM-STI-14. Washington, D.C.: Government Printing Office, 1983. An excellent nontechnical presentation of the spacecraft's characteristics. The emphasis is on the overall Salyut program, rather than particular missions. Discusses the evolution of the spacecraft, its general purpose and design, and its place in the context of the entire Soviet space program. Illustrated.

Michael Cassutt

Cross-References

The Soyuz T Program, 1495; Soyuz 29, 1503; Soyuz 32 and 34, 1511; Soyuz 35, T-1, and T-2, 1517; Soyuz T-3 and T-4, 1524; Space Centers and Launch Sites in the Soviet Union, 1592.

THE SOYUZ T PROGRAM

Date: December 16, 1979, to July 16, 1986
Type of program: Manned Earth-orbiting spaceflight
Country: The Soviet Union

Through routine crew and equipment transfers between orbiting spacecraft and Earth, the Soyuz T program demonstrated the ability to maintain a permanent manned space presence. Improvements over the old Soyuz spaceship enabled cosmonauts to make automatic, semiautomatic, and manual space station rendezvous and dockings with greater comfort and safety.

Principal personages
KONSTANTIN P. FEOKTISTOV, the Salyut design engineer and a
    former cosmonaut
A. NUZHIDIN, the deputy technical director of Soyuz T
    splashdown test operations
V. KRAVETS, the Soyuz T mission deputy flight director
PYOTR KLIMUK and
ALEXEI S. YELISEYEV, cosmonauts

Summary of the Program

The Soyuz Transport (Soyuz T) program accomplished the first operational crew transfers in the history of the Soviet space station program, demonstrating the ability to maintain a permanent manned presence in space.

Following an initial unmanned test flight (T-1) on December 16, 1979, six two-man missions (T-2, T-4, T-5, T-9, T-13, and T-15) and seven three-man missions (T-3, T-6, T-7, T-10, T-11, T-12, and T-14) using Soyuz T spaceships successfully docked with the Salyut 6, Salyut 7, or Mir space stations after attaining Earth orbit. One three-man Soyuz T (T-8) failed to dock with Salyut 7; another, a two-man spacecraft (T-10A), suffered a launchpad abort, but the emergency escape system carried the two cosmonauts away from the burning rocket to safety.

Soyuz T outwardly resembled its Soyuz predecessor, which had first seen service in 1967. Soyuz T was composed of three main modules. In launch position, the uppermost component was the orbital module, containing the radar rendezvous system, life-support equipment, television instruments, and room for the crew to work and rest. Immediately below the orbital module was the descent module, with the seats into which the cosmonauts were strapped for launch, docking, and re-entry. Finally, the instrument-equipment module, or service module, contained the service systems which supported the spaceship during independent flight and when it was a component of the space station. On the pad, these components were encapsulated within a shroud, which protected them during launch and made up part of the emergency escape system.

The emergency escape system employed a single solid-propellant motor case with twelve rocket nozzles, each with a thrust of 6,650 kilograms, mounted in a tower atop the launch vehicle. In the event of a launchpad abort, the system delivered nearly 80,000 kilograms of thrust for five seconds, exerting more than ten times the force of gravity on the crew and pulling the protective shroud with encapsulated orbital and descent modules to an altitude of 1,000 meters and at an angle away from the booster rocket and detached service module. The next three events happened almost simultaneously. Four aerodynamic breaking panels unfolded around the shroud, twenty-five small, solid-fueled stabilizing rockets ignited at the top of the escape tower, and explosive charges separated the orbital module and shroud from the manned descent module, which dropped out and away from the accelerating shroud. The descent module backup parachute was deployed, the heatshield separated, and at just under two meters the landing rockets fired. For a launchpad abort, the landing took place about three kilometers from the pad. The system, when called upon to rescue the crew of Soyuz T-10A, had performed flawlessly.

The overall length of Soyuz T in flight was 7.94 meters, of which 6.98 meters made up the main body. The maximum diameter was 2.72 meters across the service module, while the diameter of the habitable orbital modules was 2.2 meters. The span of the extended solar battery panels was 10.6 meters. Soyuz T had a mass of 6,850 kilograms at launch, and the descent module had a mass of 3,000 kilograms upon landing.

The older Soyuz was not immediately replaced by Soyuz T. In 1980, Soyuz 35 and 36 followed T-1 on two-man flights to Salyut 6 before T-2's first manned flight of the series. Soyuz 37, 38, and T-3 followed that same year. In 1981, T-4 flew, followed by Soyuz 39 and Soyuz 40, the last of the older spaceships. Cited as the reason for this simultaneous use of the two Soyuz versions was the one-and-a-half-year training time required of Soyuz T cosmonauts.

Prior to the T-1 unmanned test flight, the descent module underwent extensive practice tests for cold-water landings in stormy seas. Test subjects practiced techniques for substituting their spacesuits for thermal protective suits, and they determined the amount of time cosmonauts could remain aboard a floating spacecraft with all life-support systems shut down. While no Soviet manned spacecraft had ever made a water landing, these extensive tests underscored the fact that an operational space transportation system must be capable of handling any eventuality. All cosmonauts underwent thorough training for Soyuz T water landings.

Soyuz T boasted several major improvements over its predecessor, including a new computer complex, unified propulsion system, and solar batteries. Secondary changes expanded data transfer and communications between the spaceship and the ground. Still more changes were made to enhance crew comfort.

The Soyuz T general-purpose computer complex freed the cosmonauts from the performance of routine operations, representing a significant improvement over the conventional Soyuz. The digital complex, which utilized integrated circuits and both long-term and operative memories, consisted of a special console and visual display terminal and could be operated in either the automatic or semiautomatic mode. Manual control of Soyuz T was possible, but the computer system maintained a standby backup condition.

In automatic mode, the computer complex determined, and displayed for the crew, flight conditions and ship attitude during the mission. For the first time, direct telemetry to the ground was also possible. With the older Soyuz, ground computers processed raw flight-mode data and relayed maneuvering instructions to the crew, creating time delays blamed for previous Salyut docking failures. The Soyuz T system performed all calculations required in rendezvous and docking operations with orbiting space stations on board, including the necessary thrust of the propulsion system, and ensured the proper execution of maneuvers. During attitude control, docking, or reentry operations, the computer was simultaneously capable of making its own decision with regard to operating reserve devices which regulated the ship's performance, onboard characteristics, and equipment. To facilitate flight-crew decision making, the complex was also capable of providing short-term forecasts of anticipated flight characteristics.

In semiautomatic mode, the computer requested crew permission to perform an operation, acting only after the cosmonauts issued the proper commands. Secondary operations were possible with the computer complex deactivated.

Soyuz T also employed a unified propulsion system similar to that designed into the Salyut 6 space station, allowing the different engines to draw upon a common fuel reserve. The primary and backup main propulsion system engine, used for orbit adjustment and reentry burns, continued to use a combination of unsymmetrical dimethylhydrazine (UDMH) as a fuel and dinitrogen tetroxide as an oxidizer, which burned on contact. Soyuz T, however, did away with the use of hydrogen peroxide to power the twelve low-thrust and fourteen medium-thrust "cold gas jet" engines of the attitude control system used for orientation and docking. Instead, these engines were converted to "hot gas jet" systems, drawing from the same fuel and oxidizer supplies as the main engine. Since the old hydrogen peroxide system had also driven turbines that pumped the fuel and oxidizer to the main engine, its elimination required the change to a more efficient and reliable pressurized tank system for feeding the engines.

The Soyuz T propulsion system modifications allowed for optimal use of the total fuel supply in the event of rendezvous and docking difficulties, while the older Soyuz, unable to tap incompatible main engine fuel supplies, had been compelled to terminate docking efforts and return to Earth once its supply of maneuvering fuel was exhausted. In addition, in the event of main engine failure the de-orbit burn could be accomplished using the low-thrust maneuvering engines instead. Finally, bringing the Soyuz propulsion system in line with that of Salyut 6 provided the same in-orbit fuel exchange capability shared by the Soviet space stations and their Progress tanker spacecraft.

Soyuz T-2 was equipped with solar batteries, allowing extended flights independent of a space station. Soyuz relied on battery power during space station rendezvous maneuvers and accumulators while docked with the solar-powered station, limiting solar batteries to flights not involving space station dockings. Soyuz T's routine use of solar batteries guaranteed that spacecraft power would not severely limit available docking time should difficulties arise.

A new television system with improved performance, a modernized radio-telemetric system for relaying higher data rates to the ground, and a new radio communications system for receiving ground commands were also installed.

Flying conditions for the cosmonauts were made more comfortable by better regulating the temperature and composition of the spaceship's atmosphere. Lighter, full-pressure suits with more flexible elbow, wrist, and knee hinge designs and an improved helmet affording better vision were also introduced.

A decision to separate the Soyuz T orbital module before, rather than after, the reentry burn realized a 10 percent fuel savings, while a layered window system, with the outer layer jettisoned after reentry, solved the Soyuz problem of windows so blackened by reentry heating that visibility during and after landing was impossible. Smoother landings were made possible by enlarging the landing rockets.

Soyuz T-15 was the first to visit Mir, and the last of this second-generation Soyuz spaceship. During its flight, the first of the Soyuz Transport Modernized (Soyuz TM) series was launched unmanned. T-15 separated from Mir and proceeded to dock with Salyut 7, while TM-1 docked automatically with Mir. After six days, TM-1 separated; after about one day of independent flight, it returned to Earth. About one month later, T-15 returned to Mir, where it remained until returning to Earth and ending the Soyuz T program on July 16, 1986. Manned Soyuz TM flights began in 1987 with one two-man mission (TM-2) and two three-man missions (TM-3 and TM-4) to Mir. Two additional three-man missions were launched in June (TM-5) and August (TM-6) of 1988.

Soyuz TM offered further improvements, including the new Kurs navigation and rendezvous system for forward-port space station dockings, an emergency rescue system with lighter parachutes which allowed for carrying an additional 200 kilograms of material to and 90 kilograms from the space station, a new communications system allowing more than one cosmonaut to communicate with the ground simultaneously, and a redesigned propellant system employing a metallic membrane in place of an elastic one between the pressurization gas and propellants to prevent leakage which degraded engine performance. There were problems as well, however. In September, 1988, TM-5 was a day late returning two TM-6 crew members to Earth following a pair of reentry aborts. First, the onboard computer misread stray sunlight striking an infrared sensor as a loss of orientation during retrofire and shut down the engine; later, the computer switched to an earlier TM-5 reentry progam, and again the engine had to be stopped. Nevertheless, Soyuz TM signified a continued Soviet commitment to frequent upgradings and improvements of spaceship design.

Knowledge Gained

The Soyuz T and TM spaceships, unlike their Soyuz predecessor, were designed primarily as part of a space station transportation system rather than for independent flight and scientific data collection. Their major contributions to the Soviet space program were in the areas of engineering and design. Scientific, military, and industrial research were conducted by the crews of the spaceships only after boarding the Salyut and Mir space stations, where prolonged missions could proceed.

The Soyuz T onboard computer system reportedly provided significant benefits for the Soviet electronics industry, in addition to the enhanced capability it provided the cosmonauts during complex rendezvous, docking, and reentry maneuvers.

While the crews pursued long-duration flights and investigated the medical and psychological effects of prolonged microgravity and isolation for periods in excess of six months, the systems aboard the docked Soyuz T vehicle, which represented the crew's only means of escape to Earth in the event of a space station emergency, were carefully monitored for deterioration. While the old Soyuz vehicles had been considered dependable for flight and reentry operations for periods of only thirty days, and later spaceships in the series extended this to between sixty and ninety days, it was learned that Soyuz T's superior fuel tanks and batteries extended this orbital lifetime to periods in excess of one hundred days. The discovery was the result of a series of misfortunes which forced Soyuz T-9 to remain in space for nearly 150 days. Shorter orbital lifetimes had dictated the frequency of the short-duration missions by visiting crews, who exchange their fresh Soyuz spaceships for the ones already docked at the space station and use the older spacecraft for their return flights. Reliable lifetimes of around 124 days would provide ideal relief-flight options compatible with space station launch window opportunities and medical findings which support flights of up to 120 days as an upper limit for crew effectiveness and well-being.

Soyuz T and TM afford the option of being flown with crews of two or three cosmonauts, but their target space station must be repositioned some 50 kilometers below its normal orbit of 370 kilometers or more for its booster rocket to deliver the added mass of the third crew member. Even so, the roomier cabin of the descent module permitted crews to fly in full pressure suits, a safety feature in the event of accidental depressurization.

One major contribution to international relations was the guest cosmonaut program, which resulted in citizens from other nations, primarily but not limited to Soviet Bloc nations, to fly short-duration resupply missions to the Salyut 6, Salyut 7, and Mir space stations. Guest cosmonauts from Czechoslovakia, Poland, East Germany, Bulgaria, Hungary, Vietnam, Cuba, Mongolia, Romania, France, and India flew missions through 1987, with considerable international publicity. Such missions led to live television coverage of select space launches, greater openness in discussing ongoing and future activities, and a new eagerness to involve other nations in Soviet space projects.

Context

Soyuz T and TM were increasingly more sophisticated versions of Soyuz, the third Soviet manned program, and demonstrated the continued Soviet commitment toward a permanent manned presence in space.

Soyuz was preceded by Vostok and Voskhod, programs which had seen the first man in space, the first flight lasting longer than one day which included sleep time in microgravity, the first joint flights of two spacecraft, the first woman in space, the first two- and three-man flights, and the first tethered extravehicular activity (EVA), or spacewalk. During the six Vostok and two Voskhod flights between 1961 and 1965, ten Soviet men and one woman flight-tested spaceship life-support, navigation, propulsion, and reentry systems while obtaining the first biomedical and psychological information on spaceflight and prolonged exposure to microgravity. In contrast, between 1962 and 1963 the United States flew six one-man Mercury missions, the longest lasting more than thirty-four hours. There were no American manned spaceflights between 1963 and the beginning of the two-man Gemini flights in 1965, four days afer Voskhod 2's return to Earth.

Between the last flight of Voskhod and the Soyuz 1 mission in 1967, the United States closed the gap with ten two-man Gemini missions which included EVAs, joint flights, a record two-week flight, and the first dockings with unmanned rocket stages which boosted one Gemini to a record 1,370 kilometers.

The years predating the Apollo Moon landing were a period of intense Cold War competition in many areas, and few activities had greater visibility than politically timed, prestigious space spectaculars. The early activities of the Soyuz program were closely tied to a Soviet effort to reach the Moon before the United States. Following the tragic death of cosmonaut Vladimir Komarov, when the parachute lines of his tumbling Soyuz 1 spaceship became tangled, further Soviet manned space activities were curtailed for another year and a half. This, together with technical difficulties with booster rocket development and control system difficulties with unmanned lunar spacecraft, delayed the Soviet lunar landing effort. Following Apollo 8's manned lunar orbital flight and Apollo 11's successful landing, an attempt based upon Soyuz or a manned version of the Zond lunar flybys would have been perceived as inferior at best and was abandoned in favor of the more attainable goal of improving manned space stations.

If Soyuz began as an unsuccessful effort to reach the Moon, it quickly achieved international recognition as the prime vehicle for Soviet human exploration of near-Earth space. The Soyuz T and TM space station transport vehicles reflected modifications which better served the role of Soyuz as a transport system between Earth and space stations.

Soyuz TM and Mir operations are expected to continue into the early 1990's, when the Soviet reusable shuttle and smaller spaceplane may also begin visits to Mir and to a new, larger space station expected to be constructed in the mid-1990's. Flights by the European Hermes spaceplane to Soviet space stations are also under consideration.

Bibliography

Oberg, James E. *The New Race for Space: The U.S. and Russia Leap to the Challenge for Unlimited Rewards*. Harrisburg, Pa.: Stackpole Books, 1984. A comparative examination of the space programs of the United States and the Soviet Union, as they were in the early 1980's and as they might become in the future, by an acknowledged expert on Soviet space activities. Detailed analyses of Soyuz and Salyut missions are presented, including specifics on little-publicized Soviet unsuccessful missions. Ardent space enthusiasts will find interesting chapters detailing technical specifics on the launch vehicles of the two nations and rare material on Soviet launch centers.

Riabchikov, Evgeny. *Russians in Space*. Edited by Nikolai P. Kamanin. Translated by Guy Daniels. Garden City, N.Y.: Doubleday and Co., 1971. Prepared by the Novosti Press Agency Publishing House in Moscow and written by a Soviet journalist, this insider's account of the Soviet manned space program includes reviews of the Vostok, Voskhod, and early Soyuz and Salyut missions, useful for placing Soyuz T in historical context.

Smolders, Peter. *Soviets in Space: The Story of the Salyut and the Soviet Approach to Present and Future Space Travel*. Translated by Marian Powell. New York: Taplinger Publishing Co., 1973. In this book, written by a Dutch authority on the Soviet space program, the early Soyuz and Salyut missions are detailed. Discusses the relationship between Soyuz and the Zond lunar probes during the race to the Moon. Suitable for general audiences, this text preceded the Soyuz T flights and is therefore of limited value. Illustrated.

The Soviet Year in Space: 1987. Colorado Springs, Colo.: Teledyne Brown Engineering, 1988. This seventh annual review of Soviet space activities is suitable for advanced high school and college levels. In-depth narratives are provided on topics ranging from launch facilities and launch vehicles to the vast array of Soviet military, scientific, communications, navigation, and scientific satellites. Each of the year's Soyuz TM missions to the Mir space station is detailed. Tables of all manned and unmanned Soviet launches for the year are provided, as well as an extensive list of references. Illustrations include charts and graphs as well as some photographs.

U.S. Congress. Office of Technological Assessment. *Salyut: Soviet Steps Toward Permanent Human Presence in Space—A Technical Memorandum*. OTA-TM-STI-14. Washington, D.C.: Government Printing Office, 1983. An analysis of Salyut, Soyuz, and Soyuz T operations which also provides valuable historic perspectives back to Vostok and Voskhod. Detailed illustrations of launch vehicles, spaceships, space stations, and the Progress cargo ship are provided, and assessments of Soviet control room, cosmonaut training, and launch site operations are made.

U.S. Department of Defense. *The Soviet Space Challenge*. Item 806. Washington, D.C.: Author, 1987. Color illustrations, graphs, and photographs highlight this brief overview of Soviet space operations—including Soyuz T, Soyuz TM, and

Mir—told mostly from a military standpoint. Suitable for high school and college levels.

Richard A. Sweetsir

Cross-References

The Apollo-Soyuz Test Project, 132; Cosmonauts and the Soviet Cosmonaut Program, 273; Soviet Launch Vehicles, 742; The Mir Space Station, 1025; The Salyut Space Station, 1233; The Soyuz-Kosmos Program, 1396; Soyuz 35, T-1, and T-2, 1517; Soyuz T-5, T-6, and T-7, 1530; Soyuz T-8, T-9, and T-10A, 1537; Soyuz T-10B, T-11, and T-12, 1544; Soyuz T-13, 1551; Soyuz T-14, 1557; Soyuz T-15, 1562; Space Centers and Launch Sites in the Soviet Union, 1592; The Soviet Spaceflight Tracking Network, 1877; The Development of Spacesuits, 1917; The Voskhod Program, 2170; The Vostok Program, 2177.

SOYUZ 29

Date: June 15, 1978, to November 2, 1978
Type of mission: Manned space station flight
Country: The Soviet Union

Soyuz 29 involved the second long-term occupation of the Salyut 6 space station. The mission set a new spaceflight endurance record (139 days, 15 hours) and proved the Soviets' ability to resupply a space station as often as needed with unmanned freighters.

Principal personages
VLADIMIR KOVALYONOK, the Soyuz 29 commander
ALEXANDER IVANCHENKOV, the Soyuz 29 flight engineer
PYOTR KLIMUK, the Soyuz 30 commander
MIROSLAW HERMASZEWSKI, the Polish Interkosmos cosmonaut-
researcher aboard Soyuz 30
VALERI F. BYKOVSKY, the Soyuz 31 commander
SIGMUND JÄHN, the East German Interkosmos cosmonaut-
researcher aboard Soyuz 31
ALEXEI S. YELISEYEV, the Salyut 6 flight director

Summary of the Mission

A two-man crew commanded by Soviet air force colonel Vladimir Kovalyonok, with civilian engineer-cosmonaut Alexander (Sasha) Ivanchenkov as flight engineer, lifted off from Tyuratam atop an A-1 booster at 11:17 P.M. Moscow time on June 15, 1978. Their Soyuz 29 spacecraft was guided by ground control to rendezvous with the Salyut 6 space station; it docked at the forward docking port on June 17.

Finding the station in good working order, the crew immediately began their experimental program of Earth photography, materials processing, and biomedical research. Kovalyonok and Ivanchenkov were placed on a schedule of five work days followed by two rest days. Each day typically began at 7:00 A.M. Moscow time with about an hour and a half allowed for personal hygiene, breakfast, and a checkout of the spacecraft. The morning activities also generally included one hour of exercise and two to three hours of experimental tasks, followed by a midday meal. In the afternoon, the crew devoted about four hours to experimentation and took another hour-long exercise period. The intent then had been to allow approximately three hours in the evening for the dinner meal, a review of the next day's schedule, and free time. In practice, equipment repairs were commonly scheduled during this time, and the work day often extended until midnight.

In spite of the workload, both men reported sleeping difficulties throughout the first six weeks. These problems eventually disappeared but were replaced by severe headaches, which continued throughout most of the summer. It was suspected that a buildup of carbon dioxide in the cabin was the cause of the headaches, and more frequent changes of the air purification canisters corrected this problem.

After less than two weeks aboard Salyut 6, the Soyuz 29 crew hosted the Soyuz 30 Interkosmos mission team consisting of veteran cosmonaut Pyotr Klimuk and Polish air force officer Miroslaw Hermaszewski, the second "guest cosmonaut" to go into space in the Interkosmos series. The visiting Soyuz craft arrived at the rear port on July 29 for an eight-day stay, during which the guest crew concentrated on taking multispectral photographs of Poland with the MKF-6 camera and on conducting a series of materials processing experiments.

Soyuz 30 returned to Earth only two days before the unmanned Progress 2 supply ship lifted off at 2:26 P.M. on July 7. The freighter docked at the recently vacated rear port of Salyut 6 at 3:59 P.M. on July 9, with a cargo of propellants, food, water, film, air, air filters, some new flight instruments, and the new materials processing furnace designated Kristall (crystal). It required a full week of work for Kovalyonok and Ivanchenkov to offload and stow the 1,300 kilograms of dry cargo and then load their accumulation of waste containers and cast-off equipment into the Progress craft. Meanwhile, mission controllers on the ground directed a complicated sequence of pumping operations to transfer nearly one thousand kilograms of fuel and oxidizer into the propellant tanks for Salyut's main engines.

On July 29, the two cosmonauts conducted a 125-minute spacewalk, which set a duration record for Soviet extravehicular activity (EVA). Kovalyonok and Ivanchenkov were awakened early to prepare for their spacewalk, and by 6:55 A.M., they had already exited through the special EVA hatch in the side of the forward compartment. Their primary task was to retrieve various collection and testing devices mounted on the exterior of the Salyut station, including experiments to detect the frequency of micrometeor impacts on the hull, to measure the amount of radiation encountered, to test the deterioration of various rubber and plastic materials exposed to space for long periods of time, and to determine whether there was a danger that bacterial life riding the exterior of an unsterilized spacecraft might survive long-term exposure to space and threaten to contaminate other worlds. The collection tasks continued even after Salyut 6 traveled into the night side of Earth. The men continued to work under the glare of floodlights, which were built into the station, but at one point, they decided to rest and switched off the lights to enjoy the view. Moments later, they were the awestruck witnesses of the passage of a particularly bright meteor into the atmosphere below them. Moving again to Earth's day side, the cosmonauts used a color video camera to return spectacular views of themselves and their homeland below. Shortly before the spacecraft went out of range of the tracking station, a request came from ground control to get back inside the Salyut. Kovalyonok replied, "We would just like to take our time, since this is the first time in forty-five days that we've gone out into the street for a stroll."

Progress 2 was allowed to remain docked until after the EVA in order to take full advantage of its capacity to resupply the air and remove trash. It was separated on August 2 at 7:57 A.M. and commanded into a destructive reentry flight path. At

1:31 A.M. on August 8, its replacement, Progress 3, was launched from Tyuratam. It docked at the rear port at 3:00 A.M. on August 10, with a cargo of dry stuffs and oxygen regeneration equipment, plus Ivanchenkov's guitar. Progress 3 remained docked until August 21, when it was cleared from the rear port to prepare for another Interkosmos mission.

Soyuz 31, under the command of Valeri Bykovsky, was heralded as being a part of the Soviets' recognition of the thirtieth anniversary of the founding of the German Democratic Republic. An East German air force officer, Lieutenant-Colonel Sigmund Jähn, was aboard as the cosmonaut-researcher. In reality, the primary justification for the flight was to exchange the aging Soyuz 29 spacecraft for a fresh vehicle, since flight rules forbade the use of a Soyuz craft after ninety days in orbit. Soyuz 31 docked near midnight on August 27, bearing gifts of honey, apples, gingerbread, lemons, peppers, onions, pork, and other foodstuffs selected to combat the loss of appetite that long-duration crews typically experience. In addition to a program of materials science experiments and Earth photography of interest to the East German scientific community, the two crews had to remove the specially contoured seats from each of the Soyuz craft and exchange them, since each man's seat was fitted specially to his body. When this was done, Bykovsky and Jähn returned to Earth in the spacecraft that had brought Kovalyonok and Ivanchenkov to Salyut 6 eighty days earlier.

The new configuration of Salyut 6 (with Soyuz 31 docked at the rear port) blocked further resupply missions since the Progress freighter could only transfer propellants through connections at the rear port. To rectify this problem the two cosmonauts entered Soyuz 31 on September 7 and undocked from the Salyut, backing off to a distance of two hundred meters. Flight controllers then rotated the Salyut end for end to present its front port to the waiting Soyuz. In about the time required to orbit Earth once, Soyuz 31 was redocked at the front of Salyut 6. This tactic became a standard procedure on subsequent missions involving an exchange of Soyuz vehicles.

At 2:09 A.M. on October 4, the Progress 4 freighter was boosted into orbit. It docked at the vacant rear port on October 6 with a cargo of propellants, food, air purification equipment, and special clothing, including fur-lined boots and new "penguin suits." The latter were so named because of the odd waddle of crewmen wearing them during training on Earth. The garment was designed with special elastic tensioning, which almost duplicated the body stresses imposed by Earth's gravity and forced the cosmonaut to use muscles that would otherwise have atrophied during the prolonged exposure to weightlessness.

Kovalyonok and Ivanchenkov had now been in orbit well over one hundred days, and it was considered a high priority that they stay physically fit as they stretched man's experience with weightlessness beyond previous limits. They were ordered to wear the "penguin suits" a large part of each day, even while asleep. The fur-lined boots were a concession to the crew's complaints of cold feet, a condition symptomatic of poor lower body circulation. To help correct that problem, they were directed to wear special low-pressure trousers, called Chibis pants, at all times to counteract the tendency for blood to pool in their upper bodies.

The unloading of Progress 4 was completed in two days. Propellant transfer operations began on October 12, and then the freighter's main engine was used to boost Salyut 6 into a higher orbit, where it could be safely "mothballed" when the Soyuz 29 crew went home. On October 26, Progress 4 backed away and entered a destructive reentry flight path.

Kovalyonok and Ivanchenkov returned to Earth on November 2, landing at 2:05 A.M. Moscow time after 139 days and 15 hours in space. Their egress from the Soyuz 31 was broadcast on Soviet television, and viewers saw the two crewmen reject offers of help as they climbed out of the spacecraft on their own. Although both men experienced a weight loss of three to four kilograms, a reduction of bone calcium and heart volume, wasted muscles and general fatigue, their medical condition was considered to be excellent, and they made an unexpectedly rapid readaptation to gravity.

Knowledge Gained

Soyuz 29's biomedical research focused on maintaining crew health over prolonged spaceflights. Revisions in the diet and physical conditioning regimens were made, increasing daily caloric intake from 2,900 to 3,200 and reducing the work week. It was noted that the crew's work capacity actually increased as the mission progressed, and the fact that they returned to Earth in better health than had previous crews was attributed in part to the men's diligent adherence to their daily two-hour exercise program.

Research into the human circulatory system's response to weightlessness included expanded electrocardiograph studies. Among the experiments not present in previous flights was dynamic electrocardiography, involving the continuous recording of an electrocardiogram for twenty-four hours. Soviet spokesmen claimed that this experiment considerably broadened doctors' understanding of the heart's function in microgravity. Studies were also made of the body's ability to produce red blood cells in space. The normal life of a red blood cell is only about 120 days. Kovalyonok and Ivanchenkov had functioned for more than 19 days on red blood cells which had all been produced in space. The red cells produced in space were smaller, but the change did not significantly affect their health.

Observations of Earth produced more than 18,000 photographs of the surface, most of which were made with the MKF-6 multispectral camera for agricultural, land use, and oceanographic studies. Late in the mission, it was also revealed that the crew was using a specialized mapping camera, which was able to produce precisely calibrated topographic photographs for geodetic purposes. These images were especially useful in industrial development activities, including designing the route of a major new railroad. Soyuz 29 photography was also credited with revealing some twenty-five previously undiscovered geologic formations likely to contain important new mineral deposits.

Materials processing experiments using the Splav and Kristall furnaces were, in the main, very successful. More than fifty experiments were completed in the areas of manufacturing new semiconductor materials, metallic alloys, coatings, and extremely pure glass.

The gigantic BST 1-meter infrared/ultraviolet telescope, which dominated the aggregate equipment module of Salyut 6, was used periodically for astronomical and atmospheric studies but experienced some continuing difficulties with its liquid helium cooling system. The crew obtained successful results, however, with other astronomical telescopes aboard the Salyut, most notably in the areas of X-ray studies of pulsars and studies of the Sun.

Not all the experimental results were positive. One notable failure occurred in the effort to raise fresh vegetables in a "space garden." The cosmonauts planted garlic, onions, cucumbers, wheat, lettuce, peas, parsley, and dill, but most of the plants refused to grow and none reached the stage of producing seeds. Also, spacecraft engineers wanted to know whether the linkup of a Salyut with a Soyuz at one end and a Progress at the other was structurally stable. Unfortunately, dynamic tests conducted in orbit tended to confirm that it was not as free of vibrations as had been hoped. This conclusion led to directives curtailing certain kinds of crew activities (such as using the treadmill) during the periods when the Salyut had spacecraft docked at both ends.

Context

Although it would not be long before Soviet cosmonauts set even more impressive endurance records, the Soyuz 29 mission may be regarded as a demonstration that the Soviet manned space program had experienced a coming-of-age. With successful visits from Soyuz 30 and Soyuz 31, and from Progress 2, 3, and 4, this sequence of missions proved that the hardware had finally begun to provide reliability to the program. Any intention of operating a functional space station must rest on the dependability of flight hardware and guidance capabilities: systems that must successfully execute the complex rendezvous and docking missions necessary to provide essential and timely logistical support to the space station. It is this achievement of the Soyuz 29 mission, more than any of its other successful aspects, for which it should be remembered.

From the standpoint of manned spaceflight experience, the Soyuz 29 mission is also a landmark event because it wrested from the United States the record for total man-hours in space. Kovalyonok and Ivanchenkov alone amassed enough spaceflight time on this mission to equal nearly one-third of all the combined spaceflight time of the U.S. astronauts.

It should not be assumed that the Soviet emphasis on long-duration missions is motivated primarily by political one-upmanship; rather, it is dictated by the clear and consistent objectives of maintaining a continuous manned presence in Earth orbit and conducting a manned mission to Mars as soon as is practicable. Even before the Soyuz 29 mission ended, the Soviet news agency, TASS, had stated, "The necessity of man's prolonged stay in weightlessness is dictated to a greater extent by the future tasks of space exploration than by the present ones."

Prior to the Soyuz 29 mission, both Soviet and American space medicine experts had expressed concern about the time required by the Soyuz 26 crew (Yuri Romanenko and Georgi Grechko) to recover from their ninety-six-day mission. Although both Kovalyonok and Ivanchenkov were said to have experienced a day or two of difficulty in talking and maintaining their balance, their recovery was so rapid that they were able to take a short walk on their second day back on Earth, and they played a short game of tennis within a week. This rapid recovery signaled two important things: The changes made in the daily regimen were constructive, and the physical deterioration experienced was not necessarily in direct proportion to the length of the mission. This latter point would be studied further in subsequent Salyut missions.

Statements by two spacecraft authorities may best summarize the Soyuz 29 mission. The Salyut 6 flight director Alexei Yeliseyev said of the mission:

We are studying the margin between difficult and impossible. One thing is already clear. The Salyut 6 flight has confirmed that we have all the technical facilities and experience for making piloted expeditions practically continuous.

In Washington, the Administrator of the National Aeronautics and Space Administration (NASA), Robert Frosch, warned Congress that the Soviets were well on the way to manning a space station continuously for a year or more, and he characterized that eventuality as "serious."

Bibliography

Bond, Peter. *Heroes in Space: From Gagarin to Challenger*. New York: Basil Blackwell, 1987. A well-researched chapter on the long-duration missions of Salyut reveals the competence of the Soviet space program for conducting extended space travel, and the ability of its space medicine to overcome the debilitating effects of long-duration exposure to microgravity. The book gives warm, human interest accounts of the missions and is enriched with the actual comments of the crewmen.

Hooper, Gordon R. *The Soviet Cosmonaut Team: A Comprehensive Guide to the Men and Women of the Soviet Manned Space Programme*. San Diego: Univelt, 1986. This work lives up to its subtitle, presenting eighty-seven detailed biographies that discuss the education, flight training, mission assignments, supporting roles, family status, and political involvement of every Soviet and Interkosmos cosmonaut known to the West. Most entries include good quality photographs, and many provide quotations from wives and others who know the subjects well. Background sections discuss crew assignments, time in space, facilities, inactive personnel, and more.

Johnson, Nicholas L. *Handbook of Soviet Manned Space Flight*. San Diego: Univelt,

1980. Presents details of the hardware, flight events, and scientific experiments for Soviet missions from Vostok 1 through Soyuz 34. It includes many line drawings and photographs not seen elsewhere. More than 150 pages are devoted to the Salyuts, with references.

Oberg, James E. *Red Star in Orbit*. New York: Random House, 1981. This is a highly readable and popular account of the Soviet space program from its beginnings through the Soyuz 35 mission. Emphasis is on the more dramatic and colorful moments. Appendices include brief biographies, rosters, and an annotated bibliography. It is weak in illustrations.

U.S. Congress. House. Committee on Science and Technology. *Astronauts and Cosmonauts Biographical and Statistical Data*. Report prepared by Congressional Research Service, the Library of Congress. 99th Cong., 1st sess., rev. ed. 1985. Committee Print. This book is of interest for its chapter of comparative data on American and Soviet manned missions. It presents crew rosters, comparative flight times, numbers of individuals and person-hours by spacecraft type, number and duration of extravehicular activities, and more. The biographical information is very sketchy. Photographs are large, but many depicting the cosmonauts are of poor quality.

U.S. Congress. Office of Technology Assessment. *Salyut: Soviet Steps Toward Permanent Human Presence in Space—A Technical Memorandum*. OTA-TM-STI-14. Washington, D.C.: Government Printing Office, 1983. This is an excellent nontechnical presentation of the Salyut spacecraft that emphasizes the program rather than particular missions. The design, purposes, and evolution of the vehicle are discussed, illustrations provide a good visual impression of the vehicle, and appendices include rare insights into the flight control instruments and facilities.

U.S. Congress. Senate. Committee on Commerce, Science, and Transportation. *Soviet Space Programs: 1976-1980*. Part 1, *Manned Space Flight*. Report prepared by Congressional Research Service, the Library of Congress. 98th Cong., 2d sess., 1984. Committee Print. Discusses the launch vehicles, supporting vehicles, political goals and purposes, and the administration of the Soviet space program. Appendix 1 includes translations of many Tass releases concerning the Salyut missions, plus significant information from Western sources.

——————— . *Soviet Space Programs: 1976-1980*. Part 2, *Manned Space Programs and Space Life Sciences*. Report prepared by Congressional Research Service, the Library of Congress. 98th Cong., 2d sess., 1984. Committee Print. The Soviets' steady progress toward achieving a permanently manned space station is depicted in detail in this authoritative document. All manned spaceflights from Vostok 1 through Salyut 6 and Soyuz T-3 are treated. An eighty-one-page analysis of Soviet space life science is especially helpful and extensively footnoted. The many line drawings are of good quality.

Richard S. Knapp

Cross-References

Biological Effects of Space Travel on Humans, 188; Cosmonauts and the Soviet Cosmonaut Program, 273; Food and Diet for Space Travel, 454; Soviet Launch Vehicles, 742; Materials Processing in Space, 933; The Salyut Space Station, 1233; The Soyuz-Kosmos Program, 1396; Soyuz 25, 26, and 27, 1482; The Soyuz Interkosmos Missions, 1489; Soyuz 32 and 34, 1511; Space Centers and Launch Sites in the Soviet Union, 1592; The Development of Spacesuits, 1917.

SOYUZ 32 and 34

Date: February 25, 1979, to August 19, 1979
Type of mission: Manned space station flights
Country: The Soviet Union

The third occupation of Salyut 6 was successful, although fraught with problems. The Soviets showed a high degree of adaptability and resourcefulness in overcoming the severe difficulties. The useful life of Salyut 6 was thus extended to make possible two more long-duration missions to the space station.

Principal personages
VLADIMIR LYAKHOV, the Soyuz 32 commander
VALERI RYUMIN, the Soyuz 32 flight engineer
VLADIMIR A. SHATALOV, the head of the Soviet cosmonaut
training program

Summary of the Mission

After the second crew had left Salyut 6, the orbital space station functioned for almost four months in an automatic mode. On February 25, 1979, at 1154 Greenwich mean time (GMT), Soyuz 32 was launched with a two-man crew of Vladimir Lyakhov and Valeri Ryumin as the station's third long-stay crew. At 1330 GMT the next day, Soyuz 32 docked with Salyut 6 at the station's forward port. This was the eleventh docking with Salyut 6, seven with Soyuz craft and four with Progress craft.

The original plans for Salyut 6 had been completed by previous crews, so in order to assess the continued usefulness of the station, the "Protons" (the radio callsign of the Soyuz 32 crew) completed an extensive check and evaluation of the station's instruments and equipment. On March 1, the station's orbit was raised by about 35 kilometers, using the propulsion unit of Soyuz 32, which required less fuel to maintain. By March 5, the crew had reactivated all systems and had begun to perform medical and biological experiments and repairs on equipment.

On March 12, 1979, at 0547 GMT, the unmanned cargo supply craft, Progress 5, was launched; it docked at the aft port of the Salyut 6/Soyuz 32 complex. It brought supplies of fuel, water, food, and clothes, a linen drier, bath shampoo, standby storage batteries and six carbon dioxide detectors, a black-and-white television for two-way communications, a new tape recorder, a new system for intercrew communications, an improved Kristall furnace, sets of films and experimental materials, and personal mail and gifts. This cargo constituted about 1,300 kilograms; 1,000 kilograms of fuel was also delivered.

The previous crew of the complex had reported some problem with one of the main fuel lines of the Salyut 6 propulsion unit, resulting from a damaged membrane, which separates the liquid fuel and the nitrogen gas in one of the three fuel tanks. Although the tank was not functional, the fuel would be needed to complete the mission. On March 16, the Salyut 6/Soyuz 32 complex was spun very slowly on its transverse axis in order to create a centrifugal force. This motion would ensure the separation of the fuel and gas in the defective tank. The separated fuel was then transferred to one of the other tanks, and the residue was moved to an empty container on Progress 5. The system was then purged and vented over the course of the next few days. On March 30, using the propulsion unit of Progress 5, the orbit of the space station complex was corrected after the refueling was completed. After two more orbital corrections, on March 30 and April 2, again using the Progress 5, the cargo craft was separated from the complex and deorbited at 0104 GMT on April 5.

On April 10, 1979, Soyuz 33, with a Soviet and Bulgarian crew, was launched. The spacecraft developed a major fault in the propulsion unit, and the planned docking with the Salyut 6 complex was canceled. The consequences of this failure affected the remainder of the mission for Lyakhov and Ryumin. The problem that most concerned everyone was the state of the propulsion system on Soyuz 32 (reportedly from the same manufacturing batch as that on Soyuz 33), and further planned manned visits were postponed as modifications were made.

On May 13, 1979, at 0417 GMT, Progress 6 was launched. The Progress ferry docked at the Salyut's aft port on May 15, at 0619 GMT. The cargo included air (some eighty kilograms) and food containers, oxygen regenerators, some sleeping accessories, electric lamps, and a receiving teletype. There were also computer replacements, medical equipment, film stock, new pressure suits, and samples for experiments. Additionally, some of the Bulgarian experiments and equipment that were to have been delivered by Soyuz 33 were included. The fuel tanks of Salyut 6 were filled, and the orbit of the complex was boosted higher, using the Progress 6, in order to improve communications between the station and Earth.

With Progress 6 still attached to the complex, the Soviets launched the unmanned Soyuz 34 on June 6, at 1813 GMT. Before being undocked on June 8, the Progress 6 propulsion unit was used again to correct the complex's orbit on June 4 and June 5. Once Progress had left the complex, Soyuz 34 was docked at 2002 GMT, on the same day. The extra time taken to carry out this docking was used to evaluate fully the modifications made to the Soyuz propulsion unit. On June 9, at 1851 GMT, the Progress 6 cargo craft was deorbited into the Pacific Ocean.

This high level of activity was continued with the separation of Soyuz 32 from the complex at 0951 GMT on June 13, and its successful recovery at 1618 GMT, the same day, at a point 295 kilometers northwest of Dzhezkazgan, U.S.S.R., completing a record 109 days in orbit. Soyuz 32 brought back a variety of completed experiments and materials, totaling some 180 kilograms.

In order to free the aft docking port, the crew boarded Soyuz 34 on June 14 and, at 1618 GMT, separated from Salyut 6, which was then rotated 180 degrees. Ninety minutes later, Soyuz 34 was redocked at the forward docking port, and the crew then reboarded the complex.

One June 28, the Progress 7 cargo craft was launched, and it docked at the aft port of Salyut 6 on June 30. Its cargo included equipment for the life-support system, film, scientific equipment, food and drinking water, clothes, plants, a vaporizer experiment (Isparitel), and a radio telescope, KRT-10, which had a 10-meter dish antenna when fully deployed. On July 3 and July 4, using the propulsion unit of Progress 7, the complex was again moved into a higher, 400-kilometer, orbit, suitable for some of the planned experiments.

The KRT-10 radio telescope was delivered to the complex folded like an umbrella. Over a period of days, the crew installed the telescope along the longitudinal axis of the Progress docking unit and the aft transfer tunnel of Salyut 6. At 0350 GMT on July 18, Progress 7 was separated from the complex, allowing room for the KRT-10 to be moved, automatically, through the open docking hatch and deployed to its full 10-meter diameter. Once installed, the crew made extensive use of it on the following days. Progress 7 was deorbited at 0157 GMT on July 20, and burned during reentry over the Pacific Ocean.

The first indication that the mission was approaching its end came on August 3 and was confirmed by a formal announcement on August 4. Only Earth observations with the KRT-10 remained to be completed. The crew began regular training with the Chibis vacuum suits, which were designed to help them prepare for their return to Earth's gravity.

The smooth completion of the mission was upset when, on August 9, at the end of the work with the KRT-10 radio telescope, an attempt was made to jettison it. Vibrations in the antenna caused it to become tangled with the protruding elements at the aft end of Salyut 6. After several unsuccessful attempts had been made to shake it loose, Valeri Ryumin went out onto the surface of the complex and, using the handrails, moved along the whole length of the station. After assessing the situation with the tangled antenna, Ryumin cut it free and then pushed it clear of the station. During the 1-hour, 23-minute EVA, various pieces of equipment were removed from the surface of the station to be returned to Earth.

On August 19, 1979, at 0907 GMT, Soyuz 34 was separated from the complex and returned the crew to Earth at 1230 GMT that day, 170 kilometers southeast of Dzhezkazgan. So ended the crew's record 175 days in orbit.

Knowledge Gained

An extensive program of scientific, technical, and medical and biological research and experimentation was completed during the 175-day flight. In order to accomplish these experiments, repair and replace the faulty equipment, and sustain the crew on this record-breaking mission, a total of 4,538 kilograms of freight was delivered to Salyut 6. Also as a result of the length of the flight, medical observations were performed on a daily basis. The Polinom 2 apparatus measured the functioning of the cardiovascular system, and the Chibis vacuum suit was worn for long periods to help maintain muscle tone and circulation. Noise levels were also studied after complaints from the crew.

Biological studies included plant and microorganism growth and the study of tadpoles and drosophila. A variety of vegetables were grown, some of which provided additions to the crew's diet. The Biogravistat apparatus had a centrifuge and a stationary area, where seed growth could be studied. Because drosophila flies complete a biological cycle in two weeks, heredity studies were possible.

Earth resources studies occupied much of the crew's time, even on rest days. The crew used binoculars to observe Earth. The MKF-6M and KATE-140 cameras were fixed on the station, while two other photographic cameras were portable. The MKF-6M produced multispectral pictures with a resolution of about twenty meters. The KATE-140 was a wide-angle, stereographic, topological camera for making contour maps. The Bulgarian Spektr-15 instrument made spectroscopic surveys in fifteen spectral bands. The BST-1M submillimeter telescope was used to record data in the infrared, ultraviolet, and submillimeter ranges. It had a 1.5-meter-diameter mirror, and one of its prime uses was the study of Earth's ozone layer.

Atmospheric studies were accomplished using the Yelena gamma-ray device. Other atmospheric studies were made using the Bulgarian Duga electrophotometer, which measured the intensity of optical emissions in the upper atmosphere at various wavelengths. Astrophysical studies were carried out using the KRT-10 radio telescope, delivered by Progress 7 and deployed at the aft end of Salyut 6. The telescope was used between July 18 and August 9. Some experiments were conducted in conjunction with a 70-meter radio telescope located in the Crimea. Observations of Pulsar 0329 and mapping of the Milky Way were two prime objectives. The 70-meter radio telescope was also used extensively for Earth observations.

There were two materials processing furnaces on Salyut 6, the Splav and the improved Kristall. On March 25, experiments to obtain semiconductor crystals were begun on the Kristall unit. These experiments were later continued on both units. A large number of different materials were used in the experiments, which produced monocrystals that were later returned to Earth. The Kristall furnace was designed primarily for experiments with glass. Further, a device called "Isparitel" allowed various metals to be sprayed on to substances by vaporizing and then condensing the coating. To minimize vibrations when these devices were in use, the space station was set in a gravity-gradient mode (engines switched off, and the complex aligned toward Earth, along its longitudinal axis).

Context

This flight was the third of the so-called long-duration missions aboard Salyut 6. The two previous missions had occupied the station for 96 days and 139 days respectively. The flight of Soyuz 33 would have ferried the fourth Interkosmos visiting crew for a seven-day mission. The duration of these missions had been steadily and methodically increased and eventually led to even longer missions. The lack of any adverse, long-lasting effects on Lyakhov and Ryumin showed that humans could remain in orbit for at least six months, and confidence was being built about the ability to achieve flights lasting years rather than months. Long-duration spaceflight capability is a necessity for interplanetary travel.

In keeping with Soviet reluctance to make the results of their space missions easily available, few details on the many experiments and researches have been released. According to the Soviet Earth resources Priroda Center experts, however, benefits from Earth resources photography and observations from space between 1978 and 1981 exceeded 56 million rubles in Central Asia alone. Several hundred organizations of twenty-two Soviet ministries and departments contributed in defining the Salyut 6 Earth resources program. The Soviets claim that it took ten minutes to photograph a million square kilometers, an area that would take several years to cover using aerial photography. Direct information was supplied to farmers about crops. Ocean current boundaries were defined and accumulations of plankton observed, directly benefiting the fishing industry.

The medical research undertaken on the crew generally produced positive results. The crew's reactions and the methods applied during their flight, together with their readaptation to Earth conditions, were seen as very encouraging. Some biological results showed that seeds grew better when under the influence of artificial gravity (provided during experiments). There were a number of problems with the growth of plants in that, although the plants grew, they did not blossom or bear fruit.

Materials processing work was a high priority throughout the Salyut 6 mission, including the Interkosmos flights. A great many materials were experimented with in the Splav and Kristall furnaces, and by the end of 1980, three hundred samples had been grown, and the furnaces had been fired 181 times. At least 186 Isparitel specimens were produced. Although no specific results have been released, much has been made of the need for monocrystals of high purity and of glass with very high optical qualities.

It was made known after the flight that, during the EVA, for thirty-six of their eighty-three minutes in open space, the cosmonauts had been static, with no work being done because they were in Earth's shadow. Only one-way communications, Earth hearing the crew, was possible. Lyakhov also had some difficulty reentering Salyut 6 at the end of the EVA. That this EVA was not performed under ideal conditions testified to the growing confidence the Soviets had in dealing with unforeseen situations.

Bibliography

Cassutt, Michael. *Who's Who in Space: The First Twenty-five Years*. Boston: G. K. Hall and Co., 1987. Contains biographical sketches of cosmonauts Lyakhov and Ryumin. Gives some information on the Soyuz missions to the Salyut space stations.

Clark, Phillip. *The Soviet Manned Space Program*. New York: Orion Books, 1988. The whole Soviet manned space program is covered in well-researched detail. The material is presented in an encyclopedic and easy-to-read style. The chronological survey covers the Vostok and Voskhod flights, Soviet attempts to put a man on the Moon, the Soyuz spacecraft, and the Salyut and Mir space stations.

Future developments, including a manned Mars mission, are discussed. Illustrated with photographs and line drawings.

Johnson, Nicholas L. *Handbook of Soviet Manned Space Flight*. San Diego: Univelt, 1980. A comprehensive and finely researched book covering all aspects of the Soviet manned space program. A thorough analysis of the program is presented. The book is noteworthy for its references to other published work and detailed tables of data. Well illustrated.

Oberg, James E. *Uncovering Soviet Disasters: Exploring the Limits of Glasnost*. New York: Random House, 1988. Written by a foremost American expert in the field of Soviet space programs, this book gives rare insights into many Soviet technological catastrophes. The author uses photographs to illustrate how some accidents were covered up. Well indexed.

U.S. Congress. Senate. Committee on Commerce, Science, and Transportation. *Soviet Space Programs: 1976-1980*. Part 2, *Manned Space Programs and Space Life Sciences*. Report prepared by Congressional Research Service, the Library of Congress. 98th Cong., 2d sess., 1984. Committee Print. Covers activity on the Salyut 6 and most of the missions to Salyut 7. Although the text is very detailed, the style makes the information accessible to a nonspecialist.

Ralph Gibbons

Cross-References

SOYUZ 35, T-1, and T-2

Date: December 15, 1979, to October 11, 1980
Type of mission: Manned space station flights
Country: The Soviet Union

Beginning with a launch on April 9, 1980, the Soyuz 35 mission extended the Soviet spaceflight endurance record to 185 days and showed that intensive and complicated flight management and operations tasks could be sustained for a prolonged period. At the same time, the Soviet Union was completing a series of test flights for a greatly improved Soyuz vehicle, the Soyuz T.

Principal personages
LEONID POPOV, the Soyuz 35 commander
VALERI RYUMIN, the Soyuz 35 flight engineer
VALERI KUBASOV, the Soyuz 36 commander
BERTALAN FARKAS, the Hungarian Interkosmos research-
    cosmonaut aboard Soyuz 36
YURI V. MALYSHEV, the Soyuz T-2 commander
VLADIMIR AKSYONOV, the Soyuz T-2 flight engineer
VIKTOR GORBATKO, the Soyuz 37 commander
PHAM TUAN, the Vietnamese Interkosmos research-cosmonaut
    aboard Soyuz 37
YURI ROMANENKO, the Soyuz 38 commander
ARNALDO TAMAYO MÉNDEZ, the Cuban Interkosmos research-
    cosmonaut aboard Soyuz 38

Summary of the Missions

Soyuz T-1 was launched unmanned from Tyuratam atop an A-1 booster at 3:30 P.M. Moscow time on December 15, 1979. The timing of this launch was unusual in that it placed the T-1 in an orbit 73 minutes behind that of Salyut 6. A conventional Soyuz could not have attempted a rendezvous under such conditions because of insufficient onboard electrical power. The rendezvous was accomplished on December 19, and the T-1 was guided by ground controllers to overtake Salyut 6 and move ahead, so that a docking occurred at the front port. The maneuver showed great confidence in the guidance capabilities of the hardware. Soyuz T-1 remained docked to Salyut 6 for some weeks as engineers studied the performance of the joined craft.

On March 27, on the heels of the T-1's return to Earth, the Progress 8 unmanned freighter was launched from Tyuratam, signaling that the Soviets expected to reoccupy the Salyut in the near future. It docked on March 30 with a cargo of propellants, replacement batteries, and start-up quantities of the food, water, air, and other materials required to reprovision the space station after more than seven months of disuse.

Soyuz 35 went into orbit at 4:38 P.M. on April 9. In the commander's seat was Major Leonid Popov, a thirty-five-year-old pilot-cosmonaut, making his first trip into space. Unexpectedly, the flight engineer, Valeri Ryumin, was bound for his third visit to Salyut 6. Having already flown on Soyuz missions 25 and 32, he should not have been in line for another mission, but the designated flight engineer (Valentin Lebedev) had broken his knee one month before launch, and the backup cosmonaut had been judged too inexperienced to replace him.

When Soyuz 35 docked with Salyut 6 on April 10, the space station had already been in orbit for more than two and a half years, and a considerable amount of repair work was needed to get the vehicle back into serviceable condition. Popov and Ryumin replaced all the ship's storage batteries, replaced one of the attitude control units, and did extensive work on the communications hardware, which was simply wearing out from use.

On April 26, the Progress 8 freighter undocked and was sent into a destructive reentry. The next day, Progress 9 lifted off with another cargo for Salyut 6. The Progress vehicles normally carried two months' worth of provisions, but Progress 8 had been burdened with so much repair hardware that another mission was needed immediately to provide the necessary consumables to last through the spring. Progress 9 undocked and reentered Earth's atmosphere in mid-May for a controlled reentry burn.

Popov and Ryumin received their first guests on May 27, when the Soyuz 36 Interkosmos mission brought Valeri Kubasov and Hungarian Air Force captain Bertalan Farkas to the rear port at 10:56 P.M. Moscow time. The four men worked together on a series of twenty-one flight experiments that included materials processing and an attempt to manufacture the wonder drug interferon. On June 3, the two visiting cosmonauts departed in the Soyuz 35 vehicle, leaving the fresh Soyuz behind. The next day Popov and Ryumin boarded the Soyuz 36 and executed the now-familiar maneuver to move it from the rear to the forward docking port. This left the rear port's special fuel transfer connections accessible to future Progress vehicles.

It was not another Progress, but the first manned Soyuz T mission that made the next call on Salyut 6. Soyuz T-2 was lofted into orbit from Tyuratam at 5:19 P.M. on June 5. Lieutenant Colonel Yuri Malyshev, the commander, and flight engineer Vladimir Aksyonov were the first cosmonauts to experience a flight in the greatly improved Soyuz vehicle. Among its features was an onboard computer much larger than in any previous Soviet spacecraft, and a substantial increase in the data displays needed for the crewmen to play an active role in piloting the craft. When the two ships had closed to only a few hundred meters, Malyshev saw that the orientation was an unusual one, and that the computer was aligning for a docking approach that had never been practiced. At this point he elected to overrule the computer and took manual control, guiding the Soyuz T-2 the last two hundred meters into the

Salyut's rear port on June 6. The new guests stayed only three days and conducted a limited number of experiments with Popov and Ryumin before returning to Soviet soil on June 9.

Between the cargo handling required to unload the Progress 8 and 9 ferries, the extensive repairs program, and the hosting of two visiting crews, the Soyuz 35 team had passed their first two months in hectic activity but not extremely productive research. After the departure of the T-2 crew, they were able to concentrate on the orbital science tasks, of which a series of materials processing experiments were especially important. The extensive photography of agricultural, geologic, and oceanographic targets also continued. Official reports scarcely mentioned the use of the large, 1-meter infrared/ultraviolet telescope, which was ostensibly used for astronomical studies but which was believed by many Western observers to have been employed for reconnaissance tasks.

Progress 10 was launched on June 29 and carried the usual assortment of essential consumables plus an American-made Polaroid camera requested by the crew, who wanted to be able to take snapshots of themselves and their surroundings. The two men were in excellent health and good spirits but were vexed by instruments that had become misaligned (a result of the prolonged exposure of one side of the spacecraft to the Sun), and they were dismayed that the windows had grown cloudy, resulting from nearly three years of abrasion by micrometeoroids. Ryumin, who was already the tallest of the cosmonauts, had "grown" when his body joints had relaxed in weightlessness, and he could no longer fit into his designated sleeping space. To solve this problem, he rigged a makeshift restraint that allowed him to sleep on the floor.

The next Interkosmos mission, Soyuz 37, lifted off on July 23 with Pham Tuan, a Vietnamese Air Force officer, serving as research-cosmonaut. The commander was Viktor Gorbatko, a veteran of two previous trips into space. A week-long program of observations, concentrating on Southeast Asia, included studies of the aftereffects of the defoliants used by American forces during the war, the progress of reforestation in areas destroyed by firebombing, and coastal erosion. On July 31, Gorbatko and Tuan returned to Earth in the Soyuz 36 craft. By leaving Popov and Ryumin the fresh Soyuz 37, they made possible an extension of the mission—already 114 days long—by up to eighty days.

On August 1, Popov and Ryumin executed the standard maneuver to transfer the Soyuz 37 craft to the front port, even though no Progress freighter was expected in the near future. In fact, the mission faced a dilemma because Salyut 6 was still well stocked with dry stuffs but was running low on propellants. Flight controllers did not want to conduct another resupply mission until the need for dry stuffs made it fully justifiable. Hence, to conserve propellants, the station was allowed to drift for long periods in the attitude it assumed when gravity alone controlled its orientation. In this "gravity-gradient" mode, most of the optical instruments could not be targeted, so the scientific program suffered a setback during this time. Because the Progress freighters were also used to carry away the accumulation of trash, the dilemma led to another problem inside the station. By mid-August, the cosmonauts had resorted to ejecting the accumulated trash through a small air lock, and radar tracking images of the Salyut showed an accompanying swarm of trash containers orbiting in formation with it.

The next Interkosmos crew was commanded by Yuri Romanenko and carried Cuba's first cosmonaut, Arnaldo Tamayo Méndez, into orbit on September 18. Tamayo Méndez was the seventh Interkosmos cosmonaut and the first black to enter space. The cosmonauts conducted experiments on the crystallization of sucrose in the weightless environment, and Tamayo Méndez studied the electrical activity of the brain. The Soyuz 38 crew returned to Earth on September 26, making a pinpoint landing in the recovery zone in Kazakhstan.

On September 29, the Salyut 6 station completed three full years in orbit, having made seventeen thousand orbits of Earth in that period of time. On October 1, the crew of Popov and Ryumin passed the 175-day endurance record set by the Soyuz 32 crew; Ryumin had broken his own record.

Progress 11 was finally launched on September 28 and docked on September 30. Little of the dry cargo was required by the station's present occupants but Salyut 6 was in dire need of propellants, and while pumping operations took place under ground control, the two crewmen unloaded cargo for the fourth time. On October 8, the Progress 11 engine was used to boost Salyut 6 into a higher orbit before the freighter was undocked.

Popov and Ryumin returned to Earth in excellent physical condition on October 11, landing at 12:50 P.M., after 184 days, 20 hours, and 12 minutes in space. Ryumin had gained four and a half kilograms and Popov had gained more than three kilograms of body weight during the flight, and both men were able to enjoy a walk in the park on the day following their return to Earth.

Knowledge Gained

Popov and Ryumin confirmed the biomedical results of the previous extended Salyut missions. It appeared that the loss of bone calcium from extended weightlessness levels off after about three months in orbit. The two cosmonauts' calcium losses were each about 8 percent, which is half the amount that is considered tolerable on Earth.

The Soyuz 35 crewmen were also the first space travelers to gain weight while in orbit, indicating that important discoveries had been made in obtaining the right balance between work, physical condition, diet, and rest. As flight director Alexei Yeliseyev put it, this crew enjoyed "a well-ordered life style." In part, he was referring to the success of a new work schedule that allowed the men one day of rest after every four working days. This schedule reduced fatigue and helped considerably in avoiding "burnout" on the exercise regimen. The men were also diligent in wearing special garments designed to combat circulatory and musculature problems in microgravity. These garments included the elastic tensioned "penguin suits" and low-pressure Chibis pants used during earlier missions, plus newly introduced wrist cuffs designed to improve circulation in the hands.

Substantially more emphasis was placed on materials processing than heretofore, and hundreds of samples were produced in the Splav and Kristall furnaces. Experiments designed to combine mercury telluroids and cadmium telluroids (compounds which do not mix in Earth's gravity) resulted in large, high-quality crystals, which have great potential for the semiconductor industry. Another very successful series of materials experiments involved the application of extremely thin metallic coatings on glass, plastic, and metal plates, using the Isparitel evaporator.

A significant amount of time was devoted to observation of the oceans, with the discovery that the open sea areas hold regions of concentrated marine life that were previously thought to exist only in coastal waters. Photography with the MKF-6 multispectral camera was concentrated on Soviet agriculture and spanned the entire growing season. The KATE-140 geodetic camera produced one thousand photographs in the ongoing search for new mineral deposits and in the surveying of routes for the new Baikal-Amur railroad line. Geologist Alexander Sidprenko, Vice President of the Soviet Academy of Sciences, credited these photographs with "the discovery of phenomena that otherwise would not have been found in 50 years."

Botanical experiments continued to produce mixed results. Efforts to get vegetable seeds to germinate were as unsuccessful as in previous missions, although the cosmonauts were able to get seedlings to grow. A greenhouse containing flowering plants produced an Arabidopsis blossom after five months, but the bloom was mysteriously seedless. A group of orchids in bloom when they were carried into space promptly dropped their petals in weightlessness.

Context

Beyond any specific scientific results or the impressiveness of Popov's and Ryumin's endurance, the great achievement of the Soyuz 35 mission is its inarguable demonstration that the Soviet space program could control the flow of hardware and personnel to and from orbit with high reliability on a relentless schedule. The mission series involved ten separate launches (Soyuz T-1, 35, 36, T-2, 37, 38, and Progress 8, 9, 10, and 11), five crew recoveries (Soyuz 36, T-2, 37, 38, and 35), and two Soyuz transpositions (36 and 37). All these flights apparently took place on schedule; some even occurred on adjacent days. Only very sophisticated program management and highly reliable equipment could have met this challenge.

The Soyuz 35 mission failed to receive as much attention in the free world press as had earlier long-duration flights. In part, this was a result of the Soviets' decision to encrypt most of the transmissions to and from its spacecraft. Beginning in 1979, Western observers noted that telemetry and voice signals were routinely being encrypted, even those involving spacecraft of a nonmilitary nature. Consequently, it became more difficult to get as much detailed information about Salyut 6 events and activities.

The Soyuz 35 mission also occurred at a time of heightened tension between the United States and the Soviet Union. One way in which this affected the attention paid to this mission is seen in the way the Soyuz 37 Interkosmos mission was reported. It was widely stated in the West that the mission had been timed to coincide with the Moscow Olympic Games (which the United States had boycotted). It was also suggested that the use of a research-cosmonaut, who was a former North Vietnamese fighter pilot and claimed to have shot down an American B-52 over Hanoi, was an attempt to embarrass the United States. In reality, the orbital mechanics of rendezvous missions involve a set of very inflexible time constraints, and the Interkosmos crewmen were being flown in the Soviet alphabetical order of their countries. Pham Tuan would have flown to Salyut 6 in late July, 1980, with or without the Olympics; it cannot be denied, however, that the political circumstances that coincided with operational requirements presented the Soviet propaganda machine with an irresistible opportunity.

Adding insult to injury, the Soyuz 35 triumphs came hand in hand with a series of disappointing setbacks for the U.S. space shuttle. Already far behind schedule, the latter was plagued by a series of problems with its liquid-fueled engines, and it had now been five years since the last American went into space.

The Soviets, meanwhile, continued to emphasize the ways in which the continuing Salyut 6 mission contributed to their goals of a permanently manned space station and a manned expedition to Mars. Both Popov and Ryumin agreed that longer flights were humanly possible and said the prospects of such flights were not disagreeable to them.

Bibliography

Bond, Peter. *Heroes in Space: From Gagarin to Challenger*. New York: Basil Blackwell, 1987. A well-researched chapter on the long-duration missions reveals the competence of the Soviet space program for conducting extended space travel, and the ability of its space medicine to overcome the debilitating effects of prolonged exposure to microgravity. Above all, the chapter emphasizes crew activities and gives a warm, human interest account of the missions.

Hooper, Gordon R. *The Soviet Cosmonaut Team: A Comprehensive Guide to the Men and Women of the Soviet Manned Space Programme*. San Diego: Univelt, 1986. This work lives up to its subtitle, presenting eighty-seven detailed biographies that discuss the education, flight training, mission assignments, supporting roles, family status, and political involvement of every Soviet and Interkosmos cosmonaut known to the West. Most entries include good quality photographs and many provide quotations from wives and others who know them well. Background sections discuss crew assignments, time in space, facilities, inactive personnel, and more.

Oberg, James E. *Red Star in Orbit*. New York: Random House, 1981. A highly readable and informative account of the Soviet manned space program, from its beginnings through the Soyuz 35 mission. This is a popular work that emphasizes the more dramatic and colorful moments. Appendices include brief biographies, rosters, and an annotated bibliography. It is weak on illustrative material, and its treatment of Soyuz 35 is superficial because of publication deadlines.

U.S. Congress. House. Committee on Science and Technology. *Astronauts and Cosmonauts Biographical and Statistical Data.* 99th Cong., 1st sess., rev. ed. 1985. Committee Print. This book is of interest for its chapter of comparative data on American and Soviet manned missions. It presents crew rosters, comparative flight times, numbers of individuals and person-hours by spacecraft type, and number and duration of extravehicular activities. Biographical information is very brief. Photographs are large, but many that depict the cosmonauts are of poor quality.

U.S. Congress. Office of Technology Assessment. *Salyut: Soviet Steps Toward Permanent Human Presence in Space—A Technical Memorandum.* OTA-TM-STI-14. Washington, D.C.: Government Printing Office, 1983. An excellent nontechnical presentation of the spacecraft's characteristics. The emphasis is on the overall Salyut progam rather than particular missions. Discussions include the evolution of the craft, its general purposes and design capabilities, and its place in the development and objectives of the Soviet space program. Diagrams and photographs provide a good visual impression of the vehicle, and an appendix includes rare insights into flight control instruments and facilities.

Richard S. Knapp

Cross-References

Biological Effects of Space Travel on Humans, 188; Cosmonauts and the Soviet Cosmonaut Program, 273; Food and Diet for Space Travel, 454; Soviet Launch Vehicles, 742; Materials Processing in Space, 933; The Progress Program, 1202; The Salyut Space Station, 1233; The Soyuz-Kosmos Program, 1396; Soyuz 25, 26, and 27, 1482; The Soyuz Interkosmos Missions, 1489; The Soyuz T Program, 1495; Soyuz 29, 1503; Soyuz 32 and 34, 1511; Soyuz T-3 and T-4, 1524; Space Centers and Launch Sites in the Soviet Union, 1592.

SOYUZ T-3 and T-4

Date: November 27, 1980, to May 26, 1981
Type of mission: Manned space station flights
Countries: The Soviet Union, the Mongolian People's Republic, and the Socialist Republic of Romania

The Soyuz T-3 crew, the first three-man crew launched by the Soviet Union since the tragic loss of the Soyuz 11 crew in 1971, repaired a vital component of the Salyut station to ensure its long-term use for the Soyuz T-4 cosmonauts. With T-3 and T-4, the Soviets hosted two international flights (with crew members from Mongolia and Romania) before closing down Salyut 6 for automatic flight.

Principal personages
LEONID KIZIM, the Soyuz T-3 commander
OLEG MAKAROV, the Soyuz T-3 flight engineer
GENNADI STREKALOV, the research engineer, Soyuz T-3
VLADIMIR KOVALYONOK, the Soyuz T-4 commander
VIKTOR SAVINYKH, the Soyuz T-4 flight engineer
VLADIMIR DZHANIBEKOV, the Soyuz 39 commander
JUGDERDEMIDIYN GURRAGCHA, the Soyuz 39 flight engineer, a citizen of the Mongolian People's Republic
LEONID POPOV, the Soyuz 40 commander
DUMITRU PRUNARIU, the Soyuz 40 flight engineer, a citizen of the Socialist Republic of Romania

Summary of the Missions

Soyuz T-3 was launched from Tyuratam at 5:18 P.M. Moscow time on November 27, 1980. The crew members were Leonid Kizim (commander), Oleg Makarov (flight engineer), and Gennadi Strekalov (research engineer). Soyuz T-3 was Kizim's and Strekalov's first space mission. Makarov was on his third flight, having previously flown on Soyuz 12 and 27 and, on April 5, 1975, on the first in-flight abort of a spacecraft, when Soyuz 18A failed to reach orbit. The Soyuz T-3 crew had almost included a veteran of the Soviet space program, Konstantin P. Feoktistov. He trained with Kizim and Makarov sixteen years after his only flight, on Voskhod 1, but was replaced by Strekalov late in the training.

Soyuz T-3 docked with Salyut 6's front port at 6:54 P.M. Moscow time, November 28. At the rear of the station was an unmanned cargo spacecraft, Progress 11, which had docked on September 28 after being launched by a Soyuz rocket two days before. The cosmonauts' work included flight tests of the Soyuz T-3 spacecraft, checks of Salyut's systems, and repair and maintenance work—as well as some minor science experiments. The cosmonauts found a small bundle of bread and salt left for them as a welcoming gesture by the previous occupants of the station,

Leonid Popov and Valeri Ryumin. The two cosmonauts would converse with the three men in orbit about the work needed to be done on the station during the mission. The three Soyuz T-3 cosmonauts found adapting to weightlessness difficult, and physicians told them to exercise from their second day on the station. It was later revealed that the cosmonauts were on a short, intensive flight, so health maintenance gave way to technical work.

In order to continue manned use of the station the Soviets needed to repair a hydropump block which regulated the temperature by circulating an antifreeze fluid through piping located around the station. The pump assembly had been working continuously for three years but had at last failed. Since the station had initially been expected to fly for only about eighteen months when it was first launched in 1977, the pump assembly had not been designed for replacement. The cosmonauts had to saw off metal supports and replace the pump with a new one which had fluid in it. The operation was tricky and potentially dangerous, so great care was required to accomplish the task.

The cosmonauts also had to examine and replace several electrical components and conduct a test called "Amplitude," during which a cosmonaut jumped up and down on the station's exercise track, creating vibrations which were measured by microaccelerometers. This helped to determine the rigidity of the station, among other things. The cosmonauts used a holographic camera to record the way salt dissolved in a liquid. The three-dimensional pictures produced by the unique Soviet/ Cuban-developed camera were to be studied on Earth. Other scientific work included tending plant specimens in special greenhouse-type containers on Salyut's walls. The men also conducted some metals smelting work in a small furnace.

Progress 11 was undocked on December 9 and commanded to a destructive reentry in the upper atmosphere on December 11, as planned. It had been attached to Salyut for seventy days, a record for the series. Soyuz T-3, with the cosmonauts aboard, was undocked on December 10 and landed at 12:26 P.M. Moscow time, 130 kilometers east of the town of Dzhezkazgan in the Kazakh Soviet Socialist Republic. Medical examinations at the site revealed that Kizim and Strekalov suffered from "tension" as a result of their lack of physical exercise in orbit, while Makarov seemed in better shape because of his previous experiences.

On January 24, 1981, Progress 12 was launched from Tyuratam; it docked with Salyut two days later. Once the Progress 12 was docked, the Soviets could proceed with a long-duration flight of two men to the station. First, however, ground controllers had to solve a problem with one of Salyut's three power-producing solar battery panels. Without all three working, the station would lose power and could not be manned. One panel had become stuck, but by carefully moving the station by automatic commands the controllers contained the situation pending launch of the crew.

Soyuz T-4 was launched at 10:00 P.M. Moscow time on March 12, carrying Vladimir Kovalyonok (commander) and Viktor Savinykh (flight engineer). Savinykh became humankind's one hundredth envoy to reach space. A geodesist by training, he became involved in hardware design and flight control activities before he was selected to fly in space. The two men had trained together for only four months, a shorter period than usual.

Soyuz T-4 docked with Salyut 6 at 11:33 P.M. Moscow time on March 13, and the first activities included switching on all the station's systems. Within hours, the cosmonauts had replaced the control for the faulty panel and restored its operation. After three days of reactivation work, the men opened the hatches between the station and the Progress cargo ship and began to unload it. This process was completed by March 19, and the cargo ship was undocked and commanded to a destructive reentry the next day.

The next launch saw Soyuz 39 start out from Tyuratam at 5:59 P.M. Moscow time on March 22 with a two-man crew. The commander was Vladimir Dzhanibekov, who was on his second flight. Mongolian cosmonaut Jugderdemidiyn Gurragcha served as the flight engineer. The cosmonauts docked with Salyut's rear port the next day at 7:28 P.M. Moscow time. Over the next seven days, the four men conducted a wide range of scientific experiments (many of which had been devised by the Mongolians) in medicine, Earth observation, materials technology, and astronomy. The flight of the Mongolian, and the other international flights, generated much publicity in the Soviet Bloc. One of the purposes of these flights was to demonstrate cooperation among the Soviet states.

Dzhanibekov and Gurragcha landed at 2:42 P.M. Moscow time on March 30 in the Soyuz 39 landing cabin at a fog-bound site some 170 kilometers from Dzhezkazgan.

The first job for Kovalyonok and Savinykh after the departure of the Soyuz 39 crew was to clean the station's walls with a damp cloth to prevent the buildup of bacteria, a standard housekeeping operation that occupied the time of the cosmonauts when they were not conducting scientific work or technical operations on the station's systems. The cosmonauts also exercised for two hours each day to keep fit and help their bodies combat the effects of weightlessness. In addition, much time was spent observing areas of Earth and taking pictures for later study to search for oil and gas deposits.

The second and final crew to visit Kovalyonok and Savinykh was launched at 9:17 P.M. Moscow time on May 14. Carrying two men, Soyuz 40 was launched from Tyuratam by a Soyuz rocket; it was the last of the old Soyuz ships to fly. The commander was Leonid Popov, and the flight engineer was the Romanian Dumitru Prunariu, twenty-eight years old and one of the youngest people to fly in space. The international crew docked with Salyut's rear port at 10:50 P.M. Moscow time on May 15, and the four men conducted a weeklong joint flight on the station— performing experiments in medicine, metals smelting, and astronomy. Soyuz 40, with Popov and Prunariu, landed at 5:58 P.M. Moscow time on May 22, completing the series of international flights by Soviet Bloc countries which are signatories to Interkosmos. During their flight, the men had replaced Salyut's forward docking unit to strengthen it for a planned experiment in which a 20-metric-ton module would dock automatically with the station after the cosmonauts returned to Earth.

After the international flight departed, Kovalyonok and Savinykh began preparations for their own return to Earth. They packed into their bags all the results of the work that they had accomplished and closed the Salyut 6 station down for the last time. The two men landed safely in the Kazakh Soviet Socialist Republic, 125 kilometers from Dzhezkazgan at 4:38 P.M. Moscow time on May 26, 1981. The Soviets announced the end of the manned operations of Salyut 6, which had housed five main crews and eleven visiting expeditions over the course of nearly four years.

Knowledge Gained

The Soyuz T-3 flight proved that the repair and maintenance of even the most complex systems in a manned space station could be accomplished—this, despite the fact that the main repair job, that of the hydropump of the temperature regulation system, was not originally planned at the design stage. For the seventy-five-day stay of the Soyuz T-4 crew, whose main purpose was to keep the station active for the visits of the Mongolian and Romanian spacemen, there were a number of experiments which were follow-ups of those performed during the previous expeditions. The two cosmonauts conducted a large range of observations of Earth's surface and atmosphere using spectrometers and ordinary cameras to record a number of phenomena, such as high-altitude clouds of micrometeorite dust (caused when small rocky particles from space collide with Earth's atmosphere and disintegrate or burn up). These observations were sufficiently complex and numerous to be detailed in a book written, in part, by Kovalyonok and Savinykh. During the flight, a Soviet commentator said that the crews of Salyut 6 had spent 60 percent of their time in orbit on these studies of Earth. It was the most important priority of the Soviet program.

The completion of the Soyuz T-4 flight brought to a close the most successful period of Soviet space achievements since the early 1960's. During the flight of the station, five principal long-term crews had manned it. They had been visited by eleven shorter-duration crews and twelve cargo spacecraft. The total time the station was manned was 676 days, and during three years and eight months in orbit some thirty-five dockings had been accomplished. There were 150 types of experiments performed on the station, with some thirteen thousand pictures of Earth being returned by fixed cameras on the station, two thousand with hand-held cameras. Two hundred technological experiments and about nine hundred medical and biological ones were conducted. The latter enabled the Soviets to understand the mechanisms of the human body's adaptation to weightlessness. In short, the Salyut 6 experience provided the Soviets with the first evidence that man could stay in space permanently.

Context

While the Soyuz T-3 and T-4 missions broke no records, the first of the two missions did illustrate the Soviets' growing confidence in in-orbit repair to extend the lives of space stations. The first in-orbit repair job on a space station was in

May, 1973, when the Skylab astronauts Charles (Pete) Conrad, Joseph P. Kerwin, and Paul J. Weitz put up a sunshade over the crippled station to lower internal temperatures after a heatshield had been ripped off during launch. The Salyut 6 station was designed for many of its internal instruments to be replaced, but the repair conducted by the Soyuz T-3 crew to the heat regulation pump was special; the pump had not been designed to be replaced. This repair was an illustration of the Soviets' advancing confidence in their space station operations.

In April, 1981, between the flights of the Mongolian and Romanian cosmonaut visitors to Salyut 6 (an example of the older ballistic spaceflight technology of expendable rockets and spacecraft which could not be reused), the Americans launched the reusable space shuttle *Columbia* for its first flight. The space shuttle was supposed to make space a routine habitat for humans by ensuring a safe, quick access. There were rumors that the Soviets were developing a space shuttle similar to the American one.

Over the next five years the Americans launched the shuttle vehicles over and over again, until the *Challenger* accident in January, 1986, stopped flights by the vehicles for more than two years. After the *Challenger* accident, the Americans admitted that it had been a mistake to develop the shuttle as their sole space launcher. They began to reopen the production lines of the so-called expendable launchers. The Soviets, meanwhile, relied on the Soyuz rocket to put the old Soyuz and new Soyuz T spacecraft into Earth orbit while apparently developing their own shuttle to be used in tandem with the expendable rockets.

Bibliography

Clark, Phillip S. *The Soviet Manned Space Programme*. London: Salamander, 1988. Absolutely essential reading for anyone interested in the subject. Written by one of the leading authorities on the subject, it combines scholarly analysis with superb illustration. Suitable for high school students and undergraduates.

Gatland, Kenneth. *The Illustrated Encyclopedia of Space Technology: A Comprehensive History of Space Exploration*. New York: Crown Publishers, 1981. Covers the development of astronautics up to 1980. This large-format book is copiously illustrated in color with many cutaways of Soviet space vehicles. The book ends with a chronology of the space age. Suitable for high school students and undergraduates.

Hart, Douglas. *Encyclopedia of Soviet Spacecraft*. London: Bison Books, 1987. Provides details of most of the Soviet Union's spacecraft, manned and unmanned. Well illustrated, with color and black-and-white shots. Carries only basic details but is well organized.

Johnson, Nicholas L. *Handbook of Soviet Manned Spaceflight*. San Diego: Univelt, 1979. Excellent coverage of all aspects of the program, with black-and-white illustrations. Johnson is one of the most authoritative authors on the subject. For high school students and undergraduates.

Oberg, James E. *Red Star in Orbit*. New York: Random House, 1981. Highly readable book by an author with great knowledge and insight into the Soviet space program. Provides many interesting anecdotes concerning cosmonauts, as well as a superb annotated bibliography. Illustrated with black-and-white plate photographs. Suitable for general audiences.

Riabchikov, Evgeny. *Russians in Space*. Garden City, N.Y.: Doubleday and Co., 1971. Described by one Western author as an account of the way the Soviets wished their space program was, this book is written by a leading Soviet author close to the cosmonaut team. Despite the obvious political nature of the book and omissions of serious problems since disclosed, it does allow a glimpse into the character of the Soviet program. Includes many interesting photographs in black and white.

U.S. Congress. Senate. Committee on Commerce, Science, and Transportation. *Soviet Space Programs: 1981-1987*. Report prepared by Congressional Research Service, the Library of Congress. 100th Cong., 1988. Committee Print. Provides detailed analysis of the events of the Soviet program and also describes the hardware and the political background. Earlier volumes provide still more extensive coverage. Although quite technical, the reports do provide suitable reading for a general audience.

Neville Kidger

Cross-References

The Salyut Space Station, 1233; The Skylab Program, 1285; The Soyuz-Kosmos Program, 1396; Soyuz 25, 26, and 27, 1482; The Soyuz Interkosmos Missions, 1489; The Soyuz T Program, 1495; Soyuz 32 and 34, 1511; Soyuz 35, T-1, and T-2, 1517; Soyuz T-5, T-6, and T-7, 1530; Soyuz T-8, T-9, and T-10A, 1537; Soyuz T-10B, T-11, and T-12, 1544; Soyuz T-13, 1551; Soyuz T-14, 1557; Soyuz T-15, 1562.

SOYUZ T-5, T-6, and T-7

Date: April 19 to December 10, 1982
Type of mission: Manned space station flights
Countries: The Soviet Union and France

The Soyuz T-5, T-6, and T-7 missions carried three cosmonaut crews to the orbiting space station Salyut 7. The two cosmonauts who manned Salyut 7 in 1982 did so for a record 211 days; they were visited by two short-duration crews, which included the first representative of Western Europe, a Frenchman, and the second woman to fly into space.

Principal personages
ANATOLI BEREZOVOI, the Soyuz T-5 commander
VALENTIN LEBEDEV, the Soyuz T-5 flight engineer
VLADIMIR DZHANIBEKOV, the Soyuz T-6 commander
ALEXANDER IVANCHENKOV, the Soyuz T-6 flight engineer
JEAN-LOUP CHRÉTIEN, the researcher on Soyuz T-6, a citizen of France
LEONID POPOV, the Soyuz T-7 commander
ALEXANDER SEREBROV, the Soyuz T-7 flight engineer
SVETLANA SAVITSKAYA, the researcher on Soyuz T-7 and the second woman to fly in space

Summary of the Missions

On April 19, 1982, the Soviet Union launched a 20-metric-ton space station into a low Earth orbit by means of a massive Proton carrier rocket from Tyuratam in the Kazakh Soviet Socialist Republic. The station—Salyut 7—was to be home in space to teams of cosmonauts launched over the next few years. Salyut consisted of a stepped cylinder some 13.5 meters in length with a maximum diameter of 4.15 meters. It had two docking units, one each at the front and rear. Electrical power was supplied by three large solar panel arrays, which used solar cells to convert sunlight to electricity. The station contained facilities for the regeneration of air and water. Food supplies and supplies of fresh water would be delivered by unmanned cargo spacecraft called Progress, which were discardable. Crews would arrive in Soyuz T spacecraft and dock either at the front or at the rear of the station. The cargo ships would use only the rear port, because that was where the fuel tanks and engines were located. The cargo craft could refuel those tanks.

The first cosmonauts to man the station were Anatoli Berezovoi and Valentin Lebedev. They were launched from Tyuratam on a Soyuz carrier rocket at 1:58 P.M. Moscow time on May 13, 1982. Soyuz T-5 docked at Salyut's front unit on May 14, and the two men crossed over into the station and began activating all the systems for supporting life on the station as well as the wide range of scientific equipment that had been launched in place on Salyut.

On May 17, the men interrupted this work to launch a small communications satellite called Iskra, which was used by Soviet radio hams for amateur communications sessions. The cosmonauts placed the small satellite into an air lock normally used to expel waste bags from the station and released it into open space. After two months of operation, the satellite reentered Earth's upper atmosphere in July, 1982, and was burned, as planned.

Progress 13 arrived at Salyut 7 and docked at the rear port on May 25, after having been launched two days earlier from Tyuratam atop a Soyuz booster. It brought more than two tons of cargo, including air regenerators, water, food, scientific equipment, fuel for Salyut's engines, and personal letters from the cosmonauts' friends and families. Progress refueled the station automatically, and the two men unloaded by hand all the dry cargo. The cargo ship was undocked from the station on June 4. Two days later it was commanded to a destructive reentry into Earth's atmosphere over the area of the Pacific Ocean (any debris which did not fully burn was to fall harmlessly into the ocean).

The next stage of the flight involved the launch of a Soviet/French crew. The Frenchman was Western Europe's first representative in space. Two French pilots had been training at the Soviet training center, known as Star City, near Moscow since September, 1980. They were Jean-Loup Chrétien and Patrick Baudry. Chrétien was selected as the prime crewman to fly Soyuz T-6 with Soviets Vladimir Dzhanibekov and Alexander Ivanchenkov. The crew would conduct medical and astronomical experiments during a short flight on the station.

Soyuz T-6 was launched from Tyuratam at 8:30 P.M. Moscow time on June 24. The spacecraft was in orbit 9 minutes after launch. In keeping with standard Soviet practice, the docking was scheduled for the next day. The docking was meant to be an automatic one, but, when only 900 meters separated ship and station, a computer controlling the approach on Soyuz malfunctioned and Dzhanibekov had to control the situation manually, docking the ship at 9:46 P.M., June 25.

During a week of joint experiments, the two crews conducted tests with a unique French-made echocardiogram which allowed the men to view a television picture made by ultrasound of a section of the heart. In another test, called "posture," Chrétien assumed various bodily attitudes on a tiltable table and wore a blindfold to test the condition of the fluids in the inner ear which are disoriented in weightlessness. Many cosmonauts and astronauts suffer from a disruption of these fluids which induces a malaise similar to seasickness. The French also provided two special cameras to take photographs of stars which give off light at wavelengths that the human eye cannot see. The cosmonauts used a special electric furnace to fuse alloys of metals with different densities which gravity would cause to separate on Earth. Only in space can these alloys be made.

Soyuz T-6, with Dzhanibekov, Ivanchenkov, and Chrétien aboard, returned to Earth on July 2 at 6:21 P.M. Moscow time in an area 65 kilometers from the town of Arkalyk in the Kazakh Soviet Socialist Republic. Chrétien was showered with champagne by his backup pilot, Baudry, as he sat in a special reclining chair which the Soviets use for all returning cosmonauts, who are weak after being in weightlessness. Eight days later the Soviets launched Progress 14 toward Salyut. The new ship docked on July 12 to deliver a new cargo of food, fuel, and equipment.

On July 30 cosmonauts Berezovoi and Lebedev performed extravehicular activities (EVAs) which lasted for 2 hours and 33 minutes. During this first spacewalk from the new Salyut, the men brought into the station samples of material which had been launched on the outside of the station to determine how they were affected by prolonged exposure to the vacuum and radiation of space. Tests were also made of maintenance equipment, such as spanners, to see how they worked in open space. Progress 14, its job done, undocked on August 10 and was sent to destruction in Earth's atmosphere three days later.

The second crew to visit Berezovoi and Lebedev was launched from Tyuratam on August 19. Soyuz T-7 lifted off at 9:12 P.M. Moscow time on a Soyuz rocket with a three-person crew aboard consisting of two men and a woman. The commander was Leonid Popov, a veteran of the 1980 Salyut 6 flight, which had lasted 185 days. He was accompanied by flight engineer Alexander Serebrov and researcher Svetlana Savitskaya, the second woman to fly in space. She had been training since 1980, and her flight was clearly meant to upstage that of the first American woman, Sally Ride. The Soyuz T-7 flight served another purpose—that of switching Soyuz spacecraft in orbit so that the resident crew would have a newer spacecraft in which to return. The Soviets did not like to keep their Soyuz T spacecraft in orbit for longer than three months or so.

Soyuz docked with Salyut's rear port at 10:32 P.M. on August 20, and during the crossover into the station, Savitskaya was presented with an arabidopsis plant that had been grown on the station as part of a biology experiment. The station had also been sprayed with apple blossom and rose scents as a welcoming gesture. It is reported, however, that Savitskaya refused the offer of an apron to do the cooking. During their joint flight, the cosmonauts conducted some medical tests of Savitskaya to assess the way she adapted to weightlessness. Another important series of experiments concerned an electrophoresis unit which utilized an electrical field to separate tissue cells in a liquid. A similar system was flown on U.S. space shuttle missions between 1982 and 1985. Several series of astronomical pictures were taken with the French cameras, and observations were made of Earth's atmosphere to study its density and the effects of pollution.

On August 27, Soyuz T-5, with Popov, Serebrov, and Savitskaya, undocked from Salyut and landed 70 kilometers from Arkalyk in the Kazakh Soviet Socialist Republic at 7:04 P.M. Moscow time. Savitskaya, completing a record duration flight for a woman, was reported to be in good health after the mission. Two days later, Berezovoi and Lebedev entered Soyuz T-7, sealed themselves in, and undocked from Salyut's rear port. They backed the spacecraft away from the station while ground controllers commanded Salyut to rotate 180 degrees so that the front docking port faced Soyuz. The men then redocked and entered Salyut to continue their flight. The rear port was thus cleared for more Progress ships. For the second half of their marathon stay in space, the men were alone on Salyut. There were suggestions that the men were to have been brought home after only four months, but the flight continued past that time because of the men's good health.

Progress 15 left Tyuratam on September 18 and docked with Salyut two days later. After an unspectacular resupply flight, the cargo ship was undocked on October 14 and was commanded to destruction in the atmosphere two days later. On October 31 yet another Progress—number 16—was launched from Tyuratam and docked with Salyut two days later.

Berezovoi and Lebedev ejected another small Iskra satellite on November 18. It had been delivered by the Progress 16 ship and, like the first Iskra, had been constructed by students of a Moscow aviation college. Three days later, the men broke the official record for the longest stay in space. They were said to be ready to return home early in December. Sleeping for 12 hours each day and spending all of their time in a station which had only 100 cubic meters of living space, Berezovoi and Lebedev were becoming irritable. In order to maintain fitness and to ward off the effects of their bodies' adaptation to weightlessness, which, if not counteracted, would leave them too weak to walk upon their return to Earth, the pair exercised 2 hours per day, 6 days per week.

The cosmonauts returned to Earth on December 10 at 10:03 P.M. Moscow time. The landing was unusual in that it occurred after nightfall at the landing site 190 kilometers from the town of Dzhezkazgan in the Kazakh Soviet Socialist Republic. The landing module also landed in the midst of a thick fog and snowstorm which hampered the helicopter rescue services to the point that, after one helicopter was damaged on landing, all helicopters were called off and the recovery was effected by land vehicles. The cosmonauts were found at the bottom of a small incline. The two men who had spent 211 days in the weightlessness of space had spent their first few hours back on Earth huddled in a transport vehicle near their capsule.

Knowledge Gained

The 211-day flight of Berezovoi and Lebedev inaugurated the newest of the Soviet's Salyut stations. The Soviets had gained much knowledge about man's adaptability to prolonged weightlessness during the many flights to Salyut 6. The longest flight on that station lasted 185 days, and the flight of Berezovoi and Lebedev was illustrative of the gradual build-up of the length of time the Soviets were staying in space in preparation for the establishment of a permanent manned presence in Earth orbit and, eventually, flights to Mars. The Salyut stations had been the base for Soviet cosmonauts since 1971, while the Americans had only the single series of Skylab missions for their extended stays in space.

Generally speaking, the Soviets found that while there were some specific changes to man's physical condition in long-duration space missions (loss of calcium from the bones, for example), the use of several types of countermeasures halted these effects so that the body could reverse them once back on Earth. These countermeasures included the wearing of special elasticized suits, which exerted a pull on the long bones of the body, and a special rubberized leg garment, from which air could be vented to create a vacuum. This vacuum, reproducing the effects of Earth's gravity, caused the heart to pump blood into the lower regions of the body. In space, the blood tends to pool around the heart. The net effect of this is less blood production; thus the lower regions of the body have a net loss of blood. The inclusion of the French crew member on Soyuz T-6 aided in the medical study of the body's adaptation to the weightless state. The French supplied a measuring instrument which allowed the cosmonauts to view a cross section of their hearts on a television monitor. The flight of Savitskaya, the second woman in space, proved that the rigors of extended weightlessness could be withstood by a female.

Berezovoi and Lebedev obtained about twenty thousand photographs of Earth that were distributed to agencies across the Soviet Union to be used in a variety of sectors of the Soviet economy. The Soviets discovered that economical savings could be realized through the use of photographs of the Earth taken from space. These pictures and observations were sent back to Earth with the manned space-craft which visited Salyut 7 and by means of a television system which was used to relay Earth resources information for the first time on a Soviet space station. The cosmonauts also spoke directly to users of their data when the experts visited the mission control center near Moscow.

The men spent about seventy hours using special furnaces to melt metals samples to create alloys impossible to make on Earth and grow semiconductor crystals for use in computers and electronic devices. These crystals can be grown purer and larger in space, again because of the lack of gravity. Processing with an elec-trophoresis unit, which separates biological specimens in an electric field, was pioneered for the Soviets by the visiting Soyuz T-7 crew. In addition, the crew managed to coax a plant to produce seeds on this flight, a great advance for the biological program. The Soviets hope to be able to grow crops from seeds, on long-term flights and eventually on flights to other planets. For astronomical observa-tions, the cosmonauts used the French-made cameras to take pictures of hot stars and study their spectra, thus determining their constituent elements. They also used a large X-ray telescope to study the most violent stellar regions while other instru-ments recorded cooler stars.

Context

The flight of Berezovoi and Lebedev occurred at the same time the U.S. space shuttle's test flights were ending. While the crew of Soyuz T-5 was in orbit conduct-ing experiments for science and peace, the Americans were flying the first shuttle mission with a military payload, a fact that Soviet propagandists publicized widely. A civilian/military controversy surrounds the space programs of both superpowers. The United States accused the Soviets of flying military space missions in the Sal-yut 3 and 5 space station series, while the Soviets countercharged that the United

States was militarizing space by putting Department of Defense payloads on its shuttles.

Clearly, any space observation or experiment has both military and commercial relevance. The great volume of Earth observations which cosmonauts conducted with Salyut 7 could be used for mapping by the military; civilian commercial agencies could employ the same data for prospecting for oil and gas without the expense of field trips to investigate barren sites. Similarly, metals and crystal smelting activities could be used for high technology electronics devices with both military and civilian applications.

The launching of the two Iskra satellites also recalled the American shuttle activities—the U.S. launched two commercial communications satellites on the fifth shuttle mission in November, 1982. While the Soviets might claim to be the first to launch a satellite from a manned spacecraft in Earth orbit, the Americans could counter that eleven years before the Soviets the Apollo 15 spacecraft released a small subsatellite into orbit around the Moon.

Whereas the Soviet/French portion of the long mission was both a political and a scientific event, the inclusion of a woman for the first time in nineteen years of piloted space missions seems to have been a response to the National Aeronautics and Space Administration's selection of six women to join its astronaut corps in 1978. The Soviets, who had said earlier that a Salyut station was no place for women, began to believe that they should include women in the ranks of their cosmonaut team. Svetlana Savitskaya and Irina Pronina, her backup, were the first Soviet women to train for a spaceflight since the original five female cosmonauts (including Valentina V. Tereshkova, the first woman in space) had been disbanded from the corps in 1969. Savitskaya preceded the first American woman in space, Sally Ride, by ten months.

Bibliography

Clark, Phillip S. *The Soviet Manned Space Programme*. London: Salamander, 1988. Absolutely essential reading for anyone interested in the subject. Written by one of the leading authorities on the subject, it combines scholarly analysis with excellent illustrations.

Gatland, Kenneth. *The Illustrated Encyclopedia of Space Technology: A Comprehensive History of Space Exploration*. New York: Crown Publishers, 1981. Covers the development of astronautics up to 1980. This large-format book is copiously illustrated in color with many cutaways of Soviet space vehicles. The book ends in a chronology of the space age.

Hart, Douglas. *The Encyclopedia of Soviet Spacecraft*. London: Bison Books, 1987. Provides details of most of the Soviet Union's spacecraft, manned and unmanned. It is well illustrated, with color and black-and-white photographs.

Johnson, Nicholas L. *Handbook of Soviet Manned Spaceflight*. San Diego: Univelt, 1980. Excellent coverage of all aspects of the program, with black-and-white photographs from one of the most authoritative authors on the subject. Suitable for high school students and undergraduates.

_____ . *The Soviet Year in Space: 1987*. Colorado Springs, Colo.: Teledyne Brown Engineering, 1988. Provides exhaustive details of the events in the Soviet manned and unmanned programs over the year. It is the latest in a series from 1981. Well illustrated with line drawings and black-and-white photographs.

Oberg, James E. *Red Star in Orbit*. New York: Random House, 1981. Highly readable book by an author with great knowledge and insight into the Soviet space program. Provides many interesting anecdotes about cosmonauts. Also includes a superb annotated bibliography and black-and-white plate photographs.

Riabchikov, Evgeny. *Russians in Space*. Edited by Nikolai P. Kamanin. Translated by Guy Daniels. Garden City, N.Y.: Doubleday and Co., 1971. This highly readable book is by a leading Soviet author who is close to the cosmonaut team. Despite the political nature of the book and omissions of serious problems since disclosed, it does allow a glimpse into the character of the Soviet program. Contains many interesting black-and-white photographs.

U.S. Congress. Senate. Committee on Commerce, Science, and Transportation. *Soviet Space Programs: 1981-1987*. Report prepared by Congressional Research Service, the Library of Congress. 100th Cong., 1988. Committee Print. Provides exhaustive details and analysis of the events of the Soviet program. Contains descriptions of the hardware and the political background of the launches. Although somewhat technical, the reports do provide suitable reading for a general audience.

Neville Kidger

Cross-References

The Mir Space Station, 1025; The Salyut Space Station, 1233; The Skylab Program, 1285; The Soyuz-Kosmos Program, 1396; Soyuz 25, 26, and 27, 1482; The Soyuz Interkosmos Missions, 1489; The Soyuz T Program, 1495; Soyuz 29, 1503; Soyuz 32 and 34, 1511; Soyuz 35, T-1, and T-2, 1517; Soyuz T-3 and T-4, 1524; Soyuz T-8, T-9, and T-10A, 1537; Soyuz T-10B, T-11, and T-12, 1544; Soyuz T-13, 1551; Soyuz T-14, 1557; Soyuz T-15, 1562.

SOYUZ T-8, T-9, and T-10A

Date: April 20 to November 23, 1983
Type of mission: Manned space station flights
Country: The Soviet Union

The Soyuz T-8, T-9, and T-10A missions, all intended to carry crews to the Salyut 7 space station complex, were plagued with failures and emergencies; while postponing the realization of some Soviet spaceflight ambitions, the missions also demonstrated that the Soviet manned spaceflight program had developed a sophistication and overall flexibility which allowed it to continue in spite of its problems.

Principal personages
VLADIMIR TITOV, the Soyuz T-8 and Soyuz T-10A commander
GENNADI STREKALOV, the Soyuz T-8 and Soyuz T-10A flight
    engineer
ALEXANDER SEREBROV, the second flight engineer, Soyuz T-8
VLADIMIR LYAKHOV, the Soyuz T-9 commander
ALEXANDER ALEXANDROV, the Soyuz T-9 flight engineer

Summary of the Missions

Soyuz T-8 departed from Tyuratam on April 20, 1983, one day after the first anniversary of the launch of the Salyut 7 space station, its destination. Aboard were Vladimir Titov (commander), Gennadi Strekalov (flight engineer), and Alexander Serebrov (second flight engineer)—the first three-person crew intended for a long-duration stay aboard a Soviet space station since 1971.

Yet trouble developed almost immediately. By its second orbit it became clear that Soyuz T-8's radar antenna had not unfolded. Efforts were made to pop it open by subjecting the spacecraft to rolls and jerks, but this proved ineffectual. Under normal Soviet mission rules this failure dictated abandonment of the mission. It was decided, however, to attempt an entirely manual rendezvous and docking, something never attempted in the history of the Soviet space program.

Typically, Soyuz dockings with a Salyut space station occurred on the seventeenth orbit, after about twenty-five hours of flight, but Soyuz T-8's attempt was delayed until the nineteenth orbit. Titov relied on calculations based on Salyut 7's image size in his docking sight to determine distance from the station and on radar inputs from ground control to determine his approach speed. He soon realized that his effort had little chance of success. As it closed on Salyut 7, Soyuz T-8 began a thirty-five-minute period out of ground station range. Soon thereafter, both spacecraft moved over the nightside of Earth. At about three hundred meters, Titov shined a floodlight on the station. He could see the beam reflecting off the solar panels of Salyut 7 and the Kosmos 1443 module docked to its front port. As he drew nearer, he realized that he could not be sure of his speed relative to the station complex. Fearing a crash, he called off the attempt, firing braking thrusters to take Soyuz T-8 under Salyut 7 at a distance of 150 meters. When contact with ground control was regained, Soyuz T-8 was 4 kilometers out and moving away from Salyut 7. Ground control ordered the cosmonauts to return to Earth. Touchdown occurred at 5:29 P.M. Moscow time on April 22, near the town of Arkalyk, in Soviet Central Asia, within the usual Soyuz landing corridor.

Soyuz T-9 left Tyuratam at 12:12 P.M. on June 27, 1983. It docked with the rear port of Salyut 7 on its seventeenth orbit, at 1:46 P.M. on June 28. Aboard were Vladimir Lyakhov, commander, and Alexander Alexandrov, flight engineer. They quickly occupied the station, taking it out of the dormant state it had been in since December, 1982, and commenced an experiment program which was little noticed outside the Soviet Union.

The first excitement of the cosmonauts' stay came on July 27, when a foreign object struck one of the viewports with a loud report, creating a 3-millimeter-wide crater. The Soviets supposed that this was a micrometeoroid from a swarm through which Earth was passing at the time, though it may have been a piece of artificial space debris. Lyakhov and Alexandrov evacuated to their Soyuz T-9 space ferry until it was clear that the damage did not threaten them; then they returned to their experimental program.

On August 14, the program was interrupted by the departure of the Kosmos 1443 module, which had been launched from Tyuratam on March 2, 1983, and, after leisurely maneuvers, had docked with Salyut 7 on March 10. Kosmos 1443 weighed about 18,000 kilograms, nearly as much as the entire Salyut 7 station. When Soyuz T-9 arrived, it brought the total weight of the complex to almost 50,000 kilograms. The vehicle carried more than 2,700 kilograms of cargo to Salyut 7. Its cylindrical hull was about 13 meters long by 4 meters wide. Attached to its sides, like wings, were 40 square meters of solar panels. They generated some 3 kilowatts of electricity for the station. The vehicle docked with the front port of Salyut 7 and provided the cosmonauts with an additional 50 cubic meters of work and living space, bringing the total to about 100 cubic meters. Attached to the rear of Kosmos 1443 was a reentry module. On August 23 it separated from the free-flying Kosmos 1443 and splashed down with about 350 kilograms of disused equipment and processed materials aboard. The bulk of Kosmos 1443 was then guided to a destructive reentry on September 19.

On August 16, the cosmonauts moved T-9 to the front port to make way for the Progress 17 cargo ship, which delivered food and fuel on August 19 and was discarded September 17. While Progress 17 was docked, Lyakhov and Alexandrov experienced their second space emergency, when, on September 9, a rupture in the Salyut 7 propulsion system dumped two-thirds of their oxidizer into space. The cosmonauts fled into Soyuz T-9; it was only after exhaustive systems checks that they were allowed back into the station. Sixteen of Salyut 7's thirty-two steering thrusters and its two main engines were rendered useless, and the station entered into a drifting mode, forcing abandonment of experiments requiring its precise orientation. Lyakhov and Alexandrov did materials processing experiments, which required avoiding use of the propulsion system (most of the system had failed anyway), and awaited the arrival of a visiting Soyuz crew.

In late September, the cosmonauts learned that they would not receive visitors after all. On the ground, at Tyuratam, the crew of Soyuz T-10A had barely escaped when their booster caught fire and exploded on the launchpad, only seconds before their scheduled launch time. Commander Vladimir Titov and flight engineer Gennadi Strekalov were plucked from their burning A-2 (SL-4) booster by a solid-fueled launch escape system rocket. The Soyuz T-10A vehicle left its instrument module behind on the booster; when the solid rocket motor burned out at 950 meters, stabilizing paddles opened on the conical launch shroud. The bell-shaped descent module which contained the cosmonauts then separated from the spherical orbital module, which remained inside the shroud. A fast-opening parachute then brought the crew down safely about four kilometers from the launch site. The launchpad and neighboring facilities, possibly including a second manned spacecraft launchpad, were destroyed in the explosion.

Western newsmen believed that Lyakhov and Alexandrov were stranded in space. Their Soyuz T-9 spacecraft was more than one hundred days old. Previous missions had returned to Earth or traded craft with a visiting crew for a fresh vehicle before the four-month mark. The station was drifting and losing altitude as a result of the oxidizer leakage, and a new problem had appeared—the power system was failing. This meant that the experimental program was further compromised and that the temperature in the station dropped to about 18 degrees Celsius. Humidity ran at about 100 percent; moisture began to collect on viewports and instrument panels, endangering delicate electronics and the cosmonauts' health.

On October 20, Progress 18 arrived with replacement fuel, oxidizer, and supplies, breaking the cosmonauts' long autumn of solitude. Then, on November 1, the Soviets surprised everyone by sending Lyakhov and Alexandrov out on an unrehearsed three-hour spacewalk to augment the Salyut 7 solar panel array. Extra panels had been delivered eight months before by Kosmos 1443. These were originally intended to increase available electricity; now they would help make the cosmonauts' environment healthier. Lyakhov and Alexandrov were trained by radio. Technical information and tools were sent up on Progress 18. Soviet physicians feared that after months in weightlessness the crew would find the spacewalk too taxing. It was also feared, however, that if something were not done the station would become uninhabitable and perhaps uncontrollable.

The new 5.5-meter-long panels were hoisted along the edges of the existing arrays. A second spacewalk was performed on November 3. The cosmonauts did their work with enthusiasm. Alexandrov was clearly not worried; he was reprimanded for releasing bits of debris to watch them drift away. (It was feared that these particles would confuse the station's navigational sensors.) The Soviets called this repair the first construction work done in "raw space." Addition of the panels added 2.5 kilowatts to the station's electrical capacity.

Before it was discarded on November 13, Progress 18 was used to orient and boost the orbit of Salyut 7. On November 23, Lyakhov and Alexandrov boarded their aging Soyuz T-9 craft and returned to Earth. The Soviets claimed that their flight was no longer than originally planned, also announcing that the improved T-type Soyuz could safely withstand prolonged periods (in excess of 115 days) attached to an orbiting space station.

Knowledge Gained

Despite their many problems, the Soyuz T-8, T-9, and T-10A crews managed to make significant contributions to the world's knowledge of space. Ironically, many of these gains would not have been made if all had gone as planned on the missions. Both Soyuz T-8 and T-10A taught the West much about Soviet mission rules and emergency procedures. From T-8, Western space technicians learned that the failure of the docking antenna could ruin a mission and that the Soyuz T was limited in its ability to maneuver during rendezvous and docking. From T-10A, much was learned about Soviet abort procedures and abort procedures in general— the T-10A launchpad abort was the first of its kind. While T-8 and T-10A allowed Western analysts to understand better the often-secretive Soviet program, T-9, a qualified success, returned a wealth of scientific and engineering data. Although plagued with difficulties, the T-9 cosmonauts were able to continue with a scientific program comprising more than three hundred experiments, sometimes conducting as many as eight per day.

Earth observation, which required use of the propulsion system to orient the station, could not be carried out routinely after the oxidizer leak in September. Nevertheless, the cosmonauts were able to photograph some 300 million square kilometers of Earth's surface. The southern Soviet Union, East Germany, Hungary, India, Cuba, Mongolia, and Czechoslovakia, as well as extensive ocean areas, were photographed in great detail.

In the biological and medical fields, the Soyuz T-9 team investigated using electrical stimulation to help grow food in space. Plant growth units were used to grow tomato sprouts. Also, the cosmonauts served as guinea pigs for medical tests. These included psychological experiments. Awakening to birdsongs and having regular television and radio visits with family, friends, and celebrities helped Lyakhov and Alexandrov avoid the psychological disturbances apparent on some earlier flights, in spite of their many difficulties and discomforts.

Technological experiments were carried out as well. A special experimental device was used to perform tests of heat transfer in a vacuum. Experiments were done involving molding crystals in weightlessness, and extensive studies were made of the effects of vibration (such as that produced by air-circulating fans, steering thrusters, and the cosmonauts' movements) on materials processing in weightlessness. Pure biological substances were produced, including ampoules of an antiviral preparation ten to fifteen times purer than any which could be produced on Earth.

Context

It is easier to understand the context of the Soyuz T-8, T-9, and T-10A missions if one considers what probably would have happened if all had gone as planned. Soyuz T-8 carried three crewmen intended for a long-duration stay on Salyut 7. Other Soyuz T spacecraft had carried three crew members on visits which lasted for an average of a week; these can be seen as tests of the ability of the Soyuz T spacecraft to host three men safely. The Soyuz spacecraft was originally intended as a three-man spacecraft, but the deaths of the Soyuz 11 cosmonauts returning from Salyut 1 in 1971 forced a redesign which made it a two-man ship until the advent of the Soyuz T in 1980.

Having three crewmen available aboard a spacecraft has important advantages. Most notably, three men allow for spacewalks to be undertaken with two cosmonauts outside and the one inside wearing a pressure suit, supporting the spacewalkers by operating space station equipment and able to intervene outside in the event of trouble. Soyuz T-8's crew was trained for such a spacewalk. Kosmos 1443 carried folded solar panels for Titov and Strekalov to install on a spacewalk, with Serebrov remaining inside Salyut 7 in a support role.

The failure of the Soyuz T-8 mission probably compromised the mission of Kosmos 1443, a mysterious, large spacecraft about which there has been much speculation. The Soviets called it a modular transport craft, but it was probably much more than that. Inexplicably, it docked to the front port of Salyut 7, which is normally reserved for Soyuz manned craft. The Soviets claimed that it could transfer fuel to the Salyut 7 propulsion system, but the front port has no piping connections to allow fuel transfer. More likely, its own propulsion system was used to move the station.

The Kosmos 1443 vehicle was probably a test of several spaceflight systems. On one hand, it was a space station module, aimed at gathering information about automated assembly of independently launched large modules. On the other hand, it was a prototype man-tended free-flyer. Free-flyers carry delicate experiments, most having to do with materials processing, experiments which are compromised by the vibration of having a crew aboard. A free-flyer operates unmanned but occasionally joins with an orbiting manned space station for refurbishment and replacement of experiments. The conical cargo return module would be used to return products to Earth. This would signal the end of its usefulness—without a return module it could no longer ship its products back to Earth.

It is likely that Kosmos 1443 carried experiments which were to have been activated by the Soyuz T-8 crew. Yet it was not visited by cosmonauts until late June, 1983, by which time it had been in space for nearly four months. Its experiments and equipment may have begun to exceed their design lifetimes. In addition, it is doubtful that Lyakhov and Alexandrov could have been adequately trained to service the free-flyer, though they may have carried out a truncated test program before casting it off in August.

The solar panel extensions that Kosmos 1443 delivered were originally intended to add to the station's normally barely adequate solar arrays, not to replace them. The efficient use of Salyut 7 had been rendered impossible because of a lack of power; experiments using power-hungry apparatus could only be conducted consecutively, not simultaneously. When T-9 arrived, the solar panels were taken from Kosmos 1443 and stored, presumably to be installed on a later mission, perhaps a second attempt at a three-person crew using what became the Soyuz T-10A spacecraft. The Salyut 7 energy crunch, combined with the propellant system rupture, led first to T-10A being prepared as a two-crew panel installation mission, then to the unusual and daring spacewalks by Lyakhov and Alexandrov. The Soviets were not prepared to risk sending a three-person crew to the plagued and possibly dangerous station, nor were they prepared to abandon it, so they took a middle course.

The Soviets later admitted that Soyuz T-10A was intended to be a solar panel installation mission. Titov and Strekalov would have used the training they were given for the Soyuz T-8 mission, then would have climbed into the T-9 spacecraft and returned to Earth, leaving their fresh T-10A spacecraft for Lyakhov and Alexandrov. As it was, they could not trade ships; indeed, the explosion of their booster ruined any chance of sending an unmanned replacement Soyuz to Lyakhov and Alexandrov by destroying two of three available manned launchpads.

If all had gone as planned, the Soyuz T-8 would have fulfilled the long-held ambition of a three-person space station crew and would have augmented the Salyut power supply to allow increased productivity. At the same time, it would have tested a man-tended free-flyer in orbit. T-9 would have been a more typical two-person flight, during which time the results of the T-8 mission would have been assessed for safety and efficiency. T-10A might have carried aloft a second three-person crew, or perhaps visitors to the T-9 crew who would have returned to Earth in the T-9 craft, leaving a fresh craft for Lyakhov and Alexandrov. If T-10A had carried guests, then T-10B would have carried a second three-person crew. As it happened, T-10B carried the first three-person long-duration space station crew to Salyut 7 in February, 1984.

Bibliography

Braun, Wernher von, Frederick Ordway, and Dave Dooling. *Space Travel: A History*. Rev. ed. New York: Harper and Row, Publishers, 1985. This book was originally published as part of Wernher von Braun's tireless efforts to sell spaceflight to the American people. Frequent new editions, under several different titles, have allowed the book to keep up well with more recent events. Emphasis is on the American space program, though the Soviet program is not ignored. Good layman's introduction to the history of spaceflight, from ancient Chinese rockets to the pre-*Challenger* space shuttle era.

Furniss, Tim. *Manned Spaceflight Log*. Rev. ed. New York: Jane's Publishing Co., 1986. An invaluable reference suitable for college-level audiences. Every manned space mission from Vostok 1 to Soyuz T-15 is covered in detail through brief encyclopedic entries in chronological order. Each entry begins with a detailed summary listing important technical and biographical information. The book also contains tables comparing the achievements of the astronauts and cosmonauts.

Hart, Douglas. *The Encyclopedia of Soviet Spacecraft*. New York: Bison, 1987. Contains many good photographs of Soviet hardware not easily found elsewhere. Good layman's treatment of most Soviet programs, but tends to be cursory. The illustrations are the primary attraction.

Simpson, Theodore R., ed. *The Space Station: An Idea Whose Time Has Come*. New York: IEEE Press, 1985. A collection of essays designed to promote the construction of a large space station complex by the United States. The Soviet program is covered in essays comparing the American and Soviet space efforts. Many different viewpoints, though the majority of the authors are united in their belief that the construction of a space station in the near future by the United States is a good idea. Writing for the college-level reader, Simpson assumes knowledge of spaceflight basics but takes pains to explain technical matters related to space station operation.

Turnill, Reginald, ed. *Jane's Spaceflight Directory*. New York: Jane's Publishing Co., 1987. An endlessly fascinating, massive volume containing details on hundreds of spaceflight topics. Updated annually. Its release is eagerly awaited each year. Contains plans, photographs, and drawings unavailable elsewhere. Somewhat technical, but an excellent source of spaceflight data. Suitable for college-level audiences.

U.S. Congress. Office of Technology Assessment. *Salyut: Soviet Steps Toward Permanent Human Presence in Space—A Technical Memorandum*. OTA-TM-STI-14. Washington, D.C.: Government Printing Office, 1983. A good layman's guide to the Salyut space station program and its related spaceflight programs (Soyuz and Progress, among others). Surprisingly, it is lacking in detail, but it does present a valuable broad picture of Soviet achievements and probable future plans. Contains useful line drawings and interior plans.

David S. F. Portree

Cross-References

Biological Effects of Space Travel on Humans, 188; Cosmonauts and the Soviet Cosmonaut Program, 273; Gemini 8, 520; Soviet Launch Vehicles, 742; Materials Processing in Space, 933; The Progress Program, 1202; The Salyut Space Station, 1233; Soyuz 10 and 11, 1436; The Soyuz T Program, 1495; Soyuz T-5, T-6, and T-7, 1530; Soyuz T-10B, T-11, and T-12, 1544; Soyuz T-13, 1551; Space Centers and Launch Sites in the Soviet Union, 1592; Spacewatch: Tracking Space Debris, 1924.

SOYUZ T-10B, T-11, and T-12

Date: February 8 to October 2, 1984
Type of mission: Manned space station flights
Countries: The Soviet Union and India

These space station flights included a long-term stay aboard the Salyut 7 station—237 days, breaking the 211-day record set in 1982. Six spacewalks were performed by members of the resident crew to repair a fuel leak, and the space station was visited by a crew which included the first Indian cosmonaut and the first woman to walk in space.

Principal personages

LEONID KIZIM, the Soyuz T-10B commander
VLADIMIR SOLOVYEV, the Soyuz T-10B flight engineer
OLEG ATKOV, the researcher on Soyuz T-10B and the second
　　Soviet medical doctor to fly in space
YURI V. MALYSHEV, the Soyuz T-11 commander
GENNADI STREKALOV, the Soyuz T-11 flight engineer
RAKESH SHARMA, the researcher on Soyuz T-11, a citizen of India
VLADIMIR DZHANIBEKOV, the Soyuz T-12 commander
SVETLANA SAVITSKAYA, the Soyuz T-12 flight engineer and the first
　　woman to walk in space
IGOR VOLK, the researcher on Soyuz T-12

Summary of the Missions

On February 8, 1984, at 3:07 P.M. Moscow time, the Soviet Union launched Soyuz T-10B into orbit by means of a Soyuz launcher from Tyuratam in Kazakhstan. The Soyuz was to deliver three men to the Salyut 7 space station. The commander of the crew was Leonid Kizim, a veteran of the Soyuz T-3 flight in 1980. The flight engineer was Vladimir Solovyev, and the cosmonaut researcher was Oleg Atkov. Atkov had been graduated from one of the Soviet Union's top medical institutes and had helped develop a portable ultrasound cardiograph, used to monitor the functions of the heart, which had been tested during a record 211-day flight on Salyut 7 by two men in 1982.

Soyuz T-10B docked with Salyut's front docking port at 5:43 P.M. Moscow time on February 9. During their period of reactivation of the station the men photographed the portholes of the station and made minor repairs to the plumbing system. On February 23, an unmanned cargo spacecraft, Progress 19, docked with Salyut's rear port. It had been launched on a Soyuz rocket from Tyuratam two days earlier. Such resupply flights ensured the long-term functioning of the station by delivering food, water, and clothing—as well as fuel for the station's engines. There were about two tons of cargo on each resupply flight.

Atkov's task on the flight was to research the long-term functioning of the cardio-vascular system under conditions of weightlessness, among other things. The doctor conducted regular medical checkups on the two other men as well as on himself.

Experimental activities began with observations and photography of Earth's surface and later included photography of a comet—an interplanetary ball of rock and ice which, when near the Sun, emits a long tail of gas and dust. The photographs were part of the preparations for the study of Halley's comet, which would be close to Earth in 1986. On March 31, Progress was detached and commanded by ground controllers in Moscow to fire its engine and descend into the upper layers of Earth's atmosphere, where it was allowed to burn.

At 5:09 P.M. Moscow time on April 3, the Soyuz T-11 spacecraft was launched from Tyuratam with a three-man crew aboard. The craft carried Yuri V. Malyshev, the commander, and Gennadi Strekalov, the flight engineer—both experienced Soviet spacemen—and Rakesh Sharma, the researcher, a citizen of India. The spacecraft docked with Salyut's rear port at 6:31 P.M. the next day. During the next seven days the six men conducted a wide range of experiments which included photography of the territory of India and some unusual medical tests involving yoga: Sharma also contributed some traditional Indian dishes to break the monotony for the three cosmonauts. On April 11, the Malyshev-Strekalov-Sharma trio returned to Earth in Soyuz T-10B, leaving their newer vehicle in space for the long-duration crew. The T-10 vehicle landed at 2:50 P.M., some forty-five kilometers from the Kazakh town of Arkalyk.

On April 13, in order to free the rear port of Salyut for more cargo spacecraft, Kizim, Solovyev, and Atkov floated into Soyuz T-11 and sealed themselves in. The spacecraft was undocked and backed off from the station. The Salyut was then commanded by ground controllers to rotate 180 degrees so that the front port faced the Soyuz, which was then redocked. The men crossed over into the station to continue their flight.

A new Progress craft, Progress 20, was launched on April 15 from Tyuratam and docked at the newly vacated rear port two days later. Progress 20 delivered, in addition to the usual supplies, much equipment which the cosmonauts were to use to seal off a piece of piping that had leaked in September, 1983, and had almost ended Salyut's operation. The piping delivered an oxidizer into the combustion chamber of the engine, where it was mixed with fuel to give thrust.

When the Soviets began to plan the operation to seal off the pipe, they believed that only a few extravehicular activities (EVAs) would be necessary. The actual task, however, required an unprecedented five EVAs to accomplish. All the EVAs were performed by Kizim and Solovyev, with Atkov remaining in the main section of Salyut. The first four forays were made between April 23 and May 3. During the first EVA, the men spent 255 minutes erecting a special ladder which was on top of Progress and placing tools at the worksite at the rear of Salyut. During their second excursion, they punched a series of holes in the skin of the station and peeled back the layers of insulation to expose a conduit near the source of the leaking pipe. A pipe and valve assembly was installed. During the third EVA, a new conduit was added to the main backup oxidizer line, and the area was sealed. On their fourth spacewalk, the cosmonauts installed another conduit and temporarily called a stop to the work. Later, more work was to be done to seal off the piping, but that would require more tools and training.

Progress 20 was undocked on May 6 and destroyed the next day. Progress 21 was launched from Tyuratam in May to deliver yet more supplies. On May 10, the cargo ship delivered a new set of small solar power panels, which convert sunlight to electricity. The cosmonauts were to install these alongside the main solar panel arrays, of which Salyut 7 had three. A similar task was accomplished in November, 1983. On May 18, Kizim and Solovyev made their fifth EVA. Despite difficulties with a winch to unfold the array, the cosmonauts succeeded in erecting both panels. Once one array had been installed, Atkov commanded the main panel to rotate 180 degrees so that the other could be winched. Kizim and Solovyev succeeded in erecting two arrays in one EVA, when two EVAs had been necessary for the same task on a previous flight to Salyut 7.

On May 25, ground controllers told Kizim that his wife had given birth to a baby daughter. The proud father was to see his daughter for the first time on a video recording sent to the space station. Progress 21 departed the station on May 26 and was deorbited the same day. Two days later, Progress 22 was launched and docked on May 30. The arrival signaled the start of a six-week period of work primarily dedicated to observations of Earth. After refueling the station, Progress 22 was undocked on July 15 and sent to destruction the same day.

The next departure to the station was at 9:41 P.M. Moscow time on July 17. Soyuz T-12 carried a three-person crew which included a woman cosmonaut on her second journey into space—Svetlana Savitskaya. The commander was Vladimir Dzhanibekov, a veteran on his fourth spaceflight. Savitskaya, who had visited Salyut 7 in 1982, served as the flight engineer. The third crewman was cosmonaut researcher Igor Volk. It was later revealed that Volk was involved with the Soviet space shuttle program as chief pilot and that his T-12 trip was part of the training for that program. Soyuz T-12 docked with Salyut's rear port at 11:17 P.M. on July 18.

Despite conducting some technical and medical experiments and starting a new series of electrophoresis tests on biological substances, the Soyuz T-12 crew had flown to Salyut to conduct a new experiment in open space and brief the long-term crew about the final operation to seal the leaking pipe. On July 25, cosmonauts Dzhanibekov and Savitskaya performed an EVA lasting more than three and one-half hours to test a new device for working in open space. This new device was called the Universal Manual Tool, and it resembled a small pistol. It was hand-held and fired an electron beam at a target, coating it with a thin deposit of metal. It could also cut metal, solder, and weld. The EVA tested these functions. Savitskaya, the first woman to walk in space, was the first to test the tool in actual space conditions. Their work completed, the T-12 crew returned home at 4:55 P.M. Moscow time on July 29.

In orbit, Kizim and Solovyev made their sixth and final EVA of the mission, the fifth to repair the leak, on August 8. For five hours they again worked on the pipe and installed a special clamping device to seal it off. The hazardous series of EVAs was completed when the men removed a small section of solar panel for tests on Earth to assess the ability of materials to withstand the radiation and vacuum of space. All told, the two men had spent 22 hours and 50 minutes outside Salyut, a world record for EVA time.

The work in orbit did not end there, however, as the three cosmonauts were joined on August 16 by Progress 23, launched from Tyuratam two days earlier. As well as unloading the supplies from Progress, the men conducted an intensive series of Earth observations. Progress 23 undocked on August 26, having stayed for a shorter than usual period, and was destroyed two days later. The men continued with their Earth observations and scientific experiments. Astrophysical observations were conducted with a Soviet/French X-ray telescope which detected high-energy events in the universe.

On September 7, the three cosmonauts broke the single flight duration record set in 1982. In late September, the men finished their work and prepared for a return to Earth. Traveling in Soyuz T-11, the cosmonauts landed at 1:57 P.M. Moscow time on October 2. They had spent more than 236 days in orbit, a new record. After being examined at the landing site, the men were said to be in good health.

Knowledge Gained

The length of the Soyuz T-10B/T-11 flight meant that the most important scientific information gained concerned the condition of the cosmonauts. On their first day back on Earth, the three men had problems with their balance and needed the help of a so-called antigravity suit, which reproduced the sensation of being in space. On the second day, the men could walk a short distance with assistance from their doctors. By the fourth day after their return to Earth, the men were planting a tree at the cosmodrome, proving that light work was possible. By the third week back, Atkov was able to say that the three cosmonauts were in good health, the result of their program of countermeasures to the harmful effects of extended weightlessness. These countermeasures included wearing special elasticized suits to stress their muscles and bones while they were in space and physical exercises lasting 2 hours per day for 6 days per week.

Of equal importance to the Soviets were the cosmonauts' mental states. The crew members were in good humor both during and after the flight, mainly as a result of the psychological support they received from Earth. In this program, the specialists on Earth arranged for the men to speak to and see their families and friends on a special two-way television set on the station. The men were also encouraged to speak with experts in various scientific disciplines in which they were doing research in orbit. Poets, singers—even chess players—entertained the crew via the television hookup.

During the flight of the main crew itself, the men conducted more than five hundred experiments. More than 5,500 pictures of Earth were taken during the flight by both hand-held cameras and a special camera system which took pictures in six different lights so that they could be combined to extract different useful information about the Earth region being photographed. Using such pictures, specialists could, for example, spot diseased crops by the heat that they gave out in the infrared waveband. A healthy plant gives out far more heat than a diseased one, so the infrared output for a healthy plant is stronger.

The EVAs were also of great importance to the Soviet space program, proving that cosmonauts in orbit could go outside their station and conduct very complex and dangerous repair operations. They could even perform construction work, as evidenced when the men erected the new solar battery panel.

Context

Before 1984, Soviet EVAs had been, at best, intermittent. Following their first EVA, that of Alexei Leonov on the Voskhod 2 flight in 1965, and the Soyuz 4/5 EVA in January, 1969, made by two cosmonauts, the Soviets waited until 1977 for their next foray into raw space. Even then, the EVA, performed in order to examine a docking collar on Salyut 6, was not scientifically motivated. In the same period, the United States' astronaut corps had amassed thirty-six separate EVAs in space and another twenty-nine on the Moon. This gave the United States a total time of 265 hours and 45 minutes outside spacecraft contrasted to the Soviets' 3 hours and 52 minutes. Until 1984, the Soviets performed two additional forays into open space. Three more followed in 1982 and 1983 from Salyut 7. Therefore, the seven separate EVAs conducted during 1984 by Soviet cosmonauts effectively doubled the space-walking experience gained until that point.

Also in 1984, there were five U.S. shuttle flights, four of which featured EVAs—including the first use of a Buck Rogers type of backpack, which astronauts used to maneuver. This manned maneuvering unit, as it was called, was featured in the capture and repair of an ailing scientific satellite and the recapture in orbit of two communications satellites which had gone off course after a flawless shuttle launch earlier in the year. One EVA—that of Savitskaya—would seem to have been timed to beat that performed by American Kathryn D. Sullivan in October, 1984. The EVA work conducted by Kizim and Solovyev to repair the fuel leak and add extra solar panels closely matched the American experience in complexity. The experience also provided the springboard for other, later, complex EVAs to repair scientific instruments and even assist large ships in docking.

The inclusion of a medical physician, Atkov, on the flight showed a trend toward including specialists on orbital teams. The first doctor to fly in space was a Soviet, Boris B. Yegorov on Voskhod 1 in 1964, while the Americans flew Dr. Joseph P. Kerwin to Skylab in 1973. Beginning with the sixth shuttle flight, doctors became regular travelers in order to check the condition of astronauts in flight instead of relying on data either radioed to Earth or derived from examinations of flown crewmen.

The joint Soviet/Indian flight also highlighted another area of recent orbital flights—the inclusion of "guest" spacemen. The Soviets began this part of space exploration by flying Communist Bloc cosmonauts in Soyuz/Salyut missions in 1978. The flights, while allowing the guest country to supply some scientific equipment, provided a political spectacle. The United States, on the other hand, began flying non-Americans in November, 1983, as part of their policy of attracting business to the shuttle for commercial satellite launches. The first such guest was a German physicist working on the European Space Agency's Spacelab science module in the shuttle's payload bay. Later guests aboard U.S. shuttle flights would include a Canadian, a Frenchman, and a Saudi prince.

Bibliography

Clark, Phillip S. *The Soviet Manned Space Programme.* London: Salamander, 1988. Important for any student of the subject. Written by one of the leading authorities on the Soviet space program, it combines solid analysis with excellent illustrations.

Gatland, Kenneth. *The Illustrated Encyclopedia of Space Technology: A Comprehensive History of Space Exploration.* New York: Crown Publishers, 1981. Covers the development of astronautics up to 1980. This large-format book includes copious color illustrations with many cutaways of Soviet space vehicles. Contains much to interest the general reader.

Hart, Douglas. *The Encyclopedia of Soviet Spacecraft.* London: Bison Books, 1987. Provides details of most of the Soviet Union's spacecraft, manned and unmanned. Well illustrated with color and black-and-white photographs. Well organized and suitable for general audiences.

Johnson, Nicholas L. *Handbook of Soviet Manned Spaceflight.* San Diego: Univelt, 1980. Excellent coverage of all aspects of the program with black-and-white pictures. By one of the most authoritative authors on the subject.

_____. *The Soviet Year in Space: 1987.* Colorado Springs, Colo.: Teledyne Brown Engineering, 1988. Provides exhaustive details of the events in the Soviet manned and unmanned programs over the year in question. Illustrated with line drawings and black-and-white photographs. Suitable for high school students and undergraduates.

Oberg, James E. *Red Star in Orbit.* New York: Random House, 1981. Highly readable book by an author with great knowledge and insight into the Soviet space program. Provides many interesting anecdotes concerning cosmonauts. Also includes a superb annotated bibliography and black-and-white plate photographs.

Riabchikov, Evgeny. *Russians in Space.* Edited by Nikolai P. Kamanin. Translated by Guy Daniels. Garden City, N.Y.: Doubleday and Co., 1971. This highly readable book is written by a leading Soviet author close to the cosmonaut team. Despite the obvious political nature of the book and omissions of serious problems since disclosed, it does allow a glimpse into the character of the Soviet program. Includes many interesting black-and-white photographs.

U.S. Congress. Senate. Committee on Commerce, Science, and Transportation. *Soviet Space Programs: 1981-1987.* Report prepared by Congressional Research Service, the Library of Congress. 100th Cong., 1988. Committee Print. A detailed analysis of the events of the Soviet program, descriptions of the hardware used and the political background. Earlier volumes provide still more exhaustive coverage. Despite its technical nature, this report does provide suitable reading for a general audience.

Neville Kidger

Cross-References

The Mir Space Station, 1025; The Salyut Space Station, 1233; The Skylab Program, 1285; The Soyuz-Kosmos Program, 1396; Soyuz 25, 26, and 27, 1482; The Soyuz Interkosmos Missions, 1489; Soyuz 29, 1503; Soyuz 32 and 34, 1511; Soyuz 35, T-1, and T-2, 1517; Soyuz T-3 and T-4, 1524; Soyuz T-5, T-6, and T-7, 1530; Soyuz T-8, T-9, and T-10A, 1537; Soyuz T-13, 1551; Soyuz T-14, 1557; Soyuz T-15, 1562; Space Shuttle Mission 10: *Challenger*, 1711; Space Shuttle Mission 11: *Challenger*, 1719; Space Shuttle Mission 12: *Discovery*, 1727; Space Shuttle Mission 13: *Challenger*, 1735; Space Shuttle Mission 14: *Discovery*, 1744.

SOYUZ T-13

Date: June 6 to September 26, 1985
Type of mission: Manned space station flight
Country: The Soviet Union

The Soyuz T-13 crew boarded Salyut 7 and restored it to use after an accident had crippled the space station and sent it adrift.

Principal personages
VLADIMIR DZHANIBEKOV, the Soyuz T-13 commander
VIKTOR SAVINYKH, the Soyuz T-13 flight engineer
VALERI RYUMIN, the Salyut 7 flight director
VLADIMIR VASYUTIN, the Soyuz T-14 commander
GEORGI GRECHKO, the Soyuz T-14 flight engineer
ALEKSANDR VOLKOV, the Soyuz T-14 cosmonaut-researcher

Summary of the Mission

In the summer of 1985, Soviet cosmonauts Vladimir Dzhanibekov and Viktor Savinykh, the crew of Soyuz T-13, made history when they boarded the derelict Salyut 7 station and restored it to use.

Salyut 7 had been launched on April 19, 1982, and by December, 1984, had served as home to three teams of "expedition" cosmonauts who had inhabited it for periods of 211, 175, and 237 days successively. In addition to the usual stresses caused by launch and normal use, Salyut 7 had suffered a massive fuel leak in August, 1983, necessitating emergency repair spacewalks by cosmonauts Vladimir Lyakhov and Alexander Alexandrov.

In the winter of 1984-1985, Salyut 7 was being readied to receive its fourth crew, which was to have attempted a mission of nine to ten months' duration. In late January, 1985, however, mission controllers suddenly lost all contact with the vehicle. No one knew whether Salyut 7 had simply suffered a failure in its telemetry systems, whether its power supply had become disrupted, or whether it had been hit by orbital debris. The proposed Soyuz T-13 expedition was postponed, and an emergency flightplan was developed.

To fly the mission, which would probably require an especially difficult manually controlled approach and docking by the Soyuz T, Soviet program managers selected Vladimir Dzhanibekov, veteran of four successful Soyuz-to-Salyut dockings. Viktor Savinykh, the flight engineer of the canceled "fourth main crew"—and also one of the Salyut 7 designers—would join him. At 1040 Moscow time on June 6, 1985, they were launched aboard Soyuz T-13 into an orbit which, following early corrections, ranged from 304 to 338 kilometers.

For the next two days, Soyuz T-13 stalked the derelict Salyut. Normally such dockings occur about twenty-five hours after launch, but Dzhanibekov and Savinykh knew that Salyut 7's rendezvous and docking system would not be available to assist them; the extra time allowed Soyuz T-13 to conserve fuel for maneuvers. When the cosmonauts reached the station, their first views were discouraging: They could clearly see that the three solar panel assemblies were pointed incorrectly. After carefully circling the station, Dzhanibekov saw that the automatic guidance system had failed. At a distance of 3 kilometers, he took over manual control of his craft, and Soyuz T-13 linked up with the forward port of Salyut 7.

The cosmonauts' initial worry was that Salyut 7 might have lost internal pressure completely or that an onboard fire might have poisoned the atmosphere. By cracking a valve in the docking hatch, they were able to determine that the station held air; to protect themselves against poisons, Dzhanibekov and Savinykh donned gas masks.

As they floated through the docking tunnel, they found Salyut ominously silent. Dzhanibekov would later write that the whole vehicle smelled of "stale machine oil" and that "hoarfrost covered the windows." The cosmonauts determined that Salyut had, indeed, suffered a power failure. A short circuit in a control panel had made it impossible for Salyut's solar panels to charge its eight batteries properly.

Further complicating matters, the station's communications system was not operating, meaning that flight controllers at Soviet mission control in Kaliningrad were unable to receive telemetry from Salyut and were dependent solely on verbal reports from the cosmonauts, which had to be transmitted via the Soyuz T-13 system. Indeed, at that point some controllers wanted to abandon the station, but Dzhanibekov and Savinykh believed they could repair it, so they went to work. Their progress was hampered by extreme temperatures inside Salyut, temperatures which dipped below 0 degree Celsius.

Naturally, Dzhanibekov and Savinykh had brought a repair kit with them; because of the uncertainty surrounding the Salyut's failure—and, therefore, the impossibility of complete preparation—they possessed few tools which were immediately useful. With the encouragement of flight director Valeri Ryumin, himself an experienced cosmonaut, the cosmonauts began to improvise. Within two days, they had succeeded in linking the solar panels to the batteries again, charging six of the eight units and restoring power to the station. By June 14, communications had been restored, Salyut 7's critical life-support systems were operating again, and the cosmonauts confirmed that the station was responding to commands. The rescue had succeeded.

After a two-day rest, Dzhanibekov and Savinykh made their first attempts to do scientific work aboard Salyut 7, using Earth observation cameras (in conjunction with Kosmos and Meteor-Priroda satellites) to photograph selected areas in the Kursk region of the Soviet Union. This Interkosmos experiment was called Kursk 85. The cosmonauts also embarked on the tedious program of exercise and routine medical checks necessary for a long-duration mission.

Confident that work could be performed aboard the station, Soviet program managers launched the unmanned Progress 24 supply ship on June 21. Carrying a load of fuel, oxygen, and water in addition to more equipment for repairs, it docked with the Soyuz T-13/Salyut 7 complex two days later. Following unloading, Progress 24 was packed with garbage and debris and was separated from the complex, de-orbited, and destroyed. A new Progress-type supply ship, Kosmos 1669, later docked with the complex following its launch on July 19.

In addition to new equipment for biological and astrophysical experiments, Kosmos 1669 carried a set of solar panels. On August 2, after several days of preparations and wearing improved extravehicular activity (EVA) spacesuits, Savinykh and Dzhanibekov emerged from Salyut and attached the new units to the station's faulty third solar panel assembly. They also installed a French micrometeorite collector designed to measure dust from Halley's comet on the station's exterior. The EVA lasted five hours. Tests showed that the installation had been a success; Salyut 7 had more power.

During the rest of August, the cosmonauts concentrated on continued Earth resources studies, not only as part of Kursk 85 but also in the Gyuzian 85 program, which focused on the Azerbaijan region of the Soviet Union.

In early September, Dzhanibekov and Savinykh turned to experiments concerned with the durability of materials in space. They used a camera called an Elektro-topograf to inspect the surface of Salyut 7 in search of minute changes in the samples mounted there. The station's docking module was also temporarily depressurized to expose other samples to open space. Crystal growth experiments called Biryuza and Analiz were performed. Medical and psychological maintenance continued. The Soviet news agency, TASS, reported that the cosmonauts had succeeded in growing a strain of Central Asian cotton in Salyut 7's greenhouse.

Meanwhile, at the mission control center in Kaliningrad, near Moscow, Salyut directors prepared to relieve the crew of Soyuz T-13 in order to begin the "winter" expedition, which would extend until March, 1986, the time of the closest approach to Earth of Halley's comet.

On September 17, 1985, at 1639 Moscow time, Soyuz T-14 was launched from Baikonur. It carried commander Vladimir Vasyutin, flight engineer Georgi Grechko, and cosmonaut-researcher Aleksandr Volkov. TASS announced that Vasyutin and Volkov would join Savinykh for continued work aboard Salyut 7 while Grechko, the veteran of two previous Salyut expeditions, would accompany Dzhanibekov back to Earth. This first crew rotation would later become routine for Soviet space station crews.

Soyuz T-14 docked with the Salyut 7/Soyuz T-13 complex at 1815 Moscow time on September 18, 1985. The next week was a difficult one aboard the station. In addition to the strain placed on life-support systems by a crew of five, it was necessary to pack scientific materials, photographic film, and personal effects accumulated during one hundred days in space while also setting up housekeeping for a new crew. All of this had to take place while routine work was performed. TASS reported that at one time during this week ten different scientific instruments aboard Salyut 7 were engaged in studies of Earth's atmosphere.

Early on the morning of September 25, Dzhanibekov and Grechko bade farewell to their three comrades, boarded Soyuz T-13, and closed the hatch. After separating from the station, they performed a day of "station-keeping" exercises, then returned to Earth, landing in the prime recovery zone, about 220 kilometers northeast of the city of Dzhezkazgan, at 1352 Moscow time on September 26, 1985.

Knowledge Gained

The flight of Soyuz T-13 was, to an unprecedented extent for the Soviet manned space program, a breakthrough in space operations and engineering rather than in pure science. Observations of Earth, space manufacturing, and biomedical experiments were all in progress aboard Salyut 7 prior to the accident which turned it, temporarily, into a derelict. Most of these were simply repaired and restarted by cosmonauts Dzhanibekov and Savinykh.

A French micrometeorite collector on the exterior of Salyut 7 during the cosmonauts' August 2, 1985, spacewalk, was sufficiently important that a year later another crew was to make a special trip from the Mir space station to Salyut 7 in order to retrieve it. Dzhanibekov and Savinykh's work made that possible.

In terms of lessons learned, the mission of Soyuz T-13 was comparable to the first American manned Skylab mission in 1973, in which three astronauts docked with a malfunctioning space station and restored it to working order. Soviet mission planners had to speculate on what had gone wrong with Salyut 7 and prepare the cosmonauts for as many possibilities as they could. That meant designing and constructing special tools, developing new mission plans and writing and debugging the attendant computer software, and training the cosmonauts and control teams. All of these preparations had to be made in a very short time, since every passing day lessened the chances that Salyut 7 could be repaired.

By the summer of 1985, Soviet flight controllers had grown very sophisticated in the unsung but vital business of providing psychological support to long-duration cosmonaut teams, keeping the men in touch with their families, introducing them—via television—to authors, politicians, and musicians, and allowing them to voice private complaints and criticisms. Soyuz T-13, with its compressed and unique inflight demands, provided the psychological support team with a new challenge: how to keep Dzhanibekov and Savinykh productive and happy when the men were confronted with the staggering amount of work they needed to perform.

The psychological support team succeeded. Dzhanibekov would later say that he and his partner worked in a "trancelike" state for days on end, and that when it came time for him to return to Earth, he was glad to be going, but also sad. It is this wealth of experience in the psychological and operational demands of manned spaceflight that will make it possible for the Soviet Union to achieve a permanent manned presence in space—and future flights to the Moon and Mars.

Context

For more than twenty years, the Soviet space program treated cosmonauts either as passive observers and experimental subjects or as strictly controlled extensions of ground-based engineers, scientists, and flight directors. All spacecraft in the Vostok, Voskhod, and Soyuz series were designed to be operated from mission control and often, in fact, simply flew unmanned, usually under the Kosmos name. The role of a pilot cosmonaut was to stand by in case automatic systems failed. When technical problems arose, as they did on Soyuz 1, Soyuz 10, Soyuz 15, and Soyuz 23, among other missions, cosmonauts were forced into emergency procedures designed only to get them home safely. Missions were frequently aborted.

This system had allowed the Soviet Union to send nonpilots into space as early as 1963, with the flight of Valentina Tereshkova, a parachutist by training. Not until 1983, twenty years later, with the flight of physicist Sally Ride, was it possible for the United States to open their astronaut corps to nonpilots. What the Soviet Union gained in scientific flexibility by having engineers and physicians in space was balanced by the rigidity of mission planning. By contrast, American astronauts, on Gemini, Apollo, and Skylab missions, in particular, were forced to work around potential problems and continue their missions.

By 1979, however, with the Soyuz 32 mission of cosmonauts Vladimir Lyakhov and Valeri Ryumin aboard Salyut 6, it was clear that greater flexibility was required if cosmonauts were to operate in space for six months or longer. On Soyuz 32, Ryumin and Lyakhov had performed an unplanned spacewalk to free a scientific instrument that, no longer needed, had remained attached to the station, threatening future operations. The spacewalk occurred three months after the failure of Soyuz 33 to dock with Salyut 6 and marked a turning point in Soviet space operations: From that point onward, the Soviets would make consistent attempts to let the cosmonaut crew make judgments, attempt manual dockings, perform emergency spacewalks, even take faulty equipment apart for repairs. (Coincidentally, the next Soviet cosmonaut to take an unplanned spacewalk was again Vladimir Lyakhov, as commander of Soyuz T-9 aboard Salyut 7 in November, 1983. The Salyut 7 flight director by that time was Valeri Ryumin.)

Under previous mission procedures, those dominant from 1961 to 1979, Salyut 7 would have been abandoned and Soyuz T-13 never launched. By 1985, however, flight directors and cosmonauts had the confidence to improvise, and their confidence was rewarded: Salyut 7 was home to two more crews between June, 1985, and July, 1986, and remained in orbit for several years later as an unmanned space materials laboratory suitable for a future manned visit.

Bibliography

Bond, Peter R. *Heroes in Space: From Gagarin to Challenger*. New York: Basil Blackwell, 1987. Readable and balanced history of the first twenty-five years of manned spaceflight.

Canby, Thomas Y. "Are the Soviets Ahead in Space?" *National Geographic* 170 (October, 1986): 420-459. A well-informed survey of the Soviet manned space program "a generation after Sputnik," with special emphasis on Soyuz T-13.

Contains quotes and original drawings by Vladimir Dzhanibekov.

Cassutt, Michael. *Who's Who in Space: The First Twenty-five Years*. Boston: G. K. Hall and Co., 1987. Contains biographical profiles of cosmonauts Dzhanibekov, Savinykh, Vasyutin, Grechko, and Volkov, in addition to details on the Soyuz T-13 mission.

Clark, Philip. *The Soviet Manned Space Program*. New York: Orion Books, 1988. The first post-*glasnost* history of the Soviet manned space program, containing new revelations about early missions and additional details on the rescue of Salyut 7.

Turnill, Reginald, ed. *Jane's Spaceflight Directory*. London: Jane's Publishing Co., 1987. Updated annually, this book contains facts and figures on all manned spaceflights, with special emphasis on key missions such as Soyuz T-13.

Michael Cassutt

Cross-References

Biological Effects of Space Travel on Humans, 188; Cosmonauts and the Soviet Cosmonaut Program, 273; The Salyut Space Station, 1233; The Skylab Program, 1285; Skylab 2, 1291; The Soyuz T Program, 1495; Soyuz 32 and 34, 1511; Soyuz T-14, 1557.

SOYUZ T-14

Date: September 17 to November 21, 1985
Type of mission: Manned space station flight
Country: The Soviet Union

Soyuz T-14 carried a crew of three cosmonauts to the Soviet space station Salyut 7 to join the two Soyuz T-13 cosmonauts already aboard as part of an ongoing program to study the effects of prolonged human exposure to the space environment. The first crew rotation was accomplished when one T-13 and one T-14 cosmonaut returned aboard T-13, but the T-14 mission was cut short by a medical emergency.

Principal personages
VLADIMIR VASYUTIN, the Soyuz T-14 commander
ALEKSANDR VOLKOV, the Soyuz T-14 cosmonaut-researcher
GEORGI GRECHKO, a crew member, Soyuz T-14
VIKTOR SAVINYKH, the Soyuz T-13 flight engineer
VLADIMIR DZHANIBEKOV, the Soyuz T-13 commander

Summary of the Mission

Soyuz T-14 was launched at 1239 Greenwich mean time (GMT) on September 17, 1985, with cosmonauts Vladimir Vasyutin, Georgi Grechko, and Aleksandr Volkov aboard. The vehicle reached an initial 91.4-minute orbit between 336 kilometers and 350 kilometers, inclined 51.6 degrees to the equator. The 7,000-kilogram spacecraft pursued, rendezvoused with, and, at 1415 GMT on September 18, successfully docked with the Salyut 7 space station and the attached Soyuz T-13 spacecraft.

The Soyuz T-14 cosmonauts were greeted in space by Soyuz T-13 crew members Vladimir Dzhanibekov and Viktor Savinykh, who had been in orbit for more than one hundred days following their successful reactivation of the malfunctioning and inert Salyut 7 space station. The five cosmonauts spent the next eight days of their joint flight continuing the observations of Earth, the technical experiments, and the maintenance activities which had been initiated by the T-13 crew.

Soyuz T-13 cosmonaut Dzhanibekov and T-14 cosmonaut Grechko separated the T-13 spacecraft from the Salyut 7/Soyuz T-14 complex on September 25 and, after a day of formation-flying and approach practices, returned to Earth aboard the T-13 spacecraft at 0952 GMT on September 26, leaving T-13's Savinykh and T-14's Vasyutin and Volkov aboard the Salyut 7/Soyuz T-14 complex. The exchange resulted in the first crew rotation in the history of space exploration. For the first time in a Salyut mission, cosmonaut crews were changed without leaving a space station unmanned.

While aboard the space station, flight engineer Savinykh, researcher Volkov, and mission commander Vasyutin evaluated solar array efficiency and continued the regular schedule of maintenance work on the various station systems begun by Dzhanibekov and Savinykh to bring the once-inert Salyut 7 to full operation.

In addition to systems maintenance, the crew conducted extensive visual and photographic geophysical observations of Earth's surface. Through mid-October, geophysical studies concentrated on areas of the Black, Aral, and Caspian seas, the Caucasus region, and Central Asia. The oceans of the world came under the scrutiny of Salyut's instruments as well.

Technical experiments were conducted to investigate the characteristics of Earth's atmosphere in close proximity to the orbiting complex, with special attention to the spectral and optical characteristics of the atmosphere and of noctilucent clouds. An array of instruments also conducted remote sensing of dust and gas pollution in Earth's atmosphere and made profiles of atmospheric aerosol content.

Studies were made of heat and mass transfer processes in liquid media under conditions of microgravity. Measurements of currents of high-energy electrons and positrons, used to study these particles' mechanisms and generation in near-Earth space, were also made during the crew's stay aboard the station.

A joint Soviet-French experiment, previously installed on the outside of the station during a spacewalk by cosmonauts Dzhanibekov and Savinykh as part of the T-13 mission, completed its first stage of operations. The objective of the experiment was to collect meteoritic matter from the comet Giacobini-Zinner in the region of near-Earth space.

In the field of biology, experiments designed to cultivate higher plants under weightless conditions and under conditions of artificial gravity were performed with pepper, onion, and lettuce sprouts. A portable centrifuge was used to simulate gravitation.

Extensive medical checks were conducted on the crew to assess cardiac bioelectric activity and to determine the effects of prolonged exposure to microgravity on body mass and muscle state. The cardiovascular systems of the cosmonauts were examined frequently during the mission. In addition to the usual measurements made while the cosmonauts were at rest or undergoing exercise with various onboard devices, such as a treadmill, the cosmonauts were examined while wearing their Chibis hydrostatic pressure suits, which simulated the effects of gravity by forcing the flow of blood to their lower bodies.

At 0916 GMT on October 2, 1985, the 20,000-kilogram Kosmos 1686 satellite, launched September 27, automatically docked with the Salyut 7/Soyuz T-14 complex after a mutual search, rendezvous, tethering, and docking operation controlled jointly by the cosmonauts aboard Salyut 7 and by the ground-based flight control center. In addition to more than doubling the length of the complex, to 35 meters, Kosmos 1686 carried equipment, materials, and freight to the complex to allow for further testing of equipment, units, and structural elements of the satellite. The descent module of the satellite also carried an array of telescopes. The newly enlarged complex allowed for additional testing of control methods for sophisticated orbital complexes of large size and mass. In addition, Kosmos 1686 carried equipment which enabled the cosmonauts to conduct extensive geophysical observations of the gas composition of Earth's upper atmosphere.

The T-14 mission was terminated early, two months into the flight, because of an illness suffered by mission commander Vladimir Vasyutin. Vasyutin had apparently experienced medical and psychological difficulties almost from the beginning of the flight, requiring flight engineer Savinykh to assume most of his official duties as mission commander. Initial insomnia, anxiety, and irritability were attributed to a slow adaption to spaceflight by the novice commander, and his difficulties were not immediately reported to the ground. As the mission progressed, however, chronic pain and high body temperature further complicated Vasyutin's condition and led the crew to report his problems to the Soviet flight control center on October 28. Drugs stored aboard Salyut 7 were prescribed, and some improvement was noted. Once his condition had stabilized to a point at which ground-based flight surgeons felt confident that he could withstand reentry and landing forces, the flight was terminated. Vasyutin, Savinykh, and Volkov returned to Earth on November 21, 1985, with the descent module touching down at 0931 GMT.

Following a preliminary examination at the landing site, which indicated that Vasyutin was in satisfactory condition, further medical evaluations and recuperation took place at a clinic near Moscow until his release on December 20. While the illness was officially reported as an inner inflammation from which he may have suffered prior to launch, widespread speculation about a possible nervous disorder or breakdown was further fueled by excerpts from engineer Savinykh's diary, published on December 29, which described Vasyutin as a "bundle of nerves." Still other reports diagnosed Vasyutin as mentally unstable.

Whether his illness was physical, psychological, or a combination of both, it resulted in the first termination of a spaceflight for medical reasons and left the Salyut 7 space station unmanned once again.

Knowledge Gained

The partial cosmonaut crew exchange accomplished by Soyuz T-13 and T-14 was a major accomplishment in demonstrating a procedure for maintaining a permanent manned presence in space. It marked the first time in the history of the Soviet space program that a Salyut space station was not left unmanned for at least a brief period of time during a crew change. The partial crew exchange procedure was designed to take advantage of the experiences of the previous crew and to avoid the deactivation of experiments and space station systems between manned visitations. Even though the early termination of the T-14 mission led to another period of umanned Salyut 7 operations, the crew exchange had established procedures for future continuous manned space station operations.

Procedures for automatic docking of spacecraft and unmanned supply ships with space stations were further refined during the T-14 mission; when T-14 rendezvoused and docked with Salyut 7, T-13 separated for its return to Earth, and the Kosmos 1686 satellite joined the Salyut 7/Soyuz T-14 complex. Such multiple and automated docking techniques were considered an integral part of assembling large stations in Earth orbit and conducting future manned lunar and planetary missions.

Scientific research occupied the crew throughout the time that Soyuz T-14 was linked to the Salyut 7 space station. Extensive photographic operations were conducted during the mission using a wide-angle camera, a multispectral camera system, and other spectrometric equipment. The cosmonauts reportedly filmed 16 million square kilometers of the Soviet Union and the world's oceans. The aerosol experiment obtained new data on the optical and spectral characteristics and composition of atmospheric gases, and on the nature and triggering mechanisms of luminescent clouds. In all, four hundred sessions of scientific experiments were conducted with eighty-five different instruments and devices produced by the Soviet Union and other countries. The crew used an electronic photometer from Czechoslovakia, a spectrometer from East Germany, and additional equipment from Bulgaria, France, and other countries as part of the Interkosmos program.

The medical problems of mission commander Vasyutin, which led to the early termination of the mission, raised important questions about the effects of prolonged spaceflight under conditions of microgravity. The implications for a prolonged mission, such as would be required for a manned flight to Mars (a stated goal of the Soviet space program), were major. A physically or mentally debilitating illness could seriously jeopardize the success of such a mission and endanger the safety of crew members.

Context

Soyuz T-14 was the ninth manned spacecraft to dock with Salyut 7, and the first to dock following the rescue mission of Soyuz T-13, which successfully resurrected the inert space station following onboard electrical problems which left it without power. The T-14 mission relieved one of the two T-13 crew members; Dzhanibekov returned to Earth aboard T-13 in the company of one of the T-14 cosmonauts, Georgi Grechko. Remaining aboard Salyut 7 were T-14's mission commander, Vasyutin, and research cosmonaut, Volkov, both making their first spaceflights, and T-13's flight engineer, Savinykh, a veteran of the nearly seventy-five-day T-4 mission to Salyut 6 in 1981.

Prior to T-14's arrival, Salyut 7 had been visited by eight Soyuz spacecraft and twenty-one cosmonauts since its launch on April 19, 1982. Less than three months after the return of T-14 to Earth, the Soviet Union would launch its newest space station, Mir; although Soyuz T-15 would visit Salyut 7 in 1986, Soviet manned operations would shift to Mir after that time.

During the Soyuz T-14 mission, two United States manned spaceflights were conducted. Space shuttle mission 21, a five-man military mission for space shuttle *Atlantis* from October 3 through October 7, launched two satellites into orbit for the U.S. Department of Defense. Space shuttle mission 22 followed on October 30, with space shuttle *Challenger* carrying a crew of eight on a Spacelab mission; a satellite was also launched during that seven-day flight.

Bibliography

Bond, Peter R. *Heroes in Space: From Gagarin to Challenger*. New York: Basil Blackwell, 1987. Covers the first quarter century of manned spaceflight, including the major programs and most missions of both the Soviet Union and the United States. Includes details of the Soyuz T-13 and T-14 missions, specifically with regard to the physical and mental health of T-14 mission commander Vasyutin. Suitable for general audiences.

Cassutt, Michael. *Who's Who in Space: The First Twenty-five Years*. Boston: G. K. Hall and Co., 1987. This reference work offers biographical sketches of many cosmonauts and astronauts, as well as space planners and engineers. In addition, a capsule summary of the Soyuz T-14 mission is presented.

Furniss, Tim. *Space Flight: The Records*. Enfield, Middlesex, England: Guinness Superlatives, 1985. Includes a detailed account of manned spaceflights and their personnel. Also contains biographical information on cosmonauts, as well as mission statistics and some background material on each flight.

Miles, Frank, and Nicholas Booth, eds. *Race to Mars: The Mars Flight Atlas*. New York: Harper and Row, Publishers, 1988. A detailed examination of the status of Soviet and American spaceflight capabilities in the context of possible manned flights to the planet Mars. The psychological hazards of such a prolonged mission are considered in the light of Vladimir Vasyutin's emotional problems, which are discussed at some length. Soviet progress toward planning a manned Mars flight, which would draw heavily on the Soviet space station experience, is considered.

Turnill, Reginald, ed. *Jane's Spaceflight Directory*. London: Jane's Publishing Co., 1987. Updated annually, this indispensable reference is the most complete resource about spaceflight, manned and unmanned. It contains details on the Soyuz T-14 mission and offers information on the experiments performed on Salyut 7.

Yenne, Bill. *The Pictorial History of World Spacecraft*. New York: Bison Books, 1988. Lavishly illustrated volume describing manned and unmanned space missions chronologically. Includes a color photograph of the T-14 crew and an illustration showing the Salyut 7/T-14/Kosmos 1686 complex.

Richard A. Sweetsir

Cross-References

Biological Effects of Space Travel on Humans, 188; Cosmonauts and the Soviet Cosmonaut Program, 273; The Salyut Space Station, 1233; The Soyuz Interkosmos Missions, 1489; The Soyuz T Program, 1495; Soyuz T-13, 1551.

SOYUZ T-15

Date: March 13 to July 16, 1986
Type of mission: Manned space station flight
Country: The Soviet Union

Soyuz T-15 carried two men on the first visit to the Soviet space station Mir, launched less than a month before. Their primary mission was to activate and test the systems aboard the station in preparation for long-duration missions to the complex. During the flight, Salyut 7 was also visited and reactivated by the T-15 crew. It was the first such dual-station mission.

Principal personages
LEONID KIZIM, the Soyuz T-15 commander
VLADIMIR SOLOVYOV, the Soyuz T-15 flight engineer
VLADIMIR A. SHATALOV, a cosmonaut and the head of the
cosmonaut training program

Summary of the Mission

Soyuz T-15, the first manned mission to the Mir space station, was launched aboard a three-stage A-2 (SL-4) rocket at 1233 Greenwich mean time (GMT) on March 13, 1986, from the Baikonur cosmodrome. The launch had been announced in advance and was televised live in an impressive display of greater Soviet confidence and openness with respect to space activities. The initial 88.8-minute orbit, ranging from 193 kilometers to 237 kilometers above Earth, was adjusted frequently during the two days of rendezvous maneuvers which followed orbital insertion, and docking with Mir's forward docking port was successfully completed at 1338 GMT on March 15.

Once aboard Mir, the cosmonauts began activating the many systems housed on the third-generation Soviet space station and evaluating the performance of its various components. Among the major advantages of Mir over the earlier Soviet space stations were the improved facilities for rest and exercise, the expanded living quarters (which provided crew members with private compartments and their own viewing ports), and more sophisticated computer systems for the monitoring of station components and the rapid collection and display of scientific information gathered by the station's instrumentation. The crew tested and evaluated most of the Mir systems, some 90 percent of which were different from those aboard Salyut 7, and adjusted the station's new computers and improved communications system.

The unmanned 7,000-kilogram Progress 25 cargo spacecraft was launched on March 19, and two days later it successfully docked with Mir at the aft docking port. For the next month, the cargo vehicle remained attached to Mir while Kizim and Solovyov transferred fuel and equipment from it to the Mir station and to their own T-15 spacecraft. Once the Progress was fully unloaded, the crew stored in its lockers materials to be returned to Earth. Progress 25 was undocked on April 20 at 2224 GMT and de-orbited five hours later, leaving Mir's aft docking port available to receive Progress 26, which docked on April 26 at 2126 GMT. The crew again went through the process of unloading the supplies, fuel, and additional instruments aboard the Progress vehicle. While much of the cargo carried to Mir by the two Progress spacecrafts was slated for use aboard the space station, at least some of the fuel and instrument components were loaded into the T-15 spacecraft for later transfer to the Salyut 7/Kosmos 1686 complex. Progress 26 undocked June 22 at 1825 GMT and was de-orbited, leaving the aft docking port open for future operations. The successful twin dockings demonstrated Mir's capability to receive automated cargo vehicles smoothly and without control problems. Also, the dockings further tested the stability of large space assemblies composed of separate components.

Soyuz T-15 undocked from Mir at 1212 GMT on May 5 and began a series of manually controlled orbital rendezvous maneuvers which culminated in the successful docking at the forward docking port of Salyut 7 on May 6. The transfer between Mir and Salyut 7 (the spacecraft were separated by a distance of 3,000 kilometers) was complicated by the inability to predict accurately the mass of the additional cargo being transported; with the assistance of the onboard computer, optical instruments, and advice from ground control, the operation was completed smoothly.

The plan to have one crew visit two different space stations during the same mission necessitated extensive prior training, which at least in part dictated the selection of a cosmonaut team which had already spent much time aboard Salyut 7. Kizim and Solovyov were extensively trained in the Mir systems as well, even before Mir had been placed in orbit.

Several hundred kilograms of cargo from the two Progress vehicles were transported to Salyut 7 with the crew to replace equipment which had exceeded service lifetimes. Kizim and Solovyov resumed the work of the T-14 mission, which had been terminated early by the illness of mission commander Vladimir Vasyutin the previous November. A major objective of the cosmonauts' stay at Salyut 7 was the successful construction and testing of a large girderlike telescoping space structure. The structure, described as a hinged-lattice truss, would be used as a mount for several instruments and was considered a prototype for future construction elements from which cosmonauts would assemble orbital platforms, solar energy collecting arrays, and antennae for large telescopes. During operations with the truss, welding and soldering tasks were undertaken much as they would be during construction work on Earth, and new spacesuits which made it easier and more comfortable to work in space were tested.

More conventional experiments involving astrophysical, photographic, medical, and biological studies were also conducted, and maintenance tasks were accomplished during the cosmonauts' stay aboard the complex. The crew continued the T-14 routine of nature photography, studies of the deep space origins of high-energy electrons and positrons, upper atmospheric ozone measurements, and observations of lettuce growth in artificially created gravity. An experiment designed to overcome problems of obtaining superpure biological substances in orbit was continued, along with studies of Earth's natural resources.

While T-15 was docked with the Salyut 7/Kosmos 1686 complex, the Soviets launched the first of the improved Soyuz TM spaceships on an unmanned test flight on May 21. After a fifty-hour rendezvous approach, TM-1 successfully docked with the vacated Mir space station. The TM-1 spaceship remained at Mir only six days, undocking on May 29, but the success of the flight ensured that T-15 would be the last of the Soyuz-T series spacecraft. TM-1 continued in independent flight until May 30, when it reentered Earth's atmosphere and was recovered.

Their fifty-day stay at the Salyut 7/Kosmos 1686 complex completed, the cosmonauts undocked their T-15 spacecraft and returned to the Mir space station on June 26, carrying with them some of the equipment which had once been a part of Salyut 7. They brought back to Mir containers of plant seeds which had been aboard Salyut 7 for three years, later returning the seeds to Earth for a genetic study. Additional tests of Mir systems were conducted in the days which followed, and equipment brought back by the cosmonauts from Salyut 7 was installed and put to use in the newer space station. In late June, the crew tested Mir's temperature control system under maximum heat loads, and in early July, the cosmonauts resumed geophysical experiments—including a survey of glaciers, farmlands, and geological structures.

Kizim and Solovyev, their mission concluded, returned the Mir space station to automatic operation to await a future mission, then undocked their T-15 spaceship for the return to Earth. Their 125-day flight ended with a successful landing at 1234 GMT, July 16.

The following month, on August 22, the propulsion system of Kosmos 1686, still attached to Salyut 7, was used to place the complex into a higher orbit of some 480 kilometers, where the station, no longer planned for use as a working installation, would have its orbital lifetime extended an additional eight years. Although deactivated, the complex would be monitored for some time to come. Even after the end of its service life and the loss of radio contact, the possibility would remain that a future transfer mission from Mir or another operational space complex might be flown to Salyut 7/Kosmos 1686 to examine the long-duration lifetime and reliability of such station systems as airtight seals, tanks, and hydraulic and pneumatic systems. The retrieval of components of the space station for scientific study and the monitoring of the orbital decay rates of such a large structure would be additional options for further research.

Knowledge Gained

For the first time in manned spaceflight operations, a single crew performed work in two separate and independently orbiting space stations. The crew traveled between the two, in a demonstration of techniques described by cosmonaut Kizim as essential for servicing, performing work, and rendering emergency aid to adjacent complexes. For the first time also, future manned spaceflight operations were described in terms of orbital settlements consisting of many separate dwellings and laboratories following similar orbital paths and easily linked by transfer vehicles, rather than as a single, integrated structure of modules. The dismantling of the Soyuz structure further demonstrated the feasibility of large-scale construction projects essential to future space station operations as well as for manned ventures beyond near-Earth space.

The accumulation of record time in space, 737 days between the two cosmonauts, provided invaluable medical and psychological information on the effects of prolonged and repeated spaceflight missions. Because the same cosmonaut team had flown a previous record-setting mission, further information on the compatibility of crew members in the confines of space stations was available. While aboard Mir, the team established a fifteen-hour work day, which included time for physical conditioning and medical evaluations.

One major international project conducted during the mission involved photographing regions within East Germany as part of an experiment to study the dynamics of geosystems and the state of various ecological systems by remote-sensing equipment. Simultaneous photography from laboratory aircraft in flight and from the Kosmos 1602 satellite were correlated with the Mir data for the study; the objective was to establish measures for environmental protection planning of forest and farmland areas of member countries of the Council for Mutual Economic Assistance.

Context

Soyuz T-15 was launched twenty-two days after the successful orbiting of the new Soviet space station Mir and 111 days after the premature termination of the Soyuz T-14 mission. Two veteran cosmonauts were selected for the important mission. In addition to activating systems aboard Mir, the crew of T-15 ferried many pieces of equipment and instruments no longer needed aboard Salyut/Kosmos 1686 complex to Mir, where they were to be installed for continuing use. This ability to "cannibalize" deactivated space stations was a significant step forward in maximizing utilization of space hardware already in place, while minimizing costs that would otherwise be incurred by sending similar hardware from Earth in a separate launch.

The use of Soyuz T-15 as a space ferry was described by cosmonaut Vladimir Shatalov, head of the cosmonaut training program, as the first step in a system that would ultimately allow for the retrieval of satellites in geosynchronous orbit by unmanned robot ferry vehicles. Shatalov envisioned the use of automatic vehicles for repairs and refueling. Mir and the Progress series of tanker spacecrafts were described as potential "filling stations" for Soyuz manned and unmanned space ferry vehicles.

Spacewalks performed by Kizim and Solovyov on Soyuz T-15 brought the two cosmonauts' total experience to eight spacewalks each, for a combined time of 31 hours and 40 minutes of extravehicular activity. This experience provided Soviet scientists with valuable information on man's ability to perform important work outside the confines of a spaceship. Growing Soviet confidence in the ability to perform in "raw" space resulted in the first-ever live broadcasts of the two Soviet spacewalks on May 28 and May 31, when the cosmonauts erected a 12-meter structure on the Salyut 7 space station and attached an assortment of instruments to it.

Mission commander Leonid Kizim had previously flown the twelve-day Soyuz T-3 mission to the Salyut 6 space station in 1980 and the record-breaking 237-day Soyuz T-10/Salyut 7 mission in 1984. During the T-15 flight, Kizim shattered the world record for cumulative time in space (362 days) and three days later became the first human to accumulate a full year of space experience. At the time of Kizim's return to Earth at the conclusion of the T-15 mission, his cumulative spaceflight record was 375 days. Fellow cosmonaut Vladimir Solovyov, who accumulated 125 days of spaceflight on the T-15 mission, had previously flown with Kizim on the 237-day T-10 flight.

The Soyuz T-15 cosmonauts essentially "mothballed" the Salyut 7 space station. Shortly after T-15's return to Earth, ground controllers boosted Salyut 7 to a higher orbit for storage. With an expected lifetime of eight years, it could conceivably be reactivated for future use if necessary. Salyut 7 had been visited by ten crews of cosmonauts during its active lifetime, including two international teams which included French and Indian cosmonauts. It had been manned for a total of eight hundred days and was the station aboard which the record 237-day spaceflight had been set.

With six docking ports available to Mir for expansion into a larger complex and a demonstrated ability to do construction and repair work in space, space planners were projecting future orbital crews of six to twelve cosmonauts and up to five specialized modules at a time. These projections included permanent repair teams with all necessary materials at hand for repair and replacement of worn or malfunctioning parts. Future manned and unmanned spacecraft would only have to rendezvous and dock with the space station for repairs, servicing, and refueling before being returned to independent flight.

The T-15 mission began at a time when the American manned space program was grounded following the explosion of space shuttle *Challenger* and the loss of its seven-astronaut crew on January 28, 1986. At the conclusion of the T-15 mission, Soviet cosmonauts had accumulated a total of 104,374 hours in spaceflight, compared to the American total of 42,453 hours. The live television broadcast of the T-15 launch and later mission spacewalks pointed to a new Soviet openness at a time when competition from the world's other superpower was less threatening.

Bibliography

Bond, Peter R. *Heroes in Space: From Gagarin to Challenger*. New York: Basil

Blackwell, 1987. Covers the first quarter century of manned spaceflight, including the major programs and most missions of both the Soviet Union and the United States. Includes details of the Soyuz T-15 mission to Mir and Salyut 7. Suitable for general audiences.

Canby, Thomas Y. "Are the Soviets Ahead in Space?" *National Geographic* 170 (October, 1986): 420-459. An interesting article which sets out to answer the predominant question of the space race. It offers a survey of the Soviet manned program and discusses the achievements and failures of the Soyuz and Salyut programs.

Cassutt, Michael. *Who's Who in Space: The First Twenty-five Years*. Boston: G. K. Hall and Co., 1987. A useful work which offers biographical sketches of many key cosmonauts and astronauts. Also provides details on the Soyuz missions.

Furniss, Tim. *Space Flight: The Records*. Enfield, England: Guinness Superlatives, 1985. Detailed record of international manned spaceflights and their crews. While publication preceded the Soyuz T-15 mission, biographical sketches on cosmonauts Kizim and Solovyov and details of their prior missions provide useful background information.

Turnill, Reginald, ed. *Jane's Spaceflight Directory*. London: Jane's Publishing Co., 1987. This well-researched reference book is valuable for its capsule summaries of all manned and unmanned missions. Updated annually, it offers a complete index and some biographical information on cosmonauts.

Yenne, Bill. *The Pictorial History of World Spacecraft*. New York: Bison Books, 1988. Lavishly illustrated volume describing manned and unmanned space missions chronologically. Includes details of the T-15 mission and illustrations of possible Mir orbital complex assemblies.

Richard A. Sweetsir

Cross-References

Biological Effects of Space Travel on Humans, 188; Cosmonauts and the Soviet Cosmonaut Program, 273; The Mir Space Station, 1025; The Salyut Space Station, 1233; The Soyuz T Program, 1495.

THE SOYUZ TM PROGRAM

Date: Beginning May 21, 1986
Type of program: Manned space station flights
Country: The Soviet Union

In preparation for operations with the Mir space station, the Soviet Union developed the Soyuz TM, an upgraded version of its standard crew transport vehicle. The vehicle incorporated many improvements which extended its range and maneuverability for rendezvousing with Mir. The Soyuz TM could also remain in orbit much longer than its predecessors.

Principal personages
YURI ROMANENKO, the Soyuz TM-2 commander
ALEXANDER LAVEIKIN, the Soyuz TM-2 flight engineer
ALEXANDER VIKTORENKO, the Soyuz TM-3 commander
ALEXANDER ALEXANDROV, the Soyuz TM-3 flight engineer
VLADIMIR TITOV, the Soyuz TM-4 commander
MUSA MANAROV, the Soyuz TM-4 flight engineer
ANATOLI SOLOVYEV, the Soyuz TM-5 commander
VLADIMIR LYAKHOV, the Soyuz TM-6 commander

Summary of the Program

The existence of the TM version of the Soyuz spacecraft was first publicly revealed in connection with the unmanned test flight of the vehicle designated TM-1, launched May 21, 1986. It is possible, however, that Kosmos 1669 had been an earlier test version of the new spacecraft. Kosmos 1669 was launched July 19, 1985, and on July 21 it was docked with Salyut 7, where it remained for thirty-nine days. At the time, the Soviets described the vehicle as "similar" in appearance to the Progress vehicle (that is, it looked like a Soyuz), adding only that the craft carried onboard equipment to conduct research in autonomous flight and was "part of an orbital complex." This comment was interpreted to refer to some kind of unmanned research laboratory that would require periodic visits to a space station to have its experiments changed. Yet the description, mission characteristics, and timing are all consistent with those of the TM vehicle and are reminiscent of the way the Soyuz T vehicle was first flight-tested as Kosmos 869, 1001, and 1074. The Soyuz TM-1 mission was launched from Tyuratam by the standard Soyuz A-4 booster. On May 23, 1986, it approached the Mir station and conducted an automatic docking at the forward port, which was then vacant because the Soyuz T-15 crew had left Mir to work aboard Salyut 7 for a six-week period. Flight controllers conducted tests of the unmanned Mir/TM complex before undocking and deorbiting the TM-1 on May 30.

The next flight of a TM vehicle initiated the new design's use in manned flight operations. TM-2 was launched from Tyuratam at 12:38 A.M. Moscow time on February 6, 1987, with a two-man crew commanded by Yuri Romanenko. Alexander

Laveikin, a civilian cosmonaut, was aboard as the flight engineer. Under automatic guidance, the TM-2 took some fifty hours to rendezvous and dock with Mir. That was roughly twice the time previously taken for manned rendezvous missions but was similar to the time required by the Progress vehicles to execute their automatic rendezvous. Once in space, the craft's main engine was fired three times to achieve an orbit matching that of Mir, which circles Earth at an average height of about 350 kilometers. TM-2 docked at the forward port at 2:28 A.M. Moscow time on February 8. Progress 27 was already docked at the rear port, giving the three-vehicle assemblage a combined length of 28 meters and a total mass of 32,650 kilograms. Romanenko and Laveikin were to reactivate Mir and begin the Soviets' long anticipated "permanent presence in space" with a mission expected to last until the end of the year.

With all the long-duration missions, it is necessary to replace periodically the vehicle left docked to the space station to ensure its operational integrity. Among the improvements designed into the TM version of Soyuz were some which extended the orbital life of the vehicle from 90 to 180 days. Consequently, it was not until 4:59 A.M. on July 22 that the TM-2 vehicle's replacement was launched into orbit, carrying a three-man crew: the commander, Alexander Viktorenko; Syrian research cosmonaut Mohammad Al Fares; and the Soviet cosmonaut Alexander Alexandrov. Meanwhile, a large astrophysics observatory module called Kvant (meaning "quantum") had already expanded the basic Mir craft. When TM-3 joined the station complex at 6:31 A.M. on July 24, the elements included (from front to rear) TM-2, Mir, Kvant, and TM-3. After the docking was successfully achieved, it was announced that cosmonaut Laveikin's electrocardiograph had indicated irregularities for several weeks and that Alexandrov had been sent as his replacement. Viktorenko, Fares, and Laveikin returned to Earth in the TM-2 vehicle at 4:04 A.M. on July 29, while Romanenko and Alexandrov continued the long-duration mission aboard Mir. One of their first tasks was a transposition maneuver to relocate the TM-3 craft to the forward docking port vacated by TM-2. This routine is necessary with every Soyuz exchange because only the rear ports of the Salyut and Mir stations permit the Progress freighters to conduct automated refueling operations.

The next manned mission to Mir did not occur until the scheduled time for Romanenko and Alexandrov's replacements. TM-4 was launched from Tyuratam at 2:18 P.M. on December 21, 1987, under the command of Vladimir Titov. The flight engineer was Musa Manarov and a third crewman, Anatoli Levchenko, was designated as test pilot. Docking occurred at 3:51 P.M. on December 23, 1987. For the next six days, the five-man crew worked together until Titov and Manarov were comfortable with the effects of weightlessness. Then the command was passed from Romanenko to Titov. On December 29, Levchenko, Romanenko, and Alexandrov undocked the aging TM-3 vehicle and began their return to Earth, landing three hours and twenty-one minutes later. For Romanenko, returning to Earth ended a record-breaking 327-day stay in space. The exchange had marked the first complete crew replacement in orbit.

As early as August of 1986, plans had been announced to refly the Bulgarian Interkosmos mission in June of 1988. The first attempt (Soyuz 33) had failed to dock successfully with Salyut. TM-5 was launched on June 7, 1988, at 6:03 P.M. Moscow time. The mission was commanded by Anatoli Solovyev, with cosmonaut Viktor Savinykh as the flight engineer and the Bulgarian Alexander Alexandrov (no relation to the cosmonaut by the same name) aboard as a research cosmonaut. The docking occurred at the aft port of the Kvant module on June 9. After a week-long program of joint experiments, the three-man TM-5 crew returned to Earth in the TM-4 craft on June 17. The next day, Titov and Manarov piloted the TM-5 in the standard transposition maneuver to relocate it to the forward port.

Reports circulated that the next Interkosmos mission would occur in early 1989 and would carry a research cosmonaut from Afghanistan. The mission was rescheduled for August, 1988, because, according to the official explanation, the Afghan pilots in training for the flight already knew the Russian language and that greatly sped the training period. Western authorities believed that a more likely explanation was that the flight was rescheduled to provide a gesture of Soviet-Afghan goodwill before the Soviets completed withdrawing troops from Afghanistan in early 1989. In any case, the crew received only half of the standard twelve-month period of intensive training for the mission. TM-6 was launched on August 29 and docked two days later, carrying Vladimir Lyakhov, the commander; Valeri Polyakov, a physician cosmonaut; and Abdullah Ahad Mohamand, an Afghan research cosmonaut, to join Titov and Manarov. At 2:55 P.M. Moscow time on September 6, after six days aboard Mir, Lyakhov and Mohamand undocked the TM-5 vehicle from the forward port, leaving Polyakov to stay with Titov and Manarov for the duration of their mission.

What followed was a particularly tense episode that drew world attention to the two cosmonauts. Once free of the Mir, a returning Soyuz must jettison the spherical forward section of the craft containing the docking collar, hatch, and the guidance equipment needed to rendezvous with the station. It is discarded prior to reentry in order to reduce the mass of the vehicle. At this point, the cosmonauts are committed to a reentry and can no longer return to the space station. After accomplishing this step, Lyakhov and Mohamand programmed the onboard computer to fire the Soyuz TM-5's main engine in a braking maneuver to begin the descent to earth. What should have been a 230-second engine burn ended abruptly after 60 seconds—producing enough thrust to change the orbit drastically, but not enough to bring about a safe descent. As the cosmonauts and ground controllers worked to understand why the engine had shut down prematurely, the automatic sequencer restarted the burn. Lyakhov immediately overrode the computer with a manual command to shut the engine down again, because the opportunity to land on Soviet soil had already passed for that orbit. The spacecraft made two additional orbits before attempting another burn, probably to give flight controllers a chance to get enough data on the TM-5's new orbit to compute the best possible reentry trajectory. When the engine was again sequenced, it once more shut itself down immediately. By the time another reentry could be attempted, the Sun had set on the landing zone in Kazakhstan, and it was decided to postpone the reentry until the following day.

Supplies of air and food in the TM-5 were adequate for forty-eight hours, and the crew members seemed relatively secure about their ultimate ability to get back to Earth. Yet as the normal forty-five-minute reentry stretched into twenty-five hours, the cosmonauts were in considerable discomfort. There was a lack of onboard toilet facilities, and the men were almost immobile in their bulky pressure suits. Meanwhile, it was determined that the first engine shutdown had occurred when stray sunlight entered the field of view of the vehicle's horizon sensor, causing the computer to function as if TM-5 had lost proper orientation for reentry. The next automatic abort had occurred because an error was made in reprogramming the computer. Reentry conditions were again favorable at 4:00 A.M. on September 7, and this time the automatic equipment worked flawlessly, bringing TM-5 to a safe landing at 4:50 A.M. Had there been further problems, the cosmonauts could have attempted a manually guided reentry, but such a maneuver is considered difficult and quite risky. General Vladimir Dzhanibekov, a cosmonaut with five spaceflights to his credit, blamed the episode on a lack of attention to detail. "We lost caution. We somewhat lost vigilance," he later told the international press.

Knowledge Gained

The Soyuz TM vehicle demonstrates how successfully the Soviet space program has utilized an engineering philosophy that relies on proved technology rather than the development of state-of-the-art hardware. In terms of its performance, the TM is a much more capable spacecraft than the original Soyuz or the later Soyuz T designs. Yet it retains the structural design first put into service in 1967. The significant differences in the TM are primarily in the onboard computers and the flight instrumentation needed to execute rendezvous missions with the Soviet space stations.

When the original Soyuz vehicle was designed, the Soviets lacked the technology to miniaturize the powerful computers needed to solve complex navigational problems, so rendezvous missions were directed from the Soviets' mission control center. As advances in this technology have become available, however, they have gradually been introduced into the spacecraft to reduce the amount of data flowing between the vehicle and mission control and to simplify the management of missions involving multiple spacecraft. Using the new Kurs (course) computer, a TM craft is able to compute, simultaneously, the parameters of its own orbit and that of the targeted Mir vehicle. The TM is able to direct all the necessary maneuvers to bring about a docking.

Like the T, the TM is a three-seat spacecraft. Yet the use of newer, lightweight materials in the launch escape system and reentry parachutes permit the operational range of the TM to be extended to more than 350 kilometers in altitude, the height at which Mir typically orbits. The earlier Soyuz vehicles required the Salyut stations to maneuver to lower altitudes before a rendezvous could be attempted.

Throughout most of the Salyut program, a standing rule prevented any Soyuz vehicle remaining docked to the station for longer than one hundred days. Space planners were concerned that the inert gas used to pressurize the fuel lines would leak through the elastic membrane and contaminate the propellant and oxidizer, leading to engine failures. To rectify this problem, the TM vehicle uses metallic diaphragms in place of the elastic membranes, allowing it to stay in orbit for at least 180 days, thereby reducing the cost of station operations considerably.

Other improvements in the TM include a second air-to-ground channel to facilitate voice communications between the spacecraft, mission control, and the Mir, and the addition of a lift-generating airfoil on the reentry module to allow the craft to fly a shallower reentry path.

Context

One of the principal factors behind the design improvements in the TM was the need to upgrade the Soyuz to enable it to execute all maneuvers necessary to rendezvous and dock with a large space station which had limited mobility. In the Salyut program it had been common practice for the station to be an active participant in the maneuvering; in fact, whenever a Soyuz or Progress vehicle approached it was necessary that the Salyut adjust its orientation constantly to keep its forward end pointed at the visiting spacecraft. In this way, the smaller craft's Ilga (needle) radar could obtain the tracking information needed by its guidance program. With the prospect that Mir would eventually become a 90,000-kilogram mass involving several appendages to its six-axis docking node, designers realized that the station could not tolerate either the fuel consumption rate to permit such maneuvering or the structural stresses that would accompany it.

Some of the TM's design improvements are probably not directly attributable to engineering for the manned program alone. For example, the problem of maintaining the integrity of the liquid fuels under pressure during prolonged periods in orbit affects certain unmanned vehicles also. There is some evidence that the metallic diaphragm system utilized in the TM fuel tanks had first been developed for a family of military surveillance satellites used by the Soviets, and it is not inconceivable that the two different vehicles use identical or very similar fuel tanks.

It further appears that several of the key improvements represented in the TM had actually been brought into service on earlier vehicles. The Soyuz T-11 spacecraft was launched to Salyut 7 in April, 1984, and remained docked until early October, despite the fact that an opportunity to conduct the usual Soyuz exchange occurred at the normal ninety-day interval. A crew visited Salyut 7 in July, but there seemed to be no concern when they returned to Earth in the Soyuz T-12 vehicle that had taken them into orbit. In a similar demonstration of things to come, Soyuz T-13 was launched to Salyut 7 on June 6, 1985, and took more than forty-eight hours to achieve its docking. It followed a rendezvous approach similar to that of the Progress vehicles (and later TM vehicles) rather than what was then standard for manned missions, and it was announced that the crew was evaluating new flight controls and a new onboard computer. These examples suggest that the TM was not so much an all-new design for the Soyuz craft, but a variation that collected some of the best developments in applicable technology.

All these improvements notwithstanding, the Soyuz TM is essentially the tried and proved space vehicle that has been the mainstay of Soviet manned spaceflight for decades. Its greatest strengths are its reliability and suitability for a well-defined task—shuttling crews to and from orbit. Like the American military jeep, it lacks elegance, comfort, and sophistication, but it gets the job done well, and at a relatively small cost.

Bibliography

Furniss, Tim. *Manned Spaceflight Log*. Rev. ed. London: Jane's Publishing Co., 1986. This source provides a detailed account of all manned spaceflights to 1986. Particularly strong on the Soviet space program. Includes photographs not found readily in other sources.

Hooper, Gordon R. *The Soviet Cosmonaut Team: Comprehensive Guide to the Men and Women of the Soviet Manned Space Programme*. San Diego: Univelt, 1986. Among the most complete publications on this subject, this book contains eighty-seven detailed biographies of the Soviet and Interkosmos cosmonauts, including information about their education, flight training, mission assignment histories, and supporting roles. Most of the Soyuz TM commanders are included, but many of the secondary personnel now involved in Soviet manned missions are from the ranks of young trainees unknown to the West. In addition to the biographies, this book contains much valuable information about training facilities and mission goals. Illustrated with photographs.

Johnson, Nicholas L. *Soviet Space Programs: 1980-1985*. San Diego: Univelt, 1987. This volume is a compilation and synthesis of the information published annually by Teledyne Brown Engineering as *The Soviet Year in Space* for the period from 1981 through 1985. The publication provides an excellent overview of the status of the Soviet manned spaceflight program (and the Soviet space program as a whole) immediately prior to the introduction of the Soyuz TM and Mir vehicles.

_____. *The Soviet Year in Space*. Colorado Springs, Colo.: Teledyne Brown Engineering, 1988. This publication contains an authoritative and objective assessment of the year's developments in Soviet manned and unmanned spaceflight. Its information is derived from leading public sources, including Russian-language sources, both technical and general. The publication itself is aimed at a technically literate general audience.

Oberg, James E. *Red Star in Orbit*. New York: Random House, 1981. An excellent overview of Soviet spaceflight, with special emphasis on the political implications of certain programs and technology. Illustrations document the early Soviet policy of disinformation concerning space exploration.

Richard S. Knapp

Cross-References

Biological Effects of Space Travel on Humans, 188; Cosmonauts and the Soviet Cosmonaut Program, 273; Soviet Launch Vehicles, 742; The Mir Space Station, 1025; The Soyuz Interkosmos Missions, 1489; The Soyuz T Program, 1495; Soyuz T-10B, T-11, and T-12, 1544; Soyuz T-13, 1551; Soyuz T-15, 1562.

SPACE CENTERS AND LAUNCH SITES
IN CHINA, INDIA, AND JAPAN

Date: Beginning November 11, 1955
Type of facility: Space centers and launch sites
Countries: China, India, and Japan

Japan, China, and India were respectively the fourth, fifth, and seventh powers to orbit space satellites successfully. Their development of essential space centers and launch facilities, however, predated their satellite capabilities by years.

Principal personages
HIDEO ITOKAWA, a pioneer of Japanese space research
TU SHANCHENG, Director, Chinese Academy of Space Technology
VIKRAM A. SARABHAI, a pioneer of the Indian space program

Summary of the Facilities

With the signing of the U.S.-Japanese Peace Treaty in 1951 and the subsequent removal of restrictions on Japan's construction of aircraft and rockets, the Japanese moved swiftly into space research. Rocket testing of "Baby" and "Pencil" rockets, under the direction of Tokyo University's Hideo Itokawa, then began at the Akita Range. Located in Akita Prefecture in the northwest of Japan's main island of Honshu, the Range faces the Sea of Japan. It is served by mountainous Honshu's principal west coast highway and rail line. As the power of sounding rockets increased, however, Akita Range proved inadequate, the Sea of Japan being too narrow for safe testing.

Consequently, construction of new facilities in Kagoshima Prefecture began in February, 1962, and Kagoshima Space Center formally opened in December, 1965. It is located on Nagatsubo Peninsula at the southern extremity of Kyushu Island, and faces the Pacific. As described by launch-site experts Kenneth Gatland, Charles Vick, and Theo Pirard, Kagoshima Space Center occupies 0.72 square kilometer atop eight leveled hills, the facilities being sited at different heights. Its range control center, the dish antennae of its telemetry receivers, its radio tracking equipment, and its payload assembly shops is sited 320 meters above sea level. Its Lambda rocket center, with mobile launchpads for Kappa and S rockets, on the other hand, is sited 277 meters above sea level. The Mu complex—to which Lambda pad was later moved—is Kagoshima's largest, containing a service tower, launching and assembly shops, a blockhouse, a satellite test shop, a dynamic balance test shop, and a storehouse for propellants.

Directed by the Japanese government's Institute of Space and Aeronautical Science, Kagoshima Space Center was able to launch solid-fueled sounding rockets by 1965. By 1966, facilities were upgraded to handle more powerful Mu satellite launch vehicles. Failures marked this program between 1966 and 1969, but on February 11, 1970, a Lambda 4S-5 successfully placed Japan's first payload, the 23.8-kilogram

Oshumi satellite, into a 337-by-5,151-kilometer orbit. Since 1970, Kagoshima averages two launches per year for scientific purposes, and improvements were made during the 1980's to handle M-3S-kai-1 and -2 vehicles, which it was thought would allow Japan to participate in interplanetary exploration.

Under the administrative umbrella of the National Space Development Agency (NASDA), established in October, 1969, not only were several other space-related organizations integrated with Kagoshima Space Center, but new research and launching centers were also created. While NASDA is mainly government-funded, it does draw contributions from businesses and other organizations interested in applied space technology. Consequently, since the Kagoshima Space Center is functionally oriented toward scientific exploration, the Nii-jima Test Center, established in 1964, was devoted to research into communication, Earth observation, and maritime and aeronautical observation satellites—and to liquid propellants. NASDA's initial objective was to advance Japan's independent launch capabilities for space placement of geostationary satellites. Located 43 kilometers off the mouth of Tokyo Bay, the Nii-jima facility successfully developed multistage vehicles employed by sounding rockets with a liquid second stage. The progress realized soon rendered aspects of the Nii-jima Test Center inadequate.

Therefore, in 1966, under direction of Japan's most prestigious university, the University of Tokyo (a government institution), work commenced on advanced facilities on Tanegashima, an island in the Pacific 98 kilometers south of the Kagoshima Space Center on Kyushu. In 1968, the Takesaki site on Tanegashima was ready for the testing of small rockets. Meanwhile, north of the Takesaki site, at Osaki, NASDA completed what became Japan's largest launch base for liquid propellant rockets. Because the Japanese government decided to accelerate its entry into space by purchasing U.S. technologies (including the reliable Thor booster and a solid third stage), the Osaki site had to be adapted to handling two different rockets. As a result, along with the site's essential test range, telemetry systems, control building, blockhouse, and assembly and storage units (and its infrastructure), facilities were provided for the Q rocket with its Mu first stage and a Nippon liquid propellant as a second stage, and for the N-1 rocket. The N-1 was an American-licensed Thor supporting a Japanese second stage and an American solid-fueled third stage.

Dealing with these basic complexities yielded fruit, for in September, 1975, NASDA orbited its 83-kilogram Kiku satellite—its first payload in space. In February, 1977, the Tanegashima Space Center became the third space center in the world (using its N-1) to place a satellite, Kiku 2, in geostationary orbit. During the early 1980's, the Osaki launch site, employing American technology again in the N-2 launcher, placed a 350-kilogram geostationary satellite in position and proceeded with the development of more powerful H-1 launchers. Starting in August, 1986, H-1's lifted application satellites (for remote sensing, direct television coverage, and telecommunications) into geostationary orbit. Still more powerful H-2's, able to launch 1,980-kilogram payloads into geosynchronous orbit prospectively by 1992, mandated a massive expansion of Tanegashima. In May, 1986, construction began to transform the center into one of the world's most spectacular spaceports, providing dramatic evidence of Japan's challenge to Western nations' commercial leadership in space.

Japan's space centers and launch sites are tied together by the Tsukuba Space Center. Located about 80 kilometers north of Tokyo, Tsukuba is the nation's principal test ground for launch vehicles and satellites; equally important is its major satellite control and tracking center. For these latter purposes, it serves as the central, integrating data link with tracking and data-acquisition stations located southeast of Tokyo on the Pacific at Katsura, at Matsudo (close to Tanegashima), and at Uchinoura. Still farther downrange, tracking stations are positioned at Chichi-jima Island and on Okinawa, while a mobile station, depending upon its mission, can be sited either on Kwajalein Atoll (in the central Pacific's Marshall Islands) or farther southeastward, slightly north of the equator, on Kiritimati Atoll (Christmas Island).

Nations possessing ballistic missile technology accordingly also possess the essential technology for placing artificial satellites in orbit. The People's Republic of China (PRC) certainly had acquired the basics of modern missile rocketry by the early 1960's, although there was scant information about it for years. The PRC's ballistic rocket launch site was located in thinly populated Inner Mongolia (in Gansu Province) at the edge of the Gobi Desert. The nearest town of importance then—one, that is, with established road and rail connections—was Jiuquan. The launch test site was constructed roughly 60 kilometers northward along the banks of the generally dry Ruo Shui River. Centering on the rapidly growing town of Shuang Cheng-Tse, the site would soon be named the East Wind Center.

Facilities at the East Wind Center were first developed to accommodate short- to medium-range ballistic missiles of Soviet design. With the rupturing of relations between the PRC and the Soviet Union, however, Chinese scientists and engineers, many of them reportedly trained in the Soviet Union, the United States, and Great Britain, commenced designing their own series of missiles. The main thrust of these efforts was to furnish the PRC, which by 1966 had begun nuclear testing at Lop Nor in Zhongua Province, with a delivery system. Known by Western intelligence communities as the CSS-1, China's first liquid propellant missile was a completely redesigned Soviet SS-3 (Shyster), as photographs released by Chinese authorities showed. The East Wind Center's missile launch stand was comparable to those built during World War II for Germany's famed V-2 rockets. The CSS-1 reputedly had a range of 965 to 1,207 kilometers.

The succeeding generation of the center's ballistic missiles, which were test-flown in 1966 and 1967, were intermediate range ballistic missiles (IRBMs)—comparable in some regards to the American Jupiter IRBM or one version of the Thor—and were believed to have been fitted with nuclear warheads with 1-megaton yields. Deployment of CSS-2's in 1971 brought the developing CSS-3's on line at the center, and the Chinese are known to have made many test flights of the CSS family over distances of 644 to 1,609 kilometers.

CSS evolution meant that the preliminary phase of the center's operations ended in 1967, to be followed by the reconstruction of its facilities between 1968 and 1970. On April 24, 1970, the center placed a version of the CSS-2 (the Chinese identify it as *Chang Zheng*, or Long March, 1) into orbit with the PRC's first artificial satellite.

Having attained this level of sophistication, in addition to having deployed long-range intercontinental ballistic missiles (LRICBMs)—modified CSS-3's known to the Chinese as *Feng Bao*, or Storm Booster 1's (FB-1's)—required further extensions and redesigns of the center. Through much of the 1970's, the area embraced by center-related activities covered approximately 16,200 square kilometers. Moreover, its infrastructure—that is, paved military roads, main railways, power and water lines, as well as the launchpads, blockhouses, major industrial support, tracking, and test facilities served by the infrastructure—had been extensively augmented and upgraded. Launchpads were fitted for FB-1's for what became a series of center satellite launchings, while others were prepared for successive generations of CSS LRICBMs.

In order to test fire missiles over longer ranges, an additional test site was constructed in the Chang-bai Shan mountains in Manchuria's eastern Jilin Province. Ostensibly, this siting afforded a long-range firing of missiles 3,500 kilometers westward into Xijiang Province. Yet another Manchurian launch site, this one, in the Xiao Hinggan mountains northwest of Harbin, was established in the late 1970's to improve testing of the CSS-X-4 by firing westward over ranges of 3,220 to 4,071 kilometers. Apparently, the missiles were to impact either in central Tibet near Lhasa or in Sinkiang Uighur Province's Takla Makan Desert. Little detail is known about these sites.

When, however, the PRC's experimental CSS-X-4's had been satisfactorily tested (only after numerous delays and failures in the late 1970's), major launchings resumed at the East Wind Center. Decisions were made to fire from the center over the Pacific (instead of overflying India) to the Gilbert Islands, which autonomously straddle the equator in mid-ocean. On May 18, 1980, the PRC missile from the East Wind Center traveled 8,046 kilometers to an impact adjudged successful. Another missile, fired on May 24, 1980, fell short of its target; it nevertheless had carried 6,759 kilometers, enough again to satisfy the Chinese of its success.

Success or not, by July, 1985, decisions were forthcoming that made it appear that the East Wind Center would diminish in importance. Beijing officials announced that a new space center and launch site had been located in the rugged mountain and gorge country near Xichang, about 200 kilometers southwest of the city of Chengdu. The Cornell-trained Deputy Director of the Chinese Academy of Space Technology (CAST), Tu Shancheng, and its President, Sun Jaidong, explained in July, 1985, that the Xichang site was launching China's new heavy booster CZ-3's, which could place heavy payloads into orbit, and on which China pinned its hopes of joining the commercialization of space. Indeed, that month, a CZ-3 at Xichang lifted a 1,350-kilogram satellite into a geosynchronous transit orbit: a first for the

Chinese space program and a good augury of its accelerated pace toward the 1990's.

Helping control and support this space push during 1985 and 1986, a new ground station complex near the village of Weinan in northwest China's Shanzi Province—viewed at first hand by Craig Covault, an American aerospace authority—became operational to control the PRC's STW 1 communications satellite. In addition, 48 kilometers south of Beijing, the Rocket Testing Center, with several test stands, would attempt to improve the CZ-2/3's booster, purportedly to acquire more heavy lift capacity necessary to orbit heavier payloads.

Generally, China's space centers, launch sites, and their immediate support establishments appear less well-appointed, more "primitive," than their counterparts in the United States, the Soviet Union, and Japan. Nevertheless, they have been locations at which the PRC in little more than two decades developed and successfully orbited passive military satellites, the STW 1 and fourteen other satellites; at which it developed and deployed its LRICBMs; and at which it entered the international satellite market.

Seventh among the world's nations to put satellites in space, India has had nearly every one of a neutral, developing power's incentives to acquire facilities allowing it to make peaceful use of space. Because of its huge and growing population, it desperately needs satellite communications, for entertainment certainly but, more important, for educational purposes. With very few telephones available, it similarly needs to fill the voids in its internal communications. With so much of its economy reliant upon agriculture conducted under climatic conditions that frequently devastate the lives and livelihoods of millions of people, it needs the timely information available only through scanning and meteorological satellites.

Perception of these imperatives prompted formation of the Indian Space Research Organization (ISRO) on August 15, 1969, the national government giving it the direction of all space activities. Going still further in June, 1972, the government created a Department of Space (DOS), subject to direct control of the prime minister (at the time Indira Gandhi), and the ISRO, operating under DOS, was given responsibility for projects at all four of the country's space centers.

ISRO's centerpiece is the Vikram Sarabhai Space Center (VSSC), named in honor of the professor who founded India's space program. Located on India's extreme southwestern coast north of the city of Trivandrum, the VSSC is close to the Thumba Equatorial Rocket Launching Station (TERLS). VSSC, however, is a purely national establishment, engaged in developing sounding rockets, satellite launch vehicles (SLVs), and ancillary instrumentation. TERLS, which commenced launches with American Nike, Tomahawk, Judi, and Arcas rockets on November 21, 1963, on the other hand, operates under the auspices of the United Nations. Because its location suits it to low-altitude upper-atmosphere and ionosphere research—the magnetic equator lies just north of it—West Germany, France, the United States, Japan, the Soviet Union, and several Eastern Bloc countries use it as a sounding rocket launch site. It occupies about 2 square kilometers that contain three launch-pads capable of handling rockets up to 0.56 meter in diameter.

India's principal laboratory for developing its satellite technology—satellite design, fabrication, testing, and incorporation into spacecraft—is the ISRO Satellite Center, located near ISRO headquarters in the city of Bangalore in south central India. Aryabhata, India's first scientific satellite, was launched into orbit by a Soviet Kosmos rocket on April 10, 1975, and subsequently a number of geosynchronous, observation, and communications satellites have been developed there.

After 1975, the Sriharikota Launching Range (SHAR) became the country's preeminent launch site, principally as a result of its ability to provide launch and testing services for larger generations of multistage and satellite launching rockets. These necessitated a more extensive infrastructure of telemetry and tracking instrumentation, not to mention other support and service facilities, than was then available elsewhere.

SHAR occupies an island on India's southeastern coast about one hundred kilometers north of the city of Madras. Prior to its purchase by the Indian government for ISRO, it had been an extensive plantation for growing firewood. Despite two monsoon seasons, rainfall at the range is a launch factor only during October and November, so, like most world spaceports, it enjoys sunshine most of the year. SHAR itself covers 145 square kilometers; it became operational in October, 1971, with the launching of three Rohini 125 sounding rockets. Later additions to its facilities have included a solid propellant space booster processing plant for SLVs; a data acquisition center for the testing of solid-fueled rockets with an eye to their compatibility with SLVs; a high-altitude test facility that evaluates the ability of rockets to place satellites in their correct geostationary positions; and a static test and evaluation complex that matches different types of solid rockets to the different launch vehicles. Despite some failures, between 1980 and 1983 SHAR sent three payloads into orbit and had upgraded its capacities sufficiently to boost 40-kilogram satellites into low orbit riding on SLV-3 rockets. By 1983, in fact, plans were afoot to produce an augmented satellite launch vehicle (ASLV) to lift 150-kilogram satellites, and ISRO was ambitiously studying a polar SLV capable of putting a 500-kilogram payload into polar orbit at the rate of two per year by 1990, soon after sending 2,000-kilogram payloads on the same track.

In regard to SHAR facilities, success brought its own problems. Both SHAR and Sriharikota (or Trivandrum), unable to cope with the contemplated large, multipurpose polar orbiting satellites, have, since 1986, forced ISRO to seek new and appropriate facilities.

Context

Whether the space frontier has been viewed as a scientific and intellectual challenge or as a constellation of economic opportunities, or as a mixture of both, Japan, the PRC, and India have all made their bids to join in the conquest of space from generally different perspectives, reflecting different national resources and different commitments to utilizing and exploiting it. In the most tangible way, these differences were nowhere more apparent than in these nations' investment in and construction, maintenance, and expansion of their space centers and launch sites. That is where the complexities of placing hardware and people into space have had to be resolved in workmanlike fashion.

Yet between the late 1940's and the mid-1950's, all these countries appeared confronted with such bleak prospects on Earth that it beggared the imagination to think they could ever face bright hopes in space. Japan—devastated, defeated, and occupied—depended on its American occupiers for daily survival until peace treaties brought a lifting of restrictions in the early 1950's. For its part, China had known little except violent internal conflict during much of the twentieth century, culminating in a lengthy, bitter war against Japan made worse by an ongoing civil war which ended only in 1950, leaving immense tasks of political and economic reconstruction. India, having paid a substantial price serving in the British Empire from 1939 to 1945 and finally able to struggle for autonomy, emerged to a shaky independence that seemed, on religious, political, and nationalist grounds, more violently divisive than unifying through the 1950's.

Nevertheless, free of restrictions by the early 1950's—and constitutionally unencumbered by defense burdens—Japan moved from the relative simplicity of the Akita Range and of its tiny sounding rockets to the official opening of Kagoshima (December, 1963) and Tanegashima (October, 1969) in less than fifteen years. Its first satellite orbited Earth in 1970. The Japanese, collectively aware that they lacked significant mineral resources or great agricultural wealth, and aware that their tenuous commercial and industrial survival lies in the seas and overseas, eclectically adapting the practiced technologies of the initial space powers, have tended subsequently to view space as another limitless commercial and industrial ocean. That is the instinct represented tangibly in their space centers and launch sites, an instinct that by 1988 had allowed them, in some areas, to assume leadership.

If commercial (hence national) survival is represented by Japanese spaceports, it was the profound fear of foreign military threats, both to their cultural pride and to their revolution, that primarily shaped Chinese space policy and the character and missions of their space centers and launch sites. Urgency, secrecy, and militarism suffused the drive at the East Wind Center for more powerful and accurate IRBMs and LRICBMs, mated with the nuclear weaponry developed at Lop Nor. The aura pervaded the Manchurian launch and test centers, and more than vestiges of it remain at the Xichang Center, at Weinan, and at the Beijing Rocket Testing Center. Given their primary objectives, these Chinese launch sites produced impressive results: CSS-1 became operational in 1966; CSS-2 was deployed in 1971; East Wind Center was rebuilt and successfully orbited its Long March 1 in 1970; since Long March 1, the space centers have orbited twenty-one spacecraft, and building or sharing more powerful SLVs, they have placed their small commercial wedge in the space door.

Constrained by greater austerities, India fundamentally required different results from the work of ISRO and its launch sites. Incentives for utilizing space were less military and less commercial than either those of the PRC or of Japan. Of higher priority were the development and orbiting of meteorological, maritime, remote-sensing, and communications satellites. With these tools, old problems—of illiteracy and difficulties in spreading education, of trying to predict agricultural yields, of poor land-line communications, of the annual and deadly menaces of weather on land and sea—could be mitigated, if not prevented. Unable to marshal its directing organizations and its operational spaceports until between 1969 and 1971, India, through DOS and ISRO, developed its centers and launch sites swiftly enough to orbit its first satellite in 1975; by the early 1980's, with SHAR operational, it had begun planning for facilities that would handle more powerful boosters, heavier payloads, and more numerous scientific and commercial space ventures.

Late in the 1980's, all three of these once-unlikely space nations evinced more mixed incentives than had initially instructed the building of their centers and launch sites: The technologies in them represented the sensible and economical sharing, licensing, leasing, importing, exporting, and joint enterprising of all the space powers; the technologies of the world's scientific and commercial communities were somewhat more evident; and despite Japan's rapidly increasing expenditures on its centers and sites and some mystery about the PRC's, none reflected the far heavier expenditures of the Soviet Union, the United States, and the European Space Agency.

Bibliography

Brown, David A. "India Developing Insat Follow-on to Serve 1990's National Needs." *Aviation Week and Space Technology* 124 (May 12, 1986): 55-56. India's space programs have been minuscule compared to those of the great space powers, and as a result few publications on it exist. Brown, however, is one of the few "India watchers" with the technical competence to assess India's progress. This article is illustrated.

Brunt, Peter, and Alan J. Naylor. "Telecommunications and Space." In *The Exploitation of Space: Policy Trends in the Military and Commercial Uses of Outer Space*, edited by Michiel Schwartz and Paul Stares. London: Butterworth and Co., 1986. The authors are professional British space technologists. This substantive overview helps place some of the Japanese, Indian, and Chinese launch facilities in a broader working perspective. Clearly written for nonspecialists. Brief endnotes; no bibliography; no index. Available in good public, college, and university libraries.

"Chinese Developing Satellite for Earth Resources Exploration." *Aviation Week and Space Technology* 123 (July 22, 1985): 81-84. This authoritative periodical records, assesses, and reports aerospace and space developments with technical precision and with international coverage. All articles feature either pictures or illustrations. While intended for professionals and specialists primarily, it is written to be understood by nonspecialists.

"Chinese Modify CZ-2/3 Rocket Boosters, Focus on Commercial Launch Market." *Aviation Week and Space Technology* 123 (July 22, 1985): 77-79. Relevant for details on and pictures of Chinese launch facilities and vehicles.

Covault, Craig. "Austere Chinese Space Program Keyed Toward Future Buildup." *Aviation Week and Space Technology* 123 (July 8, 1985): 16-21. Covault, a space programs expert, personally toured the PRC's facilities, so his observations are professional, detailed, and among the few printed in English. Contains photographs and illustrations.

_____ . "Chinese Rocket Test Center to Aid Large Engine Development." *Aviation Week and Space Technology* 123 (July 22, 1985): 69-75. Continuation of an invaluable series, with photographs.

_____ . "Chinese Satellite Control Center Undergoes Broad Modernization." *Aviation Week and Space Technology* 123 (August 12, 1985): 59-61. Last of an excellent and invaluable report.

Finch, Edward Ridley, Jr., and Amanda Lee Moore. *Astrobusiness: A Guide to the Commerce and Law of Outer Space*. New York: Praeger Publishers, 1985. The authors are members of national and international aeronautical and astronautical societies and associations. While there is little technical detail—such as that in Covault's articles on China—China, India, and Japan are placed in a context that permits a better view of the work of their centers and launch sites. Written for general readers. Five excellent appendices; no illustrations or photographs; good endnotes with suggestions for further reading; useful index. Available in good public and university libraries; also available in law libraries.

Goldman, Nathan C. *Space Commerce: Free Enterprise on the High Frontier*. Cambridge, Mass.: Balinger Publishing Co., 1985. A well-published political scientist who specializes in space programs and technologies, the author usefully and clearly contributes to placing China, India, and Japan in the international context of space commercialization. Thus he gives some insight into the changing functions of their space centers and launch sites. Useful figures, tables, and appendices; good select bibliography and index. Available in larger public, college, and university libraries.

Hatanaka, Takeo. "Space Research in Japan." In *Space Research*, edited by T. M. Tabanera. New York: Macmillan, 1964. An excellent professional review of the earlier phases of Japanese development in this field. Clearly written and readily understandable by nonspecialists. Contains photographs, charts, drawings, and graphs; no notes or bibliography. Available in major college and university libraries.

Kaneda, H., K. Nishino, and Y. Ichikawa. "Operational Communication Satellite Program in Japan." In *Astronautics for Peace and Human Progress: Proceedings*, edited by L. G. Napolitano. Elmsford, N.Y.: Pergamon Press, 1979. The authors are officials of leading Japanese telecommunications companies and of NASDA. They provide a clear and detailed overview of their technical subject. Good discussion on the space centers' organization and on launch-site operations. Many illustrations, photographs, graphics, and tables. Available in major public and university libraries.

Lodgson, John M. "The Evolution of Civilian Space Exploitation." In *The Exploi-*

tation of Space: Policy Trends in the Commercial Uses of Outer Space, edited by Michiel Schwarz and Paul Stares. London: Butterworth and Co., 1986. The author was Director of Graduate Programs in Science, Technology, and Public Policy at George Washington University as well as editor of a major space journal. This article places Chinese, Japanese, and Indian programs in perspective. Useful tables; no endnotes or bibliography. Available in major public and university libraries.

Matsuura, Akiyoshi. "An Overview of Space Activities in Japan." In *Astronautics for Peace and Human Progress: Proceedings*, edited by L. G. Napolitano. Elmsford, N.Y.: Pergamon Press, 1979. The author represents Japan's NASDA, affording him a superb, clear, and detailed overview of Japanese space organization, space centers, and launch sites up to 1978. Easily understood by the nonspecialist. Contains photographs, tables, and charts. Available in major public and university libraries.

Mori, Tadahira. "Japanese Policy on Participation in the Space Station Program." In *Europe/United States Space Activities*, edited by Peter M. Bainum and Friedrich von Bun, vol. 61. San Diego: American Astronautical Society, 1985. The author was Director of the International Space Affairs, Science, and Technology Agency of Japan. This brief but clearly written article gives a good idea of why Japan was anxious to upgrade the Tanegashima Space Center. Contains drawings and diagrams, but no notes, bibliography, or index. Available in all major public and university libraries.

Williamson, Ray A. "The Industrialization of Space: Problems and Prospects." In *The Exploitation of Space: Policy Trends in the Military and Commercial Uses of Outer Space*, edited by Michiel Schwarz and Paul Stares. London: Butterworth and Co., 1986. The author was with the U.S. Office of Technology Assessment. Written for interested laymen, the article describes the environment of the mid-1980's in which the space nations—China, India, and Japan included—were glimpsing commercial prospects and reevaluating the missions of their space centers and the functions of their launch sites. Contains tables and endnotes; no appendices or index. Available in major public and university libraries.

Clifton K. Yearley
Kerrie L. MacPherson

Cross-References

The Chinese Space Program, 237; The Indian Space Program, 596; The Japanese Space Program, 655; International Private Industry and Space Exploration, 1182; National Telecommunications Satellite Systems, 1985; Maritime Telecommunications Satellites, 1991; U.S. Private and Commercial Telecommunications Satellites, 1997.

SPACE CENTERS AND LAUNCH SITES IN THE EUROPEAN SPACE AGENCY NATIONS

Date: Beginning 1950
Type of facility: Space centers and launch sites
Countries: The ESA countries

During the late 1940's and the 1950's, European nations began constructing space centers for their own national space programs. Most of these space centers were located in the Southern Hemisphere. After the formation of the European Space Agency (ESA) in 1975, the French space center at Kourou, French Guiana, became the primary European launching site.

Principal personages

ANDRÉ REMONDIERE, Director of the Centre Spatial Guyanais at Kourou, French Guiana
GILBERT RÔTROU, the Arianespace launchpad manager
MAX A. HAUZEUR, the head of the ESA office at Kourou
FRÉDÉRIC D'ALLEST, Director of Arianespace and the French Space Agency
ANDRÉ J. VAN GAVER, Ariane 4 and 5 Program Manager, the French Space Agency
WALTER G. NAUMANN, Director of ESA's Ariane Launcher Division

Summary of the Facilities

The first European rocket base established during the post-World War II period was a military test base at Woomera, Australia. Construction began in 1946. A joint project of the British and Australian governments, the Woomera base was built at a cost of more than £200 million. Located about 400 kilometers south of Adelaide and stretching approximately 2,000 kilometers across a desert section of Australia, the Woomera base was used as a test ground for the British Blue Streak intermediate range missile. It was also used to launch sounding rockets and to test pilotless aircraft.

Tests of Great Britain's Black Arrow rocket were also made from Woomera; the British Prospero satellite, placed into orbit in 1971, was one of two satellites launched by a Black Arrow from that site. During the 1970's, when Woomera became the test site for the Europa 1 rocket, a multinational project of the European Launcher Development Organization (ELDO), the Woomera base grew into a town of more than four thousand people. After the Europa project was moved to a French test base at Kourou, French Guiana, Woomera was abandoned by the successor organization to ELDO, the European Space Agency. The main reason for the change was that Woomera's location offered fewer advantages for launching satellites than the site of the French spaceport at Kourou.

Another ESA launching site located in the Southern Hemisphere is Italy's San Marco Range, located only 2° south of the equator. Operated by the Italian government since 1966, the San Marco complex consists of two offshore ocean platforms located nearly 5 kilometers off the coast of Kenya. Basically a modified oil-drilling site, the San Marco complex is supported on a sandy sea bottom by twenty-eight metal legs. More than twenty cables link the two platforms. In its first ten years of operation, the San Marco complex was the launching site for four Italian and three U.S. satellites.

Early French space launches were made from Hammaguir, a military base in Algeria's Sahara Desert. Opened during the mid-1950's, Hammaguir included a test corridor of approximately 3,000 kilometers for testing intermediate range ballistic missiles. The liquid-propellant boosters for the Diamant series of rockets, forerunners of the Ariane rockets, were developed at Hammaguir. As many as three hundred rockets, both missiles and upper-atmosphere sounding rockets, were launched from the Hammaguir complex before 1967, when Algeria gained its independence and France abandoned the base.

In 1964, the French space program was transferred to a 30-kilometer-long strip of oceanfront land in Kourou, French Guiana. The site became the major base for the launching of French, and eventually ESA, missiles. It includes the Centre Spatial Guyanais, or CSG, which provides the technical and logistic support facilities for the Ariane rockets.

A department of France with a population of less than 100,000, French Guiana saw an influx of Europeans when the space center was constructed. The launch complex covers about 90,000 hectares of land along the coast and includes a small port, shopping and recreation areas, and a residential area. In the late 1980's, the complex employed about one thousand people. Kourou's location allows launchings to the east or north without any chance that missiles would pass over land for at least 3,000 kilometers. The French Kourou site and the Italian San Marco platforms are among the southernmost launch sites still in use in the world.

The Kourou space center includes offices and payload examination facilities; a control room, located in the Technical Center, near the center of the complex; an underground blockhouse, used to supplement observations from the control room; and a series of weather radar, propellant storage, and tracking equipment buildings. Tracking stations for eastward launches are located at Natal, Brazil; Ascension Island; and Libreville, Gabon. For northward launches, the main tracking stations are in Bermuda and Wallops Island. The U.S. National Aeronautics and Space Administration (NASA) station on Ascension Island, in the middle of the South Atlantic Ocean, is a key station for receiving telemetry data on the third stage of the rockets.

The first facility at Kourou was used to launch sounding rockets. The second facility constructed was used for the Diamant rocket, which launched seven satellites into orbit from this site. The first such launching from Kourou occurred on March 10, 1970, when a foreign payload was placed into orbit.

An additional launchpad, named ELA-1 (for the French designation Ensemble de

Lancement Ariane 1), was constructed at Kourou for the testing of the Europa rocket. Before 1975, European nations were split on the question of whether Europe should build its own launchers or rely on the United States' rockets to launch European satellites. France strongly supported the building of European launchers. Therefore, when the Europa rocket was in the planning stages, the French government offered use of the launch facilities at Kourou. Consisting of a French-made first stage, a German-made second stage, and a British-made third stage, the Europa was first tested at Woomera, then transferred (as a modified version, the Europa 2) to Kourou. The Europa project was canceled in 1973, after none of eleven test launches succeeded in placing a satellite in orbit and after costs escalated from an estimate of less than $200 million to more than $700 million.

After ESA was formed, Kourou became its major launch facility. A refurbished and expanded version of ELA-1 has been used to launch the Ariane 1, 2, and 3 series of rockets, based partly on the Diamant. The first Ariane launch occurred in December, 1979; ELA-1 was the site of all following Ariane launchings until the seventeenth launch, in March, 1986.

Because the unpacking of the parts of the Ariane rockets—transported from Europe via ship or airplane—is done next to the Technical Center building, and because the rocket parts are then assembled on the launchpad itself, ELA-1 requires a long period of preparation, up to nearly a month. As a result, ELA-1 is limited to launching five rockets a year. The pad also features two auxiliary technical facilities: a propellant support zone and a liquid nitrogen and liquid oxygen plant.

ELA-2, a larger and more flexible launching area, was constructed some 500 meters south of ELA-1. While this new pad was added to the Kourou complex in 1986 partly because ESA wanted more flexible facilities, it was also specifically designed to launch the more complex Ariane 4 rocket. In fact, ELA-2 is designed to launch Ariane 2, 3, or 4 rockets.

ELA-2 features a separate assembly building located 950 meters from the actual launchpad, an arrangement which allows assembly and testing of one rocket while a second is being launched. The preparation and actual launch areas are joined by a railroad track. In the preparation zone, launcher elements are inspected and assembled, boosters are inspected, electrical and fuel connections made, and checks are made of the engine and electrical system. In the launch zone, the launchers are given final tests, the boosters are added, the payload is placed atop the launcher, the launcher is fueled, and the countdown is initiated. The launch zone includes an umbilical tower, which provides links between ground facilities and the rocket's electrical and fuel equipment. A service gantry is normally attached to the umbilical tower. Weighing nearly 1.5 metric tons, this structure forms a sealed, air-conditioned area and clean zone where the payload may be fitted on top of the launcher. When the third stage is being filled with fuel, it is pulled back 80 meters from the launcher. Up to twelve launchings per year may be made from this new site, but the pad has generally been limited to ten per year in order to allow time for periodic maintenance.

ELA-3 was planned for use by the heavy-lift Ariane 5 rocket, as well as the Hermes spaceplane that the Ariane 5 will carry into orbit. This pad was scheduled for completion by the mid-1990's at an estimated cost of $200 million. The new pad was also designed to be the launching site for rockets which would carry components for a European space station. The construction of this new facility represented a major shift in policy for ESA, which had previously cooperated with the United States on the space shuttle program. ESA-NASA cooperation includes Spacelab, a reusable spacecraft carried in the cargo bay of the U.S. space shuttle. Also, ESA astronauts and astronaut candidates have participated in NASA programs. ESA's cooperation with U.S. spaceflight now focuses on NASA's space station project. With a program called Columbus, ESA will offer the United States a combination of European-built laboratory modules, polar platforms, and manned free-flying platforms.

Designed to allow up to ten launches per year of the all-cryogenic Ariane 5, ELA-3 was planned with safety considerations in mind. Like ELA-2, the complex was designed in two parts: a launcher preparation zone and a launch zone proper, joined by a railroad track (including a siding which allows two launch platforms to pass each other). Space technicians wanted the Ariane 5 rockets, as well as the Hermes spaceplane atop them, to be completely assembled in the first zone before being transported to the second. The launcher preparation zone was designed to include a booster integration building for the final assembly of the solid-propellant boosters and a launcher integration building, where the main body of the launcher (including the first stage and second stage) is assembled atop the rocket and the fuel tanks are filled. Because of the advanced technology involved in the Ariane 5's all-cryogenic engines, the design for the ELA-3 complex includes a plant for producing liquid hydrogen, a second plant for producing liquid oxygen and nitrogen, storage facilities for all three, and additional facilities to transport and unload the sections of the rocket. A test stand for solid-propellant boosters and a factory for producing solid propellants were also planned. Preliminary tests on the rocket sections can be made at the European Propulsion Society in Vernon, France, near Rouen, where engines are also manufactured.

Whichever launchpad is in use, the CSG is responsible for coordinating activities between the base and downrange stations; for determining the position and behavior of launchers at all times; for ensuring the safety of persons on the ground or in the air, destroying errant launchers if necessary; for weather forecasting relating to launch activities; and for providing logistic support for launch areas, including storage facilities.

Also utilized by ESA is a sounding-rocket range located in Kiruna, Sweden. Operated by the Swedish Space Corporation, the range, located in northern Sweden, has since the 1970's concentrated on studies of microgravity, or diminished gravity, conditions. Such projects prepare the way for microgravity experiments aboard the ESA Spacelab and aboard ESA's European retrievable carrier (Eureca), a project which involves the use of free-flying platforms.

Context

Except for sounding-rocket launchpads, all European launch sites have been located in the Southern Hemisphere, away from Europe. Yet all the sites have been in areas with connections to Europe. Hammaguir was, and Kourou is, under French administration. San Marco is a former oil-drilling site owned by the Italian government. The Woomera launch site is located in Australia, a country which has historic ties to the United Kingdom.

While these sites are far from European nations, they are all close to the equator and far from heavily populated areas. When rockets are launched near the equator, the speed of Earth's spin (which is highest at the equator) is added to the rocket's speed. Kourou's location, for example, gives the Ariane rockets an extra 17 percent boost. Satellites launched from Kourou are more easily placed in equatorial inclination than rockets launched from the United States' Kennedy Space Center in Florida.

Such distant locations have caused some problems, however, since ESA rockets are generally designed and constructed in Europe and then shipped to southern sites via ship or airplane. The first and second stages of the Arianes 1-4 were sent to Kourou by ship. Generally, such shiploads are unpacked in the nearby port of Cayenne. If the Hermes spaceplane should land outside the Kourou area, it can be returned piggyback aboard what is called a carrier aircraft.

For the assembly of the Hermes spaceplane for launch aboard the Ariane 5, a Hermes integration building was designed in Europe. Because Hermes features an ejectable cabin for its three-person crew to use in emergencies, emergency recovery facilities were also planned at the Kourou launch base, and plans were made for recovery at sea. The solid-propellant boosters fall into the sea during launch and can be recovered for inspection. The Hermes project also requires that a series of data-relay satellites be coordinated with the central control building at Kourou, in order to provide instantaneous data on the flight of the spaceplane.

The spaceplane was to be in contact with the control center at all times via either ground stations or satellites. Use might also be made of the U.S. Tracking and Data-Relay Satellite System (TDRSS). After approximately one week in space, during which its crew might service manned space stations or flying platforms, Hermes was to reenter the atmosphere and glide to a landing on specially constructed landing strips at Kourou or at Istres, near Marseilles, France.

The advanced ELA-3 facilities, which were designed to test operations of the Ariane rocket and to produce liquid oxygen and liquid hydrogen propellants, point to ESA's continued growth. Safety was given special emphasis during the planning of ELA-3, because Arianes 1-3 had sometimes failed to perform as expected—a result of problems with their third stage, which used cryogenic technology. ESA engineers believe that they have solved earlier problems which caused liquid oxygen to solidify and block fuel lines, and they also believe that a more powerful ignition system for the third stage will make future failures unlikely. Since the Ariane 5 features cryogenic technology in all stages, however, liquid hydrogen and liquid oxygen production and test facilities occupy a significant portion of the planned ELA-3 complex.

The ELA-3 complex was also designed as the first European facility to handle recoverable spacecraft. One advantage of ESA's pre-Ariane 5 rockets has been their expendable nature; they were designed without the elaborate safety measures which would have been necessary if astronauts had been on board.

The launch and control facilities of ESA exemplify the multinational nature of the organization. Kourou is basically a French project, although the private consortium named Arianespace has responsibility for operating launchpads. A combination of thirty-six European corporations, Arianespace, which calls itself the world's first commercial space-launch company, operates the various Ariane models after they are first designed and developed at ESA facilities.

The European Space Operations Center in Darmstadt, West Germany, occupies land donated by the West German government in the late 1960's for the construction of the European Satellite Control Center. Other ESA control facilities are the European Space Research and Technology Center in Noordwijk, the Netherlands, whose employees design, develop, and test space components and vehicles, and the ESA Information Retrieval Service, located in Frascati, Italy, which allows on-line retrieval of information from major scientific data bases. The central administrative office for ESA is located in Paris.

ESA also has its own network of space vehicle and satellite tracking facilities, located in Odenwald, West Germany; Fucino, Italy; Villafranco, Spain; Gran Canaria, Spain; Redu, Belgium; Malindi, Kenya; Parkes, New South Wales, Australia; Gnangara, West Australia; and Kourou. Specialized tracking or data acquisition centers are frequently established to handle particular missions. For example, in order to track and process data from the Meteosat series of satellites, Europe's weather satellites, a data acquisition and tracking station was established in Michelstadt, West Germany.

Even before the explosion of the U.S. space shuttle *Challenger* in 1986, the Kourou facility had become the world's busiest facility for launching commercial satellites. With contracts to launch more than sixty satellites, and with substantially increasing profits, Arianespace plans to make the other ESA launch facilities some of the busiest in the world.

Bibliography

Chartrand, Mark R. "Spaceport Guiana." *Space World* U-8-248 (August, 1984): 26-29. Although brief, this article offers a fairly comprehensive account of the history of the Kourou spaceport and the physical plans of the ELA-1 and ELA-2 launchpads. In terms suitable for a general audience, it also explains the geographical advantages of using the Kourou site to launch commercial satellites. Also included are a number of photographs of the launch site and of Ariane rockets.

European Space Agency. *Reflections on Europe in Space: The First Two Decades and Beyond*. ESA BR-10. Paris: Author, 1982. This informative booklet describes the emergence of ESA as a major multinational space agency, explaining the development of its satellite programs, scientific research programs, and launcher projects. Written for a general audience, it provides insight into possible future expansion of ESA programs and space facilities, including launch sites.

Guyenne, Duc, and Norman Longdon, eds. *Twenty Years of European Cooperation in Space*. Paris: European Space Agency, 1984. Details the development of ESA's administrative structures and space centers, as well as the scientific achievements and satellite operations of the agency. Also discusses long-term plans for future projects which may require further expansion of the Kourou space center. Well illustrated.

Guyenne, T. D., and G. Levy, eds. *European Rocket and Balloon Programs and Related Research*. ESA SP-152. Paris: European Space Agency, 1980. This sizable book examines European nations' use of sounding rockets and balloons to study the upper atmosphere. Separate articles in the book examine the research programs of France, West Germany, Norway, Sweden, and the United Kingdom. The articles discuss launch sites used in these nations for sounding rockets and research balloons. Also included are summaries of knowledge gained, particularly regarding climatic changes. Suitable for a general audience.

Pfeffer, H. A. *The Future of Launchers in Europe*. Toulouse, France: Centre National d'Études Spatiales, 1982. This book, based on speeches delivered to an international conference on space vehicles, lists options for the expansion of ESA facilities. It explains ESA plans for launch systems beyond the Ariane 4, including the heavy-lift Ariane 5 rocket and Hermes spaceplane project. It also reviews existing launch facilities, particularly at Kourou. Written for a general audience.

U.S. Congress. House. Committee on Science and Technology. Subcommittee on Space Science and Applications. *Space Activities of the United States, Soviet Union, and Other Launching Countries/Organizations, 1957-1983*. Report prepared by Congressional Research Service, the Library of Congress. 98th Cong., 2d sess. Washington, D.C.: Government Printing Office, 1984. Although this book concentrates on the space programs of the United States and the Soviet Union, it includes material on the launch vehicles and launch sites of other nations and organizations, including ESA. It features tables, by country and organization, of payloads launched between 1957 and 1983. Illustrated.

Niles Holt

Cross-References

The Australian Space Program, 174; The British Space Program, 217; The European Space Agency, 372; European Space Agency Satellites, 379; The French Space Program, 461; European Launch Vehicles, 734; U.S. Launch Vehicles, 749; The National Aeronautics and Space Administration, 1032; International Private Industry and Space Exploration, 1182; Spaceplanes, 1912; The West German Space Program, 2262.

SPACE CENTERS AND LAUNCH SITES IN THE SOVIET UNION

Date: Beginning October 4, 1957
Type of facility: Space centers and launch sites
Country: The Soviet Union

From its early support for the visionary rocket designs of Konstantin Tsiolkovsky to the building of the three modern cosmodromes at Kapustin Yar, Tyuratam, and Plesetsk, the Soviet Union has demonstrated a strong commitment to developing the technology necessary for the exploration of space. Despite some major disappointments in their space program, Soviet achievements in both manned and unmanned missions have been genuinely impressive.

Principal personages

NIKITA KHRUSHCHEV, third Premier of the Soviet Union

SERGEI KOROLEV, Chief Spacecraft Designer of the early Soviet space program

VALENTIN P. GLUSHKO, Chief Designer of Engines of the early Soviet space program

YURI A. GAGARIN, a Soviet cosmonaut, the first man in space

MIKHAIL TIKHONRAVOV, Chief Theoretician of the Soviet space program

M. V. KELDISH, Chairman of the Soviet Academy of Sciences during the 1960's

ANATOLI A. BLAGONRAVOV, former President, Academy of Artillery Sciences

KONSTANTIN TSIOLKOVSKY, the Soviet scientist known as the father of Russian rocketry

LEONID SEDOV, Chairman of the Commission for Interplanetary Communications of the Soviet Academy of Sciences during the 1950's

KONSTANTIN RUDNEV, first Chairman of the State Commission for Space Exploration

VLADIMIR KIRILLIN, Rudnev's successor

Summary of the Facilities

The Soviet Union was the first government to endorse and support the goal of spaceflight. After the Russian revolution of 1917, the Bolshevik regime courted scientists and technicians in a variety of fields, offering them greater political and material encouragement than they had received from the czars. During this "golden age" of Soviet scientific recruitment, the fledgling discipline of aeronautics was not neglected.

In 1918 the new Soviet regime founded the Central Aerodynamics Institute; a year later, the Zhukovsky Academy of Aeronautics was founded. Konstantin Tsiolkovsky, the Soviet "Gravity Hater" who as early as 1903 had published the mathematics of orbital mechanics and designed blueprints for a rocket powered by liquid fuel, was elected in 1919 to the Soviet Academy of Sciences and given a lifetime government pension. Private organizations pioneering rocket research also proliferated. In 1924 the Central Bureau for the Study of the Problems of Rockets (TsBIRP) was created to disseminate information about interplanetary communications (the Soviet rubric for spaceflight) and to encourage independent study on rocketry and on the potential for military applications of rockets. The same year, a private All-Union Society for the Study of Interplanetary Communications (OIMS) was formed in Moscow, attracting 150 charter members. In 1927, the OIMS and TsBIRP cosponsored a Soviet International Exhibition of Rocket Technology in Moscow. This conference, and subsequent ones, discussed the steps needed to move from theory to practice.

The principal focal point of early rocketry research and development was the Gas Dynamics Laboratory (GDL), housed in the large military complex in Leningrad. In May, 1929, a GDL team began work on the development of electric and liquid-propellant rocket motors. Efforts to develop the electric rocket proved disappointing, but within two years the GDL group had completed designs for the ORM 1, the first working liquid-propellant engine. At about this time, GDL activity at Leningrad was expanded with the creation of two new organizations for the study of rocket propulsion systems: GIRD in Leningrad and MOSGIRD in Moscow. The deputy of the MOSGIRD organization was Tsiolkovsky's brilliant student, Friedrich Tsander. Working in a primitively equipped basement of an apartment building near the center of Moscow, Tsander and his research engineers developed the OR 2, a brass and aluminum rocket that used compressed kerosene and liquid oxygen for fuel. On November 25, 1933, just ten days before Tsander's premature death, Russian experimenters successfully launched in a wooded area near Moscow the first Soviet rocket. It was about 46 centimeters long and had a thrust of 509.74 newtons.

The eighteen-second flight of the OR 2, coupled with the subsequent firings of larger and more powerful rocket engines, attracted the attention of military experts. As the Kremlin became more aware of the potential military applications of rocketry, it substantially enlarged its commitment to rocketry research and established the Reactive Scientific Research Institute and the Jet Propulsion Research Laboratory (RNII) in Moscow. Research teams in Leningrad and Moscow worked independently over the next six years developing liquid-propellant rockets and small jet-assisted rockets. These teams recruited some of the most capable scientists in the Soviet Union, including Valentin P. Glushko and Sergei Korolev, the men who two decades later would be the chief designers of the Soviet space program. By the end of the 1930's, the Soviet researchers had succeeded in launching the world's first two-stage rocket with a ramjet engine that reached 805 kilometers per hour.

Despite these impressive accomplishments, the Soviet space program encountered difficulties. Stalinist purges of the late 1930's—purges that sent specialists such as Korolev and Glushko into *sharagas* (prison work camps for scientists and engineers) and hundreds of other less fortunate technicians to their graves— liquidated large numbers of the Soviet intelligentsia and, consequently, slowed technological advancement. Moreover, after the German invasion of the Soviet Union in 1941, main Soviet industrial centers were overrun, and research and development complexes were devastated.

The conclusion of World War II, rather than inaugurating a new era of longed-for security, was a stark reminder to the Soviets of their technological vulnerability. The German-developed V-2 rocket technology, which had rained destruction on London and Antwerp in the closing months of the war, and the U.S.-developed atomic explosives posed an enormous threat to a nation ideologically isolated from the other superpowers of the world. Already twice scourged in less than half a century and with casualties during the two wars totaling perhaps thirty million citizens, the Soviet Union emerged from World War II a paranoid victor. It was this fear that motivated it to make a maximal and largely secret effort to catch up in rocket and nuclear technology. The success of its postwar program propelled the world into the space age.

In the immediate aftermath of the war, the Kremlin tripled its research and development budget and established a department for technology, which plotted not only the traditional five-year plans but also yearly and even quarterly schedules for the deployment of new military and technology installations. In an attempt to lure the best minds into the program, the Council of Ministers resolved to double or triple the salaries of scientists. In the postwar era, as in the Leninist era that followed the revolution, Soviet scientists again found themselves a privileged class.

Between 1946 and 1953, the Soviet government also made use of some six thousand German technicians, including two hundred rocket engineers, who had worked at Peenemünde on the German V-2's during the war. Under the supervision of Helmut Gröttrup, the only major V-2 designer who went to the Soviet Union rather than the United States after Germany's surrender, this team of researchers test-launched Soviet-made V-2's, consulted on the development of a piloted, high-altitude, winged rocket (known as the Sanger project), and designed new rockets. Working at first in isolation on an island in Lake Seilger, 240 kilometers from Moscow, and later at a rocket test range at Kapustin Yar, 120 kilometers east of Stalingrad, the Gröttrup team developed a multistage R-12 intermediate-range ballistic missile (IRBM) and a single-stage, finless, alcohol- and liquid-oxygen-fueled R-14, which was designed to send a 2,995-kilogram atomic bomb 2,900 kilometers to its intended target. The Soviet Scientific Technical Council, however, made only partial use of these German designs, preferring instead the designs simultaneously being developed by Soviet scientists. For reasons both political and psychological, the Gröttrup Germans were always the "second team." In late 1953, the team was disbanded and its workers sent back to Germany.

Contrary to widespread American beliefs, Soviet space successes during the 1950's and 1960's were not fundamentally dependent on the talent of the German scientists "captured at Peenemünde." The mastermind behind advanced Soviet rocket technology was Korolev, the heroic and unrecognized scientist who emerged from a Stalin labor camp to engineer the production of the first Soviet intercontinental ballistic missile (ICBM), the R-7. Korolev's ICBM, first designed in 1952 and approved for production in 1954, was built presumably to carry an 1,800-kilogram atomic warhead 6,450 kilometers to the United States. After five years of development, however, on October 4, 1957, Korolev's missile, with its 49 million newtons of thrust, launched an 83-kilogram Earth-orbiting satellite, Sputnik 1.

Tyuratam, not Kapustin Yar, was the launch site of Sputnik 1, Earth's first artificial satellite. During the early years of R-7 development, Soviet authorities had recognized the limitations of their miniature rocket range at Kapustin Yar. This original Soviet launch facility was located in the low-lying and often misty Volga river basin, where atmospheric moisture was injurious to the sensitive instruments and equipment. Security at Kapustin Yar was insufficient, as rising rockets could be seen from excursion boats on the Volga and on the Caspian Sea. Moreover, activities at Kapustin Yar were easily monitored from a U.S. Central Intelligence Agency radar station located in nearby Samsun, Turkey. Finally, to reach the preferred orbital inclinations, rockets at Kapustin Yar had to be launched in a southeasterly direction over several populated areas where an aborted rocket lift-off could risk human life. What the Soviet Union needed was an enlarged launch facility in a drier, less populated, and more secure area that was still accessible by rail and water to the country's industrialized regions.

The launch complex begun in June, 1955, near the Aral Sea, north of the small village of Tyuratam in Kazakhstan, met all these conditions. In 1961, the Soviet Union acknowledged the existence of this facility and named it the Baikonur cosmodrome, presumably after the railroad town of Baikonur. Modern Earth survey satellites, however, place the Baikonur cosmodrome at 45.6° north latitude, longitude 63.4° east, near the rail stop of Tyuratam. The town of Baikonur, not coincidentally, is located some 375 kilometers northeast of Tyuratam along the launch trajectory of the early Soviet space flights. Western observers agree that the Soviets chose the name Baikonur as part of a disinformation campaign to hide the true location of the facility.

The Tyuratam complex, which is roughly analogous to the U.S. Kennedy Space Center at Cape Canaveral in Florida, was built in a flat, sandy, grass-covered desert valley. The scientists and technicians who run the base live in nearby Zvyezdograd (Star City), a midsized town. The initial installations within the complex consisted of a cluster of low, white buildings and concrete blockhouses that included a "cosmonaut hostel" and an underground mission control center. Mission control, with its consoles containing radarscopes, oscillographs, tape recorders, and wall-to-wall charts, closely resembled the U.S. above-ground Mercury control center at Cape Canaveral. The original launchpad was surrounded by a massive, four-pronged service structure that reached toward the top of the erected rocket. The elevator, however, stopped short of the top, thereby requiring technicians or cosmonauts to take a short flight of steps, known as the cosmonauts' walk, to the top. The early Sputnik satellites, later lunar and planet probes, and all the Soviet manned space-flights were launched from the Tyuratam facilities.

As the Soviet space program expanded, activities at the Baikonur cosmodrome became so extensive that the Soviet government saw the need for a simpler and less costly facility for the launching of routine scientific flights that did not require a large ICBM booster. To meet this need, the Soviets modified the pre-Sputnik rocket test center at Kapustin Yar. This complex, also known as the Volgograd Station, has been used for launching satellites of less than 18,000 kilograms on small B-class and C-class launch vehicles. Since its reopening in 1962, fewer than one hundred space launchings have been performed at Kapustin Yar.

In 1966, the Soviets opened a new launch facility at Plesetsk, near the Arctic Circle at 62.8° north latitude, longitude 40.1° east, about 170 kilometers from Archangel. Plesetsk is the Soviet counterpart to the U.S. Vandenberg Air Force Base launch complex. Since the majority of flights originating from Plesetsk are military in nature, the Soviet Union has attempted to maintain a veil of secrecy around the facility, officially acknowledging it only in 1983. Civilian communications, mete-orological, and scientific missions also are frequently launched at Plesetsk, making it the world's busiest spaceport. After only three years in operation, Plesetsk was launching more rockets than Tyuratam and Kapustin Yar combined, and it con-tinued throughout the 1970's to launch an average of one vehicle every five days. Because of its proximity to the Arctic Circle, missions can be flown from Plesetsk without flying over densely populated regions in the early stages of flight and placed into Earth orbits with high inclinations with respect to the equator. In 1985, Plesetsk conducted its one thousandth space launch.

In addition to the three major cosmodromes, the Soviet Union operates seven major tracking stations that support the manned space program. These stations are at Yevpatoria, Tbilisi, Dzhusaly, Kolpashevo, Ulan Ude, Ussuriysk, and Petropav-lovsk. The Soviet Union supplements these land tracking stations with a fleet of tracking ships, each ship named for a Soviet cosmonaut or spacecraft designer. The three largest ships in the fleet are the *Kosmonaut Vladimir Komarov*, the *Akademik Sergei Korolev*, and the *Kosmonaut Yuri Gagarin*. These vessels are often deployed along the length of the Atlantic and in the Western Pacific during manned space-flights. Communications with deep space probes are generally maintained by facili-ties at Yevpatoria in the Crimea and at Simeiz.

Context

Space exploration requires advanced technology, which in turn is largely depen-dent on state-funded research and development. The willingness of any superpower to funnel massive funds into such research has historically been a function of how one power perceives itself relative to the technological strength of its rivals. The pattern of broad technological pioneering on the heels of political or military insecurities is an old one. Just as it was the paranoia of the Soviet Union after World

War II that intensified its commitment to the conquest of space, so it was the paranoia of the United States after the launching of Sputnik that awakened its enthusiasm for space exploration.

The Cold War between the United States and the Soviet Union has been fought in many theaters, but none has been more important than the theater of space. The race for space was more than a simple rivalry between two great superpowers. It was perceived by both powers as a race for the loyalty of the peoples of the world, for victory in space, it was thought, would confirm the superiority of a given politico-economic system.

In the space race, both sides achieved impressive victories. Although the United States first reached the goal of sending a person to the Moon, the Soviet Union also boasted numerous significant accomplishments. During the first decade of the space age alone, the Soviet list of achievements included the first orbiting of an artificial Earth satellite, the first orbiting of a live animal, the first landing of a space vehicle on the Moon, the first photographs of the dark side of the Moon, the first orbiting of a manned spacecraft, the first woman in space, the first rendezvous of manned spacecraft, the first maneuverable satellite, and the first multiple-crew spacecraft. The Soviet Union also achieved the first spacewalk, the first soft-landing of instruments on the Moon, the first impact of a space vehicle on Venus, the first instrumented penetration of the Venusian atmosphere, and the first linking of unmanned spacecraft.

Bibliography

Johnson, Nicholas L. *Handbook of Soviet Manned Space Flight*. San Diego: Univelt, 1979. A complete, descriptive summary of Soviet manned spaceflight accomplishments. Includes numerous maps, charts, and appendices. The same author also has written *Handbook of Soviet Lunar and Planetary Exploration*, published in 1979. Both works are written for the space history buff or engineer.

Killian, James R., Jr. *Sputnik, Scientists, and Eisenhower*. Cambridge, Mass.: MIT Press, 1977. These memoirs of the first special assistant to the U.S. president for science and technology are useful for understanding American public reactions to the Soviet launching of Sputnik. Suitable for general audiences.

McDougall, Walter A. . . . *The Heavens and the Earth: A Political History of the Space Age*. New York: Basic Books, 1985. An insightful and provocative academic assessment of the impact of technology on politics in both the United States and the Soviet Union. Includes seventy-four pages of endnotes and is well indexed. Highly recommended for serious students of space-age politics.

Oberg, James E. *Red Star in Orbit*. New York: Random House, 1981. Purports to be an "inside story of Soviet failures and triumphs in space." The author is a computer analyst for NASA who has written widely on the subject of spaceflight. Includes brief biographical sketches of major Soviet space program personalities, a listing of Soviet manned spaceflights, and an annotated bibliography. Suitable for general audiences.

Romanov, Alexander Petrovich. *Spacecraft Designer*. Moscow: Novosti Press Agency Publishing House, 1976. Written in English, this is the official Soviet version of Sergei Korolev's life. Offers interesting reading. Suitable for all audiences.

Schauer, William H. *The Politics of Space: A Comparison of Soviet and American Space Programs*. New York: Holmes and Meier, 1976. A comparison of the Soviet and American space programs. Includes a thorough discussion of the politics of the space race. Written in an academic style with extensive documentation, it is suitable for advanced readers.

Shelton, William. *Soviet Space Exploration: The First Decade*. New York: Washington Square Press, 1968. A readable and insightful overview of the period from Sputnik to the death of Komarov on Soyuz 1. Includes a forty-page chronology of Soviet spaceflights and a selected bibliography. Suitable for all audiences.

Smolders, Peter. *Soviets in Space: The Story of the Salyut and the Soviet Approach to Present and Future Space Travel*. Translated by Marian Powell. New York: Taplinger, 1973. An informed and sympathetic survey of the Soviet space program. Includes numerous maps, photographs, and illustrations. Suitable for general audiences.

U.S. Congress. Senate. Committee on Aeronautical and Space Sciences. *Soviet Space Program: 1966-1970*. 92d Cong., 1st sess., 1971. The authoritative U.S. document on the Soviet space program between 1966 and 1970. Two additional volumes, which cover the years 1971-1975 and 1976-1980, were published by the Government Printing Office in 1976 and 1981, respectively. The three volumes together cover the entire Soviet space research effort through 1980. Suitable for advanced readers.

Terry D. Bilhartz

Cross-References

Soviet Biosatellites, 194; Cosmonauts and the Soviet Cosmonaut Program, 273; Soviet Earth Resources Satellites, 313; Soviet Launch Vehicles, 742; The Luna Program, 764; The Mars Program, 878; Prognoz 1-10, 1196; The Salyut Space Station, 1233; The Soyuz-Kosmos Program, 1396; The Soyuz T Program, 1495; The Soviet Spaceflight Tracking Network, 1877; The Sputnik Program, 1930; Soviet Telecommunications Satellites, 2003; The Venera Program, 2083; The Voskhod Program, 2170; The Vostok Program, 2177; Zond 1-8, 2275.

SPACE CENTERS AND LAUNCH SITES IN THE UNITED STATES

Date: Beginning 1945
Type of facility: Space centers and launch sites
Country: The United States

With the advent of the German V-2 rocket in World War II, areas separated from population centers for testing this new weapon became a necessity. As the rockets' size grew and as their purpose changed from carrying warheads to launching satellites, more and larger testing facilities were needed.

Principal personages
FORREST S. MCCARTNEY, Director, Kennedy Space Center
LAWRENCE GOOCH, Commander, Eastern Space and Missile
  Center, Patrick Air Force Base
WAYNE PENLEY, Commander, Cape Canaveral Air Force Station
THOMAS J. P. JONES, Commanding General, White Sands Missile
  Range
THOMAS W. HONEYWILL, Commander, Space and Missile Test
  Organization, Vandenberg Air Force Base
ARLEN D. JAMESON, Commander, First Strategic Aerospace
  Division, Vandenberg Air Force Base
ORLANDO C. SEVERO, JR., Commander, Western Space and
  Missile Center, Vandenberg Air Force Base
WARREN KELLER, Director, Suborbital Missions, Wallops Flight
  Facility

Summary of the Facilities

The primary launch sites for space vehicles in the United States are Kennedy Space Center, just outside Cocoa Beach, Florida, and Vandenberg Air Force Base, just outside Lompoc, California. Each lies on the coastline of an ocean, permitting relatively safe launches over large, unpopulated areas. Two other key launch sites are the U.S. Army's White Sands Missile Range, between Las Cruces and Alamogordo, New Mexico, and Wallops Flight Facility, of the National Aeronautics and Space Administration's Goddard Space Flight Center, in Virginia on the Chesapeake Bay's Eastern Shore. White Sands and Wallops are used primarily for sounding rockets, small rockets—usually from surplus military inventories—that carry scientific experiments on brief, suborbital flights. Wallops also manages the National Scientific Balloon Facility (NSBF) in Palestine, Texas, where many experiments are launched on huge balloons. Wallops supports sounding rocket and balloon campaigns worldwide, as well, using mobile facilities in locations from Andoya, Norway, to Alice Springs, Australia.

Established in the early 1960's to serve as a launch site for the Apollo lunar landing missions, Kennedy Space Center is 240 kilometers south of Jacksonville and 80 kilometers east of Orlando. Kennedy and the Cape Canaveral Air Force Station form a complex that stretches for 55 kilometers and varies in width from 8 to 16 kilometers. The total land and water area occupied by the installation measures 568 square kilometers. When fully manned, the center has a work force of approximately two thousand National Aeronautics and Space Administration (NASA) civil servant employees and between twelve and thirteen thousand personnel who work for private companies under contract to NASA.

Since the completion of the Apollo lunar landing program, Kennedy Space Center has concentrated on supporting the United States' newest launch vehicle, the space shuttle. The first space shuttle (known as STS 1, for Space Transportation System 1) was launched from Launch Complex 39A on April 12, 1981. Many other launches from the Florida site take place at Cape Canaveral Air Force Station, which is adjacent to Kennedy. All the launches using the Delta rocket, for example, are from the air force station. Kennedy Space Center also operates a Vandenberg launch site resident office, which supports NASA activities at Vandenberg Air Force Base. Vandenberg was formed when an operational site was needed to train Air Force crews to launch intercontinental and intermediate range ballistic missiles. The Department of Defense decided to use an old Army facility, known as Camp Cooke, that occupied a strip of land on the Pacific Coast of California halfway between Los Angeles and San Francisco. The site was named Cooke Air Force Base in June, 1957, and the name was changed to Vandenberg Air Force Base in October, 1958, in honor of the late Hoyt S. Vandenberg, the second Air Force chief of staff.

The first missile was launched from Vandenberg in December, 1958. In February, 1959, Discoverer 1, the first satellite to be placed in a polar orbit, was launched from the base. Discoverer 1 was a precursor to the first successful U.S. reconnaissance satellite, Discoverer 13, which was launched from Vandenberg in August, 1960. By 1988, more than sixteen hundred missiles and booster rockets of forty-eight different types had been launched from Vandenberg. Known as "America's western spaceport," Vandenberg is the only U.S. military installation that launches both land-based intercontinental ballistic missiles and space boosters.

Covering more than 396 square kilometers, Vandenberg is the third largest U.S. Air Force installation. The facilities are linked by 837 kilometers of roads, 27 kilometers of railroad tracks, 129 kilometers of gas lines, 476 kilometers of water mains, and 727 kilometers of electrical power lines.

The launch site's economic impact on the region is significant. In the fiscal year ending September 30, 1987, the base generated revenues of more than $500 million. Military and civilian employees earned $300 million, and another $181 million was paid to aerospace contractors. An estimated forty-three hundred secondary jobs were created in the area because of the base.

In the 1980's, the Air Force started development of a space shuttle launch complex at Vandenberg, spending about $3 billion in facility costs and another $400 million annually in operating costs. The facility was named Space Launch

Complex 6 (SLC 6). Because of a number of problems at the site, however, the Air Force postponed further work on SLC 6.

The original plans called for shuttle operations to be conducted both at North Vandenberg and at South Vandenberg. The runway, orbiter maintenance and check-out facility, orbiter lifting facility, thermal protection facility, supply warehouses, and most of the support personnel are at North Vandenberg. SLC 6, which includes the launch control center, payload preparation room, payload changeout room, shuttle assembly building, access tower, launch mount, mobile service tower, and three exhaust ducts, is at South Vandenberg.

The Vandenberg approach to vehicle assembly differs from the procedures used at Kennedy Space Center. At Kennedy, the shuttle's components—the orbiter, external tank and solid-fueled rocket boosters—are assembled on a mobile launch platform in the vehicle assembly building and then moved to the launch area. At Vandenberg, the components would be assembled on the launchpad.

The Army's White Sands Missile Range (WSMR), in the Tularosa Basin of southern New Mexico, is 160 kilometers long by 65 kilometers wide—larger than the states of Delaware and Rhode Island and the District of Columbia combined. The range stretches more than half the distance from El Paso, Texas, to Albuquerque, New Mexico. In area, it is the largest military reservation in the United States.

WSMR was established on July 9, 1945, as the White Sands Proving Ground; the name was changed in 1958. The first missile fired at the range was a Tiny Tim sounding rocket, in September, 1945. The facility supports missile development and test programs for the Army, Navy, and Air Force and for NASA and other government agencies.

Since 1960, WSMR has had part-time use of a 4,225-square-kilometer area adjoining the range's northern boundary. Two other areas, adjacent to the western boundary, also have been used to extend the range. Used many times a year, these areas—which total approximately 5,150 square kilometers—permit testing of longer-range missiles. When firings are scheduled in these areas, residents leave their homes, usually for a maximum of twelve hours. The ranch families are paid for the use of their land and for the hours they must spend away from home during these evacuations.

WSMR has served as an impact area for Army Sergeant and Pershing missiles launched from sites in Utah as far as 643 kilometers away. In 1982, the range added a launch complex near Mountain Home, Idaho, thereby acquiring the capability of firing the Pershing 2 missile and other test missiles with ranges of more than 1,200 kilometers.

On the northern portion of the range, on July 16, 1945, the world's first atomic device was detonated. The spot, known as Trinity Site, is in a missile impact area and is open to the public only once a year.

Several tenant organizations share the White Sands facilities. Among those organizations are the Naval Ordnance Missile Test Facility, the Atmospheric Sciences Laboratory of the Army's Electronics Research and Development Command, the

Army's Communications Command Agency, NASA, and the Air Force Range Operations Office.

The range has more than one thousand precisely surveyed instrumentation sites and approximately seven hundred sophisticated optical and electronics instrument systems. Another of its assets is the National Laser Test Facility. This installation will be used for laser lethality testing by the Army, Navy, and Air Force and by government agencies.

The Wallops Flight Facility is managed by Goddard Space Flight Center. Wallops is 64 kilometers southeast of Salisbury, Maryland, and approximately 241 kilometers southeast of Goddard, which is in Greenbelt, Maryland. Composed of a main base, the Wallops Island launch site, and the Wallops mainland, the site covers more than 25 square kilometers and has eighty-four major facilities valued at about $105 million. Approximately 380 civil service workers and 560 contractor employees staff the installation, which has an annual payroll of more than $30 million.

Development of Wallops was started in 1945 when the National Advisory Committee for Aeronautics (NACA) authorized the Langley Research Center to establish a site for research on rocket-propelled vehicles. Since then, Wallops has been used as a launching site for scientific missions as well as a facility for aeronautical research.

The Navy decided in 1958 to close its Chincoteague Naval Air Station, about eleven kilometers northwest of Wallops Island. A year later, Wallops took over those facilities, which included buildings, utilities, hangars, and an excellent airport.

Wallops is at the center of NASA's suborbital programs. Sounding rockets, balloons, and aircraft are used in NASA programs concerned with space science, applications, advanced technology, and aeronautical research.

Sounding rockets carry scientific payloads to altitudes ranging from 48 to 965 kilometers. Experiment time above the atmosphere is usually about fifteen minutes. Scientific data are collected and returned to Earth by telemetry links, and the payloads are parachuted to Earth for refurbishment and reuse. Scientific balloons carry payloads to altitudes of up to 48 kilometers and normally remain aloft for from one to sixty hours. The balloon program supports approximately forty-five launches each year. Between 1975 and 1986, 493 balloons were launched, with an overall success rate of 85 percent. In addition, more than twenty satellites have been launched from Wallops since 1961, including Explorer 9, the first satellite to be launched by an all-solid-fueled rocket.

Along with its headquarters in Washington, D.C., NASA operates nine major space centers in the United States. Ames Research Center, Mountain Home, California, was founded in 1940 and is located on 1.7 square kilometers of land adjacent to the U.S. Naval Air Station at Moffett Field. It employs twenty-two hundred civil service employees and approximately twenty-one hundred contractor employees at the main center and at a subsidiary installation, Dryden Flight Research Center, which merged with Ames in 1981.

Goddard Space Flight Center, in Greenbelt, Maryland, was established in 1959.

Goddard is 16 kilometers northeast of Washington, D.C. It has 4.45 square kilometers of land and employs approximately twelve thousand civil service and contractor employees at Greenbelt and at its subsidiary, Wallops Flight Facility.

The Jet Propulsion Laboratory, in Pasadena, California, is a government-owned facility operated by the California Institute of Technology under a NASA contract. It is 32 kilometers northeast of Los Angeles.

Johnson Space Center is about 32 kilometers southeast of Houston. The center was established in 1961 as NASA's primary center for manned spaceflight. Most of the one hundred buildings on the 6.6-square-kilometer site house offices and laboratories, some of which are dedicated to astronaut training and mission operations.

Kennedy Space Center is responsible for the assembly, testing, and launch of space shuttles and their payloads, for shuttle landing operations, and for the servicing of space shuttle orbiters between missions. Kennedy also operates a Vandenberg launch site resident office.

Langley Research Center is in the Tidewater area of Virginia between Norfolk and Williamsburg. The center occupies 3 square kilometers, one of which is used under permit from the U.S. Air Force. An additional 13.3 square kilometers of marshland near Langley are used as a model-drop zone.

Lewis Research Center is adjacent to the Cleveland Hopkins International Airport, approximately 32 kilometers southwest of Cleveland. Established in 1941, it is staffed by twenty-seven hundred civil service employees and thirteen hundred contractor personnel.

Marshall Space Flight Center, Huntsville, Alabama, is situated on 7.3 square kilometers inside the Army's Redstone Arsenal. The center has thirty-five hundred civil service employees, of whom 58 percent are scientists and engineers. Formed in July, 1960, Marshall has been most often identified as NASA's launch vehicle development center. Marshall manages two other sites: the Michoud Assembly Facility, in New Orleans, where space shuttle external tanks are made; and the Slidell Computer Complex, in Slidell, Louisiana, which provides computer service support to Michoud.

Stennis Space Center, Bay St. Louis, Mississippi, is located on the East Pearl River, which provides deep-water access to oversize cargo. Stennis occupies an area of 562 square kilometers, 54.6 of which are covered by the operational base. The center conducts static test firings of space shuttle's main engines.

Context

At the end of World War II, the United States was operating five small missile sites: one in West Virginia, three in California, and one in Texas. The maximum range of the missiles being tested at those facilities was less than 15 kilometers. To meet the greater distance requirements of the postwar era, three facilities were created in 1945. The first of these was Wallops Flight Facility, which was established by the National Advisory Committee on Aeronautics (NACA) with an 80-kilometer range. The second was the 161-kilometer-wide White Sands Missile

Range, set up adjacent to the already-established Hueco Range at Fort Bliss. The third was the Naval Air Facility, established at Point Mugu, California, with a 100-kilometer range.

Hardly were these installations established, however, before officials recognized that they were not large enough. With the development of intermediate and intercontinental ballistic missiles already under way, the need for sites with ranges of thousands of kilometers became obvious. Moreover, further expansion of the existing ranges would be extremely difficult. As a result, in 1947, a War Department research committee was established to find a suitable range for testing medium- and long-range weapons.

The committee selected three possible sites. In order of preference, they were El Centro Naval Station, in California; Cape Canaveral, in Florida; and a third site, in Washington. The selections were made based on favorable weather and the location of island chains downrange on which tracking stations could be established. El Centro was found unsuitable when Mexico refused rights to some of its islands, and the weather in the Aleutians proved a setback for the Washington site. Great Britain was more cooperative with its Bahamas, and Cape Canaveral was chosen.

In October, 1949, President Harry S Truman established the Joint Long Range Proving Ground (later known as the Air Force Eastern Test Range), a huge overwater range extending 8,000 kilometers across the Atlantic from Cape Canaveral to Ascension Island. The first launch from the Cape was conducted by a military-civilian team on July 24, 1950. The rocket was a modified German V-2 with an upper stage, and it attained an altitude of 16 kilometers. In the early 1950's, the focus turned from missile tests to satellite launches. On January 31, 1958, the United States' first satellite, Explorer 1, was launched from the Cape by a military-civilian team led by Kurt Debus, a key member of the famed Wernher von Braun rocket team. Thereafter, Cape Canaveral became the launch site for the Mercury missions and, in the 1960's, for the Gemini and Apollo missions.

Bibliography

Hartman, Edwin P. *Adventures in Research: A History of Ames Research Center, 1940-1965*. NASA SP-4302. Washington, D.C.: Government Printing Office, 1970. Published in celebration of Ames Research Center's twenty-fifth anniversary, this work captures the excitement of the persons who staffed the center in its early years. Includes appendices and references.

John F. Kennedy Space Center. *America's Spaceport*. Washington, D.C.: National Aeronautics and Space Administration, 1987. Published in celebration of the center's twenty-fifth anniversary, this comprehensive overview of the history and facilities of Kennedy Space Center is illustrated with works from the NASA art program.

Koppes, Clayton R. *JPL and the American Space Program: A History of the Jet Propulsion Laboratory*. New Haven, Conn.: Yale University Press, 1982. Discusses research at JPL during World War II and the years that followed. Describes the relationship between the California Institute of Technology and JPL and between JPL and NASA. More than half the volume is devoted to JPL's space projects.

National Aeronautics and Space Administration. *Marshall Space Flight Center 1960-1985: Twenty-fifth Anniversary Report.* Washington, D.C.: Government Printing Office, 1985. A booklet on Marshall's history and role in the U.S. space program. Includes photographs of Marshall at work, contrasting early activities with later ones, and a timeline showing the dates of major projects.

Rosenthal, Alfred. *The Early Years, Goddard Space Flight Center: Historical Origins and Activities Through December 1962.* Washington, D.C.: Government Printing Office, 1964. This commemorative manual provides a comprehensive look at the founding of Goddard Space Flight Center.

Sloan, Aubrey B. "Vandenberg Planning for the Space Transportation System." *Astronautics and Aeronautics* 19 (November, 1981): 44-50. A detailed description of the original plan for the Vandenberg shuttle complex. Provides a good history of the decision-making process involved in bringing the shuttle complex to Vandenberg. Includes illustrations, diagrams, and a useful bibliography for further study. Full of technical information, but still readable.

Wallops Flight Facility, Office of Public Affairs. *Wallops: A Guide to the Facility.* Greenbelt, Md.: Goddard Space Flight Center, 1988. This guide, prepared by the Office of Public Affairs, provides a thorough explanation of the facilities and programs at Wallops.

James C. Elliott

Cross-References

Ames Research Center, 21; The Apollo Program, 28; Cape Canaveral and the Kennedy Space Center, 229; The Gemini Program, 487; Goddard Space Flight Center, 563; The Jet Propulsion Laboratory, 662; Johnson Space Center, 669; Langley Research Center, 722; U.S. Launch Vehicles, 749; Lewis Research Center, 757; Marshall Space Flight Center, 908; The Mercury Project, 940; The National Aeronautics and Space Administration, 1032; The U.S. Space Shuttle, 1626; Vandenberg Air Force Base, 2069.

SPACE LAW
1968-1979

Date: January 1, 1968, to December 31, 1979
Type of issue: Space law
Countries: Member states of the United Nations

The first set of space laws stemming from the original space law, the Outer Space Treaty of 1967, were developed and adopted by member states of the United Nations. These laws concerned rescue of astronauts, liability of launching states, registration of space objects, and exploration of celestial bodies.

Summary of the Issue

The first space law was ratified by member states of the United Nations in 1967, one decade after Sputnik, the first artificial satellite, was put into orbit by the Soviet Union. This law, referred to as the Outer Space Treaty of 1967, established many of the fundamental principles that govern activities in outer space. Its preamble and twenty-one articles contained terminology that was imprecise or not well defined; it was hoped that the spirit of the law would be followed until terms and concepts could be refined with additional laws.

Through extensive discussions and debates within the Committee on Peaceful Uses of Outer Space (COPUOS) of the United Nations, four additional space laws were developed over the twelve years following the Outer Space Treaty. Each of these laws is related to at least one of the articles of the original treaty. The Soviet Union took much of the initiative in forming early drafts of these follow-up laws. The formal and common titles of the first treaty and the four subsequent laws are as follows: Treaty on Principles Governing the Activities of States in the Exploration and Use of Outer Space, Including the Moon and Other Celestial Bodies, or the Outer Space Treaty of 1967; Agreement on the Rescue of Astronauts, the Return of Astronauts, and the Return of Objects Launched into Outer Space, or the Rescue and Return Agreement of 1968; Convention on International Liability for Damage Caused by Space Objects, or the Liability Convention of 1972; Convention on Registration of Objects Launched into Outer Space, or the Registration Convention of 1975; and Agreement Governing the Activities of States on the Moon and Other Celestial Bodies, or the Moon Agreement of 1979.

The space laws ratified from 1968 to 1979 have a number of features in common. Like the original space law, they express a desire for the peaceful use of outer space and international cooperation in outer space activities for the benefit of all. The preamble of each law expresses the motivation of the law and refers to the applicable laws that precede it. Articles of the laws contain specifications regarding space activities, legal relationships, and procedural specifications. Although most of the articles deal with legal relationships involving responsibility, control, jurisdiction, and liability, the discussion here pertains primarily to regulations of space activity.

Undoubtedly the most important phrase to come before COPUOS is the one that appears in each law: "the peaceful use of outer space." Space technology combined with thermonuclear weapons has the potential to destroy all life on Earth; the same space technology, however, has the potential to benefit the world greatly. Consequently, much of the activity of COPUOS has been directed at space laws that encourage peaceful uses of outer space and at the application of space technology to satellites that benefit all nations.

The need for orderly regulation of activities in outer space is great, since the world is extensively affected by these activities. First, there is heavy satellite traffic in orbit about Earth. In 1981 alone, the Soviet Union and the United States launched 1,997 space systems. Also, these systems sometimes do not operate as planned, and damage results. Furthermore, member states have different outlooks on the missions of the space systems, so friction and conflict can easily result even if space activity goes as planned.

Discussion and debates within COPUOS have often been tedious and arduous. A simple analysis of the phrase "peaceful use of outer space" demonstrates some of the complexities of developing international space law. The term "peaceful" has been taken to mean devoid of weapons of mass destruction, devoid of military facilities of any type, or posing no threats to national security. The word "use" has been interpreted to mean employment, exploration, or even exploitation. The fundamental phrase "outer space" has not yet found a widely accepted interpretation; outer space can be seen as beginning 100 kilometers above sea level, where the International Aeronautical Federation assumes air space to end, but questions can be raised about even this simple delimitation. For example, do outer space laws or air space laws apply to space systems that must pass through air space during launch and reentry or satellites whose perigees are less than 100 kilometers?

The Rescue and Return Agreement of 1968 consists of a preamble and ten articles and is an elaboration of articles 5 and 7 of the Outer Space Treaty of 1967. Provisions are made in the agreement for the notification of the launching state and Secretary General of the United Nations when it is determined that astronauts are in distress or an accident or emergency has arisen. The thrust of this law, however, is to take steps for the rescue and prompt return of the astronauts and associated space system. The rescue provision is a humanitarian gesture; promptness is indicated to discourage states from detaining astronauts for interrogation or retaining space equipment for examination for espionage purposes. Humanitarian rescue is not a new legal idea; there has been a long-standing requirement for nations to rescue crew and passengers from predicaments involving maritime vessels and aircraft. The idea of rescuers returning systems associated with rescued persons, however, is a new legal idea.

In anticipation of a case when rescue from a satellite in orbit would be necessary, the United States and Soviet Union jointly participated in such a practice maneuver. In 1975 the U.S. Apollo and Soviet Soyuz space systems successfully performed a docking maneuver in which an astronaut was transferred from one satellite to another. This was not only a technological achievement but also a demonstration of the ability of the superpowers to cooperate successfully in the exploration of outer space.

The Liability Convention of 1972 consists of a preamble and twenty-eight articles and is basically an elaboration of article 8 of the Outer Space Treaty. Provisions are made in the convention for the liability of launching states when damage occurs on Earth, in air space, or in outer space. The term "damage" means loss of life, personal injury, impairment of health, or loss of or damage to property. Most of this law's articles pertain to comprehensive procedures for determining liability when multiple parties are involved and to the filing and settling of claims. Multiple parties often are involved, since the exploration and use of outer space tends to be a multinational endeavor.

The most noteworthy application of this agreement occurred in 1978, when the Soviet Kosmos 954 satellite crashed into the Canadian Northwest Territories. When the Canadians requested prompt and complete answers to questions about the nature of the satellite, the Soviets offered only a team of specialists to assist in the recovery. Eventually the Soviet Union revealed that the satellite contained a small nuclear power reactor and that some of the debris probably was dangerously radioactive. Finally, specialists from the United States were invited to join the Canadian team in the search for debris. All the debris was recovered. The Soviet Union was billed for the associated activities, but it compensated Canada for only half the bill.

The Registration Convention of 1975 consists of a preamble and twelve articles and is related to article 8 of the Outer Space Treaty. This agreement basically provides for mandatory registration and voluntary inclusion of identifying markings on space systems. Each state is to maintain its own register and file registration papers with the Secretary General of the United Nations. Information to be filed with the Secretary General includes orbital parameters and function of the satellite, time and place of the launch, and the time when the satellite will no longer be in orbit.

Nations' compliance with this agreement would guarantee orderly use of air space and outer space and encourage peaceful use of outer space. Unfortunately, many satellites are not registered, nor is their nature disclosed. In fact, it has been estimated that 75 percent of all satellites are military in nature, making outer space primarily an arena used for military purposes. This military use, especially by the Soviet Union and the United States, is in direct conflict with the promotion of peaceful use of outer space. Each of the superpowers is fearful that the other will gain a strategic edge in outer space, so there is a tendency to maintain a balance in the number of military satellites launched by each side.

The Moon Agreement of 1979 consists of a preamble and twenty-one articles and is related to articles 9 and 11 of the Outer Space Treaty. This agreement pertains to all celestial bodies in outer space but is mostly written in terms of the Moon, since this is the only celestial body besides Earth on which humans have walked. Many states have explored planets of the solar system in accordance with regulations of the Moon Agreement. These explorations have included flybys of the planets Mercury, Jupiter, Saturn, and Uranus; flybys of the moons of Mars, Jupiter, Saturn, and Uranus; probes of the outer portions of the Sun, Venus, and Halley's comet; robotic exploration of the surfaces of Mars and Venus; and direct exploration by humans of the surface of the Moon.

The agreement provides numerous guidelines for exploration of the Moon, whether through robotics or direct astronaut activity. Collection, removal, and scientific analysis of lunar material is sanctioned. Since a compelling activity for explorers is to bring back materials from the new world to be analyzed, provisions of this agreement encourage the sharing of these materials with the rest of the world. Sharing materials is a specific reinforcement of the idea, found in all the laws, that space exploration should benefit all. Exploring parties may go anywhere and may establish bases of operation, but not of a military nature. All the above activities, however, are to be conducted in such a way that the equilibrium of the Moon is not disturbed. A description of the mission is to be sent to the Secretary General, and if any new phenomenon or evidence of organic life is found, the Secretary General is to be notified of that, too.

The most innovative aspect of this agreement is the common human heritage concept, meaning that the Moon or any other celestial body is not subject to national appropriation or a claim of sovereignty by the exploring state. This idea contrasts with the age-old tradition of explorers' claiming new lands for a sponsoring sovereign by planting a flag in the soil. Although extensive explorations of the Moon by Apollo astronauts preceded this agreement, all the Apollo activities were legalized by the agreement. Among the activities sanctioned were the collection, removal, and sharing of lunar rocks and soil and excursions of Apollo 15's Lunar Rover Vehicle. The flag planted on the Moon by the Apollo 11 team was considered a celebration of first arrival rather than a claim of sovereignty. The common heritage provision does not pertain to materials of the solar system that reach Earth by natural means. Consequently, meteorites are not subject to the agreement and may be owned by individuals.

Context

Although the space laws adopted by member states have been in effect only since 1967, each law has been tested. Virtually all satellites and space vehicles conform to the Outer Space Treaty's regulations concerning noninterference with other states' space activities. Many military satellites, however, are launched without the nature of their mission having been filed with the Secretary General, which violates the Registration Convention of 1975.

Provisions of the Rescue and Return Agreement of 1968 and the Liability Convention of 1972 covered procedures for the return of Kosmos 954 debris in 1978 and reimbursement for associated expenses to the Canadians. The most important part of these two laws, however, was still untested as of 1988, since there had not been a disaster requiring rescue of astronauts or compensation for loss of life. Both the United States and the Soviet Union have lost several of their own astronauts during space exploration, but the Liability Convention of 1972 does not apply to the loss of nationals of a launching state caused by circumstances brought about by the launching state.

The Moon Agreement of 1979 has been obeyed more consistently than the other space laws. Compared with the complexities of satellite traffic in the vicinity of Earth and with the way humans have modified the surface of Earth, exploration of the solar system has been superficial. This agreement, the most far-reaching of the laws, may govern activities within the solar system, and possibly beyond, for many years to come.

The four laws discussed here have built-in flexibility. All have provisions for adoption by new member states and for withdrawal or amendments by existing member states. The Registration Convention and the Moon Agreement also have provisions for review after ten years for reevaluation of the laws in the light of new technological developments.

One of the interesting features of the space laws has been the declining numbers of nations ratifying the laws. Although 50 percent of the member states ratified the first law, only about 7 percent ratified the last law. The steady decline in ratification may be a result of the great differences in nations' levels of economic development. Developing countries may believe that significant participation in space activity is only possible in the distant future and that in the meantime, it might be more beneficial for them to make agreements among themselves without COPUOS. Advanced countries may believe that if they provide all the financing and manpower for a lucrative space exploration, they should be allowed to decide how the fortune is to be shared with the world rather than being obliged to honor other states' interpretations of the COPUOS laws.

Bibliography

Christol, Carl Q. *The Modern International Law of Outer Space*. Elmsford, N.Y.: Pergamon Press, 1982. This is one of the comprehensive publications on space law. All five space laws are extensively discussed. There are many hundreds of footnotes and references. Suitable for advanced high school or college students.

Gorove, Stephen. *United States Space Law: National and International Regulation*. 3 vols. Dobbs Ferry, N.Y.: Oceana Publications, 1982. Contains good documentation of legislation, regulations, and agreements pertinent to the U.S. space program. Suitable for advanced high school or college students.

Jasentuliyana, Nandasiri, ed. *Maintaining Outer Space for Peaceful Uses: Proceedings of a Symposium Held in The Hague, March, 1984*. Lanham, Md.: Bernan-Unipub, 1984. This is a collection of articles presented at a symposium on the demilitarization of outer space. Suitable for advanced high school or college students.

Zhukov, Gennady, and Urii Kolosov. *International Space Law*. New York: Praeger,

1984. A comprehensive text covering all five space laws. Many ideas are developed from the Soviet viewpoint. Suitable for advanced high school or college students.

Louis Winkler

Cross-References

The Apollo Program, 28; Apollo 15's Lunar Rover, 110; The Apollo-Soyuz Test Project, 132; Lunar Soil Samples, 823; The Outer Space Treaty, 1111; The Soyuz-Kosmos Program, 1396; Space Law: Ongoing Issues, 1612; Spy Satellites, 1937.

SPACE LAW
Ongoing Issues

Date: Beginning October 10, 1967
Type of issue: Space law
Countries: Member states of the United Nations

By the 1980's the United Nations was developing a second generation of space laws in an effort to regulate satellite traffic in orbit about Earth. Attention was focused on the demilitarization of outer space, remote sensing and direct television broadcasting from outer space, use of geosynchronous systems, and nuclear power sources in outer space.

Summary of the Issue

Emerging space laws are agreements about outer space that are less developed than formal space laws, which are agreements already ratified by member states of the United Nations. Emerging space laws are often collections of working papers in the Committee on Peaceful Uses of Outer Space (COPUOS) of the United Nations. COPUOS employs a variety of specialists, grouped into the Scientific and Technical Subcommittee and the Legal Subcommittee.

The five existing space laws are the Outer Space Treaty of 1967, the Rescue and Return Agreement of 1968, the Liability Convention of 1972, the Registration Convention of 1975, and the Moon Agreement of 1979. The five emerging space laws are all concerned with satellite technology. Their topics are the demilitarization of outer space, remote sensing from outer space, direct television broadcasting from outer space, the synchronous orbit-radio spectrum resource, and nuclear power sources in outer space.

International space law is such a new discipline that specific activities in outer space are often legalized many years after they begin. Spaceflight itself was legalized by a United Nations General Assembly resolution in 1961, four years after the Soviet Union had launched the first artificial satellite. Similarly, all the activities addressed by emerging space laws have existed for many years, some for the entire space age thus far.

Delays in legalizing space activity and developing space laws are consequences of the situation's complexity. Nations' outlooks differ because of their diverse cultural backgrounds, levels of development, and values. Throughout the space age, the number of United Nations member states has steadily increased, giving some of the states an opportunity to see how others have fared under various laws over the years. Also, satellite systems are highly technical, and the technology is steadily changing. The Outer Space Treaty of 1967 expresses the desire to maintain outer space for peaceful purposes. This sentiment also appears in the preamble of each of the four other space laws. Nevertheless, member states, especially the United States and the Soviet Union, have put many military satellites into orbit, and there is much apprehension that thermonuclear weapons delivered from Earth-orbiting systems can abruptly end life on Earth. Delivery of weapons from orbiting systems is judged to be inferior to delivery of weapons from conventional intercontinental ballistic missiles (ICBMs) launched from Earth's surface; if the existing precarious military balance were disturbed by additional military systems in space, however, life on Earth would be endangered. The United States and the Soviet Union, therefore, have tried to maintain parity when launching space systems of a military nature.

Military systems launched by the two superpowers are great in number and varied in scope. Thousands of satellites have been launched, and it is estimated that 75 percent of the satellites are used for military purposes. Many of them are reconnaissance satellites, using various wavelengths of the electromagnetic spectrum to sense Earth's surface. Others are communications satellites with specific tactical or strategic functions. Still others are antisatellites (ASATs) programmed to neutralize or destroy one or more of the opposition's reconnaissance or communications satellites.

Although the vast majority of the military systems in outer space have been used only for peaceful purposes, spy satellites have monitored at least two military conflicts on Earth: The Soviet Union used satellites to observe conflicts between Israel and Lebanon and between Argentina and England in the 1980's.

One of the earlier noteworthy efforts to demilitarize outer space was the proposal made by France to the United Nations in 1978 for the establishment of an international satellite monitoring agency. Under the terms of this proposal, agency satellites would be used to observe and control activities in space in accordance with COPUOS regulations designed to enforce disarmament principles.

For many years, efforts have been made to demilitarize outer space and rid Earth of missiles with thermonuclear warheads. The superpowers have not been completely successful, however, because of the problem of verification. In limited areas, however, some progress has been made; in the Strategic Arms Limitation Talks between the United States and the Soviet Union, verification in the form of remote sensing from satellites was accepted.

Perhaps the most developed multilateral, international demilitarization proposal to come from COPUOS is the ENMOD Convention of 1978, which is officially called the Convention on the Prohibition of Military or Any Other Hostile Use of Environmental Modification Techniques. In this convention, parties agree not to change the dynamics, composition, or structure of Earth or outer space. Environmental modifications represent some of the most extreme possible forms of threat.

Satellites in orbit about Earth can use various wavelengths of the electromagnetic spectrum to sense outer space and the land, sea, and atmosphere of Earth. This sensing is done either passively or actively. Passive sensing utilizes radiations emitted by Earth's features or by objects in outer space. Active sensing utilizes radiation beamed by the sensing satellite system and then reflected by what is being observed. Remote sensing from outer space has been practiced for many years and in many ways. There are communications, Earth resources, meteorological, military, and scientific remote-sensing satellites.

Member states' opinions of remote sensing depend on what is being sensed, how much detail is being revealed, and what is being done with the data. Virtually no states object to sensing limited to the ocean or atmosphere, but some states object if their territory is sensed by others, since they believe that this violates their sovereignty. Other states think that there should be no restrictions on acquiring data from outer space, since this is consistent with the Outer Space Treaty, which provides for free access to outer space for the benefit of all. Because there is so much potential benefit from remote sensing, it has been possible to find many principles on which a consensus can be reached. One of the significant working papers on this topic was developed in 1984 and is entitled "Draft Principles with Respect to the Activities of States Concerning Remote Sensing from Outer Space," or the Remote Sensing Draft of 1984.

Direct television broadcasting (DTB) involves a television signal that is broadcast from a satellite to a community on Earth. The signal from the satellite may be a relay from Earth or a program beamed through an activating signal from Earth. DTB includes direct radio broadcasting, since a television signal without video is essentially a radio signal. DTB, unlike remote sensing, is designed to influence humans directly and can be used to transmit ideas and information to shape human values and international relations. Some nations view the use of DTB as a sovereign right that can be used to promote understanding between cultures and international cooperation. Others, however, view DTB as an infringement of their national sovereignty that could result in international conflict. Because the U.S. media are run by private concerns, the United States takes the former view; because the Soviet media are run by the government, the Soviet Union takes the latter view. There also exists a view that some cultures are too fragile to be exposed to some types of DTB.

An example of a successful undertaking of DTB by two diverse cultures is the joint effort by India and the United States known as the Satellite International Television Experiment. The United States uses a geosynchronous satellite above East Africa to broadcast to India, and India provides programs on agriculture, family planning, health care, and general education subjects.

As in the case of remote sensing, there are numerous principles on which consensus can be reached on DTB. One of the more significant working papers on DTB was developed by COPUOS in 1982 and is entitled "Principles Governing the Use by States of Artificial Earth Satellites for International Direct Television Broadcasting," or the DTB Principles of 1982. One of the features of this paper is that it asks states with common cultural commitments and comparable outlooks on national security to consider developing regional agreements.

Geosynchronous satellites are highly valued for the economic benefits and military security they provide through remote sensing. At the end of 1984 there were 138 satellites in geosynchronous orbit, 80 of which were of the communications variety. Radio signals are transmitted between these satellites and ground stations.

As the number of geosynchronous satellites increases, so does the problem of radio signal interference. Consequently, there must be orderly use of orbital positions and radio frequencies. Allocations of orbital positions and radio frequencies are made by the International Frequency Registration Board at World Administrative Radio Conferences.

Allocation of the orbital radio spectrum is problematical because of the differing views of the technologically advanced and developing nations. Advanced countries favor allocation to users having present needs and capabilities; developing countries favor acceptance and approval prior to their gaining the ability to use the resources. Moreover, systems using radio frequencies already exist on land, at sea, and in the air and must be accounted for both in their frequency allocations and in their geographic positions.

One of the difficulties in getting consensus on the orbital spectrum resource proposals was created by the Bogotá Declaration of 1976, which was signed by eight countries that lie on Earth's equator. Their claim is that geosynchronous satellites exist by virtue of Earth's gravity and that the position of these satellites, at an altitude of 35,900 kilometers, is therefore not part of outer space. They claim that it follows that geosynchronous satellites above their territorial land and water are under their sovereignty. Nevertheless, while COPUOS has not been able to find a widely accepted definition or delineation of outer space, most nations agree that geosynchronous orbits are in outer space.

Nuclear energy sources for space systems have advantages over conventional sources of energy involving chemical batteries, fuel cells, or solar energy collectors. Nuclear power sources are not as limited by the amount of energy available as are chemical batteries or fuel cells, and sources using nuclear power are more compact than solar energy panels. The methods used for generating nuclear energy involve either radioactive decay of the isotope plutonium 238 or fission of enriched uranium 235 in a reactor. The power reactor system is the most efficient type of energy source when power generation is required over long periods of time or at high energy levels. Power reactor systems also constitute greater radioactive dangers to humans, animals, and the environment. These dangers can arise if a reactor malfunctions and cannot be shut down or if there is an accident and radioactive material is scattered about.

Nuclear power systems have been in use in outer space since 1961, primarily in Soviet Kosmos satellites. Although the five space laws adopted by the United Nations between 1967 and 1979 each provide regulations pertinent to the use of nuclear energy in space, none specifically addresses safety. One of the few safety standards regarding radioactive materials is found in a document of 1977 entitled "Recommendations of the International Commission on Radiological Protection."

An application of the existing space laws to nuclear power system problems occurred in 1978 when the Soviet Kosmos 954 satellite crashed in Canada's Northwest Territories and scattered radioactive debris over a wide area. For the most part, the crash was handled in accordance with general regulations of the Rescue and

Return Agreement of 1972 and the Liability Convention of 1975.

Attempts are currently being made to develop safety standards for the use of nuclear power in space. One consideration is that radiation leakage must be held to a minimum after a crash or during sustained water immersion. Also, provisions are being considered for the retention of specially trained teams that will be called on when dangerous radioactive materials from space enter Earth's atmosphere.

Context

Because of the great complexity of the five topics undergoing discussion and debate in the United Nations, there are large areas of simultaneous agreement and disagreement. There is hope that agreement on each topic can be reached, and that new space laws will eventually emerge. The most important of the topics is the demilitarization and peaceful use of outer space. Success here is most likely to be achieved if suitable verification techniques from outer space can be developed. In the late 1980's, it seemed likely that laws would be developed in the areas of remote sensing and direct television broadcasting, since there already were working systems in place that related to each area.

Geosynchronous satellites are a necessary part of military, remote-sensing, and direct television broadcasting systems. Orbital-spectrum resource problems pose the greatest technological challenges, since they involve complex radio equipment and the allocation of radio frequencies. Eight equatorial countries have claimed sovereignty over geosynchronous satellites above their territory.

Topics to be developed in the area of emerging space laws include space transportation systems, such as the space shuttle, and the construction of nearby space stations. These topics do not appear to be raising any new legal ideas, but they are of great interest since they involve activities which will be pursued intensively during the last part of the twentieth century.

Bibliography

Benko, Marietta, et al. *Space Law in the United Nations*. Dordrecht, Netherlands: Martinus Nijhoff Publishers, 1985. Contains discussions of demilitarization, remote sensing, nuclear power sources, and the orbital spectrum resource. Suitable for advanced high school or college students.

Christol, Carl Quimby. *Modern International Law of Outer Space*. Elmsford, N.Y.: Pergamon Press, 1982. One of the comprehensive publications on space law. Contains discussions of all five emerging laws. Includes hundreds of footnotes and references. Suitable for advanced high school or college students.

Fawcett, J. E. *Outer Space: New Challenges in Law and Policy*. New York: Oxford University Press, 1984. A short text that covers demilitarization, remote sensing, direct television broadcasting, and space stations. Suitable for advanced high school or college students.

Gorove, Stephen. *United States Law: National and International Regulation*. Dobbs Ferry, N.Y.: Oceana Publications, 1982. Contains good documentation of legislation, regulations, and agreements pertinent to the U.S. space program. Suitable for advanced high school or college students.

Jasentuliyana, Nandasiri, ed. *Maintaining Outer Space for Peaceful Uses: Proceedings of a Symposium Held in The Hague, March, 1984*. Lanham, Md.: Bernan-Unipub, 1984. A collection of articles presented at a symposium on the peaceful uses of outer space. Suitable for advanced high school or college students.

Zhukov, Gennady, and Urii M. Kolosov. *International Space Law*. New York: Praeger, 1984. A comprehensive text covering all five topics concerning emerging space laws. Many ideas are developed from the Soviet viewpoint. Suitable for advanced high school or college students.

Louis Winkler

Cross-References

Soviet Earth Resources Satellites, 313; Landsat 1, 2, and 3, 710; Landsat 4 and 5, 717; U.S. Military Telecommunications Satellites, 1012; The Outer Space Treaty, 1111; Seasat, 1279; Space Law: 1968-1979, 1606; Spacewatch: Tracking Space Debris, 1924; Spy Satellites, 1937; Soviet Telecommunications Satellites, 2003; U.S. Passive Relay Telecommunications Satellites, 2009.

THE SOVIET SPACE SHUTTLE

Date: Beginning November 15, 1988
Type of program: Manned Earth-orbiting spaceflights
Country: The Soviet Union

The November 15, 1988, unmanned automated test flight of the Soviet space shuttle orbiter Buran *and its Energiya booster was the most complex space mission attempted by the Soviet Union since the launch of Sputnik 1 more than thirty years earlier. The mission represented a major step toward a new flexibility in manned Soviet spaceflight operations.*

Principal personages

ALEXANDER DUNAYEV, Chief, Glavkosmos

V. FILIN, Deputy Chief Designer for the Energiya booster

G. GUBANOV, Chief Designer for the Energiya booster

VLADIMIR GUDILIN, the head of the Baikonur cosmodrome test center

OLEG MAKAROV, an engineer at the Soviet manned spaceflight control center

ALEXANDER MAXIMOV, the chief specialist in the Soviet ministry of defense for multiple-use space transportation systems

ROALD SAGDEYEV, the former head of the Space Research Institute, Soviet Academy of Sciences, and an outspoken critic of shuttle systems

Summary of the Program

The Soviet space shuttle, whose development had been a ten-year, ten-billion-dollar project, was unveiled on September 30, 1988. The first photographs released showed the shuttle orbiter *Buran* (snowstorm, in Russian), attached to its Energiya booster rocket and mounted on one of the three operational launchpads at the Baikonur cosmodrome. The Energiya-*Buran* combination is referred to in the West by the Air Force designation SL-X-18.

Buran, a near-copy of the American space shuttle orbiter, is a delta-winged spacecraft which is launched into orbit by an external booster and which lands like an airplane. There are only a few apparent differences between the Soviet and U.S. orbiters. *Buran* has no main engines, and its orbital maneuvering system engines are mounted inside the tail instead of in pods at the base of the vertical stabilizer. The Soviet spacecraft's wings and nose are more sharply angled, giving it a more pointed look than its American counterpart. The lack of main engines gives it a different center of gravity, as well. Because there is no engine weight in the back, the Soviet orbiter's wings are mounted one meter farther forward than those on American shuttles, and to preserve aerodynamic design, the Soviet shuttle is one meter shorter than the U.S. vehicle. Some of the similarities between the two orbiters were also dictated by hypersonic aerodynamics. *Buran* is 35.84 meters long and has a 24-meter wingspan; it is shorter and wider than the American orbiter, but both spacecraft have a 250-square-meter wing area. To enable *Buran* to withstand temperatures expected to reach 1,540 degrees Celsius during reentry, the arrangement of the orbiter's heat protection system and thirty-eight thousand silica tiles is identical to that on early designs for U.S. orbiters. The nose cap and leading wing edges are covered with carbon cloth coated with silicon carbide, the bottom and the windshields are covered with black tiles, and the rest of the vehicle is covered with white tiles. *Buran*'s 4.56-by-18.27-meter payload bay, the bay doors, and the door latching mechanisms are also identical to those on the U.S. orbiters.

Details of another Soviet orbiter mounted on a railcar dolly showed two 1-meter-diameter orbital maneuvering engine nozzles and a dome-shaped fuel tank protruding from the tail section, where the main engines would be on an American shuttle.

On the launchpad, the 60-meter-tall, 2,440,900-kilogram booster-orbiter combination is flanked by two tall service structures, which are surrounded by two taller lightning protection towers and four floodlight towers holding seven hundred spotlights for night operations.

For its first launch with a test payload, *Buran* weighed 101,818 kilograms. On future flights, carrying its maximum payload weight of 30,455 kilograms, the shuttle could weigh as much as 106,819 kilograms. This total weight capacity is 2,271 kilograms less than that of the U.S. orbiters; *Buran*'s payload capacity, however, is 4,545 kilograms more than that of its American counterpart, indicating that the Soviet orbiter is lighter, at 76,364 kilograms. *Buran* can also retrieve objects weighing up to 20,450 kilograms for return to Earth. Its maximum nonemergency landing weight can be as high as 83,490 kilograms.

Buran's passenger cabin is slightly larger than the U.S. orbiter's. The flight deck measures 4 by 4 meters, and the lower middeck measures 4.2 by 6 meters. Together, they supply a volume of almost 70 cubic meters. This increased volume is made possible by *Buran*'s front landing gear being placed behind the passenger cabin instead of under it, as it is on the U.S. shuttles.

Soviet space officials have said that the orbiter normally will stay in space for one week but can be equipped to spend up to four weeks in orbit. On normal missions, the shuttle will be manned by a crew of two to four persons, but it can carry up to ten cosmonauts.

Buran's Energiya booster consists of a 16.2-meter-wide core vehicle powered by four hydrogen/oxygen-burning engines which appear similar in construction to the American orbiter's space shuttle main engine. Four strap-on booster stages, each with a four-chamber engine fueled by kerosene and oxygen, provide additional thrust for lift-off.

With the orbiter attached, the four strap-on booster stages were grouped closer together than they were on the first Energiya test flight in May, 1987. This grouping allowed clearance for the orbiter's wings.

Much computer oversight is built in to the Energiya/orbiter combination. The vehicle can sustain an in-flight shutdown of one of its four strap-on boosters or one of its four core engines and still survive an aborted launch. There are three large circular structures between the Energiya and the nose of the orbiter which are believed to be separation rockets designed to push the booster away from *Buran* in case of a launch abort.

Soviet sources have announced that a second shuttle orbiter, *Ptichka* (birdie, in Russian), is complete and three more are under construction. Televised views of an orbiter under construction with its payload bay floor removed showed that the Soviet orbiter's structure is similar to the U.S. orbiter's.

The shuttle checkout building at the Baikonur cosmodrome has a design similar to the vehicle assembly building at the Kennedy Space Center in Florida, but its function is more like that of the American orbiter processing facility. The Energiya booster and the shuttle are assembled horizontally on a rail-mounted hydraulic erector and transporter. During the week of October 10, 1988, the erector carried the spacecraft to a concrete Energiya launchpad for final checkout.

The Soviet shuttle's computers take control of launch processing from ground computers eleven minutes before flight and control the sequence of countdown events up to the ignition of the Energiya's engines. The orbiter computers monitor three hundred major launch parameters every two-tenths of a second; ground-based computers monitor forty thousand parameters.

Buran's first flight was scheduled for approximately 6:23 A.M. Moscow time, October 29, 1988. This launch time coincided with a passage over the Baikonur cosmodrome by the manned space station Mir, so that its crew could observe the shuttle launch from space.

Preparations for the first launch attempt progressed well until, fifty-one seconds before Energiya booster ignition, launch processing computers detected that the crew access swing arm was not pulling away from the orbiter and terminated the countdown. Subsequent analysis revealed that the swing arm retraction had been progressing as planned, but a software error had resulted in the computers' allowing the swing arm only three seconds to retract, instead of the required thirty-eight seconds, before aborting the launch attempt. If in fact the swing arm did not pull away from the orbiter before launch, the vehicle would be destroyed.

A second launch attempt, on November 15, 1988, was successful. After the 6 A.M. lift-off, *Buran* flew a two-orbit, unmanned, fully automatic test flight which lasted three hours and twenty-five minutes. The on-time launch and apparently perfect performance of the booster-shuttle combination had followed an emergency pre-flight meeting of senior launch controllers regarding deteriorating weather conditions at the Baikonur cosmodrome launch site. Weather forecasters had warned that a cyclone was approaching the area from the Aral Sea, winds had been gusting, and the temperature had been near freezing, raising concerns that sheets of ice would form on the spacecraft. Flight managers determined that the weather was suitable, however, and the spacecraft was launched through low clouds at the opening of the "launch window" (the period in which a spacecraft can be placed in the desired orbit.)

The Soviet shuttle's test flight was as much a test of the Energiya booster as it was a test of the orbiter. The flight marked only the second launch of the heavy-lift vehicle. After ignition, the Energiya's engines required eight seconds to come to full power before lifting off with 35,190,800 newtons of thrust. Each of the four strap-on booster stages provided approximately 7 million newtons of thrust while the core stage's four engines provided a total of 5.79 million newtons of thrust. Engine performance improved with altitude until, at 60 kilometers, the vehicle had achieved a total thrust of 39.64 million newtons. At that point, the four strap-on boosters separated. (The Energiya strap-ons are designed for parachute recovery and component reuse, but recovery was not planned for this mission.)

After booster stage separation, the Energiya core stage continued to provide approximately 8 million newtons of thrust until eight minutes into the flight, where, at a velocity of more than 7,600 meters per second and an altitude of 100 kilometers, *Buran* and the core stage separated. The booster reentered the atmosphere over the South Pacific forty minutes after launch.

At that point, the shuttle was still not moving fast enough to achieve orbit. *Buran*'s orbital maneuvering system (OMS) engines were fired to increase the spacecraft's velocity by nearly 100 meters per second as it climbed past 150 kilometers altitude, thereby placing it in a 150-by-250-kilometer orbit. Forty-five minutes later, the OMS engines were fired again to achieve a circular orbit with an altitude of 250 kilometers and an inclination of 51.6 degrees.

Tracking of the shuttle was provided both by ground stations in the Soviet Union and by four Soviet spaceflight tracking ships at sea. Two ships, *Cosmonaut Vladimir Volkov* and *Cosmonaut Pavel Belyayev*, were off the west coast of Africa; two others, *Cosmonaut Georgy Dobrovolsky* and *Marshal Nedelin*, were off the west coast of South America. One Luch, one Gorizont, and two Molniya communications satellites provided continuous relay of telemetry signals from the shuttle to a new shuttle control center at Baikonur.

During its second orbit, while traveling north off the coast of Chile two hours and twenty minutes into the flight, the orbiter was maneuvered so its tail pointed toward Earth, and a three-minute OMS engine burn initiated the reentry sequence. *Buran* was then commanded to turn and assume a nose-high attitude at a 40-degree angle. This position would enable the shuttle to survive the reentry heating which would occur when it encountered the upper atmosphere at 122 kilometers above Earth, thirty minutes after the retro-rockets had fired.

The two Soviet tracking ships stationed off Senegal and Algeria were instrumental in providing data to help the orbiter's computers manage the hypersonic descent into the atmosphere.

Because *Buran*'s second orbital track had passed well west of the recovery site at

Baikonur, the shuttle had to execute a lengthy cross-range maneuver to the east, beginning at a velocity twenty-four times that of sound, to return to the launch site. Soviet officials have stated that their shuttle is capable of traveling up to 2,000 kilometers cross-range if necessary. The U.S. orbiters have a normal cross-range capability of 880 to 1,120 kilometers.

After the initial cross-range banking maneuver, *Buran* performed several additional left and right banking maneuvers at high speeds to adjust the vehicle's energy and allow it to reach the runway at Baikonur. Banking maneuvers continued as *Buran* reentered the atmosphere, flying over Morocco, Italy, and central eastern Europe. At Baikonur, the shuttle entered a 20-degree, laser-guided glide slope and executed a fully automatic landing within centimeters of the middle of the 84-meter-wide, 4.5-kilometer-long runway located only 12 kilometers from the shuttle launchpad.

Touchdown speed was 328 kilometers per hour. To help slow the landing, *Buran* held a nose-high attitude for eleven seconds before letting the nose wheel down gently. Three seconds later, three X-shaped drag chutes with an area of 75 square meters were deployed to slow the orbiter's ground speed further. The chutes were jettisoned once the vehicle had slowed to 50 kilometers per hour. Normal rollout distance for the orbiter is 3,000 meters.

Buran showed no major adverse effects from its first test flight, although reentry heating caused severe scuffing on the tiles around the windshield area, and the wings' leading edges also showed heating effects.

The first manned test flight of the Soviet shuttle was planned for 1989.

Knowledge Gained

The success of the *Buran* test has allowed the Soviets to plan manned shuttle missions that will deploy large space station modules and satellites and return heavy payloads from orbit. Extravehicular activities in the shuttle payload bay will enable Soviet cosmonauts to assemble and repair large satellites in space. Future docking with the Mir space station is also planned.

The shuttle fleet will complement the existing Soviet expendable launchers, which will continue to launch the manned Soyuz and unmanned Progress resupply spacecraft. Soviet officials have indicated that the shuttle will be used only on special occasions, because it is many times more expensive to use than expendable boosters.

The use of the Energiya booster to launch the Soviet shuttle continues the Soviet policy of using liquid-fueled propulsion systems for space launchers. This practice eliminates the dangers associated with cold-weather launches that contributed to the 1986 *Challenger* disaster in the U.S. shuttle program. The loss of *Challenger* was one of the determining factors in the Soviet decision to launch *Buran* unmanned on its first flight, a decision hotly contested by the Soviet cosmonaut corps.

The flight of *Buran* and its Energiya booster brought Soviet rocket engineers closer to using hydrogen-fueled boosters routinely. U.S. space boosters have used hydrogen fuel for twenty-five years, but the Soviet Union did not launch hydrogen-powered rockets until 1987. To increase the operational flexibility of shuttle missions, two more landing strips are being built in the eastern and western areas of the Soviet Union for shuttle recovery.

Context

The first test flight of the Soviet space shuttle represented a departure from the traditional Soviet system of relying on the evolution of tested, effective rocket systems rather than on technological revolutions. The advance public announcement and the launch of *Buran* on only the second test of the Energiya booster demonstrated a high degree of Soviet confidence in the new systems. Before the *Buran* test flight, seventeen- to twenty-five-year old Soyuz and Vostok capsule designs had been the only ones used in the Soviet manned space program.

The existence of the Soviet space shuttle was a state secret until it was officially revealed in July, 1987. Nevertheless, U.S. reconnaissance satellites had repeatedly photographed Soviet shuttle preparations over a period of several years. The first direct evidence that the Soviet shuttle existed was collected in 1983, when a full-scale orbiter was transported to the Ramenskoye Flight Test Center near Moscow atop a modified Tu-16 Bison bomber. The aircraft was forced to make an emergency downwind landing and ran off the runway, becoming stuck when the landing gear sank into the ground. Before the Soviet government could hide the accident, it was photographed by an American spy satellite.

A Central Intelligence Agency report states that the Soviet space shuttle program saved years by copying the U.S. orbiter and especially benefited from the inadvertent transfer, via unclassified data, of the technology for developing the silica reentry heat-protection tiles used on American orbiters.

Other multiple advanced technologies used aboard *Buran* were also borrowed from Western orbiter developments. They include four interconnected, fault-tolerant computers, which are able to correct errors as they occur; advanced software to operate remote controls; and the technology necessary for winged hypersonic flight, achieved for the first time by the Soviets on *Buran*'s test flight.

Although the Soviet space shuttle is a huge technical leap for Soviet space scientists, it is not viewed by Western officials as a challenge requiring an immediate response like the one that followed the launch of Sputnik 1. The launch of the Soviet space shuttle came seven years after the American shuttle's first flight.

The perfection of the Soviet shuttle represents an enormous investment of money and manpower. The Soviet space shuttle effort is comparable to the U.S. Apollo Moon-landing program of the mid-1960's, as far as commitment of personnel and equipment is concerned. Soviet officials recognize that shuttle operations are expensive, and, drawing again from American experience, believe most space operations still can be done more cheaply with expendable boosters. They say that once the Soviet shuttle system is operational, it is expected to fly only two to four times a year, on special missions that require its unique capabilities.

Bibliography

Clark, Phillip. *The Soviet Manned Space Program*. New York: Orion Books, 1988. Covers the entire Soviet manned space program in well-researched detail. The material is presented in an encyclopedic and easy-to-read style. The chronological survey covers Soviet attempts to put a man on the Moon, the development of the Soyuz spacecraft, and the Salyut and Mir space stations. Future developments, including the space shuttle and a manned Mars mission, are also considered. Illustrated with photographs and drawings.

Covault, Craig. "Soviet Shuttle Launched on Energia Booster." *Aviation Week and Space Technology* 129 (November 21, 1988): 18-21. A report on the launch of *Buran*. This issue of the aerospace industry's trade magazine contains an editorial on the Soviet shuttle, as well.

Dunayev, Alexander. "Energia: New Generation of Booster." *Soviet Life* 379 (April, 1988): 22-23. An article describing *Buran*'s launch vehicle.

Joels, Kerry M., and David Larkin. *The Space Shuttle Operator's Manual*. New York: Ballantine Books, 1982. A detailed reference work on the U.S. space shuttle system, this manual provides specifics on the shuttle, from weights and sizes to operational characteristics. It describes countdown procedures, emergency procedures, and standard operational modes. Thoroughly illustrated. An entertaining and educational source.

McDougall, Walter A. . . . *The Heavens and the Earth: A Political History of the Space Age*. New York: Basic Books, 1985. This well-researched text describes and analyzes the decisions of U.S. and Soviet leaders and their effects on the respective space programs. Includes much discussion of key political and technological leaders and relates how the American and Soviet space programs became an integral part of Cold War politics. For a general audience.

Reichhardt, Tony. *Proving the Space Transportation System: The Orbital Flight Test Program*. NASA NF-137-83. Washington, D.C.: Government Printing Office, 1983. A twenty-page educational report summarizing the U.S. shuttle system, the objectives of the four-mission test program, and the tests' results. Includes black-and-white photographs of shuttle components and diagrams of launch, orbit, and landing procedures. For general audiences.

U.S. Congress. Senate. Committee on Commerce, Science, and Transportation. *Soviet Space Programs: 1981-1987*. Part 1, *Piloted Space Activities, Launch Vehicles, Launch Sites, and Tracking Support*. Report prepared by Congressional Research Service, the Library of Congress. 100th Cong., 1988. Committee Print. A very thorough, rather technical document detailing all aspects of manned Soviet space activities. A concise history of the Soviet piloted space effort is provided. Launch vehicles, ground support, and scientific experiments are discussed. The summary and the historical section are suitable for all readers; most of the material is suitable for advanced college-level readers.

Wilson, Andrew. *Space Shuttle Story*. New York: Crescent Books, 1986. Touches on the early days of rocketry, experimental aircraft that led to the U.S. shuttle, and the development of the space shuttle concept. Highlights U.S. shuttle missions 1 through 26. Contains many color photographs, an index, and a flight summary. Suitable for the nonspecialist.

Robert Reeves

Cross-References

The Apollo Program, 28; U.S. and Soviet Cooperation in Space, 259; Cosmonauts and the Soviet Cosmonaut Program, 273; Soviet Launch Vehicles, 742; The Mir Space Station, 1025; The Soyuz-Kosmos Program, 1396; Space Centers and Launch Sites in the Soviet Union, 1592; The U.S. Space Shuttle, 1626; Space Shuttle Mission 25: *Challenger*, 1813; The Soviet Spaceflight Tracking Network, 1877; The Sputnik Program, 1930; Spy Satellites, 1937; Soviet Telecommunications Satellites, 2003; The Voskhod Program, 2170; The Vostok Program, 2177.

THE U.S. SPACE SHUTTLE

Date: Beginning January 5, 1972
Type of program: Manned spaceflight
Country: The United States

The Space Transportation System, popularly known as the space shuttle, was established to develop an economic and reusable system that could transport humans, satellites, and equipment to and from Earth orbit on a regular basis. It would also provide support for a wide range of other activities.

Principal personages
JAMES BEGGS and
JAMES C. FLETCHER, NASA Administrators
ROBERT A. SCHMITZ, Program Manager, NASA Headquarters
JOHN S. THEON, Program Scientist, NASA Headquarters
DONALD K. (DEKE) SLAYTON, Manager, Orbital Flight Test
    Program
MAXIME A. FAGET, Director of Engineering and Development,
    Johnson Space Center
ROBERT F. THOMPSON, Program Manager of the Space Shuttle
    Office, Johnson Space Center
JAMES W. BILODEAU, the chief of crew procedures for shuttle
    missions

Summary of the Program

The concept of a reusable launch vehicle and spacecraft that could return to Earth was developed early in the U.S. rocket research program. The National Advisory Committee for Aeronautics (NACA), the predecessor of the National Aeronautics and Space Administration (NASA), and NASA itself cooperated with the U.S. Air Force on early studies in the X-15 rocket research program and the Dyna-Soar hypersonic vehicle program in the late 1950's and 1960's.

In 1963, NASA and the Air Force began to work on a design for a manned vehicle that would be launched into orbit and then return to Earth. The craft was called an aerospaceplane and could take off and land horizontally in the manner of a conventional aircraft. In addition, joint tests of wingless lifting bodies, such as the M2 series, HL-10, and eventually the X-24, laid the foundations for a future craft that could safely reenter the atmosphere.

At about the same time, NASA scientists began to talk about a craft that would serve as a cargo transport to other vehicles or space stations in Earth orbit or on the Moon. Experts at NASA's Marshall Space Flight Center engaged in research on the recovery and reuse of the Saturn 5 launch vehicle. The Department of Defense and private industry also became involved in the development of a reusable transport spacecraft during the late 1960's.

In its 1967 budget briefing, NASA referred to an advanced studies program for a "ferry and logistics vehicle." The president's Science Advisory Committee agreed that developing a reusable, economic space transportation system was necessary.

Between 1969 and 1971, NASA awarded contracts to major aerospace industries to study and define such a system. After considering these findings, NASA decided in 1972 to develop the Space Transportation System (STS). Eventually, this program would be known simply as the space shuttle. On January 5, 1972, President Richard M. Nixon officially announced the inauguration of the space shuttle program. NASA's ambitious schedule called for suborbital tests by 1977 and the first orbital tests by 1979. The shuttle was scheduled to begin regular launchings by 1980.

NASA's goal was to establish a national space transportation system that was capable of substantially reducing the cost of space operations by providing support for a wide range of scientific, military, and commercial applications. Space officials hoped that the space shuttle would operate at a fraction of the cost of the expendable rockets that were in use at the time.

Designed to be a true aerospace vehicle, the space shuttle would be able to take off like a rocket, maneuver in space and attain an Earth orbit, and return to Earth and land like an airplane under a pilot's control. The four-part vehicle would include the reusable orbiter (it would be able to make one hundred launches) mounted atop the expendable external tank (ET) and two solid-fueled rocket boosters. The boosters, too, would be recoverable and reusable.

The reusable space shuttle would make spaceflight and cargo transport routine and cost-effective, thereby encouraging and enhancing the commercial use of space. The system could be used as a base from which to deploy payloads, repair and service satellites, and launch or retrieve satellites. It could also serve as a platform for scientific research and the manufacture of certain materials requiring a zero-gravity environment.

Additional advantages would be the shuttle's ability to carry large payloads, such as the Hubble Space Telescope, into orbit and to provide a vantage point from which to observe astronomical events, weather disturbances, and environmental changes on Earth. Very important, the shuttle could carry the component parts of a space station into orbit and then act as the transportation system between the station and Earth.

About the same length and weight as a commercial DC-9, the wedged-shaped orbiter could carry a crew of three to seven persons. The crew would consist of a commander, pilot, and one or more mission specialists, all astronauts. There would also be room for one to four payload specialists, nonastronauts responsible for conducting specific experiments and nominated for flight by the payload sponsor. Certified by NASA for flight, they could be chosen from the civilian population. The fact that "ordinary" people could travel on the shuttle added to the program's appeal.

A typical mission would last seven to thirty days. The crew would live and work in a shirtsleeve environment, without cumbersome spacesuits or breathing apparatuses. Maneuvering in the weightlessness of the microgravity environment would prove the biggest challenge to crew members.

In January, 1977, unmanned and manned tests of the shuttle's approach and landing capabilities began at Dryden Flight Research Center, Edwards Air Force Base, California. An orbiter prototype, *Enterprise*, was the first shuttle-type vehicle tested, and it flew successfully.

On April 12, 1981, two years behind schedule, the first of four manned orbital test flights was launched from Kennedy Space Center (KSC) at Cape Canaveral, Florida. The flight was designated Space Transportation System 1 (STS 1), and the orbiter was named "Columbia." The two-day mission demonstrated the spacecraft's ability to reach orbit and return safely. The mission provided data on temperatures and pressures at various points on the orbiter. There were also tests of the cargo bay doors, attitude control systems, and orbital maneuvering system. STS 1 landed safely at Dryden Flight Research Center.

STS 2 was launched in November of 1981. The orbiter *Columbia* was used again. For the first time, the remote manipulator system (RMS) was tested. STS 2 also marked the first time that a spacecraft had ever flown twice.

STS 3, launched in March, 1982, was the longest of the initial test flights. The spacecraft stayed in space eight days, and activities included a special test of the RMS and experiments in materials processing. This mission was the first to use the secondary landing site at White Sands Missile Range in New Mexico. (Rain at Edwards Air Force Base had prevented a normal landing at that site.)

The final test flight of this series, conducted in the summer of 1982, featured another test of the RMS, further materials processing experiments, and the launch of the first Department of Defense payload. Once these tests were completed, the space shuttle was declared operational.

From 1981 to 1983, NASA launched a total of nine STS missions. All were launched from KSC. The space shuttles *Columbia* and *Challenger* were used for the missions, and they carried a variety of payloads and experiments. Highlights included the launching of commercial and government communications satellites (the first Tracking and Data-Relay Satellite, or TDRS, was launched), the first retrieval of an object from orbit, the first shuttle-based extravehicular activity, and the launching of the first Spacelab—a portable science laboratory carried in a shuttle's cargo bay.

Beginning with the first shuttle launch of 1984, NASA began to use a new numbering system to identify the missions. The first number would refer to the year, the second number would refer to the launch site (1 for KSC, 2 for Vandenberg Air Force Base), and a letter would refer to the order of assignment in that year. The first 1984 mission, known as STS 41B, used the orbiter *Challenger* and marked the first landing on a concrete runway specifically designed for shuttle landings at KSC. The shuttle's tenth flight featured the introduction of the manned maneuvering unit (MMU), a backpack propulsion unit that allowed astronauts to maneuver in space independent of the orbiter. The next mission, 41C, was important because it demonstrated the ability of the orbiter and crew to retrieve, repair, and redeploy a malfunctioning satellite.

Throughout 1984 and 1985, the shuttle program continued. With each mission, payloads became more sophisticated, and the orbiters continued to meet NASA's expectations. Spacelab was flown two more times, and several missions were devoted to Department of Defense programs. Two new orbiters, *Discovery* and *Atlantis*, were added to the shuttle fleet.

Shuttle flights were considered so safe and routine that civilian scientists and even a U.S. senator traveled on the spacecraft. In 1984, at the suggestion of President Ronald Reagan, a national search for a candidate to be the first schoolteacher in space was started. Christa McAuliffe, a New Hampshire high-school teacher was chosen; she was scheduled to fly on STS 51L. The prospect of a civilian schoolteacher riding aboard a shuttle captured the imagination of the nation. The attention of the world, especially the world's children, was focused on the launchpad at KSC the cold morning of January 28, 1986. Seventy-four seconds after the launch, the space shuttle *Challenger* exploded, destroying the spacecraft and killing all seven crew members, including McAuliffe. The accident had been viewed by millions on television. Once the initial shock and grief passed, another kind of anguish replaced it.

President Reagan immediately appointed an independent board of inquiry headed by former Secretary of State William Rogers. Shuttle astronaut Sally Ride and former astronaut Neil Armstrong also served on the commission. NASA conducted its own inquiry, and the U.S. Congress oversaw NASA's investigation. As the committees began to probe, it became obvious that NASA was in a difficult position. It was revealed that warnings about faulty equipment had been ignored because of scheduling pressures and that there was a general lack of communication among NASA, its contractors, and the government. NASA's director, James Beggs, resigned and was replaced by a former NASA director, James C. Fletcher. The old controversy over a manned program versus an unmanned program reemerged, and the United States' thirty-year-old love affair with space exploration seemed to end. The space shuttle was put on hold, and it appeared that it might never recover from the devastating blow. In addition to the serious social and moral ramifications, the scientific and economic costs were high. A $100 million orbiter, one-fourth of the space shuttle fleet, had been destroyed, and the deployment of several expensive and important scientific projects would have to be delayed indefinitely.

In June of 1986, the official findings of the Rogers Commission were released. Failure of the O-rings, critical connecting seals in the solid-fueled rocket boosters (SRBs), was identified as the primary cause of the catastrophe. The report also revealed that there had been warnings that the rings might fail in the abnormal cold of January 28, 1986, warnings that had been ignored so that the shuttle could fly on schedule. In the wake of the report, harsh criticism fell on NASA management.

NASA began to reorganize the space shuttle program from its very foundations. Every aspect of the system was scrutinized, from the SRBs to the orbiter. More than forty major changes were made to the SRBs, at a cost of $450 million. Thirty-nine changes were made to the liquid-fueled main engines, and sixty-eight modifications were made to the shuttle itself. Perhaps the most significant changes, however, concerned the way NASA conducted business, especially with respect to safety. In July, 1986, a new safety program was instituted. NASA officials believed that their new system would safeguard against any poor or uninformed decision that could endanger the lives of shuttle crew members.

On September 29, 1988, approximately two and one-half years after the *Challenger* explosion, the space shuttle *Discovery* (STS 26) was successfully launched from KSC. On October 3, after sixty-four orbits and 2.7 million kilometers of successful spaceflight, it safely touched down on the runway at Edwards Air Force Base. The improved solid-fueled rocket boosters and modified main engines performed perfectly. NASA's goal had been reached: The space shuttle program had been reborn.

Knowledge Gained

The space shuttle is unique in its design and function. Thus, the development of the spacecraft has contributed much to the fields of aerodynamics and rocket research. Early test flights confirmed the capabilities and versatility of the vehicle that acts as rocket, spacecraft, and airplane in the course of a single mission. In addition, equipment and systems developed for the shuttle—such as the remote manipulator system, which allows for the deployment and retrieval of payloads—have raised the level of space technology and built a foundation for further advances. In fact, thousands of new products and techniques in such diverse fields as medicine and archaeology have been developed indirectly from advanced shuttle technology. The knowledge gained from the missions themselves has also covered a broad spectrum of disciplines.

The shuttle's early flights demonstrated and tested the capabilities of the craft and its systems. In addition, STS 2 carried a payload for NASA's Office of Space and Terrestrial Applications; experiments concerning land resources, environmental quality, ocean conditions, and meteorological phenomena were performed. A precedent was set for scientific study.

STS 3 carried the first Get-Away Special payloads, small, self-contained, low-cost experiments that are packaged in canisters. These payloads are available to educational organizations, industries, and governments. STS 3 also carried the first student project, an experiment designed to collect data on the effects of flight motion on insects. The first materials processing experiment was also conducted on STS 3, with the monodisperse latex reactor. The experiment produced microsized latex particles of uniform diameter for commercial use in laboratories. It marked the beginning of the shuttle program's commercial materials production capabilities.

As shuttle flights became more routine, the number and sophistication of experiments conducted in or from the orbiter increased. In 1983, STS 9 carried the first Spacelab. Spacelab 1 was an orbital laboratory and observation platform designed to remain inside the shuttle's cargo bay. When the bay doors were open, it was directly exposed to space. Spacelab 1 was funded by the European Space Agency as a major contribution to the STS program. It had the capability of performing numerous experiments in the areas of plasma physics, astronomy, solar physics, material sciences, life sciences, and Earth resources. The vast amounts of data collected in this and the subsequent Spacelab missions would take decades to analyze. The essential assumptions of the Spacelab program were proved: that non-NASA astronauts could perform as trained payload specialists working closely with a scientific command center on Earth, that the Tracking and Data-Relay Satellite System could return the information to ground stations, and that Spacelab could support complex experiments in space.

Shuttle missions also included many experiments on the effects of spaceflight, and especially of zero gravity, on human beings. It was discovered that zero gravity affects every component of the motor control system. The heart and other large muscles decrease in size because of the absence of gravity's pull. Astronauts also experienced a decrease in bone tissue and red blood cells. Certain parts of the endocrine system may be affected too. Finally, space sickness, a type of motion sickness, is not uncommon in microgravity.

These medical experiments and tests provided important data on zero gravity's effects and the ways in which those effects could be controlled. Medical experiments also raised questions about how humans would respond to long-term missions in space—missions undertaken on a space station, for example.

Over the course of the space shuttle program, hundreds of experiments and observations in almost every scientific discipline—from computers to agronomy—have been conducted. As the program moves forward and technology improves, the data base will continue to grow. The impact this scientific study will have on mankind will be overwhelming. Already, the amount of information collected is so great that it will take many years and thousands of man-hours to evaluate it all.

Context

Human technology has often been spurred by the human imagination. Nowhere has this been illustrated better than in the space shuttle program. The ability to launch manned vehicles into space, maneuver them around the universe, and return them home safely was once the exclusive province of science-fiction characters such as Buck Rogers. The space shuttle changed all of that.

Based on years of research in the fields of rocketry and aerodynamics, the flights of *Enterprise* and the later orbiters placed mankind on the threshold of a new era. The ability to conduct routine space missions had arrived. The space shuttle was the first vehicle to travel to space and return to be used again. The ramifications of that capability have been far-reaching.

Satellites have been deployed, repaired, and retrieved by shuttle astronauts. Thousands of scientific and medical experiments and hundreds of hours of solar, Earth, atmospheric, and cosmic observations have been conducted aboard the shuttle. Critical communications satellites and Department of Defense payloads have been launched from the shuttle, and the potential for the manufacture of commercial alloys, crystals, and other materials is enormous.

NASA's ambitious plans for an international space station in low Earth orbit by the end of the twentieth century depend on the shuttle's viability. After the success of STS 26, the first shuttle launched after the *Challenger* explosion, many of the more vocal critics of the shuttle program became silent. It appeared that NASA officials had learned their lesson, and the program took on a new vitality.

It is apparent that the shuttle itself will eventually become simply another step in mankind's space efforts. Already, NASA has accelerated studies on a new manned spacecraft that will replace the shuttle early in the twenty-first century. Two design concepts have been reviewed. One calls for extensive modifications to the current shuttle. The other is a design for a vehicle significantly different from the existing orbiter. Each study will be funded at $1 to $2 million. NASA has begun to define what a new U.S. manned spaceflight capability should involve so that a development program can begin.

Bibliography

Gore, Rick. "When the Space Shuttle Finally Flies." *National Geographic* 159 (March, 1981): 316-347. The article provides an in-depth look at the space shuttle program before it became operational. Written for a general audience, it includes diagrams, drawings, and color photographs.

Joels, Kerry M., and Gregory P. Kennedy. *The Space Shuttle Operator's Manual.* Rev. ed. New York: Ballantine Books, 1987. A complete guide to the space shuttle. Written from the pilot's point of view, it contains information on space shuttle systems and flight procedures. It includes checklists, diagrams, charts, and photographs. For general audiences.

National Aeronautics and Space Administration. *NASA: The First Twenty-five Years, 1958-1983.* NASA EP-182. Washington, D.C.: Government Printing Office, 1983. A chronological history of NASA and its programs. The text is designed for teachers to use in the classroom. It contains many illustrations.

Ride, Sally, and Susan Okie. *To Space and Back.* New York: Lothrop, Lee, and Shepard Books, 1986. This book offers an astronaut's insight into the living and working conditions aboard the shuttle. Contains color photographs.

Turnill, Reginald, ed. *Jane's Spaceflight Directory.* London: Jane's Publishing Co., 1987. Updated annually, this resource is invaluable for a quick overview of progress made in space exploration. Capsule summaries of manned and unmanned missions are provided, and the text is heavily illustrated with diagrams and black-and-white photographs. A helpful index is also included.

Lulynne Streeter

Cross-References

Astronauts and the U.S. Astronaut Program, 154; Biological Effects of Space

SPACE SHUTTLE LIVING CONDITIONS

Date: Beginning April 12, 1981
Type of program: Manned spaceflight
Country: The United States

Safe and comfortable living conditions in a microgravity environment must be provided for space shuttle astronauts in order to ensure the success of assigned scientific and military tasks.

Principal personages
MAXIME A. FAGET, Director of Engineering Development,
    Johnson Space Center
CHARLES A. BERRY, Director of Medical Research and
    Operations, JSC
ROBERT E. SMILEY, head of the Crew Systems Division, JSC
ROBERT F. THOMPSON, Program Manager of the Space Shuttle
    Office, JSC
JAMES W. BILODEAU, the chief of crew procedures for space
    shuttle missions
ALAN B. SHEPARD, head of the astronaut office, Manned
    Spacecraft Center

Summary of the Program

Daily life aboard the U.S. space shuttle is much more luxurious than that on the earliest manned space missions, although interior decorating is not a high priority. "The decor could be called modern metal file cabinet," according to Rick Gore of *National Geographic* magazine (March, 1981). The nose section of the shuttle orbiter contains the bilevel, pressurized crew cabin. Approximately seventy-two cubic meters of space are available for astronaut activities. Commander and pilot observe and operate shuttle functions from the upper-level flight deck, and a work area for other crew members is located behind the command center. The lower level of the cabin, known as middeck, serves as living quarters for the entire crew; experiments requiring oxygen are also housed here during some missions.

Fans force the cabin air through an array of filters. Particulates, including dust, bacteria, dead skin cells, and hair, are filtered directly; lithium hydroxide canisters remove carbon dioxide, a waste product of respiration; and activated charcoal filters remove odors. Humidity is kept low to discourage bacterial growth. The astronauts' breathing mixture is 80 percent nitrogen and 20 percent oxygen. (Earth air is 78 percent nitrogen, 21 percent oxygen, and 1 percent other gases.) Internal cabin pressure is maintained at 14.7 pounds per square inch, the pressure of Earth's atmosphere at sea level. Water—a by-product of the fuel cells that generate electricity—is provided to the crew cabin at a rate of 3 kilograms per hour. Cabin temperature is maintained by water-pipe heat exchangers which transfer heat to Freon-fueled cargo bay radiators.

Early spacefarers survived on unpalatable pastes squeezed out of devices resembling toothpaste tubes. Shuttle astronauts enjoy a wide variety of foods and even select their own menus. Each day's intake must provide 2,800 to 3,000 kilocalories and the recommended daily allowances of minerals and vitamins. Special attention is given to potassium, calcium, and nitrogen; in weightlessness, the human body loses these minerals first. Everything from scrambled Mexican eggs to candy-coated chocolates can be found among the thirty-seven beverages and ninety-two foods available.

The shuttle's galley, or kitchen, contains food lockers, which hold each day's meals in the order in which they will be consumed, a convection oven to heat precooked foods to 82 degrees Celsius, and a hot and cold water dispenser, which injects fluid into rehydratable food packages with a needle to prevent spillage. Velcro strips on lockers and walls allow food items to be fixed in place while meals are prepared. Fresh foods, including fruit, vegetables, and baked goods, are loaded shortly before launch. The galley also has a washing station for cleaning hands and utensils.

For certain special missions in which space is at a premium, the entire galley is removed and the astronauts make do with a cold water dispenser that can rehydrate a reduced menu of foods. A small, portable warmer substitutes for the convection oven. Emergency food, for unexpectedly lengthened missions, and additional snacks are stored in the pantry, which contains enough extra food to provide 2,100 kilocalories per day per astronaut for two additional mission days.

There is no refrigerator on board the shuttle because of weight considerations, so foods are prepared and packed in several ways for storage at room temperature. Freeze-dried, rehydratable food and drink come in small, sealed plastic bowls or pouches. Thermostabilized foods are heat sterilized, to discourage bacterial spoilage, and packaged in metal cans or flexible pouches. Meats are sterilized by exposure to ionizing radiation and packaged in flexible foil. Intermediate-moisture foods, such as dried apricots, dried peaches, and beef jerky, are packed in transparent plastic. Items such as nuts and cookies, designated "natural form foods," are packed in plastic containers, and condiments are provided in dropper bottles. Even salt and pepper are fluidized in water or oil to make them dispensable.

Mealtime in the shuttle may find the astronauts rooted to a surface by suction cups, sitting in a seat with meal trays strapped to their laps, upside down with trays attached to the ceiling, sitting at the small shuttle table with feet in loops, or even floating freely through the cabin. Knives, forks, and spoons three-quarters of the normal size are used for shuttle meals; their smallness helps minimize food spillage and cleanup problems for the vehicle's air recycling systems.

Keeping clean and disposing of waste is no easy task in space, but it is vital for the health of the space shuttle crew. The confined space and effects of microgravity could allow disease-inducing bacteria to multiply out of control if sanitation were not carefully maintained. The microgravity environment of low Earth orbit allows water droplets and crumbs of debris to float around the shuttle cabin, posing a threat to instrumentation and crew members.

Garbage from food preparation, used clothing, and waste from experimental activities are sealed in plastic containers for storage under the middeck floor until return to Earth. All areas of the spacecraft used by the crew are cleaned in flight with disposable wipes and disinfectant solution.

The space shuttle lavatory contains a small sink, a toilet, mirrors, and a light. Washing is performed with a minimum of water. Since fluid adheres to skin in a weightless environment, little soap or water is necessary. Crew members take short sponge baths rather than taking showers, as they did in Skylab. A fan sucks water into the basin drain, substituting for the ordinary effect of gravity on Earth. Hot water is dispensed from a gun set at temperatures from 18 to 35 degrees Celsius. Male astronauts wishing to shave must use ordinary shaving cream and safety razors, wiping the razors with disposable towels to keep whiskers from escaping into the cabin environment. Towels and personal necessities are clipped to the wall for easy access. The zero-gravity toilet drains by means of a fan, which transports the waste materials to a storage area. Originally, wastes were shredded; now, they are disinfected, deodorized, and dried for storage until return to Earth. In microgravity, to remain in place on the toilet, astronauts use a seat belt and place their feet in toeholds while holding onto handles. The toilet's cycle time is approximately fifteen minutes, so it can be used about four times in an hour. Spacesick astronauts use velcro-sealable pouches, similar to airsickness bags, which are disposed of in the commode. The same bags can be used as an alternative method of fecal collection if the zero-gravity toilet malfunctions.

Shuttle astronauts wear ordinary trousers, shirts, and jackets covered with Velcro-fastened pockets. Ordinary clothes contribute to a sense of normality and comfort as the astronauts go about their many tasks. For extravehicular activities (space-walks outside the vehicle or in the exposed cargo bay), protective spacesuits are required. Each suit is really a tiny spaceship that provides a breathable atmosphere, comfortable temperatures, and adequate internal pressure. Propulsion is provided by separate manned maneuvering units.

Shuttle suits, called EMUs (extravehicular mobility units), are much more sophisticated than those used on past space missions. In addition to offering greater flexibility and comfort, they can be put on relatively quickly without assistance. The modular suits have three primary and several secondary components, all of which come in several sizes so as to fit the exact dimensions of each astronaut. The main part of the suit consists of a hard covering for the upper torso and flexible pants, a detachable helmet with a visor, gloves, and a bag containing about twenty ounces of drinking water. The gloves are the only component that is fitted to each crew member. The torso is composed of many layers, each with an important job. A Teflon-coated outside layer resists tears and protects against damage from microme-teoroids, the next several layers of aluminized Mylar plastic reflect heat away from the suit, and the interior layers are made of insulating Dacron unwoven fabric. Inside the outer suit, a separate, water-cooled, liner garment is worn; it resembles long underwear. The small tubes sewn all over it conduct water to lower the astronaut's body temperature. Under the liner, there is a urine collection device which retains liquid waste for later transferral to the shuttle's waste management system. Physiological functions are controlled by the primary life-support system, which circulates and cools the water in the liner, absorbs carbon dioxide, supplies temperature-controlled oxygen for breathing, and maintains suit pressure. Filters remove unpleasant odors from the suit. All these complicated and vital functions are controlled by a tiny computer which displays information on the suit's chest section. Automatic checking programs test various suit functions, provide instructions for astronauts donning their suits, and sound an alarm if any suit functions begin to fail.

Sleeping accommodations vary with the demands of a particular mission. For uncrowded missions, one vertical and three horizontal bunks are available. Each sleeping pallet has storage areas, a light, pillows, a fan, a communications station, microgravity restraint sheets, and a noise-suppression blanket. For crowded missions, up to four sleeping bags attached to provision lockers are used, although some astronauts have preferred to catch naps while simply tethered to a cabin wall.

Communication among crew members in various parts of the shuttle is accomplished via simple headsets that connect to eight intercom terminals in the crew compartment. Books, tape recorders and tapes, playing cards, and other games are supplied, and a regular exercise regime prevents physiological deconditioning.

Knowledge Gained

Keeping humans alive and well in space is a tremendously complicated task. Space shuttle designers must plan each subsystem and then integrate it with the entire human systems design scheme. Shuttle missions carry up to eight astronauts for periods of seven to fourteen days; shuttle designers therefore face challenges quite different from those presented by the three Skylab missions, with their smaller numbers of astronauts and longer-duration missions.

As the Space Transportation System (STS) became operational, much was learned about problems with the various living arrangements. Solutions to these problems were gradually refined as more missions were flown. Strong odors are particularly disturbing to persons working in the confined area of a spacecraft. It was found that the odor of certain fresh fruits, such as bananas, was terribly annoying, and such items had to be stored separately or eliminated from the cargo.

Spacesickness has been a problem for a number of astronauts on the shuttle, and scientists have made considerable efforts to understand and prevent the syndrome. Senator Jake Garn experienced significant spacesickness during his 1985 voyage on *Atlantis*. He graciously offered to serve as a "guinea pig" for important studies on the symptomatology and physiology of the complaint.

The zero-gravity toilet was notoriously unreliable during many of the shuttle missions. Problems with the system were particularly demoralizing to the crew, presented a potential health hazard, and contributed to cabin odors. After the first few missions, the shredder/slinger was removed, since it did not function well in microgravity. The system was changed to allow wastes to be diverted to the side of the receiving vessel.

Debris in the cabin proved to be difficult to control, even with considerable prior planning. It is very important, for example, to have low-lint clothing and towels. During some experiments with small animals, most notably those on the April, 1985, *Challenger* mission, soiled bedding and unused food pellets escaped from the containment units and caused a major annoyance to the astronauts aboard. Such experiences have led to increasingly better designs for daily use items and experimental apparatus.

The maintenance of normal sleep cycles is very important to the crew's productivity and alertness. Schedules which keep astronauts on a regular twenty-four-hour cycle were found to be far superior to radically different schedules.

In the limited environment of a spacecraft, mealtimes become significant events. The space shuttle has the most sophisticated eating arrangements of any American spacecraft. It is possible that the preparation and consumption of food substitutes for the social and personal rituals that are lacking on board the shuttle.

Context

Just as astronauts' experiences on the three Skylab missions affected the design of the space shuttle living quarters, crew members' experiences aboard the shuttle have helped engineers to design the U.S. Space Station and the spacecraft that may go to Mars and the Moon. Human performance and well-being in space is the single largest factor determining the success of piloted space missions. It is also the area in which the United States has less cumulative experience than the Soviet Union. Setbacks in the shuttle program have slowed U.S. progress in understanding human needs in space.

The Soviet Union's piloted missions have almost all been of long duration and involved only a few astronauts at a time. Psychological stress, depression, and conflict among Soviet cosmonauts seem usually to have emerged after thirty days. As of 1988, it was not clear whether any of these symptoms arise when astronauts spend cumulatively long periods in space over the course of many missions.

The demanding work of launching and repairing satellites or recovering damaged satellites for later repair on Earth requires that the crew be in top-notch physical condition. Such projects have served as models for future situations in which spacefarers will be faced with demanding tasks under stressful conditions. The U.S. Space Station will require high performance standards in the demanding work of constructing large space structures in orbit. What scientists learn about human performance from the shuttle will be valuable in planning the activities of space station workers.

The lengthy consideration of human daily life—from sleeping, to eating, to exercising—in the alien environment of space has helped to advance the sciences of ergonomics, human performance, and stress psychology and the technologies of air and water recycling, food sterilization, and food packaging. Systems on the shuttle provide rigorous, immediate feedback on theories about human behavior and human engineering. If the designs are faulty, that is instantly apparent in the demanding shuttle environment.

Keeping human beings alive and comfortable in an environment as hostile as space shows that mankind's domain can be extended far into the solar system. Although unpiloted missions offer new perspectives on the outer planets and the universe, manned missions are the key to moving human life into the realm of space.

Bibliography

Committee on Space Biology and Medicine. *A Strategy for Space Biology and Medical Science*. Washington, D.C.: National Academy Press, 1987. A description of the biological and medical areas that are important to space planning, this book covers topics ranging from human nutrition and reproduction to the behavior of plants in microgravity and developmental biology. Some sections are accessible to general readers; some are college-level material.

Connors, Mary M., et al. *Living Aloft: Human Requirements for Extended Space-flight*. NASA SP-483. Washington, D.C.: Government Printing Office, 1985. Discusses the physical and social stresses of living in space and explores medical considerations and possible ways to deal with those stresses. Includes sections on exercise, leisure time, the need for privacy, astronaut work schedules and other aspects of human performance, the selection of crews, communications, and responses to crises. For college-level readers.

Haynes, Robert. "Space Shuttle Food Systems." In *NASA Facts*. NF-150/1-86. Washington, D.C.: National Aeronautics and Space Administration, 1986. This edition of the *NASA Facts* Educational Publications Series deals with the foods provided for the space shuttle astronauts. It is well illustrated with pictures of the various food packs, lockers, ovens, and hand-washing facilities aboard the shuttle. Includes a picture of an astronaut eating from a food tray in space. Sample menus and actual foods carried on the first four space shuttles are listed. Accessible to a general readership.

Joels, Kerry M., and Gregory P. Kennedy. *The Space Shuttle Operator's Manual*. Rev. ed. New York: Ballantine Books, 1987. A delightful book which puts the reader in the driver's seat on board the space shuttle. The reader is treated to a step-by-step tour of all the shuttle's operations from launch to landing. Chapter 2 deals with daily life in space. Most of the material is understandable to high school students. A good series of more technical appendices on specific shuttle subsystems is included.

Lattimer, Dick. *Space Station Friendship*. Harrisburg, Pa.: Stackpole Books, 1988. An entertaining fictional account of a visit to a future space station. All the problems of living in space are well covered, from acquiring food, water, and breathable air to coping with confinement and isolation. The challenges of life in space are made clear to the reader by the various characters in the story. Suitable for teenagers and adults.

McElroy, Robert D., Norman V. Martello, and David T. Smernoff. *Controlled Ecological Life Support Systems: CELSS 1985 Workshop*. NASA TM-88215. Springfield, Va.: National Technical Information Service, 1986. A compendium of ideas for life-support methods on the space shuttle, the space station, and future space missions. Discusses systems for recycling water, disposing of waste, reconstituting gases for use as breathable air, and producing food from algae, bacteria, and higher plants. College-level material.

U.S. Air Force Academy. Department of Behavioral Sciences and Leadership. *Psychological, Sociological, and Habitability Issues of Long-Duration Space Missions*. NASA T-1082K. Houston: National Aeronautics and Space Administration, 1985. This book thoroughly assesses human engineering for current and future space missions. Topics covered include work-rest cycles; astronauts' sleep needs and performance levels; the design of astronauts' garments, food, and private accommodations; and the effects of all these factors on space personnel. Advanced college-level material.

Penelope J. Boston

Cross-References

Astronauts and the U.S. Astronaut Program, 154; Biological Effects of Space Travel on Humans, 188; Cosmonauts and the Soviet Cosmonaut Program, 273; Food and Diet for Space Travel, 454; Insuring Spacecraft and Human Life, 608; The Manned Maneuvering Unit, 829; Materials Processing in Space, 933; The Mir Space Station, 1025; The Skylab Program, 1285; The U.S. Space Shuttle, 1626; Space Shuttle Mission 17: *Challenger*, 1765; Space Shuttle Mission 23: *Atlantis*, 1800; The Development of the U.S. Space Station, 1835; Living and Working in the U.S. Space Station, 1850; Modules and Nodes of the U.S. Space Station, 1857; The Spacelab Program, 1884; The Development of Spacesuits, 1917.

THE SPACE SHUTTLE TEST FLIGHTS
Enterprise

Date: September 8, 1977, to December 6, 1985
Type of mission: Manned test flights
Country: The United States

Enterprise, *the first space shuttle orbiter, tested the landing techniques of the United States' Space Transportation System. Engineers also used it for ground handling, vibration, and landing brake net tests.*

Principal personages
FRED W. HAISE,
C. GORDON FULLERTON,
JOE H. ENGLE, and
RICHARD H. TRULY, NASA astronauts
FITZHUGH L. FULTON, the shuttle carrier aircraft pilot
THOMAS C. MCMURTRY, the shuttle carrier aircraft copilot

Summary of the Missions

In September, 1976, the National Aeronautics and Space Administration (NASA) unveiled the prototype for a new class of reusable manned spacecraft. The delta-wing vehicle, *Enterprise*, was the first space shuttle orbiter, the manned component of the space shuttle vehicle. The complete space shuttle comprised the orbiter attached to a large expendable fuel tank flanked by two solid-fueled rocket boosters (SRBs). The space shuttle would be launched from a rocket, orbit like a spacecraft, then land like an airplane.

Before any of the reusable craft ventured into space, tests of the landing system had to be made; these tests were called approach and landing tests (ALTs). The first orbiter, which bore the airframe designation OV-101, was designed to undergo such tests. Construction of OV-101 began on June 4, 1974. OV-101 was not intended for spaceflight, so it did not contain many of the systems needed for an orbital craft. For example, OV-101 did not have the three rocket engines necessary for boost to space, nor did it contain any of the orbital maneuvering engines. Such spaceflight components as the star trackers, unified S-band antennae, and rendezvous radar were also not part of the design. Since OV-101 would never venture beyond Earth's atmosphere, it was not covered with any of the thermal tiles (ceramic blocks of silicon material which can withstand extremely high temperatures and insulate the orbiter's aluminum structure from the heat of reentry) needed for protection during the fiery return from space. On OV-101, blocks of polyurethane foam simulated the thermal protection tiles. Glass fiber panels on the nose cap and wing leading edges simulated the reinforced carbon-carbon structures planned for later orbiters.

On September 8, 1976, NASA Administrator James Fletcher met with President

Gerald Ford to discuss the name of OV-101. For several months prior to the meeting, fans of the science-fiction television series *Star Trek* had conducted a letter-writing campaign suggesting the name *Enterprise*, the name of the spaceship in the series. After an estimated sixty thousand letters arrived at the White House and NASA headquarters, President Ford approved the name.

Slightly more than a week later, on September 17, 1976, Fletcher, U.S. senator Barry Goldwater, Rockwell International board chairman Willard Rockwell, and about five thousand others stood outside a hangar at Rockwell International's Palmdale, California, plant. At about 9:30 A.M., as the band played the theme music from *Star Trek*, for a cheering crowd, a red, white, and blue tractor towed the *Enterprise* from behind the hangar. *Enterprise* had a wingspan of 23.1 meters, a length of 37.1 meters, and weighed 65,000 kilograms.

On January 31, 1977, NASA and Rockwell engineers moved *Enterprise* out of Palmdale, 58 kilometers to the Dryden Flight Research Center at Edwards Air Force Base. *Enterprise* made the journey, which took nearly twelve hours, on a 90-wheel trailer. At Dryden, engineers had a modified commercial passenger jet waiting to be used with *Enterprise* for the landing tests. Since the space shuttle orbiter returned from space unpowered, getting the shuttle airborne to test the landing system posed a unique challenge. The solution was to mount the orbiter piggyback on top of a large aircraft which could carry it aloft and then release it. In addition, the aircraft could ferry space shuttle orbiters for cross-country travel.

On June 17, 1974, NASA purchased a Boeing 747 from American Airlines for use as the shuttle carrier aircraft (SCA) and subsequently modified it to carry a 68,000-kilogram load on its back. All passenger accommodations—seats, galleys, and the like—were removed. Bulkheads and reinforcements had to be added to the fuselage's main deck. The 747's standard engines were replaced with higher-thrust engines. Three supports for the orbiter were added to the SCA's top, and tip fins were added to the horizontal stabilizer. Other changes to the aircraft included modifications to its trim system, air conditioning system, and electrical wiring, and the addition of an escape system for the flight crew.

On February 7, 1977, *Enterprise* was mounted atop the SCA for the first time. Eight days later, engineers began a series of taxi tests. During these, the 747 taxied along the runway at speeds just less than what was needed to become airborne. These tests showed no unusual problems, so preparations were made for the first flight of the tandem aircraft. The first five flights of the approach and landing test program were so-called captive inert flights to verify the handling of the SCA/space shuttle orbiter combination. For these, *Enterprise* did not carry a crew. The program then progressed to "captive active" flights, where *Enterprise* was "powered up" and occupied but remained attached to the SCA. Finally, there were the free flights, where *Enterprise* separated from the SCA and made an unpowered approach and landing.

For all but the last two free flights, which tried to duplicate the return from space of an orbiter as closely as possible, *Enterprise*'s aft end was covered with an aerodynamic fairing. This fairing, or tailcone, smoothed the airflow off the orbiter's base, reducing drag and buffeting on the SCA's tail. For cross-country flights with operational orbiters, the fairing also protected the three space shuttle Main Engines.

The first captive inert flight occurred on February 18. For two hours and ten minutes, Fitzhugh L. Fulton and Thomas C. McMurtry flew the SCA/*Enterprise* combination over the California desert. This flight evaluated the airworthiness of the configuration and verified the preflight stability and control predictions. Four more captive inert flights followed during the next two weeks, each exploring a different portion of the flight envelope.

After the captive inert flights, the program moved into the captive active phase. The first captive active flight was on June 18, 1977. Fred W. Haise and C. Gordon Fullerton occupied the orbiter's flight deck. During a 56-minute flight, they tested various orbiter systems and gathered additional information about buffeting of *Enterprise*'s vertical tail. Ten days later, astronauts Joe H. Engle and Richard H. Truly occupied *Enterprise* for the second captive active flight. Haise and Fullerton again occupied *Enterprise* for the final captive flight of the ALT program, a dress rehearsal for the free flights.

On August 12, 1977, *Enterprise* flew independently of the SCA for the first time. Haise and Fullerton piloted *Enterprise*, Fulton and McMurtry the SCA. About 48 minutes after takeoff, the piggyback aircraft reached an altitude of 8,650 meters. Fullerton and McMurty began a shallow dive, a maneuver called "pushover." At an altitude of 7,350 meters, Haise pushed the separation button in *Enterprise*, and seven explosive bolts fired; *Enterprise* was on its own. Fulton pitched the SCA down and rolled left to clear the free-flying space shuttle. Haise and Fullerton pitched the orbiter's nose up and gently rolled *Enterprise* to the right to clear the SCA. They straightened the craft, then eased the orbiter's nose up, practicing a landing flare maneuver. After this maneuver, the crew of the *Enterprise* executed a 180-degree turn to the left, aligning *Enterprise* with the Dryden runway. *Enterprise* touched down 5 minutes and 22 seconds after separating from the SCA.

There were some relatively minor problems encountered during the first free flight. For example, one of the general purpose computers (GPCs) stopped working at separation; however, the other onboard computers sensed the fault and automatically took the malfunctioning GPC off-line. Because Haise and Fullerton remained flexible, all mission objectives were achieved, and the handling, stability, and flight performance characteristics were as predicted.

Engle and Truly piloted *Enterprise* for its second free flight on September 13, 1977. During this flight, the pilots executed a 1.8-g turn to the left as they lined *Enterprise* with the runway, duplicating the maneuvers of an orbiter returning from space. The term "g" refers to the acceleration of gravity. Sitting still on Earth, one experiences an acceleration of 1 g, or a gravitational force of 1, the normal sensation of gravity. During periods of changing acceleration, such as a banking turn in an airplane, the so-called g-loading will change. As Engle and Truly banked the *Enterprise*, they felt as though they weighed twice as much as normal. The second flight lasted 5 minutes, 28 seconds.

Haise and Fullerton were again at *Enterprise*'s controls on September 23, 1977, for the third free flight of the ALT program. During this flight, the pilots tested the orbiter's automatic landing system. After the flight, ALT program managers decided to proceed with the tailcone-off flights, eliminating two planned missions. For these flights, the tailcone was removed, duplicating the aerodynamic characteristics of an orbiter returning from space.

The fourth free flight, also the first tailcone-off flight, occurred on October 12, 1977. Engle and Truly flew OV-101. While the SCA climbed to separation altitude, the 747's tail was visibly buffeted by the turbulence coming off the base of the orbiter. After separation, Engle and Truly flew *Enterprise* on a straight course to Dryden. Without the tailcone, the drag on *Enterprise* was much higher, and the flight lasted 2 minutes, 35 seconds.

Haise and Fullerton again piloted *Enterprise* for the fifth and final free flight on October 26, 1977. This would be the first landing on a paved runway. (All previous landings had been on dry lakebed runways.) This free flight lasted 2 minutes, 5 seconds. During landing, after making a near touchdown, the orbiter's nose suddenly rose, then settled back down. The nose rose once more, made a second touchdown, skipped off the runway briefly, then finally settled down for a third, and final, touchdown. Despite the difficulties, no further free flights were deemed necessary, so the most visible part of the ALT program ended.

After the free flights, engineers evaluated one more aspect of the space shuttle's flight characteristics: how the SCA/orbiter combination handled on cross-country ferry flights. For the ferry flights, the orbiter's front support on the back of the 747 was lowered from 4 degrees to 2 degress to reduce drag and improve the aircraft's cruise characteristics. Following a series of tests, the SCA/*Enterprise* took off from Dryden on March 10, 1978, bound for the Marshall Space Flight Center (MSFC) in Huntsville, Alabama.

At MSFC, engineers joined *Enterprise* with an external propellant tank and two SRBs in a test stand. They then applied vibrations of varying frequencies and intensities to the vehicle to see how the space shuttle reacted. These tests simulated the vibrations expected during launch.

By early 1979, the so-called mated ground vibration tests were over, and on April 10, the SCA ferried the *Enterprise* from MSFC to the Kennedy Space Center in Cape Canaveral, Florida. At the Cape, *Enterprise* was assembled with the tank and boosters atop the mobile launch platform and taken to the launchpad. This was the first time a complete space shuttle was processed for launch, and technicians tested how well all the plumbing and electrical fittings at the launchpad interfaced with the vehicle. On May 1, 1979, a space shuttle vehicle stood on Launch Complex 39A for the first time.

Following the launchpad assembly and fit checks, *Enterprise* was used for several public exhibitions. In May, 1983, NASA took the *Enterprise* to the Paris Air Show. After the French exposition, *Enterprise* was also viewed by millions of people in

West Germany, Italy, England, and Canada. The following year, from May through November, *Enterprise* was exhibited at the Louisiana World Exposition in New Orleans. For this trip, the orbiter was transported on a barge part of the way.

On November 18, 1985, *Enterprise* made its last flight, as NASA delivered it to the Smithsonian Institution at Dulles International Airport in Virginia. At a ceremony on December 6, NASA formally turned the *Enterprise* over to the Smithsonian. In June, 1987, however, NASA engineers found one more use for OV-101, as they tested an emergency net designed to keep returning orbiters from running off the runway.

Knowledge Gained

As the prototype space shuttle orbiter, *Enterprise* validated the design of a new family of spacecraft. Also, by testing the landing system, *Enterprise* proved the validity of using glide return for manned spacecraft. In the course of the flight test program, NASA engineers learned how to land a 90,000-kilogram, delta-winged spacecraft. The flights verified both pilot-guided and automatic approach and landing systems and showed that the orbiter could land on a paved runway. This had been particularly worrisome, because the orbiter lands at relatively high speeds (about 350 kilometers per hour) and tire wear is a problem. (In fact, subsequent landings by orbiters returning from space showed this to be a major problem.)

The ground vibration tests were a crucial step toward validating the entire space shuttle "stack" for launch. In the course of these tests, engineers at Marshall Space Flight Center ballasted the external tank with varying amounts of deionized water, simulating the consumption of propellants during flight. Also, the SRBs were ballasted with inert propellant for the tests. Thus, the shuttle's designers had actual measurements of the vehicle's response to dynamic flight conditions. These data were used to validate researchers' analytical math models and predictions of the space shuttle's in-flight behavior.

By taking the *Enterprise* to Kennedy Space Center for launch complex fit checks, engineers could verify that all the electrical, hydraulic, and fuel lines on the launchpad interfaced properly with the space shuttle. This was particularly important, because the shuttle used facilities originally built for the Apollo program in the 1960's. The *Enterprise* also provided a dress rehearsal for pad crews to handle and assemble a complete space shuttle before the first actual flight vehicles arrived.

Context

The idea of winged, reusable spacecraft had long appealed to engineers as the most economical means for opening the space frontier. Throughout the 1960's, NASA and military engineers discussed the possibilities of an aircraft-type space vehicle and advanced numerous designs. One of the best known was the United States Air Force Dyna Soar, a manned glider planned for launch by a Titan 3 launch vehicle. Other designs, though never built, bore such exotic names as Triamese (a shuttle comprising three identical vehicles connected for launch, one of which would reach orbit), Meteor, and Astro Rocket. By the late 1960's, NASA planners were developing a program to succeed the Apollo manned lunar missions. They finally decided on a reusable space shuttle. In April, 1972, the United States Congress approved NASA's request to proceed with the space shuttle. On August 9, 1972, NASA managers authorized North American Rockwell (later, Rockwell International) to build the space shuttle orbiter.

Engineers proposed numerous designs for the space shuttle before choosing what became the *Enterprise*. The orbiter contained a cargo bay capable of carrying payloads up to 4.5 meters in diameter, 18.3 meters in length, and 29,500 kilograms in weight. The space shuttle would lift off like a rocket, orbit like a spacecraft, then glide back for an airplane-style landing.

Winged spacecraft had existed for nearly two decades, in the form of the North American X-15. Between 1959 and 1968, three of these remarkable aircraft made 199 flights. On several occasions, X-15's took their pilots above 80 kilometers, qualifying them as astronauts. Experiences with the rocket-powered X-15 aircraft, which made unpowered, high-speed landings, were directly applicable to the space shuttle program. Yet before the plans for the space shuttle could be put into practice, particularly the notion of landing a spacecraft like an airplane, a test vehicle was needed. The *Enterprise* served that function. Thus *Enterprise* bridged the gap between the X-15 research aircraft flights and the first space flight of the OV-102 orbiter *Columbia* in 1981.

Bibliography

Grey, Jerry. *Enterprise*. New York: William Morrow and Co., 1980. This popular book on the space shuttle program deals extensively with the politics of building the space shuttle and starting the program.

Hallion, Richard P. *On the Frontier: Flight Research at Dryden, 1946-1981*. NASA SP-4303. Washington, D.C.: Government Printing Office, 1984. This volume in the NASA History Series describes flight-testing activities at the Dryden Flight Research Center from 1946 to 1981. Provides an excellent perspective on flight research activities at Dryden up to the first space shuttle mission. Also included are chapters on the X-15 and "lifting body" programs, which were precursors of the space shuttle.

Joels, Kerry M., and Gregory P. Kennedy. *The Space Shuttle Operator's Manual*. Rev. ed. New York: Ballantine Books, 1987. This book provides a description of how the space shuttle flies and includes checklists and time lines of the space shuttle landing system. Descriptions of shuttle facilities and of accessories such as the shuttle carrier aircraft are also included.

National Aeronautics and Space Administration. *Space Shuttle*. NASA SP-407. Washington, D.C.: Government Printing Office, 1976. Written on a popular level, this source provides an early look at the benefits and capabilities of the space shuttle program. Although its projections on launch frequency and ground turn-around time proved too optimistic when space shuttles began flying, this document shows the expectations that NASA managers had for the vehicle at the time *Enterprise* was being tested.

Stockton, William, and John Noble Wilford. *Space-Liner: The New York Times Report on the Columbia's Voyage*. New York: Times Books, 1981. An excellent narrative of the space shuttle program up to the first flight of *Columbia* in April, 1981. Included in the narrative are chapters devoted to the design, development, and testing of the space shuttle system, including *Enterprise*.

Gregory P. Kennedy

Cross-References

Cape Canaveral and the Kennedy Space Center, 229; Johnson Space Center, 669; Marshall Space Flight Center, 908; The U.S. Space Shuttle, 1626; Space Shuttle Mission 1: *Columbia*, 1648; Spaceplanes, 1912.

SPACE SHUTTLE MISSION 1
Columbia

Date: April 12 to April 14, 1981
Type of mission: Manned Earth-orbiting spaceflight
Country: The United States

Space Transportation System (STS) 1 was the first launch of the space shuttle. The primary objectives of this mission were to demonstrate a safe launch to orbit, test basic orbiter systems in space, achieve reentry, and land safely.

Principal personages
JOHN W. YOUNG, the commander
ROBERT L. CRIPPEN, the pilot
JOHN F. YARDLEY, Associate Administrator for Space Transportation Systems
DANIEL GERMANY, Director of Orbiter Programs
ROBERT F. THOMPSON, Manager of the shuttle program at Johnson Space Center
DONALD K. (DEKE) SLAYTON, Manager of the Orbital Flight Test Program
GEORGE ABBEY, Director of Flight Operations at Johnson Space Center
MAXIME A. FAGET, Director of Engineering and Development at Johnson Space Center
ROBERT H. GRAY, Manager of the Shuttle Projects Office at Kennedy Space Center
GEORGE F. PAGE, Director of Shuttle Operations at Kennedy Space Center
ROBERT E. LINDSTROM, Manager of the Shuttle Projects Office at Marshall Space Flight Center
MEL BURK, Shuttle Project Manager at Dryden Flight Research Center

Summary of the Mission

STS 1 was the first demonstration of a spacecraft that could take off like a rocket, fly into space, reenter the atmosphere, and land like an airplane—then be refurbished and launched again. The mission officially lasted 2 days, 6 hours, 20 minutes, and 52 seconds from launch to landing.

The first space shuttle mission was also the first of four demonstration flights, collectively known as the Orbital Flight Test Program, which were designed to test the shuttle before it would be declared officially operational. The program of more than eleven hundred carefully outlined tests and experiments was designed to verify the shuttle as a launch vehicle, living space, freight handler, instrument platform, and craft. The program was also intended to test ground operations and personnel before, during, and after each launch. In the interest of safety, the trajectory, thrust, payload weight, and other stresses on the spacecraft were deliberately kept to a minimum. The orbiter's only two payloads were associated with the flight test program.

The development flight instrumentation package consisted of strain sensors and measuring devices to gauge spacecraft performance and stresses encountered during launch, flight, and landing. The aerodynamic coefficient identification package consisted of instruments to determine air velocity, temperature, pressure, and other aerodynamic characteristics during the flight. The third experiment, not carried on board, was the infrared imagery of shuttle (IRIS). Its objective was to obtain a detailed infrared image of the orbiter's lower, windward, and side surfaces during reentry. These images were obtained using NASA's C-141 Kuiper Airborne Observatory aircraft positioned at an altitude of about 13,716 meters along the reentry path.

The first mission followed a series of taxi tests, unmanned and manned captive flight tests atop a modified Boeing 747 aircraft which concluded with free flights. Repeated problems with the *Columbia*'s three liquid-fueled main engines and the thermal tiles that protected it from reentry heat had delayed the first launch by almost three years. On November 6, 1972, the NASA Associate Administrator told the House Committee on Science and Astronautics that the first manned orbital flight was slated for March, 1978. Technical problems caused NASA to reschedule the launch several times: to June, September, November, and December, 1979; again to March 30, 1980; and to March, 1981.

NASA selected John Young, the most experienced member of the astronaut corps, as commander. His pilot, Robert Crippen, had had no spaceflight experience but was very knowledgeable about the shuttle's complex computer system and was considered one of the best astronauts.

The first space-worthy orbiter, *Columbia*, was rolled out of its hangar at Rockwell International and towed to Edwards Air Force Base on March 8, 1979. The spacecraft was missing its main engines, its orbital maneuvering system (OMS) pods, and about 7,800 heat tiles. It would be mounted on its Boeing 747 carrier aircraft and flown to Kennedy Space Center, where the remaining work would be finished. Technicians added dummy tiles held on with tape to give a clean, aerodynamic surface, but these parts fell off during a brief test flight along with one hundred real tiles. Nevertheless, the 747 took off for Florida on March 20, 1979, arriving there on March 24.

At Kennedy, the tiles were subjected to a "pull test." Many failed, and a total of 4,500 had to be removed and strengthened. Concerned that some might fall off in flight and have to be replaced, NASA sped work on its manned maneuvering unit (MMU) jet backpack so it could be used for an in-orbit repair. The plan to prepare the MMU for STS 1, however, was dropped.

The main engines were installed by the summer of 1979, while test engines at the

National Space Technology Laboratories in Bay St. Louis, Mississippi, were still giving engineers problems. An aborted firing test on November 4, 1979, revealed a problem that could have affected *Columbia*'s engines, so they were removed from the orbiter in January, 1980, for modifications. After further tests, the engines were reinstalled on the orbiter by August 3. They were removed again on October 9 and 10, then reinstalled early in November. Since the engines had never been fired as a cluster on the shuttle, NASA decided to have a 20-second test firing while the shuttle was sitting on Pad 39A. On November 3, 1980, the two solid-fueled rocket boosters were mated to the external fuel tank. The orbiter was attached on November 26, and the slow 5-kilometer trip to the pad began December 29. The engine test firing took place on February 20, 1981. Minor problems required that the target launch date be rescheduled for April 10.

With no further problems, the countdown began. About two hours before launch, Young and Crippen climbed into their seats on the flight deck. For this flight and the three to come, the *Columbia* was equipped with two rocket-propelled ejection seats. Between the time the shuttle cleared the tower and the point at which it reached an altitude of 30,480 meters, overhead panels could be blown off and the crew could be hurled to safety. Young and Crippen also wore U.S. Air Force high-altitude escape suits to provide oxygen and full-body protection at high altitudes. Ejection seats and pressure suits would be discontinued after the fourth mission.

During a built-in countdown hold at T minus 20 minutes (20 minutes prior to launch), the shuttle began to experience problems. One of the orbiter's five computers was not synchronized. Only three were needed, but NASA officials wanted all systems operational on the first launch, so the countdown was halted. It was recycled to T minus 23 minutes and held there for 28 minutes before officials restarted the clock. The timing problem happened again at T minus 16 minutes, so officials decided to postpone the launch. Correcting the problem took five hours, and the delay meant that the external fuel tank had to be emptied of its volatile propellants. A new launch was scheduled for two days later, on April 12. This time, the computers functioned normally. At 7:00 A.M. eastern standard time *Columbia*'s three main engines fired, followed seconds later by the twin boosters. They generated 6.5 million pounds per square inch of thrust to lift the 2-million-kilogram shuttle from the launchpad.

The boosters burned out in 132 seconds and were jettisoned, parachuting to the Atlantic Ocean, where they would be towed back to the launch site by recovery ships. The shuttle continued its eastward climb. At an altitude of 50 kilometers, it was moving at a speed of 4,670 kilometers per hour. It passed Mach 4 in four minutes and at seven minutes was traveling at 28,161 kilometers per hour in an elliptical orbit. It dived slightly from 135 to 117 kilometers to pick up speed. It began climbing again at Mach 25 as the engines were throttled back to provide 65 percent of the maximum thrust. The engines were shut down after 8 minutes, 34 seconds. *Columbia* was soon flying 28,161 kilometers per hour in an elliptical orbit. The tank was jettisoned to burn over the Indian Ocean. Over the next seven hours, the two

OMS engines were fired four times to attain a final, nearly circular orbit of 277 kilometers.

A major milestone after the second burn was the opening of the orbiter's payload bay doors. Had the doors not opened, *Columbia*'s final two OMS burns would have been used to position the orbiter to return to Earth after only five hours. On the fifth orbit, the doors were opened. The right door was opened and closed, followed by the left door. Then, both were opened. Young spotted dark patches on the OMS pods where thermal tiles had broken free. The loss of these tiles was not critical because they were not in an area of high reentry heat. Yet mission officials worried about whether any tiles were missing from the orbiter's underside, which the crew could not see. Some reports said that spy satellite cameras were turned toward *Columbia* to look at the bottom tiles, but neither NASA nor the U.S. Air Force would confirm those reports. At this point, the shuttle was orbiting with its open cargo hold pointing toward Earth.

The last OMS burn occurred at 7 hours, 5 minutes after launch and lasted 40 seconds. The crew conducted a long series of performance tests on the shuttle's smaller thrusters in the nose and tail of the orbiter. After their 13-hour day, the astronauts finally settled down for the night, remaining in their seats in case of an emergency. During the night, they complained of being cold, a problem traced to a malfunctioning heating valve.

The second day included more thruster tests and television transmissions, including a talk with Vice President George Bush. The attitude control system was given a workout, as the crew performed a series of yaws, rolls, and pitches. Young put the *Columbia* into a gravity-gradient attitude. Nose down and perpendicular to Earth, the ship became almost motionless, saving fuel that otherwise would have been required to maintain stability. The thrust monitoring instruments caused problems, failing to record the correct velocity. Crippen closed and reopened the doors again to determine if they had been warped during the alternately hot and cold temperatures of the 1.5-hour day/night orbits. He reported that an oxygen regulator valve was leaking slightly. Mission Control in Houston advised the astronauts that the problem was not serious as long as the valve was functioning.

During their twenty-first orbit, the astronauts donned their pressure suits and rehearsed for reentry the next day. Before going to sleep the second night, they performed a test of the inertial measurement unit in the nose. The device indicated *Columbia*'s location in space and in what direction the spacecraft was pointing by keeping track of all maneuvers made previously.

Shortly after Mission Control had signed off for the night, an alarm bell sounded on the flight deck. It had been triggered by a sudden drop in temperature in one of three auxiliary power units (APUs). Two APUs were needed to provide power for the orbiter's aerodynamic control surfaces after reentry. A cold power unit might be difficult to activate. Houston asked the astronauts to recycle the heating system switch to engage the heater. They did that and then returned to sleep, but the problem persisted. They used heaters when they woke, but the temperature continued to drop. The crew knew that they would be in no danger, unless the temperature dropped below 26 degrees Celsius.

After the thirty-fourth orbit, more than 43 hours in orbit, the astronauts donned their pressure suits for the last time and closed the payload bay doors. Young used the thrusters to flip the *Columbia* so that the OMS engines at the rear faced in the correct direction for reentry. On the thirty-sixth orbit, the two 2,270-kilogram thrust engines fired for 160 seconds to slow the orbiter and bring its path inside the atmosphere. Its orbit was now an ellipse that intercepted the ground, and its speed was reduced by 320 kilometers per hour. Young turned the ship's nose forward to prepare for the 7,081-kilometer descent through the atmosphere, the longest glide of the space program.

Columbia entered the atmosphere over the eastern Pacific Ocean and headed north to begin the descent to California, entering at a nose-up angle of 40 degrees. The tiles began to heat, surrounding the cabin with a red glow. Communications were lost for 16 seconds when the temperature rose high enough to ionize the surrounding air and block radio signals. The craft emerged from the blackout at 57.3 kilometers at Mach 10.3. Young commanded the computers to put the orbiter into a series of S-shaped maneuvers to decrease speed. The ship crossed the California coastline at Mach 6.6 and flew over the dry lake bed at Edwards Air Force Base at a 16-kilometer altitude. The spacecraft caused a double sonic boom as it dropped below the speed of sound. The landing gear came down only seconds before contact. The rear wheels touched down first, then the nose gear. It was April 14, 1:21 P.M. eastern standard time. By April 29, *Columbia* was back in the processing facility at Kennedy Space Center to prepare for the second mission, scheduled for September.

Knowledge Gained

The primary objectives of STS 1 itself were simple: a safe ascent into orbit and return to Earth. The secondary objectives were to verify the combined performance of the entire vehicle through separation and retrieval of the boosters and to gather data on the orbiter's performance in space and during reentry and landing. Potential stresses on the spacecraft were kept to a minimum. The only payloads were those associated with verifying the shuttle system.

In addition to demonstrating a safe launch and landing, STS 1 demonstrated two vital systems, the payload bay doors with their attached heat radiators and the reaction control system (RCS) thrusters used to maneuver the craft while in orbit. Opening and closing tests with the doors showed their movement to be jerkier than it had in tests on Earth, but the doors performed satisfactorily. The main engines, which had caused so many problems in development, met all requirements for start and cutoff timing, thrust direction, and flow of propellants.

The shuttle slightly overshot its path to orbit, about 3,000 meters at main engine cutoff. The inability of wind tunnel models to simulate the afterburning of hot rocket exhaust gases in the real atmosphere accounted for this miscalculation. The crew noted some momentary shaking of the ship when the main engines shut down, presumably caused by the dumping of excess fuel. That process was expected to add some velocity to the shuttle but did not. Onboard cameras showed that the external tank separated from the orbiter as predicted after engine cutoff. Ascent temperatures proved low enough during development flights that NASA decided to delete the white reflective paint on the tank to save weight.

The launchpad's water deluge system, designed to lessen the powerful acoustic pressure waves seconds before and after lift-off, had to be modified before the next mission. Sensors and microphones on STS 1 showed the acoustic shock to be up to four times the predicted values in parts of the shuttle closest to the pad. The system dumps tens of thousands of liters of water onto the pad and into the flame trenches beneath the rockets to absorb sound energy that could damage the orbiter or its cargo. In the subsequent missions, rather than dumping water into the bottom of the flame trenches, water was redirected into the exhaust plumes of the boosters just below the nozzles. Energy-absorbing water troughs were placed over the exhaust openings. The changes reduced acoustic pressures 20 to 30 percent.

On missions such as STS 1 with moderate heating and cooling requirements, engineers found the total heat stress on the cooling system to be 15 percent lower than expected. Temperatures on the surface of the payload bay insulation ranged from minus 96 degrees Celsius to a peak of 127 degrees Celsius.

Fuel usage and thrusting power of the orbiter's reaction control system performed as expected in space, with the smaller maneuvering jets more fuel efficient than predicted. Two of the four vernier jets in the tail were observed to have problems when firing downward. The exhaust hit the aft body flap, or beaver tail, and eroded some protective tiles. It also reduced the jets' effectiveness. One solution considered later was to reorient the jets slightly. In the meantime, a protective coating was applied to the tiles on the body flap.

The crew found that the orbiter was nearly impossible to stop after maneuvers without overshooting its target and coming back to the required position. A group of microphones and other sensors in the payload bay showed that noise and stress were lower than expected. After STS 1, astronauts switched to wireless headphone radios because the trailing wire proved to be a nuisance for Young and Crippen.

Upon reentry, an unplanned correction was made in the angle of the body flap. Engineers had predicted an angle of 8 to 9 degrees for the flap at high altitudes. The actual angle required to maintain the proper reentry angle was 14 degrees. Onboard computers made the adjustment automatically. The reaction control thrusters showed a greater than expected influence on the orbiter's motion in the atmosphere. It indicated that reliance on the thrusters during reentry could be reduced or eliminated entirely.

The STS 1 approach and landing was fully manual, although computers could land it automatically if necessary. Stress gauges on the landing gear and crew reports both indicated that the shuttle landing was very gentle. The length required for the orbiter to roll to a stop was well within the 4,500-meter design limit, but the actual wheel touchdown point was considerably beyond the planned point because the shuttle demonstrated a greater tendency to glide near the ground than had been expected.

When it returned to be refurbished, *Columbia* showed that it had endured the rigors of spaceflight well. Workers had to replace some three hundred of the thirty-one thousand tiles that were either missing or damaged. Yet the vehicle showed no damage from reentry temperatures as high as 1,650 degrees Celsius. With the removal of ice-forming hardware on the external tank, deletion of certain insulation on the boosters, and a general cleanup of the pad area, fewer than forty tiles needed to be replaced after the fourth mission.

Context

STS 1, the first orbital flight of NASA's Space Transportation System, was the United States' first manned space mission in nearly six years. As the first flight of an entirely new type of spacecraft, the mission set several spaceflight records.

It was the first shuttle mission, the first NASA space mission to touch down on land, and the first use of solid-fueled rocket boosters for manned spaceflight. It was also the first recovery of a booster for reuse. Unlike previous spacecraft to that time, which had used ablative heatshields, the orbiter used ceramic tiles to protect it from reentry heat. STS 1 was the first maiden flight of a spacecraft carrying a human crew. Previous spacecraft had been tested unmanned first. The shuttle was the first vehicle to provide no emergency escape for the crew during launch as part of its basic design; after the first four STS orbital flight tests, ejection seats for the pilot and copilot were omitted from the design.

For the first time, hydrogen- and oxygen-fueled engines on a launch vehicle would be fired at ground level. Previously, such engines had been confined to upper stages. The main engines were the most advanced liquid-fueled rocket engines ever built, with the highest thrust for its weight of any engine yet developed. STS 1 marked the first time a winged craft encountered the forces of maximum aero-dynamic pressure in a launch through the atmosphere. *Columbia*'s flight also marked the first time a winged spaceship reentered the atmosphere, passing through hyper-sonic and supersonic ranges to make a runway landing.

Even without its 29,484-kilogram advertised cargo capacity, the shuttle was the heaviest vehicle ever flown. The Apollo command and service modules and the lunar module placed into orbit had weighed 45,359 kilograms. Skylab had weighed 82,553 kilograms. The shuttle *Columbia* weighed 96,163 kilograms; it was the most massive vehicle flown to date. Its 37.18-meter length exceeded that of the Skylab orbital workshop by almost 11 meters. The shuttle orbiter's payload bay doors were the largest aerospace structures made of composite materials to that time.

Columbia was the first American manned spacecraft to provide a normal breath-ing atmosphere for its crew. It was an Earth-type mixture of 80 percent nitrogen and 20 percent oxygen at sea-level pressure, 14.7 pounds per square inch. The previous Mercury, Gemini, and Apollo spacecraft had provided pure oxygen at a pressure of about five pounds per square inch.

After numerous setbacks in developing the shuttle and a two-year delay in the first launch, STS 1 proved to be a morale booster for the American space program. It was the country's first manned space mission since the joint U.S.-Soviet mission, which ended July 24, 1975. Thousands of spectators viewed the launch and landing of the shuttle. The first launch renewed enthusiasm for the shuttle program and its goals. To the space agency and other shuttle supporters, the first mission represented the opening of a new era of space exploration. The shuttle was to be the United States' reusable space truck, providing routine access to low Earth orbit, not only for astronauts but also for scientists and other civilian passengers.

STS 1 raised hopes that the cost of space operations would be significantly reduced. Once normal operations began, according to the space agency, the shuttle would serve as a platform for deploying satellites, interplanetary probes, and scientific instruments such as the Hubble Space Telescope. From the shuttle, astronauts would repair ailing satellites. Research in low gravity would lead to new or reduced-cost drugs, metal alloys, and electronics materials. The shuttle was also NASA's long-awaited vehicle for shipping the parts of a permanently manned station into space.

Components of the shuttle had been tested separately, but until April, 1981, there was no proof that the shuttle system could reach orbit, perform a mission, and return for a landing. That was the goal of the orbital flight test program, which was to continue for three more missions. Design, development, test, and evaluation cost for the shuttle was $9.912 billion. Production of four orbiters, spares, ground support, and other costs would total an added $5.6 billion.

Proving the concept of a reusable winged spacecraft was more difficult than NASA had expected. The agency was at least partially vindicated by the first STS flight.

Bibliography

Allaway, Howard. *The Space Shuttle at Work.* NASA SP-432. Washington, D.C.: Government Printing Office, 1979. A look at the envisioned shuttle operations written after the initial glide tests but before first launch. Deals with an anticipated mission, uses of space, shuttle rationale, launch and landing profiles, working in space, and future uses. A seventy-six-page guide suitable for general audiences.

Chant, Christopher. *Space Shuttle.* New York: Exeter Books, 1984. Largely a picture guide. Covers initial concept through STS 14. Includes sections on the orbiter, propulsion, external tank and boosters, and ground and payload operations—as well as shuttle mission summaries. Also contains sections on future missions and principal contractors.

Kerrod, Robin. *Space Shuttle.* New York: Gallery Books, 1984. A full-color pictorial shuttle diary, covering training and ground and space operations. Also includes artist conceptions of future shuttle missions.

Lewis, Richard S. *The Voyages of Columbia: The First True Spaceship.* New York: Columbia University Press, 1984. Describes the shuttle program from concept and development to details of STS missions 1 through 9. Includes the budgetary, political, and technical debates that led to the shuttle's eventual configuration. Includes notes and index sections as well as a section with major mission statistics. Illustrated with numerous drawings and black-and-white photographs.

Reichhardt, Tony. *Proving the Space Transportation System: The Orbital Flight Test Program.* NASA NF-137-83. Washington, D.C.: Government Printing Office, 1983. A 20-page educational report summarizing the shuttle system and the objectives and results of the four mission test program. Includes black and white photos and diagrams of shuttle components. For general audiences.

Trento, Joseph J. *Prescription for Disaster: From the Glory of Apollo to the Betrayal of the Shuttle.* New York: Crown Publishers, 1987. Written in the year after the 1986 *Challenger* accident. Offers a critical postaccident analysis of the shuttle program. Describes administrative and political decisions that led to the shuttle program and subsequent developmental problems that contributed to the accident. Based on interviews with all the NASA administrators and some other key officials. Includes an index to sources and interviews.

Wilson, Andrew. *Space Shuttle Story.* Twickenham, England: Hamlyn Publishing, 1986. Touches briefly on the early days of rocketry, experimental aircraft that led to the shuttle, and the development of the shuttle concept. Includes an index and a flight summary. Illustrated with color photographs.

Martin Burkey

Cross-References

SPACE SHUTTLE MISSION 2
Columbia

Date: November 12 to November 14, 1981
Type of mission: Manned Earth-orbiting spaceflight
Country: The United States

The second flight of the shuttle Columbia *carried the first scientific experiments and tested the remote manipulator system for the first time. Although the flight was cut short because one fuel cell failed, more than 90 percent of the mission's goals were reached.*

Principal personages
JOSEPH HENRY ENGLE, the commander
RICHARD HARRISON TRULY, the pilot

Summary of the Mission

After the successful mission STS 1 in April, 1981, the National Aeronautics and Space Administration (NASA) was eager to prepare *Columbia* for another flight. NASA set a launch date in late September, 1981, for the shuttle's second trip to space. Yet there were several obstacles. First, many tiles from the heatshield had to be replaced because they had been damaged during the first flight. Then, as the rescheduled launch date of October 9 approached, nitrogen tetroxide was spilled on the tiles; some 370 of them needed to be replaced. Again, a new launch date was set, this time for November 4.

On November 4, the countdown proceeded smoothly until T minus 31 seconds, when it was stopped by a computer that detected a low pressure reading in a fuel cell oxygen tank. An attempt to override the computer manually failed. During this time, engineers who monitor the performance of the auxiliary power units (APUs) noticed that the oil pressure was higher than expected. That caused concern over the ability of the APUs to restart at the end of the mission (the APUs supplied the rudder and elevons of the shuttle with power during reentry). In addition to the problems with the oxygen and oil pressures, the weather was worsening. Once more, NASA officials decided to postpone the launch. It was rescheduled for November 12.

The problems of November 4 were corrected. The difficulty with the oxygen pressure had been in the computer software, not in the shuttle itself. The oil pressure problem was corrected by replacing the oil in the gearboxes of the APUs and by replacing the oil filters.

The countdown toward the November 12 launch proceeded smoothly until November 11, when a multiplexer-demultiplexer, an instrument which mixes data for easier transmission, failed. A replacement had to be borrowed from the shuttle

Challenger and flown to Florida from California. The unit was installed by midnight, and the countdown proceeded again. *Columbia* was lifted into space at 10:10 A.M. on November 12 in a perfect launch.

As the second of four test flights scheduled for *Columbia*, STS 2 had the primary goal of collecting data on the performance of the shuttle. This flight was the first to carry a set of scientific experiments called OSTA 1, which had been prepared by NASA's Office of Space and Terrestrial Applications. OSTA 1 was mounted on a British-made Spacelab pallet. Spacelab was designed to function in much the same way as Skylab had but with less working space and with the ability to return to Earth.

During *Columbia*'s second orbit, one of the fuel cells on board failed. The fuel cells serve a dual purpose. First, they generate the power needed to operate the electrical systems on the shuttle. Second, they provide a supply of clean drinking water for the astronauts. *Columbia* was equipped with three fuel cells. The orbiting shuttle could function well using two, and it could reenter the atmosphere with the power from only one—but the risks involved would be high.

There were some important data that the scientists at NASA needed to collect during reentry. Failure of the development flight instrumentation recorders on STS 1 had prevented the acquisition of important thermal and spacecraft maneuvering data. Failure of a second fuel cell on STS 2, or of its deterioration in power output, would cause these data to be lost for a second time. After careful evaluation of the situation, NASA officials decided to proceed with a "minimum mission" of fifty-four hours rather than the 124 hours originally scheduled for the flight. The crew was told of the decision on November 13.

Failure of the fuel cell was among the most surprising failures that could have occurred. Fuel cells have functioned well on many spaceflights, and a failure of the type that occurred on STS 2 had been seen only on test cells that had undergone hundreds of hours of operation.

Since spaceflight is such a complicated matter, NASA has attempted through the years to plan for the unexpected. The STS 2 flightplan had been written so that primary test objectives and experiments were concentrated in the first two and one-half days of the scheduled 124-hour mission. NASA had also developed a flightplan that would meet the majority of the goals in the event that the shuttle had to be brought home early. It was this plan that was used for the minimum mission of STS 2. The astronauts worked efficiently and accomplished 90 percent of the 258 priority flight objectives.

One of the major goals of the mission was the testing of the remote manipulator system (RMS). The robot arm on the RMS is also referred to by some as the Canada arm, since it was constructed in Toronto. The tests that astronaut Richard Truly performed on the arm went very well. The motions expected were observed. When Truly was using the backup system to put the RMS into its cradle for storage and landing, the shoulder of the arm would not respond, a malfunction later found to be the result of a broken wire. The arm was successfully operated in both the fully automatic and the manual modes. It was to be used on future flights to handle satellites and perform other grasping tasks in the cargo bay of the shuttle (there were no plans to use the arm to grasp a load on STS 2). A camera is mounted on the arm so that astronauts have a clear view of the area in which it is working. On this flight, the camera gave views of the cargo bay and of the astronauts displaying a sign in the window of the shuttle. The reaction control system (RCS) of the shuttle was also tested. The RCS changes the orientation of the shuttle relative to Earth. Extensive testing of the system was performed.

The scientific package OSTA 1 had several goals. One rather fundamental goal was to determine whether *Columbia* could provide a stable platform for conducting Earth surveys. Other goals included testing advanced technologies and instruments in space and gathering data about Earth's resources and environment.

The shuttle imaging radar (SIR) used all of its 1,000 meters of photographic film taking pictures of the continents that passed under *Columbia*'s path. During one pass over the Sahara Desert, SIR penetrated the Selina Sand Sheet to reveal unsuspected river channels, significant geological structures, and possible Stone Age settlements. The shuttle multispectral infrared radiometer was designed to help identify rock types such as those found by the SIR.

The ocean color experiment was designed to improve Earth sensing over deep ocean areas. Areas of the East and West coasts of the United States, the Sea of Japan, and an area extending from southern Europe down the West African coast were all scanned by the instrument. Extensive cloudiness over much of the target areas resulted in data which were less useful than had been hoped.

The measurement of pollution from satellites (MAPS) experiment charted concentrations of gases in the atmosphere. The instrument recording the data was on its first spaceflight, so all the data obtained were of a new class. Data on one pass revealed that the concentration of carbon monoxide in the middle troposphere (the layer of the atmosphere nearest Earth's surface) varied from 70 parts per billion over the Americas to 140 parts per billion over the Mediterranean.

The goal of the feature identification and location experiment was to classify Earth views into those of water, vegetation, bare ground, and snow or cloud cover automatically. Such a sensor would allow Earth resources satellites to operate with much less dependence on ground control targeting. Analysis showed that the system's data acquisition logic was effective.

The night/day optical survey of lightning collected some meteorological data, especially over Africa. Since this experiment required active participation from the crew, limited data were collected.

The Heflex bioengineering test was designed as a plant growth test. Its goal was to determine the amount of water in the soil (or other growth medium) that afforded the best plant growth. In a low-gravity environment, water gathers around a seed and can even drown it. Because of the abbreviated mission, however, only limited data could be extracted. The entire package would be relaunched aboard STS 3.

Overall, the scientific experiments worked well. The Spacelab pallet provided a stable structure on which both experiments and electrical power could be mounted. The pallet had been designed for experiments requiring a broad field of view or direct exposure to the space environment.

The shuttle's return to Earth went smoothly. *Columbia* entered the atmosphere about 40 kilometers south of the desired ground track. The position was easily corrected, although the incorrect entry position caused an experiment designed to capture an infrared (heat) image of STS 2 to fail. The data would have been used to improve thermal protection systems on future space vehicles.

A series of roll maneuvers were executed during *Columbia*'s reentry to gather data on the handling capabilities of the shuttle. Several of the maneuvers were performed manually while most of the descent was handled by the computers on board. Joseph Engle took manual control of the shuttle at an altitude of about 11 kilometers, a little higher than originally planned. (The computer had not taken into account the high winds at Edwards Air Force Base.) To compensate for the wind, Engle took the craft through a tight turn and then gradually brought *Columbia* back into alignment with the computer coordinates as the spacecraft faced into the wind at an altitude of 3.6 kilometers. The autoguidance system brought the shuttle down to 530 meters, where Engle again took control and landed *Columbia* manually. A planned crosswind landing was canceled because wind speeds were too high.

The main wheels of *Columbia* touched the runway at 4:23 P.M., November 14. Forty-two minutes later, the smiling astronauts came out to greet the ground crew and inspect their spacecraft from the outside. Their pride in a job well done was evident as they addressed a crowd of reporters and space program employees several hours later. Both men were extremely pleased with *Columbia* and the way it had flown. Truly said *Columbia* was "the real hero of the mission, really a fine machine." Engle added, "You can spread the word around: We got us a good one."

As evening came, the shuttle was turned over to the ground teams from Kennedy Space Center as they began the turnaround for the next mission, which was scheduled for March 12, 1982.

Knowledge Gained

At lift-off for STS 1, shock waves from the blast of the rocket motors had bent several of *Columbia*'s fuel tank supports. A newly developed water-deluge system installed at the base of the launchpad sprayed 1.25 million liters of water into the rocket exhaust for the STS 2 launch and damped the shock wave by more than 75 percent.

Columbia handled very well upon entry into the atmosphere. A number of pitch and roll maneuvers were needed to add to the data on the handling characteristics of the shuttle. Instrument failure on STS 1 had caused all such data on that flight to be lost. Although weather conditions were less than optimal for landing, with strong winds and low visibility, the pilot experienced no handling problems. The crew's ability to stop the shuttle after 2.1 kilometers of ground roll was encouraging to engineers at NASA as they looked foward to the use of the 4.5-kilometer runway at the Kennedy Space Center.

The robot arm of the RMS performed the movements that were expected of it. Yet the failure of one movement using the backup system for putting the arm back into its cradle was a concern to Truly. This failure was found to be the result of a broken wire in the system.

The heatshield tiles sustained much less damage than they had sustained on STS 1. This improved performance was largely the result of the water which had been sprayed into the rocket blast at lift-off. In addition, some of the tiles in higher risk areas had been strengthened.

The scientific experiments gathered much useful data. The shuttle imaging radar detected several underground features in North Africa. MAPS provided new data on gaseous pollutants in the atmosphere. The Spacelab pallet proved an excellent support for the instruments and their electrical supply. *Columbia*'s maneuverability made collection of some data from the feature identification experiment possible.

Context

STS 2 came at a time when support for space exploration and experimentation was not strong. NASA's budget was tight, and other space programs were in danger of being terminated. STS 1 had been a tremendous success, but that success had not carried into the political arena, where funding originates. The shuttle was being promoted as a reusable spacecraft that could fly on a routine basis. Not everyone was convinced that it could, or should, do that. It was important that STS 2 be a successful mission.

The scientific payload performed well, and many useful data were returned. The shuttle vehicle itself also performed well, and the crew completed 90 percent of the primary goals of the mission while flying only half the time scheduled, a sure indication that STS 2 was indeed a success. The only significant failure occurred in a component (the fuel cell) that had an excellent record in space as well as in the test laboratory. Clearly, the second test flight of the space shuttle *Columbia* contributed significantly to the success of subsequent flights of the shuttles.

Bibliography

Allen, Joseph P., and Russell Martin. *Entering Space: An Astronaut's Odyssey*. New York: Stewart, Tabori and Chang, 1984. A description of a typical flight of the space shuttle, although other aspects of the exploration of space are included. Illustrated with excellent photographs.

Bond, Peter. *Heroes in Space: From Gagarin to Challenger*. Oxford: Basil Blackwell, 1987. A history of spaceflight which focuses on the astronauts and cosmonauts. Its last two chapters give details of the shuttle flights. Well written.

Cassutt, Michael. *Who's Who in Space: The First Twenty-five Years*. Boston: G. K. Hall and Co., 1987. A comprehensive biographical work covering manned spaceflight. Includes essays on programs, biographical profiles organized by nationality, a summary of all manned flights from April, 1961, to April, 1986, and a chronological log of flights. Suitable for the lay reader.

Collins, Michael. *Liftoff: The Story of America's Adventure in Space*. New York: Grove Press, 1988. A survey of the U.S. space program that includes a chapter on the space shuttle. Speculation on future flights is included. Contains many line drawings but few photographs.

Cross, Wilbur, and Susanna Cross. *Space Shuttle*. Chicago: Children's Press, 1985. A summary of the shuttle and its intended use, Mission Control, the astronauts, and the future of the shuttle program. Contains many color photographs. Written for children but suitable for adults.

Furniss, Tim. *Manned Spaceflight Log*. Rev. ed. London: Jane's Publishing Co., 1986. Contains a summary of each spaceflight from Vostok 1 in April, 1961, to Soyuz T-15 in March, 1986. Data include flight name, crew, launch site, and significant accomplishments of the mission.

National Aeronautics and Space Administration. *NASA: The First Twenty-five Years, 1958-1983*. NASA EP-182. Washington, D.C.: Government Printing Office, 1983. Highly condensed information about the space missions of the United States, including the first ten STS flights. Written for a general audience.

Time-Life Book Editors. *Life in Space*. Boston: Little, Brown and Co., 1984. Contains a pictorial as well as a written history of the first six shuttle flights. Also contains histories of the other major space programs of the United States. Includes color photographs.

Vogt, Gregory. *The Space Shuttle: Projects for Young Scientists*. New York: Franklin Watts, 1983. The goal of the author is to encourage young scientists (primarily high school students) to consider becoming involved in space research by designing a project to fly in space. Examples of successful projects are given, and steps to follow in developing the project are discussed.

Yenne, Bill. *The Encyclopedia of U.S. Spacecraft*. New York: Exeter Books, 1985, reprint 1988. Contains a section covering the first seventeen shuttle flights as well as a general description of the vehicle and its function.

Dennis R. Flentge

Cross-References

SPACE SHUTTLE MISSION 3
Columbia

Date: March 22 to March 30, 1982
Type of mission: Manned Earth-orbiting spaceflight
Country: The United States

The third test flight of the shuttle Columbia *began only one hour after its scheduled lift-off time. Although several pieces of equipment failed, the mission was highly successful: Thermal testing of the orbiter was accomplished, the remote manipulator system successfully moved a plasma diagnostics package, and several scientific experiments were monitored.*

Principal personages
JACK ROBERT LOUSMA, the commander
CHARLES GORDON FULLERTON, the pilot

Summary of the Mission

At 11:00 A.M. eastern standard time, March 22, 1982, *Columbia* began its third trip to space only one hour after its scheduled launch time. The launch followed the smoothest countdown in the brief history of the space shuttle program. For the first time, *Columbia* flew the normal shuttle launch trajectory that follows a continuous ascending line into orbit. STS 1 and STS 2 had followed a path that took them through an initial climb, a short dive, and then another climb to reach orbit. The shuttle had carried less weight during the first two flights than on the third and had had excess performance capability available in order to power it back to the Kennedy Space Center if the mission needed to be aborted during the early stages of flight. STS 3 did not have that excess performance capability available, so the normal ascent trajectory was adopted.

About four minutes into the flight, Charles Gordon Fullerton noticed that the temperature of the oil in the third auxiliary power unit (APU) was rising. After about seven minutes the temperature alarm from the APU was acknowledged, and thirty seconds later the APU was deactivated. (The auxiliary power units swivel the rocket engines during launch and operate the rudder and elevons during the return through the atmosphere, when the shuttle flies like an aircraft.) The shuttle can operate safely with only two of the APUs functioning properly. All three APUs worked well when *Columbia* returned to Earth.

As the third of four test flights of the shuttle, STS 3 was to collect much information on the shuttle itself. The development flight instrumentation, designed to inform flight engineers on exactly how *Columbia* operates under various flight conditions, was carried on this flight just as it had been on STS 1 and STS 2. The data from this equipment were collected as *Columbia* entered the atmosphere and glided to a landing in White Sands, New Mexico.

Columbia underwent passive thermal tests to determine its response to the varying temperatures found in space. Smaller objects can be tested in Earth-based laboratories which simulate space conditions, but the size of the shuttle does not allow for such testing on the ground. The tail was aimed at the Sun for thirty hours, the nose for eighty hours, and the cargo bay for twenty-six hours. The entire shuttle was rotated like a rotisserie (a maneuver known as the barbecue mode) for ten hours. *Columbia* demonstrated that it could tolerate the extremes of space well. The only difficulty came after the cargo bay doors had been on the dark, cold side of the shuttle. The doors could not be closed because of a frozen latch. When the shuttle was rolled over and the doors were heated by the Sun, the latch worked well and the doors closed securely.

The maneuvering and attitude thrusters were successfully fired after long "cold soaks." (A cold soak is an extended period of time during which an object is exposed to low temperatures.) The temperatures on the surface of *Columbia* ranged from +93 degrees Celsius to −66 degrees Celsius. The engines tested were responsible for final insertion of the shuttle into orbit, for adjusting orbits, and for slowing the shuttle for return to Earth.

The remote manipulator system (RMS) had received limited testing on the abbreviated STS 2 flight. The robot arm, manufactured in Toronto and called the Canada arm by some, was first scheduled for several hours of testing without a load. In the initial testing, the astronauts met all of their objectives, and the RMS worked very well. Yet during this session, six data acquisition cameras, the arm's wrist camera, and the aft starboard payload bay camera failed. Without the wrist camera and the payload bay camera, the larger of the two payload packages to be handled could not be grasped. Although manipulating the 360-kilogram contamination monitor would have been a better test of the arm's capabilities, the 160-kilogram plasma diagnostics package (PDP) provided a good load for the arm to handle.

The reaction of the arm was minimal when the orbiter's primary thrusters were fired. In the most severe conditions of this test, the arm was fully extended above the cargo bay with the PDP on the end. Firing the roll jet caused a motion of less than thirty centimeters, which dissipated quickly. Replacing the PDP into its Spacelab pallet retention mechanism was expected to be difficult: about thirty minutes were allocated to complete the task. The actual task required only five minutes.

A Get-Away Special payload canister made its first trip into space on STS 3. Experiments sent to space in these canisters must be entirely self-contained, except for a switch that activates them. The first experiment measured temperature, vibration, noise, and pressure continuously through launch and at ten-minute intervals during the entire flight.

The OSS 1 scientific payload prepared by NASA's Office of Space Science and Applications (for which it is named) contained nine experiments. Some of the experiments provided data for immediate use while some were so-called pathfinder experiments for more detailed studies to be conducted on future flights. Four of the experiments dealt with the environment surrounding the orbiter. The induced environment contamination package was a set of ten instruments that sampled whatever pollution *Columbia* generated. The shuttle induced atmosphere package studied the effects of gases and vapors on the optical quality of the space near the orbiter.

The plasma diagnostics package measured the characteristics of the rarefied gases in space. It measured the electric and magnetic fields within 13.7 meters of the orbiter. The vehicle charging and potential experiment was designed to indicate whether the shuttle builds static charges as it sweeps through space.

Experiments in space require protection from the temperature extremes found there. The thermal canister was a sophisticated array of heat pipes designed to heat and cool instruments without moving parts. Heat pipes are long, narrow chambers with internal fluids and wicking that pump heat from one location to another. Results from this experiment would contribute to the thermal design of future instruments.

Two experiments studied the Sun. The X-ray polarimeter studied X rays emitted during solar flare activity on the Sun. These data aid astronomers in determining how flares develop. The second experiment studied the ultraviolet radiation emitted from the Sun. Yet an instrument malfunction limited the data collected. The overall goal of the experiment was to study the ultraviolet radiation during an eleven-year sunspot cycle. A correlation of ultraviolet radiation intensity and long-term climate changes on Earth is of great interest to scientists.

The last of the OSS 1 experiments studied the effects of low gravity on the production of lignin in plants. Lignin is a polymer that provides strength for plants to grow upward against the pull of gravity. While it is essential for plant growth, it can interfere with the extraction of wood fibers that make paper and chemical cellulose. Analysis of the plants for lignin was completed soon after STS 3 returned to Earth. It was hoped that the data would help in utilizing Earth resources in the future.

Sheets of aluminum foil bonded to Kapton plastic created an instrument to study micrometeorites passing the spacecraft. Analysis of the craters and residues left on the foil would provide information about the number of micrometeorites in the region just above Earth's atmosphere.

A small-scale manufacturing experiment produced 20-micron monodisperse (identical size) polystyrene latex microspheres. (One micron is one-millionth of 1 meter.) These microspheres are useful in medical research.

Electrophoresis is a process that uses an electrical charge to separate cells. On Earth, gravity causes the cells to settle out of the mixture, and separation is not easily accomplished. The cells separated quickly in the low-gravity environment of the shuttle, but the samples were ruined when a storage freezer failed.

The Heflex bioengineering test (HBT) had first flown into space on STS 2. Yet the shortened mission had caused the experiment to fail. Dwarf sunflower seeds were planted in pots with varying amounts of moisture in the growth medium. Analysis of the experiment was based on the amount of growth measured in the plants compared to the amount of growth measured in plants grown on Earth using the same moisture conditions. In low gravity, moisture gathers around the seeds and can drown them. The goal of the experiment was to determine the amount of soil moisture that promotes the best plant growth. These data would be used in later Heflex experiments carried on Spacelab 1.

Along with the varied experiments developed by professional scientists for STS 3 was an experiment developed by Todd Nelson, an eighteen-year-old senior from Southland Public School in Adams, Minnesota. Nelson was one of ten finalists in the first national Shuttle Student Involvement Project (SSIP). SSIP was cosponsored by NASA and the National Science Teachers Association (NSTA) and was intended to stimulate the study of science and technology in the nation's secondary schools by providing access to research on the space shuttle. Nelson's experiment, the insects in flight motion study, was to examine the effects of a low-gravity environment on the flying activities of the velvet bean caterpillar moth, the housefly larva, and adult honeybee workers. After several days in space, most of the insects walked on the chamber walls instead of flying (or floating).

Several minor problems arose during the flight. Jack Lousma developed space-sickness, with accompanying nausea and vomiting, early in the flight. The shuttle's toilet did not function properly, causing some inconvenience to Lousma and Fullerton. In addition, there were temperature control problems in the cabin and radio static interfered with sleep. Also, the loss of three communications links on March 26 reduced data transmission to Earth but did not affect the safety of the crew. Several changes in the flightplan, however, allowed for some easing of the work load and helped the astronauts accomplish their major goals easily in spite of these setbacks.

After seven days in space, the crew was ready to come home. Yet forty minutes before the retrofire was to occur, the astronauts were told that they would have to wait. The runway at White Sands, New Mexico, was being subjected to strong winds, and visibility there was limited because of blowing sand. It was only the second time in American space history that a flight had been extended. On March 30, Lousma and Fullerton brought *Columbia* safely home. During the descent, the shuttle was taken through a set of maneuvers to provide the engineers with more data to use in analyzing the flight capabilities of the shuttle.

Touchdown occurred at 11:04 A.M., 8 days and 4 minutes after lift-off and after a journey of almost 5,400,000 kilometers. The mission had accomplished its goals, and, apart from a few minor problems, the shuttle had performed beautifully. NASA had taken another step toward bringing the space shuttle into routine operation.

Knowledge Gained

STS 3 was the first shuttle flight to be launched on its scheduled date, with only a one-hour delay during the late stages of the countdown. The date of March 22, 1982, was announced on November 14, 1981, shortly after *Columbia* had landed from its second mission. Knowledge gained in making the seven-month turnaround between STS 1 and STS 2 had been applied in preparation for STS 3. The turnaround time from STS 2 to STS 3 was 114 days. Additional knowledge and skills in handling the shuttle would result in a turnaround time of 78 days between the end of STS 3 and the start of STS 4.

Thermal testing of the shuttle showed that the engineering design and materials withstood the temperature extremes of space very well. The failure of the cargo bays to latch properly after a cold soak was easily corrected by exposure of the doors to the Sun. Engineers did, however, check the system when it returned so that improvements could be made that would eliminate the problem. The shuttle's orbital maneuvering system (OMS) engines worked well after extended cold soaks. The tests had simulated the worst-case conditions for starting the OMS engines in orbit.

The autoguidance system was given a test as *Columbia* neared the runway at White Sands. Lousma switched control of the shuttle to the autoguidance system at an altitude of 3,700 meters and allowed the system to control *Columbia* down to an altitude of less than 40 meters. He then landed the shuttle manually. Lousma later commented, "I never felt like I was going to have to take it over," when describing the autoguidance system's performance.

The OSS 1 scientific package brought back information that sent the scientists to their laboratories to prepare for future experiments in space. Although the samples from the electrophoresis experiment were ruined, the performance of the instruments in space had been successful; thus, an OSS experiment would fly on STS 4. Eventually, the electrophoresis work would develop sufficiently to have a mission specialist dedicated to the electrophoretic work as part of the crew on the twelfth space shuttle mission. Manufacture of monodisperse polystyrene latex microspheres on STS 3 also demonstrated the viability of materials processing in space.

An unexpected discovery came when the astronauts photographed the shuttle glowing in the dark. They were using high-speed film and long exposures in their effort to photograph an electron beam being used in the vehicle charging experiment. The glow was not discovered until the film was processed on Earth. The glow could present problems for future experiments that require detection of very low intensity radiation.

The RMS worked especially well. It handled the plasma diagnostics package effectively and performed much as it had in its tests on Earth. The failure of some television cameras meant that testing the heavier load had to be postponed until a later mission, but this failure was not expected to affect future mission plans significantly.

Context

The third test flight of *Columbia* was successful from almost all perspectives. For the first time, the shuttle launch occurred on the originally scheduled date. Its experimental payload collected large quantities of useful data. Initial steps toward materials processing succeeded, and the electrophoresis experiment laid the groundwork for experiments that would repeatedly ride the shuttle. The first experiment designed by a high school student was used on the flight and generated good data.

NASA was still in the process of convincing the U.S. Congress that the shuttle was a workable, economical space vehicle. Preparation time for the shuttle work crews had dropped from 750 calender days for STS 1 to 198 for STS 2 and to 114 for STS 3. (The preparation time would be cut to 78 calendar days for STS 4.) A launch on the appointed day and the success of the seven-day mission were crucial to gaining acceptance for the program.

The problems that arose during the mission were minor and had no effect on the accomplishments of the crew and the shuttle. Although the press discussed difficulties such as unreliable radios, faulty television cameras, and the malfunctioning toilet rather than the successes of the mission, when the mission was completed the accomplishments were readily evident. Even before the flight, public interest was turning toward the shuttle. In fact, the largest crowd since the Apollo lunar missions had gathered at the Cape to watch *Columbia* climb into the sky for the third time. There was good reason for NASA to be gaining confidence as it prepared for STS 4, which would be the last test flight for *Columbia*.

Bibliography

Allen, Joseph P., and Russell Martin. *Entering Space: An Astronaut's Odyssey*. New York: Stewart, Tabori and Chang, 1984. This book describes a typical space shuttle flight in addition to other aspects of space exploration. Includes excellent illustrations. Intended for a general, nontechnical audience.

Bond, Peter. *Heroes in Space: From Gagarin to Challenger*. Oxford: Basil Blackwell, 1987. This historical overview of spaceflight covers the various missions up to the January, 1986, *Challenger* explosion. Its focus is on the astronauts and cosmonauts who risk their lives in space. The last two chapters provide details on shuttle flights. This well-written text is suitable for the lay reader.

Cassutt, Michael. *Who's Who in Space: The First Twenty-five Years*. Boston: G. K. Hall and Co., 1987. A comprehensive work covering manned spaceflight, this book includes essays on various programs, biographical sketches organized by nation, and capsule summaries of all manned flights from April, 1961, to April, 1986.

Cross, Wilbur, and Susanna Cross. *Space Shuttle*. Chicago: Children's Press, 1985. Although intended for children, this book is also suitable for adult readers. A summary of the shuttle and its many uses, it focuses on Mission Control, astronauts, and the future of the space program. Includes color photographs.

Furniss, Tim. *Manned Spaceflight Log*. Rev. ed. London: Jane's Publishing Co., 1986. Informative summaries of each manned spaceflight from Vostok 1 to Soyuz T-15. The information includes crew members, launch sites, and the significant accomplishments of each mission.

Hitchcock, Barbara, ed. *Sightseeing: A Space Panorama*. New York: Alfred A. Knopf, 1985. An excellent collection of eighty-four photographs from the NASA archives. The editor selected the photographs that she believed would best communicate the beauty of space.

National Aeronautics and Space Administration. *NASA: The First Twenty-five Years,*

1958-1983. NASA EP-182. Washington, D.C.: Government Printing Office, 1983. This slick booklet contains highly condensed information on the space missions NASA has undertaken from 1958 to 1983. Included are photographs and short entries on the first ten space shuttle flights.

Time-Life Book Editors. *Life in Space*. Boston: Little, Brown and Co., 1984. In addition to general coverage of other major U.S. spaceflights, this book details the first six space shuttle missions. Illustrated.

Vogt, Gregory. *The Space Shuttle: Projects for Young Scientists*. New York: Franklin Watts, 1983. In keeping with the goal of encouraging high school students to become involved in the exploration of space, this book provides examples of successful experiments designed by students. Step-by-step project development is discussed.

Yenne, Bill. *The Encyclopedia of U.S. Spacecraft*. New York: Exeter Books, 1985, reprint 1988. The section on the space shuttle covers the first seventeen flights. Includes a general description of the vehicle and its many functions. Suitable for the lay reader.

Dennis R. Flentge

Cross-References

Astronauts and the U.S. Astronaut Program, 154; Biological Effects of Space Travel on Humans, 188; Cape Canaveral and the Kennedy Space Center, 229; The Get-Away Special Experiments, 550; Johnson Space Center, 669; U.S. Launch Vehicles, 749; Materials Processing in Space, 933; The National Aeronautics and Space Administration, 1032; The U.S. Space Shuttle, 1626; Space Shuttle Living Conditions, 1634; The Space Shuttle Test Flights: *Enterprise*, 1641; Space Shuttle Mission 1: *Columbia*, 1648; Space Shuttle Mission 2: *Columbia*, 1657; Space Shuttle Mission 4: *Columbia*, 1670; Spaceplanes, 1912.

SPACE SHUTTLE MISSION 4
Columbia

Date: June 27 to July 4, 1982
Type of mission: Space shuttle orbital flight test
Country: The United States

Space Transportation System 4 was the last of four orbital flight tests that demonstrated the space shuttle's capabilities. It also carried the first military payload for the shuttle program and several other important secondary payloads.

   Principal personages
      DONALD K. (DEKE) SLAYTON, Manager, Orbital Flight Test
         Program
      THOMAS K. (KEN) MATTINGLY, the mission commander
      HENRY W. HARTSFIELD, the mission pilot
      DAVID YOEL, the Get-Away Special integration manager,
         University of Utah

Summary of the Mission

   The space shuttle Orbital Flight Test (OFT) program initially comprised about six flights, but shortly before the program started two of those flights were eliminated from the plan. The primary objective of the fourth OFT (which, like the previous three, used the spacecraft *Columbia*) was to put the shuttle through the harshest conditions it could endure in routine operations. The flight would test the remote manipulator system (RMS), fly with portions of the spacecraft aimed at space to test the "cold-case" attitude, measure contaminants around the spacecraft with a monitor, measure spacecraft reactions through a package of development flight instrumentation (DFI) designed to measure vehicle responses to flight, and, by way of an induced environmental contamination monitor (IECM), determine whether the shuttle polluted its own environment.

   Medium-size payloads were also flown starting with Space Transportation System (STS) 2 to test the shuttle as an experiment platform. The payload for STS 4 was not selected until after the OFT program started and was ultimately given to the United States Air Force, a major user of the shuttle. Officially, the payload was known only as DOD 82-1 (meaning the first Department of Defense payload in fiscal year 1982), and the Air Force sought to keep all details classified. This decision, however, was not made until after a number of professional papers had been released by scientists working on the program, and several news agencies were able to piece together what was generally conceded to be an accurate portrait of the payload. In addition, the shuttle carried the first Get-Away Special payload and the first major materials science experiments for the shuttle program. Operation of these payloads was considered secondary, although DOD 82-1 was designed to quantify the shuttle environment for that agency's prospective users and to provide its managers with actual mission experience.

Launch originally was scheduled for early 1982 but was postponed several times because of difficulties in the preceding shuttle missions. It was finally scheduled for June 27, 1982, with the landing to take place on July 4. Launch was almost postponed one more time when a freak storm pelted Kennedy Space Center with rain and hail, but a quick survey of the shuttle revealed no major damage. The heatshield tiles, however, were found to have four hundred small dents and were calculated to have absorbed some 200 kilograms of water. The heatshield tiles are coated with a commercial waterproofing agent to prevent water absorption, but the pits created new openings. Although the water would not impair the mission, engineers were concerned that the water would boil out during reentry and crack tile surfaces open, requiring extensive replacement after the flight. It was decided to proceed with the mission and to dissipate the water by pointing the belly of *Columbia* at the sun for an extended period of time. The small pits in the tiles were repaired by applying a slurry of ground tile by hand. This was completed an hour before propellant loading started.

The *Columbia* was launched at 11:00 A.M. eastern daylight time, June 27, 1982. The ascent trajectory was some 2,500 meters too low one minute into the flight because of a slightly lower-than-normal impulse from the twin solid-fueled rocket boosters. The trajectories on STS 1 and STS 2 had experienced some "lofting" when the boosters burned hotter than planned, so the trajectories of STS 3 and STS 4 were adjusted downward. This depression delayed milestones in the remainder of the ascent by as much as 15 seconds, and the main engines had to burn 2 seconds longer than planned to compensate. (This would have cost 900 kilograms of payload in a fully loaded flight.) In addition, there was a problem unrelated to the low trajectory: The two boosters were lost during recovery. Their parachutes deployed late and were still partially reefed when they struck the water at 549 kilometers per hour, causing their casings to spring and allowing them to leak and sink.

The two maneuvering engines were fired to insert *Columbia* into its final orbit, the first raising its orbit to 62 by 241 kilometers and the second circularizing it at 241 kilometers. The craft initially went into the "gravity-gradient" attitude, with its tail pointed to Earth, in order to allow the DOD 82-1 payload to scan the horizon, but *Columbia* developed a tendency to drift out of position. This behavior was later attributed to the slight motion of the shuttle as water evaporated from its tiles. A third engine firing of 17 seconds on July 1 raised the orbit to 299 by 316 kilometers to set up the entry trajectory for specific tests.

During the flight, the mission commander, Thomas K. Mattingly, and the pilot, Henry W. Hartsfield, continued experiments started on the STS 1, 2, and 3 missions. Each flight carried the shuttle through a series of more rigorous environmental tests. Where STS 3 had conducted "hot-case" tests, STS 4 conducted "cold-case" experiments, exposing selected portions of the shuttle to deep space for extended periods to determine the effects of such exposure. These were accomplished by flying in various positions such that the nose and payload bay would be shaded from the Sun. (The direction a spacecraft points is immaterial, except when a certain orientation is necessary to expose solar cells to the Sun and direct telescopes at targets, among other things.) The bottom of the spacecraft was exposed to the Sun for 33 hours in order to evaporate water that had been absorbed in the preflight hailstorm. National Aeronautics and Space Administration (NASA) officials announced that a mass spectrometer verified that the evaporation was working as planned, but NASA did not reveal that the data came from the Air Force mass spectrometer.

One result of extended cold-case testing was that the payload bay doors became misaligned and would not close. The orbiter apparently had warped slightly from uneven heating, an expected effect. Rotating the shuttle for several minutes, like a barbecue, evened the heat distribution and allowed the doors to close. Another test measured how long hydraulic fluid could be left static in its lines without periodic warming for recirculation; that would affect how much electrical power had to be reserved for spacecraft housekeeping.

Four thrusters had to be turned off on the first day when one developed a leak, but there were enough backup thrusters so that this was no real problem. The thrusters were turned on later in the mission and did not malfunction again.

Payload operations probably were similar to those of STS 3 in many respects, since the crew was operating a similar suite of plasma physics instruments. Payload control, in this case, was the U.S. Air Force Satellite Control Facility in Sunnyvale, California. The Big Blue Cube, as it is known, served as mission control for several classified Air Force satellite projects. The 82-1 payload was comparable in size and capability to the single-pallet Spacelab payloads carried on STS 2 and STS 3, although a different experiment support structure (ESS) was used. This one was made up mainly of large tubing that held a boxlike structure with standard mounting points for instruments. These instruments included cryogenic infrared radiance instrumentation for the shuttle (CIRRIS), the horizon ultraviolet program (HUP), the space experiments with plasmas in space (SEPS), the sheath and wake charging (SWC) experiments, a solar coronagraph, and an autonomous navigational aid called a space sextant. The payload's mass was 11,021 kilograms.

CIRRIS 1 was a liquid-helium-cooled, 15.2-centimeter telescope sensitive to the 2.5-to-25-micron spectral range of the infrared spectrum. Its objective was to provide fine-resolution spectral data on the constituents of the upper atmosphere by scanning Earth's limb (horizon) from a 30-to-300-kilometer altitude. It was mounted in a single-axis gimbal, allowing it to slew along the shuttle orbiter's nose-to-tail axis. CIRRIS 1 carried a low-power laser to illuminate (as a reference point) the portion of the atmosphere being surveyed. HUP had a similar objective but was designed as a smaller instrument since it did not have to be cooled to cover the ultraviolet spectrum from 110 nanometers (short wavelength) to 400 nanometers (the edge of visible, violet light). Together, these two instruments were part of a larger military program conceived to understand the space environment as it affects sensors used in a variety of spacecraft and what could be expected when observing targets near the horizon and in deep space.

The plasma instruments in the SEPS/SWC configuration, and the solar coronagraph, were designed to study the space environment. SEPS/SWC included ion and neutral mass spectrometers to analyze the environment directly and plasma probes of various types to measure electrical charging effects that might hamper experiments. The coronagraph was used as a means of photographing particles near the shuttle by "back-lighting" with sunlight. This would provide a measure of particulate contamination around the craft.

The space sextant received its field test on the *Columbia*. With two telescopes operating like a mariner's handheld sextant, it would fix a spacecraft's position to within 250 meters and its attitude to within 0.5 degree, without the need for contact with the ground.

For both HUP and the CIRRIS telescope, *Columbia* needed to fly in gravity-gradient mode so the two instruments could scan the horizon and measure light being filtered through them at various angles. News reports during and after the mission alleged that the lid on CIRRIS never opened, despite repeated attempts to pry it open with the remote manipulator system. NASA considered having Mattingly or Hartsfield perform a contingency extravehicular activity (EVA) to pry it open manually but ruled that out for safety reasons. After a few days, the question was moot, as the helium coolant had finally evaporated from its container.

Orientation toward Earth was also used for the night/day observations from space of lightning (NOSL) experiment, which used a modified Bolex motion picture camera with a special light sensor to observe lightning from above the cloud tops. The sensor turned the flash produced from lightning, which includes infrared signals, into an audio cue so the crewman would know when to run the camera. The crew also took a number of photographs from the aft payload bay windows using a 35-millimeter film camera equipped with an image intensifier in an attempt to collect data that would aid in an understanding of the shuttle glow phenomenon observed on STS 3.

Also, during the flight the crew performed the first operations on two promising materials processing facilities, the continuous flow electrophoresis system (CFES) and the monodisperse latex reactor (MLR), both located in the middeck for crew operation.

CFES was designed to separate biological materials by setting up an electrical field at right angles to the flow of a buffer solution containing cells or proteins and enzymes. As the buffer flows through the chamber, the field pulls with different strengths on the components, and they separate according to mass and charge. The technique is limited on Earth because the electric field also heats the fluid and causes convection currents which remix the separated components.

The MLR carried chemical reactors used to heat and mix styrene solutions that would form microspheres of one size, depending on ingredients and conditions. The microspheres are used for calibrating electron microscopes, filters, and pores in cells, among other things. Their size is limited, as larger microspheres become buoyant and will form a sort of cream on the surface.

The Get-Away Special experiment was the first of its kind to be carried by a shuttle. It had been purchased for use by students at Utah State University, the University of Utah, and other colleges in the state. GAS 1, as this one was known, included experiments on seed germination, brine shrimp growth, composite curing, oil-water mixing, soldering, fruit fly growth, and metals alloying. Unfortunately, GAS 1 could not be activated after repeated attempts. Although it would be flown again, its failure on STS 4 frustrated the students who had built it. After analyzing possible problems, NASA finally gave the crew permission to hot-wire a section of shielded cabling going into the payload bay, and an "on" signal was received on the flight deck. To protect the biology experiments, power was left on until after landing rather than being shut down in flight.

A remote manipulator system, first flown on STS 2, was used again on STS 4. This time it picked up the 394-kilogram induced-environment contamination monitor and held it at 92 programmed "pause and flyby points," where it collected samples and analyzed the environment for postflight study. Stereo cameras photographed dust floating in the region. The handling of the monitor also provided data on how it behaves when loaded.

Reentry was scheduled for July 4, with the shuttle landing at Edwards Air Force Base, where President Ronald Reagan and his wife, Nancy Reagan, would be watching. The angle of attack at entry was 40 degrees, a few degrees higher than most missions would use, in order to generate new data. *Columbia* also flew one of the greatest cross-range entries, 930 kilometers. The crew engaged the automatic landing system at an altitude of 3 kilometers, returning to manual controls at an altitude of 600 meters to allow sufficient time to regain full control and drop the landing gear. Touchdown occurred at 3:09 A.M., Pacific daylight time, at Edwards, the first hard-surface landing for the shuttle.

Knowledge Gained

Much of what was learned from the STS 4 mission was in the form of engineering data, since this was the last of four missions intended to clear the shuttle for routine operations. The mission established a modest set of boundaries within which the vehicle could safely operate. All systems were validated and shown to operate as designed despite a number of minor problems, the most serious being the loss of the boosters. Postflight studies showed that the same defect existed in all four booster sets flown by NASA; STS 4 was simply the first to fly in hot weather, which aggravated the boosters' malfunction. Oil in an altimeter that activated the parachute release system was more fluid in the summer, altering its operation to give a false reading of a higher altitude and delaying parachute deployment. Earlier flights had taken place in cooler weather, which causes the oil to be more viscous.

Some orbiter systems had minor problems. The low-thrust vernier reaction control system thrusters had to be replaced when two showed abnormally high wear on a thermal protection coating. The payload bay liner showed minor discolorations and deposits that required its replacement so that the cleanliness of future payloads would not be compromised. The remote manipulator arm, however, functioned with precision when commanded to carry a payload (the contamination monitor) to a number of programmed points.

The contamination monitor recorded no exhaust from the solid-fueled rocket boosters (which spew aluminum oxide and hydrochloric acid) but did record water vapor as the main contaminant in orbit. The vapor largely came from the heatshield as it was baked out and from thruster firings (for which it is one of several exhaust products). One set of measurements recorded pollutant patterns around the payload bay, but a second set, showing thruster exhaust pressures, was lost as a result of electrical problems.

For the most part, the materials science experiments proceeded as planned. The CFES separated human liver and kidney cells in the first run and rat and egg albumins in the second; each lasted about seven hours. McDonnell Douglas, the developer of the CFES, claimed that the system produced high-purity samples with a density 463 times greater than what could be produced by similar systems on Earth.

The MLR produced quantities of latex microspheres of great uniformity in two of four reactors. About 55 percent of the chemicals reacted as planned, forming batches of microspheres 7.9 and 10.8 microns wide, double the sizes of their seeds. These were later used as seeds for experiments on growing even larger microspheres on later flights.

The Get-Away Special experiment did not function. Although it was activated and the computer ran, no data were recorded because the tape recorder failed. It apparently had been dropped and damaged during integration before the flight. Most of the other experiments failed as well. Some were found to have blown fuses or lost batteries before launch, and some were frozen by the extended bottom-sun attitude, which caused payload temperatures to drop lower than anticipated.

The NOSL experiment produced several minutes of film showing lightning from above the cloud tops. Results from the Air Force instruments were largely classified. The handheld photography of the shuttle glow effect returned a number of photographs of the tail surfaces of the shuttle glowing at night. The photographs were partially censored to prevent the Air Force payload from being seen.

Context

STS 4 confirmed the space shuttle's capability to operate as a reusable spacecraft. That the system was maturing was evidenced by the fact that the management team conducting the T minus 2-day flight readiness review had only nits and other small items to handle; there were no major issues (the rainstorm came the night before launch).

The long bottom-sun attitude confirmed that the shuttle indeed warps slightly with uneven heating. Although the effect was observed on STS 3 during top-sun studies, some engineers had believed that foreign matter had been jamming the doors. With the flight of STS 4, the heat-warping theory was proved. The solution in any event was the same: The orbiter is slowly rolled for 15 minutes to even out the heat load. This procedure is now standard in pre-entry preparation.

The failure of the Get-Away Special experiment demonstrated that even though the program may seem amateur to NASA, it still required as much careful handling and testing as any "professional" experiment in order to work properly in space. More important, the experience gained by the students showed it to be a valuable tool for educating students about careers in space. GAS 1 also set the pattern for many of these payloads to be purchased by civic and professional groups and given to students.

The CFES purification runs confirmed that the absence of gravity's effects would eliminate convective flow caused by electrical currents. In like manner, the MLR showed that a commercially salable material could be manufactured in space, although the value had to be high to justify the small quantities that could be accommodated.

Data from the shuttle glow photography were somewhat inconclusive but showed the need for further investigation. The spectral grating over the camera lens showed that the shuttle glow phenomenon grows stronger toward the infrared end of the spectrum. The shuttle windows, however, are designed with a strong infrared cutoff to prevent sunlight entering the windows from overloading the environmental system. Thus, the photographs were cut off just at the point where they may have supplied useful data. They did, however, reveal that the glow was brightest on the "ram" side, where the exposed surfaces of the shuttle struck the thin upper atmosphere.

Bibliography

Baker, David. *The History of Manned Space Flight*. New York: Crown Publishers, 1982, rev. ed. 1985. A comprehensive history of manned missions, this large volume is generously illustrated. It offers the beginner an overview of human spaceflight and includes a helpful index.

Covault, Craig. "Shuttle Gears Towards Operational Era." *Aviation Week and Space Technology* 117 (July 5, 1982): 18-19. Detailed article highlighting operational aspects of the STS 4 mission. Written for those familiar with spaceflight.

Dooling, Dave. "Space Shuttle Columbia Passes Its Final Exam." *Space World*. 5-10-226 (October, 1982): 10-13. General article on the STS 4 mission with day-by-day summaries of activities. Written for the educated reader with an interest in space.

_____ . "USAF Cargo for Space Shuttle." *Space World*. 5-6-222 (June/July, 1982): 9-11. Provides overview of U.S. Air Force plans for payloads to fly aboard the space shuttle.

Yenne, Bill. *The Encyclopedia of U.S. Spacecraft*. New York: Exeter Books, 1985, reprint 1988. Offers an overview of the nature and function of the space shuttles. Intended for the lay reader, this volume is well illustrated.

Dave Dooling

Cross-References

The Get-Away Special Experiments, 550; The U.S. Space Shuttle, 1626; Space Shuttle Mission 1: *Columbia*, 1648; Space Shuttle Mission 2: *Columbia*, 1657; Space Shuttle Mission 3: *Columbia*, 1663; Spacewatch: Tracking Space Debris, 1924.

SPACE SHUTTLE MISSION 5
Columbia

Date: November 11 to November 16, 1982
Type of mission: Manned Earth-orbiting spaceflight
Country: The United States

The fifth flight of Columbia *was the first operational flight of the shuttle and the first flight to carry mission specialists. Two communications satellites were successfully launched, but the planned extravehicular activity had to be canceled because of faulty spacesuits.*

Principal personages
VANCE DEVOE BRAND, the commander
ROBERT FRANKLYN OVERMYER, the pilot
WILLIAM BENJAMIN LENOIR and
JOSEPH PERCIVAL ALLEN, mission specialists

Summary of the Mission

After four very successful test flights of the space shuttle *Columbia*, the National Aeronautics and Space Administration (NASA) had high hopes for the first commercial flight of *Columbia*. The mission carried the first two satellites to be launched into orbit from the space shuttle (rather than from Earth using an expendable booster). Also aboard STS 5 were three experiments designed by high school students, a Get-Away Special sponsored by West Germany, and more engineering tests on the shuttle's performance.

This flight also marked the first time that four astronauts were launched into space simultaneously. It was also the first flight for a new type of astronaut—the mission specialist. Mission specialists are trained in satellite deployment, payload support, extravehicular activity (EVA, or walking in space), and operation of the remote manipulator system (RMS). (The RMS was not used on this flight.)

The countdown for the November 11 launch proceeded exceptionally well despite a few setbacks. Two power supplies failed, a backup helium regulator developed a leak, and the prime radar altimeter failed during a built-in self-test. The power supplies were repaired, and the altimeter was replaced. Since the leak in the helium regulator was small and would not be a problem during the launch, the system was deactivated. None of these difficulties affected the launch time, and STS 5 began at 7:19 A.M., November 11, 1982.

Ascent to orbit went smoothly. The solid-fueled rocket boosters had not performed as well as expected on STS 4, so the method for projecting their power output was revised for STS 5. The revised value for performance was lower than the original value, so the computer program that controlled the throttle on the main engines had to be changed to compensate for the lower output. Even with the revised estimate of burn rate, the rocket boosters did not perform up to expectations, and the main engines had to carry the extra load necessary for boosting *Columbia* into a 296-kilometer circular orbit.

One of the most important tasks was the deployment of the two satellites. The SBS 3 communications spacecraft owned by Satellite Business Systems (SBS) was scheduled to be deployed by astronauts Joseph Allen and William Lenoir on the sixth orbit, approximately eight hours after lift-off. During the six hours that preceded the launch of the satellite, the altitude, velocity, inclination, and other information about the orbital path of the shuttle were sent to the SBS control center in Washington, D.C., which in turn sent refined information to the shuttle about the exact time and location for insertion of the satellite into orbit.

As deployment time approached, the shuttle was oriented so that its right wing pointed toward Earth and its payload bay doors faced away from its orbital direction. Then the thermal shield of the satellite was opened, and a turntable was spun to give SBS 3 a fifty-revolution-per-minute spin. This spin stabilizes a satellite and keeps it from tumbling randomly in space. It also helps to keep the temperature on all the surfaces of the satellite relatively constant. Finally, at 3:17 P.M. explosive bolts which were holding down a powerful spring were fired, and SBS 3 was launched from the shuttle at a speed of about one meter per second. The shuttle then turned its well-protected underside toward the satellite and changed its orbit slightly. The satellite was now under the control of SBS, not the crew of the *Columbia*.

Forty-five minutes later, the Payload Assist Module's solid rocket motor was fired, and SBS 3 was carried into a highly elliptical orbit. On November 13, the satellite's apogee kick motor was fired, putting SBS 3 into a circular geosynchronous orbit. In such an orbit, the satellite appears stationary relative to Earth's surface.

The second satellite, Canada's Anik/Telesat, was successfully deployed using the same technique on November 12. Astronaut Allen reported to Earth, "Two for two. We deliver." The crew posed for a picture during a public telecast and displayed a sign: "Ace Moving Co. We deliver. Fast and courteous service."

Although satellite deployment was among the more visible tasks undertaken during the flight, there were other experiments that yielded valuable data. There were three Shuttle Student Involvement Project (SSIP) experiments conducted on STS 5. The primary goal of SSIP, a program cosponsored by NASA and the National Science Teachers Association, was to encourage talented young people to become involved in scientific research in space and ultimately to become scientists and engineers.

D. Scott Thomas of Johnstown, Pennsylvania, designed an experiment to study surface tension convection. Surface tension is often described in terms of the "skin" on the surface of a liquid. For example, a needle will float on water (if placed there carefully) as a result of surface tension. Convection is a circulation pattern in a heated fluid. Large-scale convection currents in Earth's atmosphere give rise to wind as warm air rises and cool air moves under it to take its place. A liquid such as oil will exhibit the convection currents when heated. Near Earth's surface, the effects of gravitational convection make it very difficult to observe the convection that takes place on the surface, in the "skin" of the liquid. In the low-gravity environment of space, these surface effects can be more easily studied than on Earth.

Aaron K. Gilette of Winterhaven, Florida, proposed a study of the reaggregation of cells of particular sponges. In seawater on Earth, these sponge cells reassemble themselves into perfect sponges. Gilette wanted to determine if the absence of gravity would change the way in which the sponge cells performed. The reaggregation is triggered by calcium and magnesium ions. The cells were transported into space in water that had no calcium or magnesium. Once in space, the triggering ions were inserted into the solutions. Later, a substance was injected that would preserve the sponges that formed.

Michele A. Issel of Wallingford, Connecticut, designed an experiment to determine if geometrically perfect crystals of triglycine sulfate can be grown in microgravity. Gravity is thought to cause defects in crystals grown on Earth.

The Ministry of Research and Technology of West Germany purchased a Get-Away Special which studied the behavior of a molten mixture of mercury and gallium. On Earth, the mixture separates into liquid mercury and liquid gallium. The experiment used X rays to study the effects of low gravity on dispersion of mercury droplets into gallium and particle movement resulting from convection, as well as other properties of the mixture. The Get-Away Special program offers researchers the opportunity for safe, scientific, peaceful experiments to be performed in space. Each experimental unit must be entirely self-contained, except for the switch the astronauts use to activate it. Get-Away Special experiments are flown on a first-come, first-served, space-available basis.

A study of spacesickness was conducted during STS 5. Since half the crew of the first four flights suffered some degree of spacesickness, its effect on the productivity of a mission could be significant. Astronaut Allen wore electrodes that recorded his eye motion during launch, both Allen and Lenoir attached the electrodes during the time of adjustment to low gravity, and Lenoir wore them during reentry. Eye movement data provide some indication of the nervous system's adaptive reactions to a lack of gravity. Astronauts Lenoir and Robert Overmyer suffered from spacesickness, and the commander, Vance Brand, felt some discomfort. Allen was unaffected. The motion sickness caused some rearrangement of schedules for the astronauts who were performing at less than maximum capacity.

Allen and Lenoir were to participate in the first EVA of the space shuttle program. The activity was postponed from Sunday to Monday because of Lenoir's spacesickness early in the flight. Problems developed soon after the astronauts put on their spacesuits. A fan in Allen's life-support pack started to cause undue amounts of noise, and Lenoir's pack held a pressure that was more than 10 percent too low. Both suits could have been used if an EVA had been necessary for successful completion of the flight. Yet, since a spacewalk was not essential for completion of STS 5, mission managers decided to cancel the EVA. The failure in Allen's suit was apparently caused by moisture that had penetrated a seal. Lenoir's suit failed because two small plastic inserts for mounting screws had been omitted when the unit was assembled. This omission had escaped the eye of a quality control inspector.

Photographs taken on STS 3 had shown that the orbiter glowed in the dark. STS 5 studied the glow that covered the tail section, engine pods, and other shuttle features during the flight. Scientists were concerned about the effect this glow could have on faint effects measured by optical instruments mounted in the payload bay.

During reentry, a set of instruments collected more data on the handling characteristics of the shuttle and on the autoguidance system. An automatic landing using the autoguidance system had been canceled several weeks before the flight, because the system had not been giving consistent results for two craft in which it was being used. The reentry and landing on the hard-surface runway at Edwards Air Force Base went very well. In fact, the landing, which took place on November 16, was so smooth that Brand asked, "Are we on the ground yet?"

Knowledge Gained

An important goal of the mission was the successful deployment of the two satellites. The first use of the deployment equipment provided valuable information on the performance characteristics of that equipment and of the shuttle. STS 3 was released from the shuttle within 1,500 meters of its target, and Anik/Telesat within 150 meters. Both of these values were well within the margin of error which had been predicted.

Data on motion sickness was collected throughout the mission. The two astronauts studied provided the extremes of no effect (Allen) and vomiting (Lenoir). In addition, initial testing of the new spacesuits gathered valuable data for future flights. Although the spacewalk was canceled, the suits were tested in low-pressure situations and worked well.

Experiments from SSIP provided useful data about convection within the surface of a heated liquid, about the cellular communication process that causes separated sponge cells to group together to form sponges, and about crystal formation in space. The last experiment was expected to provide information useful in commercial processing of materials in space.

Data were collected that would improve the performance of the shuttle on future flights. The braking system was deliberately given a severe test after the shuttle had landed.

Context

As the flights of the shuttle *Columbia* began in April, 1981, there had been many who were skeptical about the value of a reusable space vehicle and many who believed that the goals of the shuttle program could not be achieved. STS 1 had been extremely successful. Performance of crews preparing the shuttle for its next flight improved with each fight. Launch on the scheduled day at the scheduled time was achieved. Yet, even after the four successful test flights of *Columbia*, many people were not committed to the shuttle program. Even President Ronald Reagan had not become an enthusiastic supporter of the program.

STS 5 was probably the most significant manned spaceflight for the United States (and for NASA) since the landing of men on the Moon in 1969. The successful deployment of two satellites was a forceful rebuttal to the critics who had once said that no meaningful cargo would be hauled by the shuttle, that no one would buy space on it, and that it would not perform as predicted.

In spite of the importance of the mission, STS 5 passed relatively quietly. There were several reasons for its modest reception. First, there were no significant problems in the countdown, and the launch proceeded uneventfully. Second, neither the shuttle nor the crew had major difficulties during the flight. Third, shuttle flights were becoming more common, and general interest of the news media and the public was not as intense as it had been for STS 1.

Each of these factors was considered positive by NASA. The long-range goal of the shuttle program was to have a fleet of shuttles fly every two weeks. Routine, uneventful shuttle missions had to become a reality before the fleet could be built to its desired size. Clearly, STS 5 was a major step in the direction of routine shuttle flight.

Bibliography

Allen, Joseph P., and Russell Martin. *Entering Space: An Astronaut's Odyssey*. New York: Stewart, Tabori and Chang, 1984. Allen describes a typical shuttle launch, in addition to detailing other aspects of space exploration. This book includes excellent photographs and is aimed at a general, nontechnical audience.

Bond, Peter. *Heroes in Space: From Gagarin to Challenger*. Oxford: Basil Blackwell, 1987. A refreshing change from more technical overviews of the space program, this book focuses on the personal aspects of spaceflight: the men and women who risk their lives in space. Biographical profiles of astronauts and cosmonauts, as well as essays on space programs and a summary of all manned spaceflight from 1961 to the spring of 1986.

Cross, Wilbur, and Susanna Cross. *Space Shuttle*. Chicago: Children's Press, 1985. An informative summary of the shuttle vehicles, their many uses, Mission Control in Houston, the astronauts who fly the vehicles, and the future of the space shuttle program. Written with children in mind, this text is also appropriate for the adult lay reader.

Furniss, Tim. *Manned Spaceflight Log*. Rev. ed. London: Jane's Publishing Co., 1986. With a summary of each of the world's manned space missions from Vostok 1 to Soyuz T-15, this reference is extremely useful. Contains information on the crew, launch sites, and accomplishments of each mission.

Hitchcock, Barbara, ed. *Sightseeing: A Space Panorama*. New York: Alfred A. Knopf, 1985. A breathtaking collection of photographs from the NASA archives, this book conveys well the special views space travel affords.

National Aeronautics and Space Administration. *NASA: The First Twenty-five Years, 1958-1983*. NASA EP-182. Washington, D.C.: Government Printing Office, 1983. A visually appealing booklet featuring capsule summaries of NASA missions. Included is information on the first ten shuttle flights. Intended for a general audience.

Time-Life Book Editors. *Life in Space*. Boston: Little, Brown and Co., 1984. Features a pictorial as well as a written history of the first six shuttle flights. Also contains information on other major spaceflights of the U.S. space program. Illustrated with color photographs.

Vogt, Gregory. *The Space Shuttle: Projects for Young Scientists*. New York: Franklin Watts, 1983. Includes step-by-step directions on developing a scientific experiment to fly in space. Although this book is intended for the high school science enthusiast, it is useful as an example of how space research has evolved to include projects designed by students.

Yenne, Bill. *The Encyclopedia of U.S. Spacecraft*. New York: Exeter Books, 1985, reprint 1988. A useful reference for all aspects of the U.S. space program. Catalogs spacecraft alphabetically. The section on the shuttle covers the first seventeen shuttle flights, with complete descriptions of the vehicles and their function.

Dennis R. Flentge

Cross-References

Astronauts and the U.S. Astronaut Program, 154; Biological Effects of Space Travel on Humans, 188; Cape Canaveral and the Kennedy Space Center, 229; U.S. Launch Vehicles, 749; Materials Processing in Space, 933; The National Aeronautics and Space Administration, 1032; International Private Industry and Space Exploration, 1182; U.S. Private Industry and Space Exploration, 1187; The U.S. Space Shuttle, 1626; Space Shuttle Living Conditions, 1634; The Space Shuttle Test Flights: *Enterprise*, 1641; Space Shuttle Mission 1: *Columbia*, 1648; Space Shuttle Mission 2: *Columbia*, 1657; Space Shuttle Mission 3: *Columbia*, 1663; Space Shuttle Mission 4: *Columbia*, 1670; Spaceplanes, 1912; The Development of Spacesuits, 1917.

SPACE SHUTTLE MISSION 6
Challenger

Date: April 4 to April 9, 1983
Type of mission: Manned Earth-orbiting spaceflight
Country: The United States

Space Transportation System mission 6, the maiden voyage of the space shuttle
Challenger, *deployed the first Tracking and Data-Relay Satellite. The extravehicular
mobility unit, used for the first time, permitted two astronauts to work in space
unencumbered by oxygen hoses and communication lines attached to their spacecraft.*

Principal personages
PAUL J. WEITZ, the mission commander
KAROL J. BOBKO, the mission pilot
F. STORY MUSGRAVE and
DONALD H. PETERSON, mission specialists

Summary of the Mission

The "shakedown cruise" of the space shuttle *Challenger*, Space Transportation
System (STS) 6 was designed to test the second orbiter in the National Aeronautics
and Space Administration (NASA) fleet and to deploy a satellite which would be
the first link in a continuous communications system for future missions. The flight
marked the first time a manned mission was flown without a flight-tested vehicle
and with no means of escape if a problem arose during launch.

The commander of STS 6 was Paul Weitz, a retired Navy captain who was
selected with the fifth group of astronauts in April, 1966. The only experienced
member of the crew to have flown in space, he had been the pilot of the 28-day
Skylab 2 mission, which was launched May 25, 1973. The STS 6 pilot was United
States Air Force colonel Karol J. Bobko. He was transferred from the Air Force's
canceled Manned Orbiting Laboratory program in September, 1969. He served in a
support capacity for the Skylab and Apollo-Soyuz programs, as well as for the
shuttle approach and landing tests.

Two mission specialists were on the flight, Dr. Story Musgrave and retired U.S.
Air Force colonel Donald Peterson. Musgrave became an astronaut in 1967, served
as backup science pilot for Skylab 2, and was the capsule communicator for the second and third Skylab missions. He participated in the design and development of all
space shuttle extravehicular activity (EVA) equipment, including life-support systems, spacesuits, air locks, and manned maneuvering units. Peterson became an astronaut in September, 1969, and served on the astronaut support crew for Apollo 16.

The major payload for the flight was the Tracking and Data-Relay Satellite
(TDRS), the largest privately owned telecommunications satellite ever built.

TDRS-A was the first of three identical spacecraft planned for the Tracking and Data-Relay Satellite System (TDRSS) to be placed into geosynchronous orbit (that is, an orbit where the satellite's velocity and altitude make it appear to hover over one spot on Earth's surface). TDRS-B would be placed into orbit by STS 8, while TDRS-C would be deployed by STS 12 and would be an in-orbit spare which could be moved to replace either of the other satellites.

The two operational satellites would be in orbit 130 degrees apart to permit the use of a single ground station (located in New Mexico), instead of the two needed if they were 180 degrees apart. Initially, the TDRSS was used to support space shuttle flights, providing a communications link for about 98 percent of each orbit. Without the TDRSS, only about 30 percent of an average orbit is covered, because of the scarcity of ground tracking stations. Later, TDRSS would support other spacecraft, including Landsat and the space station *Freedom*.

Challenger, designated STA-099, was built as a static test article in 1976. It was named for the American research vessel that made extensive oceanographic cruises of the Atlantic and Pacific oceans between 1872 and 1876. Being ships of the new ocean of space, each of the orbiters was named for a famous oceangoing vessel. In addition, *Challenger* was the name of the last lunar module to land on the Moon during the Apollo 17 mission. The spacecraft are designated as orbiter vehicles, or OVs. Thus *Enterprise*, the first orbiter vehicle to be built, is designated OV-101, *Columbia* is OV-102, *Discovery* is OV-103, and *Atlantis* is OV-104. Although *Enterprise* was designated as an orbiter vehicle, it was never designed to go into space. Instead, it was used to test the gliding and landing characteristics of the orbiter's design.

Early in 1978, *Challenger* was completed and rolled out from Rockwell International's main orbiter assembly plant in Palmdale, California, to the Lockheed-California test building across the road. There, engineers bonded approximately 2,700 pads to *Challenger*'s aluminum structure so that load jacks could apply stresses which simulate the complex dynamic environment that the orbiter would experience during the different phases of flight. Stresses up to 140 percent of the design limits could be applied, but researchers limited the stress they applied to 120 percent. They wanted to test the structure and still ensure a safe margin so that *Challenger* could be used for actual space missions. In order to save the expense of building a fifth orbiter, something not provided for in NASA's budget, NASA and Rockwell agreed to move STA-099 back to its assembly bay. During 1979, modifications were made to equip it for spaceflight. On June 30, 1982, *Challenger* (redesignated OV-099) was rolled out of the Palmdale plant, transported overland to the nearby NASA Dryden Flight Research Facility at Edwards Air Force Base, loaded atop the Boeing 747 shuttle carrier aircraft, and flown to the Kennedy Space Center in Florida. STS 6 was scheduled for launch on January 27, 1983, having been stacked and rolled out to Launch Complex 39A at Kennedy Space Center in late November. Serious problems with the space shuttle main engines (SSMEs), however, delayed the launch until April, 1983.

Prior to the first flight of any orbiter, the SSMEs are qualified by means of a flight readiness firing (FRF). The three SSMEs, each providing 1,670 kilonewtons of thrust at lift-off, burn for approximately 8 minutes during launch. The FRF is a 20-second test, performed with the shuttle on the launchpad, which ensures that the SSMEs are functioning properly. The FRF also allows for a complete rehearsal of the activities leading to a launch, without involving the crew or igniting the solid-fueled rocket boosters (SRBs).

After the FRF, which took place on December 18, 1982, engineers found a high concentration of hydrogen gas near the aft end of the orbiter, where the SSMEs are located. Liquid hydrogen is the fuel for the SSMEs and the presence of the gas after the firing indicated a possible leak in one or more of the engines. A second FRF was ordered for January 26, 1983.

After this second firing, a crack was found in the hydrogen line of one of the engines. In order to fix the problem, the engine had to be replaced, causing a one-month delay. A liquid oxygen leak was discovered in the replacement engine. This delayed the launch until mid-March. In early March, cracks were found in the hydrogen lines of *Challenger*'s other two main engines. At the same time, several strong storms blew into the area, causing the TDRS to become contaminated with dust and sand. Cleaning of the satellite and repair of the engines pushed the launch date back to April 4.

On April 4, 1983, at 1:30 P.M. eastern standard time, *Challenger* was launched. The launch went flawlessly and, after two short burns of the orbital maneuvering system engines, STS 6 was safely in a circular orbit at an altitude of 265 kilometers. Preparations for the deployment of TDRS and its Inertial Upper Stage (IUS) propulsion unit were immediately begun. Ten hours after lift-off, the 22-meter-long, 17,000-kilogram combination was raised 59 degrees. Small springs gave the TDRS/IUS a gentle push and sent it on its way as *Challenger* was 2,300 kilometers east of a point above Rio de Janeiro.

The TDRS deployment plan called for the first stage of the two-stage IUS to burn for 2 minutes and 31 seconds, placing the high point of the orbit (the apogee) at 35,888 kilometers. This stage would be dropped and the second stage would burn for 1 minute and 43 seconds, circularizing the orbit at the apogee. Once in its geosynchronous orbit, *Challenger* would jettison its second stage, and TDRS would open up like an awakening butterfly.

Approximately 80 seconds into the second-stage burn, an oil-filled seal on the steering mechanism of the stage's engine deflated. This caused the engine to remain at an extreme angle and sent the spacecraft tumbling. Quick action by the controllers allowed TDRS to be separated from the IUS before the gyrations tore the spacecraft apart. TDRS was left nearly powerless, in an orbit 35,021 kilometers by 22,013 kilometers.

In the meantime, *Challenger* continued on its successful flight. On April 7, the first shuttle extravehicular activity (EVA), or spacewalk, began with Musgrave exiting the orbiter through the air lock on the lower deck at 4:21 P.M. He and Peterson had donned their extravehicular mobility units (EMUs), or spacesuits, and spent 3.5 hours in the air lock breathing oxygen to purge nitrogen from their blood. After floating out into *Challenger*'s payload bay, they attached tethers to wires running the length of the bay on either side. These would prevent the pair from accidentally drifting off into space. Handrails along the perimeter of the bay were used to travel to various workstations. All planned tasks for the EVA were successfully performed, and the EVA was completed at 8:15 P.M.

The final full day in orbit was spent stowing equipment and experiments for reentry and landing. Of the thirty test objectives scheduled for the flight, only one could not be accomplished. The de-orbit burn to slow *Challenger* down for reentry was performed on schedule, and the spacecraft glided in for a landing on the dry lake bed at Edwards Air Force Base in California.

At 11:54 A.M. Pacific standard time on April 9, 1983, *Challenger* rolled to a stop some 12 kilometers beyond where its main wheels had touched down. STS 6 had come to an end. The flight had lasted 5 days, 23 minutes, and 42 seconds and covered some 3.4 million kilometers in orbit.

Knowledge Gained

The successful deployment of the TDRS showed that large payloads could be transported to low-Earth orbit by the shuttle. This would prove valuable for satellites too big for conventional launch vehicles. Despite the problems TDRS had after deployment, the crew of STS 6 had released it at the proper time and place.

About six hundred of the bulky heat-resistant tiles that cover the upper surfaces of *Columbia* had been replaced by advanced flexible reusable surface insulation (AFRSI) blankets on *Challenger*. Each blanket is made of a sewn composite quilted fabric with the same silica material as the tiles sandwiched between the inner and outer layers. By replacing the bulky tiles, technicians could reduce the overall weight of the spacecraft by approximately 900 kilograms. This decrease in orbiter weight allowed for heavier payloads to be taken up to orbit and returned.

The cockpit featured new "heads up" visual displays, which project essential flight control information for landing onto a clear screen between the pilots and the front windows. This setup permitted them to monitor the information while continuing to watch where they were going.

The 4 hours and 10 minutes that the two mission specialists spent in *Challenger*'s cargo bay gave the new spacesuits an excellent test. The suits, unlike the ones used in prior space programs, are not custom-made for each astronaut. Instead, they are "off the rack." Their main components—the hard-shell torso, helmet, flexible arms and gloves, pants, and boots—come in various sizes. An individual's suit is fitted to him or her, allowing hundreds of different suit combinations and saving millions of dollars in building customized suits for each astronaut; this approach also permits every astronaut the opportunity to perform a spacewalk.

The two spacesuits performed perfectly, adjusting for increased activity and, consequently, increased oxygen consumption. Even though the suits were pressurized, they were still flexible enough to permit freedom of movement without overexertion. Tools could be used easily, and hardware such as screws, nuts, and bolts could be removed and replaced. These spacesuits would make possible the in-orbit repair of satellites and, if necessary, the repair of an orbiter itself.

One of the experiments carried on board *Challenger*, the continuous flow electrophoresis system (CFES), verified that the device would separate materials to purity levels four times higher than those possible on Earth. The CFES works on the principle that molecules of substances with different structures and sizes contain different electrical charges and, therefore, can be separated within an electrical field. Although electrophoresis can be performed under normal Earth gravity, heavier molecules tend to settle to the bottom of the device. In the microgravity of orbital flight, there is none of this settling.

Another experiment, the monodisperse latex reactor (MLR) experiment, used near weightlessness of spaceflight to study the feasibility of making monodisperse (identically sized) spheres of a plasticlike substance called latex. These spheres may have major medical and industrial research applications.

Context

STS 6 was the sixth flight of the Space Transportation System, the second operational flight and the first flight of an operational orbiter. For its first five missions, *Columbia* was an experimental spacecraft, requiring heavy ejection seats (available for use only on the first four flights) and structural supports for such things as the landing gear doors, main engine thrust frames, and propellant tanks. These heavier items were necessary because of the uncertainty of the stresses to which the orbiter would be subjected. As an operational spacecraft, *Challenger* could do away with these heavy structures, thereby trimming 1,128 kilograms.

Ground controllers were able to save TDRS through a series of maneuvers over a 58-day period. Small thrusters on the satellite, designed only for small orbital corrections, were fired thirty-nine times for a total of 40 hours of burn time. By performing the maneuvers at precisely the right point in the orbit, the *Challenger* crew could raise the lowest point of its orbit (perigee) to equal the apogee. TDRS was in place and was used during STS 9 to relay data and voice communications to and from ground stations. The IUS problem was resolved—but not in time to permit the launch of the second TDRS on STS 8. (The IUS problem also caused the postponement of the STS 10 flight, a Department of Defense mission which would use the IUS to deploy a military satellite. Eventually, the STS 10 mission was flown, and the IUS performed perfectly.) TDRS-B was scheduled for the STS 51E mission, but the flight had to be canceled because of internal problems with TDRS; the TDRS-B was in the payload bay of *Challenger* for the ill-fated STS 51L flight.

In thirty-three months of service, *Challenger* flew ten missions, traveling more than 41 million kilometers in orbit. In addition to the work done on STS 6, *Challenger* accomplished many impressive feats. STS 7 saw the first flight of an American woman in space in June, 1983. In August, STS 8 featured the first black astronaut and the first night launching and landing of the shuttle (which was also the first night landing of any American manned spacecraft).

Challenger's fourth mission, STS 41B, in February, 1984, included the first use of the manned maneuvering unit (MMU). The MMU is the Buck Rogers-style backpack that astronauts use during an EVA to travel to and from the orbiter and other spacecraft. At the conclusion of this mission, *Challenger* made the first landing at Kennedy Space Center. It was the first time a spacecraft landed at the same location from which it had been launched.

On its next flight, STS 41C, *Challenger*'s crew used the MMU to fix the Solar Maximum Mission satellite (better known as Solar Max). This was the first time an ailing satellite had been retrieved, repaired, and replaced into orbit. STS 41G marked the first flight of a seven-person crew, including two women astronauts, Sally Ride (becoming the first American woman to fly twice into space) and Kathryn Sullivan (who performed the first EVA by an American woman).

Three Spacelab missions were flown on *Challenger*: in April, 1985, in July, 1985, and the first German Spacelab mission, in October, 1985. Spacelab was built by the European Space Agency and consists of interchangeable modular units. By combining these units, different experiments can be performed in the shuttle's payload bay. Most of these experiments are too large to be run inside the crew compartment.

Challenger's last and, unfortunately, its most memorable flight was STS 51L. On January 28, 1986, the spacecraft and crew of seven were lost when a leak in one of the joints of its right-hand SRB caused the vehicle to break up during launch.

Bibliography

Allen, Joseph P., and Russell Martin. *Entering Space: An Astronaut's Odyssey*. New York: Stewart, Tabori and Chang, 1984. This personal account of a space shuttle flight describes the tension of the countdown and launch, the fun and difficulties of living and working in space, the awe-inspiring views of Earth from above, and the fiery return to the ground. Included are more than two hundred color photographs taken during many shuttle and pre-shuttle spaceflights. The experiences of other astronauts are presented in an effort to present a balanced view of space travel. Written for general audiences.

Furniss, Tim. *Manned Spaceflight Log*. Rev. ed. London: Jane's Publishing Co., 1986. A complete, nontechnical look into each manned spaceflight since Yuri Gagarin was launched into space in April, 1961. The book presents a concise look at flights by American astronauts, Soviet cosmonauts, and space travelers from the other nations who have flown with them. Each flight is listed with specific data, black-and-white photographs, and an unbiased account of the major events of the mission.

_____ . *Space Shuttle Log*. London: Jane's Publishing Co., 1986. An in-depth look at the space shuttle and its first twenty-two flights, from STS 1 through STS 61A. The first part of the book examines the design concepts for the Space Transportation System and provides an overview of the space shuttle systems. The remainder gives a concise account of each shuttle flight, along with black-and-white photographs from the missions.

Hallion, Richard. *On the Frontier*. NASA SP-4303. Washington, D.C.: Government Printing Office, 1984. Part of the NASA History Series, the book explores the experimental aircraft which provided the necessary research for the development of the space shuttle. It is very readable and contains many photographs of these pioneer aircraft. The author chronicles the evolution of these craft from the first plane to break the sound barrier through the space shuttle orbiter. A complete annotated listing of the flights of each of the vehicles, as well as an extensive bibliography, completes this authoritative work.

Kerrod, Robin. *Space Shuttle*. New York: Gallery Books, 1984. Written for general audiences, this book is full of color photographs of the space shuttle. The author includes very little text because the illustrations convey so well the essence of this marvelous vehicle and the people who fly it. The components of the Space Transportation System are detailed, and highlights of the first dozen missions are presented. Also included is some speculation on the future of space exploration.

Otto, Dixon P. *On Orbit: Bringing on the Space Shuttle*. Athens, Ohio: Main Stage Publications, 1986. The author takes a look at the early designs of the space shuttle and how they developed into the actual flying machine. Then he gives an account of each of the first twenty-five flights, including the names of the crew members, the principal payloads, and the objectives of the flight. The book contains many black-and-white illustrations to highlight each mission.

Smith, Melvyn. *An Illustrated History of Space Shuttle: X-15 to Orbiter*. Newbury Park, Calif.: Haynes Publications, 1986. A concise, highly detailed look at the space shuttle and the experimental aircraft which led to its design, the book spans the period from 1959 through 1985. Written for the general audience, it contains many rare photographs of the early lifting bodies, which help to show how the shuttle orbiter came to look as it does today. Organized chronologically.

Wilson, Andrew. *Space Shuttle Story*. New York: Crescent Books, 1986. More than one hundred color photographs are used to trace the history of the space shuttle from the early days of rocketry to the destruction of *Challenger*. This clearly written book is aimed at a general audience. Little detail is given on the technical aspects of the shuttle; the emphasis is on the men and women who fly the spacecraft.

Yenne, Bill. *The Astronauts*. New York: Exeter Books, 1986. This book, directed toward a general audience, presents an account of the manned space programs of the United States and the Soviet Union. It is illustrated with several hundred color and black-and-white photographs taken aboard the two countries' spacecraft. It also tells about the non-American and non-Soviet passengers who flew as guests on some of these flights. The book does not give the complete personal backgrounds of each astronaut and cosmonaut, but it does provide an intriguing insight into the human aspect of space travel.

_____ . *The Encyclopedia of U.S. Spacecraft*. New York: Exeter Books,

1985. A complete, nontechnical reference on the manned and unmanned spacecraft built and launched by the United States. Photographs of each of the spacecraft, most of them in color, accompany the text. The book gives details of the spacecraft, as well as launch dates. It also provides details of the American launch vehicles and a glossary of acronyms and abbreviations.

Russell R. Tobias

Cross-References

Astronauts and the U.S. Astronaut Program, 154; Skylab 2, 1291; The U.S. Space Shuttle, 1626; Space Shuttle Living Conditions, 1634; Space Shuttle Mission 7: *Challenger*, 1692; Space Shuttle Mission 8: *Challenger*, 1699; Space Shuttle Mission 10: *Challenger*, 1711; Space Shuttle Mission 11: *Challenger*, 1719; Space Shuttle Mission 13: *Challenger*, 1735; Space Shuttle Mission 17: *Challenger*, 1765; Space Shuttle Mission 19: *Challenger*, 1780; Space Shuttle Mission 22: *Challenger*, 1793; Space Shuttle Mission 25: *Challenger*, 1813; The Development of Spacesuits, 1917.

SPACE SHUTTLE MISSION 7
Challenger

Date: June 18 to June 24, 1983
Type of mission: Manned Earth-orbiting spaceflight
Country: The United States

On its second trip into orbit, the space shuttle Challenger *carried the first five-person crew, including the United States' first woman astronaut, Sally Ride. During their seven-day mission, the crew deployed two communications satellites and the first retrievable satellite, the Shuttle Pallet Satellite. Later, they picked up the free-flying Shuttle Pallet Satellite and returned it to Earth.*

Principal personages
ROBERT L. CRIPPEN, the mission commander
FREDERICK H. HAUCK, the mission pilot
JOHN M. FABIAN,
SALLY K. RIDE, and
NORMAN E. THAGARD, mission specialists

Summary of the Mission

Much attention was paid to Sally Ride when she was assigned to be the first woman to ride the shuttle. It had been twenty years since the first woman, Soviet cosmonaut Valentina Tereshkova, had flown into space aboard Vostok 6. Although she flew as part of a double flight, with Valeri Bykovsky being launched first in Vostok 5, more emphasis was placed on her presence in space. The time lapse between Tereshkova's flight and that of the second Soviet spacewoman, Svetlana Savitskaya in Soyuz T-7 in 1982, seems to add credence to the common belief in 1963 that Tereshkova's flight was another of Nikita Krushchev's attempts to outshine the United States. Bykovsky had set a record during his flight, spending nearly five days in orbit alone, a fact lost in history.

Ride, an astronaut since 1978, had been capsule communicator (capcom) for Space Transportation System (STS) 2 and STS 3. In the eyes of the news media, Ride's presence on STS 7 overshadowed the rest of the crew, as well as the goals of the mission. At preflight press briefings, reporters would usually stray from important questions about the payload and flight expectations. One asked whether Ride was going to take makeup with her and whether she felt uncomfortable spending a week in the cramped crew compartment with four men. Those who knew Ride were aware that she did not care very much for all this attention. She preferred to be considered simply as one of the crew, doing her job as anyone else would.

The commander of the flight was United States Navy captain Robert L. Crippen, the only veteran astronaut of the crew, having been the pilot on the first space shuttle mission in April, 1981. He became a National Aeronautics and Space Administration (NASA) astronaut in 1966, transferring from the canceled United States Air Force Manned Orbiting Laboratory program. His pilot was U.S. Navy Captain Frederick H. Hauck. He and the rest of the crew were selected as astronauts in 1978. In addition to Ride, two other mission specialists were aboard, U.S. Air Force colonel John Fabian and a medical doctor, Norman Thagard.

After the successful landing of STS 6, *Challenger* was examined, and its payloads were secured. Then it was lifted atop the special Boeing 747 shuttle carrier aircraft for the trip back to the Kennedy Space Center in Cape Canaveral, Florida. There, the *Challenger* was examined in more detail, and consumables (food, water, and the like) were replaced. Minor repairs to the spacecraft's heat tiles were made. It was then fitted with the payload for STS 7, brought into the vehicle assembly building, hoisted into the air and mated with the external tank and solid-fueled rocket boosters (SRBs). After the final test, *Challenger* was rolled out to the launchpad.

Challenger blasted off from Launch Complex 39A at 7:33 A.M. eastern daylight time, on June 18, 1983. The shuttle dropped its SRBs on schedule and continued on its journey powered by the three main engines. At 8 minutes and 20 seconds into the flight, the engines were shut down. Eighteen seconds later, *Challenger* separated from the external tank. During the spacecraft's first orbit of Earth, its orbital maneuvering system (OMS) engines, located near the shuttle's main engines, performed two maneuvers and placed the orbiter in a nearly circular 297-kilometer orbit. The payload bay doors were opened, and the radiators were extended to permit the heat built up by onboard systems and the crew to be radiated into space.

The main activity for the first day was the launching of the Canadian Anik/ Telesat, a telecommunications satellite tucked inside *Challenger*'s bonnet-shaped sunshield. When *Challenger* was at the proper position in space, small springs gave Anik a gentle push, and it was on its way through the opened shield at 5:02 P.M. *Challenger* maneuvered away from the satellite, and preparations began for the firing of Anik's Payload Assist Module, Delta class (PAM-D). Forty-five minutes after deployment, the first stage of the McDonnell Douglas PAM-D engine fired, raising its apogee (the high point in its orbit). Three days later, the second-stage engine placed the Anik into geosynchronous orbit (that is, an orbit where the satellite's velocity and altitude make it appear to hover over one spot on Earth's surface).

On the second day of the mission, the Indonesian Palapa-B communications satellite was successfully deployed at 9:33 A.M. and placed into geosynchronous orbit. Palapa, like Anik, was deployed from the orbiter within 0.15 degree of its planned location, well within the orbiter specification of 2.0 degrees. Once Palapa was well on its way, the remote manipulator system (RMS) arm and the Shuttle Pallet Satellite (SPAS-01) were prepared for their upcoming activities.

Early the third day, communications tests with the Tracking and Data-Relay Satellite (TDRS) deployed on STS 6 were successfully conducted. Later, experiments with SPAS attached to the RMS were conducted, as were other experiments carried in the orbiter's middeck and in the payload bay. SPAS was the first satellite tailored specifically to the reusability of the shuttle. It was developed by a West German firm and carried ten experiments furnished by West Germany, the European Space Agency (ESA), and NASA. The SPAS-01 structure was 4.2 meters long, 1.5 meters tall, and 0.7 meter wide. Fully equipped, it weighed 1,500 kilograms. It contained its own stability control system, which used four blocks of three reaction control thrusters.

In *Challenger*'s cargo bay was the OSTA 2 (sponsored by NASA's Office of Space Science and Applications and named for the acronym of that office's predecessor organization, the Office of Space and Terrestrial Applications). OSTA 2 was the first NASA materials processing payload to fly in the shuttle's payload bay and was a cooperative project with the West German Ministry of Research and Technology. It was completely automated and comprised four instrument packages containing six experiments designed to study fluid dynamics, transport phenomena, and metallurgy. The instrument packages were attached to a framelike structure called a mission-peculiar equipment support structure (MPESS).

Three German materials processing payloads included in OSTA 2 were in Get-Away Special (GAS) canisters. Two of the canisters contained "stability of metallic dispersions" experiments, while the third held the "particles at a solid-liquid interface" (PSLI) experiment. The NASA materials processing payload element—the materials experiment assembly (MEA)—contained two general-purpose rocket furnaces and the single-axis acoustic levitator (SAAL).

The next day, the continuous flow electrophoresis system (CFES) completed three runs to separate materials to purity levels four times higher than those possible on Earth. The CFES functions on the principle that molecules of substances with different structures and sizes contain different electrical charges and, therefore, can be separated within an electrical field. While electrophoresis can be performed under normal Earth gravity, heavier molecules tend to settle to the bottom of the device. There is none of this settling in the microgravity of orbital flight.

Activities on the fifth flight day began when SPAS-01 was gently lifted from its berth in the payload bay and deployed. Once it had deployed the satellite, *Challenger* moved away to fly in formation with it. For the next 4.5 hours tests were conducted, first with SPAS-01 about 300 meters away and then at distances of about 60 meters. During these activities, 16-millimeter, 70-millimeter, and television cameras mounted on SPAS were used to photograph *Challenger*, providing the first pictures of an entire orbiter in space. The RMS arm had been left in a position such that it formed the number seven, in honor of the flight's mission number.

During the last full day in orbit, the final RMS tests were performed, the Ku-band antenna (used for communications through the TDRS) was stowed, and stowage of equipment inside the crew cabin was begun in preparation for the return to Earth. *Challenger*'s flight control systems were checked for the first time since just before launch. The orbiter could not be guided to the landing site safely if these systems were not functioning properly.

On the seventh day, all the experiments were powered down and the payload bay doors closed. *Challenger* was scheduled to make the first landing at Kennedy Space Center, but poor weather conditions there resulted in a decision to delay the landing for two orbits. The landing took place at 6:57 A.M. Pacific daylight time on the runway at Edwards Air Force Base in California. The *Challenger* and its crew had spent 6 days, 2 hours, 23 minutes, and 59 seconds in flight and traveled more than 4 million kilometers.

Knowledge Gained

Thagard's main objectives for the mission were to gather information on motion sickness and cardiovascular deconditioning countermeasures. Although NASA offers no details, many of the astronauts and cosmonauts who have flown in space suffer from a malady similar to seasickness. After a few days, they become accustomed to the weightless conditions and can function normally. Having a disabled crew member for two or three days, however, could prove disastrous in case of an emergency. Thagard had worked on many different theories of the causes and cures for spacesickness and was given a chance to test these theories. Experiments on spacesickness have been flown on subsequent shuttle flights and, although a "cure" has not been found, methods of lessening its effect on crewmen have worked. One such remedy is to have the crewman move slowly and deliberately, while using visual cues for establishing "up" and "down."

When a person has been in space for a while, the cardiovascular system (heart, veins, and arteries) becomes "lazy" since it does not have to fight gravity as it does on Earth. Thagard conducted experiments to find ways of keeping the system in shape. These experiments, along with those conducted on subsequent shuttle flights, have shown that exercise is necessary even in space. By walking on a treadmill, an astronaut can give his cardiovascular system a workout and resume his duties with renewed energy.

Evaluation of the OSTA 2 flight hardware and experiments showed that the payload's objectives were met. The MPESS was demonstrated to be a very effective carrier for both shuttle payload integration and flight operations. The MEA and experimental furnaces functioned as expected and provided good specimens in the NASA materials processing investigations. The SAAL malfunctioned and was only a partial success. It was designed to process up to eight samples which are injected sequentially by a carousel mechanism into a furnace chamber and levitated by an acoustic energy field to hold the sample free of the container. The German materials processing payloads were evaluated and considered to have performed satisfactorily. These experiments help scientists better understand how a variety of metals and liquids react to the environment of space, an understanding which will aid in the development of structures and propellants for future spaceflight, as well as newer and better medicines, materials, and energy sources to be used on Earth.

As on STS 6, the monodisperse latex reactor (MLR) experiment was carried in the middeck area of *Challenger*. It used the weightless conditions of spaceflight to study the feasibility of making monodisperse (identical size) spheres of a plasticlike substance called latex. These spheres may have major medical and industrial research applications. They can also be manufactured larger and more economically in space once an MLR is placed permanently in orbit aboard the space station *Freedom*.

Context

Materials processing experiments carried aboard *Challenger* in future Spacelab missions would begin making some of the spage-age products only thought possible before STS 7. Spacelab is built by the European Space Agency and consists of interchangeable modular units. By combining these units, different experiments can be performed in the shuttle's payload bay. Most of these experiments are too large to be run inside the crew compartment.

All the astronauts on board STS 7 flew on other missions, including Sally Ride. In October, 1984, Ride became the first American woman to go into space twice, this time riding aboard *Challenger* on STS 41G. Physiologically speaking, Ride faired as well as, if not better than, some of her male companions. On neither of her flights did she report any spacesickness.

Crippen became the first astronaut to fly the shuttle into space four times. In addition to STS 1 and STS 7, he commanded STS 41C in April, 1984 (which featured the first in-orbit repair of an ailing satellite), and STS 41G. The latter marked the first flight of a seven-person crew, including two female astronauts, Ride and Kathryn Sullivan (who performed the first spacewalk by an American woman).

STS 7, the second flight of *Challenger*, showed the reliability of the Space Transportation System. In a little more than two months since its first flight (STS 6), the orbiter was cleaned, refurbished, and fitted with new experiments and payloads. Two months after completing the STS 7 mission, *Challenger* was launched on STS 8, which featured the first black astronaut and the first night launching and landing of the shuttle. With a fleet of four or five orbiters and two launch complexes at Kennedy Space Center, and an additional one at Vandenberg Air Force Base in California, NASA's goal of a shuttle launch every two weeks seemed achievable.

Time would show, however, that meeting this goal would be costly both in materials and in personnel. On *Challenger*'s last flight, the spacecraft and its crew of seven were lost when a leak in one of the joints of its right-hand SRB caused the vehicle to break up during the launch of STS 51L. According to a presidential commission which investigated the accident, NASA managers may have placed schedule before safety. In the wake of the accident, nearly three years were lost and more than fifty missions had to be canceled or rescheduled. Plans for launching from Vandenberg were terminated, and NASA's decision-making process was scrutinized very carefully. The space shuttle was supposed to be NASA's "truck," making access to space routine and affordable. It would fly again, but it would never be viewed as "routine."

Bibliography

Allen, Joseph P., and Russell Martin. *Entering Space: An Astronaut's Odyssey*. New York: Stewart, Tabori and Chang, 1984. The personal account of a space shuttle flight brings to life the anxiety and exhilaration of a shuttle mission. Includes more than two hundred color photographs. The experiences of other astronauts are given in an effort to present a balanced view of space travel. Written for general audiences.

Furniss, Tim. *Manned Spaceflight Log*. Rev. ed. London: Jane's Publishing Co., 1986. This comprehensive, nontechnical volume covers spaceflight since Yuri Gagarin's mission in April, 1961. Presents a concise profile of flights by astronauts, cosmonauts, and space travelers from the other nations. Contains black-and-white photographs.

_____ . *Space Shuttle Log*. London: Jane's Publishing Co., 1986. An in-depth look at the space shuttle and its first twenty-two flights. Design concepts for the Space Transportation System, as well as an overview of the space shuttle systems, are covered in the first sections. Also included is a concise accounting of each shuttle flight, along with photographs from the missions.

Hallion, Richard. *On the Frontier*. NASA SP-4303. Washington, D.C.: Government Printing Office, 1984. Part of the NASA History Series, this volume explores the experimental aircraft which provided the necessary research for the development of the space shuttle. In addition to tracing the evolution of these aircraft, the author includes a complete annotated listing of the flights of each of the vehicles, as well as an extensive bibliography. Contains black-and-white photographs.

Kerrod, Robin. *Space Shuttle*. New York: Gallery Books, 1984. Written for general audiences. This book is replete with color photographs of the space shuttle which convey well the essence of this marvelous vehicle and the people who fly it. The components of the Space Transportation System, and highlights of the first dozen missions, are presented, as well as a fanciful look toward the future of space exploration.

Otto, Dixon P. *On Orbit: Bringing on the Space Shuttle*. Athens, Ohio: Main Stage Publications, 1986. Dixon examines how the early designs of the space shuttle developed into the actual flying machine and gives an account of each of the first twenty-five flights. Included are the names of the crew members, the principal payloads, and the objectives of each flight. The book contains a large number of black-and-white illustrations to highlight each mission.

Ride, Sally, with Susan Okie. *To Space and Back*. New York: Lothrop, Lee and Shepard Books, 1986. The personal account of life aboard the space shuttle during STS 7, this book is directed to a younger audience. Readers of all ages will find the color photographs breathtaking. The adventure begins on the morning of launch and uses photographs from many shuttle flights for illustration. A glossary of terms is provided to make the reading easier.

Smith, Melvyn. *An Illustrated History of Space Shuttle: X-15 to Orbiter*. Newbury Park, Calif.: Haynes Publications, 1986. A concise, highly-detailed overview of the space shuttle and the experimental aircraft which led to its design, the book spans the period from 1959 through 1985. Contains many rare photographs of the early shuttle lifting bodies which help to show how the shuttle orbiter came to look as it does. Information is presented chronologically.

Wilson, Andrew. *Space Shuttle Story*. New York: Crescent Books, 1986. Through more than one hundred color photographs, the space shuttle's history from the early days of rocketry to the destruction of *Challenger* is told. Aimed at a general audience, this volume emphasizes the men and women who fly the spacecraft.

Yenne, Bill. *The Astronauts*. New York: Exeter Books, 1986. Directed toward the general audience, this volume details the manned space programs of the United States and the Soviet Union. It is illustrated with several hundred color and black-and-white photographs taken aboard the spacecraft. Although the book does not give the complete personal backgrounds of every space traveler, it does provide insight into human travel in space.

—————————— . *The Encyclopedia of U.S. Spacecraft*. New York: Exeter Books, 1985, reprint 1988. A complete, nontechnical reference of spacecraft built and launched by the United States. Contains photographs of each of the spacecraft, most of them in color. The book gives details of the spacecraft, as well as launch dates and the disposition of the craft. Also covers the American launch vehicles and contains a glossary of acronyms and abbreviations.

Russell R. Tobias

Cross-References

Astronauts and the U.S. Astronaut Program, 154; Biological Effects of Space Travel on Humans, 188; The U.S. Space Shuttle, 1626; Space Shuttle Living Conditions, 1634; Space Shuttle Mission 1: *Columbia*, 1648; Space Shuttle Mission 8: *Challenger*, 1699; Space Shuttle Mission 11: *Challenger*, 1719; Space Shuttle Mission 13: *Challenger*, 1735; Space Shuttle Mission 25: *Challenger*, 1813; U.S. Private and Commercial Telecommunications Satellites, 1997; Vostok 5 and 6, 2212.

SPACE SHUTTLE MISSION 8
Challenger

Date: August 30 to September 5, 1983
Type of mission: Manned Earth-orbiting spaceflight
Country: The United States

STS 8 was the first space shuttle mission to launch and land at night. The crew performed experiments concerning spacesickness and zero-gravity drug processing. This mission also tested the Tracking and Data-Relay Satellite System for shuttle communications and featured the first spaceflight of a black American.

Principal personages
RICHARD H. (DICK) TRULY, the mission commander
DANIEL C. BRANDENSTEIN, the mission pilot
DALE A. GARDNER,
GUION S. (GUY) BLUFORD, and
WILLIAM E. THORNTON, mission specialists

Summary of the Mission

The eighth flight of the space shuttle, STS 8, was the third flight for the orbiter *Challenger*. The mission would mark the first night launch and landing of a shuttle. Crew commander for STS 8 was United States Navy captain Richard H. (Dick) Truly, making his second spaceflight. Truly had been an astronaut with the National Aeronautics and Space Administration (NASA) since 1969 and was the pilot on STS 2 in November, 1981. U.S. Navy commander Daniel C. Brandenstein was the STS 8 pilot, making his first spaceflight. Brandenstein was selected as a NASA astronaut in 1978 and had served as capsule communicator (capcom) between the shuttle orbiter and Mission Control in Houston on STS 1 and STS 2. U.S. Navy lieutenant commander Dale A. Gardner was also making his first spaceflight as a mission specialist. Gardner was selected as a NASA astronaut in 1978 and had served on the support crew for STS 4. U.S. Air Force lieutenant colonel Guion S. (Guy) Bluford, who became an astronaut in 1978, would make history by becoming the first black American to fly in space—although he was not the first black chosen to be an astronaut. (The first black to be chosen as an astronaut was Robert Lawrence, who died in an aircraft accident in 1967; Lawrence's widow would be at Cape Canaveral for the STS 8 launch.)

Rounding out the STS 8 crew was William E. Thornton, a medical doctor, making his first spaceflight as a mission specialist. He was selected as a NASA scientist-astronaut in 1967. At fifty-four, Thornton would become the oldest person to fly in space up to that time. He was a support crew member for the three Skylab missions and was a crew member on the Skylab medical experiments altitude test (SMEAT), a 56-day Skylab simulation mission made in 1972 to collect medical data and evaluate equipment.

STS 8 was scheduled for lift-off at 2:15 A.M. eastern daylight time, August 30, 1983. It would be only the second night launch in the history of the United States' manned space program. Apollo 17 had been launched at night in 1972. The launch window, or period in which the shuttle could lift off, was only 34 minutes. NASA would need almost all of that time.

As the original lift-off time neared, a cold front had settled on Cape Canaveral, Florida. Thunderstorms menaced Launch Complex 39A, where *Challenger* stood, and a planned 10-minute hold on the countdown at the T-minus-9-minute mark was extended to give NASA time to evaluate the weather. The rain stopped, and the visibility increased sufficiently to allow for the launch 17 minutes into the launch window, at 2:32 A.M.

Night turned to day for a short time as *Challenger* lifted from its launchpad. A beautiful sight in daylight, this nighttime shuttle launch was simply magnificent. The two solid-fueled rocket boosters (SRBs) and three main engines lit the area enough for viewers to read a book at the press site, some 5 kilometers away. When *Challenger* entered a cloud formation one minute after launch, the entire cloud glowed a brilliant orange. The view from inside the shuttle was spectacular as well, with Brandenstein reporting that it was like being inside a bonfire. It was anticipated that viewers as far as 800 kilometers away would be able to see the launch, but poor weather prevented that.

The ascent itself was perfect: *Challenger* entered a 277-kilometer circular orbit with an inclination to the equator of 28.45 degrees. Only after the flight was it discovered that the carbon lining in one of the two SRB nozzles had come dangerously close to burning completely through. Had this occurred, hot gases would have escaped through the hole in the nozzle, which could have sent *Challenger* veering off course. STS 8 had come very close to disaster. This problem would have to be corrected before the next shuttle flight.

During the first orbit, the crew communicated with Mission Control through the Tracking and Data-Relay Satellite (TDRS), which had been deployed on STS 6, for the first time ever. The quality of communications through TDRS was reported to be as good as any in the shuttle program. *Challenger* would test TDRS throughout the mission. TDRS would be vital for transmitting the large volumes of data anticipated during the first Spacelab flight late in 1983. The completed TDRS system would consist of three nearly identical satellites and would provide the shuttle with communications, both audio and video, over approximately 80 percent of its ground track.

The only deployable payload of the mission was the Indian National Satellite (INSAT 1B), built by Ford Aerospace and Communications Corporation in Palo Alto, California, and owned by the Indian government. It provides radio and television communications and carries data collection equipment for weather surveillance and forecasting. INSAT 1B, with a seven-year lifetime, is controlled by the Satellite Control Center in Hassan, India.

Guy Bluford pressed the buttons to deploy INSAT 1B at 3:49 A.M., August 31, using a Payload Assist Module, Delta class (PAM-D). PAM-D worked perfectly, placing the INSAT into a geosynchronous orbit at 74 degrees east longitude.

During the first two days in orbit, Guy Bluford and Dale Gardner operated the continuous flow electrophoresis system (CFES), which was being flown on its fourth shuttle mission. CFES is a commercial project sponsored by McDonnell Douglas, in conjunction with Johnson and Johnson. Electrophoresis is a process of separating materials by passing them through an electrical field. In zero gravity, electrophoresis results in much purer materials. For the first time, on STS 8, live cells were used as samples. Six samples were run through CFES—two each of kidney, pituitary, and pancreas cells. The samples were removed from the shuttle immediately after landing for analysis.

During the third and fourth days in flight, the crew maneuvered the payload flight test article (PFTA) at the end of the remote manipulator system (RMS), or shuttle robot arm. The PFTA, which resembled a large dumbbell, was 6 meters long and 4.7 meters wide. Weighing 3,855 kilograms, it was the heaviest object to be lifted thus far by the RMS. The tests went well, with the crew observing how the elbow, wrist, and shoulder joints of the robot arm functioned with a large mass at the end of it. As had been the case on earlier shuttle missions, the arm worked perfectly. The PFTA was not released from the RMS, however, as it was a passive object with no propulsion system to control it.

A student experiment involving the ability to use biofeedback techniques in zero gravity was conducted by Thornton. During four tests, his skin-surface temperature, heart rate, skin response, and muscle activity were measured. Six rats were carried into space in the animal enclosure module (AEM), which was being tested for the first time. The purpose of the test was to demonstrate the ability of the AEM to support live animals without compromising the health or comfort of the crew. The rats behaved well and remained healthy throughout the flight. Four small, self-contained Get-Away Special payloads flew in the payload bay. These included a cosmic-ray experiment designed to help determine the effect of these rays when they pass through memory cells. A photographic emulsion experiment evaluated the effect of the orbiter's gaseous environment on film emulsion. This would be important for future missions requiring highly sensitive cameras and films. A Japanese snow crystal experiment which did not function properly on STS 6 flew on this mission; the experiment was designed to determine whether snow can be made in space. A contamination monitor was flown to test the reaction of different materials to atomic oxygen molecules which exist just outside Earth's atmosphere.

Eight Get-Away Special canisters in the payload bay carried approximately 260,000 United States Postal Service philatelic covers commemorating the twenty-fifth anniversary of NASA. These covers were sold to collectors by mail order after the flight. The money from the sale of the covers was split evenly between NASA and the U.S. Postal Service.

Thornton conducted tests throughout the flight concerning space adaptation syndrome, or spacesickness. These tests involved monitoring brain waves and observing the nervous system, the eyes, and fluid shifts within the body. NASA was trying to determine why so many astronauts suffer from spacesickness and why ailments vary from person to person.

After six days in orbit, *Challenger* landed at Edwards Air Force Base in California; it was the first night landing of the shuttle program. Xenon floodlights illuminated runway 22 at Edwards as Truly and Brandenstein brought *Challenger* to a pinpoint landing at 12:40 A.M. Pacific daylight time, on September 5, 1983. An infrared camera provided a spectacular view of the landing, showing the nose cap of the orbiter glowing from the heat of reentry. *Challenger* had proved itself durable in flying three missions in six months, while also demonstrating the feasibility of night operations for shuttle launches and landings.

Knowledge Gained

Above all, STS 8 demonstrated the capability of launching and landing the space shuttle at night. During the landing, Truly and Brandenstein used a precision approach path indicator for the first time to give visual cues as to whether they were on the correct glide path.

Also on STS 8, the continuous flow electrophoresis system separated live cells for the first time. Guy Bluford operated the system, separating cells from the pancreas, pituitary glands, and kidneys. The results of cell purification have become essential to medicine. Insulin from the pancreas is used to aid diabetes, growth hormones from the pituitary gland can be used to treat burns, and an enzyme from the kidney can dissolve blood clots.

India's INSAT 1B, launched on the second day of the mission, was properly deployed in geostationary orbit despite problems after leaving *Challenger*'s payload bay. The folded solar array would not deploy as planned after the satellite reached its orbit. After its initial difficulties, however, the solar array was properly unfolded. (Engineers thought it may have been struck by debris immediately after release from *Challenger*.)

The Tracking and Data-Relay Satellite System (TDRSS) tested well for the first time, although there were problems with ground equipment in White Sands, New Mexico. The S-band link was used for voice, commands, and telemetry data. The Ku-band link provided high-quality television pictures.

The animal enclosure module was tested successfully with six rats carried aboard. The rats seemed to adjust well to their new environment, although no tests were run on the animals. Their food consisted of nutrient bars developed at Ames Research Center, and their water was obtained through raw potatoes.

Thornton's medical tests designed to collect data on physiological changes associated with space adaptation syndrome recorded symptoms ranging from dizziness and mild nausea to vomiting. The spacesickness usually subsided in a day or two, but sick time in flight is extremely expensive. The hope was that enough would be learned about spacesickness to find ways to prevent it in the future.

Context

By the time STS 8 flew in August, 1983, the Space Transportation System had already proved valuable. Since NASA had scheduled many space shuttle missions requiring precise launch times, not all of which would occur during daylight, researchers needed to test the shuttle's ability to launch and land at night. In the history of American manned spaceflight, only once before had a launch occurred at night. With a flawless night launch and landing, STS 8 paved the way for future missions and gave NASA a boost of confidence that the shuttle was, indeed, a flexible vehicle. The ability to schedule launches regardless of lighting constraints was a major step forward in the shuttle program.

Furthermore, the testing of the TDRS was the first step toward elimination of the costly ground stations located around the world along the orbital path of the shuttle. With one TDRS, *Challenger* was able to receive and transmit high-quality data continuously for more than 40 minutes at a time. With a second TDRS placed in orbit, shuttle communications would be continuous for more than 80 percent of each orbit. An improved version of the TDRS would be vital for transmitting and receiving an even greater amount of data.

Guy Bluford became the first black American to travel into space, although he was not the first black in space. A Cuban black, Arnaldo Mendez, had flown on Soyuz 38 in 1980. Although as the first black American to travel in space Bluford did not garner as much attention as had Sally Ride two months earlier as the first American woman in space (on STS 7), his flight was another step forward in making spaceflight accessible to all. Although Bluford downplayed his role as the first black American to fly, a barrier had been broken, as the image of the test pilot broadened to include all races.

William Thornton, by becoming the oldest person to fly at age fifty-four, broke another barrier. Age apparently is not a factor in spaceflight, provided the person is in good health. Thornton was not affected by spaceflight any more or less than his younger colleagues. He downplayed any rigors associated with flying in space. Again, space was being opened up to many people regardless of age.

In flying STS 8, NASA had cut the time between flights drastically. Although the originally planned flight rate of one every two weeks was unrealistic, NASA was learning how to process the space shuttle efficiently, thus increasing the frequency of flights. In two years, the turnaround time dropped from seven months between STS 1 and STS 2 to about two months for STS 8. With these advances, STS 8 took the Space Transportation System one step closer to its ultimate goal as the reusable space vehicle of the future.

Bibliography

Bond, Peter. *Heroes in Space.* New York: Basil Blackwell, 1987. A fast-paced, readable account of every manned space mission up through the *Challenger* explosion. Contains few illustrations, but the appendix lists all American and Soviet manned spaceflights through May, 1987. A good primer for anyone first learning about manned spaceflight.

Braun, Wernher von, Frederick I. Ordway, and Dave Dooling. *Space Travel: A History*. Rev ed. New York: Harper and Row, Publishers, 1985. A broad history of manned and unmanned spaceflight with heavy emphasis on the German rocket scientists and the early days of rocketry. Contains many rare early photographs as well as photographs from more recent spaceflights. Although technical in some areas concerning rocketry, it is suitable for general audiences.

Furniss, Tim. *Space Flight: The Records*. London: Guinness Superlatives, 1985. A listing of every Soviet and American manned spaceflight in chronological order, with a paragraph synopsis of each flight. Also contains Guinness records on spaceflight and a detailed account of every person who had flown in space. through May, 1985.

Kerrod, Robin. *The Illustrated History of NASA*. New York: Gallery Books, 1986. Covers mostly NASA achievements but also discusses important Soviet space activities. Containing more than two hundred photographs, many full page and mostly in color, this volume is a beautiful pictorial history of both manned and unmanned spaceflight. The text is lively and devotes half of its 240 pages to the shuttle program.

Otto, Dixon P. *On Orbit: The First Space Shuttle Era, 1969-1986*. Athens, Ohio: Main Stage Publications, 1986. Beginning with approval of the shuttle design in 1972, this book covers every shuttle flight through the *Challenger* explosion. Includes a few color and many black-and-white photographs. Mission objectives—along with crew members, launch date, landing date, duration, orbits, and cargo weight—are listed for each flight. Suitable for general audiences.

Christopher F. Dickens

Cross-References

SPACE SHUTTLE MISSION 9
Columbia

Date: November 28 to December 8, 1983
Type of mission: Manned Earth-orbiting spaceflight
Country: The United States

STS 9 marked the first flight of Spacelab, a pressurized space laboratory built by the European Space Agency and housed in the shuttle payload bay. During the ten-day mission, the six-man crew operated seventy-two experiments ranging from astronomy and solar physics to life sciences and materials sciences.

Principal personages
JOHN W. YOUNG, the commander
BREWSTER H. SHAW, JR., the pilot
OWEN K. GARRIOTT and
ROBERT A. PARKER, mission specialists
BYRON K. LICHTENBERG and
ULF MERBOLD, payload specialists

Summary of the Mission

The ninth space shuttle mission, STS 9 saw the first flight of Spacelab, built by the European Space Agency (ESA). It also marked the return of the orbiter *Columbia* to space after a year of modifications following the STS 5 mission. Spacelab itself, costing approximately $1 billion, was housed in the payload bay of the shuttle orbiter. The module was 4 meters in diameter and 7.5 meters in length. The crew entered through a connecting tunnel 1.1 meters in diameter that led from the airlock module of the orbiter to the Spacelab, where crewmen could work in their shirtsleeves because of the module's pressurized environment.

Columbia was originally scheduled to launch Spacelab 1 on October 28, 1983. Following the STS 8 mission in early September, however, the National Aeronautics and Space Administration (NASA) discovered a problem with insulation in one of the recovered solid-fueled rocket booster (SRB) nozzles. A hole was almost burned through the rocket nozzle. If that had occurred, the vehicle could have veered off course with disastrous results. When the problem was discovered, STS 9 was already on Launch Complex 39A at the Kennedy Space Center. The SRBs were closely checked, and a similar problem was discovered on one of the STS 9 nozzles. The decision was made to roll *Columbia* back to the vehicle assembly building to replace the suspect nozzle assembly, as a precaution. The rollback caused a two-month delay of the launch.

Spacelab 1 would mark the first American spaceflight to conduct twenty-four-hour around-the-clock operations. The six-man crew was split into the red shift and the blue shift, each working twelve-hour days. The red shift was led by John W.

Young, making a record sixth spaceflight. He had flown on Gemini 3, Gemini 10, Apollo 10, and Apollo 16 and had commanded the first shuttle mission, STS 1. He was also chief of the astronaut office. Joining Young on the red shift was mission specialist Robert A. Parker, making his first spaceflight. Selected as an astronaut in 1967, Parker had been a support-crew member for Apollo 15 and Apollo 17 and had served as a program scientist for the Skylab missions. Payload specialist Ulf Merbold from West Germany was the third member of the red team. He became the first non-American to fly aboard an American spacecraft. Merbold was a materials engineer in Stuttgart, West Germany. He was selected as a payload specialist by the ESA in 1978.

The blue shift was led by U.S. Air Force major Brewster H. Shaw, the mission's pilot, who was making his first spaceflight. He had become an astronaut in 1978 and had served as a capsule communicator on STS 3 and STS 4. Mission specialist Owen K. Garriott joined Shaw on the blue team. Garriott was making his second spaceflight, having spent 59 days in space aboard the second Skylab mission in 1973. The third blue team member was payload specialist Byron K. Lichtenberg of the Massachusetts Institute of Technology. He had been selected as a payload specialist in 1978 and was making his first spaceflight.

STS 9 lifted off on schedule from its launchpad at Cape Canaveral, Florida, at 11:00 A.M. eastern standard time, November 28, 1983. The ascent was perfect, and *Columbia*, with Spacelab aboard, was placed into a 250-kilometer circular orbit inclined to the equator at 57 degrees. Less than two hours after launch, Garriott, Merbold, and Lichtenberg floated through the tunnel to begin activating Spacelab and its experiments.

Once Spacelab was activated, control of the mission switched from the Johnson Space Center in Houston, Texas, to the Marshall Space Flight Center in Huntsville, Alabama. On the first day, a problem developed that could have seriously hampered the mission. A remote acquisition unit (RAU 21) would not send data from four instruments connected to it to the main experiment computer. This problem did not affect data going to the experiments—simply the transfer of those data. The problem occurred only when the RAU 21 was hot from operating or from exposure to sunlight, leading to the suspicion that a loose connection was opening when heated. The problem was soon traced to heat-sensitive resistors.

This first Spacelab mission would test out the module in five major science areas: Earth studies, space physics, astronomy, life science, and materials science. Tests on human physiology and biology occupied most of the first two days, with much time spent studying the human body and its ability to adapt to weightlessness. The main experiments in this area involved a crew member placing his head in a dome with a pattern of rotating dots giving him the sensation of spinning. (It is believed that vestibular responses to body movement and acceleration are associated with rotational eye movements.) The crew member's eye rotation was measured and recorded in the dome. Eye rotation was also measured while a subject was spinning in a device called a body restraint system.

Another experiment, known as the "hop and drop," tested the influence of weightlessness on basic postural reflexes normally experienced on Earth. This experiment was done by placing elastic cords connected to the floor around a crew member's shoulders and having him hop up and down while blindfolded, in an effort to determine changes in the inner ear. The "drop" portion of the experiment involved falling with the aid of elastic cords pulling the subject toward the floor, while nerves in his lower leg were electrically stimulated. The subject's physiological responses to this stimulation were monitored and recorded, providing data on responses to brief periods of acceleration during weightlessness.

Materials processing began on the third flight day, with Merbold switching on three high-temperature furnaces. A materials sciences facility contained equipment shared by investigators from ten European countries. Two of the furnaces had to be repaired by the crew, but all three brought back excellent data on the study of crystal growth, fluid physics, and the processing of metals and glass in space.

A movable camera experiment to photograph cloudlike structures in the upper atmosphere—at the 85-kilometer level—was saved when Young and Shaw maneuvered the shuttle to compensate for a mechanical failure which kept the camera from pointing properly. A metric camera experiment nearly failed when a film magazine jammed, but Parker repaired it by hand and the crew took advantage of the high orbital inclination by taking high-resolution pictures of areas of Earth never before photographed from space.

The far ultraviolet space telescope did not work as expected because of fogging on its film. It was at first believed that the fogging was caused by the shuttle glow phenomenon—which occurs when the shuttle itself gives off light interference—but it was later determined that two bands of ionized oxygen circling the globe caused the problem. These bands were first photographed from the Moon by an ultraviolet camera aboard Apollo 16 in 1972. A wide-angle camera photographed deep-space targets, including a thin band of stars and gas between the Magellanic Clouds. An X-ray spectrometer observed the Perseus cluster of galaxies and measured X-ray emissions from the Cassiopeia A supernova remnant.

The flight was proceeding so well, and the data return was so massive, that NASA officials extended the mission by one day. The crew spent part of the extra day conducting experiments, and then they packed and stowed equipment in preparation for return to Earth.

Columbia was originally set to land at Edwards Air Force Base at 7:59 A.M. Pacific standard time on December 8, 1983. Four hours before the de-orbit burn to bring *Columbia* home, two of the orbiter's five onboard computers shut down. One computer failed during a nose-reaction-control-jet firing, with a second computer shutting down 4 minutes later when another nose jet fired. Some 40 minutes after the problems occurred, the crew restored the second computer to operation. The first computer remained off for the rest of the mission. NASA wanted time to study the problem, so the landing was delayed. Studies concluded that the problems were isolated to those two computers and were not related to the thruster firings, so the landing was rescheduled for eight hours later than planned.

On orbit 166, *Columbia* finally performed the de-orbit burn to bring it back to Earth. Because of the delay, the shuttle made its first-ever descent to Edwards from the north. The reentry took *Columbia* northward over eastern China and the Soviet Union, then over the Aleutian Islands at Mach 23, or 23 times the speed of sound. Young and Shaw piloted the heaviest landing payload of the shuttle program to a perfect touchdown on runway 17 at Edwards Air Force Base at 3:47 P.M. Pacific daylight time, December 8, 1983. When the orbiter's nosewheel touched down, the second computer shut down again. Hydrazine fuel leaks around two of the orbiter's three auxiliary power units (APUs) ignited small fires immediately after landing. The crew was in no danger, and the fires were quickly extinguished.

Knowledge Gained

Columbia and its Spacelab 1 cargo gathered two trillion bits of digital scientific data, more than twenty million frames of television data, and several thousand photographs to document the flight's science output. The Spacelab module itself proved to be a flexibile tool for a multitude of science studies. STS 9 was really an experimental flight to determine how useful Spacelab could be.

The Tracking and Data-Relay Satellite System (TDRSS), tested on STS 8 but fully utilized for the first time on this mission, was instrumental in allowing the crew to send long transmissions of real-time data to ground scientists. With communication continuous for up to 40 minutes at a time, the crew and ground controllers were able to converse at length concerning the experiments on board. This resulted in more data and allowed the crew to receive instructions on the maintenance and repair of some equipment which had malfunctioned.

A grille spectrometer, used for the first time in space, detected gases thought not to be present at certain upper levels of the atmosphere. Carbon dioxide in the thermosphere and water vapor in the mesosphere were discovered. The materials processing experiments produced protein crystals several hundred times larger than those possible to manufacture on Earth. In the area of vestibular experiments, tests using the rotating dome revealed that humans rely heavily on vision for orientation in space. As the body adjusted to space, the motion in the dome gave the person the impression he was moving in the opposite direction.

The most startling data of the mission involved tests concerning the inner ear. Researchers varied the temperatures of a subject's ears and discovered that, with his ear temperatures varied, a subject experiences the sensation of rotating when he is actually sitting still. Earlier, the Austrian physician Robert Bárány had theorized that different ear temperatures created convective motions in the fluid of the inner ear, causing the subject to believe that he is in motion. This response had been measured by observing the subject's eyes twitch as his brain tried to follow what it perceived to be rotating head motions. Thermal convection, which is caused by variation in density and temperature in fluids interacting with gravity, is not a factor in zero gravity, and tests on Ulf Merbold showed that the eye motions continued with different temperatures, even when convection was not a factor. That finding contradicted data that had helped Bárány win a Nobel Prize in 1914.

In addition to the scientific experiments, engineering tests were run on the Spacelab itself. The orbiter was turned at different angles toward the Sun to bake and cool the Spacelab in an effort to see how the module reacted to temperature variation. The crew also participated in a fire drill, scrambling quickly out of Spacelab in a test to determine how much time would be needed to evacuate the module in case of emergency. Both crew and ground personnel learned much about around-the-clock operations—including ways to accommodate sleeping crew members while still accomplishing work.

Context

Prior to STS 9, no manned spaceflight had ever been attempted which required so much interaction among different countries. During STS 9, a laboratory built by the ESA was flown inside a spacecraft built by the United States. Although the flight was not controlled in Europe after the science operations began, as would be the case with later Spacelab flights, the amount of planning and execution for the multitude of experiments on Spacelab ushered in a new era of international cooperation in space.

Spacelab 1 was an introduction to permanent scientific laboratories in space. Future space stations will undoubtedly use the lessons learned in Spacelab concerning everything from the types of experimental payloads to the coordination of twenty-four-hour work schedules. The space shuttle was stretched to its endurance limits—especially since its mission was extended by one day. The ten-day STS 9 mission was the longest shuttle mission up to that time and came close to the maximum duration possible for a shuttle flight without extensive modifications to the orbiter. Despite computer problems prior to the de-orbit burn, *Columbia* demonstrated the shuttle's flexibity by flying five extra orbits and still executing a perfect landing.

The value of having a crew on board was demonstrated on STS 9. The crew was called upon repeatedly to repair equipment and alter procedures to ensure proper data collection. The fluid physics module, high data rate recorder, materials science rack, and metric camera were all repaired by the crew—in addition to the computers. The interaction between crew and ground in devising methods of fixing equipment was essential to the success of the mission.

The Spacelab program was created in December, 1972, by the European Space Research Organization (ESRO), predecessor to the European Space Agency. In August, 1973, Spacelab became a confirmed ESRO program and an integral part of the Space Transportation System. Ten years later, the planners saw their dreams come to fruition as the concept of a space laboratory worked in a manner never before demonstrated. Spacelab, a prelude to future space stations, was now a viable concept for space science, representing a first step toward a permanent human presence in space.

Bibliography

Bond, Peter. *Heroes in Space*. New York: Basil Blackwell, 1987. An accessible account of manned space missions. A good introduction to the topic, suitable for general audiences. Contains an appendix of all American and Soviet manned spaceflights through May, 1987. Illustrated with black-and-white photographs.

Braun, Wernher von, Frederick I. Ordway, and Dave Dooling. *Space Travel: A History*. Rev. ed. New York: Harper and Row, Publishers, 1985. This volume offers a broad history of spaceflight with heavy emphasis on the German rocket scientists and the early days of rocketry. Covers both manned and unmanned missions. Although technical in some areas, it is suitable for general audiences. Contains many photographs, both black-and-white shots of early rockets and color shots of modern spaceflight.

Kerrod, Robin. *The Illustrated History of NASA*. New York: Gallery Books, 1986. Covers mostly NASA achievements, but also discusses important Soviet space activities up through the *Challenger* explosion. Half of the text's 240 pages are devoted to the shuttle. For general audiences. Contains more than two hundred photographs of both manned and unmanned missions.

Otto, Dixon P. *On Orbit: Bringing on the Space Shuttle*. Athens, Ohio: Main Stage Publications, 1986. Beginning with approval of the shuttle design in 1972, this overview of the space shuttle program covers every shuttle flight through the *Challenger* explosion. Provides information on mission objectives, the crew members, launch dates, landing dates, duration, orbits, and cargo weight. Illustrated.

Christopher F. Dickens

Cross-References

Apollo 16, 116; Cape Canaveral and the Kennedy Space Center, 229; The European Space Agency, 372; The French Space Program, 461; Johnson Space Center, 669; Marshall Space Flight Center, 908; Materials Processing in Space, 933; The Skylab Program, 1285; Space Shuttle Living Conditions, 1634; Space Shuttle Mission 5: *Columbia*, 1678; Space Shuttle Mission 8: *Challenger*, 1699; Space Shuttle Mission 17: *Challenger*, 1765; Space Shuttle Mission 19: *Challenger*, 1780; Space Shuttle Mission 22: *Challenger*, 1793; The Development of the U.S. Space Station, 1835; International Contributions to the U.S. Space Station, 1843; The Spacelab Program, 1884; Spacelab 1, 1891; Spacelab 2, 1898; Spacelab 3, 1904; The West German Space Program, 2262.

SPACE SHUTTLE MISSION 10
Challenger

Date: February 3 to February 11, 1984
Type of mission: Manned Earth-orbiting spaceflight
Country: The United States

STS 41B, the tenth mission of the space shuttle, displayed the operational poten-tial of the Space Transportation System. Although it was not the first operational flight, STS 41B could be considered one of the most important. The crew not only returned from space to land for the first time where they were launched, at Kennedy Space Center, Florida, but also demonstrated the ability of astronauts to maneuver in space.

Principal personages
   VANCE D. BRAND, the commander
   ROBERT L. (HOOT) GIBSON, the pilot
   RONALD E. MCNAIR,
   BRUCE MCCANDLESS II, and
   ROBERT L. STEWART, mission specialists

Summary of the Mission

The National Aeronautics and Space Administration (NASA) launched *Challenger* on Space Transportation System (STS) mission 41B at 8:00 A.M. February 3, 1984, from Launchpad 39A at Kennedy Space Center, Florida. The space shuttle carried five astronauts, two communications satellites, and a variety of scientific payloads into a circular orbit 305 kilometers above Earth. Vance Brand was the commander of STS 41B. Brand had also commanded STS 5, the fifth flight and first operational flight of the space shuttle, in November, 1982. Robert L. (Hoot) Gibson, making his first spaceflight, was the pilot. Bruce McCandless, Ronald McNair, and Robert Stewart, also making their first flights, were mission specialists. STS 41B was the fourth flight of the orbiter *Challenger*.

Approximately eight hours into the mission, at 3:59 P.M. February 3, a Western Union communications satellite, Westar 6, was deployed from the payload bay while the space shuttle was passing over the far western Pacific Ocean on its sixth orbit. As planned, the satellite and its attached Payload Assist Module, Delta class (PAM-D), rocket motor were set spinning on a turntable in the payload bay and released by springs to coast away from the orbiter. Also as planned, the PAM-D's perigee kick motor fired 45 minutes later to boost the satellite toward its intended circular orbit 35,900 kilometers above Earth. The solid-fueled rocket, however, burned for only 16 seconds of the normal 85-second burn period, and although the satellite was working properly, it ended in an orbit which was both too low and too elliptical.

The failure prompted NASA to delay the deployment of a nearly identical satellite owned by the Republic of Indonesia, Palapa B2, from the second day until the fourth day of the mission, February 6. Palapa B2 was also deployed normally, but a PAM-D failure robbed it of the thrust necessary to reach the proper orbit. Both satellites were retrieved and returned to Earth by space shuttle astronauts on STS 51A in November, 1984.

Palapa B2, the Indonesian national telecommunications satellite, was the second Palapa to be deployed by *Challenger*. The first was deployed on STS 7. Palapa B2, built by Hughes Communications International of Los Angeles, California, was to provide a communications network to Indonesia and the Association of Southeast Nations, which includes the Philippines, Thailand, Malaysia, Singapore, and Papua, New Guinea. Palapa B2 and its PAM-D booster weighed 4,366 kilograms. In orbit, the satellite weighed 630 kilograms. With its antennae deployed, it was 6.8 meters in height and 2.16 meters in diameter.

Westar 6, built by Hughes Aircraft Company of El Segundo, California, was the third advanced Western Union communications satellite to be placed in space and was the first Westar to be deployed from the space shuttle. The Westar system provided continuous video, facsimile, data, and voice communications service throughout the United States, Puerto Rico, and the Virgin Islands. Westar 6 was similar in size and weight to Palapa B2.

Much of STS 41B was devoted to practicing for *Challenger*'s next flight, a mission to retrieve and repair the Solar Maximum Mission (SMM) satellite (sometimes called "Solar Max"). The satellite's attitude control system, the computerized system which maintains a spacecraft's posture in orbit, failed shortly after SMM was launched to study the Sun in 1980. The STS 41C rescue mission would require *Challenger* to fly within 90 meters of the spinning satellite while an astronaut wearing a manned maneuvering unit (MMU) docked with and held the satellite so that other crew members could grasp it with the space shuttle's 15-meter remote manipulator arm.

On the second day of the STS 41B mission, February 4, the crew members tried to inflate the integrated rendezvous target (IRT), a Mylar balloon 2 meters in diameter which they would use to practice maneuvering *Challenger*. The orbiter was to move about 14.5 kilometers from the balloon, close back to about 9.7 kilometers, move out again, then drift to a distance of slightly more than 225 kilometers before closing back to only 244 meters. The IRT burst, however, and the crew used radar to track pieces of the thin, aluminum-like material as it floated into space.

Also on the second day, Bruce McCandless and Ronald McNair (who would die aboard *Challenger* on STS 51L in January, 1986) used two 35-millimeter motion-picture cameras with "fish-eye" lenses to begin filming portions of their mission for a documentary being developed in a 360-degree format especially for planetarium viewing. They used the cameras on the sixth day. Cinema 360, a consortium of planetariums, later produced the film *The Space Shuttle: An American Adventure* in cooperation with NASA.

In addition to the two satellites that it deployed—Palapa B2 and Westar 6—*Challenger* carried the West German Shuttle Pallet Satellite (SPAS-01A) and a variety of minor payloads in its bay and crew cabin. SPAS-01A carried eight scientific experiments and served as a substitute for the Solar Maximum Mission satellite when the STS 41B crew members practiced retrieval and repair procedures on the seventh day. The experiments operated automatically, and most, with the exception of those on SPAS-01A, were activated by the crew on the second day. Five Get-Away Special (GAS) canisters in the payload bay contained small physics, biology, technology, and materials science experiments designed to investigate or take advantage of the low-gravity environment in space. Three materials processing experiments and a life-sciences experiment with rats were carried in the pressurized cabin.

On the fifth day, at 5:25 A.M. February 7, McCandless and Stewart became the first people to take an untethered spacewalk. They wore MMUs, 136-kilogram jet-propelled backpacks that allow free, detached flight. Of their six hours outside the orbiter, McCandless and Stewart spent more than two and one-half hours testing the MMUs. Spacewalkers normally breathe oxygen for an extended period to remove nitrogen from the bloodstream before beginning their extravehicular activity (EVA). By lowering the orbiter's cabin pressure, McCandless and Stewart achieved the same goal. They abbreviated the "pre-breathe" period and gave themselves more time to test the MMUs.

To test his MMU maneuvering capabilities, McCandless flew about 15 meters from the orbiter, returned, flew 96 meters away, and returned while being tracked by *Challenger*'s radar. McCandless also practiced docking himself with another spacecraft. To perform this feat, he latched himself to an equipment box in the payload bay with a portable tool called a trunnion pin acquisition device. Meanwhile, Stewart practiced using a manipulator foot restraint. The restraint is a set of straps at the end of the armlike remote manipulator system (RMS) that creates for astronauts a stable working platform similar to the "cherry pickers" used by telephone line technicians. Later, McCandless and Stewart traded positions and repeated the routines.

The crew spent most of the next day working with SPAS-01A and the eight scientific experiments it carried. Built by a West German firm, SPAS-01A was the first satellite ever to be refurbished and flown again. It had been released as a free-flying space platform during STS 7; during STS 41B, however, the satellite remained attached to *Challenger*. SPAS-01A weighed 1,448 kilograms. It was 4.8 meters long, 3.4 meters high, and 1.5 meters wide.

On the seventh day, February 9, SPAS-01A stood in for Solar Max while Stewart and McCandless conducted the mission's second EVA. SPAS was to have been hoisted outside the payload and set spinning slowly on the remote manipulator arm while McCandless used the trunnion pin acquisition device to dock with it. An electrical problem in the arm's wrist joint made hoisting impossible, so McCandless practiced docking with SPAS in the payload bay.

During their EVA, which began at 3:40 A.M., McCandless and Stewart practiced more free-flight maneuvers in the MMUs. They practiced stopping precisely, holding a steady position, and controlling speed and direction. Stewart tested a tool being developed for fueling satellites inside the payload bay. The second spacewalk lasted more than six hours and was captured on film by the Cinema-360 cameras.

The eight-day STS 41B mission ended on schedule, milliseconds past 7:17 A.M., February 11, on *Challenger*'s 128th orbit. The mission had lasted 7 days, 23 hours, 15 minutes, and 54 seconds. *Challenger* had traveled more than 5.3 million kilometers. Brand landed the orbiter, gliding faster than 350 kilometers per hour, less than 6.5 centimeters off the center line of runway 15 at Kennedy Space Center, with 690 meters of pavement to spare.

Knowledge Gained

The STS 41B mission turned Buck Rogers-type fantasies into reality and set the stage for the space shuttle to mature into a reliable, increasingly economical tool for research and commerce. Despite the fact that equipment problems prevented the completion of several tasks that would have provided valuable information about the space shuttle and its capabilities, STS 41B demonstrated that untethered EVAs are feasible.

In spite of several equipment failures on hardware launched from the space shuttle during the missions, most of the major test objectives of the flight were accomplished. Among their tasks, the five-member crew deployed two commercial communications satellites and practiced satellite repair procedures.

Westar 6, owned by Western Union, and Palapa B2, owned by the Republic of Indonesia, did not reach proper orbit because their PAM-D rocket motors failed. A failure investigation committee appointed by the manufacturer of the payload assist modules—McDonnell Douglas Astronautics Company of Huntington Beach, California—released its detailed findings in a final report in September, 1984.

Exhibiting their prowess with MMUs in the Solar Maximum Mission satellite repair rehearsal, McCandless and Stewart gave their fellow astronauts and the public a preview of mission tasks which were expected to become typical of future space shuttle flights. Their satellite repair practice led to the successful rescue of SMM on the next mission, STS 41C in April, 1984.

For the scientists who flew the variety of experiments aboard *Challenger*, STS 41B revealed valuable information about microgravity and its potential benefits for society, ranging from specialized manufacturing to biomedical therapy. The small, automatic GAS experiments included studies of how proteins crystallize, how liquids move, how light scatters, how cosmic rays affect memory, and how radish seeds sprout in microgravity; other tests had commercial applications, such as that aimed at the development of an energy-efficient arc lamp. These experiments were sponsored by GTE Laboratories, the U.S. Air Force, NASA's Goddard Space Flight Center in Greenbelt, Maryland, and high school and college students from Utah and the University of Aberdeen in Scotland.

The monodisperse latex reactor (MLR) payload was one of three materials processing payloads flown inside the pressurized crew cabin. MLR, carried on four previous space shuttle flights, was designed to develop monodisperse, or identically sized, beadlike rubber particles for use in medical and industrial research. Another materials processing payload, the acoustic containerless experiment system (ACES), was activated on the second day; it tested a materials processing furnace. The third materials processing payload, the isoelectric focusing (IEF) experiment, tested electrophoresis, a process for separating protein fluids by their diverse electric charges.

STS 41B was the second mission to carry live rats for scientific experimentation. On this flight, six rats were the subject of a student experiment to study whether weightlessness relieves the symptoms of arthritis. Dan Weber, who designed the experiment while he was attending Hunter College High School in New York City, flew three healthy rats and three arthritic rats in a life-support cage called an animal enclosure module (AEM). Before the rats were launched, Weber injected Freund's adjuvant, a substance used to induce arthritis, into the animals' hind paws. After the flight, the rats were killed and Weber conducted autopsies, comparing the space shuttle rats with twelve controls—six healthy and six arthritic rats.

The results of the rat experiment were inconclusive, partly because the flight was not long enough to allow arthritis to develop fully in the animals. During postflight examination, Weber found no significant differences in the degree of swelling between the flown rats and the ground controls, and reported that spaceflight did not inhibit the development of arthritis. The flight crew, however, observed that the arthritis spread less extensively in the space shuttle rats than in rats they examined in earlier ground-based tests—an indication of possible beneficial effects of weightlessness.

Six experiments on SPAS-01A were sponsored by West Germany's Ministry of Research and Technology. Materialwissenschaftliche Autonome Experiments Unter Schwerelosigkist (MAUS) 1 and 2 investigated materials processing in microgravity. MAUS 1 mixed bismuth and manganese, two metals that are difficult to combine on Earth, in an attempt to create a new permanent magnetic alloy. MAUS 2 was a basic crystal-growth experiment. Another experiment, with friction loss, studied how pneumatic or air-operated conveyor systems operate in the absence of gravity. An electronic remote-sensing camera, the modular optoelectric multispectral scanner (MOMS), was used to scan land masses on Earth. The Bonn neutral mass spectrometer measured the intensity and composition of gaseous contaminants in and around *Challenger*'s payload bay. Another experiment studied heat transfer in microgravity.

Two experiments on SPAS-01A were sponsored by the European Space Agency. The first measured the yaw, or drift, of a stabilized spacecraft, with the goal of gathering information to help simplify attitude control systems. The other measured solar power cells in direct sunlight to set calibration standards for systems on Earth.

NASA learned how much more easily it would be to maintain space shuttle flight schedules with routine Florida landings. *Challenger*'s unprecedented touchdown at Kennedy Space Center's 4.8-kilometer-long Shuttle Landing Facility (SLF) eliminated the need for a cross-country ferry from one of NASA's other landing sites and enabled crews to prepare the orbiter for another flight in fifty-five days. The return-to-launch-site landing allowed the shortest turnaround time for a space shuttle orbiter to that date and demonstrated the effectiveness of a design characteristic which had been unproved until then.

Context

With its disappointing equipment failures, STS 41B was far from the most successful of the first twenty-five space shuttle missions at accomplishing predeter-mined tasks. Nevertheless, the mission was full of spectacular "firsts" for the United States' space program. Happily for NASA, those historical events—and breathtaking film footage from the motion-picture cameras—were enough to leave a lasting impression of mission success. STS 41B included the first untethered spacewalks in program history, the first flight of an astronaut wearing an MMU, the first use of foot restraints mounted on the RMS, the first EVA without an extended "pre-breathe" period, and the first space shuttle landing at Kennedy Space Center, Florida.

The tenth space shuttle mission was an important educational and political tool for NASA, which continually found itself in battles with the U.S. Congress over funding. For lawmakers who might be questioning the need for a space shuttle, the mission demonstrated program continuity. For example, during the satellite repair practice, crew members not only rehearsed procedures that would be used on the next flight but also tested equipment and techniques that eventually would be used to build and service a space station. A few days before *Challenger* was launched, President Ronald Reagan had announced plans for a space station in his "State of the Union" address. Reagan had reaffirmed the shuttle's convenience and necessity as a "truck" to carry parts of the space station into orbit. By the time *Challenger* was launched, almost three years had passed since the first space shuttle, *Columbia*, blasted into orbit. News media coverage, often a determinant of public interest in the space shuttle program, had begun to wane. In the Cinema-360 project, NASA had seen an effective means of communicating its goals to the American public. STS 41B produced approximately 914 meters of film, 80 percent of which was of high quality. The footage was incorporated into a 32-minute documentary and shown at planetariums across the country. The film gives its audience a striking vantage point—unprecedented, undistorted, and unobstructed views of Earth and space. Through *The Space Shuttle: An American Adventure*, NASA was able to document its reusable spaceship as the necessary predecessor to a permanently manned space station.

STS 41B was the first of sixteen flights to take place under a coded designation. The mission was designated as *4* (for 1984, the fiscal year of the launch), *1* (for Kennedy Space Center, one of two launch sites), and *B* (for the second launch scheduled in the fiscal year). In the past, NASA had numbered missions one through nine consecutively, beginning with STS 1. The new alphanumeric system, instituted as interest in the space shuttle as a commercial transport peaked, supported the belief that the space shuttle truly was a reliable and increasingly economical way to put payloads into orbit. The new system was intended to reduce the public confusion created when numerically designated missions flew out of order because of payload changes or cancellations.

Bibliography

Braun, Wernher von, et al. *Space Travel: A History*. Rev. ed. New York: Harper and Row, Publishers, 1985. This is the fourth, updated edition of *History of Rocketry and Space Travel*. Von Braun, a German rocket pioneer, was a key figure in the development of the U.S. space program. One of his collaboraters, Ordway, worked with von Braun at the Army Ballistic Missile Agency, the forerunner of NASA's Marshall Space Flight Center in Huntsville, Alabama. Suitable for general audiences, this illustrated edition takes the reader from the rocketry of the ancient Chinese and Greek civilizations through the space shuttle eras of the United States and the Soviet Union.

Furniss, Tim. *Space Shuttle Log*. New York: Jane's Publishing Co., 1986. This book covers the first twenty-two missions of the space shuttle program. The design concepts for the entire Space Transportation System are reviewed, as well as specific data on each flight. Black-and-white photographs from each mission accompany the summaries.

Kerrod, Robin. *Space Shuttle*. New York: Gallery Books, 1984. Components of the space shuttle vehicles and highlights from the first dozen missions are detailed in this well-illustrated volume. Its full-color photographs are perhaps this book's greatest asset.

National Aeronautics and Space Administration. *Mission 41-B: Alone in Space*. MR-41B. Washington, D.C.: Author, 1984. A summary of the tenth space shuttle mission. With general information about payloads aboard orbiter *Challenger*, the failed deployment of two commercial satellites, and two precedent-setting untethered spacewalks. Suitable for general audiences.

_____ . *NASA Activities: March, 1984*. Washington, D.C.: Government Printing Office, 1984. Official monthly publication for employees of the National Aeronautics and Space Administration. Contains STS 41B mission facts and a pictorial chronology from prelaunch preparations through landing.

Beth Dickey

Cross-References

Astronauts and the U.S. Astronaut Program, 154; Biological Effects of Space Travel on Humans, 188; Cape Canaveral and the Kennedy Space Center, 229; The French Space Program, 461; Galaxies Beyond the Milky Way, 474; U.S. Launch Vehicles, 749; Materials Processing in Space, 933; The Milky Way, 1018; The New Astronomy and the Study of Electromagnetic Radiation, 1066; Soyuz T-5, T-6, and

SPACE SHUTTLE MISSION 11
Challenger

Date: April 6 to April 13, 1984
Type of mission: Manned Earth-orbiting spaceflight
Country: The United States

Space shuttle mission 11 (STS 41C) launched into low Earth orbit the Long-Duration Exposure Facility to study materials degradation. The crew then performed a repair on the Solar Maximum Mission satellite, achieving the first in-orbit repair of a serviceable free-flying spacecraft.

Principal personages
ROBERT L. CRIPPEN, the commander
FRANCIS R. SCOBEE, the pilot
TERRY J. HART,
JAMES D. VAN HOFTEN and
GEORGE D. NELSON, mission specialists
FRANK J. CEPOLLINA, Multimission Modular Spacecraft and
Flight Support System Project Manager, Goddard Space Flight
Center
FRANCIS J. LOGAN, Deputy Project Manager
PETER E. O'NEILL, Mission Manager
WILLIAM N. STEWART, Mission Operations Manager
GERALD P. KENNEY, Payload Integration Manager
JAY H. GREENE, Flight Director
JOHN B. BIBATTISTA, Long-Duration Exposure Facility Experiment
Manager
WILLIAM H. KINARD, Long-Duration Exposure Facility Chief
Scientist

Summary of the Mission

To give an account of the Solar Maximum Repair Mission, one must begin with the launch of the Solar Maximum Mission (SMM, or Solar Max) observatory, which employed for the first time a serviceable multimission modular spacecraft. Launched on February 14, 1980, from the Cape Canaveral Air Force Station, the vehicle achieved an altitude of 576 kilometers, with an inclination of 28.5 degrees. The SMM scientific payload consisted of seven instruments designed to make in-orbit measurements of solar phenomena—including flares, the corona, and the total solar output—during a period near the height of maximum solar activity. These operations were successfully completed during the first eight months of Solar Max's lifetime.

Prior to the launch of the SMM observatory, all nations with space programs had designed their low-orbit, free-flying spacecraft as expendable vehicles; when the spacecraft's operational life was over or when it experienced failure, it was abandoned, left to decay or burn up in Earth's atmosphere. The multimission modular spacecraft was conceived as a multipurpose, low-cost, reusable spacecraft. It was an assembly of modular subsystems that would be individually replaceable in the laboratory and in space. These modules are the attitude control system, the communications and data handling subsystem, the modular power system, and the propulsion module. The multimission modular spacecraft and its SMM experiment payload were cooperatively designed by the National Aeronautics and Space Administration (NASA), American industry, and American and foreign experimenters for several years of operation.

During the fourth to seventh months of orbital operations, the coronagraph/ polarimeter instrument in the payload section experienced successive failures of two four-stage integrated circuits, causing its main electronics box (MEB) to fail. (The main purpose of the MEB was to create television-type pictures of the occulted solar corona for transmission to Earth.) A few months later, the spacecraft suffered a series of three failures because of a long-term fuse derating problem. This problem caused the loss of precise three-axis stabilization of the satellite, rendering selected viewing of regions on the Sun impossible. Engineers managed to devise a system which would allow three of the solar instruments to continue limited measurements, but extensive repairs were definitely necessary.

Under the direction of Frank Cepollina, a plan for the retrieval of SMM by the space shuttle using the so-called flight support system was changed to an orbital repair plan. Engineers estimated that for an expenditure of $45 million, in addition to launch costs, the SMM observatory, whose replacement cost would have been $235 million, could be restored to nominal operation. At launch, the SMM observatory, including the development of the serviceable multimission modular spacecraft, had cost NASA $79 million. In August, 1982, the U.S. Congress gave NASA permission to plan the rendezvous with and repair of the SMM spacecraft. These measures would be taken after more than four years of space operations; the observatory would thus be operational during the period of minimum solar activity in the eleven-year solar cycle.

The Solar Maximum Repair Mission was scheduled to fly with the Langley Research Center's Long-Duration Exposure Facility. Use would be made of the Space Transportation System (STS), more popularly known as the space shuttle, with the multimission modular spacecraft's spare attitude control system module, a new main electronics box, tools for extravehicular activity (EVA), the flight support system, and the Long-Duration Exposure Facility installed in its cargo bay. The flight support system would be used to berth and service the malfunctioning solar observatory. This mission would be the eleventh flight of the space shuttle, scheduled for April 4, 1984. Other experiments would be performed in the crew cabin, including a nineteen-year-old student's separate middeck honeybee experiment to determine bees' adaptability to weightless conditions. Also included in the payload were a 360-degree camera in the shuttle bay and a 70-millimeter camera for making exposures through the portholes in the aft flight deck. Mission planners agreed that the Long-Duration Exposure Facility would function as an excellent secondary payload because it required the same 28.5-degree launch inclination and close to the same altitude that the Solar Maximum Repair Mission required.

Mission planners were confident about the schedule and the flightplan. An available Landsat D attitude control system module was chosen to replace Solar Max's malfunctioning module. This spare would still serve to support the Earth resources Landsat D spacecraft through their launches. After the building and testing of a new coronagraph/polarimeter main electronics box, engineers determined that substituting it for the faulty system aboard Solar Max would restore six of the seven SMM instruments to full operational capability. Numerous training simulations were performed on the ground with various elements of the servicing mission. These simulations indicated the practicality of performing the required servicing activities during two six-hour EVA periods.

On the morning of April 6, following the usual prelaunch preparations at the Kennedy Space Center, the space shuttle *Challenger* was launched for the STS 41C mission—two days later than scheduled. A direct-ascent burn was employed, and the external tank was separated from the shuttle and left to burn up over the southern tip of Hawaii. Upon arrival at the desired 28.5-degree, 491-kilometer-apogee orbit, the space shuttle cargo bay doors were opened. The remote manipulator system and the flight support system were tested before they were used for deployment of the Long-Duration Exposure Facility and the SMM berthing and repair operations.

On April 7, mission specialist Terry J. Hart released the Long-Duration Exposure Facility using the Canadian-built remote manipulator system. This huge 9,707-kilogram payload, designed for gravity-gradient orientation, stabilized perfectly upon release. With the secondary payload deployed, the space shuttle performed maneuvers to increase its altitude to 502 kilometers to rendezvous with Solar Max.

On April 8, James D. van Hoften and George D. Nelson donned their EVA spacesuits in the air lock and went into the cargo bay. Nelson put on the manned maneuvering unit and, untethered, flew his planned ten-minute, sixty-meter flight to approach Solar Max. The plan called for the astronaut to put the maneuvering unit controls into an autopilot mode to stop the spiraling spacecraft. The space shuttle would be maneuvered to approach Solar Max and use its remote manipulator system to grasp a fixture located on the satellite. Although the maneuvering unit flew perfectly and synchronized with the spin rate of the satellite, after three attempts at increasing velocities, the shuttle failed to lock onto a spacecraft trunion located between the two solar arrays. Yet another unsuccessful attempt was made to grasp the uncontrolled, tumbling observatory with the remote manipulator. A last, desperate attempt failed when Nelson held onto a solar array panel and the spacecraft structure and attempted to stabilize the SMM using the manned maneuvering unit. As the maneuvering fuels were running low, Commander Robert Crippen ordered Nelson to return to the shuttle.

Directed by William Stewart, the SMM Payload Operations Control Center at Goddard and worldwide ground stations performed a difficult feat in regaining attitude control of the observatory before the SMM batteries lost too much power. Alternate magnetic control programs were loaded into the spacecraft's computer memory and commanded to develop about one-half the previous spin rate. Engineers on the ground wanted to achieve the rates used in backup computer simulations of the remote manipulator system capturing a spinning SMM.

Over the next sixteen hours on April 9 and 10, space planners at Goddard took measures to improve the power and thermal situation in the observatory. On June 10, after the desired SMM spin rate was established and the latest space shuttle approach maneuver was attempted, Crippen performed a fuel savings maneuver to rendezvous with the observatory. Fortunately, Terry Hart was able to grasp the SMM on his first attempt. The SMM was then berthed to the flight support system for the planned series of repair operations.

On April 11, van Hoften and Nelson again went into the cargo bay and compressed nearly two days of scheduled EVA activities into one. Riding the manipulator foot restraint attached to the remote manipulator, van Hoften, assisted by Nelson, used a battery-powered module service tool to remove the spacecraft's attitude control module and put it onto a temporary holding conical nut on the side of the flight support system. He removed the replacement module from a holding fixture and installed it on the observatory. The faulty module was next stowed onto the holding fixture on the side of the flight support system.

A second repair was performed within four minutes by van Hoften, with a gloved-hand installation of a 0.5-kilogram plasma baffle over a small rectangular propane exhaust port in the X-ray polychromator instrument panel. This repair corrected an interference in that instrument's data output.

For the third repair, the failed main electronics box was removed by van Hoften, who used a specially adapted, battery-powered screwdriver and other EVA hand tools. Nelson then removed a new main electronics box from a storage locker and performed the delicate installation. The complicated electronics box, which has 365 connections through eleven electrical connectors, had been built and tested on the ground after the coronagraph/polarimeter instrument failure. The new box had never operated with the rest of that instrument until it was installed in space. A thirty-page EVA sequence had been written by space planners for this complicated exchange.

The cargo bay activities were performed so smoothly that the astronauts were able to complete their work earlier than planned, giving van Hoften an opportunity to don the manned maneuvering unit and perform a familiarization flight down the cargo bay. A planned space shuttle maneuver to reboost Solar Max to a 528-kilometer altitude, in order to extend its orbital lifetime, was canceled when the shuttle's maneuvering fuel became so low that the maneuver would have jeopardized the safe reentry of the shuttle and its crew. Only four short burns were performed to circularize the shuttle's orbit before SMM was released.

Before the conclusion of the Solar Max repairs, its computer memory was loaded and the spacecraft was examined carefully. On April 12, once it had been determined that the attitude control system module and the new electronics box appeared to be working satisfactorily, the remote manipulator was used to engage the spacecraft and hold it suspended while the high-gain antenna system was deployed. This system would be used with the new Tracking and Data-Relay Satellite System. The observatory redeployment went smoothly at the space shuttle's altitude of 502 kilometers, and Solar Max was tested yet again by the ground stations while the space shuttle was still in the vicinity. Upon final ground confirmation of the successful observatory repairs, the crew closed the shuttle, and *Challenger* returned to a landing at Edwards Air Force Base on April 13. (The plan had originally called for a landing at the Kennedy Space Center, but weather there was hazardous.)

The retrieved attitude control module was returned to Goddard Space Flight Center for measurement of the degradation of its mechanical, electrical, and thermal components. Technicians planned to refurbish it and possibly fly it on a subsequent scientific mission. The faulty electronics box was also returned to Goddard, where technicians from the High Altitude Observatory in Boulder, Colorado, examined it. Three circuit boards were reworked by installing a new counter chip on each board. The fifteen individual boards, groups of boards, and the entire box were retested using automated computer programs. Engineers determined that this unit could have been reflown. A report was prepared following the completion of a number of degradation studies, which used the retrieved SMM attitude control module main electronics box components, materials, and surfaces. The general condition of the retrieved electrical and mechanical parts led engineers to believe that long-life operation of space components can be expected with use of proper design techniques.

Knowledge Gained

With STS 41C, for the first time the space shuttle used a direct-ascent burn to orbit, followed by the release of its external tank to burn up at high altitude. This mode of higher-than-usual orbital injection allows for more efficient servicing of free-flying spacecraft above the area of residual atmospheric drag of the shuttle's parking orbit.

At an altitude of 491 kilometers and an orbital inclination of 28.5 degrees, the space shuttle successfully deployed the Long-Duration Exposure Facility. This satellite was designed for a series of in-orbit studies of materials degradation. The satellite's low-cost, twelve-sided open structure, outfitted with experiment trays, was easily deployed by the shuttle's remote manipulator system; it was designed to operate unattended for years before its recovery.

The space shuttle crew demonstrated the ability to rendezvous with and retrieve Solar Max at an altitude of about 502 kilometers, using the remote manipulator system in a backup capture mode. This maneuver was followed by the successful forty-two-minute exchange of an attitude control subsystem module, proving that repairs could be made on a serviceable spacecraft in orbit. In addition, the mission showed that with considerable planning, replacement hardware and tool development, simulations, and crew training, some EVA repairs can be made on payload instruments not designed for in-orbit servicing. To ensure successful servicing in orbit, however, work areas must be well within astronauts' operational constraints.

One of the most serious problems during the mission arose because of the lack of a secondary, manual means of triggering the trunion pin attachment device during attempts to capture the free-flying observatory. Also, the astronauts were forced to adjust the shuttle's fuel consumption and drift control during various rendezvous modes.

For an in-orbit repair mission to proceed in a timely and economical manner, good photographs and other documentation of the free-flyer must be available prior to launch. Replacement units and spare components must also be available. Proper repair planning and sufficient use of simulations are essential for an in-orbit repair to be successful. Planned alternate backup modes were found necessary during several contingency situations during STS 41C. The mission specialists' limited EVA time during this mission indicated the need for additional power tools and servicing aids to increase astronauts' productive servicing time in orbit.

In addition to the highly successful in-orbit repairs of Solar Max at less than 20 percent of its replacement cost, the return to Earth of the malfunctioning observatory hardware opened the possibility of ground repair, refurbishment, and subsequent reuse of space resources. Returned materials and components were evaluated and generally found to be in excellent condition, except for degradation of thermal blanket materials and a high micrometeoroid count. The results of these studies, which followed SMM's four years of in-orbit operations, are aiding the design and operation of long-life serviceable spacecraft, scientific instrumentation, and applications payloads.

Context

In late 1969, Joseph Purcell, Project Manager for the Orbiting Astronomical Observatories, developed the concept of a modular spacecraft that could be reconfigured to handle various types and sizes of payloads. With the advent of the space shuttle, Frank Cepollina advocated extending the modular concept to include the capacity for in-orbit replacement of the modules. The idea for modular and serviceable spacecraft was adopted after an intercenter competition for new space exploration concepts. After several years of refinement, the multimission modular spacecraft was adopted as the spacecraft to support the Solar Maximum and Landsat D missions. Following SMM's successful launch and nine months of operation before the attitude control failure, the Solar Maximum Repair Mission demonstrated the space shuttle's capability to rendezvous with, capture, repair, and redeploy a malfunctioning spacecraft.

After winning the approval of Congress and undergoing two years of intense preparations, the STS 41C Solar Maximum Repair Mission was performed. This pathfinder mission first proved the capability of the space shuttle to deploy the large, passive Long-Duration Exposure Facility and then to perform the repairs on Solar Max, extending the observatory's scientific investigations. The astronauts, employing in-orbit EVA and intravehicular activity servicing techniques, proved the practicality of exchanging an attitude control system module designed for servicing. The difficult exchange of the 12.4-kilogram coronagraph/polarimeter main electronics box was also accomplished, showing the possibility of in-orbit repair of payload instruments not specifically designed for in-orbit servicing.

The successful stable deployment of the Long-Duration Exposure Facility demonstrated that a low-cost, passive spacecraft could be orbited by the space shuttle, permitting the performance of long-term materials degradation experiments in space. The student honeybee experiment indicated that, after an initial difficulty with adaptation, the honeybees were able to make a honeycomb while in a weightless state—proving that, with certain environmental conditions controlled, lifeforms can adapt to the space environment.

While scientists are very concerned about the amount of scientific data returned, they are also conscious of the need for timely return of data to the investigators who spend so much time designing and building experiments for space. By the time a new replacement spacecraft and payload can be funded, produced, and qualified for flight (which usually takes from three to seven years), the experiment aboard a malfunctioning spacecraft could become outdated. In this context, in-orbit repair and servicing of payloads is clearly valuable to the experimenters.

The STS 41C mission demonstrated the technical, scientific, and economic benefits of using the space shuttle to retrieve, repair, and redeploy free-flying spacecraft that were designed for routine servicing. The mission also demonstrated the more limited capability of repairing payload instruments not intended for in-orbit servicing. More nations are expected to use these techniques of designing spacecraft and their payloads for routine servicing and repairs, thereby extending the benefits derived from their nations' initial investments.

Bibliography

Allen, Joseph P., and Russell Martin. *Entering Space: An Astronaut's Odyssey*. New York: Stewart, Tabori and Chang, 1984. A personal account of space travel aboard a U.S. space shuttle, with details of the experience of launch, the work accomplished in and around the spacecraft, and the thrilling return to Earth. Illustrated with color photographs.

Chaikin, Andrew. "Solar Max: Back from the Edge." *Sky and Telescope* 67 (June, 1984): 494-497. This article provides an overview of the Solar Maximum Repair Mission, recounting its successes and failures for the general reader.

Furniss, Tim. *Space Shuttle Log*. London: Jane's Publishing Co., 1986. An in-depth history of the space shuttle and its flights, from STS 1 through STS 61A. Features details about the design of the space shuttle vehicle and an overview of the shuttle systems. A concise account of the shuttle flights is provided, along with black-and-white photographs from each mission covered.

McMahan, Tracy, and Valerie Neal. *Repairing Solar Max: The Solar Maximum Repair Mission*. Washington, D.C.: Government Printing Office, 1984. Describes the preparations for the Solar Max repair and the people who worked on STS 41C. Tells of the successful operations and the problems encountered. This reference also discusses the new era of orbital repairs of spacecraft.

Maran, Stephen P., and Bruce F. Woodgate. "A Second Chance for Solar Max." *Sky and Telescope* 67 (June, 1984): 498-500. This article offers two astronomers' views of the SMM repair and the promise it held for future repair missions.

Robert E. Davis

Cross-References

Cape Canaveral and the Kennedy Space Center, 229; Solar Explorers, 440; Goddard Space Flight Center, 563; International Sun-Earth Explorers, 620; The Interplanetary Monitoring Platform Satellites, 631; Johnson Space Center, 669; Pioneer Missions 1-5, 1116; The Skylab Program, 1285; The Solar Maximum Mission, 1353; The U.S. Space Shuttle, 1626; Space Shuttle Mission 10: *Challenger*, 1711; The Spacelab Program, 1884; The Stratospheric Aerosol and Gas Experiment, 1957.

SPACE SHUTTLE MISSION 12
Discovery

Date: August 30 to September 5, 1984
Type of mission: Manned Earth-orbiting spaceflight
Country: The United States

STS 41D/F, the maiden flight of Discovery, *featured the first deployment of three communications satellites, including the Leasat. Leasat was the first satellite designed to be launched exclusively by the shuttle.*

Principal personages
    HENRY W. HARTSFIELD, the mission commander
    MICHAEL L. COATS, the mission pilot
    RICHARD M. MULLANE,
    STEVEN A. HAWLEY, and
    JUDITH A. RESNIK, mission specialists
    CHARLES D. WALKER, a payload specialist

Summary of the Mission

STS 41D/F, the twelfth space shuttle flight, saw the maiden voyage of the orbiter *Discovery*. *Discovery*, designated orbiter vehicle 103 (OV-103), was named for Captain James Cook's British ship which made voyages of discovery in the Pacific Ocean in the 1770's. He and his crew discovered the Hawaiian Islands and explored southern Alaska and western Canada. In addition, *Discovery* was the name of Henry Hudson's ship, which in 1610 and 1611 searched for a northwest passage between the Atlantic and Pacific oceans and discovered Hudson Bay.

Discovery rolled out of the Palmdale, California, plant of Rockwell International on October 16, 1983, weighing about 300 kilograms less than its sister ship, *Challenger*. Its weight savings resulted from the replacement of additional low-temperature tiles with "advanced flexible reusable surface insulation" (AFRSI) blankets. Each blanket was made of a sewn composite quilted fabric with the same silica material as the tiles sandwiched between the inner and outer layers. In addition, graphite epoxy replaced some internal aluminum spars and beams in the spacecraft's wings and payload bay doors.

The orbiter was placed atop the modified Boeing 747 shuttle carrier aircraft and transported to the Kennedy Space Center in Florida, where its systems were given a final check. *Discovery*'s cargo of satellites and other experiments were loaded aboard, and the orbiter was mated to the external tank and twin solid-fueled rocket boosters. On May 19, 1984, the completed stack was moved majestically to the pad at Launch Complex 39A for its scheduled flight on June 25.

The crew for the mission was commanded by Henry Hartsfield, a veteran astronaut who had served in a support capacity for the Apollo 16 lunar landing mission and for the three Skylab orbital flights. He had been the backup pilot for STS 2 and STS 3 and had made his first trip into space as the pilot of STS 4. For STS 41D/F, the pilot was U.S. Navy commander Michael Coats, who had become an astronaut in 1978. The three mission specialists for the flight were from the same astronaut class, U.S. Air Force lieutenant colonel Richard Mullane, Steven Hawley, and Judith Resnik.

Joining them on the flight was payload specialist Charles Walker, chief test engineer for the McDonnell Douglas project on electrophoresis operations in space (EOS). He was the first nonprofessional astronaut to fly into space under a NASA policy that allows major space shuttle customers to have one of their own people on board to operate their payloads. His major role on the flight was to operate one of the experiments carried on board, the continuous flow electrophoresis system (CFES). It was a modified version of the device flown on STS 4, STS 6, STS 7, and STS 8, and verified that materials would be separated and purified to levels four times higher than those possible on Earth.

The CFES works on the principle that molecules of substances with different structures and sizes contain different electrical charges and, therefore, can be separated within an electrical field. Although electrophoresis can be performed under normal Earth gravity, in that environment heavier molecules tend to settle to the bottom of the device. In the microgravity of orbital flight, there is none of this settling. Walker's presence was needed because the device had been changed significantly to operate continuously for about one hundred hours during the flight.

In addition to the CFES, *Discovery* would carry Leasat 1, a communications satellite, which measures 4.26 meters in diameter and 6 meters in length when deployed. The Leasat, designed by Hughes Aircraft Company, is unique in that it does not require a separately purchased upper stage for deployment. All the other communications satellites launched from the shuttle required a Payload Assist Module, consisting of a one- or two-stage solid rocket motor, to take them to geosynchronous orbit (that is, an orbit where the satellite's velocity and altitude make it appear to hover over one spot on Earth's surface).

The worldwide Leasat (short for leased satellite) system is operated by Hughes under a contract with the Department of Defense, with the U.S. Navy acting as the executive agent. The system operates with five satellites (one is a spare) in geostationary orbit and associated ground facilities. The armed forces have access to the spacecraft through mobile air, surface, subsurface, and fixed ground stations.

A major experiments package on board *Discovery* was the OAST 1, sponsored by the Office of Aeronautics and Space Technology (OAST), part of the National Aeronautics and Space Administration (NASA). OAST 1 consisted of three major experiments: the solar array experiment, the dynamic augmentation experiment, and the solar cell calibration facility. The experiments were carried aboard a frame-like structure called the mission-peculiar equipment support structure (MPESS). Attached to a second MPESS was the large format camera, a high-altitude aerial metric stereographic mapping camera. The 408-kilogram camera can produce 2,400 negatives from 31.7 kilograms of film, including two types each of black-and-white and color.

A problem with one of *Discovery*'s general purpose computers (GPCs) caused the June 25 launch to be canceled nine minutes before lift-off was to occur. There are five GPCs on the orbiter (one is a spare) which control all the automatic functions of the spacecraft from launch to landing. That evening, the external tank was drained of propellants and the faulty GPC was replaced. The countdown was recycled, and the launch was rescheduled for June 26, at 8:43 A.M. eastern daylight time.

The countdown proceeded on schedule and the go-ahead for redundant set launch sequence (RSLS) start was given at T minus 31 seconds. At this point, the four primary GPCs took over main control of the launch. Only one further command would be needed from the ground, "Go for main engine start," at approximately T minus 6 seconds. The GPCs, operating in redundant sets, based on the onboard clock, began to issue commands to the vehicle. The ground launch sequencer, which had been issuing the orders up to this point, continued to monitor several hundred launch commit criteria and could call a hold if a discrepancy were observed.

Everything proceeded normally, and the space shuttle main engines (SSMEs) were given the firing command. The engines are ignited in sequence, SSME 3 (engine number 3) first, followed by SSME 2 and SSME 1, at 120-millisecond intervals. SSME 3 ignited and so did SSME 2, but an indication of irregular operation of the main fuel valve of SSME 3 during the start transient (from ignition to full thrust) caused the engine to be shut down by the RSLS. SSME 2 was commanded off and SSME 1 was never given the command to start. All of this occurred within 0.08 second of the ignition command to SSME 3. The launch vehicle systems were made safe, and the crew exited the vehicle.

As a result of the aborted launch, the vehicle was unceremoniously moved back to the vehicle assembly building, and SSME 3 was replaced. A decision was made to remanifest the mission, using the same flight crew but combining the payloads from STS 41F with STS 41D (thus, the mission is known as STS 41D/F). Launch was set for August 29. Leasat 1 was replaced by Leasat 2 at the request of Hughes and scheduled to be launched by STS 51A. The large format camera was replaced by the two STS 41F communications satellites, Telstar 3 and SBS (Satellite Business System) 4. These are two of the smaller Hughes HS-376 satellites, similar to ones deployed on previous missions.

After a one-day delay because of a timing problem between the onboard computer command software and the ground-based master events controller, STS 41D/F was launched on August 30, 1984, at 8:41:50 A.M. The ascent was normal in all aspects, and *Discovery* was placed in a nearly circular orbit at 297 kilometers. The flight proceeded well, with each of the three communications satellites being deployed on time and in the correct location. Subsequently, all three attained geosynchronous orbit. The solar array experiment was extended and tested on two separate days.

On the fourth day of the mission, a review of data from the orbiter's supply water dump system indicated that ice had formed on the dump nozzle which opens to space on the side of the spacecraft. There were also indications that ice had collected around the wastewater dump nozzle, but it was believed that the ice did not stay there. The remote manipulator system (RMS) was deployed, and the television camera located at the end of the RMS arm showed a large column of ice over the supply nozzle. A wastewater dump, attempted during the television coverage, showed ice built up around that nozzle. The dump was terminated.

Although all systems functioned properly on the fifth day, concern over the ice buildup continued. A television scan showed that the amount of ice was considerably smaller than the day before. Several firings of the orbiter's reaction control system jets proved unsuccessful in dislodging the ice. The crew compartment was depressurized somewhat to allow for a spacewalk, if necessary.

Early on the sixth day, the crew began to stow onboard equipment and experiments in preparation for rentry. The RMS was then used to break off most of the ice from the supply nozzle, but the ice remained on the wastewater dump nozzle. Later, a last look at the ice showed that extended Sun exposure and repeated nozzle heater cycles had solved the problem.

The de-orbit burn by the orbital maneuvering system engines slowed *Discovery* down, and it began its long glide to Earth. The flight of STS 41D/F ended after 6 days, 56 minutes, and 4 seconds with touchdown of the main landing gear on the dry lakebed at Edwards Air Force Base in California. The spacecraft rolled for approximately 3,130 meters and came to a complete rest at 6:38:54 A.M. Pacific daylight time.

Knowledge Gained

All fifteen of STS 41D/F's test objectives were met, yet only 85 percent of the CFES samples were processed. Payload specialist Walker proved his value on the flight when he performed in-flight maintenance on the unit and operated the control system manually when difficulties developed in the automated system. Walker returned from orbit with quantities of an unidentified processed hormone to be used in human clinical tests relating to the treatment of diabetes. Unfortunately, the samples later proved to have been contaminated.

The solar array experiment consisted of a thin blanket of plastic material called Kapton, which was made into 84 panels that fold accordion-style when the structure is retracted. It was deployed by extending an epoxy-fiberglass mast stored in a canister. When fully extended, the 4-meter-wide array stood 31.5 meters tall; it was folded into a package only 17.78 centimeters thick for storage during launch and landing. The solar array, the forerunner of solar energy collection panels for satellites and the space station *Freedom*, carried active solar cell modules located on panels near the top. All other solar array panels carried dummy cells. It was neither necessary nor cost effective to cover the entire array with active cells. A solar array of this size, however, fully populated with active solar cells, would be capable of producing 12.5 kilowatts of power.

The array extensions and retractions to both the 70 percent and 100 percent levels were successful. The dynamic augmentation experiment showed that the array was able to dampen deflections introduced, well within desired ranges. Calibration of the solar cells by the solar cell calibration facility was satisfactorily completed.

The successful deployment of the Telstar and SBS 4 satellites once again displayed the ability of the Space Transportation System to deliver its payloads on time and with pinpoint accuracy. The problems with the Payload Assist Modules which had prevented previous satellites from reaching geosynchronous orbit had been fixed.

The capability of carrying a large satellite within the payload bay and then gently releasing it was demonstrated. The deployment method was unique, too, for the satellite was mounted horizontally in the orbiter's payload bay. Ejection of the satellite was initiated when locking pins at four contact points were retracted. An explosive device then released a spring that ejected the spacecraft in a motion not unlike the throwing of a Frisbee. This motion gave the satellite the momentum to separate from the shuttle and gyroscopic stability during the forty-five minutes between deployment and ignition of its first-stage motor. The HS-376 satellites were stabilized by spinning them on a platform before ejecting them.

Context

With the completion of its twelfth space shuttle mission, NASA's Space Transportation System fleet of orbiters numbered three. Eventually, *Discovery* was assigned to flight operations at Vandenberg's shuttle launch facility. There, it would be used to launch Department of Defense payloads into polar orbits. The loss of *Challenger* and the subsequent cancellation of shuttle launch activities at Vandenberg freed *Discovery* to return to duty at Kennedy Space Center. *Discovery* was chosen to make the first shuttle flight after the *Challenger* explosion.

Prior to the first flight of any orbiter, the SSMEs are qualified by means of a flight readiness firing (FRF). The three SSMEs, each providing 1,670 kilonewtons of thrust at lift-off, burn for approximately eight minutes during launch. The FRF is a twenty-second test performed with the shuttle on the launchpad, which ensures that the SSMEs are working properly. The FRF also allows for a complete rehearsal of the activities leading to a launch, without involving the crew or igniting the solid-fueled rocket boosters. After the FRF for STS 41D, which took place on June 2, 1984, engineers found debonding in a fuel preburner shield on SSME 1. A heat-shield was bonded to the wall of the hot gas manifold to protect the pressure vessel in case of overheating. The SSMEs operate on a staged combustion cycle, first burning fuel-rich oxygen and hydrogen in the preburner. Exhaust gases from the combustion process are ducted through the high-pressure fuel turbopump turbine, actuating the turbine that drives the high-pressure fuel pump. *Discovery*'s SSME 1 was duly replaced by an engine which had flown twice before on *Challenger*.

Inspection of SSME 3 after the RSLS abort of June 26 revealed slightly damaged insulation on one of the engine fuel ducts directly above the main fuel valve actuator, leading to speculation that liquid nitrogen leaked on the valve actuator. Single-engine tests at the National Space Technology Laboratories in Bay St. Louis, Mississippi, could not confirm that the insulation damage caused the failure. No exact cause of the failure was revealed, leading NASA officials to believe that it was a momentary clog which led to the shutdown. A year later, during the attempted launch of the STS 51F/Spacelab 2 mission, another "stuck" valve was found, this time in one of *Challenger*'s main engines; the problem was blamed on an overly sensitive sensor which detected the sluggishly opening valve and sent an abort signal to the RSLS.

Judith Resnik, who spent a few terrifying moments during the abort, would be aboard the ill-fated STS 51L. Charles Walker would fly with the CFES on two more flights (STS 51D and STS 61B) before operations were temporarily suspended in the wake of the *Challenger* accident. Henry Hartsfield would command the STS 61A flight, and Steven Hawley would be aboard *Columbia* for STS 61C, the mission launched sixteen days before STS 51L.

Bibliography

Allen, Joseph P., and Russell Martin. *Entering Space: An Astronaut's Odyssey*. New York: Stewart, Tabori and Chang, 1984. Describes the tension of a shuttle countdown and launch, the challenges of living and working in space, the views of Earth from space, and a shuttle landing. Although this book is essentially a personal account, the experiences of other astronauts are presented in an effort to give a balanced view of space travel. Written for general audiences. Illustrated with photographs.

Furniss, Tim. *Manned Spaceflight Log*. Rev. ed. London: Jane's Publishing Co., 1986. An overview of spaceflight since Yuri Gagarin's pioneering mission in April, 1961. The book covers the flights by American astronauts, Soviet cosmonauts, and space travelers from the other nations who have flown with them. Includes an unbiased account of the major events of each mission.

_____ . *Space Shuttle Log*. London: Jane's Publishing Co., 1986. An examination of the space shuttle and its first twenty-two flights. Reviews the design concepts for the Space Transportation System, as well as an overview of the space shuttle systems. Also gives a concise accounting of each shuttle flight, along with black-and-white photographs from each mission.

Hallion, Richard. *On the Frontier*. NASA SP-4303. Washington, D.C.: Government Printing Office, 1984. Part of the NASA History Series. Explores the experimental aircraft which provided the necessary research for the development of the space shuttle. Very readable, containing photographs of these pioneer aircraft and a complete annotated listing of the flights of each of the space shuttle vehicles. An extensive bibliography completes this work.

Kerrod, Robin. *Space Shuttle*. New York: Gallery Books, 1984. Written for general audiences, Kerrod's book includes color photographs of the space shuttle. The photos illustrate well this marvelous vehicle and the people who fly it. The components of the Space Transportation System, and highlights of the first dozen missions, are presented.

MacKnight, Nigel. *Shuttle*. Nottingham, England: MacKnight International, 1985. A history of the space shuttle, this copiously illustrated book traces the design of the vehicle and the various aspects of a typical mission. The author, a British journalist, takes the reader on a tour of the Kennedy Space Center in Florida and shows a shuttle vehicle being prepared for flight, from the stacking of the solid-fueled rocket boosters to the vehicle rollout to the launchpad. Articles about and interviews with astronauts help to emphasize the personal side of each flight.

Otto, Dixon P. *On Orbit: Bringing on the Space Shuttle*. Athens, Ohio: Main Stage Publications, 1986. Covers the early designs of the space shuttle. An account of each of the first twenty-five flights is given, including the names of the crew members, the principal payloads, and the objectives of each flight. Illustrated.

Smith, Melvyn. *An Illustrated History of Space Shuttle: X-15 to Orbiter*. Newbury Park, Calif.: Haynes Publications Inc., 1986. A highly detailed overview of the space shuttle and the experimental aircraft which led to its design, the book spans the period from 1959 through 1985. Written for the general audience, it contains many rare photographs. Information is presented chronologically.

Wilson, Andrew. *Space Shuttle Story*. New York: Crescent Books, 1986. Traces the history of the space shuttle from the early days of rocketry to the *Challenger* disaster. Aimed at a general audience, Wilson's book contains little detail; the emphasis is on the men and women who fly the shuttle. Contains more than one hundred color photographs.

Yenne, Bill. *The Astronauts*. New York: Exeter Books, 1986. This book presents an account of the manned space programs of the United States and the Soviet Union. Illustrated with several hundred photographs taken aboard the two countries' spacecraft, it also tells about the non-American and non-Soviet passengers who flew as guests on some of these flights. While Yenne does not give the complete personal background of each astronaut and cosmonaut, he does provide an in-triguing insight into the human aspect of space travel.

_____ . *The Encyclopedia of U.S. Spacecraft*. New York: Exeter Books, 1985, reprint 1988. A valuable reference for learning about spacecraft built or launched by the United States. Photographs of each of the spacecraft, most of them in color, accompany descriptions and launch data. Also provided are details on the American launch vehicles and a glossary of acronyms and abbreviations.

Russell R. Tobias

Cross-References

Astronauts and the U.S. Astronaut Program, 154; Materials Processing in Space, 933; The U.S. Space Shuttle, 1626; Space Shuttle Living Conditions, 1634; Space

Shuttle Mission 4: *Columbia*, 1670; Space Shuttle Mission 16: *Discovery*, 1759; Space Shuttle Mission 22: *Challenger*, 1793; Space Shuttle Mission 23: *Atlantis*, 1800; Space Shuttle Mission 24: *Columbia*, 1806; Space Shuttle Mission 25. *Challenger*, 1813; U.S. Private and Commercial Telecommunications Satellites, 1997.

SPACE SHUTTLE MISSION 13
Challenger

Date: October 5 to October 13, 1984
Type of mission: Manned Earth-orbiting spaceflight
Countries: The United States and Canada

STS 41G obtained valuable data on Earth resources from a variety of experiments carried in the payload bay of the orbiter. The record seven-person crew obtained measurements from photographic and radar instruments which were used to perform new interpretations of geological and oceanographic features and in making new maps for detailed studies of Earth's resources.

Principal personages
ROBERT L. CRIPPEN, the spacecraft commander
JON A. MCBRIDE, the pilot
SALLY K. RIDE,
KATHRYN D. SULLIVAN, and
DAVID C. LEESTMA, mission specialists
MARC GARNEAU and
PAUL SCULLY-POWER, payload specialists
JOHN T. COX, the lead flight director
EUGENE F. KRANZ, Director of Mission Operations

Summary of the Mission

The Space Transportation System (STS) 41G mission was flown as the seventeenth U.S. space shuttle flight and the sixth for the orbiter *Challenger*. The mission was also the first time seven persons had been launched on one spacecraft, the crew consisting of five men and two women, another new feature. Commanding the eight-day flight in Earth orbit was shuttle veteran Robert L. Crippen of the National Aeronautics and Space Administration (NASA), on his fourth spaceflight. The pilot was Jon A. McBride, making his first flight into space. The three mission specialists were Sally K. Ride, America's first woman in space, flying her second mission; Kathryn D. Sullivan, on her first flight; and David C. Leestma, also on his first mission. Sullivan and Leestma were to perform an extravehicular activity (EVA, or spacewalk) during the mission. Two payload specialists were also assigned to this flight: Marc Garneau of the National Research Council, the first Canadian in space, and Paul Scully-Power, an Australian by birth but now a U.S. citizen, a civilian oceanographer employed by the U.S. Navy.

The NASA crew had been selected in November, 1983, and had begun specific mission training for the 41G mission. Initially Crippen did not train with the four NASA astronauts as he was also assigned to fly as commander of STS 41C before his flight in 41G. He finally joined the 41G crew full-time in late May, 1984. Meanwhile, the crew had increased in size by the selection of the two payload specialists. Garneau had been named to be the first Canadian in space on March 14, and he was soon assigned to the 41G crew. Scully-Power was assigned on June 13.

While training progressed smoothly, elements of the hardware to be used for the 41G mission were being prepared at the Kennedy Space Center in Florida. The orbiter to be used on the mission was orbiter vehicle 099 (OV-099), named *Challenger*. The *Challenger* had previously flown on five space missions and had arrived back at the Cape on April 19 on top of the shuttle carrier aircraft (SCA), a converted Boeing 747 airliner. *Challenger* spent a total of 69 days in bay 2 of the orbiter processing facility (OPF), where work was completed in removing the remaining payload from the 41C mission and ground maintenance was performed. Major work included replacement of a general purpose computer (GPC) which was removed and placed on *Discovery*, and a series of changes in the space shuttle main engines (SSMEs) after inspections had revealed several malfunctions.

The payload for 41G was lowered into the payload bay of *Challenger* on August 9, 1984, and consisted of an Office of Space and Terrestrial Applications package (OSTA-3), which included the shuttle imaging radar (SIR-B); the large format camera; the measurement of air pollution from satellites (MAPS) payload; the feature identification and location experiment (FILE); the Earth Radiation Budget Experiment (ERBE), which included the ERBE Satellite, the ERBE non-scanner and scanner, and the Stratospheric Aerosol and Gas Experiment (SAGE) 2; eight Get-Away Special (GAS) canisters; and the orbital refueling system (ORS) experiment. Following a series of compatibility checks between the payload and the orbiter, *Challenger* was towed to the vehicle assembly building (VAB) to be mated with the rest of the 41G components on September 8.

Work in the VAB had begun in June with the stacking of the twin solid-fueled rocket booster (SRB) components on the mobile launch platform on June 4. Fifteen days later, on June 19, the huge external tank (ET) was mated to the twin SRBs. This work was originally intended for the subsequently canceled 41F mission but was reassigned to the 41G mission. Once checked, *Challenger* was hoisted up vertically and mated to the ET/SRB combination and completed the 41G configuration.

After five days in the VAB, the vehicle was rolled out, on September 13, to Pad 39A, where it waited for the next twenty-three days, undergoing a series of prelaunch tests and the final countdown for launch. After one of the smoothest countdowns on record, the thirteenth flight in the shuttle series began at 7:03 A.M. eastern standard time, October 5, 1984. The vehicle performed a nominal ascent profile with a 57-degree heading alignment over the Atlantic. All stages of the ascent profile went according to plan, with normal separation of the twin SRBs and their subsequent ocean recovery and separation of the ET before the orbital maneuvering system (OMS) performed two burns to place *Challenger* and its crew of seven into its planned orbit. Following the opening of the payload bay doors, the crew inspected the slight damage to the thermal protection system from the aft flight deck. The damage posed no serious problem to the crew, and despite an additional problem with the failure of one of the smaller onboard thrusters very early in the mission, the crew prepared for their week of orbital activities.

Initial activities included the activation of the scientific payload in the payload bay and the checkout of the robot arm. The remote manipulator system (RMS, or "the arm") was checked out by Ride, who, after completing a series of tests on the system, maneuvered the arm to grapple the ERBE satellite for deployment. Ride lifted the satellite clear of the bay to prepare for its release nine hours into the flight. It was during this period that a problem with the satellite's solar array panels was first noticed. When the solar arrays failed to unfold as programmed, it was assumed that the deployment mechanism had become frozen in the extreme low temperature of space. The solution was for Ride to point the satellite at the Sun, and after four attempts to defrost the panels they eventually unfurled successfully. The satellite was deployed by the RMS 11 hours and 15 minutes after launch. The orbiter was then maneuvered away from the satellite to monitor its separation burn to place it in its required operational orbit. With the deployment of the satellite behind them, the crew settled down to conduct the rest of their program of activities aboard *Challenger*.

During the second flight day, Garneau began his series of experiments, and oceanographer Scully-Power continued his visual observations of the world's oceans. The crew experienced difficulty in directing the onboard Ku-band antenna drive mechanism to lock on to Tracking and Data-Relay Satellite (TDRS) A in order to relay important scientific data obtained by the Earth-pointing instruments in the payload bay back to Earth. Faced with a serious problem which threatened to erase most of the data that had been collected, the crew finally succeeded in working around the problem by maneuvering the whole orbiter to allow the antenna to lock on to the TDRS, thereby saving the all-important data.

Several minor problems plagued the crew during their flight, but none was serious enough to hamper their performance. The problems with the Ku-band antenna forced postponement of the planned EVA from flight day 5 to flight day 7 to allow extra time for data gathering by the SIR-B antenna and the LFC. The SIR-B equipment was not functioning as planned and the delay in the EVA helped overcome this problem by extending the data collection time allocated to this experiment.

Both Garneau and Scully-Power and the NASA members of the flight crew conducted extensive visual observations of geological and ocean features during the mission, in particular Sullivan, a qualified geologist, who complemented the observations of oceanographer Scully-Power and the onboard instruments.

On flight day 7, the crew completed their planned EVA, delayed from flight day 5. After putting on their spacesuits and life-support backpacks, Leestma and Sullivan entered the air lock in *Challenger*'s middeck to depressurize for exit. Leestma was first out, followed by Sullivan, who became the first American woman to conduct a spacewalk. Her EVA came only three months after Soviet cosmonaut Svetlana Savitskaya became the first female to conduct an EVA, nineteen years after the first spacewalk by Soviet cosmonaut Alexei Leonov.

Once outside, the two astronauts busied themselves with their tasks, which had been supplemented with a manual reconfiguration of the Ku-band antenna so that it could be stowed in its correct position for reentry, below the starboard payload bay door hingeline. The crew would also manually latch the folding SIR-B antenna structure, which had earlier proved difficult to achieve automatically, even when the crew had used the RMS to push it shut.

The two astronauts spent the next three and one-half hours working in the open payload bay of *Challenger*, mostly at the aft bulkhead with the equipment that was being developed for future satellite refueling missions. Leestma performed the majority of this work with Sullivan assisting him and taking photographs to record his activities. The rest of the crew followed their activities from the aft flight deck, and television views of the two astronauts were transmitted to Earth via payload bay and RMS cameras.

Leestma and Sullivan also successfully reconfigured the troublesome Ku-band antenna and inspected the SIR-B antenna. After Leestma performed a somersault from the middle of the payload bay to retrieve a dislodged air lock safety valve cover, the two astronauts stowed equipment and moved back into the air lock, completing their EVA of 3 hours, 27 minutes. Once post-EVA operations had been completed, the crew conducted further simulated fuel transfer experiments.

The crew spent the next day resting and performing stowage for their return to Earth. The two payload specialists also took advantage of the final full day in space to complete their individual research programs. Finally, on flight day 9 (October 13, 1984), all was set for entry and landing, it was hoped at the Cape, using the shuttle landing facility (SLF), near the launch complex, where the mission had begun. As the crew received the weather reports from Mission Control, it appeared that, at the third attempt, Crippen would at last make a landing at Kennedy Space Center. (His previous landings of shuttles 7 and 11 had been redirected to Edwards Air Force Base as a result of poor weather at the Cape.) Fears of hurricane Josephine diverting the landing were dispelled when the weather reports forecast perfect landing conditions at the Cape.

The orbital ground track of *Challenger* dictated that the crew perform an entry profile that took the vehicle over central Canada and the central United States for the first time. That these are some of the most highly populated areas of the continent indicated NASA's growing confidence in the shuttle entry and landing phase of a mission.

During the descent, the flight crew of Crippen and McBride performed a series of entry maneuvers providing them with spectacular views of the continental United States. *Challenger* finally touched down on runway 13, at the Kennedy Space Center, at 12:26 P.M. eastern daylight time, achieving wheelstop fifty-nine seconds later. The mission's duration had been logged at 8 days, 5 hours, 23 minutes, and

33 seconds. The vehicle had completed 132 orbits of Earth, landing during the 133d. Challenger had traveled 4.3 million miles, or nearly 7 million kilometers.

Knowledge Gained

Mission 41G was a science-oriented flight, with a broad range of observations and experiments. Despite the cramped confines of the flight deck and middeck, the crew were able to obtain significant results.

As a result of reduced operating time, the SIR-B experiment was able to provide only 40 percent of the images planned. A total of 50 hours of data collection had been planned, which would cover 47 million square kilometers of the surface of Earth. Actual data recording time totaled only 9 hours during the mission because of equipment failure, coupled with the need to point the orbiter and equipment at the target manually. Nevertheless, the black-and-white images produced from millions of microwave radar pulses recorded by the eight panels on the 11-by-2-meter array were far superior to the images produced by SIR-A on STS 2 in 1981. Signals recorded by the instruments identified the unique signature of reflected surfaces, which then turned the radar "pictures" into detailed computer-generated black-and-white photographs for interpretation. The most important feature of the equipment was in its ability to record data during both daytime and nighttime passes, regardless of weather conditions on Earth. The 41G experiment covered the deserts of Egypt and the Sudan, southwest Africa, India, the western coast of Peru in South America, the Gobi desert in China, Saudi Arabia, the Great Western and central deserts of Australia, and the Mojave Desert in California, where Edwards Air Force Base is located. The images were used for identifying ancient river formations, 5 to 40 million years old, for locating evidence of earlier human habitation, and in ground-water prospecting.

Radar photographs of several areas of Earth were obtained during the flight, which included the discovery of mosquito-breeding ponds in the jungles of Bangladesh, the remains of very early settlers in Kenya's Rift Valley; medieval road systems in Sweden; coastal landforms of Holland; Canadian meteor-impact craters; vegetation in North America, South America, New Zealand, Australia, and Europe; tropical rainforests in Brazil; acid-rain damage in Germany; agricultural crop monitoring in Japan, the United States, and Australia; and several mountain ranges around the world.

The SIR-B instrument also recorded oceanic phenomena, including extreme wave patterns and currents in the South Atlantic, sea ice around Antarctica, icebergs off the Labrador coast, and oil pollution in the North Sea and the Pacific Ocean.

The large format camera recorded 2,300 photographs of every continent on Earth and provided 23-by-46-centimeter photographs which assisted environmentalists and geologists looking for pollution and new sources of minerals around the globe. In addition, several important photographs were taken of the town of Kyshtym in the Soviet Union, where, during the winter of 1957-1958, a nuclear accident had occurred.

The MAPS experiment provided important information on what effects industrial wastes have on the air after they are released into the atmosphere, taking measurements of the ozone layer from orbit and measuring levels of carbon monoxide in the troposphere. The FILE project continued experiments designed to assist in the production of more reliable and efficient remote-sensing instruments on later satellites and spacecraft.

The ERBE satellite provided data on the levels of solar energy absorbed over the different regions of Earth, as well as levels of thermal energy which the Earth returned to space. This information will provide an understanding of how the natural balance of thermal energy is affected by volcanic dust and industrial and aerosol pollution.

While the instruments on *Challenger* recorded data, the two payload specialists gathered additional information from their research programs. Garneau busied himself mainly with the effects of zero gravity on the human organism—himself. Scully-Power, a trained oceanographer, reported enthusiastically on his observations from space on the features of the world's oceans. He observed many new and interesting features, including an unsuspected system of giant eddies in the Mediterranean Sea.

In a demonstration of the large ground support needed for such flights, a NASA team from the Goddard Space Flight Center was in the jungles of Bangladesh as *Challenger* flew overhead and, by placing metallic reflectors on the jungle floor, made it possible for the SIR-B to identify these spots on the recorded images. This proved that the radar could "look" through cloud cover and trees and vegetation to reveal the ground beneath. Pictures revealed ponds of breeding mosquitoes and low spots which flood during the monsoon season; the images were recorded during the rainy season for the first time.

Context

The STS 41G mission was the thirteenth shuttle mission and the sixth for shuttle *Challenger*. The mission was preceded by several missions which concentrated on the deployment of satellites rather than scientific investigation and Earth observations. The wholly scientific Spacelab 1 mission in 1983 did fly a pressurized laboratory, but it was the first of a planned series of Spacelab missions and its role was multidisciplinary, whereas STS 41G was specifically oriented toward Earth observations.

From the early stages of the program and from earlier flights in the Mercury, Gemini, Apollo, and Skylab series, it had been recognized that spacecraft could provide valuable information on the resources and phenomena of Earth's surface and climate and that the shuttle, with its open payload bay, capable of supporting a variety of specialized experiments, could provide the first orbital platform to be monitored by an astronaut crew in order to make real-time evaluations of changes in the data collection from the instruments.

The observations from 41G proved that the shuttle was a valuable and reliable platform from which to conduct Earth-observation experiments for up to ten days in duration (the limit of the orbital life of the orbiter). The crew's ability to overcome hardware failures also ensured the success of the flight and once again demonstrated the value of having a human crew on hand to repair and operate equipment. Earlier operations from shuttle missions 2 and 3 established guidelines for this type of mission, but it was 41G that finally secured the plans for other Earth resources data-gathering flights later in the program.

Information from the instruments flying on the vehicle was also supplemented by the trained observations of the NASA crew and payload specialists such as ocean-ographer Scully-Power. The NASA astronaut could not possibly specialize in one area of research for one flight. Flying specialists on the mission made it possible to make expert observations and gather specific data.

The orbital refueling system experiment was also an important step in future refueling operations in space using the shuttle as a space tanker to extend the operational usefulness of satellites in Earth orbit. The Landsat 4 satellite was the first satellite targeted for such a fuel transfer, and the 41G experiments proved in practice what had been in the planning stages for several years. In addition, the flying of a mixed and international crew in the cramped confines of the orbiter provided valuable information to the designers of the U.S. Space Station and to planners of later Spacelab missions.

Crippen's return to flight after the 41C mission was useful in determining the optimum level of training needed by a crew commander between flights, as a step toward more frequent flying of the shuttle's crew. Determining the desirability of exchanging crews as opposed to flying a core crew who would remain together as a team on different missions (as the Soviet space station crews do) was another purpose of the experiment.

Despite the fact that the mission was over in less than nine days, these results from the experiments and crew observations were to keep the postflight evaluation team and scientists busy for several years.

Bibliography

Cooper, Henry S. F., Jr. *Before Lift-Off: The Making of a Space Shuttle Crew.* Baltimore: Johns Hopkins University Press, 1987. An account of the preparations undertaken by a group of astronauts and training officers, which results in a crew for a space shuttle mission. The author obtained special permission to document the training program of the 41G crew, from their selection to just after the mission, and a vivid text which records in detail the arduous training program was the result. The text identifies the problems and successes of the training program and follows the crew, their training team, and development of the mission itself from the autumn of 1983 through to the fall of 1984. Suitable for a general audience.

Furniss, Tim. *Manned Spaceflight Log.* Rev. ed. London: Jane's Publishing Co., 1986. This updated edition offers a brief history of manned spaceflight, from Yuri Gagarin's historic flight in April, 1961, to the tragic *Challenger* disaster and the

Soviet Mir mission of 1986. Presented in chronological order, 115 manned U.S.
and Soviet spaceflights are covered, as well as the thirteen X-15 missions of the
1960's. The STS 41G mission is listed as spaceflight 114, the fifty-seventh American spaceflight, and is located within a summary of world manned spaceflights.
Illustrated.

_____, ed. *Space Shuttle Log.* London: Jane's Publishing Co., 1986. A
collection of reports on the first twenty-two shuttle flights, providing mission
data, a summary of the missions (including the most notable events during each
flight), and a collection of biographical information on the shuttle astronauts.
Entries are in chronological order providing useful information on the place of
41G within the program as a whole. Suitable for both general and younger
readers.

Gurney, Gene, and Jeff Forte. *Space Shuttle Log: The First Twenty-five Flights.*
Blue Ridge Summit, Pa.: Tab Books, 1988. A collection of chapters summarizing the first twenty-five missions of the Space Transportation System program,
covering the operational flight time of April, 1981, to January, 1986, the first five
years of the flight program. Each entry, from STS 1 through STS 25, covers information on the crews, payloads, launch preparations, the launch, orbital operations, and landing phases of the flight. A mission summary and text are accompanied by a selection of black-and-white photographs for each flight. The entry
for the 41G mission provides information on the scientific investigations of the
flight.

Shayler, David J. *Shuttle Challenger: Aviation Fact File.* London: Salamander
Books, 1987. A book devoted to the career of orbiter vehicle 099, *Challenger.* A
comprehensive text covers the role of *Challenger* in the shuttle program, the
construction of the vehicle, its missions, the STS 51L tragedy, and the astronauts
and payloads *Challenger* carried during its career. The coverage of the 41G
mission includes information on launch preparations, the launch, orbital
activities, reentry, landing, and postlanding activities on the vehicle. A mission
data and flight log information block is provided, with additional flight data on
hardware and achievements in a series of tables at the rear of the book. This
large-format book is suitable for students as well as a general readership.

David J. Shayler

Cross-References

Astronauts and the U.S. Astronaut Program, 154; The Australian Space Program,
174; Biological Effects of Space Travel on Humans, 188; The Canadian Space
Program, 222; Cape Canaveral and the Kennedy Space Center, 229; Johnson Space
Center, 669; Landsat 1, 2, and 3, 710; Landsat 4 and 5, 717; U.S. Launch Vehicles,
749; U.S. Meteorological Satellites, 999; The National Aeronautics and Space Administration, 1032; Space Shuttle Living Conditions, 1634; Space Shuttle Mission 2:
Columbia, 1657; Space Shuttle Mission 9: *Columbia,* 1705; Space Shuttle Mission

SPACE SHUTTLE MISSION 14
Discovery

Date: November 8 to November 16, 1984
Type of mission: Manned Earth-orbiting spaceflight
Country: The United States

STS 51A was the first space retrieval mission. Using techniques devised on the spot, the crew captured and returned to Earth two errant satellites. The impressive success of this flight was an excellent demonstration of the value of people working in space.

Principal personages
FREDERICK H. HAUCK, the commander
DAVID M. WALKER, the pilot
JOSEPH P. ALLEN,
ANNA L. FISHER, and
DALE A. GARDNER, mission specialists

Summary of the Mission

When five astronauts were assigned to Space Transportation System (STS) 51A in late 1983, they expected their mission to be a routine cargo-hauling trip into space. Yet after the first flight of 1984, STS 41B, it became apparent that STS 51A might involve more unusual tasks. The crew members of STS 41B saw perfect deployment of their payload of two communications satellites, Indonesia's Palapa B2 (*palapa* is Indonesian for "fruit of the effort") and Western Union's Westar 6. In both cases, however, the rocket motors designed to take the satellites from the space shuttle *Challenger* to their orbital destinations 35,900 kilometers above Earth shut down prematurely. The two satellites were left in useless orbits about 1,000 kilometers high.

During 1984, the crew of STS 51A prepared for the retrieval of these two satellites. Meant for orbits out of reach of the space shuttle, the satellites had not been designed for recapture, but, with the help of ingenious engineers and astronauts, an apparently workable solution was devised. While plans were being formulated and equipment manufactured, ground controllers gradually lowered the orbits of the two satellites to an altitude the space shuttle orbiter could attain.

On November 8, 1984, *Discovery* began its second trip into space, less than one-tenth of a second after the scheduled time of 7:15 A.M. eastern standard time. This fourteenth mission of the Space Transportation System was commanded by Frederick Hauck. His pilot was David Walker, and the mission specialists were Joseph Allen, Anna Fisher, and Dale Gardner. As soon as *Discovery* was settled into its orbit 302 kilometers above Earth, the astronauts began preparing for their job in space.

The task of rendezvousing with an orbiting spacecraft is very complicated. In addition to getting to the right point in space to meet the target, it is essential to be in the same orbit as the targeted object. Many fine adjustments are required to make the entire orbits match and not simply intersect at one point. Matching orbits exactly ensures that the two spacecraft will stay together once they meet. It would require a total of forty-four carefully timed burns of the *Discovery* rocket engines to bring the shuttle to its first quarry and still allow it to be in the correct positions at the correct times to deploy its payload of two communications satellites.

The first satellite the *Discovery* crew was to deploy was owned by Telesat of Canada. It was the third Canadian communications satellite taken into space by the space shuttle. This one was designated Anik D2 (*anik* is Inuit for "brother"), or Telesat H. After confirming that the satellite was in good condition, the crew deployed it on schedule at 4:04 P.M. on November 9. *Discovery*'s engines were then fired so that the shuttle could keep a safe distance. Forty-five minutes later, the Anik fired its rocket engine, and, unlike the satellites being pursued on this mission, it went smoothly to its targeted orbit.

The second satellite on board was to be leased to the United States Navy. The manufacturer, Hughes Aircraft Company, called it Leasat 1. It was released from the payload bay on November 10 at 7:56 A.M. and successfully attained its correct orbit.

After completing the delivery of the two satellites, the crew could devote full attention to the retrieval plans. While *Discovery* continued to pursue Palapa on November 10, Allen and Gardner tested the spacesuits they would use for their extravehicular activities (EVAs, or spacewalks).

As Hauck and Fisher completed the rendezvous with Palapa on November 12, Walker helped Allen and Gardner into their bulky spacesuits. By the time the two suited astronauts had exited the air lock and entered *Discovery*'s payload bay, the orbiter had closed to within 9 meters of Palapa. Allen donned the manned maneuvering unit (MMU). With its small thrusters, this backpack allowed him to maneuver in space. Gardner helped him attach the 2-meter-long "stinger" to the front of his MMU. The stinger was a pole with extendable fingerlike probes and would be used to dock with Palapa.

Palapa was a cylinder 2.7 meters in height and 2.1 meters in diameter. At one end was the nozzle of the spent rocket engine, and at the other the fragile antennae that would have been put into service had the satellite reached its intended orbit. The astronauts would have liked to capture the satellite with the orbiter's 15-meter mechanical arm (the remote manipulator system), but the satellite's smooth surface presented nothing for the arm to snag. It was the job of the EVA astronauts to attach something for the remote manipulator to hold and then to stop the satellite from rotating so that it could be captured.

After confirming that all of his equipment was working as intended, Allen waited until an orbital sunrise and used his MMU to move to the nozzle end of Palapa. He slowly approached the satellite and inserted the stinger rod into the nozzle of the rocket engine. With a control lever, he opened the rod's "fingers" inside the engine. The force of the extended prongs against the interior of the satellite provided a connection between the astronaut and the spacecraft. Allen had successfully docked with the errant satellite.

At that point, Allen began rotating with the satellite. By using the gyroscopic stabilization system in his MMU, he was able to stop both himself and the satellite from spinning. Fisher was then able to guide the remote manipulator to a fixture on the side of the stinger. The *Discovery* crew finally had control over Palapa.

To secure the satellite in the payload bay, it would be necessary to connect the nozzle end to a cradle in the bay. The antennae made the other end too fragile. Therefore, the next goal was to attach a temporary fixture (the antenna bridge structure, or ABS) over the antennae so the remote manipulator could hold it by that end. Allen and Gardner then would connect mounting brackets to the satellite that would allow it to attach to the cradle waiting in the payload bay, and the mechanical arm would lower it into place.

While Allen relaxed in his position at the bottom of the satellite (still connected to it with the stinger), Fisher positioned the entire assembly so that Gardner could attach the ABS. To Gardner's surprise and frustration, a small protrusion on the spacecraft prevented the ABS from fitting properly. He struggled but was unable to make the critical connection. Without it, the remote manipulator would not be able to place Palapa into its cradle.

After some quick discussion, the crew, with the concurrence of mission controllers, chose a backup procedure that had been practiced briefly before the flight. With Walker orchestrating the operations from inside *Discovery*, Allen detached himself from the stinger and returned the MMU to its station. He positioned himself in a foot restraint attached to the side of the payload bay, and Fisher used the remote manipulator to hand him the 597-kilogram Palapa. He took it by the antennae end and held it while Gardner worked at the other end.

In raw space, objects have essentially no weight. They do, however, have mass. Allen found that he was able to control the huge mass of the satellite through slow, careful movements. He was in an uncomfortable position, with the satellite above his head, but he endured long enough for his coworker to complete the necessary tasks. For one orbit of Earth, lasting ninety minutes, he held the satellite while Gardner removed the stinger from the nozzle and attached the bracket for the cradle. This chore had been planned for the two crewmen working together, but because Allen was now performing the function of the ABS, Gardner had to do the job alone. The two men then managed to position the satellite in its holder and lock it into the payload bay.

The astronauts collected their tools and finished the EVA six hours after it had begun. Palapa, despite some difficulty, was finally secured in the payload bay. Yet there was no time for celebrating. The crew members would spend the next day pursuing the second errant satellite, and Allen and Gardner would need to recharge their spacesuits in preparation for capturing that satellite. The crew was clearly aware of the possibility that there might be an interfering protrusion on Westar as there had been on Palapa. With Palapa berthed in the bay, the working space would be more crowded. Furthermore, keeping the satellite positioned for Gardner had exhausted Allen. The crew had no choice but to devise an alternate plan.

On November 14, with Westar rotating only 9 meters from the *Discovery*, Gardner flew his MMU/stinger combination to the nozzle end of the satellite. He docked with it and stopped its rotation exactly as Allen had done two days earlier. Instead of guiding the remote manipulator to the grapple target on the stinger, Fisher used it to hold a foot restraint. Allen fixed himself in it as if he were on a cherry picker, and Fisher positioned him so he could grab the antennae end of Westar. While he held it, Gardner removed and stowed his MMU. With the remote manipulator holding Allen and Allen holding Westar, Gardner attached the mounting bracket. Allen was in a more comfortable position than he had been in when he held Palapa, and Gardner had the benefit of his experience as he attached the mounting bracket by himself once more. Five hours and forty-three minutes after it had begun, the EVA ended, with both satellites safely in the payload bay awaiting return to Earth.

The next day, the proud crew prepared for the return to Earth and held a press conference. At 5:55 A.M. on November 16, while above the Indian Ocean, the crew fired *Discovery*'s engines for 184 seconds to bring them back to Earth. Thirteen minutes after sunrise, at 6:59 A.M., the orbiter touched down at Kennedy Space Center.

Discovery had begun its 5.3-million-kilometer journey only 5 kilometers away with two satellites to deploy and a hopeful crew. The mission ended with two satellites retrieved and a jubilant crew.

Knowledge Gained

The two communications satellites that *Discovery* delivered into space attained their intended orbital positions. At the altitude of both satellites (39,500 kilometers), a full Earth orbit takes twenty-four hours. The orbital speeds then match Earth's rotational speed, and each satellite appears stationary in the sky. Many communications satellites are placed in such geosynchronous orbits, where they can act as relay antennae in continuous view of widely separated ground stations.

The Anik D2 was stored in orbit for almost two years before being used. Telesat had wanted to launch it while launch costs were still relatively low. Also, it was then available in space should there have been a need to use it earlier than expected. Anik D2 was brought into service on November 1, 1986, and formed part of a network of communications satellites serving Canada. It is located above the equator at longitude 110.5° west. The Leasat assumed duties immediately after it was tested in orbit and has continued to function as expected, aiding in communications for the Navy. It is stationed in orbit over the Atlantic Ocean at longitude 15° west.

Shortly after the *Discovery* reached orbit, the crew activated the diffusive mixing of organic solutions experiment. This experiment ran throughout the flight with little attention required from the astronauts; it was designed to study the growth of crystals from organic compounds in the near weightlessness of space. The failure of some valves prevented some of the chemicals from crystallizing, but other samples produced hundreds of crystals. As scientists had hoped, the crystals grown in space, without the distorting effects of gravity, were larger and purer than those produced in Earth-based laboratories. The detailed analysis of their properties is expected to shed light on the complex process of crystal formation and aid in producing better crystals both on Earth and, when space manufacturing becomes a reality, in large space laboratories.

The knowledge that astronauts could manipulate extremely massive objects in space was an unexpected benefit of STS 51A. If everything had worked according to plan, the need would never have arisen. After Allen held the satellites and was able to position them wherever Gardner needed him to, space planners realized that this ability could be applied to many other situations.

Context

The ability to handle large, massive objects in orbit did indeed prove very useful for the National Aeronautics and Space Administration (NASA). Relying on the results of STS 51A, the crew of STS 51I successfully captured the malfunctioning Leasat 3 that had been deployed on STS 51D. It was the confidence and experience gained from STS 51A that made it possible to develop a plan for having the astronauts hold and move this 6,890-kilogram satellite. The demonstration that the direct handling of massive objects was possible is expected to permit great flexibility in future space retrieval and construction tasks.

The failure of Palapa and Westar to reach their targeted orbits after their deployment on STS 41B, although not NASA's fault, did tarnish the agency's image. The recovery of the satellites restored NASA's excellent reputation. The mission also served as a demonstration of the value of manned missions, as the recovery was clearly beyond the realm of remotely controlled machines.

Palapa had been purchased by the Indonesian government to help unite its many isolated regions. Westar was built for Western Union's use in its commercial work. Both satellites belonged to insurance underwriters after their rocket failures. Insurers had paid $180 million to the original owners, and, by paying a total of $10.5 million for the recovery operation, they hoped to resell the satellites and recoup their losses. The failures of these satellites occurred in a year in which spacecraft insurers paid out almost $300 million in claims, and there was great concern over the size of these payments. The retrieval helped to minimize those concerns.

The recovery agreements had specified that the two salvaged satellites would be relaunched with the Space Transportation System. After the reevaluation of the United States' space policy in the wake of the STS 51L accident (in which the space shuttle *Challenger* exploded), it was decided that commercial communications satellites would no longer be taken into space on these manned flights. There were, however, not enough expendable launch vehicles in the nation's inventory to launch all the satellites that were ready, and the unexpected hiatus in the capability of the United States to launch satellites caused long delays in the relaunching of Palapa and Westar.

The commander of STS 51A, Frederick Hauck, gained much experience from the complexity of the flight. His next trip into space was as commander of the very successful STS 26R, the first flight after the failed STS 51L. After the *Challenger* was destroyed and the crew killed on STS 51L, the Space Transportation System underwent many changes, and greater emphasis was placed on missions requiring people in space rather than routine cargo-hauling trips. STS 51A continues to stand as a stellar example both of the kind of mission that requires people in space and of the ability of NASA to accomplish impressive and valuable tasks.

Bibliography

Allen, Joseph P., and Russell Martin. *Entering Space: An Astronaut's Odyssey.* New York: Stewart, Tabori and Chang, 1984. This exquisite book was written by one of the STS 51A mission specialists and includes a firsthand account of the flight. Suitable for all audiences, it describes the experiences of spaceflight, both the routine chores and the excitement of being in space. Contains more than two hundred color photographs of the beautiful views available in space as well as of the activities performed by astronauts.

Cooper, Henry S. F., Jr. *Before Lift-Off: The Making of a Space Shuttle Crew.* Baltimore: Johns Hopkins University Press, 1987. The long process of training astronauts for a flight on the space shuttle is described by following the crew of STS 41G, the flight immediately preceding STS 51A. Although the astronauts discussed trained for a specific mission, the book contains many interesting insights into the difficulty and importance of the preflight training for any mission. All readers will gain an appreciation of the challenges that precede a space shuttle flight.

Furniss, Tim. *Manned Spaceflight Log.* Rev. ed. London: Jane's Publishing Co., 1986. Covers every manned mission into space through Soyuz T-15 in March, 1986. This well-written book provides the essential facts from each flight.

Joels, Kerry M., and Gregory P. Kennedy. *The Space Shuttle Operator's Manual.* Rev. ed. New York: Ballantine Books, 1987. This book contains a wealth of information on space shuttle systems and flight procedures. It is written as a manual for imaginary crew members on a generic mission and will be appreciated by anyone interested in how the astronauts fly the orbiter, deploy satellites, conduct spacewalks, and live in space. The book contains many drawings and some photographs of equipment.

Powers, Robert M. *Shuttle: The World's First Spaceship.* Harrisburg, Pa.: Stackpole Books, 1979. Despite its having been written before the first flight of the Space Transportation System, this book contains excellent descriptions of the space shuttle systems and the types of missions that would be conducted. There are very good explanations of why and how the environment of space is used for a variety of scientific and technological applications. Includes many paintings and drawings, a glossary, and an index.

Marc D. Rayman

Cross-References

Astronauts and the U.S. Astronaut Program, 154; The Canadian Space Program, 222; Cape Canaveral and the Kennedy Space Center, 229; Insuring Spacecraft and Human Life, 608; U.S. Launch Vehicles, 749; The Manned Maneuvering Unit, 829; Materials Processing in Space, 933; U.S. Military Telecommunications Satellites, 1012; The National Aeronautics and Space Administration, 1032; Space Centers and Launch Sites in the United States, 1599; The U.S. Space Shuttle, 1626; Space Shuttle Living Conditions, 1634; The Development of Spacesuits, 1917; U.S. Private and Commercial Telecommunications Satellites, 1997.

SPACE SHUTTLE MISSIONS 15 and 21
Discovery and *Atlantis*

Date: January 24 to October 7, 1985
Type of mission: Manned Earth-orbiting spaceflights
Country: The United States

STS 51C (space shuttle mission 15), Discovery, *was the first space shuttle mission entirely dedicated to a classified U.S. Department of Defense payload and marked the first time that details of a manned U.S. mission, including the scheduled time of launch, were not revealed to the public before the mission. STS 51J (space shuttle mission 21), the maiden flight of* Atlantis, *featured the deployment of two military communications satellites during the second classified American manned spaceflight.*

Principal personages

THOMAS K. (KEN) MATTINGLY, STS 51C mission commander
KAROL J. BOBKO, STS 51J mission commander
LOREN J. SHRIVER, STS 51C mission pilot
RONALD J. GRABE, STS 51J mission pilot
ELLISON S. ONIZUKA and
JAMES F. BUCHLI, STS 51C mission specialists
DAVID C. HILMERS and
ROBERT L. STEWART, STS 51J mission specialists
GARY E. PAYTON, payload specialist for STS 51C
WILLIAM J. PAILES, payload specialist for STS 51J

Summary of the Missions

According to the National Aeronautics and Space Act of 1958,

> The aeronautical and space activities of the United States shall be conducted so as to contribute . . . to the expansion of human knowledge of phenomena in the atmosphere and space. The [National Aeronautics and Space] Administration shall provide for the widest practicable and appropriate dissemination of information concerning its activities and the results thereof.

Unlike its Soviet counterpart, the National Aeronautics and Space Administration (NASA) opted to make public all of its activities relating to manned spaceflight. This would allow the budding agency a chance to showcase its greatest accomplishments, as well as to lay open to criticism its shortcomings.

The chief personnel within NASA understood politics and budgets. They knew that the amount of money they would be allocated by the U.S. Congress would, for the most part, be dictated by the will of the American public. If the citizens believed that a project was worthwhile (for example, landing an American on the Moon before the Russians landed a cosmonaut on the Moon), NASA would be given support to accomplish the goal. From Mercury-Redstone 3, the first manned spaceflight, in May, 1961, through the spectacular retrieval of two stranded satellites by the STS 51A crew in November, 1984, every manned journey into space was duly publicized. Information about the crew and mission was presented well in advance of the launch, and every aspect of flight, from lift-off to landing, was broadcast live around the world.

This open policy came to an end, at least temporarily, for the fifteenth flight of the space shuttle, STS 51C, the first flight of a dedicated Department of Defense (DOD) payload. Since the DOD was in the habit of deploying secret satellites, the flight of 51C would be shrouded in mystery. At least, that was the plan.

The history of STS 51C is long and involved but can well illustrate how even minor changes in one mission can result in major changes for another. Through the first nine shuttle missions, NASA relied on a simple numbering system for designating each flight. The first would be Space Transportation System flight 1 (STS 1), and the rest would follow similarly. By the time the first shuttle mission was ready for launch in April, 1981, forty-four flights had been assigned various payloads, and each was given a flight designation. Later, launch dates would be assigned along with flight crews.

The flight which became STS 51C was originally manifested as STS 10, to be flown in December, 1983. Its major payload would be a classified satellite, launched into geosynchronous orbit (that is, an orbit in which the satellite's velocity and altitude make it appear to hover over one spot on Earth's surface) by the Inertial Upper Stage (IUS). The IUS is a two-stage solid propellant payload booster which can be taken into low Earth orbit by either an expendable launch vehicle, such as the Titan, or the space shuttle.

The military crew for STS 10, announced in October, 1982, included veteran Ken Mattingly, who had flown previously as command module pilot of Apollo 16 and commander of STS 4. He would be the commander of this flight. His pilot would be Loren Shriver, and the mission specialists would be Ellison Onizuka and James Buchli. The payload specialist, a U.S. Air Force manned spaceflight engineer, would be named at a later date.

Following the failure of the IUS on STS 6 to place the first Tracking and Data-Relay Satellite (TDRS-A) into geosynchronous orbit, the Air Force asked NASA to delay the launch of STS 10 until the problem had been resolved. Immediately, NASA officials found themselves in a public relations dilemma. Should they call the flight after the STS 9 mission STS 11, as it was originally designated, or should they call it STS 10 and renumber all of the remaining flights? Would they do this each time a flight had to be delayed or rescheduled?

The answer to that seemed clear to NASA. They would simply have to devise another numbering system, one which could be rearranged, if necessary, without additional confusion. Basically, a mission would be designated by its payload and not by its launch sequence. Each payload would be given an alphanumeric designation.

A three-character designation was used, consisting of two numbers and a letter.

The first character, a number, indicated the fiscal year in which the payload was scheduled to be launched. NASA's fiscal year ran from October 1 through September 30. The second number was a numerical designator of the payload's launch site—*1* for the Kennedy Space Center (KSC) and *2* for Vandenberg Air Force Base (VAFB). Finally, a letter suffix would reflect the originally scheduled order of launch for the payload within a fiscal year. Thus, the first payload to be launched from KSC during fiscal year 1984 would be "STS 41A" (the designation for STS 9). STS 11 was now STS 41B, and STS 10 would be given a new designation when its payload was remanifested.

At the beginning of 1984, the crew for STS 10 (which now included Gary Payton) and its payload were designated STS 41E and scheduled for launch on July 7, 1984, aboard *Challenger*. In addition, the STS 12 crew and its payload were named STS 51C and set for launch aboard *Discovery* on December 20, 1984. STS 14 would now be called STS 41D, and its payload would be flown on *Discovery* June 6, 1984.

In April, 1984, however, a new manifest revealed a few changes. Missions that were scheduled to be launched were delayed, requiring a change in their denotation. Letters and numbers became so jumbled that the new system was no longer useful. It is understandable that after the STS 51L accident, NASA reverted to the original numbering system, and the first mission after resumption of flights would be called STS 26.

When *Challenger* returned from its STS 41G mission, loose tiles were found all over its skin. Nearly four thousand of them had to be replaced before the spacecraft could be reflown. NASA decided to use *Discovery*, just back from STS 51A, for STS 51C. This would push the launch back to January, 1985.

NASA announced that the launch of STS 51C would take place between 1:15 and 4:15 P.M. eastern standard time on January 23, 1985; the administration would not reveal the exact launch time until the countdown resumed after its last scheduled hold at nine minutes before launch. No information about the military payload would be released. On December 18, *The Washington Post* revealed that the payload for STS 51C was an electronic monitoring satellite, the advanced Signal Intelligence Satellite (SigInt). Although many in the DOD came close to calling the announcement an act of treason, *The Washington Post* had not actually given any details about the satellite.

On January 23, the mission was delayed for twenty-four hours because of what NASA called "extreme weather conditions." This was the first time a manned spaceflight had been postponed because of cold weather. At 11:40 A.M. eastern standard time on January 24, the crew transfer van carrying the astronauts arrived at Launch Complex 39A. The crew usually arrived two and one-half hours prior to launch, but that mark passed and the public countdown clocks remained blank. Suddenly, at 2:41 P.M., a NASA launch commentator announced, "T minus nine minutes and counting."

Discovery was launched at 2:50 P.M., 1 hour and 35 minutes into the 3-hour launch window. Two problems involving orbiter systems caused the delays, but each was corrected on its own. All systems performed normally during launch, and the orbiter was placed into an orbit of 332 by 341 kilometers. NASA announced only that the shuttle was in orbit and that everything was going well. Status reports were given every eight hours thereafter.

Although never confirmed officially, at about 7:00 A.M. on January 25, the SigInt satellite was deployed along with its IUS. The IUS fired about forty-five minutes later and placed the satellite into its proper orbit. Later, the DOD announced that the IUS had been deployed and had successfully completed its mission.

At 12:23 P.M. on January 27, NASA announced that *Discovery* would be landing at 4:23 P.M. the next day. Prior to the flight, NASA had indicated that it would announce the landing time sixteen hours before it was to take place. The de-orbit burn took place at 3:18 P.M. over the Indian Ocean, and *Discovery* began its long glide back to KSC. At 4:23:23 P.M., its main landing gear touched down 792.48 meters beyond the threshold on runway 15, bringing the mission to an official end after 3 days, 1 hour, 33 minutes, and 23 seconds. There was no postflight interview of the astronauts, who were quickly whisked away for debriefing.

The fourth of NASA's shuttle orbiters, orbiter vehicle 104 (OV-104) was almost identical to its sister ship *Discovery*. *Atlantis* was named for the Woods Hole Oceanographic Institute research ship used from 1930 to 1966. It was the first American-operated vessel designed especially for oceanic research. The space shuttle *Atlantis* was rolled out of Rockwell International's Palmdale, California, orbiter assembly plant on April 6, 1985. It was transported overland to Edwards Air Force Base, placed atop the Boeing 747 shuttle carrier aircraft, and flown to KSC. After spending only four months in the orbiter processing facility, *Atlantis* was moved to the vehicle assembly building, mated with its external tank and solid-fueled rocket boosters, and rolled out to Launch Complex 39A. The flight readiness firing was performed on September 12.

The commander of STS 51J was Karol Bobko, a veteran of two previous shuttle flights. He was the pilot of *Challenger* for STS 6 and the commander of *Discovery* for STS 51D. The remainder of the crew included Pilot Ronald Grabe, Mission Specialists David Hilmers and Robert Stewart, and Payload Specialist William Pailes. Stewart was the only other veteran, having test-flown the manned maneuvering unit on STS 41B.

The security surrounding STS 51J was tighter than that surrounding STS 51C; the DOD was not going to tolerate the leaking of any information regarding the payload. NASA imposed the same restrictions about flight details that it had on STS 51C. The cargo for the flight was reported to be two military communications satellites known as Defense Satellite Communications System 3 (DSCS 3). The DSCS 3 was built by General Electric Company, which had released unclassified information about it in 1981. The "jam-proof" satellites were deployed piggyback from the orbiter aboard a single IUS. Each satellite was 2.07 meters long, 1.96 meters tall, and 1.93 meters wide and weighed 893 kilograms. With its solar panels deployed, it had a span of 11.63 meters.

The twenty-first space shuttle mission was launched at 11:15:30 A.M. eastern daylight time on October 3, 1985, with very little notice. All systems worked as planned during the launch phase, and *Atlantis* was placed in a shuttle record-high orbit of 469 by 476 kilometers. Almost immediately, its secret payload was deployed. NASA remained silent about the progress of the flight until twenty-four hours before the planned landing. STS 51J was landed successfully on October 7, 1985, as *Atlantis* touched down on runway 23 at Edwards Air Force Base. The mission had lasted 4 days, 1 hour, 44 minutes, and 38 seconds.

Knowledge Gained

Although neither the U.S. Air Force nor NASA has given specific information about the military payloads flown aboard the two Department of Defense missions, it is generally believed that the satellites were each placed into geosynchronous orbit and performed as designed. The IUS, which had proved troublesome on the STS 6 mission, worked as planned. There were other experiments flown aboard the flights, and some information about them has been released.

One of the experiments aboard *Discovery* was an Australian experiment concerning blood. The package, known as the "aggregation of red blood cells" experiment, was flown in two canisters in the middeck of the orbiter. Eight individuals, including patients afflicted with cancer, blood disease, heart disease, kidney disease, and diabetes, were on hand at the Kennedy Space Center so that blood samples could be drawn twenty-four hours before lift-off and loaded aboard *Discovery*.

A computer controlled the experiment, which involved the passing of all eight donors' blood between two glass sheets so that cameras and a digital data system could assess how the blood aggregates in the near-weightless conditions of orbital spaceflight. The glass plates were only about 12 microns apart. Since blood aggregates differently in persons with disease from the way it aggregates in those who are free from disease, researchers can understand better how blood circulates by viewing its activities under controlled conditions. Additional tests are planned for future shuttle flights to provide enough data to begin testing various drugs on diseased blood cells; these tests would examine what effect, if any, they have in eliminating the symptoms and causes of the diseases.

A NASA experiment called Bios, designed to study the damage to biological materials from high-energy cosmic rays, was positioned in the middeck area of *Atlantis*. A solid-state dosimeter was used to survey the interior of the orbiter to identify the areas most likely to be affected by such radiation. The experiments help to ensure that astronauts (and other biological passengers) are not exposed to potentially hazardous radiation from the Sun and other celestial bodies. In addition, the data are useful in the design of the space station and future space vehicles.

Context

In the wake of the *Challenger* accident, NASA was ordered to discontinue using the space shuttle to launch commercial satellites. Its primary mission would be to carry scientific experiment packages such as Spacelab. Spacelab, built by the European Space Agency, consists of interchangeable modular units. By combining these units, different experiments can be performed in the shuttle's payload bay. Most of these experiments are too large to be run inside the crew compartment.

Naturally, the shuttle plays an active role in the assembly of the space station *Freedom*. It is designed to be used as a ferry for equipment and personnel and for accomplishing repairs on the station and ailing satellites. Geosynchronous satellites will have to be brought down to the low-operational altitude of the shuttle to be fixed and then boosted back to their original positions.

The only satellites to be launched by the orbiter fleet would be the Tracking and Data-Relay Satellites, which are necessary to ensure adequate communications during the missions and military ones. Many have expressed concern about turning the Space Transportation System into a military machine; most tend to forget that the majority of the money for shuttle flights has always come from the Department of Defense. It is reasonable to assume, with a definite decrease in the number of annual shuttle flights, that the DOD will want to get the most for its dollar.

In comparison to its sister ships, *Atlantis* had a quick and spectacular debut. It spent only six months on the ground awaiting its first launch. *Challenger* and *Discovery* suffered through main engine troubles during the nearly ten months each spent between rollout and launch. *Columbia*, the first orbiter, waded through two years of problems before shaking her earthly bonds.

Atlantis came back from orbit virtually unscathed, a far cry from the various damaged parts and nonworking systems the others brought back. More than anything, experience gained from the previous twenty missions contributed to the success of *Atlantis*. Major changes included improved construction materials and electronic hardware, lighter thermal protection systems, and provisions for carrying a Centaur high-energy booster. The Centaur, a liquid propellant vehicle, was the upper stage of the Atlas and Delta launch vehicles. It was to be used to boost several large deep space probes from the shuttle, including the Galileo probe to Jupiter. Like the orbiter's main engines, Centaur used liquid hydrogen and liquid oxygen for propellants. After the *Challenger* accident, the Centaur program was canceled, because the vehicle was considered too hazardous to be carried in the shuttle's payload bay.

STS 51C, which had been delayed in getting off the ground because of cold weather, landed a year and a day before the next flight to be seriously affected by the cold, STS 51L. Ellison Onizuka would be on that tragic mission, too. After that cold morning in January, 1986, the space shuttle program would forever change. Never again would a flight be attempted in freezing weather.

Bibliography

Allen, Joseph P., and Russell Martin. *Entering Space: An Astronaut's Odyssey*. New York: Stewart, Tabori and Chang, 1984. In this personal account of a space shuttle flight, Allen describes the difficulties and the joys of living and working in space. The experiences of other astronauts are examined in an effort to present a balanced view of space travel. Includes more than two hundred full-color photographs taken during the many shuttle and preshuttle flights.

Furniss, Tim. *Manned Spaceflight Log*. Rev. ed. London: Jane's Publishing Co., 1986. This reference provides a nontechnical overview of manned spaceflight since its beginning. Covers the flights of American astronauts, Soviet cosmonauts, and space travelers from other nations who have flown with them. Accounts of each flight are accompanied by black-and-white photographs.

——————— . *Space Shuttle Log*. London: Jane's Publishing Co., 1986. From STS 1 through STS 61A, the space shuttles are covered in depth. Furniss discusses the design concepts for the Space Transportation System and provides a concise account of each shuttle flight. Includes black-and-white photographs from the missions.

Hallion, Richard. *On the Frontier*. NASA SP-4303. Washington, D.C.: Government Printing Office, 1984. Part of the NASA History Series, this source takes as its subject the experimental aircraft on which the development of the space shuttle rests. The author traces the evolution of these craft from the first plane to break the sound barrier, the Bell X-1, through the space shuttle orbiter. Contains a complete annotated listing of the flights of each of the vehicles, as well as an extensive bibliography.

Kerrod, Robin. *Space Shuttle*. New York: Gallery Books, 1984. Most valuable for its beautiful color photographs of the space shuttle, this volume conveys the essence of the Space Transportation System vehicles and the people who fly them. Highlights of the first dozen missions are presented, as well as a fanciful look at the future of space exploration.

MacKnight, Nigel. *Shuttle*. Nottingham, England: MacKnight International, 1985. This well-illustrated book covers the design of the space shuttle and the various aspects of a mission. MacKnight, a British journalist, tours the Kennedy Space Center and observes the shuttle being prepared for flight. Interviews with astronauts help to reveal the human side of the missions.

Otto, Dixon P. *On Orbit: Bringing on the Space Shuttle*. Athens, Ohio: Main Stage Publications, 1986. Early designs of the space shuttle are discussed. Also presents an account of each of the first twenty-five flights, including the crew, the payloads, and the flight objectives. Illustrated in black and white.

Smith, Melvyn. *An Illustrated History of Space Shuttle: X-15 to Orbiter*. Newbury Park, Calif.: Haynes Publications, 1986. A concise overview of the space shuttle and the experimental aircraft which led to its design. Spanning the period from 1959 through 1985, the book was written for the general reader. Illustrated with many photographs of the early lifting bodies, which help to show how the shuttle orbiter came to look as it does today. Arranged chronologically.

Wilson, Andrew. *Space Shuttle Story*. New York: Crescent Books, 1986. Traces the history of the space shuttle from the early days of rocketry to the *Challenger* disaster. Furnished with more than one hundred color photographs, this volume provides little detail but emphasizes the men and women who fly the spaceplane to and from orbit.

Yenne, Bill. *The Astronauts*. New York: Exeter Books, 1986. Directed toward the lay person, this book presents an account of the manned space programs of the United States and the Soviet Union. Illustrated with several hundred color and black-and-white photographs taken aboard the two countries' spacecraft, it also examines the non-American and non-Soviet passengers who flew as guests on some flights.

_____ . *The Encyclopedia of U.S. Spacecraft*. New York: Exeter Books, 1985, reprint 1988. A complete, nontechnical reference work listing U.S. manned and unmanned spacecraft and launch vehicles. Photographs of the spacecraft, most of them in color, accompany the text. Supplemented by a glossary of acronyms and abbreviations.

Russell R. Tobias

Cross-References

Apollo 16, 116; Astronauts and the U.S. Astronaut Program, 154; U.S. Military Telecommunications Satellites, 1012; Space Shuttle Living Conditions, 1634; Space Shuttle Mission 4: *Columbia*, 1670; Space Shuttle Mission 6: *Challenger*, 1684; Space Shuttle Mission 16: *Discovery*, 1759; Space Shuttle Mission 25: *Challenger*, 1813.

SPACE SHUTTLE MISSION 16
Discovery

Date: April 12 to April 19, 1985
Type of mission: Manned Earth-orbiting spaceflight
Country: The United States

STS 51D, the sixteenth space shuttle mission, launched the Telesat 1 and Syncom IV-3 satellites. The first flight to have an unscheduled space-walk (in an attempt to repair a malfunctioning Syncom), STS 51D was also the first to carry a nonpilot, nonscientist astronaut, U.S. Senator Edwin Garn of Utah.

Principal personages

KAROL J. (BO) BOBKO, the mission commander
DONALD E. WILLIAMS, the mission pilot
JEFFREY A. HOFFMAN,
S. DAVID GRIGGS, and
MARGARET (RHEA) SEDDON, mission specialists
CHARLES WALKER, a payload specialist
EDWIN JACOB (JAKE) GARN, a U.S. senator and payload specialist
B. RANDY STONE, the lead flight director
T. CLEON LACEFIELD, the "orbit-one" (first half of crew day) flight director
JOHN T. COX, the "orbit-two" (second half of crew day) flight director

Summary of the Mission

The mission of STS 51D, *Discovery*'s fourth flight, got off to a shaky start but clearly demonstrated the overall flexibility of the space shuttle program. Originally, the crew of 51D was supposed to fly STS 51E, on *Challenger*, in early March, 1985. Only six days before launch, severe problems were discovered with the primary payload: the second Tracking and Data-Relay Satellite (TDRS-B), used for extended shuttle mission communications, which would finally fly nine months later on *Challenger*'s last mission, STS 51L. The flight, already delayed five times previously, was finally canceled outright. In order to keep to schedule as much as possible, a revised STS 51D mission was quickly assembled, to be launched a mere six weeks later. The new payload would be the Telesat 1 (Anik C) satellite from 51E, and the Hughes Communications Syncom IV-3 Navy communications satellite originally scheduled for 51D.

All but one of the original crew members would fly: French payload specialist Patrick Baudry was replaced by Charles Walker from McDonnell Douglas as a result of payload requirements. This was the second flight for Walker, his first having been STS 41D, about ten months earlier. The commander, Karol (Bo)

Bobko, would be making his second flight as well. He first flew as the pilot on STS 6, the maiden voyage of *Challenger*.

One of the other notable elements of this flight was that it would be the first mission to have a nonscientist, nonpilot crew member, Senator Edwin Jacob (Jake) Garn of Utah. As the chairman of the Housing and Urban Development and Independent Agencies Subcommittee, Senator Garn had control over funding for the space program. Much was made of the senator's participation, considered by some to be a public relations stunt, but he participated in valuable medical experiments, particularly in the area of motion sickness. Motion sickness commonly plagues most astronauts, causing many to have violent fits of nausea lasting up to two days. Because of the costs and short duration of the missions, the last thing needed is a sick crew, so extreme care was taken to avoid the malady. Since Garn had no active roll in the payload deployment or piloting of the spacecraft, he was the ideal candidate to get sick deliberately, offering the crew physicians important data without jeopardizing the mission.

The fourth flight of *Discovery* got off the ground on April 12, 1985, at 8:59 A.M., four years to the day after STS 1. After a normal ascent and orbital insertion, the crew successfully launched the Telesat communications satellite at about nine and a half hours into the mission.

Early on the second day the Syncom satellite was deployed successfully, using the "Frisbee" technique. Normally the satellites were seated vertically in the shuttle's payload bay, spun up like tops (the technique used for the Telesat), and shot straight out. The Syncom was much larger, however, being a squat cylinder 5 meters in diameter, 4 meters high, and weighing about 6,800 kilograms. It was therefore stowed on its side and practically "rolled" out of the spacecraft such that it resembled a giant Frisbee being thrown (hence the name "Frisbee deployment"). While the physical deployment was on time and apparently correct, the "omni" antenna on top of the satellite did not erect itself, as it was supposed to do about a minute after release. Furthermore, the kick motor used to boost the spacecraft into its final orbit did not fire at the intended 45-minute mark after deployment.

Immediately a special analysis team was formed; it decided that the on/off lever on the side of the satellite had not been switched to "on" at the time of deployment. This lever was supposed to activate an internal sequencing timer which in turn would deploy the antenna and fire the engine.

Several options were discussed, the main ones calling for an unplanned extravehicular activity (EVA) to throw the switch manually. Astronaut Bruce McCandless from the STS 11 mission had rehearsed this scenario in the one-gravity trainer at Johnson Space Center. The maneuver required a crewman to throw the switch using a small screwdriver-like tool. Astronauts Sherwood C. Spring and Jerry L. Ross had taken the procedure a step further when they had simulated the proposed EVA in a giant water tank simulating zero gravity. As a result, it was determined that it would be too risky to have an astronaut at the end of the arm coming into contact with a spinning seven-ton satellite. The other main option would have the two EVA crewmen attach snaring devices on the end of the robot arm, or remote manipulator system (RMS). Afterward, the snares would be used in an attempt to trip the lever once the astronauts were safely inside. Astronaut Sally Ride rehearsed this maneuver using the snares in the one-gravity RMS simulator with a high degree of success. It was this option which was finally selected.

Because of the change in plans, the mission was extended by two days. The normal flightplan was followed on the third and fourth days, while ground crews put the finishing touches on the EVA schedule and designed the snaring devices. The capsule communicator (capcom) radioed up descriptions of the snares, one termed a "flyswatter" and the other a "lacrosse stick," for the objects they resembled. The crew constructed them out of tape, plastic pages from their onboard documents, and "swizzle sticks" used by the crew to reach distant switches while strapped into their seats. Dr. Margaret (Rhea) Seddon used her onboard surgical equipment to construct the devices, assisted by Senator Garn.

The flyswatter consisted of a long plastic sheet with three large square holes in a vertical row, looking much like a small ladder with three rungs a few centimeters wide. The object would be to snag the lever with one of these rungs; if the flyswatter missed or broke a rung, the lever would likely hit a second. A single stick would attach it to the RMS. The lacrosse stick looked much like the swatter, except that it had a loop of wire across the top and was supported by two sticks on either side so as to give it slightly more strength.

Although most flights do not have spacewalks scheduled, flight rules dictate that there always be two crew members trained for emergency operations. Such emergencies might include repair of the delicate tiles, releasing a satellite stuck in the payload bay, or manually cranking the payload-bay doors closed. On this mission, Jeffrey A. Hoffman and S. David Griggs were the two trained in EVA operations. Rhea Seddon would assist them in manipulating the RMS as required. The EVA took place on the fifth day of the flight and lasted slightly more than three hours. Only one hour was required to attach the devices to the end of the arm, with the rest of the time used in various housekeeping duties and making sure that the devices were safe while the arm was berthed. At one point the crew members were asked by Mission Control to wait until the next television would be available over Hawaii in about forty minutes. Hoffman responded an understandable "I'm sure you know how tough that's going to be!" Once the EVA was completed, preparations were begun for the following day's rendezvous with Syncom and snaring of the switch.

Visual sighting first took place while the Syncom was about 70 kilometers distant in the early morning hours of April 17. In about 75 minutes it was rotating slowly at only about 300 meters away. The spin rate was noted at one revolution every 36 seconds. The distance narrowed to only 15 meters in another 30 minutes. By now the crew could clearly see the separation lever, and that it was apparently thrown as it should have been originally. This meant either that there was an internal failure of the timer or that the switch needed only a tiny bit of motion to trip it, since the internal microswitches were activated in only the last few degrees of movement.

The actual "swat window" would be only 6 minutes long at the beginning of the fifth day of the mission on orbit 69. Rhea Seddon positioned the arm only a meter or two away from the spinning satellite. Television transmissions to ground controllers showed the reflection of the arm, snares, and Earth in the mirrored solar cells in the side of the spacecraft. At 5 days, 13 minutes into the flight, Seddon was given the go-ahead. She slowly moved the arm toward the center of the satellite, exactly where the lever would be when it passed by. Viewers on the ground could clearly make out the lever each time it slipped by the view. At one time it could be seen slicing one of the rungs. Another time, the arm appeared to bump up against the Syncom. Six minutes later the window was closed, and the crew reported that they got "a hard physical contact on at least two occasions." With that, *Discovery* separated from the satellite for the last time and maneuvered to an attitude from which the crew could observe any possible firing of the kick motor. No such firing was seen, and the satellite was left dormant in a useless 300-by-416-kilometer orbit for the possibility of a rescue mission sometime later (this would happen on the STS 51I flight four and a half months later).

Landing took place on Friday morning, April 19, 1985, at the Kennedy Space Center. As if enough had not happened during the flight, the landing was plagued by more troubles. First, the weather delayed reentry by one revolution. Next, during landing, crosswinds gusting to 15 knots blew the vehicle off the centerline of the runway. Bobko tried to correct this with "moderate" braking. As a result, both right brakes locked, with only a few meters left until the vehicle was to stop. With only 1.5 meters to go, the inboard tire blew out, and all tires were rendered unusable. Later investigation also revealed that a tile had fallen off during ascent, exposing bare aluminum to the heat of reentry, 650 degrees Celsius. More than 120 other tiles were damaged as a result, requiring replacement.

Knowledge Gained

Many of the shuttle missions are primarily targeted toward delivery of satellites; some have few if any major experiments. That was the case with STS 51D. Vital experience was gained in on-the-spot planning for the unscheduled EVA, verifying that the current systems of training and mission planning did work.

On board the shuttle were two "Get-Away Special" canisters, ("GAS cans," used for low-cost experimental units requiring little crew intervention). G035 was an experiment sponsored by the Asahi National Broadcasting Corporation of Japan to test the surface tension, viscosity of fluids, and solids and alloy furnaces, and was activated and deactivated on schedule.

G471, the capillary pump loop priming experiment, was from the Goddard Space Flight Center. A malfunction prevented the experiment from being conducted.

Payload specialist Charles Walker operated the McDonnell Douglas continuous flow electrophoresis system (CFES), which was flying for the sixth time. The CFES was used to develop techniques required for generating a pure pharmaceutical material. McDonnell Douglas reported that "all samples were processed and no contamination of the product was observed." What exactly the product was, however, was kept secret.

The problems encountered during the landing illustrated weaknesses in the shuttle braking system. These were further explored and enhanced in simulations conducted at Ames Research Center in California.

On the lighter side was the "Toys in Space" project. This served to demonstrate the behavior of more than thirty miniature mechanical systems in zero gravity. Films were taken of the crew which would later be used in classroom science discussions. Common toys, such as Slinkies, paper airplanes, jacks, yo-yos and paddleballs were all used.

Context

The flexibility of the space shuttle system was decisively demonstrated in the first-ever unplanned EVA. The ability of ground personnel combined with the contingency training of the flight crew made for a successful operation even though the satellite was not activated. The space program was seen to have reached a new level of maturity. Senator Garn's presence served to emphasize that space travel was becoming increasingly routine.

The failure of the Syncom was the third of a shuttle-launched satellite. In February, 1984, the kick motors of both satellites launched from STS 41B misfired, sending the satellites into unusable orbits. Eight months later, astronauts Joseph P. Allen and Dale A. Gardner performed two complicated EVAs to capture and return the satellites back to Earth, paving the way for an eventual go-ahead with a Syncom rescue mission.

After two scrubbed launch attempts, STS 51I lifted off on August 27, 1985, to "hot-wire" the Syncom. (The physical design of the Syncom precluded any return to Earth unlike the design of the two failed satellites.) Four days later, astronauts James (Ox) van Hoften and William F. Fisher left *Discovery* to snare the satellite manually and return it the payload bay. There Fisher installed the Hughes-designed Spun Bypass Unit to bypass the failed sequencer. Once the unit was installed, Fisher threw four switches, bringing the $90 million machine back to life. Using handles which he had installed in the side of Syncom, van Hoften spun it up by hand to two revolutions per minute and "launched" it back into its own orbit.

The success of this flight, along with STS 51D, deflated the arguments of those who claimed that manned spaceflight was a mere luxury and that robots could do all that was necessary.

While no future rescue missions were expected, routine servicing was planned for the Space Station and the Hubble Space Telescope. Other long-duration vehicles could now be designed with servicing in mind, making them less expensive and more flexible in the long run.

Bibliography

Allen, Joseph P., and Russell Martin. *Entering Space: An Astronaut's Odyssey*. New

York: Stewart, Tabori and Chang, 1984. This is the view of spaceflight as seen by astronaut Joseph P. Allen. Allen flew on STS 5, the first "operational" mission, and again on STS 51A, helping to rescue two satellites. An accomplished photographer, Allen illustrated the book with many of his own photographs. All aspects of living and working in space are covered. Not strong on technical content, but highly recommended for casual browsing.

Joels, Kerry M., and David Larkin. *The Space Shuttle Operator's Manual.* New York: Ballantine Books, 1982. A simplified version of astronaut training manuals, this volume gives the reader a look at the operational side of a shuttle mission. Topics covered include everything from launch profiles and checklists to how to use the shuttle's stove. Contains foldouts of the control panels, sample mission time lines, and many crew cabin photographs. Of particular interest to the reader of this article is the section on extravehicular activity and robot arm operations.

Kerrod, Robin. *The Illustrated History of NASA.* New York: Gallery Books, 1986. A good general history of NASA starting in 1958. This is a lavishly illustrated work, oriented toward the general reader. Both manned and unmanned flights are covered through the *Challenger* tragedy.

National Aeronautics and Space Administration. "Mission Report: 51D." *World Spaceflight News.* August, 1985: 2-3. *World Spaceflight News* is a semiregular publication oriented toward anyone with an interest in specific shuttle missions. Official NASA timelines are reprinted ahead of each mission, along with charts, payload diagrams, crew biographies, and detailed flight descriptions.

Yenne, Bill. *Space Shuttle.* New York: Gallery Books, 1986. A large-format picture book which covers the shuttle in the most general fashion, from construction to operations. Sections are devoted to history, manufacture, and mission profiles. A brief flight log is included in the back.

Michael Smithwick

Cross-References

Biological Effects of Space Travel on Humans, 188; Robotics and Automation, 1227; Space Shuttle Mission 11: *Challenger*, 1719; Space Shuttle Mission 14: *Discovery*, 1744; Space Shuttle Mission 20: *Discovery*, 1787; Space Shuttle Mission 25: *Challenger*, 1813; Air and Space Telescopes, 2014; Tracking and Data-Relay Communications Satellites, 2042.

SPACE SHUTTLE MISSION 17
Challenger

Date: April 29 to May 6, 1985
Type of mission: Manned Earth-orbiting spaceflight
Countries: The United States, France, and India

STS 51B carried the Spacelab 3 science payload into orbit, including rats and monkeys as well as human beings. The results of life science and microgravity experiments would provide a wealth of information with applications to technology on Earth as well as to living and working in space.

Principal personages
ROBERT F. OVERMYER, the spacecraft commander
FREDERICK D. GREGORY, the mission pilot
DON L. LIND,
NORMAN E. THAGARD, and
WILLIAM E. THORNTON, mission specialists
TAYLOR G. WANG, the payload specialist in fluid mechanics
LODEWIJK VAN DEN BERG, the payload specialist in materials science
GARY E. COEN, the lead flight director
ROBERT A. SCHMITZ, Program Manager, NASA Headquarters
JOHN S. THEON, Program Scientist, NASA Headquarters

Summary of the Mission

The STS 51B mission, carrying the Spacelab 3 scientific payload, was the seventeenth flight in the shuttle series. The primary areas of investigation for this mission were the life sciences and microgravity (the weightless environment and its effects on humans, animals, and properties of matter).

The astronauts assigned to STS 51B were selected in stages. On February 22, 1983, the National Aeronautics and Space Administration (NASA) crew was announced. The commander was Robert F. Overmyer, who had previously flown on the fifth shuttle mission as pilot in 1982; his pilot on STS 51B was to be Frederick D. Gregory, who was on his first shuttle mission. Three NASA mission specialists were named: Don L. Lind, who was making his first flight after a wait of nineteen years (he had been selected in 1966 for the Apollo program but was not assigned to a flight crew); Norman E. Thagard, who had flown previously on shuttle mission 7; and William E. Thornton, who was on his second flight, having flown on shuttle mission 8, and who, at age fifty-six, was the oldest person to date to have flown in space. In addition to their experiences as career astronauts, the three mission specialists called on other professional experience: Lind was a physicist, and both Thagard and Thornton were trained medical doctors with special interests in the adaptation of the human organism to spaceflight. On June 8, 1984, the two payload specialists for the mission were selected from a group representing the scientific interests of the mission: Taylor G. Wang, a fluid mechanics expert and a principal investigator in one of the Spacelab 3 investigations, and Lodewijk van den Berg, a materials science expert. During the mission, these crew members were to work in twelve-hour shifts: The "gold" (day) shift would consist of Overmyer with Lind, Thornton, and Wang. The "silver" (night) shift would be commanded by Gregory with Thagard and van den Berg. Though no spacewalk (EVA) was planned, Gregory and Thagard were trained as contingency EVA crew members.

Although the selection of the flight crew was resolved without much difficulty, the preparations of the hardware took longer. The payload and area of investigation for Spacelab 3 had been finalized several years before launch, and as a result of development difficulties with Spacelab 2, as well as several launch delays within the program, the manifest placed the launch of Spacelab 3 (which had been designated the first "operational" flight of the Spacelab series) before the Spacelab 2 flight.

The orbiter *Challenger* was manifested as the carrier vehicle for Spacelab 3. Following shuttle mission 41G in October of 1984, the orbiter had been returned to the orbiter processing facility (OPF) to undergo payload change and turnaround activities prior to its next launch, the military 51C mission. While in the OPF, the orbiter underwent detailed inspections that revealed damage to the thermal protection system, the tiles used to protect the delicate skin of the orbiter from heat damage. *Challenger* was therefore reassigned to the 51E mission, which allowed extra time to correct the tile problem. As preparations for 51E continued in the early months of 1985, serious problems with the Tracking and Data-Relay Satellites (TDRSs)—both TDRS-A, in orbit, and TDRS-B, scheduled to be deployed by mission 51E— eventually forced a cancellation of the mission and the reassignment of *Challenger* to the 51B mission early in March, 1985.

Challenger arrived back at the OPF on March 7 and underwent payload exchange, from the TDRS-B Inertial Upper Stage (IUS) to Spacelab 3. The long module element of Spacelab's pressurized compartment had previously flown on Spacelab 1 in 1983 and had been outfitted with the experiment racks for the Spacelab 3 mission through 1984. The module was finally lowered into *Challenger*'s payload bay, on March 27. The stacking of the twin solid-fueled rocket boosters (SRBs) for 51B began in the vehicle assembly building (VAB) at the Kennedy Space Center on November 28, 1984. The external tank (ET) for 51B was mated to the SRBs on January 9, 1985.

After thirty-three days of processing in the OPF, *Challenger* was towed to the VAB on April 10 to be mated to the SRBs and the ET. After five days in the VAB, *Challenger* was moved to Launch Complex 39, Pad A, where for the next fifteen days final preparations for its launch were made. The countdown for 51B proceeded without major incident, and its life science payload—two monkeys and twenty-four rats—was installed in the holding facility twenty-four hours before launch, allowing the animals to become accustomed to their new home.

At 12:02 P.M. eastern standard time, the engines of *Challenger* had built up sufficient thrust to lift the vehicle from the launchpad. A nominal ascent profile for the mission was flown, with only minor incidents occurring—none that threatened the safety or success of the launch. Fifteen minutes after launch, *Challenger* was safely in orbit once again, after the successful burning of the orbital maneuvering system (OMS) engines. Following a second OMS burn, the payload bay doors of *Challenger* were opened and the crew prepared for their week of data gathering and research in Earth orbit.

The crew's first major activity was to deploy two small satellites from Get-Away Special (GAS) canisters in the payload bay. In order to ensure successful deployment and efficient battery power, it had been decided to deploy these satellites on flight day 1. The Northern Utah State Satellite (Nusat) was deployed by spring ejection 4 hours and 14 minutes into the mission; the Global Low-Orbiting Message Relay (GLOMR) satellite, which was to have been deployed some 14 minutes later, did not eject from its canister, though the GAS door did open. It was returned to Earth for reassignment to a later flight.

Challenger was then maneuvered into a gravity-gradient stabilization attitude with the tail toward Earth and *Challenger*'s port wing pointing in the direction of flight. The rest of the first day of the flight was spent in activating Spacelab and its experiments. For the next few days, the crew of STS 51B worked hard to gather as much information as possible from their experiments, as well as tackling a series of hardware problems that plagued the crew during the mission—none of which, however, seriously hindered their performance.

Difficulties with the French "very wide field camera" (VWFC) were encountered some eight hours into the flight, when Lind had trouble using Spacelab's air lock in connection with the camera. A bent handle in the air lock forced ground controllers to decide against using the system for the rest of the flight, and the VWFC had to be abandoned with almost no data obtained. The camera had been reassigned from Spacelab 1 in 1983, when unfavorable night-pass viewing conditions were encountered as a result of the delayed STS 41A mission (space shuttle mission 9).

On the whole, the crew members kept to their flightplan well, but only with much effort. Problems with the toilet system plagued them, and Berg experienced difficulties with his crystal-growing experiments during the second day of the flight. The animals, however, adapted well to their strange new environment. As time in orbit increased, thoughts of extending the mission were aired, a move that would enable the crew to complete research that had been slowed by the need to repair faulty equipment: Berg had to shut down his experiment while he tried to repair its equipment, which he succeeded in doing during flight day 3, and Thagard had to repair the urine-monitoring system experiment and the "atmospheric trace molecules spectroscopy" (ATMOS) experiment. These efforts were worth the trouble: The ATMOS experiment, for example, yielded some spectacular results despite operating for only three days and obtaining only 19 of 60 planned data takes.

Throughout his twelve-hour shifts in the Spacelab, Lind was able to obtain excellent photographs and record precise visual descriptions of auroral displays, which had been of scientific interest to him for years, especially after a period of intense solar activity on April 30.

As the crew gained experience in their orbital workplace, the facility with which they were able to gather data from their experiments and their ability to repair faulty equipment improved as well. A fine demonstration of the value of the human presence in space appeared in the untiring efforts of Wang, whose "drop dynamics fluid mechanics" experiment failed to work early in the flight because of an electrical malfunction. Determined not to return home unsuccessful, Wang almost completely rewired the machine himself, finally getting the experiment to function after several days' work. Another example of the importance of the "human factor" occurred when one of the two monkeys refused to eat for several days, apparently suffering from a bout of spacesickness; Thornton was able to encourage the animal to eat by hand-feeding him, probably saving his life.

Some of the most widely publicized problems stemmed from the reported leakage of feces from the animal holding facility. In reality, the items found in the flight deck were bits of food pellets, which nevertheless were dangerous, as they might have damaged *Challenger*'s delicate instruments and thus jeopardized the lives of the crew members. As a result of this mishap, much thought was given to the design of later facilities for animal storage in the Spacelab.

The last full day in space was spent in stowing experiments and equipment in preparation for reentry into Earth's atmosphere. After some difficulty in closing the payload bay doors, which resulted in a contingency EVA to secure them, all was readied for the landing on flight day 8, May 6, 1985.

The orbital flight path of *Challenger* dictated almost no communications with the spacecraft during the reentry phase. The vehicle was flown by Overmyer and Gregory from near the Antarctic north over the Pacific, and eventually over Los Angeles at Mach 4. *Challenger* completed three S-turns for deceleration. A series of flight-test maneuvers was deleted from the entry profile as doubts were raised about the integrity of the closed payload bay doors.

Challenger touched down on runway 17 at Edwards Air Force Base after an uneventful descent at 09:12:03 Pacific daylight time, May 6, 1985, and rolled to a wheelstop 47 seconds later. The shuttle had traveled more than 4 million kilometers (2.5 million miles) in 7 days, 8 minutes, and 46 seconds, and had completed 108 orbits of Earth with a landing achieved during orbit 109.

Knowledge Gained

The scientific objectives of the STS 51B Spacelab 3 mission could be divided into four areas: materials processing, environmental observations, fluid mechanics, and life sciences. Out of fifteen experiments, the crew had gained useful data from fourteen, resulting in 250 billion bits of scientific data which could fill 44,000 two-hundred-page volumes, and 3 million video pictures, thousands of still and motion-picture camera frames, and miles of audiotape commentary. Investigators would be busy studying these data for years after the completion of the mission.

Preliminary data from the Spacelab 3 experiments were described as excellent by Mission Scientist George Fichti. The research on the first operational Spacelab mission continued work that had begun on earlier missions, such as Skylab in 1973 and 1974, Spacelab 1 in 1983, and, in a more indirect way, the Gemini, Apollo, and Apollo-Soyuz missions between 1965 and 1975.

In the materials science experiments, a mercury iodide crystal about the size of a sugar cube was grown from a seed crystal in the vapor crystal growth system over a period of 104 hours, using a vapor transport technique. Postflight analysis determined its quality and properties as an X-ray and gamma-ray detector for future applications in the fields of medicine, scientific research, and industry.

For the first time in space, a fluid transport technique was used to grow two triglycerine sulfate crystals in the fluid experiment system. The crystals underwent postflight analysis to determine their qualities as sensitive infrared detectors. The vapor crystal growth and fluid experiment systems, in combination with the unique capabilities of the Spacelab hardware, provided the first opportunity to observe in detail crystal growth in a microgravity environment and to determine the difference between growth on Earth and in orbit. The samples obtained from the French mercury iodide crystal growth experiment were returned to France for analysis. Cartridges of seed-type crystals were examined to provide data on the beginning of crystal growth from samples of different properties.

A total of 102 hours of geophysical fluid flow cell operations were completed on the flight and recorded information on convective flows on rotating spherical bodies. In experiments to understand convection on the Sun, in planetary atmospheres, in Earth's oceans, and in basic fluid physics, approximately 46,000 images were recorded on the flight by the crew. All planned experiments were completed in 84 hours, and a bonus of thirteen unscheduled experiments were conducted.

After untiring efforts by Wang to repair the drop dynamics module, the first experimental data on the behavior of a free-floating fluid in a microgravity environment were obtained. Several unexpected results came from the investigations. For the first time, both solid and liquid samples were acoustically positioned and maneuvered in weightlessness; drops of varying sizes and viscosities were formed, rotated, and oscillated. In addition, studies were made on compound drops (drops formed within drops). Examination of photographs of these experiments has helped scientists to postulate the principles of fluid mechanics in weightlessness.

The ATMOS experiment obtained nineteen sequences of more than 150 independent atmospheric spectra, each containing more than 100,000 individual measurements used to analyze Earth's stratosphere and mesosphere at altitudes between 10 and 150 kilometers. In addition, high-resolution infrared spectra of the Sun were obtained during five calibrations and provided some surprising evidence about the molecular constituents of the Sun.

A total of eighteen auroral imaging experiment observations were carried out during the flight, with significant data recorded on each pass. Videotape images and the visual observations of the crew, especially Lind, provided sufficient data to evaluate three-dimensional images of auroral structures and motion from eighteen out of twenty-one planned passages, with half a million video images and an undetermined number of 35-millimeter frames exposed. Evaluation of data obtained allowed for accurate measurements of the vertical extent and dimension of the auroral forms, and initial data revealed that the height of the aurora is the function of local time more than it is of geomagnetic substorm time.

Mounted outside the pressurized module, the "ionization of solar and galactic cosmic ray heavy nuclei" experiment (IONS) recorded data on high-energy particles emitted from the Sun and other, more distant galactic sources. Tracks in the detector were analyzed to determine specific intensity, energy, arrival time, and direction of the rays.

The life science experiments revealed that all the animals could successfully adjust to spaceflight conditions, although one of the monkeys did suffer from space adaptation syndrome, recovering in a manner similar to human recovery. The primary purpose of the animal holding facility was to provide in-flight engineering data for evolution and design baselines for larger, more complex systems planned for the U.S. Space Station.

Context

The flight of 51B provided scientists with their first real opportunity to investigate the science of fluid mechanics on an American manned spaceflight since the Skylab missions of 1973 and 1974. It was an opportunity to reestablish experimental conditions used on Skylab to reaffirm and develop results gained on America's first space station and to provide significant baseline data to aid in planning for large manufacturing facilities on the U.S. Space Station in the 1990's.

The growing of crystals in space has significant applications in the world of microelectronics, military systems, telescopes, cameras, and infrared monitors. The important link between the crew and ground teams was demonstrated in the work of Wang, who for the first time operated and repaired his own equipment in space, recovering the experimental facility and achieving almost all preflight goals, despite a late start in the mission.

The Spacelab 3 module, flown as the first operational vehicle in the Spacelab series, verified the performance of the hardware begun by Spacelab 1 in 1983. The use of Spacelab as an experiment platform within the orbiter vehicle continued the varied and multirole performance of the STS system. The Spacelab hardware provided a vital link between the pioneering efforts of early manned spaceflights in the Mercury-Apollo series, including the Skylab series, and the U.S. Space Station program. A significant number of Spacelab 3 research tasks were aimed at future programs and at evaluating the baseline requirements for Space Station habitation hardware. In addition, results from the round-the-clock operations on STS 51B provided vast amounts of new data to complement the results obtained prior to the mission. For example, the ATMOS experiment gathered more data on one flight than previously obtained in decades of similar research with balloon-borne high-altitude sorties.

The flying of principal investigators allowed them to refine their own hardware and to experience at first hand the operation of their experiments. What they learned was of great importance in the development of follow-up experiments. An understanding of the effects of spaceflight on hardware and the difficulties and advantages of the microgravity environment allowed Wang and van den Berg to make plans for more efficient and productive experimental hardware for later flights and use by other crews.

The flight of STS 51B provided NASA with pre-Space Station experience in areas of research in which the Soviet Union had been working on their Salyut space stations since 1971. The lack of a long-term space platform for extended scientific research by manned crews in the U.S. program is offset by missions such as 51B which fly specialists into the experimental environment and operate equipment around the clock for maximum scientific return from each flight.

Bibliography

Furniss, Tim. *Manned Spaceflight Log*. Rev. ed. London: Jane's Publishing Co., 1986. This updated version of the first edition (1983) provides a comprehensive history of manned spaceflight from Yuri Gagarin in April of 1961 to the tragedy of STS 51L, *Challenger*, and the triumph of the Mir space station in 1986. In addition to 115 manned U.S. and Soviet spaceflights, Furniss covers thirteen U.S. X-15 aircraft astroflights of the 1960's. STS 51B is listed as spaceflight 118, the sixty-first U.S. flight, the seventeenth shuttle mission, and the seventh for *Challenger*. Illustrated.

——————————, ed. *Space Shuttle Log*. London: Jane's Publishing Co., 1986. A collection of highly readable reports on the first twenty-two shuttle missions, providing flight data and a summary of the most notable events of each mission, as well as biographical data on the astronauts. The inclusion of 51B among the first twenty-two flights invites interesting comparisons between this flight and others in the series. Suitable for general and younger readers.

Gurney, Gene, and Jeff Forte. *Space Shuttle Log: The First Twenty-five Flights*. Blue Ridge Summit, Pa.: Tab Books, 1988. A collection of chapters summarizing the first twenty-five missions of the Space Transportation System program, covering the operational flight time of April, 1981, to January, 1986, the first five years of the flight program. Each entry, from STS 1 through STS 25, lists information on crews, payloads, launch preparations, launches, orbital operations, and landing phases. A mission summary and text are accompanied by a selection of black-and-white photographs for each mission.

National Aeronautics and Space Administration. *Spacelab 3*. NASA EP-203. Washington, D.C.: Government Printing Office, 1984. This NASA publication provides a preflight overview of the 51B mission and the scientific investigations planned for Spacelab 3. Background chapters on the flight crew, mission planning, and each of the major areas of scientific research are included, along with diagrams and color photographs, providing a handy summary of preflight objectives.

Shayler, David J. *Shuttle Challenger: Aviation Fact File*. London: Salamander Books, 1987. A book devoted to the career of space shuttle orbiter OV-099, the *Challenger*. The text covers the role of *Challenger* in the shuttle program, the construction and components of the vehicle, its missions (including the 51L tragedy), the astronauts who flew it, and the payloads it carried. The coverage of the 51B mission includes information on the long preparations for the flight from 41G in October, 1984, to 51B in April, 1985, as well as data on launch preparations, the launch phase, orbital activities, reentry, the landing, and postlanding activities. A mission data and flight log information block lists additional data on hardware and achievements in a series of tables at the rear of the book. This large-format volume is suitable for students and general audiences.

David J. Shayler

Cross-References

Biological Effects of Space Travel on Humans, 188; Soviet Biosatellites, 194; U.S. Biosatellites, 204; U.S. Launch Vehicles, 749; The Skylab Program, 1285; Skylab 2, 1291; Skylab 3, 1298; Skylab 4, 1303; The U.S. Space Shuttle, 1626; Space Shuttle Living Conditions, 1634; Space Shuttle Mission 13: *Challenger*, 1735; The Development of the U.S. Space Station, 1835; Living and Working in the U.S. Space Station, 1850; The Spacelab Program, 1884; Spacelab 1, 1891; Spacelab 2, 1898; Spacelab 3, 1904.

SPACE SHUTTLE MISSION 18
Discovery

Date: June 17 to June 24, 1985
Type of mission: Manned Earth-orbiting spaceflight
Countries: The United States, France, and Saudi Arabia

STS 51G, the eighteenth flight of the space shuttle, was one of the most successful of the series. Four satellites were released, one was retrieved, and many important technological and scientific investigations were completed.

> *Principal personages*
> DANIEL C. BRANDENSTEIN, the commander
> JOHN O. CREIGHTON, the pilot
> STEVEN R. NAGEL,
> JOHN M. FABIAN, and
> SHANNON W. LUCID, mission specialists
> PATRICK BAUDRY and
> SULTAN SALMAN ABDELAZIZE AL-SAUD, payload specialists

Summary of the Mission

Despite a lightning strike on the 24-meter-tall lightning mast the night before, the fifth flight of *Discovery* began with a perfect lift-off at 7:33 A.M. eastern daylight time on June 17, 1985. The ride to orbit for the international crew of seven initially suffered from a low thrust from the solid-fueled rocket boosters, but the space shuttle main engines made up the difference by burning longer than planned. Some 8 minutes and 46 seconds after leaving Kennedy Space Center's Launchpad 39A, *Discovery* was in orbit.

Upon reaching the desired orbit, the crew began preparing for a seven-day mission which would see the release of a record four satellites from the space shuttle orbiter, the retrieval of one of them, and a variety of experiments ranging from studies of human biology to measurements of the emissions of distant galaxies. The crew of astronauts from the National Aeronautics and Space Administration (NASA) comprised the commander, Daniel C. Brandenstein; the pilot, John O. Creighton; and mission specialists John M. Fabian, Shannon W. Lucid, and Steven R. Nagel. While the crew was preparing the orbiter for its stay in space, Patrick Baudry began a series of measurements to study the flow of blood in his body. A payload specialist, Baudry was a French space traveler who had served as backup for his countryman Jean-Loup Chrétien on Soyuz T-6. The French echocardiograph experiment (FEE) that Baudry was using within three hours of launch was very similar to the equipment Chrétien had used on Salyut 7.

Both Patrick Baudry and the other payload specialist, Sultan Salman Abdelazize Al-Saud, were on board to conduct specific experiments from scientists in their countries. Al-Saud's participation was sponsored by Saudi Arabia and was permitted because the twenty-two-member Arab Satellite Communications Organization was hiring NASA to deploy a satellite from the space shuttle. NASA policy allowed customers to include a passenger in such cases. Neither Baudry nor Al-Saud had any responsibilities directly related to the principal goals of the flight.

Keeping with the international flavor of STS 51G, the first important goal in orbit was to release the Morelos-A communications satellite belonging to Mexico. Stored under one of the three protective sunshields in the payload bay, Morelos was destined for orbit 35,900 kilometers above the equator at a longitude of 113.5 degrees west. At this altitude it would take 24 hours to circle Earth, matching Earth's own rotational speed. It would then appear stationary to observers on Earth, and as with so many other communications satellites positioned in geosynchronous orbit, provide a convenient relay point for widely separated ground transmitters and receivers. The astronauts confirmed that the satellite was functional, and it was ejected into space only 8 hours and 5 minutes after *Discovery* itself was launched. *Discovery* fired its own jets to move away from the free-floating satellite, and after 45 minutes a timer on the Morelos activated its rocket engine to propel itself to the desired orbit.

Although the Arabsat 1B release was scheduled for the next day, that satellite demanded attention when ground controllers received a signal indicating that one of its solar panels (used to convert sunlight into electricity for the satellite) had partially opened under the sunshield. The crew could see no evidence of this defect, so the next day the remote manipulator system (RMS) arm was used to get a closer view of the satellite. The RMS is a 15-meter-long "robot arm" in the orbiter's payload bay and is controlled by the astronauts. A camera at the "wrist" of the RMS allowed a detailed inspection of the solar array, and it was determined that the indicator was faulty. The array was correctly tucked against the side of the satellite. The release of the Arabsat took place on schedule and without difficulty on the second day of the mission, at 9:36 A.M. The successful deployment of the Telstar 3D occurred at 7:20 A.M. on June 19 and completed the delivery of communications satellites to orbit.

With the three satellites on their way, the crew had time to turn to other activities. A chocolate cake was on board to celebrate Steven Nagel's becoming the one hundredth American in space. Patrick Baudry continued with the FEE and the French postural experiment, both designed to improve understanding of the body's adaptation to the near weightlessness of orbit. He was assisted by Lucid and Al-Saud, who also spent time photographing his home country and performing experiments on the mixing of oil and water without the effects of gravity.

While various small experiments ran throughout the mission with minimal attention required from the astronauts, who were busy with the satellite deployments during the first days, some important activities remained. One of these was the high-precision tracking experiment (HPTE), an unclassified test in collaboration with the Strategic Defense Initiative Office (SDIO). The purpose was to evaluate various schemes for training a laser on an Earth target over a period of time. Earth's turbulent atmosphere makes this very difficult. The plan called for the astronauts to install a special 22-centimeter mirror in one of the windows. When a low-power laser at Mount Haleakala in Maui, Hawaii, was directed toward *Discovery*, the mirror would send some of the light back to the ground station, which could then measure how accurately the laser had "hit" the orbiter.

The astronauts entered the location of the ground-based laser into the computers so that the orbiter could orient itself correctly to ensure that the mirror would reflect the laser back to the ground test facility. Shortly before 3:00 P.M. on June 19, immediately before the test, the astronauts reported that the window was not pointing toward Hawaii, but was pointing into space instead. The astronauts were able to see the blue-green light from the laser (it covered an area on the spacecraft about 9 meters in diameter), but the mirror was not in a position to return any of the light. It was soon determined that the location of the laser transmitter was entered into the computer as being at an altitude of 3,046 meters (9,994 feet) above sea level. The computer had been programmed to receive the number in nautical miles (1 nautical mile is equivalent to 1.86 kilometers) instead of feet, so it aimed the window at a site 9,994 nautical miles (about 18,500 kilometers) above sea level. The orbit of the *Discovery* was only 370 kilometers high. Thus the computer miscalculated the laser's location. By the time this error was discovered, it was too late to correct it.

Before another attempt to perform the tracking experiment was made, the last satellite release had to be undertaken. The shuttle-pointed autonomous research tool for astronomy (SPARTAN) was designed to conduct observations independently of the space shuttle for as long as two days. This first test flight had instruments for measuring the X rays emanating from the center of the Milky Way galaxy and from the galaxies clustered in a group known as Perseus. Shannon Lucid used the RMS to remove SPARTAN 1 from its cradle in the payload bay and point it so that its own systems would be directed toward the Sun and the star Vega. This orientation would allow the satellite to establish and maintain its own direction in space so that it could aim its instruments at the preprogrammed targets. The satellite, about the size of a telephone booth, was gently released at 12:03 P.M. on June 20. In order to minimize the cost and complexity of the SPARTAN, no communications equipment was built into it, so, to inform the crew that all of its systems had passed a self-test, the free-flying spacecraft performed a "pirouette." Satisfied that everything was working as planned, the astronauts directed *Discovery* away from the satellite to allow SPARTAN's observations to proceed without interference from the orbiter. The distance between the two craft would slowly grow to more than 190 kilometers.

On June 21, another attempt to perform the laser tracking experiment was planned. This time it was the weather, not the finicky computer, that threatened the experiment. Winds in excess of 65 kilometers per hour blew at the test site in Hawaii, where the upper limit on acceptable wind speeds for the test had been set at

48 kilometers per hour. Just before the test was to begin, the winds abated, and the experiment was performed successfully.

On June 22, the crew members began a twenty-hour, thirteen-orbit chase to recover the SPARTAN. When they were still 58 kilometers and 4.5 hours from retrieving it, they were able to see it. Finally, shortly after 9:00 A.M., when they were fewer than 50 meters away from the satellite, they could see that it was not in the correct orientation. It was stable, but the fixture that the RMS needed to attach itself to was not on the side facing *Discovery*. The orbiter closed to within 10 meters of the craft, and John Fabian manipulated the RMS expertly to reach behind the SPARTAN and pluck it from its independent orbit. He then returned the satellite to its resting place in the payload bay so that scientists and engineers on Earth could evaluate both the data from its astronomical observations and the overall performance of the new, reusable satellite.

The next day was devoted to preparations for the end of the mission and to a press conference with an international press corps. On June 24 at 8:07 A.M., the retrograde engines of *Discovery* were fired one final time for this mission to slow the craft enough to return it to Earth. As with virtually every phase of this eighteenth mission of the Space Transportation System, the actual entry and landing matched the plan almost perfectly. Commander Brandenstein landed *Discovery* on the dry lake bed at Edwards Air Force Base about one hour after the de-orbit burn. The spacecraft rolled for 40 seconds before stopping, the final part of its 4.7-million-kilometer journey marred only by the left main landing gear digging 15 centimeters into the ground as *Discovery* came to a halt. The orbiter incurred minimal damage, however, and STS 51G concluded with the same level of success it had demonstrated since it began.

Knowledge Gained

The flight of SPARTAN 1 yielded important scientific and technical results. The primary objective of mapping the X-ray emissions from the central region of the Milky Way and the complete Perseus cluster of galaxies was achieved, although problems with the satellite allowed only about one-half of the planned observations to be completed. The measurements of the Perseus cluster extended over a larger region of space than did previous X-ray data, and the strong X-ray emission at large distances from the center of the cluster suggested that some "missing mass" (matter whose presence is inferred from its gravitational effects but which has not been detected directly with radio or visible observations) may be there. The X rays detected emanate from matter at temperatures in excess of 5 million degrees Celsius, a finding that may yield a better understanding of the nature of the matter and the overall structure of the galaxies. Data on the center of the Milky Way added pieces to the poorly understood puzzle of how the hot matter there fits into the overall structure and composition of that region.

Along with the astrophysical observations, an important goal in the flight of SPARTAN 1 was to evaluate the spacecraft itself. This first flight did encounter an unexpected problem. The gyroscope system, which was used to help stabilize the satellite, did not function properly. The result was that the small jets used to change its orientation had to fire more than had been planned. Therefore, the supply of argon gas used for these jets was consumed more quickly than it otherwise would have been. When the computer detected the level of gas to be low, the observations were terminated and the SPARTAN was switched into a gas-conservation mode. The spacecraft virtually turned itself off, except for a timer. It tumbled randomly in its orbit, until the timer indicated that its retrieval by *Discovery* was nearing. Some of the systems were then reactivated, and the dwindling supply of gas was used to stabilize SPARTAN 1 so that the RMS could capture it. Naturally, having been turned off, it could not reestablish its previous orientation. Thus the satellite floated aimlessly until John Fabian could capture it.

The French experiments on the adaptation to spaceflight and the readaptation to normal gravity completed all the planned tests. The results of Baudry's measurements of the cardiovascular system and other systems in the body added to a small but growing data base on the effects of gravity (or its absence) on living organisms. These experiments would be flown repeatedly to gather statistically significant data.

One of the other experiments conducted throughout the mission was designed to shed light on the process of convection in the melting of certain materials. Operated automatically while the astronauts slept (so that their movements about the orbiter would not cause disturbances in the sensitive experiment), it melted samples for later study to examine to what extent the absence of gravity reduced convection. The postflight analysis revealed the surprising fact that convection plays a very important role in solidification even when gravitational effects are greatly reduced.

Context

STS 51G was described by NASA as being more than 100 percent successful, because all the principal objectives of the flight were met and the crew was often ahead of schedule. The mission took place as NASA was working to increase the number of shuttle flights per year, and the successes and smooth operation of this flight gave NASA a boost in its description of the Space Transportation System as an "operational" system.

The three communications satellites sent into orbit by *Discovery*'s crew all reached their appointed slots in geosynchronous orbit. The Morelos was the first Mexican communications satellite, and its use to provide telecommunications to remote parts of that nation is an example of the increasing use of sophisticated space technology by nations throughout the world. Morelos helps bring educational television, commercial programs, telephone and facsimile, and data and business transmissions to virtually every area in Mexico. An earthquake later in 1985 damaged some of the nation's ground communication facilities, and financial constraints prevented them from being repaired immediately. Therefore, the second satellite in the Morelos system (successfully deployed on STS 61B) could not be used to complete the communications network as soon as Mexican officials had hoped.

SPARTAN's flight demonstrated the capabilities of a new family of free-flying spacecraft. With minimal reliance on the orbiter, the satellite was able to conduct observations for many hours. Prior to this flight, similar astrophysical observations were conducted from sounding rockets, which simply flew an arc into space before returning to Earth. Such flights generally provide up to fifteen minutes of experiment time. After diagnosing the problem with the gyroscopes, engineers were confident that SPARTANs could provide up to two days of observations on future space shuttle flights. Furthermore, the retrieval of the satellite demonstrated the value of returning it to Earth, where the problems with it could be analyzed and repaired before the next use of the spacecraft.

The high-precision tracking experiment provided experimenters with about 2.5 minutes (more than twice as long as needed) of data on the performance of different tracking techniques. It was the first SDIO experiment conducted with the space shuttle, and more were planned to follow.

The error in the altitude data on the laser source proved a foreshadowing of future problems. The experiment had been added late in the crew-preparation schedule, and there was not enough time to simulate the test during preflight training. After the failure of STS 51L, the mission which ended in the explosion of the *Challenger*, the importance of not modifying plans late in the training sequence was raised. Fortunately, the error on STS 51G had caused no serious problems.

Bibliography

Allen, Joseph P., and Russell Martin. *Entering Space: An Astronaut's Odyssey*. Rev. ed. New York: Stewart, Tabori and Chang, 1984. Allen is a veteran of two space shuttle missions. He and Martin include more than two hundred color photographs displaying beautiful views from space as well as the activities performed by astronauts. Suitable for all audiences, this book describes the experiences of spaceflight, both the routine chores of living and working and the excitement of being in space.

Cooper, Henry S. F. *Before Lift-Off: The Making of a Space Shuttle Crew*. Baltimore: Johns Hopkins University Press, 1987. The long process of training astronauts for a flight on the space shuttle is described by following the crew of STS 41G. Although it covers the training for a specific mission, the book provides interesting insight into the difficulty and importance of preflight training for any mission. All readers will gain an appreciation of the challenges that precede a space shuttle flight and how difficult an astronaut's work is.

Furniss, Tim. *Manned Spaceflight Log*. Rev. ed. New York: Jane's Publishing Co., 1986. Containing a description of every manned mission into space through Soyuz T-15 in March, 1986, this book is entertainingly written and should be enjoyed by general audiences. It provides the essential facts from each flight and allows the reader to understand any flight in the context of the human effort to explore and work in space.

Joels, Kelly Mark, Gregory P. Kennedy, and David Larkin. *The Space Shuttle*

Operator's Manual. New York: Ballantine Books, 1982. This book contains a wealth of information on space shuttle systems and flight procedures. It is written as a manual for imaginary crew members on a generic mission and will be appreciated by anyone interested in how the astronauts fly the orbiter, deploy satellites, conduct experiments, and live in space. Heavily illustrated with drawings and some photographs of equipment.

Powers, Robert M. *Shuttle: The World's First Spaceship.* Harrisburg, Pa.: Stackpole Books, 1979. Despite being written before the first flight of the Space Transportation System, this book contains excellent descriptions of the space shuttle systems and the types of missions planned. There are very good explanations of why and how the environment of space is used for a variety of scientific applications. The book includes many illustrations, a glossary, and an index.

Marc D. Rayman

Cross-References

The Manned Maneuvering Unit, 829; The U.S. Space Shuttle, 1626; Space Shuttle Mission 11: *Challenger*, 1719.

SPACE SHUTTLE MISSION 19
Challenger

Date: July 29 to August 6, 1985
Type of mission: Manned Earth-orbiting spaceflight
Country: The United States

On shuttle mission 51F, better known as the flight of Spacelab 2, astronauts conducted experiments in solar and space plasma physics and astrophysics.

Principal personages
DAN SPICER, the program scientist
LOUIS J. DEMAS, the program manager
ROY C. LESTER, the mission manager
EUGENE W. URBAN, a mission scientist
CHARLES GORDON FULLERTON, the commander
ROY D. BRIDGES, the pilot
ANTHONY W. ENGLAND,
F. STORY MUSGRAVE, and
KARL G. HENIZE, mission specialists
LOREN W. ACTON and
JOHN-DAVID F. BARTOE, payload specialists

Summary of the Mission

The nineteenth space shuttle mission returned important data on the Sun, the stars, and the space environment with an advanced array of sophisticated instruments. The mission also demonstrated the instrument pointing system (IPS), designed as part of the Spacelab science system for the shuttle. Although the flight itself was designated Space Transportation System (STS) 51F, it is best known by its primary payload, Spacelab 2. Its scientific objectives were to scan the sky and to analyze the near-space environment around Earth.

The first attempt to launch mission 51F, which would use the space shuttle *Challenger*, was aborted on the launchpad. Apparently, an engine had been slow in starting only three seconds before lift-off on July 12, 1985. Tests conducted later revealed that the backup computer for the Spacelab payload had failed. Because replacement required removing the shuttle from the launchpad, officials from the National Aeronautics and Space Administration (NASA) decided to take the risk of flying with only two main Spacelab computers operable (that would not affect the shuttle's own flight computers).

The launch was reset for July 29. After a ninety-minute delay caused by flight computer problems, *Challenger* lifted off at 4:00 P.M. eastern daylight time. Ascent was normal until 5 minutes and 45 seconds after lift-off, when the center engine was automatically shut down by its computer. That forced the crew to implement a procedure known as "abort to orbit." The remaining two engines would use the rest of the propellant to burn one minute longer in order to achieve orbit. Although called an "abort," this maneuver actually allows the mission to proceed by placing the spacecraft in an orbit lower than the one that had been planned. *Challenger*'s engines were, in fact, performing as designed, but a pair of temperature sensors on a turbopump gave erroneous high readings and the computer deactivated the engine. A flight controller saw that all other engine readings were normal. When sensors on a second engine functioned the same way, the crew was instructed to override the computer's automatic command to deactivate this second engine.

Although *Challenger* was successfully inserted into an orbit 322 kilometers (instead of 385 kilometers) high, extensive mission replanning was immediately required because the time line, or flightplan, was dependent upon the Sun and other targets rising and setting at certain times. A lower orbit meant that these events would occur more frequently. "Fly-around" activities with a deployable science package were severely curtailed as well, because most of *Challenger*'s onboard maneuvering rockets had to be fired to lighten the vehicle of almost 2,000 kilograms of fuel. The engine failures caused no further problems for the mission, since the main engines are only used during launch.

Because energy was conserved during the flight, Mission Control could extend the mission by one day to allow the solar science team to recover part of the experimental time lost when the instrument pointing system was malfunctioning. The mission ended at 3:45 P.M., when *Challenger* landed at Edwards Air Force Base in California.

Instruments in the Spacelab payload were designed to return data in the fields of astrophysics and solar and space plasma physics; experiments in the areas of atmospheric physics, technology development, and the life sciences were also on board. These were assembled on three U-shaped Spacelab pallets and on a special structure carried in *Challenger*'s payload bay.

The solar and atmospheric physics instruments were attached to an instrument pointing system designed to aim telescopes at the Sun, the stars, Earth, and other targets as the shuttle flew through space. Spacelab 2 had been delayed for several years because of problems in developing this highly sophisticated system.

Four solar instruments were mounted on the forward pallet of the instrument pointing system: the high-resolution telescope and spectrograph (HRTS), the solar optical universal polarimeter (SOUP), the coronal helium abundance experiment (CHASE), and the solar ultraviolet spectral irradiance monitor (SUSIM). Only the first three were considered to be true solar physics instruments, since the SUSIM was designed to support studies of Earth's atmosphere. The SUSIM had flown earlier on the STS 3 mission in 1982.

The HRTS and the SOUP were complementary instruments designed to return data on active regions of the visible surface of the Sun. The SOUP consisted of a 30-centimeter telescope, complete with a tunable filter system and film and video cameras. The filters allowed scientists to view the Sun in specific wavelengths (from

480 to 700 nanometers) and polarizations which, in turn, could be related to gas temperature, velocity, and magnetic field strength and direction. Investigators on Earth could observe through video cameras and then take high-resolution film images. It was hoped that the SOUP would help produce photographs of individual magnetic field activities within granules (convective eddies rising to the Sun's surface) during their 5- to 20-minute lives and within supergranules during their 20- to 40-hour lives. The HRTS would aid scientists in their study of the outer layers of the solar atmosphere, especially the transitional region between the chromosphere and the corona. The instrument's 30-centimeter ultraviolet telescope used a slit spectrograph to build images of the Sun in ultraviolet light (120 to 400 nanometers) for video and film cameras. It had extremely high spectral resolution.

Astrophysics instruments were mounted on pallets and structures through the remainder of the payload bay. These were the X-ray telescope (XRT), the small, helium-cooled infrared telescope (IRT), and the elemental composition and energy spectra of cosmic-ray nuclei (CRNE) instrument. The XRT actually consisted of two telescopes of similar design; each used a pinhole mask to project images of the sky in high-energy X rays. This device worked much like a pinhole camera except that there were multiple pinholes to allow many X rays to enter. Computers were used to aid scientists in their evaluation of the images. The IRT used liquid helium to cool the detectors at the focal plane of a 15-centimeter telescope in order that cold objects in the 1- to 120-micron wavelength range, such as stellar nurseries and nebulae, could be observed. The telescope itself scanned at right angles to the shuttle's line of flight to construct images line by line. The CRNE, also called the "Chicago egg" because of its shape and its origin (the University of Chicago), was the largest cosmic-ray instrument placed in orbit (it was conceived for the High-Energy Astronomical Observatory program). Its design allowed for detection of extremely heavy cosmic rays at energies between 400 and 4,000 gigaelectronvolts. Cosmic rays are not actually rays but atomic and subatomic particles released after the explosion of stars and other such violent events.

Two plasma physics instruments shared pallet space with the IRT: the ejectable plasma diagnostics package (PDP) and the vehicle-charging and potential experiment (VCAP). Both the PDP and the VCAP had been flown on STS 3 in 1982. The PDP carried several instruments in an ejectable package that the shuttle was to circulate in order to help scientists determine the effects of large vehicles on the space environment. The VCAP comprised complementary instruments, including an electron gun to probe the plasma environment while the PDP measured responses. A third investigation, designed to return data on plasma depletion for ionospheric and radio astronomical studies, had no special equipment aboard *Challenger*. Instead, it used the shuttle's thrusters to burn "holes" in the ionosphere.

One technology experiment, whose subject was the properties of superfluid helium in zero-gravity, was carried on the pallet. Superfluid helium, in which electrical resistance disappears, behaves according to the laws of quantum mechanics. Two life sciences experiments were carried in the shuttle cabin to measure the effects of weightlessness on life; the first focused on the normal cycles in human bones, and the second focused on the production of lignin (a tough cellulose) in mung bean and pine seedlings.

The operation of most instruments proceeded normally throughout the mission. The instrument pointing system, however, frustrated flight and ground crews almost from the start. Its "fine-track" mode was ineffective when the instrument was pointed at the Sun. In a week of intense troubleshooting, engineers uncovered four defects in the Spacelab software, including one that had the IPS trackers programmed to "look" for an object much brighter than the Sun. In the meantime, the crew was able to operate the IPS by using trackers mounted within the instruments. Solar observations did not start until the third mission day, and normal IPS operations were not possible until the seventh mission day.

Additional frustration was caused by the SOUP telescope, which stopped functioning more than three hours after the crew had activated it. Engineers tried many software changes throughout the mission. At the very end of the mission, their last software change coincided with a thruster firing that may have caused some contaminant to break loose. Although it was near the end of the mission, the crew was able to use all the 12,800 frames of film in only sixteen hours (fifty hours of observations had been planned). In addition, two sounding rockets carrying solar telescopes to complement Spacelab 2 were unsuccessful. One was destroyed in flight, and the other was canceled after a lightning strike. The HRTS, meanwhile, operated as planned and shot more than four thousand frames of film. The CHASE data were degraded, because the instrument required a higher altitude to detect helium isotopes in the solar corona, but the SUSIM performed well.

At one point, the IRT appeared to be operating in a cloud. Repeated observations showed that it was focused on a hot cloud of material which, like a fog, prevented it from detecting the stars. Water vapor and dust particles from the spacecraft were believed to be hanging around the vehicle like a cloud, and an infrared observatory in Hawaii reported that the shuttle looked like a bright comet as it passed overhead. Television images taken from the robot arm, however, showed that a strip of insulation had become loose and was dangling in front of the telescope aperture.

The PDP was retrieved by the robot arm on the third mission day. It was then released so the shuttle could retreat to a point a few kilometers away and maneuver around it for six hours (about half the time initially scheduled for the maneuver). Some of these activities required expert flying by the crew to place the shuttle and the PDP on the same magnetic field lines. Four of the eight in-orbit rocket firings planned for the plasma depletion experiments were also canceled because of the fuel expenditure made during ascent.

Knowledge Gained

Although most of the mission objectives were achieved, the scientific results from Spacelab 2 were not all useful. Many of the HRTS images were fogged by overheating when the payload bay liner reflected more sunlight than expected.

Nevertheless, scientists have called some of the images remarkable. They have discovered jet or explosive events in the solar corona, possibly where the solar magnetic field is perpendicular to the surface. Magnetic activity may also have been observed in superspicules, jets of hot gas rising to 15,000 kilometers above the solar surface and lasting three to five minutes. The HRTS also observed smaller spicules that match known spicules observed for some time in white light.

The CHASE instrument did not return useful data on helium ratios because of time constraints and because of internal instrument problems. Although the SOUP film was shot quickly, the experiment yielded more than six thousand striking, high-resolution images showing unusual evolution of granular structures. As the SOUP helped scientists discover, granules explode or break into bright rings that fade or they are destroyed by interaction with granules that have exploded. Also, the granules were found to be absent where solar magnetic activity is most intense.

The twin XRTs produced images of the center of the Galaxy and other stellar objects in a broader energy range than had previously been observed. The IRT provided useful data at short and long infrared wavelengths, including images of the center of the Galaxy, despite the cloud problem. Data collected in the midrange, though, were useless. The CRNE detected millions of low-energy events and some ten thousand high-energy events of interest. A few registered as high as 10 teraelectron volts, and a gamma-ray burst was detected by the secondary particles it created when it hit the detector shell.

Results from the plasma experiments were substantial. The most striking was the opening of a "hole" in the ionosphere through which the radio telescope at Hobart, Tasmania, could observe stars on wavelengths that normally are reflected by the electrified upper atmosphere. The "hole" was actually an area depleted of electrons and ions and thus transparent to those wavelengths for a few minutes, until the ionosphere regenerated itself. A similar "hole" was generated over New England and persisted for only fifteen minutes. The plasma wake left by the shuttle was found to be complex and turbulent. Thruster firings, water dumps, gas leaks, and other emissions from the shuttle generated a large cloud of neutral gas that expanded around the vehicle and altered the ionosphere. Water ions not normally present at the shuttle's orbiting altitude were detected in large quantities to a distance of several hundred meters from the shuttle, especially in the plasma wake. The PDP fly-around activity placed the shuttle and PDP on the same magnetic field line four times and showed that electrostatic noise (first detected on STS 3) extends far "downstream" from the shuttle but only a short distance "upstream."

Context

Like Spacelab 1 and Spacelab 3, Spacelab 2 advanced space science in several areas and demonstrated that the shuttle/Spacelab combination is an effective platform for conducting space science experiments. Observations made with the cluster of solar instruments marked the first time since Skylab's Apollo Telescope Mount in 1973-1974 that a manned solar observatory had been operated in space.

Despite the problems with the IPS, the data from the HRTS and SOUP telescopes were outstanding. Results from both experiments revealed details of solar activity which had been suspected but unobserved because Earth's atmosphere blocks the view. The images from the SOUP will provide a better understanding of the evolution and importance of granules (discovered only two centuries ago) in transporting energy to the solar surface. The HRTS images of superspicules show that that particular spicule phenomenon is larger than previously believed and plays a greater role in the transport of mass and energy from the solar surface into the transitional region where temperatures rise rapidly. A raster survey of 25 percent of the solar disk would help establish global properties of the fine structures of the solar surface. The SUSIM provided measurements of the solar ultraviolet output, with an accuracy of 6 to 10 percent. The SUSIM flown on Spacelab 2 was the beginning of a long-term program to collect data with respect to the influence of the Sun on the terrestrial environment, including the ozone hole. The value of these data will become known as SUSIM-type instruments are reflown over the next few decades. X-ray and infrared images of the skies, and cosmic-ray data, are adding to scientists' understanding of celestial objects.

The shuttle's utility as a scientific platform was demonstrated with mixed results. The "abort to orbit" demonstrated a need for performance margins for experiments and for less intense mission planning. After Spacelab 2, infrared observations aboard the shuttle were perceived as risky at best, based on the IRT results. The plasma experiments, however, provided a wealth of data, as scientists were able to disturb the plasma environment in a controlled way and observe the effects with a nearby craft. Although the scientific results were generally good, the operation of the setup would need refining.

Bibliography

Covault, Craig. "*Challenger*'s Spacelab Telescopes Gather Solar, Deep Space Data." *Aviation Week and Space Technology* 123 (August 5, 1985): 14-16. A mid-flight review of launch and initial activities on Spacelab 2. Technical but informative.

_____ . "Most of Spacelab 2 Mission Objectives Achieved Despite Early Problems." *Aviation Week and Space Technology* 123 (August 12, 1985): 25-28. An overview of science activities during the Spacelab 2 mission.

Kolcum, Edward H. "Shuttle Delayed by Software Error, Flies Without Backup Computer." *Aviation Week and Space Technology* 123 (August 5, 1985): 19. A description of the countdown and the problems preceding the launch of Spacelab 2.

National Aeronautics and Space Administration. Marshall Space Flight Center. *Spacelab 2*. NASA EP-217. Washington, D.C.: Government Printing Office, 1985. This educational publication describes the instruments aboard Spacelab 2 and the planned scientific experiments. Written for reporters covering the mission.

Smith, David H., and Thornton L. Page. "Spacelab 2: Science in Orbit." *Sky and*

Telescope 72 (November, 1986): 438-445. An extensive survey of scientific results from the Spacelab 2 mission. Well written and well illustrated with color photographs and charts. For the educated reader interested in astronomy.

Dave Dooling

Cross-References

Biological Effects of Space Travel on Humans, 188; The European Space Agency, 372; Marshall Space Flight Center, 908; The U.S. Space Shuttle, 1626; Space Shuttle Living Conditions, 1634; The Spacelab Program, 1884; Spacelab 1, 1891; Spacelab 2, 1898; Spacelab 3, 1904.

SPACE SHUTTLE MISSION 20
Discovery

Date: August 27 to September 3, 1985
Type of mission: Manned Earth-orbiting spaceflight
Country: The United States

STS 51I was the twentieth flight of the United States' space shuttle program. In addition to deploying three communications satellites, crew members captured a malfunctioning satellite (which had been launched by a previous shuttle), repaired it successfully, and returned it to orbit. It was the second such in-orbit satellite repair in history.

Principal personages

A. D. ALDRICH, Manager, Space Transportation System
JOE H. ENGLE, the mission commander
RICHARD O. COVEY, the pilot
JAMES VAN HOFTEN,
JOHN M. LOUNGE, and
WILLIAM F. FISHER, mission specialists

Summary of the Mission

STS mission 51I marked the sixth spaceflight of the orbiter *Discovery*. The seven-day mission proved the extraordinary versatility of the space shuttle as a manned delivery and repair platform.

The first launch date scheduled for mission 51I was August 24, 1985, from Kennedy Space Center's Launch Complex 39A. The launch was rescheduled for the next day because of thunderstorms. During the second attempt, on August 25, 1985, an onboard computer malfunctioned during the countdown. The malfunction was described by National Aeronautics and Space Administration (NASA) engineers as a "GPC 5 byte fault." GPC 5 is general purpose computer number 5, located inside the space shuttle orbiter. This computer contained backup flight system software essential to the shuttle's launch. Engineers reinitialized the software after the error was found, but the error appeared again only 11 minutes later. The flight was postponed again, this time for two days, so GPC 5 could be removed and replaced.

The third countdown, on August 27, 1985, proceeded smoothly. *Discovery* and its five-member crew were launched without significant delays at 6:58:01 A.M. eastern daylight time from Pad 39A. The launch proceeded normally in all respects. The solid-fueled rocket boosters separated without any problems 2 minutes and 1 second after lift-off. The three main engines were shut down 6 minutes and 27 seconds later, 18 seconds before the large external tank was jettisoned. (It later burned in the atmosphere over the Indian Ocean.)

For many missions it is necessary to fire the orbital maneuvering system (OMS) rocket engines twice to refine the orbital parameters. In this mission, however, the ship was flown in an ascent mode called a "direct insertion ascent trajectory," which precluded the necessity to initiate the first scheduled OMS firing. Exactly 40 minutes and 21 seconds after lift-off, the OMS engines were fired for 3 minutes and 3 seconds, placing the orbiter in a nearly circular orbit approximately 306 by 306 kilometers above Earth. At 10:41 A.M. on August 27, 1985, *Discovery* was safely in orbit.

Immediately following the OMS burn which placed *Discovery* in its orbit, the orbiter's payload bay doors were opened, exposing the satellites in the bay. At 2 hours and 2 minutes after lift-off, the sunshield covering the Australian satellite (Aussat) in the payload bay was commanded to open so that the satellite's systems could be checked prior to deployment from *Discovery*. The sunshield, however, did not fully open. It was determined that the shield was probably binding on an antenna bracket located on top of the satellite. Two hours after the problem was discovered, ground engineers authorized the crew to use the remote manipulator system (RMS), sometimes called the robot arm or the Canada arm, to help push the sunshield open and expose the satellite.

During these operations, the RMS "elbow joint" did not respond to computer commands. Fortunately, the arm had a backup system, and that backup system was used for the remainder of the mission. Yet the failure caused the cancellation of some operations involving use of the RMS-mounted video cameras, such as the monitoring of satellite engine burns and a wastewater dump from the orbiter.

Aussat was finally deployed at 6.5 hours into the mission. Three days later, the satellite reached its station in orbit 35,800 kilometers above Earth, propelled by an engine attached to it called the Payload Assist Module, Delta class (PAM-D). Aussat is used to provide communications relay services for Australia and its off-shore islands. A second satellite, American Satellite Company 1 (ASC 1), was deployed at 11 hours and 9 minutes into the mission. Its deployment was successful, and ASC 1 reached its orbit on August 31. ASC 1 is a communications satellite for American business and government agencies.

The second day onboard *Discovery* was much more relaxed than the first. It was spent performing experiments with an experimental package called PVTOS, for physical vapor transport of organic solids, a package sponsored by the 3M Company and designed to collect data from chemistry experiments conducted in the weightless environment of space. The second day was also used to check out the third satellite still in the payload bay and prepare it for deployment on the third day.

The third satellite, synchronous communications satellite IV-4 (Syncom 4, also called Leasat 4), was deployed as scheduled on August 30. It reached geosynchronous orbit, at 35,800 kilometers in altitude, successfully. At such an altitude, satellites rotate at the same speed as Earth so that they appear to remain stationary in the sky. Unfortunately, for unknown reasons, all communications with the satellite were later lost.

Meanwhile, *Discovery* was effecting orbital corrections to rendezvous with

Leasat 3, which had been launched by STS 51D (also from *Discovery*) some four and one-half months earlier. Leasat 3's booster rocket, which would have placed it in a high, geosynchronous orbit, had failed. The *Discovery* crew planned to maneuver the malfunctioning satellite into the payload bay and repair it.

The fourth day in space was spent preparing for the encounter with Leasat 3. Two rendezvous maneuvers were performed while the crew members tested their extravehicular mobility units (EMUs, or spacesuits). That included charging their batteries and checking out the remote power unit (RPU), whose batteries had been charged on the second day. They would use the RPU to repair the satellite.

The following day, *Discovery* maneuvered to within a few meters of the ailing satellite. Crew members William Fisher, a physician, and James van Hoften, a researcher, exited the orbiter by way of the air lock into the payload bay. With the help of the RMS and some muscle, they captured the satellite and locked it into place in the payload bay to begin the long task of repairing it. Fisher and van Hoften's extravehicular activity (EVA) set a record for the longest spacewalk of the shuttle program: 7 hours and 10 minutes. During that time, Fisher and van Hoften worked to repair the satellite by replacing the parts needed to fire the satellite's booster rocket.

The sixth day was used to finish the repair work on the satellite in an EVA lasting 4 hours and 20 minutes. The crew members reentered the *Discovery*, and Leasat 3 was deployed. Days later, ground controllers successfully fired its troublesome booster rocket; the satellite attained the proper geosynchronous orbit and began normal service.

The seventh day of the flight was used to prepare for reentry. During this time, the crew members pressurized the cabin to sea level pressure. They tested the forward thrusters and the flight control systems using an auxiliary power unit (APU), which provides the flight control systems with power during reentry. They also dumped wastewater into space and stowed all loose items in the cabin for reentry.

Early on the eighth day of flight, the payload bay doors were closed. The crew fired their OMS engines for 4 minutes and 9 seconds to reduce the orbiter's speed. Thirty minutes later, *Discovery* had descended from 305 kilometers to 126 kilometers, where it encountered the "atmospheric interface," or the upper, relatively dense portion of Earth's atmosphere. *Discovery* reentered Earth's atmosphere at twenty-five times the speed of sound (Mach 25). Thirty minutes after reaching the atmosphere, the spacecraft touched down at Edwards Air Force Base in California, at 9:16 A.M., September 3, 1985. The mission had lasted 7 days, 2 hours, and 18 minutes.

Knowledge Gained

The success of STS 51I underscores many of the general aims of the United States' space shuttle program. The system delivered multiple large satellites to orbit. As a manned system, it was able to correct relatively simple payload problems in space (the failure of the sunshield to open, for example) that probably would have resulted in the loss of an unmanned payload. Its own systematic problem (the failure of an RMS mode) was overcome because crew members were able to evaluate the situation. Also, perhaps most important, *Discovery* was able to perform an in-orbit repair.

The RMS system was used in a unique way on this mission, to assist in the capture and stowing of an in-orbit satellite. Since the RMS required the help of a backup system, the crew expanded the knowledge of RMS capabilities and just how far the RMS could be pushed beyond its design.

The capture and repair of Leasat 3 incorporated a body of knowledge into the Space Transportation System that would be used in future repair missions and even eventual space construction. In the weightlessness of space, the crew members were able to maneuver the massive satellite and its attached PAM-D booster, weighing thousands of kilograms on Earth, into the spacecraft's restraints in the cargo bay. They were then able to anchor it into place for the repair work, releasing it later for boosting into its final orbit. Using the crew's experience, researchers would be better equipped to design tools for the most efficient methods of construction in weightlessness.

The repair provided valuable knowledge about bypassing complex electronic systems with alternate circuits and externally modified systems. It required assessing the problem from ground telemetry, working up a probable scenario of the circuitry involved, and designing a system to bypass the troubled circuits. Ground researchers had accomplished this over the span of a few months, and the astronauts were trained and sent into orbit to effect the repairs. All these activities provided a baseline of experience and knowledge that could be used repeatedly as a successful example of how such in-orbit repair missions could be effected in the future.

The seven-hour EVA set a very important precedent for work activities in space. It proved the ability of man to work in space for long periods and established that spacesuits and life-support systems are functional under extremely rigorous conditions.

The PVTOS experiment provided knowledge of the transport of organic solids by vaporizing organic materials in what were called "reactor cells" within the experimental package. Data were obtained and stored in a special computer storage system that was a part of the PVTOS package itself. The exact data and parameters obtained were returned to the 3M Company as proprietary information; the data concerned chemical reactions that can only be performed in weightlessness.

Context

Prior to this *Discovery* mission, deployment of satellites from the shuttle system had become, for all practical purposes, commonplace. Twenty-four satellites had been deployed from the shuttle on previous missions. All deployments had been successful; yet, after leaving the shuttle payload bay, several had malfunctioned in orbit—which was not the fault of the shuttle delivery system.

The in-orbit repair of satellites, however, was not common at all. Although the single previous attempt, STS 41C, had been successful, such repair missions incorporated many uncertainties. For example, the exact cause of the malfunctioning spacecraft could only be narrowed down to a list of possibilities, since the system could not be examined directly. Then the satellite engineers were required to manufacture a solution to cover the entire range of possibilities, plan how these could be installed in space by the crew, and assist the mission planners in training the astronauts to execute the repairs. The pilot and commander of the shuttle, meanwhile, were required to train in rendezvous maneuvers in simulators while other mission specialists trained in the use of the RMS, which would help maneuver the satellite into the payload bay. All of these were mere contingencies; the spectrum of the training program would also have to cover any unplanned events.

NASA engineers had been designing a system whereby an Orbital Maneuvering Vehicle (OMV) would ascend to higher orbits, retrieve malfunctioning spacecraft, and transport them down for repair in lower orbits. Yet that system was not available to mission 51I.

As STS 51I flew, the Soviet Union was at least two and one-half years away from the first launch of their shuttle system, and the Europeans had hardly released word of their planned shuttle-type system, Hermes. Hence, the United States was the only nation at the time to have such capability of launching and repairing spacecraft in orbit from a manned vehicle.

Unfortunately, the United States' shuttle system would fly only four more times before the tragic loss of the orbiter *Challenger*. Not only would the United States lose its lead in the operation of shuttle-type systems, but the program itself would emerge fundamentally changed after that paralyzing tragedy.

Bibliography

Allen, Joseph P., and Russell Martin. *Entering Space: An Astronaut's Odyssey*. New York: Stewart, Tabori and Chang, 1984. A copiously documented volume depicting the United States' space shuttle program. It describes the shuttle's movements from processing at the Kennedy Space Center to launch, orbital activities, and landing. The book is one of the most beautifully photographed and illustrated of all the books on the shuttle program.

Clarke, Arthur C. *Ascent to Orbit*. New York: John Wiley and Sons, 1984. This work is a compilation of many of Clarke's works from his early material (1930's) to his work of the mid-1980's. It is most effective in presenting the "history of conception" of space systems, from communications satellites to the distant future of space exploration. A mixture of technical and purely entertaining essays that can be appreciated by most readers with any interest in the space sciences. Illustrated.

Joels, Kerry M., and David Larkin. *The Space Shuttle Operator's Manual*. New York: Ballantine Books, 1982. This manual is a detailed space shuttle system reference work. It gives specifics on the space shuttle system, from weights and sizes to operational characteristics. It enumerates countdown procedures, emergency instructions, and standard operational modes. Written for a general audience, this book serves as an entertaining as well as an educational reference work. Illustrated.

Nova: Adventures in Science. Reading, Mass.: Addison-Wesley Publishing Co., 1982. A collection of essays and photographs from the public television series *Nova*. Includes several essays on space exploration, with details on the United States' space shuttle system. The book discusses the role of science in daily life, making it an especially valuable tool for referencing the space program and the shuttle's link with everyday existence. It is aimed toward the general reader.

O'Neill, Gerard K. *Two Thousand and Eighty-one: A Hopeful View of the Human Future*. New York: Simon and Schuster, 1982. Princeton physicist, founder of the Space Studies Institute, and "father" of the space colony, Gerard K. O'Neill has pieced together a thoughtful look at the year 2081. The book speculates on future shuttle systems in an insightful way that reveals the grand vision of today's missions. Illustrated and directed toward the general audience with an interest in the future and in space exploration.

Dennis Chamberland

Cross-References

Astronauts and the U.S. Astronaut Program, 154; The Canadian Space Program, 222; Cape Canaveral and the Kennedy Space Center, 229; The Commercial Use of Space Program Innovations, 253; The European Space Agency, 372; Insuring Spacecraft and Human Life, 608; U.S. Private Industry and Space Exploration, 1187; Space Shuttle Mission 5: *Columbia*, 1678; Space Shuttle Mission 6: *Challenger*, 1684; Space Shuttle Mission 11: *Challenger*, 1719; Space Shuttle Mission 14: *Discovery*, 1744; Space Shuttle Mission 16: *Discovery*, 1759; The Development of Spacesuits, 1917; U.S. Private and Commercial Telecommunications Satellites, 1997.

SPACE SHUTTLE MISSION 22
Challenger

Date: October 30 to November 6, 1985
Type of mission: Manned Earth-orbiting spaceflight
Countries: The United States and the ESA countries

STS 61A, the twenty-second space shuttle mission and the ninth Challenger *flight, was the first spaceflight to have its control, once the shuttle was in orbit, centered outside the United States or the Soviet Union. Spacelab D-1, which it carried, was an international mission dedicated to various scientific and technological investigations.*

Principal personages
HENRY W. HARTSFIELD, the spacecraft commander
STEVEN R. NAGEL, the pilot
ERNST W. MESSERSCHMID,
REINHARD FURRER, and
WUBBO J. OCKELS, payload specialists
HANS-ULRICH STEIMLE, Spacelab D-1 mission manager
PETER R. SAHM, Spacelab D-1 mission scientist
BONNIE J. DUNBAR,
JAMES F. BUCHLI, and
GUION S. BLUFORD, mission specialists

Summary of the Mission

The year 1985 was a busy year for National Aeronautics and Space Administration (NASA) shuttle operations, with nine manned missions flown. By the time STS 61A took to the air, the media interest in reporting shuttle missions had dropped considerably; thus, this mission carrying the Spacelab D-1 payload was notable not only for the largest crew ever launched into space by one vehicle but also for the low-key coverage the general media devoted to the science mission.

The largest crew ever to be launched into space on one vehicle was commanded by shuttle veteran Henry W. Hartsfield, who had flown on the fourth shuttle in 1982 and the twelfth shuttle in 1984. His pilot was Steven R. Nagel, who had flown on the eighteenth shuttle in 1985. In fact he had only completed his first mission, the first *Discovery* (STS 41D/F) mission, 128 days before the launch of STS 61A, setting a new world record. Mission specialists for STS 61A included Bonnie J. Dunbar, who had degrees in ceramic and biomedical engineering and who was on her first spaceflight, James F. Buchli, who had flown on the fifteenth shuttle earlier in 1985, and Guion S. Bluford, the first black American in space, who had flown on the eighth shuttle in 1983. In addition, three European payload specialists were members of the crew: Ernst W. Messerschmid and Reinhard Furrer, both from West Germany, and Wubbo J. Ockels, a Dutch national from the European Space Agency

(ESA). The astronauts had been selected in stages. The two Germans were named to the flight on December 17, 1982; Ockels was assigned the same day. On February 14, 1984, Nagel, Dunbar, and Bluford were assigned to the crew, and on August 3, 1984, Hartsfield and Buchli were named.

As with all Spacelab missions, the crew members were to alternate in twelve-hour shifts to operate the experiments in the Spacelab module. The blue shift was led by Nagel with Dunbar and Furrer; the red shift was led by Buchli with Bluford and Messerschmid. Hartsfield and Ockels were not assigned to a team and worked with either team as required. Buchli and Dunbar trained as contingency extravehicular activity (EVA) crew members.

Preparations for the launch of Spacelab D-1 began years before the actual launch in 1985. Work on the scientific payload began in West Germany in the mid-1970's, and discussions between Germany and NASA on a German mission began in the late 1970's before the shuttle had even flown in space. Experiment racks and the special equipment needed to support them were developed and integrated in West Germany; they were flown to the United States on April 30, 1985. Using the long module configuration of Spacelab hardware, technicians checked the experiment racks and installed them in the habitable module during the summer of 1985.

Challenger was towed to the Orbiter Processing Facility (OPF) on August 12, 1985, following the nineteenth shuttle mission. Its cargo from that flight, the Space-lab 2 pallets, were removed and equipment was installed to support the Space-lab D-1 hardware, which was installed between September 18 and 20, 1985, while the vehicle was in OPF Bay 1. Modifications to the vehicle included the installation of an eighth seat to accommodate the record crew.

Stacking the twin solid-fueled rocket boosters (SRBs) for the mission began on Mobile Platform 1, High Bay 1, of the vehicle assembly building (VAB) on September 13, followed by the mating of External Tank 24 on September 23. *Challenger* itself was transferred from the OPF to the VAB on October 12 after sixty-one days in the OPF. Four days later, the shuttle *Challenger,* mated to the SRBs and external tank that were to power it into space, was moved to Launch Complex 39A to undergo the final preparations for launch.

Despite a few minor problems, the countdown for STS 61A was one of the smoothest and most trouble-free of the program to date. With eight astronauts aboard, *Challenger* left the pad exactly on time, at noon eastern standard time on October 30, 1985. All stages of the ascent were nominal and close to predicted values. Successful separation and recovery of the twin SRBs was followed by the separation of the external tank and the firing of the orbital maneuvering system engines (OMS) to secure the orbital flight path of the spacecraft. Once the orbit had been achieved, the payload bay doors were opened, and a week of orbital science experiments began for the crew.

Three hours after launch, the crew floated into Spacelab to activate the experiments and equipment. Two hours later, this task was completed, and the control of payload operations was transferred from NASA Mission Control in Johnson Space

Center, Houston, Texas, to the West German Space Operations Center in Ober-pfaffenhofen, near Munich, a facility operated by the Federal German Aerospace Establishment (DFVLR).

As soon as Spacelab was activated, the crew split into its two shifts, one team settling down for a sleep period, the other beginning the round-the-clock work in the science module. Initial radio communication problems finally cleared up some twenty-four hours into the flight. English was used as the standard language, though the Europeans did lapse into German when they considered it necessary to explain in detail their operations and observations; their words were then translated into English. The crew fell some forty-five minutes behind schedule early in the flight, but they soon caught up and worked ahead of schedule for most of the flight. The delay was attributed to the complicated and demanding task of moving into place the equipment needed for orbital operations. The television cameras showed that the novice astronaut Dunbar experienced a certain amount of disorientation early in the flight, but soon she adapted to her new surroundings and, like the rest of the crew, displayed adequate control and speed in moving through the spacecraft.

Once the launch phase had been successfully completed and the orbital operations begun, the coverage of the mission began to decrease, an indication of how routine shuttle flights had become. Meanwhile, the crew successfully deployed the Global Low-Orbiting Message Relay (GLOMR) satellite, which had failed to deploy on the seventeenth shuttle five months before. During the week in space, seventy-three experiments out of a projected seventy-six were successfully activated, and their data were recorded.

Several problems plagued the flight, as with most missions, but the crew was able to work around most of them. With the cooperation of the ground controllers, several experiments and items of equipment were repaired in order to obtain useful information. These included the repair of the mono-ellipsoid mirror heating facility (ELLI) within the materials science experiment (MEDEA) furnace, solving a synchronization problem with the navigation experiment communications investigations by unplugging a cable which linked the experiment to the shuttle's universal time clock; the repair of several small leaks; and the investigation of several false-alarm calls during the mission. Initial difficulties with the vestibular sled early in the flight were overcome when a decision was made to complete experiments on the sled and the materials processing experiments at the same time.

Several of the experiments were conducted as forerunners to a planned Spacelab D-2 and the U.S. International Space Station, then planned for the early 1990's. One experiment by Ockels investigated a new sleep restraint designed to alleviate the sensation of floating in space and therefore disturbing sleep cycles. Tubes in the restraint were inflated to apply pressure to the body. More important was a demonstration of the capability of a crew of eight to work together in the confined environment of the Spacelab module and shuttle flight and middeck areas. The facts that the crew was international and that it included a woman helped habitability engineers in their plans for later flights of the space station.

On November 6, 1985, the crew successfully initiated the deorbit burn to bring *Challenger* back from orbit for what later proved to be the last time. Flying a planned program of aerodynamic braking maneuvers as he descended, Hartsfield brought *Challenger* home. After a nominal descent trajectory, *Challenger* landed on Runway 17 at Edwards Air Force Base just before 9:45 A.M. Pacific standard time and began its rollout down the runway to a wheelstop. During the 2,560-meter rollout, Hartsfield completed the last experiment of the flight with the nose wheel steering test. Crews of several previous missions had experienced difficulty in controlling the orbiter during the runway rollout, and therefore new instrumentation had been fitted to *Challenger* for this flight to investigate the nose wheel steering inputs the pilot conducts during the rollout. Hartsfield successfully moved *Challenger* first to the left of the central line, then to the right, before moving back to the central line for a wheelstop.

Challenger had logged 7 days and 44 minutes in space and traveled more than 4 million kilometers in 111 orbits, landing during the 112th. Despite the signs of wear on its thermal protection system that were noticed after the landing of STS 61A, mission planners were looking forward to seeing *Challenger* fly at least five more times in 1986.

Knowledge Gained

The Spacelab D-1 shuttle 61A mission flew a scientific package consisting of seventy-six investigations, of which only one failed to work during the flight. The one that failed had to do with mixing two different types of saline solution; the experiment could not achieve any results because the mixing chamber did not achieve the required level of heat. The experiments undertaken on the flight involved fluid physics, solidification, biology, medicine, space-time interaction, GLOMR satellite deployment, flight test maneuvers during descent, and the steering wheel test during rollout. In the fields of biological and life sciences, the ground-based scientists were able to evaluate their data almost in real time, to confirm their findings and determine the success or failure of each experiment. The samples from the materials science experiments were evaluated over a longer period of several months after the conclusion of the mission.

From the materials science double rack with the isothermal heating facility, mirror heating facility, gradient heating facility with its quenching device, and fluid physics module, a total of 75 to 125 percent positive runs and stored data flows were obtained. From the process chamber with the holographic interferometric apparatus and the Marangini convection experiment in an open boat, a recorded level of 90 percent positive runs was achieved. Following early operational difficulties, from the MEDEA payload element carrying the multipurpose ELLI and the gradient furnace with a quenching device, a 110 percent success rate was achieved during the flight. From the life sciences experiments, success levels of 95 and 100 percent were recorded for the investigations. In addition, the vestibular sled, which was flown for the first time on this flight, achieved 120 percent test-run success. Among the navigation experiments, the clock synchronization and one-way distance measurement experiments were 100 percent successful.

In all, Spacelab D-1 provided a vast wealth of scientific data from experiments and investigations that had been years in the making; these data made planning for the D-2 mission much easier.

Sixty percent of the crew's time was spent performing life sciences experiments, so that the crew was constantly occupied with the collection of data, their evaluation, and their conversion into preliminary results in real time. The crew was praised for its dedication and commitment to its scientific tasks and for overcoming language barriers. In the MEDEA experiments the crew continued this enthusiasm for work and obtained the most data possible during each twelve-hour shift.

The success of the data gathering of Spacelab D-1 was even more remarkable when one remembers that only 40 percent transmission time could be achieved from the spacecraft to Earth because only one Tracking and Data-Relay Satellite was operational instead of the planned two.

Context

The flight of Spacelab D-1 on STS 61A was the result of years of cooperative efforts of West Germany, the United States, and ESA, begun long before the shuttle program began its flight operations. Experimental results from the flight were significant for later forays into space, as was the fact that STS 61A had carried the largest crew ever on one space vehicle, and an international crew at that. The flight provided a valuable baseline for further research by NASA and West German research groups into life sciences and materials processing.

The mission provided a valuable link for the Americans between the early biomedical and materials experiments carried out on the earlier Apollo and Skylab missions in the 1970's and the planned flights on the space station in the 1990's. The Spacelab D-1/STS 61A mission continued the scientific investigations carried out on the Spacelab 1 and 3 long module missions in 1983 and earlier in 1985. Before the *Challenger* tragedy in 1986, a series of life and materials sciences shuttle Spacelab missions had been planned as a follow-up to D-1, and discussions were well under way for a Spacelab D-2 and possibly a D-3 and D-4. Following the loss of *Challenger*, these talks continued for revised payloads in the new manifest so that the work begun by the D-1 crew would not be lost and the results obtained not wasted by the enforced grounding of the shuttle.

Cooperation with NASA was also beneficial to West Germany in further cooperation with ESA and, in time, the Soviet program with a view toward flying post-D-1 experiments on the European Columbus and Hermes programs and possibly on the Soviet Mir space station as well as the NASA space station.

From the human point of view, the flight of a crew of mixed sexes, races, and nationalities pointed the way to international cooperation on the space station and talks on the need of a united program of exploration of Mars in the next century. The effective use of the confined habitable quarters of the shuttle during D-1 allowed spacecraft designers to determine the most efficient, pleasing, and functional interior designs of the space station and future spacecraft. The Soviets have gone a long way toward spacecraft habitability with their Salyut and Mir series. As crews increase in size and missions increase in duration, with the added complications of mixed sexes, religions, and races, suitable internal designs of spacecraft are an important element in planning. Spacelab D-1 represented a milestone in this ongoing aspect of the space program.

Another important, though largely ignored, value of STS 61A was the fact that with the completion of this mission *Challenger* had become the undisputed leader of mission-logged time by a manned spacecraft on more than one flight. *Challenger* had logged 1,495 hours, 55 minutes, and 2 seconds on nine missions, a record for the fleet. Several other craft, including Skylab Apollo command modules and Soviet Soyuz ferrycraft, had remained docked to space stations for one hundred days or more, but mostly powered down and only on one flight. *Challenger* had maintained fifty-three astronauts during nine missions for a length of time totaling almost sixty-three days of continuous operation in space. This workload resulted in the visible weathering of *Challenger,* but it remained the astronauts' favorite orbiter as the ground crews prepared it for the next mission, STS 51L, which was to carry an American schoolteacher.

Bibliography

Cooper, Henry S. F., Jr. *Before Lift-Off: The Making of a Space Shuttle Crew.* Baltimore: Johns Hopkins University Press, 1987. The author obtained special permission to document the training program of a shuttle crew from its assignment to the mission to just after the mission. A vivid text which records in detail the arduous training program to which each shuttle crew is subjected. The text identifies the problems and successes of the training program.

Furniss, Tim. *Manned Spaceflight Log.* Rev. ed. London: Jane's Publishing Co., 1986. This updated version of the 1983 first edition covers in a minihistory the world's manned spaceflights in chronological order, from Yuri Gagarin's historic first flight in April, 1961, to the *Challenger* tragedy and the triumph of Mir in 1986, twenty-five years later. Presented in launch order, 115 manned spaceflights from the United States and the Soviet Union are described, along with thirteen X-15 Astro flights of the American research aircraft of the 1960's. The STS 61A mission is listed as Spaceflight 125, the sixty-sixth American and the twenty-second shuttle flight, the ninth for *Challenger*. The STS 61A report is part of a complete history of the first twenty-five years of manned spaceflight. Places the flight in context with the flights that preceded it and those that followed it the next year. Illustrated. Supplements the *Space Shuttle Log* (below) by the same author.

_____, ed. *Space Shuttle Log.* London: Jane's Publishing Co., 1986. A collection of highly readable reports on the first twenty-two shuttle flights, from April, 1981, to the *Challenger* mission of October/November, 1985. The text provides a useful mission summary and data on each flight in sequence, as well as a collection of biographical sketches of shuttle astronauts up to 1985. The STS 61A section includes a brief summary of the facts of the flight and provides an interesting account of the flight from the perspective of the whole program through the fall of 1985, prior to the loss of *Challenger* on mission twenty-five. Suitable for general readers.

Gurney, Gene, and Jeff Forte. *Space Shuttle Log: The First Twenty-five Flights.* Blue Ridge Summit, Pa.: Tab Books, 1988. A collection of chapters summarizing the first twenty-five missions of the space shuttle program, covering the operational flights from April, 1981, to the loss of *Challenger* in January, 1986. The entry on each mission covers data on crew and payload and flight records; the main text describes launch preparations and experiments and investigations on each flight. A collection of black-and-white photos from all the missions accompanies the text. The STS 61A chapter provides interesting information on the technical research tasks performed on that mission.

Joels, Kerry M., and David Larkin. *The Space Shuttle Operator's Manual.* New York: Ballantine Books, 1982. A highly simplified version of astronaut training manuals, this book gives the reader a look at the operational side of a shuttle mission. Topics covered include everything from the launch profile and checklists to how to use the shuttle's stove. Foldouts show the control panels and sample mission timelines.

Shayler, David J. *Shuttle Challenger: Aviation Fact File.* London: Salamander Books, 1987. A book devoted to the career and achievements of space shuttle orbiter OV-099, *Challenger.* This comprehensive text covers the role of the *Challenger* in the shuttle program, the construction and components of the vehicle, and its missions—including an account of the STS 51L accident and summaries of all the astronauts and payloads *Challenger* carried into space on its ten missions. A selection of tables logging accumulated time and hardware data completes the work. The STS 61A entry covers launch preparations, launch phase orbital activities, and landing and post-landing activities. Includes a selection of color photographs. A large-format book, this commemorative work on *Challenger* is aimed at a general readership.

David J. Shayler

Cross-References

SPACE SHUTTLE MISSION 23
Atlantis

Date: November 26 to December 3, 1985
Type of mission: Manned Earth-orbiting spaceflight
Countries: The United States, Mexico, Australia, and Canada

During the twenty-third flight of the space shuttle, astronauts launched three communications satellites and practiced assembling large structures in space, in preparation for the assembly of space stations.

Principal personages

BREWSTER H. SHAW, JR., the mission commander
BRYAN D. O'CONNOR, the mission pilot
MARY L. CLEAVE,
SHERWOOD C. SPRING, and
JERRY L. ROSS, mission specialists
RUDOLFO NERI VELA and
CHARLES D. WALKER, payload specialists

Summary of the Mission

On November 26, 1985, STS 61B, the twenty-third shuttle mission, began with the lift-off, at 7:29 P.M. eastern standard time, of the orbiter *Atlantis*. During the weeklong flight, the second one for *Atlantis*, the crew deployed three communications satellites and demonstrated the techniques needed for building large structures in space. The three satellites were the American Satcom 2, the Mexican Morelos 2, and the Australian Aussat 2.

Brewster H. Shaw commanded the mission. Bryan D. O'Connor was the pilot. National Aeronautics and Space Administration (NASA) astronauts Sherwood C. Spring, Jerry L. Ross, and Mary L. Cleave were mission specialists on the flight. They were accompanied by McDonnell Douglas engineer Charles D. Walker and Mexican engineer Rudolfo Neri Vela, payload specialists. Vela was present to observe the deployment of the Morelos communications satellite, to operate several Mexican-built medical experiments, and to photograph areas of Mexico from space.

The 7:29 P.M. lift-off was the second night launch of the space shuttle program and the third in the history of U.S. manned spaceflights. *Atlantis* provided a spectacular sight and was visible from South Carolina to Cuba. At the Kennedy Space Center launch site, it could be seen for more than six minutes before it disappeared behind a cloud bank. Although first planned for a morning lift-off, the mission was changed to the night launch to accommodate a change in Mexico's space plans following the September, 1985, earthquake which had devastated much of the country's capital city. Mexican officials found that they could not use the Morelos satellite for about two more years. NASA was charging the Mexican government

$10 million to launch Morelos, considerably less than it would cost to store the craft on Earth. Thus, it was decided to place the craft in a parking orbit which would allow it to drift into its final position. This necessitated a different deployment location, forcing the change in launch time.

In addition to the trio of satellites, *Atlantis* carried several payloads in its crew compartment. Among these was the continuous flow electrophoresis system (CFES), a commercial payload built by McDonnell Douglas. Electrophoresis is a process for separating cells using weak electrical charges. All living cells have a small negative charge on their surfaces; different types of cells have different charges, and in solution it is possible to separate them because of these differences. On Earth, such separation is difficult because the charges are extremely small and gravity causes sedimentation and convection. In the microgravity environment of orbital flight, however, such separation can be more easily accomplished. STS 61B was the seventh flight to carry the CFES. Charles Walker, the payload specialist selected by McDonnell Douglas to operate the experiment, was on his third flight into space with the payload. Walker also operated a handheld protein growth experiment, a device to study the feasibility of crystallizing enzymes, hormones, and other proteins. Again, trying to crystallize such materials on Earth is extremely difficult. Nevertheless, successful crystallization permits the study of their three-dimensional atomic structure—important knowledge for enhancing or inhibiting certain functions of the proteins in the development of improved pharmaceuticals.

Other payloads in the crew compartment included the diffusion mixing of organic solution (DMOS), an experiment built by the 3M Corporation to try to grow large organic crystals for optical and electrical uses. As with electrophoresis, the microgravity of orbital flight enhances this activity. Scientists at 3M wanted to see if larger, perfect crystals could be grown in space. Such crystals could be used for optical switches and computers which process information with light rather than electricity. This device also had cells to observe the mixing of fluids in weightlessness.

In the payload bay, *Atlantis* carried several attached payloads. One of these was an IMAX camera. IMAX, a Canadian large-format camera, had flown in the crew compartment on three previous space shuttle missions. The footage collected from these was used for a film first shown at the National Air and Space Museum in Washington, D.C. This marked the first time an IMAX camera was placed in the payload bay. *Atlantis* also carried a small, self-contained payload, or Get-Away Special experiment, for Telesat of Canada. The result of a national competition among high school students in Canada, this experiment, designed by Daniel Rey and Jean-François Deschenes of the École Secondaire Charlebois of Ottawa, Canada, sought to fabricate better mirrors than those made on Earth by placing gold, silver, and aluminum coatings on quartz plates.

Atlantis flew a direct-ascent trajectory into its 352-kilometer-high initial orbit. In direct-ascent launches, the crew fires the orbital maneuvering system engines only once to reach orbit instead of the usual two times. After reaching orbit, the crew opened the doors covering *Atlantis'* 18.3-meter-long payload bay. Spring and Ross conducted diagnostic checks of the three satellites in the bay and closed the sunshields which protected the spacecraft prior to their release. Also, early in the flight (within three hours of launch) Cleave activated the 3M DMOS experiment and Walker turned on the CFES. On STS 61B, the CFES was producing erythropoietin, a red blood cell stimulant. McDonnell Douglas officials hoped to obtain enough of the material on this flight to begin animal and clinical testing.

The first satellite deployment of the mission, the Morelos 2, came only seven hours after launch, at 1:47 A.M. central standard time. Just before releasing the satellite, Shaw asked Mission Control in Houston, Texas, to verify that *Atlantis* was in the proper orientation (the crew had not been able to simulate the new attitude before launch). Spacecraft communicator Sally K. Ride confirmed that *Atlantis* was oriented properly, and the crew released the satellite. About forty-five minutes later, the Payload Assist Module (PAM) attached to the satellite fired and moved it on a trajectory toward its eventual geosynchronous orbit. Later that same day, at 7:20 P.M. central standard time, the crew released Aussat 2. The third and final satellite release of the mission, Satcom 2, occurred on Thursday, November 28.

After the satellite deployments, the crew prepared for the next major mission activities, a pair of extravehicular activities (EVAs). During the EVAs, or spacewalks, as they are sometimes popularly called, Spring and Ross would build a 13.7-meter-tall tower and a 3.7-meter-wide tetrahedron in *Atlantis'* payload bay. These two structures represented the culmination of nearly a decade of research on large space structures.

The tower, designed and fabricated by engineers at the Langley Research Center in Hampton, Virginia, was called "assembly concept for construction of erectable space structures," or ACCESS. The other structure, developed jointly by the Marshall Space Flight Center and the Massachusetts Institute of Technology, was named "experimental assembly of structures in extravehicular activity," or EASE.

Each structure required a different assembly technique. EASE was a geometric structure resembling an inverted pyramid and comprised a few large beams and connecting nodes. ACCESS, by comparison, was a high-rise tower consisting of many small struts and nodes. ACCESS could be assembled from a fixed workstation in the payload bay, while EASE required the astronauts to move about the structure during assembly. Both were anchored on a special pallet which bridged the payload bay.

The first EVA began at 3:45 P.M. central standard time on November 29. For five and a half hours, Spring and Ross practiced assembling the structures. They first built the ACCESS tower. During preflight underwater simulations, they had taken an average of 58 minutes to build the tower. For the orbital EVA, mission planners had allotted two hours for the task. After only fifty-five minutes, however, they were finished. Spring and Ross disassembled the tower, and by 5:11 P.M. they were about an hour ahead of schedule. They stowed the ACCESS components away and began working with EASE.

The pair assembled and disassembled the tetrahedron eight times during the first EVA. For the first four times, Ross acted as low man, handing beams to Spring and later putting them back in their storage rack. After the third assembly, Spring indicated that his hands were tired and his fingers were getting numb. By the fourth time, fatigue was beginning to set in, so Spring and Ross traded places for the remaining assemblies. Ross was supposed to perform only two assemblies from the upper position, but the process went fast enough that he had time for four. The first EVA provided fundamental information on space construction.

The second EVA, on December 1, explored specific space station assembly tasks and evaluated the use of the shuttle's manipulator arm in these operations. For the arm tests, the astronauts attached a portable foot restraint to the arm. Spring and Ross assembled the ACCESS tower. Then, while Ross stood on the foot-restraint platform, Cleave moved the arm to various work locations from inside *Atlantis*. While attached to the arm, Ross assembled one bay of the ACCESS tower's struts and nodes. Then, as Cleave maneuvered him along the tower, he attached a simulated electrical cable to its length, demonstrating a common space station assembly task. For the next test, Spring released the tower from its assembly jig in the payload bay, and Ross then maneuvered it by hand, demonstrating manual movement and positioning of large space structures. After Ross put the ACCESS tower back in its jig, he and Spring exchanged positions on the end of the arm. Spring then practiced removing and replacing tower struts. He also moved the 13.7-meter tower by hand.

The astronauts then turned their attention to the EASE pyramid and assembled it while Spring was on the end of the arm, a different assembly technique from the one used during the first EVA. Ross then exchanged positions with Spring and tried moving the completed tetrahedron by hand. Following the conclusion of these tests, the astronauts disassembled the structure, stowed the components, and reentered *Atlantis'* air lock. The EVA had lasted six and a half hours.

On December 3, the crew brought *Atlantis* back to Earth. Mission Commander Shaw landed *Atlantis* at Edwards Air Force Base, California, at 1:33 P.M. Pacific standard time. This was the first shuttle landing on a paved runway in six missions. (The last such landing had been *Discovery* on April 19, 1985, after the STS 51D mission. On that flight, *Discovery*'s tires and brakes were damaged while landing.) Following *Atlantis'* landing, Shaw applied only light braking, allowing the orbiter to roll 3,279 meters.

Knowledge Gained

The ability to alter the STS 61B launch time relatively late in the mission-planning cycle was an impressive demonstration of the maturity of space shuttle operations. Although the change was introduced and the Morelos launched without giving the crew an opportunity to simulate the specific ejection target, because of the extensive ground simulations of other flight ejection targets, mission planners believed that they could accommodate the change.

The mission introduced a new satellite upper stage, the PAM-D2. All three satellites used the PAM, as had many of the satellites released during previous shuttle missions. The 61B satellites, however, used an improved, more powerful version of the motor. PAM-D2 could propel satellites weighing 1,900 kilograms to geosynchronous orbit, while earlier PAM-D motors had only a 1,270-kilogram capacity. In fact, Satcom 2, with a weight of 1,860 kilograms, was the heaviest payload ever propelled by a PAM.

Nevertheless, the most significant results of the mission were from the two EVAs. During twelve hours outside *Atlantis*, Spring and Ross had demonstrated many of the techniques needed to build space stations and other large space structures. With ACCESS, they showed how to construct a long, thin tower structure from a fixed workstation with an assembly jig. EASE, on the other hand, required one of the crew to be free-floating as they assembled the large, pyramid-shaped structure.

During the second EVA, Spring, Ross, and Cleave showed that astronauts inside the spacecraft could work in concert with astronauts outside the vehicle. Cleave maneuvered the two EVA astronauts on the manipulator arm along the lengths of both EASE and ACCESS. She positioned her fellow crewmembers precisely at predetermined work locations. Working with Cleave, Ross attached a length of rope along the tower. This demonstration showed that it was possible to construct a structural framework in space, then route cables and electrical leads along it. Ross and Spring also showed that a spacesuit-clad astronaut could move large structures manually and could position them precisely by hand.

Context

STS 61B was the twenty-third flight of the space shuttle and the fifty-fourth American manned spaceflight. It came at a time when NASA managers were selecting the configuration for the International Space Station, which they planned for the mid-1990's. Validating the concept of EVA construction by in-flight experience was important as they made their decisions.

The EVAs were the culmination of nearly a decade's development and testing. On Earth, astronauts can simulate weightlessness in large tanks of water. Wearing spacesuits, the astronauts are ballasted so they neither sink nor rise, instead floating motionless in a state of "neutral buoyancy." Neutral buoyancy simulators, as the tanks are called, exist at the Marshall Space Flight Center in Huntsville, Alabama, and the Johnson Space Center in Houston, Texas. Engineers used the one in Huntsville, which is 22.9 meters in diameter and 12.2 meters deep and holds 4.9 million liters of water, to test the EASE and ACCESS hardware. Engineers and astronauts were testing in-flight assembly concepts in the tank in mid-1978. Later that year, officials at the Langley Research Center announced their plans to develop the technologies required for assembling large space structures. For the next seven years, designs for the first in-space construction were refined, and hardware was developed.

During this period of hardware development, crewmen aboard shuttle missions were demonstrating an amazing capability for EVA operations. The first space shuttle EVA was performed during STS 6 in April, 1983. One year later, astronauts repaired the ailing Solar Maximum Mission satellite during the STS 41C mission. In November, two communications satellites which had been placed in incorrect orbits were retrieved and returned to Earth for refurbishment and relaunch. In August, 1985, the Leasat 3 satellite, which failed just after being released from the orbiter *Discovery* some four months earlier, was jump-started in space. Thus, by the time the EASE and ACCESS experiments flew on *Atlantis*, American astronauts had considerable experience in on-orbit satellite servicing and retrieval. The STS 61B mission added experience with in-space construction.

Bibliography

Allen, Joseph P., and Russell Martin. *Entering Space: An Astronaut's Odyssey*. New York: Stewart, Tabori and Chang, 1984. This account describes all prelaunch, launch, flight, and landing experiences from the perspective of a shuttle astronaut. Includes more than two hundred color photographs of all phases of various shuttle missions.

Hallion, Richard. *On the Frontier*. NASA SP-4303. Washington, D.C.: Government Printing Office, 1984. This book surveys the research that went into the development of the space shuttle; includes accounts of all the experimental aircraft that were used. Contains many black-and-white photographs of the various pioneer craft and an extensive bibliography.

Joels, Kerry M., and Gregory P. Kennedy. *The Space Shuttle Operator's Manual*. New York: Ballantine Books, 1987. This work describes the flight, satellite deployment, and extravehicular activities of the space shuttle.

Yenne, Bill. *The Astronauts*. New York: Exeter Books, 1986. Presents an overview of the Soviet and American space programs and tells of the international passengers carried on various missions. Illustrated with several hundred photographs taken in both countries.

Gregory P. Kennedy

Cross-References

The Australian Space Program, 174; Langley Research Center, 722; Marshall Space Flight Center, 908; The U.S. Space Shuttle, 1626; Space Shuttle Living Conditions, 1634; Space Shuttle Missions 15 and 21: *Discovery* and *Atlantis*, 1751; The Design and Uses of the U.S. Space Station, 1828; The Development of the U.S. Space Station, 1835; Living and Working in the U.S. Space Station, 1850; The Development of Spacesuits, 1917.

SPACE SHUTTLE MISSION 24
Columbia

Date: January 11 to January 18, 1986
Type of mission: Manned Earth-orbiting spaceflight
Country: The United States

During STS 61C, the twenty-fourth flight of the space shuttle, astronauts aboard Columbia *launched a commercial communications satellite, tested a new payload carrier system, and photographed Halley's comet.*

Principal personages
ROBERT L. (HOOT) GIBSON, the mission commander
CHARLES F. BOLDEN, JR., the pilot
GEORGE D. (PINKY) NELSON,
STEVEN A. HAWLEY, and
FRANKLIN R. CHANG-DIAZ, mission specialists
ROBERT J. CENKER and
C. WILLIAM (BILL) NELSON, payload specialists

Summary of the Mission

On January 11, 1986, Space Transportation System (STS) mission 61C began with the predawn lift-off of the space shuttle *Columbia*. The 6:55 A.M. (eastern standard time) launch was the twenty-fourth space shuttle mission and the seventeenth flight for *Columbia*. In its payload bay, *Columbia* carried the RCA Satcom K-1, thirteen Get-Away Special cannisters, the Hitchhiker payload carrier, a materials science laboratory, and an infrared imaging experiment. Inside the crew compartment, the astronauts operated the initial blood-storage experiment, the Comet Halley Active Monitoring Program, and three Shuttle Student Involvement Program experiments. *Columbia* also carried special flight instrumentation to determine more precisely orbiter aerodynamic and reentry heating characteristics.

Veteran astronaut Robert L. (Hoot) Gibson commanded *Columbia*. This was his second trip into space. The STS 61C pilot was Charles F. Bolden, Jr., making his first spaceflight. The crew also included three mission specialists: Franklin R. Chang-Diaz, Steven A. Hawley, and George D. (Pinky) Nelson. RCA engineer Robert J. Cenker and Florida congressman C. William Nelson, served as payload specialists.

STS 61C was the first mission for *Columbia* since the STS 9 flight in late 1983. Following that mission, National Aeronautics and Space Administration (NASA) managers returned *Columbia* to Rockwell International in Palmdale, California, for an eighteen-month overhaul. The hundreds of changes made to the first orbiter to fly in space included updating its navigation system, adding a cylindrical housing to its vertical stabilizer, and building a new nose cap to house the shuttle entry air data system (SEADS). For its first flight in two years, *Columbia* also carried instrumentation to sample air at its surface in the upper atmosphere and pressure transducers on the top and bottom sides of the wings to determine wing loading during ascent and reentry. *Columbia* originally had 90 wing load sensors. During its overhaul, engineers added 200 more.

The RCA Satcom was the only deployable payload aboard *Columbia* for the STS 61C mission. The satellite cost $50 million, and RCA paid NASA $14.2 million to launch it from the shuttle. It was a Ku-band communications satellite to provide voice, television, facsimile, and data services to commercial customers throughout the forty-eight states. As with all earlier communications satellites carried aboard space shuttles, the RCA Satcom was attached to a booster motor which would propel it from low-Earth orbit to a higher, geosynchronous orbit. The motor attached to the Satcom was called the Payload Assist Module D2 (PAM-D2). Satellites which orbit at an altitude of 36,000 kilometers are in a geosynchronous orbit; that is, at that altitude, it takes twenty-four hours to complete one orbit. Thus, a satellite orbiting 36,000 kilometers above the equator will remain fixed in space with respect to an observer on the ground. Ground stations can receive broadcasts from geosynchronous satellites with fixed antennae.

This was the second of three planned vehicles for the RCA American Domestic Satellite System. The first RCA Satcom had been launched during the STS 61B mission. RCA Satcom is a version of the RCA 4000 series of three-axis stabilized satellites. It carries sixteen operational transponders and six spares, each with an output of 45 watts. These are powerful enough to permit ground stations to receive their transmissions with antennae as small as one meter in diameter. The RCA Satcom system can provide direct-to-home television program distribution and television service to hotels, apartment houses, and other large institutions.

Early in the space shuttle program, NASA created the Get-Away Special (GAS) program. Get-Away Specials are small, self-contained payloads carried in the orbiter's payload bay which may be flown in space at a cost of as little as $3,000. GAS experiments must be entirely self-contained. That is, they must have their own power and data-recording systems. All an astronaut will normally do with a GAS experiment is turn it on and off during the flight. They are flown on a space-available basis and are accessible to private individuals, foreign governments, and corporations. NASA provides standardized GAS containers for mounting in the payload bay. The containers are about 85 centimeters tall and 50 centimeters wide.

STS 61C was the maiden flight of a new piece of GAS support equipment: the GAS bridge. The GAS bridge was an aluminum structure which spanned the width of the shuttle's cargo bay and could accommodate up to twelve GAS containers. A thirteenth GAS cannister was attached to the inside wall of the cargo bay near the GAS bridge. It contained instrumentation to measure the environment of the bridge during launch and landing. Prior to this flight, all GAS cannisters had been attached to the inside wall of the cargo bay. By the time *Columbia* flew the first space shuttle mission, NASA had sold more than two hundred GAS reservations. At the time of the STS 61C flight, the backlog was even greater. Engineers at the Goddard Space Flight Center in Greenbelt, Maryland, devised the GAS bridge as a means of carrying large numbers of GAS payloads on individual shuttle missions to reduce the backlog.

Hitchhiker, a new payload carrier system, was also tested on STS 61C. Like the GAS experiments, Hitchhiker was devised as a method of providing researchers with rapid and economical access to space. Hitchhiker can support scientific, technological, and commercial payloads. It has limited instrument pointing and data processing capabilities. Developed as a payload-of-opportunity carrier, Hitchhiker uses cargo space remaining after the space shuttle's primary payload has been accommodated. Unlike the autonomous GAS cannisters, Hitchhiker payloads are connected to the orbiter's communications and power systems. Communications with the payload are provided through a payload operations control center at Goddard, enabling real-time customer interaction and control.

NASA developed two separate Hitchhiker systems. Engineers at Goddard developed Hitchhiker-G, the type flown on STS 61C. It was mounted on the front wall of the orbiter payload bay and could accommodate up to four experiments with a combined weight of up to 340 kilograms. The other system, Hitchhiker-M, was developed at the Marshall Space Flight Center in Huntsville, Alabama. It was a structure similar to the GAS bridge which could carry payloads heavier than those carried by Hitchhiker-G. Hitchhiker was created to support payloads too large for GAS and too small for the Spacelab carrier.

U.S. congressman Bill Nelson accompanied the crew as a payload specialist and congressional observer. He was the chairman of the House of Representatives' Space Science and Applications Subcommittee. Nelson represented the Eleventh Congressional District in Florida. During the mission, he operated the handheld protein crystal growth experiment. This experiment sought to use the weightless environment of space to produce protein crystals of sufficient size and quality to allow their nature and structure to be analyzed. Nelson also participated in detailed studies for NASA's Biomedical Research Institute. These studies provided additional data on the effects of spaceflight on the human body.

The flight of STS 61C was canceled four times before the *Columbia* was launched on January 11, 1986. During the early part of the ascent, cockpit instruments indicated that one of *Columbia*'s engines had a helium leak. The situation was serious enough to threaten a shutdown of one of the orbiter's three main engines. If such a malfunction had occurred at that point in the flight, the mission would have been aborted. Pilot Bolden took immediate action to correct the problem, and the mission proceeded according to schedule. Thirty seconds after lift-off, *Columbia* entered the area of maximum dynamic pressure, or "max Q." (This pressure is the product of air density times velocity squared.) After reaching a maximum during the first minute of flight, the aerodynamic forces on the vehicle decreased as the shuttle climbed higher.

The ascent profile flown by *Columbia* was deliberately selected to place greater stresses than ever before on the vehicle. Because actual stresses on the craft are greater than what is predicted based on wind-tunnel testing and other experiments, launch profiles that were less stressful (and therefore less capable of testing the shuttle's full payload capability) had been flown on past missions. STS 61C was one of three flights planned to collect data that would explain the difference between actual flight results and wind-tunnel predictions. Once acquired, the new information could lead to a relaxation of ascent load constraints, allowing space shuttles to carry heavier payloads.

After the main engines finished their nine-minute burn, and after two firings by the orbital maneuvering system (OMS) engines, *Columbia* was in a 323-kilometer-high circular orbit. Nine hours after launch, during the seventh orbit, the crew opened the sunshield, which protected the Satcom in the cargo bay, and released the satellite from its launch cradle. Forty-five minutes later, the PAM-D2 motor fired and placed the satellite into a highly elliptical orbit which took it to 36,000 kilometers. On January 15, another rocket motor contained in Satcom fired and circularized the orbit at geosynchronous altitude.

During their first day in space, the crew also activated the material science laboratory 2 (MSL 2). MSL 2 comprised three experiments in the cargo bay to study the behavior of materials in microgravity. Two of the experiments studied how melted materials solidify; the third observed liquid behavior in zero gravity. MSL 2 experiments continued throughout the mission.

The astronauts observed Halley's comet on the second day of the mission. The equipment used for this experiment, called the Comet Halley Active Monitoring Program, included a 35-millimeter handheld camera system provided by the University of Colorado. For this experiment, crew members photographed the comet using standard filters to obtain images and spectra. Unfortunately, an intensifier which boosted the light-gathering power of the camera malfunctioned, so the experiment returned only very limited results.

Another payload, an infrared imaging experiment, was operated by Cenker, the RCA payload specialist. Developed by RCA, this was one of two experiments aboard STS 61C which supported the Strategic Defense Initiative (SDI) and future space-borne surveillance systems. This experiment was mounted on the aft wall of the cargo bay. As he operated the setup, Cenker observed aircraft to measure their infrared signatures. The exact location and types of aircraft were classified. Cenker also used the system, which has possible applications for civilian remote-sensing systems, to observe such unclassified targets as cities and volcanoes.

The other SDI-related payload was carried by Hitchhiker. Developed by the United States Air Force, it was called the particle-analysis camera system (PACS.) It comprised two 35-millimeter cameras and a strobe light to take photographs every 120 seconds, recording the amount and type of floating debris surrounding the space shuttle orbiter.

The STS 61C mission was scheduled to land at the Kennedy Space Center (KSC) in Florida. This was the first landing scheduled for KSC since the STS 51D mission in April, 1985. During that flight's landing, the orbiter *Discovery*'s right main landing tire experienced a blowout. After that landing, orbiters had landed on the dry lakebed of the Dryden Flight Research Center until mission 61B. The STS 61B flight concluded with a landing on the paved runway at Dryden. Following this successful landing, NASA managers opted for the shuttle to land at KSC. The weather at KSC, however, prevented a landing there on either January 16 or 17, so *Columbia* returned to Dryden on January 18 instead. The duration of the mission was 6 days, 2 hours, and 4 minutes. During reentry and atmospheric flight, infrared sensors in a housing on top of *Columbia*'s stabilizer measured the temperatures on the craft's upper surfaces. Other instruments in *Columbia* studied the composition of the upper atmosphere and provided precise measurements of the craft's flight attitude.

Knowledge Gained

The six-day STS 61C mission demonstrated the utility and versatility of the space shuttle. On a single mission, NASA flew a diverse group of payloads. Major crew activities during the mission included deploying one commercial satellite, testing new payload support equipment, evaluating new space-based Earth imaging systems, and conducting materials processing experiments in space. *Columbia* also carried instrumentation which provided high-resolution infrared images of the top of the orbiter's left wing to create detailed maps of aerodynamic heating during reentry.

The one deployable payload was the RCA Satcom K-1. This was the second of three Ku-band communications satellites. Most previous communications had operated in the C-band frequency range, which can interfere with terrestrial microwave systems. Because the Ku-band frequencies are not shared with microwave traffic, antennae served by the RCA Satcoms can be located inside major metropolitan areas. Also, most C-band satellite transponders emit a signal strength of 12 to 30 watts. The RCA Satcom transponders transmit 45 watts of power. This makes direct reception from the satellites possible with antennae of less than 1 meter in diameter.

The Hitchhiker payload system, first demonstrated on this mission, promised to provide researchers with low-cost and rapid access to space. From its inception, the system was designed for simplicity and economy. It incorporated such features as standardized interfaces with orbiter systems and reusability to reduce hardware costs. In addition, with the introduction of the Hitchhiker, NASA reduced the level of paperwork and documentation normally required for shuttle payloads.

Another new piece of payload support hardware tested on this flight was the GAS bridge. Engineers at Goddard devised the GAS program as a means of providing researchers access to space at the lowest possible cost. Through this program, individuals and organizations, both public and private from all countries, have an opportunity to send experiments into space aboard the space shuttle.

This was also the second flight to have a congressional observer as a payload specialist. The first such flight of an elected official was the STS 51D mission in

April, 1985. On that flight, Senator Edwin Jacob (Jake) Garn flew aboard *Discovery*. Providing flight opportunities for appropriate congressional leaders gave them first-hand experience with spaceflight which they could use when evaluating proposed programs. In addition, they provided NASA physicians with an opportunity to evaluate the effects of spaceflight on individuals who were not career astronauts.

Context

The STS 61C mission was the twenty-fourth flight of the Space Transportation System Program and the last space shuttle mission before the loss of *Challenger* in January, 1986. STS 61C demonstrated the flexibility of shuttle payload scheduling by mixing deployable and attached payloads on *Columbia*.

Columbia was the first space shuttle orbiter to orbit Earth. On April 12, 1981, *Columbia* lifted off for the first time. Seven months later, it made its second voyage into space, becoming the first manned spacecraft to be reused. *Columbia* made four more spaceflights after that, then was temporarily removed from service for an overhaul. As the first operational orbiter, *Columbia* did not have many of the refinements which were built into subsequent vehicles. These included a "heads-up" display for the commander and pilot to use during landing, improvements in the thermal protection system, and structural changes. During its eighteen-month stay at the Rockwell International plant in Palmdale, California, engineers made these and hundreds of other modifications to *Columbia*.

While these modifications were under way, the other three orbiters made fourteen flights into space. Payloads included commercial satellites, classified Department of Defense experiments, scientific laboratories, and research satellites. The flight of STS 61C combined many of these types of payloads into a single mission.

Bibliography

Couvalt, Craig. "Delays in Columbia Mission Complicate Shuttle Scheduling." *Aviation Week and Space Technology* 124 (January 20, 1986): 20-22. This article provides an overview of the launch and early flight results of the STS 61C mission. It also discusses the impact of this mission's launch delays on the flight schedule planned prior to the loss of *Challenger*.

Joels, Kerry M., and Gregory P. Kennedy. *The Space Shuttle Operator's Manual.* Rev. ed. New York: Ballantine Books, 1988. This book provides a description of how the space shuttle flies. It contains information on shuttle payload types, including Get-Away Specials and deployable satellites. It also contains data on the Payload Assist Module.

Microgravity Science and Applications Division, Office of Space Science and Applications. *Microgravity: A New Tool for Basic and Applied Research in Space.* NASA EP-212. Washington, D.C.: Government Printing Office, 1984. Written for a general audience, this document provides an overview of NASA's space materials processing programs.

Nelson, Bill. "Ascent." *Final Frontier* 1 (July/August, 1988): 18-21, 57. In this article, Congressman Nelson provides a firsthand account of the first 8.5 minutes of the STS 61C mission.

Nelson, Bill, with Jamie Buckingham. *Mission*. New York: Harcourt Brace Jovanovich, 1988. This is a personal account by Congressman Bill Nelson of his flight aboard STS 61C.

Gregory P. Kennedy

Cross-References

Cape Canaveral and the Kennedy Space Center, 229; The Get-Away Special Experiments, 550; Goddard Space Flight Center, 563; Johnson Space Center, 669; Materials Processing in Space, 933; The U.S. Space Shuttle, 1626; Space Shuttle Living Conditions, 1634; Space Shuttle Mission 1: *Columbia*, 1648; Space Shuttle Mission 2: *Columbia*, 1657; Space Shuttle Mission 3: *Columbia*, 1663; Space Shuttle Mission 5: *Columbia*, 1678; Space Shuttle Mission 9: *Columbia*, 1705; U.S. Private and Commercial Telecommunications Satellites, 1997.

SPACE SHUTTLE MISSION 25
Challenger

Date: January 28, 1986
Type of mission: Manned Earth-orbiting spaceflight
Country: The United States

STS 51L, the twenty-fifth mission of the U.S. space shuttle, was to have launched the second Tracking and Data-Relay Satellite and a scientific mission called Spartan-Halley into Earth orbit; additionally, Teacher-in-Space Christa McAuliffe was to have broadcast a series of lessons to schoolchildren throughout America. STS 51L exploded, however, only 73 seconds after launch, killing its crew and completely destroying the space shuttle Challenger and its satellite cargo. In the wake of the STS 51L disaster, the United States space program was severely set back, and the shuttle did not fly again for almost three years.

Principal personages
FRANCIS R. (DICK) SCOBEE, the mission commander
MICHAEL J. SMITH, the mission pilot
ELLISON S. ONIZUKA,
RONALD E. MCNAIR, and
JUDITH A. RESNIK, mission specialists
GREGORY B. JARVIS, a payload specialist
S. CHRISTA MCAULIFFE, the first teacher in space
WILLIAM P. ROGERS, the chairman of the Presidential
Commission on the Space Shuttle *Challenger* Accident

Summary of the Mission

Preparations for the Space Transportation System's (STS's) twenty-fifth mission, STS 51L, began more than eighteen months before launch. When the flight crew was originally selected, on January 27, 1985, 51L's launch was scheduled for the summer of 1985. Delays and a series of cargo changes, however, postponed the flight to mid-January, 1986. Because of these delays, both the detailed flight planning process and the crew's training were interrupted.

The major payloads carried on STS 51L were the second National Aeronautics and Space Administration (NASA) Tracking and Data-Relay Satellite (TDRS) and the Spartan-Halley comet research observatory. In addition to these payloads, several small experiments were carried in the crew cabin, and the flight was to include the "teacher-in-space" activities of Christa McAuliffe.

According to preflight planning, mission 51L was to last six days. During this time the crew would launch the TDRS satellite, activate and launch Spartan, conduct astronomical and medical experiments, recover Spartan from orbit, and broadcast lessons to students on the ground.

The planned 1986 shuttle launch schedule was very tight, and several very high-priority missions were to take place in the early part of the year. Within NASA, plans were discussed to skip 51L if the launch date slipped beyond February 1 and proceed with the rest of the schedule. The purpose of this move would have been to clear the pad for the next launch (an important mission scheduled for March) and to begin readying *Challenger* for its planned launch of an international mission to explore Jupiter and the Sun.

An afternoon launch was originally planned for 51L. Although scientists leading the Spartan project argued for retaining this time for scientific reasons, NASA mission planners insisted on changing the lift-off to mid-morning. NASA's reasoning for a morning launch was based on safety concerns. Were the vehicle to suffer an "engine-out" during its ascent from Cape Canaveral, it would have to glide to an emergency landing site at Casablanca on the west coast of Africa. Casablanca's runway was not equipped with lighting for night landings. It was decided therefore that the shuttle would be launched in the morning, eastern standard time, so that there would still be light in Casablanca, 6,400 kilometers to the east.

The countdown for STS 51L began on January 24, but weather forecasts caused the launch to be postponed to January 27. The crew spent the extra time reviewing flightplans and watching the Super Bowl football game from their quarters. During this period, pressures within NASA to launch 51L mounted. The Spartan satellite required a launch before January 31. With flights of even higher priority on NASA's schedule, the prospect of canceling 51L became greater. Every effort was made to make sure the shuttle would be ready on the twenty-seventh, when the weather cleared.

On January 27, the vehicle was fueled and the crew had boarded when high wind conditions forced NASA to reschedule the launch once again, this time for January 28.

During the evening of January 27 and the early morning hours of the next day, a series of meetings were held among intermediate-level managers from NASA's Marshall Space Flight Center and the shuttle program's major industrial contractors, Rockwell, Morton Thiokol, and Martin-Marietta. Marshall had final responsibility for the solid-fueled rocket boosters (SRBs). The purpose of these meetings was to assess the status of the launch. Such meetings take place during every countdown.

During these prelaunch meetings, concerns were expressed about the possible effects of a cold weather front approaching the Cape. Three concerns were expressed by some engineers from Thiokol, the manufacturer. In particular, Thiokol engineers Roger Boisjoly and Alan McDonald thought it possible that the booster's hot exhaust could "blow-by" (get past) its protective seals, called O-rings. The reason the O-rings might be bypassed was that they would become stiff in the cold. Once stiffened, the O-rings (which are supposed to be resilient) would not act to seal the SRBs. Without a good seal, exhaust would then leak from the booster's side, rather than from the nozzle, and the booster would be likely to explode or rupture—ending the mission in catastrophe. In one conversation, Alan McDonald went so far as to say that if anything happened, he would not want to have to explain it to a board of inquiry. McDonald noted that no shuttle had ever been launched at a temperature below 53 degrees Fahrenheit (12 degrees Celsius), and that even at that temperature the SRBs had experienced some exhaust blow-by.

The possibility of severe blow-by raised concerns and was the reason for many of the meetings that were held that night. Unfortunately, no actual tests of the boosters had ever been made at low temperatures; therefore, there was no clear case for what would happen. Thiokol's engineers recommended the launch be delayed until later in the day, or perhaps until January 29. NASA managers, however, feeling increasing pressure to launch, pressed for a firm decision from Thiokol. In testimony to the Rogers Commission, NASA managers later stated that the probability of an O-ring failure was believed to be low because each O-ring was backed up by another for increased protection, in case blow-by did occur.

Perhaps sensing the impatience of some NASA officials, Thiokol managers overruled their own engineers and signed a waiver form, stating that the SRBs were safe for launch. Without such a signature, the launch could not have occurred.

During the final hours before the launch of STS 51L, all *Challenger*'s mechanical and electrical systems were checked. The crew was awakened at 6:00 A.M. At 8:36 A.M. the astronaut crew arrived at the pad and boarded the shuttle. Because there was a buildup of ice on the launchpad and some delays in fueling the huge external tank, the launch was delayed first from 9:38 to 10:38, and then to 11:38. These intermittent delays were unusual in the STS program. Several of the onboard scientific experiments required launch times earlier than 10 A.M. on any given day in order to have the right lighting conditions in orbit. These experiments were sacrificed in order to get the flight launched that morning. The countdown proceeded.

As the final few minutes passed, Pilot Mike Smith powered up *Challenger*'s turbines for flight. Only two minutes before launch, Commander Scobee called to crew members McNair, Jarvis, and McAuliffe on the shuttle's lower passenger deck, "Two minutes, downstairs. Anybody keeping a watch running?"

At launch minus thirty seconds, *Challenger*'s onboard computers took control. First, the orbiter's three powerful main engines were pressurized, then thousands of electronic checks were performed to verify the engines were ready to start. At minus 6.6 seconds, the main engines were ignited, one at a time, about a second apart. When 90 percent of flight-level thrust was reached on all three, the command was sent to ignite the SRBs. Both SRBs ignited simultaneously at exactly 11:38:01 A.M., and the vehicle rose from the pad. On board, astronaut Judy Resnik exclaimed, "Aaall riiight," as *Challenger* began its long-awaited push to orbit. In the launch control center three miles away, Thiokol engineers Boisjoly and McDonald relaxed a bit—apparently the O-rings had held. The ambient air temperature was 36 degrees Fahrenheit (about 2 degrees Celsius), 15 degrees colder than that of any previous shuttle launch.

Less than a half-second after the SRBs ignited, the first of eight small but ominous puffs of black smoke swirled from one of the lower joints in *Challenger*'s right booster. These puffs were not obvious to onlookers (no one is allowed within five kilometers of the launchpad) but were recorded by cameras filming the launch. Later analysis by technical experts working with the Rogers Commission revealed that a primary O-ring had failed to seal in the right SRB and that its backup O-ring had failed as well. Blow-by had occurred. Engineering analyses have since indicated that either propellent residue or O-ring soot plugged this leak about two and one-half seconds into the flight.

For nearly a minute, the ascent went as planned. *Challenger* rolled to put itself on the proper flight path, thousands of electronic checks of onboard systems showed everything performing "nominally" (according to plan), and the vehicle properly throttled back its engines when aerodynamic forces increased.

About fifty-nine seconds into launch, however, trouble began. A review of film from ground cameras recording the launch detected flames coming from the right SRB. *Challenger* was being buffeted by a combination of high-altitude winds and the aerodynamic stresses of the launch. In response the vehicle flexed slightly and began to steer its engines to counteract the wind. In combination, these forces probably reopened the hole in the right SRB caused by the blow-by at ignition. Over the next five seconds the plume of flame grew and grew. By sixty-four seconds into the flight, a gaping hole was formed in the casing of the SRB. The thrust escaping through this hole exerted a force of 45,000 kilograms on the shuttle, greater than the thrust of many jetliners. *Challenger*'s computers interpreted this force as unusually strong winds. To counteract the 45,000-kilogram side-force, the shuttle automatically swung its engines slightly to the left. Inside the cockpit, the crew was jolted around by a combination of actual wind gusts, engine steering, and the thrust escaping from the breeched SRB. Pilot Mike Smith remarked, "Looks like we've got a lot of wind here today."

At 72 seconds into the flight, the searing exhaust from the right SRB either tore or burned loose the attachment strut between the SRB and the external tank. In the final second of flight, computers on board *Challenger* detected a fuel line break caused by the widening explosion and shut down each of the shuttle's three main engines. A moment later, the SRB slammed into and tore off *Challenger*'s right wing, then careened into the tank, setting off a massive explosion that destroyed the orbiter. Simultaneously, the cockpit voice recorder taped the first and last indication that anyone on board knew of the serious trouble—Pilot Michael Smith, either seeing the SRB veering toward him through his window or noting the red main engine shutdown lights on his control panel said, "Uh oh." At an altitude of 48,000 feet (14,600 meters) and a speed of Mach 2 (twice the speed of sound), *Challenger* exploded.

On the ground, some spectators realized that the SRBs had separated too early. Others, unfamiliar with shuttle launches, thought this was the normal staging of SRBs. Soon, however, it was clear to all that the shuttle was nowhere to be seen in a widening fireball, and that the SRBs were wildly spinning off on their own, still under thrust.

At Mission Control in Houston, telemetry signals suddenly stopped. At first, having seen no indications of trouble during the launch, flight controllers believed that either the tracking station or the shuttle's radios had failed. Within seconds, however, radar tracking detected hundreds of pieces of debris following *Challenger's* trajectory. Noting this, Flight Dynamics Officer Brian Perry, a veteran shuttle flight controller, confirmed the tracking data and reported the explosion to the flight director.

The explosion that destroyed *Challenger* (NASA's second and most experienced space shuttle) also destroyed the two satellites carried in its hull. Her crew, Commander Francis (Dick) Scobee, Pilot Michael Smith, mission specialists Ellison Onizuka, Judith Resnik, and Ronald McNair, payload specialist Gregory Jarvis, and spaceflight participant Christa McAuliffe, were all killed.

In the days that followed the *Challenger* disaster the nation mourned. President Reagan eulogized the crew both in a nationally televised speech and at a memorial ceremony at NASA's Johnson Space Center in Houston, Texas.

Within hours of the explosion that destroyed the *Challenger*, calls were made for an official investigation. At NASA, Dr. Jesse Moore, the official in charge of the shuttle program, set up a task force to carry out a technical investigation of the cause, or causes, of the explosion. Moore's all-NASA team impounded all data relating to the flight and initiated a salvage effort to recover as much of the wreckage as possible from the ocean. The wreckage would provide physical evidence which would be available to help pinpoint the disaster's cause.

There were calls for a non-NASA investigation. Such an investigation, it was said, would more likely be freer of bias than any investigation carried out by NASA. Heeding these calls on February 3, 1986, President Reagan appointed a group of thirteen distinguished engineers, test pilots, and scientists to investigate the *Challenger* accident. This group was officially known as the Presidential Commission on the Space Shuttle *Challenger* Accident. The commission's chairman was William Rogers, a former secretary of state, former U.S. attorney general, and an accomplished lawyer. Other members of the commission included Neil Armstrong, the first man to walk on the moon; Sally Ride, an astrophysicist and the first American woman in space; and Richard Feynman, a physicist and Nobel Prize winner. Like the Apollo 1 investigating committee, the Rogers Commission was charged with carrying out a full assessment of all aspects of the accident and the shuttle program; unlike the Apollo investigation, the *Challenger* inquiry was performed publicly, by a basically non-NASA group.

The Rogers Commission took testimony from more than 160 individuals involved in the shuttle program and *Challenger's* last flight. More than twelve thousand pages of sworn testimony were taken, and more than sixty-three hundred documents relating to the accident were reviewed. More than six thousand engineers, scientists, technicians, and other individuals participated in the commission's work. On

June 6, 1986, the Rogers Commission released its final report, fixing the immediate cause of the accident as well as discussing the contributing factors that had led to the decision to launch *Challenger* on January 28, 1986. The Commission's report also made recommendations to improve the design of the space shuttle and to prevent future accidents.

Using facts uncovered by the Rogers Commission, as well as supporting evidence and eyewitness accounts of the accident and the salvaged wreckage, it is possible to reconstruct the flight of STS 51L and the crucial events that led to its ill-fated launch.

Context

The Rogers Commission made a methodical study of all the events leading up to the flight of STS 51L. Also evaluated were flight records radioed to the ground, debris recovered from the ocean, and films of the flight taken by long-range cameras. Many individuals were interviewed, and a great number of technical studies were performed to test theories concerning the in-flight events of January 28.

The commission considered many things that could have caused *Challenger's* destruction. Possible causes which were investigated included a failure of the main engines, a rupture of the huge external fuel tank, a problem in one of the payload rockets (such as the ignition of the TDRS's upper stage), a failure in one of the SRBs, premature ignition of the shuttle's emergency destruct system, and sabotage. As the evidence mounted, many of the possible causes were eliminated from the list. By early February, only weeks after the launch, the investigators were already focusing their entire attention on the right SRB. Much of the reason for this early narrowing of the possibilities came about because films from automatic cameras developed after the flight clearly showed black smoke seeping from SRB joints at ignition. The films also depicted bright flames jetting from the rocket casings about fifty-eight seconds after launch. Engineers and technicians working for the commission considered propellant cracks, cracks in the rocket motor case, and O-ring seal problems as possible causes of the SRB failure.

In its final report, the commission pinpointed the cause of the accident and made several recommendations for improvements in the shuttle and its management. From a technical standpoint, the cause of the disaster was quite clear. The commission found that the cause of the accident was a failure of the O-ring pressure seal of the right solid rocket motor. In reaching this conclusion, many possible SRB failure modes had been evaluated. Once the O-ring was identified as the cause, the commission went on to determine what specifically caused the O-ring to fail.

Had the O-ring been improperly installed or tested? Had sand or water got into the O-ring joint to prevent it from sealing? Had the cold been to blame? Had the elastic putty used in the O-ring joint failed to seal? Again, more tests were performed, and the flight data and debris were reanalyzed. The commission did not, however, draw a definite conclusion about this cause of the accident. Too much of the evidence had been destroyed in the explosion. Although it was certain that the right SRB had experienced a failure in one of its joints, it was possible that one or more of the above causes were to blame. The commission did, however, conclude that the SRB design was prone to certain failures, including the one that destroyed *Challenger.*

The Rogers Commission's findings went far beyond a determination of the immediate cause of the accident. The commission also concluded that there had been "serious flaws in the decision-making process" leading to 51L's launch. In particular, it concluded that exceptions to established rules had been granted "at the expense of flight safety" and that Morton Thiokol's management "reversed its position and recommended launch . . . contrary to the views of its engineers in order to accommodate a major customer."

It was found that previous ground tests and blow-by problems experienced on past flights should have alerted NASA and Thiokol to the serious deficiencies in the SRBs. The commission also found that the Marshall Space Flight Center had not properly passed evidence of SRB problems up the chain of command within the shuttle program but had instead "attempted to resolve them internally." The commission stated in its report to the president that this kind of management "is altogether at odds with . . . successful flight missions."

After analyzing the cause of the *Challenger* disaster, the Rogers Commission made a number of recommendations to NASA. These recommendations fell into several categories, including the design of the SRBs and shuttle management. The goal of the recommendations was to improve the reliability of the entire shuttle.

The commission recommended that the SRBs be redesigned and recertified to solve the numerous problems inherent in their O-ring joints. The redesign specifically called for an SRB that in future flights would "be insensitive to" environmental factors, including the cold and rain as well as "assembly procedures." Further, the commission called for a design that would have joints as strong as the rocket casings themselves. To verify the integrity of the new design, the commission recommended testing full-size boosters before the new SRBs were committed to actual flight. These tests began in the summer of 1987.

The commission also made specific recommendations relating to other potential problem areas in the shuttle. They insisted that the shuttle's brakes be improved (a long history of brake problems had occurred over many flights) and that a reevaluation of crew abort and escape mechanisms be undertaken to determine if launch and landing problems could be made "more survivable." Finally, the commission insisted that the rate of shuttle flights be controlled to maximize safety. Such a policy had not been implemented in the past, the commission said.

Beyond technical matters, the Rogers Commission also recommended a number of sweeping changes in the shuttle program's management structure. These were designed to prevent the problems that led to a "flawed decision-making process" regarding the launch of 51L. These specific recommendations included the establishment of a safety panel with broad powers reporting directly to the manager of the shuttle program and the establishment of the Office of Safety, Reliability, and

Quality Assurance within NASA reporting directly to the NASA Administrator, with broad powers to investigate and demand solutions to safety-related issues.

Additionally, it was recommended that a full review take place of all critical safety items in the space shuttle before the next flight. Finally, the commission recommended that astronauts be more fully involved in the shuttle program's management. This recommendation came in response to the anger expressed by some astronauts during the investigation that they, who were at greatest risk in each flight, had not been informed of the O-ring blow-by and erosion problems prior to the accident. In response to this call, NASA placed senior astronauts—Robert Crippen, Sally Ride, Paul Weitz, and others—in key advisory roles.

The *Challenger* disaster brought the United States space program to a halt. Within months of the accident, two unmanned launchers failed as well. With no way of launching satellites until either these rockets or the shuttle was recertified for flight, both NASA and the military were "pinned down." New research in space could not be conducted. Replacement military and weather satellites could not be launched. Planned space missions stagnated, awaiting the availability of a launcher. More than a dozen scientific payloads were canceled, and seventy more were delayed for years. Space planners were forced to buy dozens of expendable Titan and Delta rockets to supplement the grounded shuttle program.

Bibliography

Durant, Frederick C., III, ed. *Between Sputnik and the Shuttle: New Perspectives on American Astronautics, 1957-1980.* San Diego: Univelt, 1981. A comprehensive history of American manned spaceflight from 1957 to 1981. This book contains an excellent description of the origins of the Space Transportation System program.

Lewis, Richard S. *Challenger: The Final Voyage.* New York: Columbia University Press, 1988. A factual account of the *Challenger* disaster, this book relates the events of January 28, 1986. A popular version of the Rogers Commission Report.

Report of the Presidential Commission on the Space Shuttle Challenger Accident. Washington, D.C.: Government Printing Office, 1986. Contains the full text of the official report of the Rogers Commission. Technical in its content, this volume details both the immediate and root causes of the STS 51L accident.

Stern, Alan. *The U.S. Space Program After Challenger.* New York: Franklin Watts, 1987. A detailed look at the *Challenger* disaster and its ramifications for the future of the United States space program.

Trento, Joseph J. *Prescription for Disaster: From the Glory of Apollo to the Betrayal of the Shuttle.* New York: Crown Publishers, 1987. Though somewhat biased, the author gives a detailed account of the *Challenger* accident and its root cause. Trento advances the theory that the events at Cape Canaveral on January 28, 1986, were the culmination of the decline of the U.S. space program since the early 1970's.

Washington Post Editorial Staff. *Challengers.* New York: Simon and Schuster, 1986.

A touching and personal series of biographies of each of the seven crew members of the ill-fated STS 51L mission.

Alan Stern

Cross-References

Apollo 1-6, 37; Astronauts and the U.S. Astronaut Program, 154; Halley's Comet Probes, 569; The U.S. Space Shuttle, 1626; Tracking and Data-Relay Communications Satellites, 2042.

SPACE SHUTTLE MISSION 26
Discovery

Date: September 29 to October 3, 1988
Type of mission: Manned Earth-orbiting spaceflight
Country: The United States

Space Transportation System (STS) 26R was the first shuttle flight following the catastrophic explosion of the space shuttle Challenger *thirty-two months before. STS 26R successfully returned the United States' manned space program to an active flight status. During the flight, a communications satellite vital to the U.S. space program was launched into geosynchronous orbit.*

Principal personages
FREDERICK H. (RICK) HAUCK, the commander
RICHARD O. (DICK) COVEY, the pilot
GEORGE D. (PINKY) NELSON,
DAVID C. HILMERS, and
JOHN M. (MIKE) LOUNGE, mission specialists

Summary of the Mission

Space shuttle mission 26R was the first U.S. manned spaceflight following the loss of the space shuttle *Challenger* and its seven-member crew on January 28, 1986. Because of the protracted recovery time of thirty-two months, STS 26R became widely regarded as America's return to space. In fact, the National Aeronautics and Space Administration (NASA) officially designated the mission "Return to Flight."

Not since the fatal launchpad fire of Apollo 1 on January 27, 1967 (which killed astronauts Virgil Grissom, Edward White, and Roger Chaffee), had there been such an extensive reworking of an American spacecraft. Following the loss of *Challenger*, a thirteen-member investigative commission was appointed by President Ronald Reagan and headed by former Secretary of State William Rogers. Called the Rogers Commission, the panel issued its report to the president on June 9, 1986. More than four hundred changes in a $2.4-billion program were advocated to improve the shuttle and help ensure the safety of future flights. These changes included a complete redesign of the O-ring system connecting the solid-fueled rocket booster segments, the system that was blamed for the *Challenger* explosion.

Problems encountered after the initial launch date was set for February, 1988, caused a series of delays. Space planners wanted to be certain that the tests of the solid-fueled rocket boosters were completed successfully. Finally, on July 4, 1988, after the redesigned joints had been approved, the assembled vehicle was rolled from the vehicle assembly building at the Kennedy Space Center to Launchpad 39B. *Discovery* was poised for launch.

Even with the shuttle positioned on the pad, NASA officials waited before setting another launch date, ostensibly to evaluate the assembled system further and to receive the results from yet more booster tests. The media proved especially critical of the space agency in the wake of the *Challenger* disaster and these frequently shifting launch dates. After the final flight readiness review panel met, the launch date was set for Thursday, September 29, 1988.

The media gave as much attention to the upcoming launch as to any other space launch in American history, including the Apollo Moon flights. NASA had instituted a new launch management system to prevent a recurrence of what the Rogers Commission had called "a flawed decision-making process" for shuttle launches. Heading a launch management team was active astronaut Robert L. Crippen, pilot of the first shuttle, who would make the final launch decision. In the glare of world attention, NASA and the U.S. space program could ill afford a problematic launch or mission.

The countdown proceeded smoothly on September 29. Many predictions prior to the launch held that the new and untested safety and management systems were so bulky that there would likely be days of delays, holds, and reconsiderations before STS 26R could be launched. These predictions proved unfounded. After a delay of only one hour and thirty-eight minutes, caused by high-altitude winds that were lighter than predicted, *Discovery* was launched from Pad 39B at 11:37 A.M. eastern daylight time (EDT).

The launch was normal in every respect. The redesigned solid-fueled rocket boosters were jettisoned on schedule and dropped by parachute into the ocean off the coast of Florida. Subsequent inspection proved that they had come through the flight in pristine condition. The shuttle's three main engines performed well enough to preclude an initial burn of the orbital maneuvering system (OMS) engines to achieve stable orbit. Later, an OMS burn was performed in order to place *Discovery* in a 348-kilometer orbit above Earth.

Aside from the principal function of proving viability of the extensively reworked shuttle system, the four-day mission was to include eleven scientific experiments and the deployment of a vital NASA communications satellite. The satellite, a $100-million Tracking and Data-Relay Satellite (TDRS), was to replace the one lost on *Challenger*. With a mass of 2,268 kilograms, the TDRS was one of the largest communications satellites ever launched; it was so massive that it could fit only in the shuttle's payload bay. The TDRS was successfully deployed by a spring-loaded platform from *Discovery*'s payload bay six hours into the mission. After the astronauts maneuvered the orbiter to a safe 72 kilometers away, the TDRS automatically boosted itself 35,800 kilometers above Earth into geosynchronous orbit. (Satellites in geosynchronous orbit rotate at the same speed as Earth rotates and thus appear to remain at a fixed point in the sky.)

The purpose of the TDRS system is to provide a three-satellite communications constellation for NASA missions. The TDRS system would enable nearly constant communications between Earth and other orbiting spacecraft such as the orbiter fleet, the U.S. space station *Freedom*, and the Hubble Space Telescope.

One of the first problems the crew encountered on STS 26R was the partial failure of a cooling device called a flash evaporator, which is used to cool the crew cabin and the equipment. During lift-off, the evaporator became frozen with ice and operated at less than its optimal capacity. To assist in melting the ice, ground engineers allowed the temperature in *Discovery* to rise to 29 degrees Celsius for the first two days of the mission. The evaporator would malfunction again briefly during reentry, but it never endangered the crew or *Discovery*'s systems.

The Ku-band antenna, used to communicate with Earth-based stations, malfunctioned on the first day of the mission. The antenna failed to align itself properly for broadcast of signals to Earth, and it wobbled erratically on its mount. On the second day, the malfunctioning antenna was finally stowed back in the shuttle's payload bay; consequently, the flow of communications between *Discovery* and the ground for the remainder of the flight was reduced.

Eleven scientific experiments were carried on board the shuttle. Protein crystal growth experiments were conducted for use in the development of complex protein molecules that could be utilized in medicines and other chemical solutions. One of the crystals being examined was critical to the study of the acquired immunodeficiency syndrome (AIDS) virus and how it replicates. Two experiments investigated medicinal properties unique to weightless space. Two other experiments were designed to investigate molten metal resolidification and crystallization for development of stronger metal alloys. Also on board was an experiment involving crystal growth on a semipermeable membrane (the results could ultimately help reduce medical X-radiation doses). Yet another was designed to produce thin films of organic material and study their properties.

Two meteorological investigations were conducted on STS 26R. One photographed lightning and the other the glow of Earth's horizon near sunrise and sunset. This last experiment was remarkably similar to one of the first scientific investigations ever conducted by man in space.

At 11:34 A.M. EDT on October 2, 1988, *Discovery*'s crew fired the OMS engines for two minutes and fifty seconds in the de-orbital maneuver. Forty minutes later, *Discovery* reentered Earth's atmosphere. Twenty-one minutes after reentry, at 12:37 A.M. EDT, the shuttle and its crew landed safely at Edwards Air Force Base in the high desert of Southern California. The duration of mission 26R had been four days and one hour.

Knowledge Gained

The primary goal of mission 26R was to prove the safety of the redesigned shuttle system and return American manned spaceflight to an active status. The successful return of the crew with all major mission objectives met fulfilled that goal. Precise details of the success of each redesigned element would take many weeks of detailed analysis, but all major redesigned components were proved sound.

The newly designed O-ring system appeared to perform flawlessly. According to engineers who examined the system after it was recovered from the ocean following the launch, the boosters appeared in better condition than any recovered from any other mission.

The three main engines had undergone forty significant design changes in a $100-million program that included strengthening of the engine's high-speed pump components. These components also appeared to have performed well, although one engine apparently experienced an oxidizer leak near the end of the main combustion chamber.

The orbiter's tires, brakes, and nosewheel steering system had all undergone extensive modifications. These systems absorb the monumental energies of landing when the shuttle orbiter touches down at speeds of more than 350 kilometers per hour. *Discovery*'s landing speed was said to have been 381 kilometers per hour. The vehicle required only 2,337 meters to stop, indicating a very good braking (energy absorption) efficiency when compared to that of past missions.

The performance of these critical systems indicates the viability of these redesigns. The ability of space planners to identify and produce the necessary redesigns gave NASA the confidence to incorporate future changes as they may be required in the shuttle program. One manifestation of this newfound capability was the redesign of a drogue chute braking system to be installed on all orbiters to absorb touchdown energies further and enhance the safety of landings.

Although overshadowed by the mission's main goal of returning the U.S. space program to flight status, the scientific experiments aboard STS 26R represented one of the primary reasons the space shuttle program was first conceived. The extensive study of protein crystal growth provided data for vital chemical studies that may have far-reaching implications. Crystal growth on membranes may one day reduce dosages of medical X-radiation, which account for the single largest source of ionizing radiation exposure for the American public. The experiment designed to study the AIDS virus also proved valuable. Information gathered from the experiment may lead to the development of medications.

Most important, STS 26R proved the ability of the space agency to recover from catastrophe and unprecedented tragedy in space to fly again. The system emerged from the flight of 26R fundamentally changed, with a better spacecraft and a baseline of knowledge that, unfortunately, might not have been obtained under other circumstances. From those hard-won lessons, the space program gained a clearer vision that would guide the United States into the next century.

Context

Mission STS 26R flew as the twenty-sixth space shuttle mission, the fifty-seventh United States manned mission, and the twenty-second manned mission of the operational shuttle system. During the thirty-two-month period of rebuilding, NASA had been heavily criticized by the Rogers Commission and the world media for a lack of proper management and a poor decision-making process. The space agency worked ceaselessly during this long hiatus to regain the confidence of the American public, the confidence they had enjoyed since their formation by Congress in 1958.

NASA took various measures to help ensure a successful 26R mission. The agency reviewed the cause of the *Challenger* accident and corrected the flawed O-ring system. It reviewed all shuttle systems, identifying and modifying any which could cause future problems.

Space planners at NASA also restructured the agency's management system, strengthening safety, quality, and reliability by making improvements in training and personnel. Finally, NASA reduced the planned flight rate and removed altogether the somewhat artificial dependence on civil payload manifests which had resulted in an overloaded system.

The crew selected to fly the 26R mission was an all-veteran crew; NASA wanted to maximize the experience available on this important return to space. Hauck and Nelson had both flown twice before, and Covey, Hilmers, and Lounge had flown once before—making the STS 26R crew one of the most experienced ever to fly on a shuttle mission.

The space agency and the nation approached the launch with an apprehension which attracted much attention. The shuttle's systems were tested and retested as though *Discovery* had never flown before. The orbiter sat on the pad undergoing tests some thirteen weeks before launch, the longest launchpad preparation period since the earliest shuttle launches. Clearly, the launch was approached with maximum caution.

Just before the launch, crowds gathered at Kennedy Space Center. The atmosphere was reminiscent of that preceding the early Apollo Moon launches. Unlike the previous launch of mission STS 51L, which was attended by relatively few and virtually dismissed by the press as "routine," the mission of 26R was anything but ordinary.

More than at any other time in history, the fate of the Western world's future in space was on the line. If STS 26R had failed, the manned space effort would have suffered another catastrophic setback, perhaps giving way to critics' calls for the abandonment of the manned program in favor of mechanical, robotic exploration. With the string of ongoing successes by the Soviets, another U.S. failure would have meant abdicating superiority in space exploration. The United States had only three shuttle orbiters left in its active fleet. The loss of another of these multibillion-dollar national resources would have been disastrous.

The success of STS 26R held an implicit significance for the continuance of manned spaceflight. Without question, it was the mission that had to succeed. Succeed it did, brilliantly restoring the United States to its competitive position in space. The tragedy of mission 51L and all it entailed had been replaced by triumph. All space projects were suddenly possible again: the Hubble Space Telescope, Magellan to Venus, Galileo to Jupiter, and the space station *Freedom*. The United States had regained its foothold in space.

Bibliography

Allen, Joseph P., and Russell Martin. *Entering Space: An Astronaut's Odyssey.* New

York: Stewart, Tabori and Chang, 1984. This heavily documented work describes the United States space shuttle program. It details the stages of a typical mission, from processing at the Kennedy Space Center to launch, orbital activities, and landing. The book is aimed toward all readers and is one of the most beautifully photographed and illustrated of all books on the shuttle.

Baker, David. *The History of Manned Space Flight*. New York: Crown Publishers, 1982. This book offers a precise chronology of the history of manned spaceflight, heavily oriented toward the United States effort. It is a detailed work which chronicles the U.S. manned space effort from its beginning to the start of the space shuttle program. Includes analyses of U.S. spaceflights, beginning with the Mercury missions of the 1960's.

De Waard, E. John, and Nancy De Waard. *History of NASA: America's Voyage to the Stars*. New York: Exeter Books, 1984. A colorful pictorial essay on the history of NASA. It does not go into great detail on every flight but does include many color photographs of the various U.S. manned programs.

Joels, Kerry M., and Gregory P. Kennedy. *The Space Shuttle Operator's Manual*. Rev. ed. New York: Ballantine Books, 1987. This manual is a detailed space shuttle system reference work. It provides specific information about the space shuttle system, from weights and sizes to operational characteristics. It enumerates countdown procedures, emergency instructions, and standard operational modes. Thoroughly illustrated.

McConnell, Malcolm. *Challenger: A Major Malfunction*. Garden City, N.Y.: Doubleday and Co., 1987. This work offers the author's unflattering, unapologetic view of what happened to the U.S. space program from the closing days of the Apollo program to the *Challenger* disaster. It offers an often-bitter appraisal of the compromises that led to tragedy and the pressures that caused the NASA management system to fail. While some of the author's charges have not been entirely supported by formal investigations, the book does provide a baseline of information from which the reader may form his own opinions.

Dennis Chamberland

Cross-References

Apollo 1-6, 37; The Commercial Use of Space Program Innovations, 253; Materials Processing in Space, 933; The National Aeronautics and Space Administration, 1032; U.S. Private Industry and Space Exploration, 1187; The U.S. Space Shuttle, 1626; Space Shuttle Mission 1: *Columbia*, 1648; Space Shuttle Mission 25: *Challenger*, 1813; Tracking and Data-Relay Communications Satellites, 2042.

THE DESIGN AND USES OF THE U.S. SPACE STATION

Date: Beginning May 20, 1982
Type of program: Manned space station
Countries: The United States, Japan, Canada, and the ESA nations

The U.S. Space Station has been designed to be a permanently orbiting space platform. It will consist of a collection of specialized modules for scientific experimentation, for industrial research and manufacturing, and for the construction of spacecraft.

Principal personages

RONALD REAGAN, the U.S. president who directed NASA to develop the U.S. Space Station

JAMES BEGGS, NASA Administrator from 1981 to 1986

JAMES C. FLETCHER, NASA Administrator beginning 1986

ANDREW J. STOFAN, NASA Associate Administrator for the Space Station, beginning 1986

Summary of the Program

The U.S. space station *Freedom* is designed to be an orbiting scientific and industrial research laboratory. It will be able to accommodate eight crew members, including command astronauts, engineers, astronomers, technicians, and other flight specialists. These men and women will be selected from the international scientific and business community, and each will spend as long as three months in orbit before being relieved by new crew members.

The idea of a permanently manned space station in Earth orbit was first developed by Edward Everett Hale in 1869, in an article in *The Atlantic Monthly*. Hale's "station" was made of brick and carried a crew of thirty-seven. A more realistic model was conceived by Russian space pioneer Konstantin Tsiolkovsky, in 1911, and developed into its modern form by Hermann Oberth in his 1923 book *The Rocket in Interplanetary Space*. Oberth envisioned that such a space station might be used for global communications, weather prediction, and as a docking point for other manned spacecraft.

Almost from its inception in 1958, the National Aeronautics and Space Administration (NASA) has speculated about and studied the possibility of a permanent manned presence in space. Throughout the 1960's, NASA conducted engineering and conceptual studies of possible space station designs. These studies were relegated to the background by President John F. Kennedy's directive stating that the U.S. space program's goal in the 1960's would be a manned lunar landing. This goal was achieved in 1969. The post-Apollo space program of the 1970's focused on the development of the reusable orbiter that would eventually become the space shuttle. The Space Station Program was delayed until the shuttle program became operational. In 1984, in his State of the Union address, President Ronald Reagan directed that NASA undertake the development and construction of a permanently manned space station and that the task be completed in a decade.

In April, 1983, a group of U.S. aerospace companies under contract to NASA completed a set of detailed studies on the requirements and possible uses of a manned space station. The Space Station Task Force, established on May 20, 1982, expanded on those studies. The Space Station Task Force was divided into several working groups, each of which handled some aspect of the station's design. The work was conducted by various NASA centers and by private contractors.

The task force and contractor studies resulted in two basic station designs. Each design was based on modules that could be constructed on the ground and assembled in orbit. The fundamental components included a large, rigid framework to which laboratory, manufacturing, and habitat modules could be attached; external platforms for scientific instrument, construction, and space shuttle docking; and a self-contained power generating system. Also included in the plans were two or more free-flying platforms which could be serviced by the space station crew but would be launched independently.

The two space station designs being seriously considered for implementation were known as the baseline configuration, or "dual-keel" design, and the reference configuration, or "power-tower" design. The former was being developed by Lockheed and McDonnell Douglas, the latter by Grumman Aerospace.

The dual-keel design called for a rectangular framework 110 meters long and 44 meters wide. The longer sides were known as keels and were always to point toward Earth's center. The shorter sides of this frame were called booms and would always be parallel to Earth's surface. A third boom, 153 meters long, would be mounted across the keels near their center. This transverse boom would carry the experimental and habitat modules. The keels and booms were to be constructed from a lattice of graphite epoxy tubing, similar in appearance to ordinary construction scaffolding, and were to be erected by space shuttle and space station astronauts. The main advantages of the dual keel were the uniform microgravity environment that could be achieved inside the laboratory modules and the high pointing accuracy for scientific instruments made possible by the structure's rigidity.

The power-tower design's advantages were ease of initial construction, ease of later expansion to include additional modules, and orbital stability. The tower was designed to be a 122-meter, reinforced truss structure. One end would always point toward Earth's center. The slender design and the slightly greater mass at the tower's lower end would provide greater orbital stability. The various pressurized modules and instrument platforms would be attached to points along the length of the tower. The modules would be arranged end to end.

In 1986, the dual-keel configuration was chosen as the space station's blueprint. That structure, station engineers decided, would provide more safety for crew members and a better environment for experiments. The scientific laboratories, industrial research and manufacturing modules, crew habitat modules, and many of the station's technical components will be designed and constructed by members of an international partnership in the Space Station Program. The nations involved include Japan, Canada, and a scientific consortium of European nations known as the European Space Agency (ESA), which counts among its members the United Kingdom, West Germany, France, Spain, Italy, Austria, Belgium, Denmark, Switzerland, Norway, the Netherlands, Sweden, and Ireland. ESA will supply a pressurized laboratory module that will be permanently attached to the station and will also develop a detachable, pressurized module that will have crude manuvering capabilities and so can be used independently of the main station. Such a module will be useful for delicate experiments that might be disturbed by general crew or instrument activity. In addition to those two modules, ESA will develop a free-flying instrument platform which will be launched into a polar Earth orbit (an orbit that passes over Earth's poles rather than remaining near the equatorial plane).

Japan will test and operate a general-purpose experimental module called the Japanese Experiment Module (JEM). The JEM will be pressurized to allow crew members to work there comfortably. It will be modeled on the ESA module and will carry a flat instrument platform at one end.

Canada is constructing a mobile servicing facility that will be able to move along the superstructure of the station to reach most of the external equipment and instruments. This facility will be equipped with a remote manipulator arm, similar to the space shuttle's, to be used for fabrication and repair. In addition, Canada will develop a solar energy array to power individual modules and to serve as an auxiliary power source for the station as a whole.

Two power generating mechanisms are under consideration; they will probably be hybridized in the final station design. The first of these is a standard photovoltaic solar array system, which generates electric power directly from sunlight. The energy gathered by the solar array will be stored in a system of batteries for later use. The other mechanism for power generation uses a working fluid which is heated by concentrated solar rays. The working fluid turns turbines to generate electric power in a manner similar to hydroelectric power plants on Earth.

Current plans allow for three laboratory modules and one habitat module, each 13.6 meters in length and 4.2 meters in diameter. In the tower configuration, the modules are linked end to end; in the dual-keel configuration, the modules are clustered near the center of the superstructure. The modules will be connected by dumbbell-shaped sections called nodes. Each node consists of a tunnel with small chambers at either end that serve as entrances to modules. The node chambers will also function as air locks, allowing crew members to enter and exit the station, and as storage space for equipment and supplies.

At least two detachable logistics modules will be used as ferries to remove waste materials and return supplies. The logistics modules will be rotated with each space shuttle supply visit, at intervals of approximately three months.

The free-flying platforms are envisioned as manned, independent orbiters which will carry equipment and experiments that are either too delicate or too dangerous to be performed on the main station. At least two such platforms will be used with the U.S. Space Station. One will orbit parallel to the main station and will carry advanced detectors for astronomical research, materials development equipment, and other scientific instruments. The other will be placed in a high-altitude polar orbit more suited to Earth observation. A major advantage of free flyers is that they may be developed by individual nations or even by private corporations, subject only to the limitation that each be capable of being launched as a unit by the space shuttle. The platforms may be serviced by the shuttle directly or may be taken to the space station for servicing. The platforms orbiting parallel to the station may be retrieved and serviced by the space station crew without the shuttle's assistance. There may be as many as eight free-flying platforms when the space station is in full operation.

Knowledge Gained

Unlike the Apollo program, whose primary goal was a manned lunar landing, the Space Station Program has many, equally important goals. These goals, however, were not defined at the outset of the program; in fact, as late as 1983, both the National Research Council (the president's primary science advisory board) and the Department of Defense stated publicly that the scientific justification for a manned space station had not been established to their satisfaction. In response, the Space Station Task Force, along with private firms under contract to NASA, produced reports which identified more than 250 space station missions in the fields of scientific research, technology research and development, and space manufacturing.

The reports produced by the Space Station Task Force in April, 1986, pointed out several deficiencies in the program. They called for more experience with extended manned missions; a complete review of the safety standards followed by flight crews and in component manufacturing; a system that could quickly transport samples of delicate or perishable materials, such as medicines, to the ground; a greater number of space shuttle flights per year and shorter periods between successive flights; and finally, a reexamination of station design in the light of crew utilization and comfort.

Some of the knowledge necessary to correct these deficiencies had been acquired in early NASA manned space programs. The Mercury, Gemini, and Apollo programs were valuable in this regard, but more important were the Skylab and Spacelab programs, during which astronauts actually performed complex experiments. During the Skylab mission, three crews were rotated at various intervals, and one crew remained in orbit for eighty-four days. Skylab, operational for approximately nine months in 1973 and 1974, also demonstrated that astronauts can perform sophisticated tasks effectively even after long periods in orbit; that humans can successfully undertake spacecraft assembly and repair tasks, including those requiring extravehicular activities (EVAs); that direct and frequent communications between flight and ground crews is vital to mission efficiency; and that longer continuous missions with single crews were desirable, as they would allow more extended experiments to be conducted. The Spacelab program was a joint effort of NASA and ESA to place a manned laboratory in Earth orbit. Spacelab was first placed in orbit by the U.S. space shuttle in November, 1983, for a ten-day mission. Although Spacelab's scientific capability greatly exceeded that of Skylab, Spacelab was limited to orbital missions lasting less than two weeks because of its design and inherent dependence on the space shuttle. The *Freedom* space station is designed to provide greater flexibility of use than either of those early projects.

The space station missions as outlined in the task force report fall into the following catagories: scientific research; technological research and development; commercial product development; terrestrial observation for weather research and geological surveying; astronomical research; resupply and maintenance of spacecraft; docking and launching of space vehicles of all types; and fabrication of spacecraft and other orbital facilities too large to be launched from the ground.

Context

The historical development of the space station concept in general, and of the U.S. space station *Freedom* in particular, has been long and uneven. The program's timeliness and effectiveness have undoubtedly suffered from a lack of resolution on the part of Congress, which must approve program funding, and on the part of the president, who must apply considerable pressure to see such a massive program through to a successful conclusion. Unlike the space station and the space shuttle programs, the Apollo program of the 1960's received consistent governmental support.

President Kennedy successfully put the goal of placing an American on the Moon at the top of the national agenda and kept it there. No such constant guidance and nurturing have been forthcoming for the Space Station Program, even though the potential economic and political gains are great.

The Soviet Union has developed a manned space program that is more focused than that of the United States. The Soviet program must be considered more successful in terms of achieving the goal of operating a permanently manned space station. While the U.S. space program was preparing for the deployment of the space shuttle, the Soviet Union proceeded with its Salyut and Mir manned orbiting laboratory programs, both of which have been strikingly successful. Soviet cosmonauts, as a group, have spent much more time in space than American astronauts.

The 1984 presidential directive to develop the U.S. Space Station and the 1986 report of the Space Station Task Force helped to focus and better define the program. The inclusion of other nations in the project, despite occasioning some minor disagreements, has also helped to give definition to the tasks that must be accomplished to ensure the station's success.

Several design decisions and changes were introduced as a result of the 1986 task force report. The first of these involved crew safety. The baseline, or dual-keel, configuration was chosen for the basic station design because it arranged the modules in an irregular polygon, which allows any one module to be sealed off from the main station while leaving the remaining modules accessible. It was also determined that this configuration would provide a better environment for microgravity experiments. After the *Challenger* accident, space station designers added an escape vehicle that would transport the crew members to Earth if the space shuttle was unable to reach them for a very long time. The space shuttle is an integral part of the Space Station Program; without a reliable shuttle fleet, the Space Station Program would be doomed.

If the Space Station Program realizes even a fraction of its potential, the effect could be tremendous. In essence, the world in which humans live and work will have been expanded to include regions of near-Earth orbit. Eventually, the demand for space station manufacturing facilities may justify additional stations of greater capacity and capabilities that will require larger crews. The space stations of the future will be used as tools to extend the human sphere of influence even farther, to the Moon, to Mars, and beyond.

Bibliography

Bekey, Ivan, and Daniel Herman, eds. *Space Stations and Space Platforms: Concepts, Design, Infrastructure, and Uses*. Vol. 99 in *Progress in Astronautics and Aeronautics*. New York: American Institute of Aeronautics and Astronautics, 1985. This book gives the history of space station development. Discusses the role of the space station in the U.S. space program. Included are reviews of economic, military, and industrial uses of space platforms. Suitable for advanced high school and college readers.

Boston, Penelope J., ed. *The Case for Mars*. Washington, D.C.: American Astronomical Society, 1984. A monograph in support of a manned expedition to Mars. The space station plays a major role in most planned programs for Mars exploration. Somewhat biased but presents convincing evidence. Illustrated. Accessible to a general audience.

Braun, Wernher von. "Crossing the Last Frontier." *Collier's* 129 (March 22, 1952): 24-29. In this article, von Braun voices support for an American space station. He provides a complete account of the design, building, and operation of such a station. The applications outlined here are surprisingly similar to those listed in modern space station studies. Suitable for general audiences.

Froehlich, Walter. *Space Station: The Next Logical Step*. NASA EP-213. Washington, D.C.: Government Printing Office, 1984. Provides a brief layperson's introduction to the U.S. Space Station Program. Outlines the program's origins, organization, and goals in nontechnical language. Illustrated with color prints from Apollo and space shuttle missions and with drawings of proposed space station designs. A highly accessible work.

Hargrove, Eugene C., ed. *Beyond Spaceship Earth: Environmental Ethics and the Solar System*. San Francisco: Sierra Club Books, 1987. A popular exposition of the social, commercial, environmental, and even theological aspects of a permanent manned presence in space. Topics are far-ranging, including the military implications of space colonization and the possibility of interaction with extraterrestrial life. This book is highly recommended; would make an excellent supplement to more advanced references.

O'Leary, Brian. *The Fertile Stars: Man's Look to Space as the New Source of Food and Energy*. New York: Dodd, Mead and Co., 1981. This book offers ideas on the economic and social potential of space exploration. The vital role played by the space station is addressed briefly. Of particular interest here is the section on the use of space resources for energy production. Suitable for all audiences.

Simpson, T. R., ed. *The Space Station: An Idea Whose Time Has Come*. New York: IEEE Press, 1985. A collection of articles on all aspects of space station development, this volume includes reviews of the history and justification of space station concepts. Also included are chapters on various station designs and the long-term potential of space station programs. Contains numerous line drawings of historical and modern space station designs. Suitable for general audiences.

U.S. Congress. Office of Technology Assessment. *Civilian Space Stations and the U.S. Future in Space*. OTA-STI-241. Washington, D.C.: Government Printing Office, 1984. Contains published proceedings from several workshops sponsored by Congress on space station development. Designed to be a reference source for those interested in specific technical or administrative information on space station program planning and management. For advanced high school or college-level readers.

Chris Godfrey

Cross-References

THE DEVELOPMENT OF THE U.S. SPACE STATION

Date: Beginning May 20, 1982
Type of program: Manned space station
Countries: The United States, Japan, Canada, and the ESA nations

The United States' space station Freedom *was conceived as a manned spacecraft in permanent Earth orbit. Plans for the space station include several connected modules—habitats for station personnel, scientific laboratories, spacecraft docking facilities, unmanned platforms, and manufacturing plants.*

Principal personages

RONALD REAGAN, the fortieth President of the United States, who in 1984 directed the National Aeronautics and Space Administration (NASA) to develop the space station
JAMES BEGGS, Administrator, NASA, 1981 to 1986
JAMES C. FLETCHER, Administrator, NASA, beginning in 1986
WERNHER VON BRAUN, the former director of the Marshall Space Flight Center and an early advocate of manned spaceflight

Summary of the Program

The U.S. Space Station is designed to be a permanently manned orbiting platform to support a variety of activities. These activities include terrestrial and astronomical observations, zero-gravity manufacturing of medical and other high technology materials, and deep space missions launched from orbit.

The term "space station" was coined by Hermann Oberth in 1923. Oberth visualized the space station as an aid in establishing a global communications network, as a tool for harnessing solar power for terrestrial use, and as a base for solar system exploration. Prior to World War II, however, the technology to create rockets capable of launching a space station did not exist. Great advances in rocketry were made in the United States and particularly in Germany during World War II. These developments paved the way for active space programs that included plans for a space station.

In the years from 1947 to 1955, the most vocal and well-known advocate of manned spaceflight, and of a manned space station in particular, was Wernher von Braun. He had come to the United States from Germany after the war and eventually became the director of the U.S. Army's rocket development program. In a magazine article entitled "Crossing the Last Frontier" (1952), von Braun described in detail the construction of a space platform in the shape of a torus, or ring, more than 60 meters in diameter. Spokes connecting the ring to a central hub would serve as passageways. In this design, artificial gravity is provided as the ring rotates slowly about the hub axis. The possible uses of such a station, according to von Braun, included weather observation and prediction and military surveillance. He also envisioned the station as a launching platform for lunar expeditions and, possibly, nuclear weapons. The design popularized by von Braun became the subject of science fiction books and films. Yet the space station planning projects first commissioned by the National Aeronautics and Space Administration (NASA) in the 1960's demonstrated that the spinning ring was not a practical design.

The most detailed study of the feasibility of space station programs performed in the early 1960's was conducted at the NASA Langley Research Center in Virginia. One result of these studies was a plan for a Manned Orbital Research Laboratory (MORL), produced by Douglas Aircraft Corporation contractors and Langley researchers between 1963 and 1966. Several configurations of the MORL were given consideration. The MORL was designed to be a minimum-sized, zero-gravity station. Two methods were developed for producing artificial gravity, which might be needed for certain experimental or manufacturing processes or to counter the effects of zero gravity on the crew. The first provided the MORL station with an internal rotating chamber, or centrifuge, in which gravity could be simulated. The second involved attaching the MORL to a Saturn 4B rocket via cables. If the cables were reeled out and the MORL spun slowly, then Earth's gravity could be simulated with cables approximately 30 meters in length. The MORL station was 3 meters in diameter and about 8 meters in length. It would carry a crew of nine and be launched aboard a Saturn 1B rocket.

The development of the MORL project emphasized that the technical capabilities to design and build a space station had developed before the engineers had determined exactly how to utilize a space laboratory. What experiments were to be done and how were they to be conducted? To address these questions, NASA commissioned several large-scale studies of space station experimental programs. The results of these studies were published in a set of documents known as "Blue Books." These documents provided basic references for rocket and satellite payload development for two decades.

The major thrust of the U.S. space program in the 1960's, as outlined by President John F. Kennedy in May of 1961, was to achieve a manned lunar landing within the decade. Plans for a manned orbiting platform, however, continued to be studied, particularly by the Department of Defense (DOD). The Douglas Aircraft Corporation was awarded a DOD contract to develop the Manned Orbiting Laboratory (MOL) in 1966.

The MOL was a small experimental station for a crew of two. The crewmen would work in a zero-gravity environment for periods of up to thirty days. The MOL project was canceled in 1969 because of federal budget cuts and the lack of a clearly defined military need for a manned space platform.

In 1967, NASA announced plans for the Apollo Applications Program (AAP), which would include as a major mission a manned space station. The AAP was to be the major post-Apollo space program at NASA. Later, the program was scaled down as a result of funding limitations. In February, 1970, the project was officially renamed Skylab. The major goals of the program were redefined as being the scientific exploration of space.

Skylab was placed in orbit on May 14, 1973, utilizing a Saturn 5 launch vehicle. The Skylab station consisted of a laboratory and habitat module, the Apollo Telescope Mount, and air lock and spacecraft docking modules. The complete payload weighed 90,720 kilograms, making it the largest spacecraft ever launched. The three-man crew, launched aboard a separate Saturn 1B vehicle, used the Apollo command module to rendezvous and dock with Skylab.

In September, 1969, the NASA Marshall Space Flight Center in Huntsville, Alabama, initiated studies for a larger manned space station project. These plans included development of a new, reusable space transportation system, or space shuttle. The plan to use the shuttle to transport and assemble the space station put restrictions on the station design. The contractors for the project, the McDonnell Douglas Corporation and North American Rockwell, concentrated on modular designs. The modules were to be about 4 meters in diameter, to be accommodated by the shuttle cargo bay. Engineers designed the station with a four-month resupply schedule in mind. Each module had a maximum weight limit of some 9,000 kilograms, and the setup would be powered by a solar panel electrical system. A single Research Applications Module (RAM) based on these studies eventually led to Spacelab, developed by the European Space Agency in cooperation with NASA. The first three Spacelab flights were launched by the space shuttle in November, 1983.

Space station design studies in the 1970's focused on an expanded platform built around a basic module similar to Spacelab. Actual development of the station, however, was deferred until after completion of the development phase of the space shuttle program because of budget restraints.

In 1975, the McDonnell Douglas Corporation conducted a manned orbital systems concept study for NASA and produced a space station design based on Spacelab-like modules. The basic facility consisted of a four-module system supporting a four-man crew.

In 1979, the Johnson Space Center developed a concept for a space operations center. The center was to be a platform dedicated to construction and servicing of space vehicles and satellites. These activities were deemed to be the most economically promising.

In the light of the success of the early space shuttle missions, NASA's administrator, James Beggs, established the Space Station Task Force on May 20, 1982, staffed by senior scientific and administrative personnel from throughout the agency. The task force conducted concept studies for the space station; these studies became known as Phase A of the program. They basically addressed the questions: What would a space station do, and what should it be like?

The efforts of this task force led to a directive from President Ronald Reagan. Delivered during the president's State of the Union address on January 25, 1984, the directive ordered NASA to proceed with the development of a permanently manned space station and to complete it within a decade.

The space station moved from the planning stage to the definition and construction design stage (known as Phase B) on April 19, 1985. Phase B unfolded under the guidance of four individual working groups that made up the Space Station Task Force. The Mission Requirements Working Group was responsible for defining potential space station missions and integrating them into the overall project planning. The Systems Working Group was responsible for identifying and developing spacecraft and ground-based systems requirements. The Planning Working Group was established to manage the program if and when it won approval. Finally, the Concept Development Working Group was assigned the job of presenting scientific and economic justification to Congress for approval of the program. This last group would also serve to coordinate the efforts of the other working groups.

In Phase C of the program, detailed engineering blueprints for computer hardware and software, living quarters, scientific and manufacturing facilities, and energy and life-support systems are to be prepared. These preparations will continue until a critical design review is conducted, at which time the design will be finalized. Phase D is the spacecraft development phase, during which contracts are awarded for the construction, outfitting, and testing of the space station components. Phase E calls for the establishment of a permanent manned presence by 1995, and for the station to be fully operational by 1997.

Knowledge Gained

The lengthy development process of the U.S. Space Station *Freedom* has produced a variety of technical, political, and administrative advances in space program formulation. It became apparent early in the development process that the form of a complex spacecraft such as the space station should follow its function. The technological capability to design an advanced space station facility developed in the United States in the late 1960's and early 1970's. This capability preceded a careful and complete consideration of the applications of such a facility. A space station could be built, but for what purpose?

The lack of a clearly defined set of goals during the last two decades led to unnecessary false starts, delays, and redundancy in effort for the space station program. Although Phase A, the concept definition phase of the program, had begun in 1982, as late as mid-1983 the DOD stated that it saw no need for a manned space station. This view was spurred by the DOD's concerns about diversifying its space defense strategy as opposed to relying on the possibly vulnerable space station. In November of 1983, the views of the DOD were echoed by the National Research Council, which saw no pressing scientific justification for a manned space platform until after the turn of the century. A series of detailed applications studies were undertaken by members of the Space Station Task Force to address these reservations. The results led to modifications in the basic design and overall scope of the space station mission.

The needs of the scientific community and the DOD differ significantly. Defense needs call for spacecraft in high-altitude orbits that are less vulnerable to attack from the ground. The orbit should be polar as opposed to near-equatorial so that targeted regions of Earth's surface would be more frequently and exclusively accessible (for more effective military surveillance). Scientific payloads are best placed in lower-altitude, equatorial orbits, from which frequent communication of instrument data and spacecraft telemetry to ground stations is possible. These diverse requirements needed to be addressed if the space station program was to gain broad-based support outside NASA.

The decision by NASA in the early 1970's to make the space shuttle the sole launch vehicle for major payloads strongly affected the development of the space station. The shuttle is limited in the size—and, more important, in the weight—of individual components that it can deliver into orbit (the weight limit is approximately 9,000 kilograms). The Saturn launch vehicles used in the Apollo program are capable of lifting payloads many times heavier than the payload capacity of the shuttle.

Safety of the station crew members has been an important consideration in many aspects of space station planning and design. The shocking explosion of the space shuttle *Challenger* on January 26, 1986, underscored the importance of administrative and technical planning for all extended manned spaceflight. The *Challenger* accident grounded the shuttle fleet for more than two and one-half years. It became painfully clear that the shuttle could not be an absolutely dependable rescue vehicle for the space station crew.

Context

The second major report of the Space Station Task Force, a report which addressed U.S. Space Station uses, was produced in April of 1986. It outlined more than three hundred possible missions and payloads. Included in these considerations were commercial applications, military missions, technology development, and terrestrial and space science.

The design plan for the space station has evolved into a dual-keel configuration. In this configuration, two keels 110 meters in length are connected at each end by transverse booms 45 meters long. A central boom crosses the keels and is 153 meters in length. The central boom will carry the crew habitat, laboratory, and logistics modules. The upper and lower transverse booms will carry astronomical and terrestrial study instruments respectively. This basic design was adopted on May 14, 1986.

To satisfy the need for a polar orbit for military payloads, and for scientific and research and development payloads that must be isolated from the disturbances produced by crew movements, a number of free-flying platforms are planned. These platforms will be launched into orbits parallel to the station or into polar orbits (on separate shuttle flights). The platforms would be serviced by shuttle visits and could be docked with the space station for long or complicated repairs. These "free-flyers" provide an extremely versatile component to space station operation.

The grounding of the shuttle fleet following the *Challenger* disaster pointed to the need for a vehicle in which crew members could return to Earth in emergency situations. Although definite plans for an escape vehicle have not been formulated, one suggestion is to refit spare Apollo command modules for that purpose. Such a retrofit would provide a timely, workable, and inexpensive solution to the problem of crew safety.

These design decisions and changes address shortcomings in early space station planning. Yet serious technical problems have surfaced as a result of the overall direction taken by the U.S. manned space program from its first missions. U.S. manned spaceflight in the 1980's has consisted of short, single-payload missions. As a result, Americans have woefully inadequate experience and technical data on long-term spaceflight. This problem has been made all the worse by overdependence on the shuttle, with its technical and safety problems, and the dismantling of rocket launch vehicle manufacturing facilities in the United States since the mid-1970's. During this period, the Soviet Union has pushed forward in manned space research with the launching of the Mir space station. Although modest compared to the planned U.S. Space Station, Mir has been a tremendous success, setting numerous manned spaceflight records. Clearly, the Soviet Union has won the "space station race."

The development, deployment, and operation of the space station will dominate the U.S. manned space program well into the twenty-first century. The ultimate success of the program, however, is not assured. Major space programs have always been prey to funding cuts—as well as delays and pressures as a result of the political climate. If the space station is to become a reality, it will require a firm and steadfast commitment to the program from the president and from the Congress.

Bibliography

Bekey, Ivan, and Daniel Herman, eds. *Space Stations and Space Platforms: Concepts, Design, Infrastructure, and Uses*. New York: American Institute of Astronautics and Aeronautics, 1985. This book outlines the history of the development of a permanent space habitat and presents current thinking on the relationship between space platforms, the space station, and the overall space program. Included are reviews of economic, military, and industrial uses of space platforms. Suitable for advanced high school and college reading levels.

Boston, Penelope J. *The Case for Mars*. San Diego: Univelt, 1984. A monograph outlining the political, sociological, and economic reasons for mounting a manned expedition to Mars. The space station plays a major role in most programs for the exploration of Mars. Although this book is somewhat one-sided, it does present its case convincingly. Includes many photographs and artists' conceptions of space stations and manned spacecraft for interplanetary travel. Written for general audiences.

Braun, Wernher von. "Crossing the Last Frontier." *Collier's* 129 (March 22, 1952):

24-29. This article was the first to give national exposure to the concept of a manned space station. In addition to its historical importance, the article gives an early yet complete account of the design, building, and operation of such a station. The applications outlined here are largely the same as those listed in modern space station studies.

Froehlich, Walter. *Space Station: The Next Logical Step*. NASA EP-213. Washington, D.C.: Government Printing Office, 1984. This booklet provides a brief introduction to the U.S. Space Station program for the layman. It outlines the program's origin, organization, and goals in nontechnical language. The work is illustrated with color photographs from Apollo and space shuttle missions, as well as artists' conceptions of proposed space station designs. Suitable for general audiences.

Hargrove, Eugene C., ed. *Beyond Spaceship Earth: Environmental Ethics and the Solar System*. San Francisco: Sierra Club Books, 1987. A popular exposition of the social, commercial, environmental, and even theological aspects of a permanent manned presence in space. Topics are far-reaching, including the military implications of space colonization, the effect of space habitations on artistic endeavors, and possible interaction with extraterrestrial life. This book is highly recommended. It is suitable for general readership and would make an excellent supplement to more advanced references.

O'Leary, Brian. *The Fertile Stars: Man's Look to Space as the New Source of Food and Energy*. New York: Dodd, Mead and Co., 1981. This book offers ideas on the economical and social potential of space exploration. The vital role played by the space station is addressed briefly. Of particular interest here is the use of space resources for energy production. Suitable for all audiences.

Simpson, T. R. *The Space Station: An Idea Whose Time Has Come*. New York: IEEE Press, 1985. A collection of articles on all aspects of space station development, this volume includes reviews of the history and justification of space station concepts. Also included are chapters on current designs and long-term potential of space station programs. Contains numerous line drawings and artists' conceptions of historical and modern space station designs. Suitable for general audiences.

U.S. Congress. Office of Technology Assessment. *Civilian Space Stations and the U.S. Future in Space*. OTA-STI-241. Washington, D.C.: Government Printing Office, 1984. This volume contains published proceedings from several workshops on space station development sponsored by the U.S. Congress. It is designed to be a reference source for those interested in specific technical or administrative information on space station program planning and management. Suitable for the advanced high school or college-level audience.

Chris Godfrey

Cross-References

The Apollo Program, 28; The Apollo-Soyuz Test Project, 132; Astronauts and the U.S. Astronaut Program, 154; Biological Effects of Space Travel on Humans, 188; The European Space Agency, 372; Langley Research Center, 722; Marshall Space Flight Center, 908; The Mir Space Station, 1025; The National Aeronautics and Space Administration, 1032; The Skylab Program, 1285; The U.S. Space Shuttle, 1626; The Design and Uses of the U.S. Space Station, 1828; International Contributions to the U.S. Space Station, 1843; Living and Working in the U.S. Space Station, 1850; Modules and Nodes of the U.S. Space Station, 1857; The Spacelab Program, 1884.

INTERNATIONAL CONTRIBUTIONS TO THE U.S. SPACE STATION

Date: Beginning May 20, 1982
Type of program: Manned space station
Countries: The United States, Japan, Canada, and the ESA nations

The United States' space station Freedom *has been designed to be a permanently manned orbiting space platform. The station is planned as an international facility, with various experimental modules built by the United States, Japan, and member nations of the European Space Agency.*

Principal personages

RONALD REAGAN, the U.S. president who directed NASA to develop the U.S. Space Station
JAMES BEGGS, NASA Administrator, 1981 to 1986
JAMES C. FLETCHER, NASA Administrator, beginning 1986
ANDREW J. STOFAN, NASA Associate Administrator for the Space Station, beginning 1986

Summary of the Program

In January, 1984, in his State of the Union address, President Ronald Reagan directed the National Aeronautics and Space Administration (NASA) to build a manned space station that would be operational within a decade. The goals of the program immediately outlined included an emphasis on international cooperation on the development of the peaceful uses of space. To this end, NASA Administrator James Beggs was asked to enlist and encourage the cooperation and participation of Canada, Japan, and the European Space Agency (ESA) nations in the development and implementation of the Space Station Program. Beggs offered the following list of space station capabilities and functions to potential partners: a launching platform for future deep space missions; a servicing facility which would repair malfunctioning communications and scientific Earth satellites; an international space laboratory for the development and study of new industrial, scientific, and medical technologies; an assembly facility for constructing even larger structures in orbit; a microgravity manufacturing facility; and permanent astronomical and terrestrial observatories which would provide data on space environments and Earth respectively.

The development of the Space Station Program, like all large projects at NASA, would be effected in various phases. During Phase A, the concept phase, the basic objectives of the program are outlined along with designs of the hardware necessary to complete those objectives. Phase A officially began with the creation by NASA of the Space Station Task Force on May 20, 1982. The second phase, Phase B, is the definition phase, during which preliminary designs are proposed and technical data are collected. Phase B began on April 19, 1985, and lasted for two years, after which a specific design was chosen as the one best suited to fulfill mission requirements. Contractors were then chosen to participate in Phase C, the detailed design phase. Phase C, begun in late 1987, involves the production of plans and blueprints for mechanical, electrical, and computer systems required for the basic space station design.

Final decisions on system configuration are made during the Critical Design Review. The development phase, Phase D, involves the awarding of major contracts for the construction of space station components, the training of technicians to assemble and operate the ground-support systems, and the selection and training of crew members for the space station. The final development phase is the operations phase, Phase E. An operational station was scheduled to be in orbit by 1993, with permanent manning to begin two years later.

The station would be placed in low Earth orbit, at an altitude of 460 kilometers. The orbit would be inclined at an angle of 28 degrees to Earth's equator. A two-man crew would occupy a station composed of five modular sections by the end of 1993. By 1997, the station would be fully operational, with a crew of eight occupying as many as fifteen modules. In addition to the main space station structure, two free-flying unmanned platforms would be launched into Earth orbit. One free-flyer would orbit in parallel with the station and would carry instruments that would monitor the activities of the station crew. The other would follow a polar orbit to facilitate studies of Earth's atmosphere.

The basic design of the station developed along two different routes. One design is known as the "tower," or reference configuration, and the other design is known as the "dual-keel," or baseline configuration.

The reference configuration consists of a 122-meter-long tower, one end of which would always point toward Earth. The tower end closest to Earth would carry instruments for terrestrial observation and research. The center section would serve as the anchor point for a solar panel array for the generation of electrical power. The upper end of the tower would carry astronomical instruments. Docking facilities for the space shuttle orbiter, together with scientific and manufacturing laboratories and living quarters for the station crew, would be located well away from the bulky power-generating systems. One major advantage of the reference configuration is its inherent gravitational and structural stability. The addition of crew modules or instrument platforms is easily accomplished in this design. The tower design, as originally developed by Grumman Aerospace Corporation, was adopted as the offical space station design after an initial three-year (Phase A) study.

In October, 1985, the tower configuration design was withdrawn, and in May, 1986, it was replaced by the baseline configuration. This concept was developed primarily by Lockheed and McDonnell Douglas. It offers as a major advantage a more nearly gravity-free environment needed for delicate manufacturing processes and scientific experimentation, activities which are not possible with the tower configuration. The baseline station consists of two vertical keels 110 meters long, connected by horizontal booms (each with a length of 44 meters). The experimental laboratories and modules for manufacturing and crew living quarters would be carried on a 150-meter-long central boom. The upper and lower horizontal booms would carry astronomical and terrestrial scientific apparatus, and the ends of the central boom would serve as supports for the power-generating system.

The research and crew modules would be arranged in the form of a polygon, so that any one module could be closed without affecting the use of others. This capability was considered by many to be a necessary safety feature. To test the effectiveness of safety measures, and to facilitate the assembly of the station, the first three to five years of station operation would be "man-tended" rather than permanently manned.

Assembly of the baseline configuration was scheduled to begin as early as 1993 and would require at least fourteen shuttle flights for completion. Permanently manned operations would begin as early as 1996. The assembly process would take place in orbit at an altitude of 400 kilometers. From there, the completed station would be boosted to an operating altitude of 460 kilometers.

Two additional shuttle flights would be required to place into orbit two free-flying space platforms. These were envisioned as instrument platforms that could be serviced directly by the space shuttle or taken to the space station for more extensive work. The platforms are necessary because the orbital path of the space station would be unsuited for some purposes, such as weather observation and forecasting and military surveillance.

The need for separate free-flying platforms, the modular design of the station as a whole, and the almost prohibitive costs of development, testing, and deployment of the space station and its components led NASA to seek international sponsorship of the program in 1983. A major partnership, which includes the United States, Japan, Canada, and the ESA nations, has resulted.

NASA and ESA reached agreement on the program involvement of ESA in August, 1986. The contribution of ESA to the program would require an expenditure of $2.1 billion through 1995. The specific hardware developed by ESA includes a pressurized laboratory module to be permanently attached to the baseline station and a free-flying platform to be placed in polar orbit (an orbital path which passes over the geographic poles rather than remaining near the equator). In addition, it was agreed that NASA and ESA would collaborate on the development of a pressurized free-flying module that could be detached from the baseline station. This detachable module would then be available to the international community for experiments requiring particular orbits or especially stable microgravity environments and could be used as a standard station laboratory module when these special conditions were not required. The inclusion of the detachable free-flyer is an attempt to satisfy the various and sometimes conflicting needs and wishes of the international scientific community that would eventually utilize the station.

Canada, by an agreement signed with NASA in April, 1985, would fund the program in the amount of $450 million. As part of this arrangement, Canada would develop a mobile module designed for in-orbit construction and equipment servicing that incorporates necessary tools, module controls, and a remote-controlled manipulator arm that can handle the tasks of station assembly and maintenance. The mobile servicing device would have the capability to move along the central transverse boom to reach instruments of equipment to be serviced.

Japan would spend $1.1 billion to outfit a multipurpose Japanese Experiment Module (JEM). The design for the JEM includes an instrument platform to be serviced by a remote manipulator arm (perhaps identical to that being developed by Canada). The module itself would be supplied by ESA. Taken together, the laboratory modules developed by Japan, the ESA nations, and the United States were designed to offer a complete range of experimental, research, and commercial capabilities, with little or no overlap.

Knowledge Gained

International agreements are generally difficult to reach, and agreements concerning the development, deployment, and use of the space station have been no exception. Originally the station was to have been a truly international facility, with all laboratory and manufacturing modules available for use by all countries involved. In February of 1987, however, NASA issued statements that the United States would require 50 percent use of the Japanese and ESA's modules and that the U.S. module would not be available for use by other countries. In addition, it was stated that all use of the station would be supervised by the United States. The primary reason for this change was a decision on the part of the U.S. Department of Defense to claim some space station resources for military research and development. This announcement drew swift and strong protests from ESA, Japan, and Canada.

The single largest barrier to the Space Station Program is cost. The originally estimated budget for the entire program was $8 billion in 1984. In 1988, the total bill was estimated at $22 billion, not including operating costs of approximately $1 billion per year and not incorporating the expense of design changes.

The tragic explosion of the U.S. space shuttle *Challenger* in 1986 resulted in a safety review of all NASA programs. Life-threatening situations on the space station were originally to be handled by providing a module equipped with life-support, power, and communications systems which could be sealed from the rest of the station. In an emergency, the crew could take refuge in this module until a shuttle could reach the station and effect a rescue. A space shuttle orbiter and launch vehicle would be kept in a state of preparation for this purpose. Yet the loss of the *Challenger* and thirty-month grounding of the shuttle fleet have shown that the shuttle is less than 100 percent reliable. The solution agreed upon was to equip the space station with a reentry vehicle capable of transporting the crew back to Earth if necessary. The cost of this "lifeboat" would be approximately $1 billion.

Several other important design decisions were made at the beginning of Phase C of the Space Station Program. To minimize vibrational disturbances, the station would drift downward approximately 60 kilometers before being reboosted to the nominal orbit of 460 kilometers. The reboosts would occur every three months. The space station power system would be a combination of photovoltaic solar collectors, which generate electricity directly, and a heat engine, in which the Sun's rays would heat a working fluid which would in turn operate a turbine to generate electricity. It has also been decided to use expendable launch vehicles to launch some of the space station component payloads. Although that would make station assembly more complex, it would also ease payload size limitations (currently payloads are limited by the size of the shuttle cargo bay) and give more flexibility to the crowded shuttle launch schedule.

Context

Part of NASA's mission since its inception in 1958 has been to cooperate with other nations in the peaceful use of space. There are many advantages to international participation in space exploration—including the sharing of scientific and technical expertise, the sharing of expense, the wider range of activity, the prevention of duplication of effort, and the social and cultural ties that develop from such partnerships.

The largest international scientific collaboration in history, prior to the space station, was Spacelab. The member nations of the ESA designed, built, and operated Spacelab, an advanced orbiting laboratory for scientific and industrial research. Ulf Merbold, a West German physicist with ESA, became the first foreigner to be a crew member of an American spacecraft when Spacelab was launched by the space shuttle in 1983. Spacelab was a marvelous demonstration of the capabilities for which the space shuttle was originally designed and built.

After the *Challenger* disaster, international cooperation developed quickly into a healthy and fortuitous competition. The shuttle fleet was grounded for more than two years, and the United States was without adequate satellite payload launch capabilities. ESA's unmanned Ariane launcher took over the profitable business of launching satellites for military and private communications.

Spacelab and an earlier U.S. program known as Skylab both pointed to the scientific and economic need for a permanent equipment platform in Earth orbit. The U.S. Space Station was planned to allow larger and more massive equipment to be used in space for longer experiments. The equipment will be set in place, tended, and repaired by crew members if necessary. For these reasons, the space station is the next logical step for the U.S. space program.

The first need of the international community to be addressed by the space station is telecommunications. In the late 1980's, there were more than eighty operational communications satellites in orbit, with several being added each year. With the emergence of Third World nations into the age of satellite communications the demand for these services should result in a 250 percent increase in the number of such satellites by the year 2000. Satellites allow connection to regions that are geographically isolated or inaccessible. Throughout the United States and Europe, and in major cities worldwide, obsolete telephone equipment is being replaced in part by new equipment utilizing communications satellites. These new telecommunications systems offer new capabilities for data as well as voice transmission.

The potential economic returns on the commercial exploitation of space are tremendous. The vacuum and microgravity laboratory facilities available on the space station will be ideal for production of ultrapure metal alloys, medicines, and crystalline substances. Yet the potential profitability means that competition for this kind of production will be severe. The Soviet Union has an edge in the space station race, having achieved much success with the Salyut and Mir space stations. The United States, Europe, Japan, and Canada are in jeopardy of being locked out of these high-technology markets. The space station *Freedom* is an international effort to ensure that these nations remain competitive into the twenty-first century.

Bibliography

Bekey, Ivan, and Daniel Herman, eds. *Space Stations and Space Platforms: Concepts, Design, Infrastructure, and Uses*. Vol. 99 in *Progress in Astronautics and Aeronautics*. New York: American Institute of Aeronautics and Astronautics, 1985. This book traces the development of a permanent space habitat and describes the relationship between space platforms, the space station, and the overall space program. Summarizes economic, military, and industrial uses of space platforms. Suitable for advanced high school and college reading levels.

Boston, Penelope J., ed. *The Case for Mars*. Washington, D.C.: American Astronomical Society, 1984. A monograph outlining the political, sociological, and economic reasons for mounting a manned expedition to Mars. The space station plays a major role in most programs for the exploration of Mars. Although this book is somewhat one-sided, it does present its case convincingly. Includes many photographs and artists' conceptions of space stations and manned spacecraft for interplanetary travel.

Braun, Wernher von. "Crossing the Last Frontier." *Collier's* 129 (March 22, 1952): 24-29. This article was the first to give national exposure to the concept of a manned space station. In addition to its historical importance, the article gives an early yet complete account of the design, building, and operation of such a station.

Froehlich, Walter. *Space Station: The Next Logical Step*. NASA EP-213. Washington, D.C.: Government Printing Office, 1984. Provides a brief introduction to the U.S. Space Station Program for the lay reader. Outlines the program's origin, organization, and goals in nontechnical language. Illustrated with color prints from Apollo and space shuttle missions, as well as artists' conceptions of proposed space station designs.

Hargrove, Eugene C., ed. *Beyond Spaceship Earth: Environmental Ethics and the Solar System*. San Francisco: Sierra Club Books, 1987. A popular exposition of the social, commercial, environmental, and even theological aspects of a permanent manned presence in space. Topics are far-ranging, including the military implications of space colonization and the possible interaction with extraterrestrial life. This book is highly recommended. It is suitable for a general readership and would make an excellent supplement to more advanced references.

O'Leary, Brian. *The Fertile Stars: Man's Look to Space as the New Source of Food and Energy*. New York: Dodd, Mead and Co., 1981. This book offers ideas on the economical and social potential of space exploration. The vital role played by the space station is addressed briefly. Of particular interest here is the use of space resources for energy production.

Simpson, T. R., ed. *The Space Station: An Idea Whose Time Has Come*. New York: IEEE Press, 1985. A collection of articles on all aspects of space station development, this volume includes reviews of the history and justification of space station concepts. Discusses space station designs and the long-term potential of space station programs. Well illustrated.

U.S. Congress. Office of Technology Assessment. *Civilian Space Stations and the U.S. Future in Space*. OTA-STI-241. Washington, D.C.: Government Printing Office, 1984. This volume includes the published summaries of the work of several groups organized to develop space station concepts. Designed for those interested in specific technical and administrative details concerning the U.S. Space Station Program.

Chris Godfrey

Cross-References

Astronauts and the U.S. Astronaut Program, 154; Biological Effects of Space Travel on Humans, 188; The European Space Agency, 372; The Japanese Space Program, 655; Langley Research Center, 722; Marshall Space Flight Center, 908; The Mir Space Station, 1025; The National Aeronautics and Space Administration, 1032; The Skylab Program, 1285; The U.S. Space Shuttle, 1626; Space Shuttle Mission 25: *Challenger*, 1813; The Design and Uses of the U.S. Space Station, 1828; The Development of the U.S. Space Station, 1835; Living and Working in the U.S. Space Station, 1850; Modules and Nodes of the U.S. Space Station, 1857; The Spacelab Program, 1884.

LIVING AND WORKING IN THE U.S. SPACE STATION

Date: Beginning May 20, 1982
Type of program: Manned space station
Country: The United States, Japan, Canada, and the ESA nations

The development of a space station in which humans can live and work safely, comfortably, and efficiently for long periods is the principal challenge for the U.S. space program.

Principal personages
RONALD REAGAN, the U.S. president who directed the National Aeronautics and Space Administration to develop the U.S. Space Station
JAMES BEGGS and
JAMES C. FLETCHER, NASA Administrators
ANDREW J. STOFAN, NASA Associate Administrator for the space station

Summary of the Program

The idea of humans traveling through space, living and working in a permanent artificial environment that is safe and comfortable, was once considered the province of science-fiction writers. In the twenty-first century, however, permanent human space colonies may become a reality.

The National Aeronautics and Space Administration (NASA) has long considered the construction of a permanently manned space station. Early U.S. and Soviet missions proved that humans could survive and perform in spacecraft for short periods in extremely uncomfortable circumstances. It was obvious, however, that cumbersome spacesuits, food in squeeze tubes, and a lack of hygiene facilities would not do for long-term missions. These conditions had to be addressed before humans could be expected to live and work in space for long periods and remain mentally and physically healthy.

NASA's Skylab program in the 1970's was a step in that direction. Among other things, NASA hoped to show that humans could live and work safely and comfortably in space for extended periods. The biological data collected by astronauts and by equipment on the three manned Skylab missions provided a wealth of information that NASA experts could apply to plans for a permanently manned space station.

In a "shirt-sleeves environment," Skylab crews conducted dozens of medical experiments on human adaptability to microgravity. They proved that humans could live in space for extended periods (the longest Skylab mission lasted eighty-four days, eleven hours) and could perform a wide range of tasks in the spacecraft. The insights gained into the physical and psychological needs of humans in a microgravity environment were invaluable.

Skylab was judged a success in all areas, and by 1982 NASA was ready to push ahead with the development of a manned space station. Major aerospace industries contracted with NASA to study every aspect of a space station, including crew safety and comfort. The following year, studies showed that a space station design of component parts would best meet the proposed program's needs.

At that time, NASA formed the Concept Development Group to integrate the results of the studies and produce a basic set of architectural concepts on which a space station design could be based. The group produced four versions of a space station blueprint so that the best cost and schedule estimates could be determined.

The official signal that the U.S. Space Station program was under way took place on January 25, 1984, when the newly reelected president, Ronald Reagan, called for NASA to develop, launch, and man a permanent space station by 1994. The space station, he said, would be called "Freedom."

Other nations have been invited to participate in the space station program. The United States' share of the project is to build the station's framework and to develop two pressurized station modules that will include crew quarters and a research laboratory. The United States will also provide two logistics modules for replenishment of the station's consumables.

Plans call for a dual keel craft, approximately 100 by 90 meters, that can be placed into a low Earth orbit. Broken into component parts that can fit into the space shuttle's cargo bay, the station will be ferried into position about 400 kilometers above Earth. Crews of six to eight will rotate every ninety days.

The space station is designed to contain a proper mix of humans and machines. Humans will provide creativity, flexibility, and the ability to adjust to the unforeseen. Machines will provide reliability and precision in the performance of routine or dangerous tasks.

The station will be multifunctional, serving as a laboratory for scientific experiments, a base from which to explore the universe, a factory in which to develop new processes and manufacture new materials, a facility for the assembly of antennae and other large structures, and a satellite servicing, retrieving, and refueling center.

When contracts were let in 1987, Grumman Aerospace was assigned the responsibility of finding ways to make the space station habitable. Grumman engineers have studied factors such as command and control systems, sanitation, environmental control, airflow, exercise, nutrition, crew efficiency, and crew morale.

For example, to combat the effects of spacesickness and improve the morale of free-floating crew members, the modules will have a clearly defined ceiling and floor. Work and safety paths will be short and simple. Areas near the walls, ceilings, and floors will be used for human traffic. Handholds, foot restraints, and push-off areas will be incorporated into the space station's architecture, and fully adjustable body restraints will be used to anchor crew members to their workstations. Many of the routine housekeeping activities will be performed by computers.

Work activities will include servicing customer projects, spacewalks, docking with the shuttle, and launching and refurbishing satellites. The normal workweek will consist of six days on and one day off. A typical day will comprise eight to ten hours of work with a lunch break, eight hours of sleep, and four to six hours of free time.

A payload specialist or station specialist will be able to relax in the lounge or in the exercise area. The latter will be equipped with radio and television to help relieve boredom during the long hours of exercise required to offset the effects of microgravity. The exercise area will be situated away from the crew quarters to protect the quiet and privacy of that area.

Each of the crew members will have a "room" containing about 4.25 cubic meters of space—as much space as there is in a large closet—with a wall-mounted sleeping bag; an audiovisual entertainment center; storage for clothing, books, and personal items; a desk; and a bulletin board. Each room will have separate lighting, ventilation, and temperature controls, and wall and room configurations will be rearrangeable. Throughout the living and working areas, attractive colors and textures will make the crew feel at home.

In addition to crew quarters, there will be a health management facility complete with pharmaceuticals, physical examination equipment, a diagnostic imaging system, and an infirmary. It will also include a laboratory to analyze routine respiratory, cardiovascular, microbiology, immunology, hematology, and urine tests.

Because there will be no room for extra or disposable clothes, a laundry will be located near the galley. The galley design will feature a refrigerator and a microwave oven, which will allow crew members to prepare a wider variety of foods than ever before. The crew will clean up with the help of a dishwasher and trash compactor.

Hygiene will be handled with a combined toilet/shower. Drinking water will be processed through a closed-loop system, and a separate system will process shower, hand washing, and laundry water.

Designers have speculated that disappearing walls, inflatable furniture, and receding tables will eventually be used to provide a more pleasing environment. The ultimate goal is to make living and working in space comfortable and appealing as well as safe and productive.

Knowledge Gained

Early in the U.S. space program, every effort was made to learn as much as possible about the effects of the space environment on humans. Small mammals and primates were launched in spacecraft, and manned balloon experiments were conducted to study the effects of space travel. Still, many questions remained unanswered until the manned missions of the 1960's, which proved that humans could safely travel in space and return to Earth with few ill effects. It was not until the Skylab missions, however, that American scientists had the chance to collect data on the effects of long-term space travel.

Living conditions for the astronauts on Skylab were much freer and more comfortable than the conditions endured by their predecessors. The crew was not constrained by awkward spacesuits and could float freely around the roomy cabin, and food and hygiene arrangements were greatly improved. In general, the crew enjoyed good health, but extensive medical monitoring showed some important physiological changes.

Skylab crews occupied the craft for more than 171 days. The physiological and psychological data gained from the missions were essential to scientists' plans for a more ambitious, permanently manned space station. It was noted that the longer crew members stayed in space, the longer it took for them to recover from the effects of weightlessness. Postflight examinations revealed that microgravity had an impact on every facet of the motor system, from muscle mass to motor control. Calf muscle strength dissipated, and astronauts experienced a marked inability to stand up straight after a flight. The mineral density of bones decreased, and heart rates tended to increase.

Faces flattened and cheeks rose to give the astronauts a rounded appearance. Their spines lengthened and they temporarily grew taller in space. They complained of having too much routine, dull work. It appeared that the changes the crews experienced were significant and should be addressed, but it also seemed that the effects disappeared once the astronauts returned to Earth.

It was found that in a microgravity environment, sinuses congest, blood volume is reduced, hormone levels change, and the muscles and heart shrink. Based on these findings, space medicine experts determined space motion sickness, cardiovascular deconditioning, red blood cell loss, and bone mineral loss to be of greatest concern.

Information gained through Skylab was applied to the space shuttle program, which in turn increased scientists' understanding of how humans respond to life in space. In designing the space station, engineers and technicians have tried to plan an environment for work and play that will be as similar as possible to normal settings on Earth.

Context

A permanent station in space is perceived by NASA as the next logical step in an orderly progression of manned spaceflight activities. Since the era of the manned Mercury, Gemini, and Apollo missions, NASA planners have prepared for the day when a manned space station would be launched. The idea received new impetus from the successful development of the space shuttle. The two projects seemed to complement each other: The shuttle would serve as the reliable method of transport to the station, a permanently manned base where materials processing, satellite servicing, and scientific research could be conducted in a microgravity environment.

The Skylab program was a step toward the implementation of such a space station. Skylab, a temporarily manned station, offered many opportunities for learning about the effects of space on humans over the long term. Skylab's success and the wealth of data that the mission generated inspired NASA scientists and technicians to press forward in developing a more sophisticated station.

In 1982, NASA issued a series of contracts to several aerospace firms in the

United States. Their task was to define the basic needs and architecture of a space station. Data gleaned from Skylab and other manned programs were to be incorporated into the designs. Later, NASA would choose one contractor to develop each of the work packages.

Governmental support seemed enthusiastic when, in 1984, President Reagan called for the building and manning of a space station by 1994. Unfortunately, an enormous federal deficit and an unforeseen disaster threatened the foundations of the U.S. manned space program and the ambitious plans for an international space station.

On January 28, 1986, the explosion of the space shuttle *Challenger* and the death of the seven crew members on board left the American people and the world grieved and angry. In the wake of the devastating accident, questions and issues were raised and answers received that undermined American confidence in the federal government, NASA, contractors, and further manned space programs in general. Discouraged and disillusioned, Americans at all levels began to say that the cost of a manned space program was too high a price to pay in terms of human life and economic resources. The ambitious and expensive plans for an international space station that would depend on a reliable space shuttle fell under immediate fire. Even the president's enthusiasm seemed to wane.

In April, 1987, amid investigations into space contractors and sharply rising cost estimates, President Reagan ordered NASA to scale back the space station program dramatically. Earlier that year, Congress had already directed NASA to adapt its space station design to a drastically shrinking budget.

NASA persevered and announced a new plan to develop and deploy the space station in two phases. The dual keel design was modified, the satellite servicing capability was omitted, and one of two solar power systems was eliminated. Phase 1, it was estimated, would cost about $12.2 billion, a significant increase over the original 1984 estimate of $8 billion for the entire program.

In December, 1987, NASA selected four industry teams to build the space station under contracts valued at $5 billion. Boeing Aerospace, McDonnell Douglas, Rocketdyne Division of Rockwell International, and General Electric's Astrospace Division were chosen to build various components of the modified space station. In theory, this set in motion the largest U.S. space program ever funded, but budgets for the contracts had not been approved, and even tighter funding restrictions were expected in the coming years.

In February, 1988, negotiations with the international partners concluded amid unsettled questions on military use and technology. By September, the European Space Agency (ESA), Japan, and Canada had signed an intergovernmental agreement among the cooperating nations. ESA and Canada also signed a memorandum of agreement among the space agencies appointed to carry out the program.

Budget disputes between NASA and Congress continued. In June, the House and Senate appropriations committees approved legislation that would automatically end the space station program early in 1989 if it was not directly and quickly endorsed by the winner of the 1988 presidential election. In a budget analysis titled "The NASA Program in the 1990's and Beyond," the Congressional Budget Office noted that if the federal budget deficit impelled Congress to hold NASA's budget at the then-current $9 billion level indefinitely, space station construction could be postponed well into the twenty-first century.

With an overall program cost estimate ranging from fourteen to sixteen billion dollars and a rising deficit, some top-level officials expressed doubts about the space station program. A perception persists that the United States is perhaps not committed to carrying out the lengthy project to its finish. Some experts have said that if funding and governmental support are not forthcoming, the United States will sacrifice the tremendous economical, technological, and political benefits of a permanently manned space station. Some have even gone so far as to predict that if the project is allowed to wither, the United States will be admitting that it is dropping out as a major contender in the race to settle and utilize space.

Bibliography

Anderton, David A. *Space Station*. NASA EP-211. Washington, D.C.: Government Printing Office, 1985. A thirty-page, color booklet that explains the history of the space station program at NASA through the mid-1980's. Color photographs highlight the text. Good background information is provided in layman's terms.

Canby, Thomas Y. "Skylab." *National Geographic* 146 (October, 1974): 441-503. An excellent overview of conditions on the Skylab missions, with special emphasis on the astronaut's point of view. Many color photographs enhance the very readable text.

Froehlich, Walter. *Space Station: The Next Logical Step*. NASA EP-213. Washington, D.C.: Government Printing Office, 1985. A fifty-page booklet that discusses the design, development, and mission of the U.S. Space Station program. Contains photographs, artists' drawings, and quotes from national and international leaders and scientists.

Heppeheimer, T. A. *Colonies in Space*. Harrisburg, Pa.: Stackpole Books, 1977. The author, a planetary scientist, discusses the desirability of human colonization of space. He develops social, economic, and philosophical arguments in support of space colonization. Includes photographs, drawings, an index, and a bibliography.

National Aeronautics and Space Administration. *NASA: The First Twenty-five Years, 1958-1983*. NASA EP-182. Washington, D.C.: Government Printing Office, 1983. A chronological history of NASA and its programs. Contains information on Skylab and the space shuttle. The text is designed for teachers to use in the classroom. Many photographs, charts, and drawings are included. Two appendices list NASA launch dates and educational services.

Nicogossian, Arnauld E., and James F. Parker, Jr. *Space Physiology and Medicine*. NASA SP-447. Washington, D.C.: Government Printing Office, 1982. A general technical reference for persons engaged in or concerned with space medicine. The authors discuss the technical medical data gathered in manned space missions. There are sections on spaceflight systems, physiological adaptation to spaceflight, and health maintenance of astronauts. Includes tables, charts, and an index. Suitable for college-level readers.

Lulynne Streeter

Cross-References

The Apollo Program, 28; Astronauts and the U.S. Astronaut Program, 154; Biological Effects of Space Travel on Humans, 188; The Canadian Space Program, 222; Cosmonauts and the Soviet Cosmonaut Program, 273; The European Space Agency, 372; Food and Diet for Space Travel, 454; The Gemini Program, 487; The Japanese Space Program, 655; The Mercury Project, 940; The Mir Space Station, 1025; The National Aeronautics and Space Administration, 1032; The Salyut Space Station, 1233; The Skylab Program, 1285; The U.S. Space Shuttle, 1626; Space Shuttle Living Conditions, 1634; The Design and Uses of the U.S. Space Station, 1828; The Development of the U.S. Space Station, 1835; International Contributions to the U.S. Space Station, 1843; Modules and Nodes of the U.S. Space Station, 1857; The Spacelab Program, 1884.

MODULES AND NODES OF THE U.S. SPACE STATION

Date: Beginning May 20, 1982
Type of program: Manned space station
Countries: The United States, Japan, Canada, and the ESA nations

The U.S. Space Station Freedom *is designed to take on a permanent crew. The station's modules and nodes will be mounted on the base and linked together to make a pressurized area where the crew will work and live.*

Principal personages
RONALD REAGAN, the U.S. president who directed NASA to develop the U.S. Space Station
JAMES BEGGS, NASA Administrator, 1981 to 1986
JAMES C. FLETCHER, NASA Administrator, beginning 1986
ANDREW J. STOFAN, NASA Associate Administrator for the Space Station, beginning 1986

Summary of the Program

The U.S. space station *Freedom*'s manned base is the centerpiece of the Space Station Program. In addition to instruments mounted outside the station on the truss structure and separately orbiting platforms that look toward Earth, the Sun, or deep space, instruments and experiments will be mounted inside the station in the pressurized modules and nodes. These instruments will be used to conduct experiments in fields such as life sciences, materials processing, microgravity sciences, physics, and chemistry.

Initially, four modules will be linked together by nodes to form a pressurized area of approximately a thousand cubic meters; eight astronauts will be able to work in this shirtsleeve environment. Two of the modules will be supplied by the United States, and two will be supplied by international partners in the space station effort. All the modules and the connecting nodes will be delivered to orbit by the U.S. space shuttle.

The modules will be equipped to supply electrical power, environmental control, data handling and communications, and other support for the international, eight-person crew. The excess heat generated by people and equipment on the inside and the Sun's shining on the outside will be carried by a cooling system to radiators located outside the modules.

The United States' habitation module is scheduled to be the first module launched. The habitation module will be a pressurized accommodation area for resting and active crew members and will include facilities for health services, recreation, personal hygiene, and other daily activities. It will be 13.6 meters long and 4.45 meters in diameter. In comparison, the first U.S. space station, Skylab, was made from the upper stage of a Saturn 5 rocket and was 8.2 meters long and 6.7 meters in diameter. The habitation module will weigh approximately 19,945 kilograms with all of its equipment. It will contain crew quarters, wardrooms, the galley, exercise and recreation areas, storage units, a shower, and an area for human physiological research and medical treatment.

The laboratory module, also to be built by the United States, will be the second module launched to the station. It is designed to accommodate projects which need the lowest possible levels of gravity. Such projects include materials research and development and experiments in basic biology, physics, and chemistry. It will be the same size as the habitation module and will weigh about 31,460 kilograms when complete. Once the laboratory module is in place, the station will be able to support a visiting space shuttle crew for short periods.

The duration of experiments performed in the laboratory module will vary greatly. Some experiments, such as those that concern the effects of the space environment on the crew, will be continuous. Others may take only a few minutes, hours, or days, depending on their objectives. The time between changes of experiments (the space shuttle will periodically deliver new equipment) is called a mission increment. The mission increment is the station's primary planning interval and will last approximately six months.

Objects in Earth orbit are subject to microgravity. The movement of the crew and Earth's proximity will have slight but measurable effects on the gravity level on the space station. The low gravity required by experiments in the laboratory module will be provided by maintaining the station's center of mass in that module most of the time. The laboratory may also have special provisions for vibration isolation so as to minimize the effects of motion on the sensitive experiments. The level of gravity in the laboratory will be extremely low—one-millionth of the strength of Earth's gravity at sea level—but only in certain locations and for limited periods.

The laboratory module will house several life science, microgravity, physics, and chemistry experiments and payloads. The largest single piece of equipment will be a 1.8-meter centrifuge. Centrifugal force can simulate gravity in space. The station's centrifuge will be used to subject biological specimens, such as plants and small animals, to normal Earth gravity levels so that they can serve as experimental controls. The specimens also may be spun at slower speeds to simulate weaker gravity levels, such as that of Mars, to determine the effects of various gravity strengths on living organisms. The centrifuge might also be used to test the effects of partial gravity on physical or chemical processes, such as crystal formation or the mixing of fluids.

The Columbus module, to be supplied by the European Space Agency (ESA), will be a multipurpose laboratory module designed primarily for research in the fields of fluid physics, life sciences, and materials processing. Columbus is slightly smaller than the U.S. modules—approximately 4.2 meters in diameter and 12 meters in length—and will weigh 23,300 kilograms with its equipment. It will be constructed from four Spacelab elements. (Spacelab is an ESA-provided modular laboratory which fits into the cargo bay of the U.S. space shuttle.)

The Japanese Experiment Module (JEM), to be supplied by Japan, is a 20,800-kilogram facility measuring 4.2 meters in diameter and 10 meters in length. It will accommodate general scientific and technological research activities, including microgravity experiments. In addition, the Japanese module will provide an area, unpressurized and exposed to space, for the attachment of external payloads, and a remote manipulator arm, similar to the one used on the space shuttle, that will maneuver those payloads.

The pressure inside the modules will be maintained at Earth's sea-level pressure of 14.7 pounds per square inch. Oxygen and nitrogen will be mixed in the same proportions as those of Earth's atmosphere. Living conditions will thus be kept as safe and comfortable as possible for the crew, who may stay at the station for as long as six months at a time.

Nodes are the connectors between the modules that allow the crew to move from one module to the next and provide a buffer between the modules for isolation and safety. The nodes are 3.2 meters in diameter and have six 1.98-meter portholes so that modules and other nodes can be attached from any direction for flexibility and future growth.

There will be four nodes. One will link the ends of the U.S. laboratory module and the ESA Columbus module, and another will link the ends of the U.S. habitation module and the Japanese Experiment Module. These two nodes will also be linked together to allow passage through the center of the cluster. Once these first two nodes are in place, the station will be capable of housing a permanent crew; until then, the station will be manned only while the space shuttle is visiting it. The two other nodes will be on the opposite ends of the U.S. modules and will also be linked together. The result will be a large U-shaped system that will allow easy passage among the modules. The space shuttle will dock at a porthole on one of these outside nodes.

The nodes will be more than simple passageways. They have been designed with fairly large spaces inside where equipment can be mounted, especially equipment that does not need the constant attention of the crew. Their function as corridors, however, is not trivial; great care has been taken to design the configuration without "dead ends" where crew members could be trapped in an emergency.

Modular mounting frames, or "racks," will be used to mount and organize pieces of equipment inside the modules and nodes. Approximately one meter wide by two meters tall (exact measurements will depend on where it is installed), a rack will be able to accommodate several payloads, station systems, or storage lockers. Of the 165 racks planned for the station, about a hundred will be used for the crew's effects, subsystems, storage units, and other housekeeping equipment, leaving about sixty-five racks for user payloads. There will be four rows of racks in each module: one along the "floor," one along the "ceiling," and one along each "wall."

When equipment and payloads destined for the pressurized area of the station are delivered by the space shuttle, they will already be housed in their racks. The racks will be brought into the station by the crew and installed in the module or node.

Later, as equipment is replaced, racks of new equipment will replace the racks of outgoing equipment, which will be taken back to Earth on the shuttle.

Because ESA countries, Canada, and Japan are contributing hardware to the station, a portion of the station is reserved for these countries' payloads. The apportionment is based on each nation's level of contribution to the station as a whole. The United States is entitled to 71 percent of the station's space and resources, the European Space Agency and Japan are entitled to 13 percent each, and Canada is entitled to 3 percent. (Canada is providing hardware for the servicing of payloads mounted on the outside of the station.) These resources can be sold or bartered to other partners as desired; for example, ESA may trade away its 13 percent for one mission increment so that it might use 26 percent for another.

The United States has been allocated 46 percent of the space in both the Japanese Experiment Module and the ESA Columbus module, though this space can also be bartered or sold. In accordance with their wishes, neither ESA nor Japan has been allocated any space in the U.S. laboratory module. Their shares of their own modules are thus maximized. Only the United States and Canada, then, will use the U.S. laboratory module.

This method of sharing resources allows each partner the right to send a certain number of its own crew members to the station. In essence, then, 13 percent of the crew will be from ESA countries and 13 percent from Japan, or approximately one person each in each eight-person crew, and 3 percent will be from Canada. This right can also be bartered to allow Japan, for example, to have no crew members on one mission but two on another and to allow Canada to send one astronaut on about every fourth mission. Since the station is planned to be operational for as long as thirty years, crew and resource distributions will balance out in the long run to match the exact percentages allocated.

At various places inside the modules where work is to be performed, standardized computer terminals, or workstations, will be provided for the crew to interact with payloads, onboard computers, and ground-based computers and personnel. Each workstation will have access to the common communications and data management systems, allowing communications with Earth-based scientists who will be able to monitor onboard experiments.

Knowledge Gained

Payloads which may play a part in early space station experiments include a facility to study the growth of crystals in microgravity; machines to mix substances without the use of containers, so that extremely pure compounds can be made; chambers used to study the effects of weightlessness on plant growth; systems to study the crew, such as equipment for collecting samples of blood and urine and for obtaining data on cardiac output, lung capacity, and the ability to perform complex tasks; and equipment to study the behavior of fluids. Fluid research is particularly important. Scientists wish to learn how different fluids mix and how to measure and manipulate fluids in the low gravity of space. These studies will affect space-based materials processing, life-support systems, and propulsion systems.

A primary goal of life sciences research on the space station will be to understand the effects of microgravity on living organisms. This interest is focused in three directions: research into how gravity affects physiological processes; research into phenomena such as space adaptation syndrome and osteoporosis, which may provide insight into similar illnesses on Earth; and research into the long-term effects of weightlessness, especially negative effects, so that means to counter problems caused by microgravity can be developed.

Although considerable knowledge about the human body's adaptation to a weightless environment has been gained from Skylab and some recent shuttle experiments, much still needs to be learned about the mechanisms and limits of human adaptation to prolonged spaceflights. The development of countermeasures for the undesirable effects of microgravity is a major research goal.

Context

The facilities for life sciences research on the *Freedom* space station are designed for specific studies in space medicine and space biology. Scientists hope these studies will shed light on the effects of long-term human exposure to the low gravity and high radiation levels in space. The continuous research, which will be performed on the station's crew and on plants and animals, will also help provide answers to questions about Earth's environment and the possibilities for exploration and colonization of other worlds.

Crew members' interaction with one another and their environment will be studied to gain important information about the dynamics of living and working in an enclosed, isolated, and sometimes dangerous environment. Could a crew tolerate a three-year mission to Mars? Research performed on the space station will help to answer this and other vital questions.

Experiments on materials will help to determine the best way to create substances that cannot be created on Earth. Ultrapure drugs can be manufactured and brought back for use on Earth; high-speed computer chips made from large, perfectly formed crystals grown in space might lead to breakthroughs in computers.

Earth and ocean observations made from orbit provide vast amounts of information on Earth's environment and its resources. There is a great need for continuously gathered, worldwide, remotely sensed data on weather, oceanographic, and navigational hazards to ocean-going vessels. Industries such as shipping, fishing, and oil and gas exploration depend on the accuracy of such data. Similarly, land data are required by agricultural firms, geologists, urban land use planners, and environmentalists. Data about the atmosphere will help scientists to study the effects of the depletion of the ozone layer; to understand the "greenhouse effect," or the warming of Earth's climate; and to make more accurate weather forecasts.

Bibliography

Bekey, Ivan, and Daniel Herman, eds. *Progress in Astronautics and Aeronautics.*

Vol. 99, *Space Stations and Space Platforms: Concepts, Design, Infrastructure, and Uses*. New York: American Institute of Aeronautics and Astronautics, 1985. This book outlines the history of the development of a permanent space habitat and presents current thinking on the relationship between space platforms, the U.S. Space Station, and the entire U.S. space program. Included are reviews of economic, military, and industrial uses of space platforms. Suitable for advanced high school and college-level readers.

Boston, Penelope J., ed. *The Case for Mars*. San Diego: Univelt, 1984. A monograph outlining the political, sociological, and economic reasons for mounting a manned expedition to Mars. The *Freedom* space station plays a major role in most proposed programs for the exploration of Mars. Although this book is somewhat one-sided, it presents its case convincingly. Includes many photographs and artists' conceptions of space stations and manned spacecraft for interplanetary travel. Written for general audiences.

Braun, Wernher von. "Crossing the Last Frontier." *Collier's* 129 (March 22, 1952): 24-29. This article was the first to give national exposure to the concept of a manned space station. It provides an early yet complete account of the design, building, and operation of such a station. The applications outlined here are largely the same as those listed in modern space station studies. Suitable for general audiences.

Froehlich, Walter. *Space Station: The Next Logical Step*. NASA EP-213. Washington, D.C.: Government Printing Office, 1984. This booklet provides a brief introduction to the U.S. Space Station Program for the layperson. It outlines the program's origins, organization, and goals in nontechnical language. The work is illustrated with color photographs returned from Apollo and space shuttle missions and with artists' conceptions of proposed space station designs. Suitable for general audiences.

Hargrove, Eugene C., ed. *Beyond Spaceship Earth: Environmental Ethics and the Solar System*. San Francisco: Sierra Club Books, 1987. A popular exposition of the social, commercial, environmental, and even the theological aspects of a permanent manned presence in space. Topics are far-ranging, including the military implications of space colonization and the possibility of interaction with extraterrestrial life. This book is highly recommended. It is suitable for a general readership and would make an excellent supplement to more advanced references.

O'Leary, Brian. *The Fertile Stars: Man's Look to Space as the New Source of Food and Energy*. New York: Dodd, Mead and Co., 1981. This book discusses the economic and social implications of space exploration. The vital role played by the U.S. Space Station is addressed briefly. The work focuses on the use of space resources for energy production. Suitable for all audiences.

Simpson, T. R. *The Space Station: An Idea Whose Time Has Come*. New York: IEEE Press, 1985. A collection of articles on all aspects of space station development, this volume includes reviews of the history and justification behind various space station concepts. Also included are chapters on current designs and the long-term potential of space station programs. Contains numerous line drawings and artists' conceptions of historical and modern space station designs. Suitable for general audiences.

U.S. Congress. Office of Technology Assessment. *Civilian Space Stations and the U.S. Future in Space*. OTA-STI-241. Washington, D.C.: Government Printing Office, 1984. This volume contains published proceedings from several Congress-sponsored workshops on space station development. It is designed to be a reference source for those interested in specific technical or administrative information on space station program planning and management. Written for an advanced high school or college-level audience.

Randy Cassingham

Cross-References

Biological Effects of Space Travel on Humans, 188; The European Space Agency, 372; Materials Processing in Space, 933; The Mir Space Station, 1025; The Skylab Program, 1285; The U.S. Space Shuttle, 1626; The Design and Uses of the U.S. Space Station, 1828; The Development of the U.S. Space Station, 1835; International Contributions to the U.S. Space Station, 1843; Living and Working in the U.S. Space Station, 1850; The Spacelab Program, 1884.

THE SPACE TASK GROUP

Date: November 5, 1958, to November 1, 1961
Type of organization: Space agency
Country: The United States

The Space Task Group was the United States' first civilian agency for manned spaceflight. It was the core team responsible for the Mercury, Gemini, and Apollo projects, and it was the seed from which grew the Manned Spacecraft Center, now the Johnson Space Center, near Houston.

Principal personages
ROBERT R. GILRUTH, Manager and Director, Space Task Group
CHARLES J. DONLAN, Assistant Manager, STG
MAXIME A. FAGET, Chief Designer, STG

Summary of the Organization

Unofficially established by the brand-new National Aeronautics and Space Administration (NASA) on October 8, 1958, the Space Task Group (STG), created by a memorandum bearing thirty-five names and dated November 5, 1958, was destined to place the first humans on the Moon.

The thirty-five scientists from the old aeronautical laboratory at Langley Field, Virginia, and the ten additional professionals soon to join them from Lewis Research Center in Cleveland, Ohio, foresaw the possibilities that might arise from combining aviation with rocket and missile technologies. Their initial charge was simply to create a team of humans and machines for manned space exploration, and their early projects involved one-man ballistic and orbital spaceflight. Soon, however, they were responsible for a two-man maneuverable spacecraft and for three-man circumlunar and lunar-landing vehicles.

In the mid-1950's, well before Soviet Sputniks 1 and 2 spurred the creation of NASA from the National Advisory Committee for Aeronautics (NACA), certain farsighted engineers within and outside the government were studying rockets' potential to send humans beyond Earth's atmosphere. The U.S. Air Force had long been interested in expanding its flight regime into space, and NACA's X-15 rocket research airplane was another example of future-oriented work. Perhaps the most vigorous group of aerospace visionaries, however, was gathered around Robert R. Gilruth and his Pilotless Aircraft Research Division (PARD) at Langley Field and Wallops Island in Virginia. Another group at the NACA Lewis Propulsion Laboratory, led by Abe Silverstein, also vied for attention, but when NACA became NASA in October, 1958, President Dwight D. Eisenhower appointed T. Keith Glennan as the first NASA administrator, and Glennan needed Silverstein's assistance. They delegated authority to Gilruth's group to proceed with a manned satellite program. Officially designated Project Mercury on November 26, 1958, the manned satellite program began the first American series of flights into space.

During the spring and summer of 1958, a series of competitive planning conferences around the country gradually led NACA engineers to a consensus that the best proposal for a method of manned spaceflight was the one championed by Maxime A. Faget and his colleagues at Langley, near Norfolk. After years of experience with Gilruth's PARD testing drones and guided missiles, Faget and his associates advocated a wingless, nonlifting, nose cone configuration for the first manned satellite. Rather than follow the pattern of the X-15 rocket research airplane, they wanted to adapt a small, inhabitable cockpit to the first operationally tested intercontinental ballistic missile (ICBM). This idea was at first received without enthusiasm by the Air Force and by General Dynamics/Astronautics, whose Atlas ICBM was the only viable candidate at that time for the job of launching a person into orbit. While the orbital flight plan rapidly took shape at the field centers, NASA headquarters expanded and helped STG to complete preliminary designs, to issue specifications, to choose the prime contractors, and to manage the entire project. Criticism abated as creative engineering activities moved ahead rapidly.

At the beginning of 1959, McDonnell Aircraft Corporation in St. Louis was chosen, out of a competitive bidding group of a dozen companies, to manufacture a dozen manned satellite capsules according to the Faget concept. John F. Yardley of McDonnell quickly assumed leadership in the development of the Mercury hardware. He and his corporation, together with Faget and his STG colleagues, became the core of the Mercury team. By midyear, when seven military test pilots, to be called astronauts, joined the project, most of the basic decisions as to how NASA would try to put a human in space were firm.

Three central principles guided the Mercury program: Use the simplest and most reliable approach, attempt a minimum of new developments, and conduct a progressive series of tests. In the hope of saving time and money and ensuring safety, NASA's policymakers tried to minimize trial and error. Five approaches to major aspects of the project were determined as soon as the government-industry team began to cooperate: The manned satellite capsule would be launched into orbit by the Atlas ICBM; it would be equipped with a tractor escape system, in case the booster malfunctioned; it would be a frustum-shaped vehicle with an attitude control system; it would be braked in orbit by retro-rockets; and it would be slowed on descent by parachutes. Although these plans and the mission profiles were remarkably well laid, nearly all the details of their implementation were yet to be incorporated and verified.

Patents for inventions made in the course of work on Project Mercury were conferred only after the designs were proved in practice, so that official awards tended to obscure the actual process of innovation. Seven men were credited by NASA with designing the Mercury spacecraft: Faget, Andre J. Meyer, Jr., Robert G. Chilton, Willard S. Blanchard, Jr., Alan B. Kehlet, Jerome B. Hammack, and Caldwell C. Johnson. For their conceptual designs and preliminary tests of components, these members of Faget's team were recognized some eight years later in the issuance of U.S. Patent 3,270,908. In addition, Faget and Meyer were credited with the tractor-pylon emergency rocket escape system, and Meyer was credited with the parachute and jettison system design; along with Faget, William M. Bland, Jr., and Jack C. Heberlig were recognized for the pilot's contour couch. Later still, R. Bryan Erb and Kenneth C. Weston shared honors with Meyer for the ablation heatshield, and Matthew I. Radnofsky and Glenn A. Shewmake were recognized for their inflatable life rafts and radar reflectors.

McDonnell employees, led by Raymond A. Pepping, Edward M. Flesh, Logan T. McMillan, John F. Yardley, and, later, Walter F. Burke, took an active and at times initiating role in the creation of the Mercury spacecraft. NASA's policy of retaining ownership of inventions was highly controversial at first, but it did not stanch industrial initiative; STG grew from thirty-five to more than 350 members within its first nine months of existence, but the industrial team grew even faster.

Many subcontractors and third-tier vendors, as well as the prime contractor working with STG, suggested and completed systems engineering studies and components for the Mercury project. Especially noteworthy examples were the McDonnell "pig-drop" impact studies of the aluminum honeycomb shock absorber, the research work of Brush Beryllium Company and of Cincinnati Testing Laboratories on the heat sink and ablation heatshield, and the extraordinarily careful design and development of the environmental control system by AiResearch Manufacturing. The contractors were not limited to hardware development; new techniques and procedures, notably human factors engineering led by Edward R. Jones of McDonnell, originated as often from contractors as from NASA workers.

Because of concerns over weightlessness and its effects on humans and mechanical parts in orbit, the automation experts held sway over the development of Mercury during 1959. By the end of 1960, however, the automatons had failed so often and the astronauts had been trained so well that Mercury's managers were beginning to place more reliance on men than on machines for mission success. At all critical points, redundant, automatic safety features were built in, but the pilots were given manual control over their vehicle wherever feasible. Missile and aircraft technology were rapidly converging.

Meanwhile, STG was continuously testing each part and the whole Mercury configuration in the laboratory and in flight. Three levels of testing had originally been specified: development, qualification, and performance. To these were added, in mid-1960, reliability tests of many varieties to ascertain the life and limits of all the systems. Most dramatic was the extensive flight testing program, which used the unique Little Joe boosters for several tests and the Atlas booster for a single Big Joe shot that demonstrated reentry capability. The Big Joe mission was accomplished successfully on September 9, 1959, and so paved the way for a series of seven more Little Joe missions during the next two years.

By the beginning of 1960, a presidential election year, Gilruth's STG was in high gear and accelerating. Military liaisons had been established, a worldwide tracking and data network was being arranged, an industrial priority rating for Mercury was obtained, a class of seven military test pilots had been chosen and were undergoing astronaut training, and intensive studies and renovations were under way to "man-rate" the booster rockets (that is, to make them safe enough for humans). Politically, however, 1960 was to be a rough year. STG's personnel roster contained about five hundred names, and its prime contract with McDonnell, already modified in more than 120 particulars, was nearing $70 million and rising. Gilruth's group, still housed and hosted by Langley, was supposed to be moving to the new Goddard Space Flight Center being built at Beltsville, Maryland, between the capital and Baltimore. It was unclear, however, whether construction would go forward on the Marshall Space Flight Center at Huntsville, Alabama, which would be occupied by Wernher von Braun's team of rocket experts, at work on the Saturn series of engines and boosters. Political rhetoric about the so-called missile gap, the U-2 incident in May, continuing Soviet launches of dogs and robots in orbital spacecraft, and several widely publicized failures of NASA flight tests in October and November helped make 1960 a most suspenseful year.

The appointments of a number of senior engineers, who distinguished themselves further as Gilruth's group evolved, added to STG's strength during this critical year. Walter C. Williams, Kenneth S. Kleinknecht, Robert O. Piland, James A. Chamberlin, and G. Merritt Preston were a few of the managers. George M. Low and others at NASA headquarters decided between administrations, in January, 1961, to make STG separate from the Goddard center. By then, STG employed 680 persons.

After monkeys had survived flights in boilerplate spacecraft propelled by Little Joe solid rockets, the McDonnell-built spacecraft were mated to Atlas and Redstone liquid-fueled rockets for their combination qualification flight tests. The first two attempts at mated flight failed, because of the boosters more than the capsules. By February, 1961, however, successful flights of both the Mercury-Redstone (MR) and the Mercury-Atlas (MA) combinations had gone far toward man-rating the machines. The performance and recovery of the chimpanzee Ham in MR-2 seemed to indicate that a human could make a similar suborbital hop. On April 12, 1961, however, Yuri Gagarin orbited Earth in 108 minutes aboard the Soviet Union's Vostok 1. Thus the parabolic test flights in May of Alan B. Shepard, Jr., in *Freedom 7* (MR-3), and in July of Virgil I. (Gus) Grissom, in *Liberty Bell 7* (MR-4), set no world records, but merely tested the ability of the Mercury men and machines to work in space for a few minutes. Shepard and Grissom did prove, however, that STG had designed and developed a primitive spacecraft and not merely a manned bullet.

By mid-1961, the tiny Mercury spacecraft encasing forty thousand components and eleven kilometers of wiring was widely publicized around the world. Designed for a reference mission of three orbits, the basic systems in Mercury were advertised openly and often described as falling into ten categories: heat protection, mechanical, pyrotechnical, control, communication, instrumentation, life support, electrical, sequential, and network. Some sixteen major subsystems were novel and critical enough to worry reliability experts and STG managers. STG was upstaged again when, on August 6 and 7, 1961, the Soviet cosmonaut Gherman S. Titov made a seventeen-orbit, day-long circumnavigation of Earth in Vostok 2. In contrast to Mercury, the details of the Vostok spacecraft were shrouded in secrecy.

Difficulties and delays in manufacturing the Mercury capsule and in man-rating its boosters had afforded the seven American astronauts more than an extra year of training. Because they were active as consulting engineers as well as test pilots, the Mercury astronauts contributed to quality control, mission planning, and operational procedures before they ventured into space. Their specialty assignments indicated another way of categorizing the most critical features of the Mercury program. Shepard became the expert on tracking and recovery operations, Grissom studied the complicated electromechanical spacecraft control systems, and John H. Glenn, Jr., worked on the cockpit layout. M. Scott Carpenter specialized in the communications and navigation systems, Walter M. Schirra, Jr., handled the life-support systems and spacesuits, and L. Gordon Cooper, Jr., and Donald K. Slayton analyzed the Redstone and Atlas boosters.

For all the exotic training and trips undergone by the astronauts, only three activities proved to have been indispensable: weightlessness conditioning, accomplished through flights of Keplerian parabolas; acceleration endurance tests in human centrifuges; and, most important, the overlearning of mission tasks in McDonnell-built capsule procedures trainers. Many other training aids were helpful in bolstering the astronauts' confidence that they could endure and overcome any eventuality, but they were confident men; learning to live and work within the pressure suits and within the sealed pressure vessels was an exceedingly difficult job in itself.

At times in 1960 and 1961, all members of the Mercury teams were stymied by some recalcitrant system, process, or device. The recurrent balkiness of the smaller thrusters in the reaction control system, the overassigning of pilot tasks in flight planning, and difficulties with the Department of Defense in scheduling support operations typified tendencies that threatened to become permanent. Both STG and McDonnell underwent several reorganizations of personnel and divisions of labor to meet changing program situations. Moving to the Cape Canaveral launch site, establishing an operations team, responding to new hardware integration needs, and riding the tide of a new political administration all caused confusion and elicited new organization.

Nevertheless, the flight test series began to experience success. By late 1961, it was obvious that STG was to become institutionalized as a permanent, separate NASA installation devoted to the long-term development of manned spaceflight and space exploration. John Glenn was ready to fulfill the Mercury mission, the capsule had evolved from a container into a spacecraft, and the boosters had been refined to the point of deserving to be called man-launching vehicles.

On May 25, 1961, President John F. Kennedy called upon Congress to approve a decade-long lunar landing-and-return program. Already funds had been approved for a site selection process. STG itself proposed a manned spacecraft development center. On September 19, NASA announced that a site near Houston, Texas, had been selected, and by October 13, NASA headquarters had approved construction plans for at least eighteen buildings. More important, STG's responsibility for Project Mercury had escalated into responsibility for the Apollo spacecraft Mercury Mark 2, soon to be renamed Gemini. Thus it was no surprise when on November 1, 1961, STG personnel, now numbering about one thousand, learned that "the Space Task Group is officially redesignated the Manned Spacecraft Center."

Context

The Space Task Group, headquartered in Virginia from 1958 to 1961, fulfilled its initial mission with Glenn's three-orbit flight in *Freedom 7* (MA-6) on February 20, 1962. By that time, the STG that had become virtually synonymous with Project Mercury was anticipating relocating under its new name, the Manned Spacecraft Center (MSC), to southeast Texas around Houston and Galveston Bay. There, its members would design, develop, manage, and control the missions for several new generations of spacecraft. The influence of Faget's flight systems design team and Gilruth's directorship pervaded the next decade of U.S. spacecraft developments, as attested by the similarities in the Mercury, Gemini, and Apollo command modules. In addition to twelve men brought back to Earth safely after six lunar landings, fifteen astronauts had circumnavigated the Moon and returned in Apollo command modules by the end of 1973. On February 17 of that year, the MSC was officially renamed the Lyndon Baines Johnson Space Center (JSC).

A space task group of a different sort passed quickly into obscurity during this period. In January, 1969, President Richard M. Nixon appointed his vice president, Spiro Agnew, to chair a special advisory committee on future directions for manned spaceflight. This commission was formed in the wake of celebrations of mankind's first circumnavigation of the Moon, in Apollo 8, and met amid the excitement of the Apollo 9, 10, and 11 achievements. In September of 1969, it published a report titled *Post-Apollo Space Program: Directions for the Future*. The group advocated manned missions to Mars, but it was so marred by the political scandals that soon enveloped its chairman that its recommendations were quickly forgotten.

Bibliography

Brooks, Courtney G., James M. Grimwood, and Loyd S. Swenson, Jr. *Chariots for Apollo: A History of Manned Lunar Spacecraft*. NASA SP-4205. Washington, D.C.: Government Printing Office, 1979. This is the semiofficial history of the initial achievements of the Apollo spacecraft as seen from Houston. Part of the NASA Historical Series, the work is a sequel to two earlier books which cover the Mercury and Gemini programs. Its stops short of considering the Apollo 12 through 17 missions. Several more volumes in the series deal with other aspects of the Moon-landing program.

Ertel, Ivan D., and Mary Louise Morse. *The Apollo Spacecraft: A Chronology*.

Vol. 1, *Through November 7, 1962*. NASA SP-4009. Washington, D.C.: Government Printing Office, 1969. This first of four volumes covering the Apollo program chronicles key events from the 1920's through the lunar orbital rendezvous decision of November 7, 1962. Includes a foreword by Robert O. Piland as well as forty-four illustrations, abstracts of key events, seven appendices, and an index.

Ezell, Linda Neuman. *Programs and Projects*. Vol. 2 in *NASA Historical Data Book, 1958-1968*. NASA SP-4012. Washington, D.C.: Government Printing Office, 1988. This reference work complements the volume by Van Nimmen, with five chapters documenting launch vehicles, manned spaceflight, space science and applications, advanced research and technology, and tracking and data acquisition. Charts, tables, maps, diagrams, and drawings abound, but there are no photographs.

Grimwood, James M. *Project Mercury: A Chronology*. NASA SP-4001. Washington, D.C.: Government Printing Office, 1963. This is the first of a series of historical chronologies and programmatic accounts of U.S. manned spaceflight projects. Features a preface by K. S. Kleinknecht and a foreword by Hugh L. Dryden. Includes sixty-eight illustrations, ten appendices, and a good index.

Grimwood, James M., Barton C. Hacker, and Peter J. Vorzimmer. *Project Gemini, Technology and Operations: A Chronology*. NASA SP-4002. Washington, D.C.: Government Printing Office, 1969. Focuses on the technology and operations of Gemini, from its concept and design in April, 1959, to its abolition and the summary conference in February, 1967. This book would serve as a good introduction to *On the Shoulders of Titans* (see below). The foreword is by Charles W. Mathews. Includes 131 illustrations, eight appendices, and a thorough index.

Hacker, Barton C., and James M. Grimwood. *On the Shoulders of Titans: A History of Project Gemini*. NASA SP-4203. Washington, D.C.: Government Printing Office, 1977. A volume in the NASA Historical Series, this work is a history of the Gemini program. It describes how the Mercury Mark 2 became a first-class maneuverable spacecraft, suitable for rendezvous and docking in orbit.

Rosholt, Robert L. *An Administrative History of NASA, 1958-1963*. NASA SP-4101. Washington, D.C.: Government Printing Office, 1966. With an interesting foreword by James E. Webb, this book presents a political scientist's analysis of the first five years of NASA administration. It is heavily documented but poorly illustrated, and it focuses almost exclusively on NASA headquarters.

Swenson, Loyd S., Jr., James M. Grimwood, and Charles C. Alexander. *This New Ocean: A History of Project Mercury*. NASA SP-4201. Washington, D.C.: Government Printing Office, 1966. This 681-page narrative is the first program history to be published in the NASA Historical Series. Organized in three parts— "Research," "Development," and "Operations"—this book is the semiofficial account of the Mercury program. It emphasizes the history of Mercury's technology and field management. Profusely illustrated and fully documented, the work was designed as a model for NASA spaceflight histories and is aimed at the intelligent layperson.

Van Nimmen, Jane, Leonard C. Bruno, and Robert L. Rosholt. *NASA Resources*. Vol. 1 in *NASA Historical Data Book, 1958-1968*. NASA SP-4012. Washington, D.C.: Government Printing Office, 1976. This reference work traces the growth of NASA over its first decade, with six topical chapters and two appendices. With a brief foreword by George M. Low, the book presents tabular and graphical data on NASA's facilities, personnel, finances, procurement, installations, awards, and organization. The largest section is chapter 6, which details basic facts about NASA's fourteen largest field installations.

Loyd S. Swenson, Jr.

Cross-References

Astronauts and the U.S. Astronaut Program, 154; Biological Effects of Space Travel on Humans, 188; Food and Diet for Space Travel, 454; Funding Procedures of U.S. Space Programs, 468; The Gemini Program, 487; Gemini 3, 494; Gemini 4, 501; Gemini 5, 507; Gemini 6A and 7, 514; Gemini 8, 520; Gemini 9, 9A, and 10, 527; Gemini 11 and 12, 533; Insuring Spacecraft and Human Life, 608; U.S. Launch Vehicles, 749; The Mercury Project, 940; The Development of the Mercury Project, 947; Mercury-Redstone 3: *Freedom 7*, 953; Mercury-Redstone 4: *Liberty Bell 7*, 960; Mercury-Atlas 6: *Friendship 7*, 967; Mercury-Atlas 7: *Aurora 7*, 973; Mercury-Atlas 8: *Sigma 7*, 979; Mercury-Atlas 9: *Faith 7*, 985; The National Aeronautics and Space Administration, 1032; Saturn Launch Vehicles, 1240; Spaceplanes, 1912; Titan Launch Vehicles, 2036; The Van Allen Radiation Belts, 2065.

THE SPACEFLIGHT TRACKING AND DATA NETWORK

Date: Beginning in 1972
Type of organization: Tracking network
Country: The United States

The Spaceflight Tracking and Data Network is a network of fifteen ground communications and tracking stations, located in countries around the world, that provide data relay, data processing, communications, and command support to the U.S. space shuttle program and to other orbital and suborbital spaceflights.

Principal personages
DANIEL A. SPINTMAN, Division Chief, Ground and Space
    Networks, Goddard Space Flight Center
VAUGHN E. TURNER, Chief, NASA Communications Division,
    GSFC
ROBERT T. GROVES, Chief, Flight Dynamics Facility, GSFC
JOHN T. DALTON, Chief, Data Systems Technology Division,
    GSFC

Summary of the Organization

The Spaceflight Tracking and Data Network (STDN) is part of a complex and rapidly changing group of programs designed to provide a two-way communications and command link between flight control centers on the ground and manned and unmanned space missions. In the 1980's, STDN also provided primary support for U.S. space shuttle missions.

As of July, 1988, STDN operated fifteen tracking stations located in Fairbanks, Alaska; Goldstone, California; Kauai, Hawaii; Wallops Island, Virginia; Merritt Island, Florida; Rosman, North Carolina; Ascension Island; Bermuda; Canberra, Australia; Guam; Madrid; Quito, Ecuador; Santiago, Chile; Winkfield, England; and Greenbelt, Maryland, at Goddard Space Flight Center (GSFC). Major computing interfaces for the system are operated at GSFC's Network Control Center and Flight Dynamics Facility; the Western Space and Missile Center, at Vandenberg Air Force Base in California; the White Sands Missile Range, White Sands, New Mexico; and the Eastern Space and Missile Center at Cape Canaveral Air Force Station, Cape Canaveral, Florida.

STDN ground stations are equipped with ultrahigh-frequency and television hardware, with 4.3-, 9-, and 26-meter S-band antenna systems, used for radio transmissions, and with C-band radar systems, used for tracking objects by radar. Department of Defense facilities are frequently used to supplement existing STDN hardware with additional S-band and C-band equipment. About 2,500 persons work at STDN tracking stations or are involved in STDN functions at GSFC.

STDN operates in cooperation with the National Aeronautics and Space Administration (NASA)—specifically, with NASA's Communications Division (NASCOM) and the Flight Dynamics Facility at GSFC. NASCOM is the communications link for launch and landing sites, for mission and network control centers, and for all U.S. spacecraft. It provides voice, low- and high-speed telemetry, and television transmissions to more than a hundred NASA facilities. The Flight Dynamics Facility receives the tracking data relayed by STDN and calculates the information necessary to orient the spacecraft being tracked.

By 1988, STDN was providing tracking, communications, and command services to a total of nineteen scientific, weather, communications, and environmental U.S. satellites in Earth orbit. STDN also has the capability to support European, Soviet, and Chinese satellites with similar services.

Part of STDN and other NASA tracking networks, the NASA Ground Terminal at White Sands, New Mexico, would serve as a backup space shuttle mission control facility if Johnson Space Center, in Houston, were rendered inoperative for any length of time. GSFC would serve as an interim mission control center while the flight control personnel transferred from Houston to White Sands.

Each STDN station is able to track and communicate with a spacecraft only during the period when the spacecraft's orbit brings it into the station's "line of sight," or when Earth's curvature does not block direct radio and radar contact. Each station can track or remain in contact with a spacecraft for a maximum of approximately 15 percent of its orbit. When one station loses contact, responsibility for tracking and communications passes to the next ground station in the network.

Knowledge Gained

STDN provides a vital link between scientists and experts on Earth and the manned and unmanned spacecraft in Earth orbit. STDN allows NASA to have virtually instantaneous contact with and control of the functions of a spacecraft, wherever it flies. In many cases, for both manned missions and unmanned probes, this communications lifeline between Earth and space has made the difference between failure and success.

On both manned and unmanned missions, the data received by STDN give mission managers and technicians a complete picture of the health and reliability of the spacecraft in orbit, something that the astronauts on manned missions often do not have the time or opportunity to do. The information lets the mission managers on Earth serve as "extra crew members" who can help prevent or overcome problems with the spacecraft.

The space shuttle *Challenger*'s launch of the first Tracking and Data-Relay Satellite (TDRS) in April, 1983, demonstrated the interaction between ground control and spacecraft made possible by STDN. TDRS-A was successfully released from the space shuttle on April 5, 1983, but the booster rocket attached to the satellite failed to fire, leaving it in a uselessly low Earth orbit. STDN allowed TDRS mission managers to assess TDRS's situation and devise an alternate way for it to reach a geosynchronous orbit (an orbit wherein a satellite travels once around Earth every twenty-four hours) 35,900 kilometers above Earth. Sending commands via STDN, ground control workers used the satellite's tiny reaction control thrusters to move it slowly to the proper altitude.

STDN and other NASA-operated tracking networks have allowed the United States to participate in the growth of the international space community by providing launch and data tracking support for the French Ariane rocket program. STDN is also capable of providing support to other foreign satellites.

Context

STDN works in conjunction with the Deep Space Network, which is controlled by the Jet Propulsion Laboratory, in Pasadena, California, and the Tracking and Data-Relay Satellite System (TDRSS), made up of satellites in geosynchronous orbit.

STDN is part of an effort to develop U.S. communication and tracking capabilities that began in the earliest days of the nation's space program. In 1958, as part of the country's plan to launch an artificial satellite into orbit as the United States' contribution to the eighteen-month International Geophysical Year (July 1, 1957, to December 31, 1958), NASA took over the U.S. Naval Research Laboratory's Minitrack network of ground stations. These facilities were designed only to track satellites and receive data and did not have the capacity to transmit commands to spacecraft from the ground.

There were only ten stations in the Minitrack system when NASA first began using the network; by 1963, however, eighteen ground facilities were in use. Their locations were San Diego; Goldstone, California; Blossom Point, Maryland; Fort Meyers, Florida; East Grand Forks, Minnesota; Fairbanks, Alaska; Rosman, North Carolina; Antigua, West Indies; Quito, Ecuador; Lima, Peru; Autofagasta and Santiago, in Chile; Canberra and Woomera, Australia; Saint John's, Newfoundland; Winkfield, England; and Eselen Park and Johannesburg, in South Africa.

During the years that the Minitrack network was in operation, NASA began expanding the technological capabilities of its ground stations, adding new and more powerful antennae and better data retrieval and processing systems. With additions in 1963 of 12- and 26-meter antennae to several Minitrack stations, the system was renamed the Satellite Network. By 1964, NASA had brought into use the Satellite Telemetry Automatic Reduction (STAR) system, which provided not only better tracking and data processing but enabled ground stations to issue commands to unmanned satellites. The improved network, which operated from 1964 to 1972, was known as the Space Tracking and Data Acquisition Network (STADAN). STADAN operated ten ground stations at former Minitrack locations, with an additional station at Tananarive, Madagascar.

In 1962, NASA had separated tracking and communications functions into a satellite division and a manned division, creating the Manned Space Flight Network (MSFN), which operated concurrently with the STADAN satellite-tracking system. In addition to land-based stations, MSFN used eight aircraft and five ships to provide a comprehensive network of facilities that could communicate with Mercury, Gemini, and Apollo astronauts, receive telemetry signals, and command both manned spacecraft and unmanned target vehicles such as those used during Gemini flights 8 through 12.

A total of twenty-two MSFN ground stations were located in White Sands, New Mexico; Corpus Christi, Texas; Eglin Air Force Base and Merritt Island, in Florida; Point Arguello and Goldstone, in California; Kauai, Hawaii; Antigua; Ascension Island; the Canary Islands; Bermuda; Canton Island; Grand Bahama Island; Grand Turk Island; Guam; Canberra, Carnarvon, and Muchea, in Australia; Guaymas, Mexico; Kano, Nigeria; Madrid; and Tananarive, Madagascar. In 1972, the STADAN and MSFN systems were unified to create the STDN system.

Because of the complexities of receiving data from manned and unmanned spacecraft and relaying data among the several STDN facilities, NASA inaugurated the TDRSS system with the 1983 launch of TDRS-A, which became TDRS 1 when it was successfully placed in orbit. TDRS-B was on board the space shuttle *Challenger* when it exploded shortly after launch on January 28, 1986. TDRS-C was the payload on the space shuttle *Discovery*, launched in September, 1988. TDRS-D and TDRS-E were scheduled to be launched in January, 1989, and July, 1990, respectively.

The TDRSS network was designed to replace STDN as NASA's primary tracking system, using satellites in geostationary orbits above the equator to receive data from other spacecraft and relay them to the White Sands Ground Terminal. At least six STDN stations—those in Ascension Island, Santiago, Guam, Hawaii, Dakar, and Canberra—were planned to be closed when TDRSS was fully operational.

Bibliography

Elliott, James C. *Goddard's Worldwide Communications Network Set to Provide Support for STS-26 Mission*. NASA News Release. Washington, D.C.: National Aeronautics and Space Administration, 1988. This news release details the role of STDN and TDRSS in the 1988 flight of the space shuttle *Discovery*. It includes a list of the times during the mission when *Discovery* was in contact with Goddard Space Flight Center through STDN.

_____ . *NASA/Goddard Space Flight Center*. NASA Release 88-43. Washington, D.C.: National Aeronautics and Space Administration, 1988. This brochure gives an overview of the activities and functions performed by Goddard Space Flight Center. It was written to help reporters and broadcasters better communicate information about Goddard, STDN, and other NASA organizations.

_____ . *Questions and Answers on the Space Flight Tracking Data Network (STDN)*. NASA Release 88-47. Washington, D.C.: National Aeronautics and Space Administration, 1988. This news release, written in easy-to-understand language, looks at the changing nature of STDN and its future after TDRSS.

Furniss, Tim. *Manned Spaceflight Log*. Rev. ed. London: Jane's Publishing Co., 1986. This is a concise, fact-filled listing of the primary mission objectives and results of all manned spaceflights up to Soyuz T-15. The book provides a broad overview of the progress made in space exploration. One of the best books for the beginning space enthusiast.

National Aeronautics and Space Administration. *Entering the Era of the Tracking and Data Relay Satellite System: NASA Facts/Goddard Space Flight Center*. Washington, D.C.: Author, 1987. This brochure introduces STDN and TDRSS to the layperson. It also discusses the importance of ground stations to the success of both manned and unmanned space missions.

Rosenthal, Alfred. *The Early Years, Goddard Space Flight Center: Historical Origins and Activities Through December 1962*. Washington, D.C.: Government Printing Office, 1964. This commemorative manual provides a precise and comprehensive look at the founding of Goddard Space Flight Center, the Minitrack Network, and the beginnings of the Satellite Network.

Eric Christensen

Cross-References

Cape Canaveral and the Kennedy Space Center, 229; The Deep Space Network, 280; Goddard Space Flight Center, 563; The Jet Propulsion Laboratory, 662; Johnson Space Center, 669; Space Shuttle Mission 6: *Challenger*, 1684; Space Shuttle Mission 26: *Discovery*, 1822; The Soviet Spaceflight Tracking Network, 1877; Tracking and Data-Relay Communications Satellites, 2042; Vandenberg Air Force Base, 2069.

THE SOVIET SPACEFLIGHT TRACKING NETWORK

Date: Beginning October 4, 1957
Type of organization: Tracking network
Country: The Soviet Union

The spaceflight tracking network of the Soviet Union has been in operation since the launch of Sputnik 1. It is designed to track objects in orbit, provide orbital data, and support communications between ground stations and manned and unmanned flights.

Principal personages
ALEXANDER M. LOZINSKY, the head of the Satellite Observation Laboratory of the Soviet Academy of Sciences
ALLA G. MASSEVICH,
M. K. ABELE, and
K. K. LAPUSHKA, members of the Soviet Academy of Sciences
VALERI RYUMIN, Director of the Kaliningrad Flight Control Center
VLADIMIR SOLOVYOV, Deputy Director of the Kaliningrad Flight Control Center

Summary of the Organization

The Soviet spaceflight tracking network sprang from the Soviets' desire to set up communications with its first satellite, Sputnik 1, launched on October 4, 1957. The network at that time consisted of receivers and theodolites located in various parts of the Soviet Union, usually based at universities. These instruments would receive signals transmitted and determine the satellite's orbit. In addition to processing their own observations, the Soviets encouraged foreign observers to forward to Moscow any information on the satellite they might have gathered. This command and measurement complex was first called the KIK, for Komanda Izmerenie Kompleks (command measurement complex). The successor to the KIK is the NAKU, for Nazemny Avtomatizirovanniy Kompleks Upravleniya (ground automated control complex).

To augment radio tracking of objects, and to assist in refining, or upgrading, the orbits of inactive payloads and rocket stages, the Soviet Union started to create a network of optical tracking stations across the country. Optical tracking is performed by observing a satellite either visually or photographically in the night sky. A satellite moves between the stars as a point of light, being illuminated by the Sun and reflecting light off its surface. The equipment used for these observations was an adapted wide-angle, fast-action camera, used for aerial photography.

In 1965, new cameras were designed at Riga University which could track objects as far away as 3,500 kilometers; they were placed at Riga, Uzhgorod, Zvenigorod, and Juzhno-Sakhalinsk, in the Soviet Union. They were also stationed overseas in

Ondrejov, Czechoslovakia; Havana, Cuba; Sofia, Bulgaria; Ulan Bator, Mongolia; Baja, Hungary; Cairo, Egypt; Afgoi, Somalia; the Kerguelen Islands; and Mirnyy in Antarctica. The FAS camera is basically a more stable version of the same system; these cameras were installed in 1969 at Riga, Zvenigorod, Uzhgorod, Pulkovo, and Juzhno-Sakhalinsk.

At the same time, the world's largest camera, known as the VAU, was being constructed at the Zvenigorod site. Its mounting allows a satellite to be followed in any part of the sky and at any velocity. One project the camera has undertaken is the tracking of space probes in flight from Earth, a task previously performed by optical telescopes located at the Crimean and Burakan observatories. Two further VAU systems were installed in 1970 at Dushanbe and Yerevan. Yet even the VAU was superseded; in 1985, at Zvenigorod, the VAU was replaced by the 25-ton Maksutov-Sobolev telescope. This telescope is used to observe objects 36,000 kilometers from Earth and can track in any direction.

Closely related to optical tracking is the observation of satellites by lasers. This method of observation is effective only on objects equipped with special reflectors to bounce the laser beam back to the ground station, similar to the way a "cat's-eye" reflector in the road works when illuminated by a car headlight. This technique is used to track the height of an orbit to a few centimeters. Soviet laser stations are located in the Soviet Union and overseas—in Cuba, Bolivia, and India. One of the most active is located at Potsdam, East Germany, where a laser tracking station works with Western stations in an observing program coordinated by the National Aeronautics and Space Administration (NASA). A newer laser was installed at Riga in 1980 and is capable of tracking objects 6,000 kilometers in space with an accuracy of 20 centimeters (somewhat less accurate than Western lasers, which are capable of tracking objects with an accuracy of 5 centimeters or less).

Even though optical tracking is one of the most accurate ways to determine an object's orbit, it is restricted by good weather and the satellite must pass at night, illuminated by the Sun. Consequently, the bulk of space tracking work depends on radar, operable around-the-clock and in all weather. The Soviet system incorporates both missile and space tracking, in the same way the American system does, though in a different format. The prime radar systems suited to space tracking and the identification of objects in orbit are based throughout the Soviet Union at Pechora, Irkutsk, Lyaki, Skrunda, and Kamchatka. These systems are known in the West as the "Hen House" radars; there are eleven of them, all designed in the late 1950's. The details of the Hen House radars are scarce, but it is believed that they are used for a combined role of missile and space tracking. The antennae used are 300 meters long and 20 meters high, with a range of 6,000 kilometers. They are able to scan in different modes at the same time for enhanced coverage.

The Hen House radars are of the type known as phased-array radars. That means that the radar beam is steered electronically from one direction to another in a split second instead of using a conventional radar dish, which is used to track and detect objects by steering the beam mechanically. Because a phased-array radar needs no moving parts to alter the beam direction, a greater area can be covered in less time than that required by dish radar.

A newer phased-array radar was built in 1982 at Pushkino, near Moscow. This instrument—25 meters in height—has four active radar faces, to provide all-around, 360-degree coverage. Additional phased-array systems were built in Pechora, Komsomolsk, Kiev, Lyaki, and Mikhailovka; they became operational in the early 1980's. These radars are 30 meters tall, 100 meters long, and consist of a separate transmitter and receiver building. The sixth of the series is under construction at Krasnoyarsk in Siberia, and more radars are planned for Skrunda, Mukachevo, and Baranovichi. Yet another system, called the "Hen Roost," has been reported, but details of this radar are sketchy. It is possible that the Hen Roost radars are actually the same phased-array radars located at Pechora and associated sites.

After launching a satellite, researchers receive its data and send it updated instructions. Ideally such communications can be sustained for a satellite's entire orbit around the globe. The information is then processed at a control center to assess the flight and to determine how the mission should proceed. In the case of manned Soviet missions, the primary control center is located at Kaliningrad, on the outskirts of Moscow. This facility was built for the Apollo-Soyuz Test Project (ASTP) flight in 1975 and resembles Mission Control at the Johnson Space Center in Texas. It has a large central operations room with television displays of the cosmonauts' activities in orbit and a map of the world with the position of the spacecraft superimposed on it. Twenty-four flight controllers are based in this room, with adjacent rooms used for various support activities and certain phases of the missions. The five hundred consoles in the whole complex were used to monitor one thousand readings on the Soyuz spacecraft one hundred times per second, and double this quantity on the Salyut and Mir missions.

Apart from controlling the mission and communicating with the crew, the center maintains contact with the ground stations tracking the spacecraft and issues instructions via these stations' antennae to be sent back up to the crew. The call sign used on past missions was Zaria (dawn), but the Mir crews referred to the center as TsUP (the acronym for Tsentr Upravleniya Poletom, Russian for "flight control center").

Before the center at Kaliningrad was built, the mission control center had been based at Yevpatoriya in the Crimea, where the deep space antennae which track interplanetary probes are located. It is believed that this center is still involved in unmanned flights, both interplanetary and Earth orbiting, and that it serves as a backup mission control for manned flights. For the ASTP mission, Kaliningrad was used, while the concurrently orbiting Salyut 4/Soyuz 18 flight was controlled from Yevpatoriya. Unlike Mission Control at Houston, Kaliningrad only has the capacity for handling one mission at a time. Both Vega flights to Comet Halley were controlled from Kaliningrad for at least parts of the missions, mainly at critical times, such as during the flybys.

The majority of unmanned flights launched each year by the Soviet Union are controlled from undisclosed sites. As most of these missions are military, their locations are unlikely to be announced. Similarly, the ground stations used to track these missions are unknown to the public, along with the stations involved with the manned flights. As part of the ASTP mission, the Soviets did announce their stations as Yevpatoriya, Tbilisi, Dzhusaly, Kolpashevo, Ulan-Ude, Ussurisk, and Petropavlovsk. These are the equivalents of the NASA Spaceflight Tracking and Data Network (STDN), located within the United States and overseas. No foreign tracking stations are used in the Soviet manned program, but it is believed that certain bases outside the Soviet Union are involved with unmanned flights. Flights of an international nature have used ground stations in Bulgaria and Czechoslovakia.

In order to keep contact with the manned crews, the Soviets rely not on stations based in foreign countries but on a fleet of Soviet registered ships equipped to perform the same task. This fleet came into service in the late 1950's, using converted cargo vessels to act as simple gap fillers over the world's oceans. Initially, the boats in service were the *Illichevsk* and *Krasnodar*, to be followed by the *Dolinsk*, *Bezhitsa*, *Ristna*, *Morzhovets*, *Keogstrov*, *Nevel*, *Borovichi*, and *Aksay*. These were slowly decommissioned, until only the *Nevel*, *Morzhovets*, *Borovichi*, and *Kegostrov* remained. The equipment carried is used to support voice communications and data links with the Soyuz spacecraft and the Salyut and Mir space stations, through shortwave relay used for communications with flight control.

The fleet in use during the mid-1980's consisted of the four small vessels mentioned above, three larger boats, unique in their design, and four medium-sized boats constructed in the late 1970's. The ships are manned by civilians and are controlled by the Soviet Academy of Sciences as space and atmospheric research vessels. The flagship of the fleet is the *Kosmonaut Yuri Gagarin*, constructed in 1970 at the Baltic shipyard in Leningrad. The vessel is an adaptation of a supertanker. Its displacement is 45,000 tons, it has a length of 236 meters, and it carries an abundance of antennae. The main dishes, 25 meters in diameter, are used to track interplanetary craft after they have been launched from Earth. Two smaller, 12-meter dishes are used for tracking and control and for relay of data from spacecraft being tracked via satellite to Kaliningrad. That means that flight control is able to communicate directly with the crew aboard a spacecraft via satellite relay and the vessel's antennae. Further relays of data and general day-to-day operations are sent over shortwave.

The *Akademik Sergei Korolev* is a smaller vessel; it has a displacement of 21,465 tons and a length of 182 meters. The large, 25-meter dish antennae are not carried, but the two 12-meter dishes perform the same functions as on the *Kosmonaut Yuri Gagarin*, along with the shortwave antennae and the standard very high frequency (VHF) voice antennae, which are to be found on all the tracking ships. A small, 2-meter dish is carried in a dome, which is also used for tracking and control. The *Akademik Sergei Korolev* was built in 1970 at Nikolayev on the Black Sea, near its home port of Odessa.

The third of the large vessels assigned to space tracking work is the *Kosmonaut Vladimir Komarov*, built in 1966. The VHF voice antennae and shortwave equipment are carried on this ship, along with two 8-meter dishes kept under 18-meter-diameter domes. A smaller 2-meter dish is also used for tracking.

The most modern of the tracking ships used today are those of the Belyayev class, named after deceased cosmonauts. They have a displacement of 9,000 tons and are 122 meters in length, converted from standard timber carriers in the Vytegrales class. The equipment carried on board is the standard VHF and shortwave antennae, plus a satellite relay dish and a clover-leafed, four-dish antenna used for tracking and control. Built in 1977 in Leningrad, the *Kosmonaut Pavel Belyayev*, *Kosmonaut Viktor Patsayev*, *Kosmonaut Georgi Dobrovolsky*, and *Kosmonaut Vladislav Volkov* are used worldwide primarily for Mir and Salyut communications.

The prime locations for Mir support have been Nova Scotia, the Gulf of Guinea, the Gibraltar Straits, Montevideo, and the Caribbean. Usually the *Kosmonaut Yuri Gagarin* or the *Akademik Sergei Korolev* is stationed off Canada, with the *Kosmonaut Vladimir Komarov* residing in the Mediterranean. The Belyayev-class ships cover the African and South American coasts, with the smaller vessels in the Caribbean and also off South America. For specific missions, Belyayev-class ships have assisted in places such as the Middle East and Singapore, but that is not a common occurrence.

Context

The Soviet space network is the only system outside the Western world capable of tracking and communicating with spacecraft in orbit. From its basic beginning as a support arm of the Sputnik 1 flight, when ordinary equipment was used to follow the spacecraft, it has developed, in many ways, as a counterpart to NASA's STDN. The Soviet optical tracking network is the largest in the world; while this type of tracking has gone out of fashion in other countries, the Soviet Union still makes much use of it. The development of new Soviet tracking cameras is an indication that the Soviets do not intend to lose this capability, although it could be argued that these systems' data do not compare with the data produced from the U.S. Ground-Based Deep Space Electro-Optical System now being deployed worldwide.

It is thought that the Soviets' use of radar for space tracking is keeping pace with the upgrades the United States is now implementing. The laser tracking network is becoming more open, with increased cooperation between East and West in the tracking of satellites used to determine continental drift and to analyze the shape of Earth.

The space tracking fleet, which has served the manned and unmanned programs admirably since the late 1950's, is being augmented. New vessels are under construction, as acknowledged openly by the Soviet Union. The vessels at sea have had to extend their periods of duty in order to support the ever-growing trend of longer stays aboard the space stations (for one particular mission, the *Akademik Sergei Korolev* was away from the Soviet Union for ten months). Although it is unclear whether these new boats will replace any older vessels, the growth of the fleet indicates that the policy of not locating tracking stations on foreign soil still holds, even with increased cooperation between the Soviets and the Americans. The Soviets are, however, receiving assistance from NASA in tracking their Phobos probes to Mars, using the capability of the U.S. dishes to assist their own tracking network—a cooperative system which has been successful in the past.

Behind each launch and mission is the bread-and-butter routine of communicating daily with spacecraft, tracking objects in orbit, analyzing the data received, and ensuring each mission's success. The Soviets have constructed a competent system that has sufficed since the start of the space age and which will continue to meet their requirements.

Bibliography

Bussert, Jim. "Whose Phased-Array Radars Violate the ABM Treaty?" *Defense Electronics*, April, 1987: 116. Gives a good assessment of Soviet radars, their history, capabilities, and functions. A comparison is made between the Soviet and U.S. systems. Also provides illustrations of the systems. Very accurate.

Jane's Fighting Ships, 1988-1989. London: Jane's Publishing Co., 1988. Contains all statistical data and illustrations concerning the civilian tracking fleet and naval vessels involved with missile tracking. Western designations of the Soviet antennae are provided, although the purposes of some of the dishes are inaccurately identified.

National Aeronautics and Space Administration. *An Overview of the Kaliningrad Spaceflight Control Center*. NASA TM-87980. Washington, D.C.: Author, 1986. This article is a translation of a Soviet document and is suitable for the general reader. Explains the operations that are carried out in Kaliningrad and what missions are controlled from that facility. Includes good photographs of the center and the antennae used, both on land and at sea, to communicate with Flight Control.

U.S. Congress. Senate. Committee on Commerce, Science, and Transportation. *Soviet Space Programs: 1976-1980*. Part 1, *Manned Space Flight*. Report prepared by Congressional Research Service, the Library of Congress. 98th Cong., 2d sess., 1984. Committee Print. This volume covers the ground stations of the Soviet Union, along with details about the tracking fleet. Includes description of Flight Control.

_____ . *Soviet Space Programs: 1981-1987*. Report prepared by Congressional Research Service, the Library of Congress. 100th Cong., 1988. Committee Print. The most comprehensive guide available to the general reader on the Soviet tracking systems and the Soviet space program as a whole. Contains good material on the control centers and detailed analysis of the tracking ships. Highly recommended.

Max White

Cross-References

The Apollo-Soyuz Test Project, 132; The Deep Space Network, 280; The Mir Space Station, 1025; The Salyut Space Station, 1233; Space Centers and Launch Sites in the Soviet Union, 1592; The Spaceflight Tracking and Data Network, 1872.

THE SPACELAB PROGRAM

Date: Beginning August, 1973
Type of program: Manned space shuttle experiment facility
Countries: The ESA nations and the United States

Spacelab is a major space shuttle payload designed to provide scientists with facilities approximating those of a terrestrial laboratory.

Principal personages
JAMES FLETCHER, NASA Administrator
ALEXANDER HOCKER, Director General of ESRO
ROY GIBSON, Director General of ESA
DOUGLAS R. LORD, Spacelab Program Manager
T. J. LEE and
JOHN THOMAS, Spacelab project managers
JAMES DOWNEY and
JESSE MOORE, Spacelab missions managers

Summary of the Program

Because Spacelab was designed to operate within the payload bay of the space shuttle orbiter, configuration interface between it and the concurrently designed shuttle was sometimes problematic. Components of Spacelab often had to be redesigned in order to meet changing shuttle requirements. In particular, a major redesign of Spacelab's instrument pointing system was required. Starting in 1974, Spacelab passed through many tests and design reviews as hardware was planned and built. These led to final acceptance reviews in 1981 and 1982, when the elements of what was termed Flight Unit 1 were delivered to the National Aeronautics and Space Administration (NASA).

Meanwhile, NASA had organized the management of Spacelab within its network of facilities. Marshall Space Flight Center (MSFC) in Huntsville, Alabama, was to oversee the work of the European Space Agency (ESA) on Spacelab and assure that agency's compliance with shuttle standards. (Later, MSFC was given responsibility for developing additional missions and for providing the hardware to other NASA centers which also prepare and conduct Spacelab missions.) NASA issued an "announcement of opportunity" to space scientists, asking them to propose experiments that might be performed aboard the first two Spacelab missions. Since these were verification flights, NASA tried to accommodate as many scientific disciplines as possible. The payload mass was allocated equally between NASA and the ESA for Spacelab 1, while Spacelab 2 was primarily an American mission (but European scientists were invited to propose experiments). Researching a path for the complete Spacelab, NASA flew engineering models of Spacelab pallets on the STS 2 and STS 3 shuttle missions in 1981 and 1982. As part of the exercise, the pallets carried science instruments that gathered useful data.

The final configuration for Spacelab comprised pressure modules and open pallets in addition to equipment designed to join these components and provide supports for the experimental gear they would carry. Spacelab is controlled by crew members operating a computer either in the module or in the aft flight deck of the shuttle.

The module was designed with core and experiment components. Each segment is 2.70 meters wide and 2.88 meters long. With end cones, a short module measures 4.27 meters in length and a long module 6.96 meters in length. The interior arrangement includes a floor to cover the support systems, equipment racks placed on each side of the module, overhead storage areas, and a small access science port. Designed as "singles" and "doubles," the racks were 1.48 centimeters wide and capable of holding up to 290 and 580 kilograms of experimental gear respectively.

In the Spacelab core module, the two forwardmost double racks were dedicated as the control station (starboard) and the workbench (port). That left two double racks and two single racks (one each, port and starboard) for use by experimenters. The experiment segment added another four double racks and two single racks.

Additional experiments can be accommodated by an optical quality viewport mounted over the core segment and a small science air lock in a similar position in the experiment segment. The viewport has a removable exterior cover so that it is protected from the space environment and shuttle contamination, except when used by medium-sized cameras mounted by the crew. The air lock allows the payload crew to expose equipment up to 1 meter long and 0.98 meter wide into space.

Linking the module to the shuttle cabin is the transfer tunnel, 1.02 meters in diameter. It is assembled from a set of cylindrical sections to match different module lengths and locations. It also has flexible sections to allow for slight bending in the airframe during ascent and entry.

The other major element of the Spacelab system is the pallet, a U-shaped platform that provides an interface between experiment hardware and the shuttle itself. Each pallet is 4 meters wide and 2.9 meters long and, like the modules, can be joined with other similar components. Each pallet is made up of five angular U-shaped frames joined by longitudinal members and covered with metal plates. The inner plates have a pattern of bolt holes in a 14-by-14-centimeter grid for mounting lightweight hardware; twenty-four hard points are provided for heavy equipment. The pallets also provide routing for cooling equipment, electrical cables, and other support services.

Both the pallets and the modules are held in the payload bay by sill and keel trunnions, 8.25-centimeter pins which are locked down by special clamps bolted to the orbiter structure. The modules and pallets can be grouped in almost a dozen configurations depending on mission needs. The module can be flown "long" or "short," with or without one to three pallets. Up to three pallets may be joined in a train, and up to five may be flown at once.

Spacelab is totally dependent upon the space shuttle for electrical power, environmental control, and life support. Power and environmental gear provided in Spacelab's subfloor area is designed to assist the shuttle in that respect. Spacelab does have its own command and data management system (CDMS) through which the crew may control experiments. The CDMS commands experiment apparatus and collects data from them by way of remote acquisition units (RAUs), which function somewhat like sophisticated telephone exchanges. The rapid advance of microelectronics in the late 1970's, however, has relegated the CDMS to the role of traffic controller for the various experiments, which often have their own microprocessors. The Spacelab CDMS actually comprises three central processing units: one to operate Spacelab proper, one to operate the experiments, and a third held as a manually selected backup. In missions using the module, the CDMS is housed in the starboard forward double rack. For pallet-only missions, it is housed in a pressurized container, the "igloo," mounted on the forwardmost pallet. The igloo provides a sea-level environment for the CDMS, thus eliminating the need to prepare the computer for the environment of raw space.

For pointing large telescopes or telescope clusters at targets, an instrument pointing system (IPS) is provided. The IPS has three electrically driven gimbals that can point the IPS payload within extremely close range of a target. The IPS is mounted on a support framework on a pallet, and, in turn, provides a large, circular equipment platform for the payload. Payloads can weigh up to 7,000 kilograms and can be several meters long. Not all payloads requiring pointing can justify use of the IPS, so experimenters have developed smaller pointers tailored to their investigations.

Assembly of a Spacelab mission is a long, complex process involving several levels of effort. After the science community has identified important investigations, NASA performs a preliminary study of the kinds of instruments that might satisfy this need. Instruments generally fall into two classes, the principal investigator and the facility. In the first, an individual scientist or science team develops an instrument for a narrow investigation. In the second, NASA and a contractor develop an instrument that can serve a number of scientists on many missions. Experiments on Spacelabs 1, 2, and 3 were developed from announcements asking specifically for them. In 1978, NASA issued a broader announcement soliciting instruments in physics and astronomy. Forty instruments were selected, some of which were grouped for Spacelab or other missions and some of which were later canceled. Other announcements were issued for life-science missions and facility-class instruments.

After the science investigations are selected, an investigators' working group (IWG) is formed from the lead scientists. NASA appoints a mission manager and mission scientist from its own ranks. The IWG and NASA engineers work closely together to develop the flightplan and details of how and when each investigation is to be conducted during the mission. It is not unusual to discover that some experiments will not fit in or will be late. This normally results in an instrument's being moved to a later mission rather than it being canceled.

As it becomes ready, experiment hardware is delivered to Kennedy Space Center, Florida, for integration into the complete Spacelab. The first step in the process is to install the experiment elements in racks or on pallets. The racks and floor are then fitted into the module, the module is closed, and the module and pallets are physically and electrically joined. The complete assembly is placed inside the cargo integrated test equipment (CITE) stand, where all the components are exercised as they would be in flight. Finally, the complete Spacelab is installed in the space shuttle, and an "end-to-end" test is conducted to validate all links from the experiment to the control center.

Typically, a Spacelab mission includes three types of crew members: pilot astronauts, the mission commander and pilot, who fly the shuttle itself; mission specialists, career NASA scientist astronauts who have overall responsibility for the payload; and payload specialists, members of the IWG selected to fly on the mission and to conduct the experiments. Two payload specialists, prime and alternate, are selected for each flight opening.

The inclusion of payload specialists on the Spacelab missions was a major point used by NASA in selling Spacelab and the shuttle to the science community. Previously, scientists could only listen or watch from the ground while their experiments were conducted by career NASA astronauts. With the routine operations to be provided by the shuttle, scientists could fly, almost passenger-like, with the experiments that they had developed. The process has turned out to be slightly more complex, but the basic philosophy holds.

Spacelab missions start a few hours after the shuttle achieves orbit and last until about four hours before reentry. When the shuttle's in-orbit time is shorter than originally planned—for example, ten days instead of thirty—mission activities are intense and go around the clock. Typically, there will be a six- or seven-man crew which operates in three-man, twelve-hour shifts.

Spacelab missions are directed from two control centers. The first, Mission Control at Johnson Space Center, retains overall control of and responsibility for the completion of the flight. For the most part, Mission Control defers to the Payload Operations Control Center (POCC), where the science phase of the mission is directed. Thus, Spacelab is heavily dependent on the Tracking and Data-Relay Satellite System (TDRSS) to relay telemetry from the experiments to the POCC and commands back from the POCC.

Knowledge Gained

Spacelab has proved a versatile and useful facility for conducting space science research. Spacelabs 1, 2, 3, and D-1 (this last set of experiments were sponsored by West Germany)—and the various single-pallet payloads flown on STS 2, 3, and 41G—were all successful. Unfortunately, in the view of many scientists, NASA has made use of the facility too difficult. In fact, in the era preceding the 1986 *Challenger* tragedy, the agency replaced its own science payloads with commercial and military equipment. Thus, scientists soon found themselves in a sort of inflationary spiral where the cost of a mission required extreme efforts to guarantee success, which, in turn, raised the cost of the mission.

To combat this problem, NASA conducted a Spacelab mission integration cost analysis and developed a concept known as the dedicated discipline laboratories (DDL). Each DDL would comprise a group of experiments with similar or complementary mission requirements. For example, it would be logical to carry astronomical instruments and solar instruments on one mission, since they would have similar pointing requirements during a mission. One would not, perhaps, think to carry materials and life-science experiments together until one compared their needs: heavy electrical power demands and intermittent tuning for materials experiments, and intense manpower and low-power demands for life sciences. Yet procedures often required of biomedical experiments can be disruptive to crystal-growth and other fluid experiments. Thus, carrying them together would require innovative scheduling to avoid conflicts.

At the very least, the DDL concept would reduce the integration cost of Spacelab missions by reducing the analysis and paperwork required for each mission. At the best, much work could be avoided by allowing clusters of instruments to remain intact until their next flight. Even requests to upgrade instruments were disregarded in order to cut costs.

The Spacelab and shuttle experiences have also contributed to a better understanding of what is required to support a vigorous experiment program. This knowledge led to the development of intermediate payload carriers between Spacelab and the Get-Away Specials, an innovative payload system. The effort required to replace even a single rack inside the module affected the design of the U.S. space station, so its racks are now better designed for easy replacement in orbit.

Context

Spacelab has proved difficult for scientists from some disciplines to use. Materials scientists need as smooth a ride as possible so that samples are not jostled (excessive motion disrupts the formation of crystals and the study of fluid flows). These required conditions are at odds with necessary crew exercise periods and even with pumps and fans that cool Spacelab. Early shuttle missions discovered a phenomenon known as "shuttle glow," an eerie luminescence that peaks in the infrared spectrum. The cause remains under debate but appears to be some chemical reaction between the shuttle itself and rare molecular species in the upper atmosphere. The shuttle glow hampers observations in the infrared and low-light levels under certain conditions.

Spacelab grew out of a 1969 invitation by NASA for the European Space Research Organization (ESRO) to become involved in the post-Apollo space program. European involvement in U.S. space activities had been commonplace since the origins of NASA but rarely had been larger than limited partnerships on small satellite projects. The European Space Conference in 1970 authorized studies with the United States in the post-Apollo area. In 1972, NASA selected the space shuttle program as its major effort for the 1970's.

As conceived, the space shuttle was to have a reusable third stage, called the Space Tug, to carry satellites to and from geostationary orbit and other destinations. ESRO was very interested in developing this vehicle, which it saw as having potential uses aboard European launch vehicles then under study and possibly providing more jobs for the European aerospace industry. Yet because the shuttle also was to serve a number of U.S. military payloads, the Department of Defense opposed any foreign role in the Space Tug, especially since ESRO might try to veto launches of defense satellites it found objectionable. In 1972, both the Department of Defense and the State Department formally denied ESRO a role in the Space Tug, and an alternate was sought by NASA and ESRO. The two possibilities were structural elements of the shuttle orbiter and a science lab that would fit in the payload bay. Of the two, ESRO found the latter more attractive because it would provide research opportunities for European scientists and provide the community with direct experience in manned spaceflight.

NASA had for some time been studying a research and applications module (RAM), which would function as a lab facility and turn the shuttle into a temporary space station. Since a permanent space station was on indefinite hold, that was seen as necessary to continue manned space research.

Between December, 1972, at the ministerial meeting of the European Space Conference, and August, 1973, NASA and ESRO officials conducted concept and definition studies of the laboratory facility, soon called Spacelab. An intergovernmental agreement was reached in August, 1973, and a memorandum of understanding was signed by NASA Administrator James Fletcher that month and the ESRO director general, Alexander Hocker, in September.

Under the terms of the memorandum, ESRO would design and build a complete Spacelab flight unit for use by NASA and ESRO aboard the space shuttle "for peaceful purposes," and NASA agreed to buy a second flight unit at a price to be negotiated later. Although the term "peaceful purposes" is subject to debate, it has been interpreted by NASA and ESRO (later ESA) as permitting Department of Defense research missions but not weapons missions. In 1974, a West German consortium was selected as the prime contractor for Spacelab. In keeping with ESRO's international nature, contracts were awarded to ESRO member nations in proportion to their contributions to Spacelab. In this manner, each nation recouped most of the money that it had invested in Spacelab. Finally, in 1975, ESRO merged with the European Launcher Development Organization (ELDO) to become the European Space Agency.

ESA's experience in developing Spacelab, and in flying it less often than expected, led that agency to assume a tougher negotiating stance on participation in the space station missions and to demand treatment as an equal partner in the space community. It has also provided the basis for ESA's own Columbus program to develop a human-tended station.

Bibliography

Dooling, Dave. "Future Spacelab Missions." *Space World* T-10-238 (October, 1983): 33-37. Describes efforts by NASA to reduce the cost of future Spacelab missions and plans for dedicated discipline laboratories. Written for the general reader. Illustrated.

_____. "Spacelab 1." *Space World* T-8-9-236/237 (August/September, 1983): 8-14. This article provides an overview of how a Spacelab mission is developed and traces the plans for Spacelab 1. Describes preliminary results from the Spacelab pallets carried on STS 2 and STS 3.

Froelich, Walter. *Spacelab: An International Short-Stay Orbiting Laboratory.* NASA EP-165. Washington, D.C.: Government Printing Office, 1983. A booklet designed for teachers and students. Describes the development of Spacelab and the work required to assemble a mission. Includes color illustrations.

National Aeronautics and Space Administration. *Spacelab 1.* NASA MR-009. Washington, D.C.: National Aeronautics and Space Administration, 1984. A NASA publication written for teachers and reporters, with color illustrations and capsule summaries of experiments. It includes a discussion of how an IWG functions and how the mission was conducted.

Shapland, David, and Michael Rycroft. *Spacelab: Research in Earth Orbit.* New York: Cambridge University Press, 1984. A broad description of the development of Spacelab through the first mission, with descriptions of various scientific disciplines it can serve. Written for a general audience.

Dave Dooling

Cross-References

SPACELAB 1

Date: November 28 to December 8, 1983
Type of mission: Manned scientific mission
Countries: The ESA nations and the United States

In addition to achieving scientific successes, Spacelab 1 broke new ground in the degree and speed of political communication among participating nations. The first Spacelab mission also tested the design and structural integrity of the spacecraft, its instrumentation, and crew operations.

Principal personages
ERIK QUISTGAARD, Director General of ESA
IAN PRYKE, Manager of ESA, Washington, D.C., office
U. JOHN SAKSS, Acting Chief of the International Affairs Division, NASA
JAMES C. HARRINGTON, Spacelab Program Director, NASA
ALFRED L. RYAN, Chief, Integration and Testing, NASA
MICHAEL J. SANDER, Director of the Spacelab Flight Division, Office of Space Science and Applications, NASA
ULF MERBOLD, a West German payload specialist
BYRON K. LICHTENBERG, a U.S. payload specialist
OWEN GARRIOTT and
ROBERT PARKER, NASA mission specialists
JOHN YOUNG, the mission commander
BREWSTER SHAW, the mission pilot

Summary of the Mission

Spacelab 1 was the most ambitious international mission conducted up to that time and contained the most experiments of any spaceflight. Launched aboard the shuttle *Columbia* (STS 9) at 2:30 P.M. eastern standard time on November 28, 1983, the Spacelab 1 mission immediately assumed a 250-kilometer orbiting altitude. Of the seventy-one experiments on board, fifty-eight were conducted by Europeans, twelve by Americans, and one by Japanese—all in ten days' flight time using thirty-eight instruments.

Contained within a shuttle orbiter, the Spacelab system is designed to accommodate two different kinds of scientific experimentation. In an enclosed cylindrical laboratory module, scientists work in a shirtsleeve environment. A series of U-shaped pallets, usually located behind the module in the orbiter cargo bay, holds experiments which can be exposed to the harsh space environment. Taken together, the two separate constructions constitute a versatile system; the laboratory module exists in two sizes, long and short, and the pallets can be used singly or in conjunction with the module. One can envision the module together with one, two, or three pallets, depending on whether the long or short module is used, or without the module at all, in which case it is possible to position five pallets in a row using the entire length of the cargo bay.

Spacelab offers several unconventional arrangements of experiment equipment, such as those which could not be used on a satellite. It is capable of carrying and housing many experiments in one concentrated mass. It provides power and thermal control for the experiments, as well as a computerized system to manage the support subsystems, and it allows for humans to operate and monitor the experiments and equipment. By combining these capabilities, Spacelab allows scientists to conduct experiments in an environment similar to that of a ground laboratory, such as the American Skylab or the Soviet Salyut. It is carefully designed, using new equipment engineered specifically for the Spacelab system.

Spacelab 1 measured 2.7 meters and was set between two end cones. The short module was about 4.3 meters in length, the long module about 7 meters in length with the end cones in place. The diameter of the cylinders measured 4 meters. The experiment equipment was located in the 2.7-meter core segment; if more space were needed, a second segment was added to the core segment. All the experiment equipment was of a modular design, set in standard-sized single racks or double racks stacked on top of one another. A cylindrical tunnel between the orbiter and the Spacelab was created so that a scientist could pass from inside the shuttle orbiter to inside the Spacelab module without being exposed to the outside space environment. A total communication system linked orbiter astronauts and Spacelab payload specialists, and the environment temperature and pressure were equalized throughout the orbiter-tunnel-Spacelab complex. The Spacelab system of pressurized laboratory and open pallets was fixed solidly to the floor of the orbiter.

Spacelab derives its versatility from the combinations of configurations used— module only, module and pallets, pallets only. The Spacelab 1 mission consisted of a long module and one pallet. In addition, Spacelab was pressurized like a commercial airplane at 1 atmosphere so that the astronauts could breathe the same way they breathed on the ground. The module was fitted with handholds and foot restraints inside as well as outside for easy crew mobility. Normal and emergency lighting was easily controlled by crew members, who also had access to a full complement of tools (wrenches, pliers, screwdrivers, and the like) to repair equipment. Just inside the entrance to the cylindrical module was the Spacelab control center, where all the experiment equipment and subsystems could be monitored. Special cooling equipment in the form of fans and heat exchanger plates kept the interior temperature constant.

In the ceiling of the core segment was a viewport, as well as a vent system to dump unwanted gases. An air lock was fitted to the roof of the equipment section for specialized experiments, to permit an astronaut to pass outside the Spacelab or to attach a specialized piece of equipment that needed to be exposed to the space environment. The laboratory was fitted throughout with warning and safety devices to protect the crew from dangerous changes in temperature or the presence of toxic gases, and the module temperature was kept at a pleasant 22 degrees Celsius with about 50 percent humidity.

Spacelab 1 involved six crew members: two National Aeronautics and Space Administration (NASA) astronauts in the orbiter's flight deck to operate and navigate the shuttle orbiter, two NASA astronaut mission specialists to operate the orbiter resources for the Spacelab as well as assist with experiments, and two payload specialists responsible for the onboard operation of scientific experiments. Mission specialists and payload specialists were responsible for the execution of the Spacelab flightplan. All six crew members for the Spacelab 1 mission were trained by the mission manager at the Marshall Space Flight Center, in addition to the European Space Agency's training pertaining to its experiments in Spacelab.

Data transfer from Spacelab 1 to the ground was accomplished by NASA's Tracking and Data-Relay Satellite System (TDRSS), at 50 million bits per second, and by the NASA Spaceflight Tracking and Data Network (STDN), at 192,000 bits per second, using S-band antennae. Both of these systems are connected to the Payload Operations Control Center in Houston, Texas. The shuttle orbiter fuel cells generate electricity by oxygen-hydrogen conversion, converting to alternating and direct current at either 150 or 200 volts. A high-rate data stream can handle data from sixteen sources, transmitted either in real time or after recorder storing. Spacelab 1 carried three identical general-purpose computers, each dedicated to a specific function and controlled by software programs, and an 8-million-word mass memory unit of coded instructions which was fed into the computer system before each flight.

During the launch of STS 9, the astronauts and mission and payload specialists rode inside the shuttle orbiter. Some three and one-half hours into the flight, the huge shuttle opened its cargo bay doors to expose the Spacelab system, and the laboratory module structure was made operational. Personnel could float through the tunnel and enter the Spacelab facility at will. Spacelab crews worked in shifts, dividing their time between duties in the Spacelab and rest time or additional duties inside the shuttle orbiter. The remote manipulator system, a flexible arm 15 meters long, was permanently attached to the shuttle and could be used to operate or move instruments about on the exposed pallets. Fitted with elbow and wrist-type joints, and with an elbow-joint television camera, the remote manipulator system was controlled from inside the shuttle orbiter. Personnel could see what was happening by looking out the aft shuttle cockpit windows or by watching a television screen. At the end of the mission, Spacelab personnel returned to the shuttle crew compartment, and the cargo bay doors were closed and locked, firmly sealing the Spacelab module and the pallets in the cargo bay.

A reusable system designed to make up to fifty spaceflights, the Spacelab is refitted and modified after each mission; completely new equipment is sometimes added to allow experimenters to investigate new subjects of inquiry. All stored onboard data are brought back and shared with interested scientists.

Knowledge Gained

While it is impossible to review all seventy-one of the scientific experiments conducted on Spacelab 1, several of the more spectacular achievements deserve mention. In general, the Spacelab experiments fall into six categories: verification flights (also known as shakedown missions), materials processing, space plasma physics, life sciences, astronomy and solar physics, and atmospheric physics and Earth observation.

Since no in-space tests of the Spacelab configuration had been made before the Spacelab 1 flight, the verification flight of the Spacelab 1 mission was critical to test all the hardware operations and compatibilities of the Spacelab system structures. The Spacelab 1 mission, especially, was a test to make certain that all the equipment functioned as designed.

When heavy metals are melted and mixed on Earth, the heaviest settle before the mixture cools to a solid state. Reduced gravity allows the materials to remain in a uniform mixed condition. Also, in a weightless environment, incompatible substances can usually be mixed together into new combinations of materials. Materials processing experiments were conducted to test uniform combining, purer mixtures, and new materials created from mixing new combinations of existing materials. In tests of the reverse phenomenon, materials separation was accomplished with ease. Also, studies were made of containerless materials, materials which must be contained on Earth but which were found to hold together in space without being confined by a container. Liquids and near liquids both were tested. The process of solidification was studied to determine rates and uniformity of congealing, turning liquids and gases to solids.

To accomplish various tests, Spacelab 1 was fitted with several well-designed instruments: a gradient heating facility to study crystal growth, a fluid physics module to study weightless fluids, an isothermal heating facility for the study of solidification of metals and alloys, a mirror heating facility which concentrated heat from a filament upon a single element, and six other pieces of specialized equipment. A materials science double rack was specially constructed to hold this new equipment.

Astronomy and solar physics instruments included a new Faust telescope for far ultraviolet imaging, a very wide field camera for making a general ultraviolet survey of the cosmos on a large scale, and a spectroscopy unit to study detailed features of cosmic rays. Other instruments measured the total solar radiation and the energy output of the Sun, detected faint optical emissions, observed the effects of charged particle beam injections into Earth's upper atmosphere, measured the magnetic field surrounding the orbiter while in flight, measured the wavelengths in the airglow spectrum, and surveyed Earth's atmosphere between 15 and 150 kilometers.

In the life sciences area, instruments were devised to detect radiation penetration to the inside of Spacelab and measure the influence of the space environment on various biological specimens. Researchers studying spacesickness designed experiments that would detect changes in spinal reflexes and posture during prolonged weightlessness, investigate the vestibular functions of the inner ear, help determine the effect of weightlessness on the body's immune response, and measure changes in the circulating red blood cell mass. Data were collected on changes in the distribution of body fluids and minerals, as well as mass discrimination perception in space. Plant growth in Spacelab was compared with plant growth on Earth.

Spacelab 1 made a significant contribution to space science and to human living and working conditions in the space environment. Both NASA and ESA shared equal payload availability; NASA's concentration during the mission was on atmospheric phenomena, while ESA concerned itself mostly with materials processing. Spacelab 1 experiments were activated after 2.5 hours into the mission, and the crew entered the facility about one hour later. At the end of the mission, the entire Spacelab structure was found to be without a single leak. Both the viewing window and the triple-glass viewports functioned perfectly. The Spacelab facility was monitored by more than fifty strain gauges and thirty accelerometers throughout the flight, and the facility was found to respond to the normal expected stresses. No gases or toxic fumes, no unwanted or unexpected sounds, and no interior water condensation were detected during the flight. Relative humidity was kept below 40 percent, and the air temperature was kept at about 20 degrees Celsius. Most of the data obtained during the mission confirmed the correct planning of procedures.

Earth observation experiments were carried out using two instruments: a metric camera, responsible for more than five hundred color and black-and-white images during the flight, and a microwave remote sensing instrument which failed because its transmitter did not operate. Most of the experiments, however, functioned as expected. The crew demonstrated its ability to operate equipment with ease and precision and went beyond planned experiments by modifying computer software, repairing broken equipment, and even improvising a photography darkroom. On occasion they devised new investigations, demonstrating once again (as in the earlier Skylab missions) the value of thinking humans in space to react and respond to unplanned situations.

Context

Ongoing space research and experimentation through the use of the Spacelab system allow scientists of many nations to glean important data from all the experiments conducted. The missions following Spacelab 1 were possible because of the successful record of the Spacelab 1 crew and their dedicated work. New knowledge increased at an enormous rate as a result of the Spacelab 1 mission, much faster than scientists on the ground expected considering the multiplicity of disciplines and detailed experiments.

In all, four separate missions of the Spacelab system were launched from November, 1983, to September, 1985. The first three—Spacelabs 1 through 3—were undertaken primarily for the European Space Agency; the fourth was prepared and manned by West Germany and reserved entirely for its universities, industries, and research institutions. All four flights were successful beyond expectations and resulted in significant contributions to space science, space systems management, and spaceflight.

The Spacelab system is able to take advantage of the characteristics of spaceflight which offer prolonged weightlessness (microgravity), large sweeping views of Earth regions, a view of the universe free from an obstructing atmosphere, a high and nearly complete vacuum, and access to cosmic phenomena near Earth. In this sense, the Spacelab system represented a new and highly useful tool enabling humans to work at the very doorstep to the universe, high above the restrictions of an earthbound environment.

Spacelab is inextricably linked to the destiny of the shuttle orbiter because it was specifically designed to fit the shuttle cargo bay. There are, however, numerous possible ways to change the Spacelab module to fit other configurations; placing it on the surface of some of the planets or having it serve as a science module attached to a space station or free-flying orbiting platform are two such possible setups. As a protective habitat for human space exploration, Spacelab has, within its design limits, the capacity to furnish a mobile space laboratory for use beyond the normal ties to Earth. Because of the unqualified success of Spacelab 1, space engineering and science investigation entered a new phase of sophistication.

In a political sense, the Spacelab system proved to be a giant step forward in the continued development of the European Space Agency and European scientific research, attesting the ingenuity of European engineers and scientists determined to establish themselves in a position of leadership in space. Spacelab is an important example of European creative engineering and cooperative scientific investigation and has made the ESA nations more determined to develop a common philosophy of space exploration. It is impossible to assess Spacelab's enormous impact on the development of worldwide space projects for human benefit.

Bibliography

Baker, David. *The History of Manned Space Flight.* New York: Crown Publishers, 1981. A large volume with many illustrations, this book offers a complete overview of the manned space programs undertaken by various nations from the first dreams of space travel to the flights of 1981. Included are sections on Spacelab.

Froehlich, Walter. *Spacelab: An International Short-Stay Orbiting Laboratory.* NASA EP-165. Washington, D.C.: Government Printing Office, 1983. Filled with definitive information on every conceivable aspect of the Spacelab system and illustrated with sometimes lavish color and excellent black-and-white photographs and diagrams, this marvelous booklet explains NASA's role in the Spacelab project.

National Aeronautics and Space Administration. *Spacelab 1.* NASA SP-1-46. Washington, D.C.: Government Printing Office, 1982. This full-color thirty-page booklet covers the personnel, design, purpose, and equipment of the first Spacelab mission. Photographs and line drawings provide further details on the mission.

_____ . *Spacelab 2.* NASA EP-217. Washington, D.C.: Government Printing Office, 1985. This booklet recounts the aims and achievements of the second flight of Spacelab. Illustrated.

Shapland, David, and Michael Rycroft. *Spacelab: Research in Earth Orbit.* New York: Cambridge University Press, 1984. If this is not the only standard reference work on Spacelab, surely it is the best and most comprehensive. Well written, this book explains the concept of the ESA Spacelab system in charts, diagrams, photographs, and anecdotal material. Organized logically, from the original conception of Spacelab to the complexities of space research in orbit.

Thomas W. Becker

Cross-References

Biological Effects of Space Travel on Humans, 188; The European Space Agency, 372; Food and Diet for Space Travel, 454; The Salyut Space Station, 1233; The Skylab Program, 1285; Skylab 2, 1291; Skylab 3, 1298; Skylab 4, 1303; Space Law: Ongoing Issues, 1612; The U.S. Space Shuttle, 1626; Space Shuttle Living Conditions, 1634; Space Shuttle Mission 9: *Columbia*, 1705; The Development of the U.S. Space Station, 1835; International Contributions to the U.S. Space Station, 1843; Living and Working in the U.S. Space Station, 1850; Modules and Nodes of the U.S. Space Station, 1857; The Spacelab Program, 1884; Spacelab 2, 1898; Spacelab 3, 1904.

SPACELAB 2

Date: July 29 to August 6, 1985
Type of mission: Manned scientific mission
Country: The United States

Spacelab 2 collected important new data in the scientific disciplines of infrared astronomy, high-energy astrophysics, solar physics, plasma physics, physics of the upper atmosphere, the life sciences, and space technology.

Principal personages
DAN SPICER, the program scientist
LOUIS J. DEMAS, the program manager
ROY C. LESTER, the mission manager
EUGENE W. URBAN, a mission scientist
CHARLES GORDON FULLERTON, the commander
ROY D. BRIDGES, the pilot
ANTHONY W. ENGLAND,
F. STORY MUSGRAVE, and
KARL G. HENIZE, mission specialists
LOREN W. ACTON and
JOHN-DAVID F. BARTOE, payload specialists

Summary of the Mission

Spacelab 2 was an engineering test flight of the Spacelab system. This mission marked the first time all the major equipment and experiments were mounted in the payload bay of the space shuttle orbiter. Since there was no manned module in the bay, as there had been for Spacelabs 1 and 3, the experiments were operated from the aft flight deck in the orbiter, immediately behind the commander's and pilot's seats. Conducting these experiments was, in fact, an engineering objective of the mission, since it was the most definitive way to demonstrate the value of the new Spacelab approach to conducting science in the space shuttle. Operation of the precise instrument pointing system (IPS), which carried four solar telescopes, was another engineering objective of the mission, as was a test of the orbiter's ability to release, maneuver, and recover a subsatellite. The crew of seven consisted of the commander; the pilot; three mission specialists, who operated the orbiter and Spacelab equipment; and two payload specialists, who operated the experiments.

The thirteen Spacelab 2 experiments were selected in 1977 from more than two hundred proposals submitted to the National Aeronautics and Space Administration (NASA). They were primarily astrophysics and solar physics investigations but included plasma experiments and atmospheric and life sciences experiments as well. Most were newly developed systems, but three had previously been flown in the space shuttle. These three were included to demonstrate the value of the repeated reflight capability provided by the shuttle.

The various experiments on board had greatly differing observation requirements. One experiment required pointing solar telescopes at specific points on the Sun for many minutes at a time—and doing so several times throughout the eight-day mission. Others involved scanning an infrared telescope over the entire sky except the Sun, the Moon, and Earth; pointing an X-ray telescope at astronomical targets for long periods; and releasing a plasma physics experiment package overboard, flying the orbiter around it while the package measured the local plasma environment, then recovering the package. Some of the experiments, particularly the solar experiments and two biological experiments, were controlled by the onboard payload specialists and mission specialists, who were scientists and scientist-engineers.

All the experiments' operations had to be carefully planned in advance to ensure that the orbiter would always be oriented properly for the particular experiment which was operating, that the proper astronomical targets were in view, that adequate electrical and cooling power was available, and that the appropriate crewman was on duty and ready to act. This planning process was an ongoing one, because the Spacelab 2 launch date was delayed many times and other conditions changed constantly. Furthermore, it was essential that the entire scientific operation could be replanned during the mission, in case the orbital conditions were not as expected or some experiment did not work as designed. Also, if a new observation made it necessary to change scientific priorities the experiments could then be rearranged. This replanning activity was practiced repeatedly before Spacelab 2 was launched, and the science and operations teams were trained to conduct replanning every twelve hours.

Spacelab 2 was to have been launched on July 12, 1985, for a seven-day flight. On that date, the Moon was new, or dark, which aided several of the experiments. Three seconds before lift-off, a technical problem caused a launch abort. The flight was rescheduled for July 29. A launch at 2:23 P.M. on July 29 would have enabled the Spacelab crew to follow most of the detailed experimental time line which had been prepared for the July 12 launch. By that date, however, the Moon was full, so some experimental changes were unavoidable.

On July 29, it was necessary to delay the launch from 2:23 until 4:00 P.M. eastern daylight time. Then, as the *Challenger* was ascending, one of its three main engines shut down prematurely. The shuttle reached Earth orbit but was forced to jettison a large mass of the liquid fuel which was to have been used for maneuvering and attitude control.

The *Challenger* finally attained a circular orbit some 300 kilometers high, shortening the orbital period somewhat and also restricting the usable viewing time of one of the solar experiments. Since the Spacelab 2 orbital period was about ninety minutes, the launch delay of 1 hour and 37 minutes shifted all the planned operations, astronomical targets, and Sun-observing opportunities. All these factors meant that the previously planned observation program was no longer valid. Immediate and extensive replanning was begun, and it continued intensively and very successfully throughout the mission. Through careful use of electrical power and propellant resources, Spacelab 2 was able to stay in orbit for an eighth day. Because of the well-rehearsed and highly cooperative scientific and operations team effort, most of the experiments acquired as many or more data than had been anticipated.

The onboard instruments included a large, egg-shaped cosmic-ray nuclei experiment mounted in the aft end of the orbiter bay which, at 1,968 kilograms, was the heaviest single instrument to be carried into space up to that time. It was designed to detect and measure high-energy charged particles from deep space which cannot be directly detected from the ground. An infrared telescope, which was cooled to a temperature of 3 Kelvins by superfluid liquid helium, scanned back and forth across the sky to map cool and diffuse dust and gas clouds in star-forming regions of the Milky Way. A dual X-ray telescope on a two-axis gimbal generated images of clusters of distant galaxies and of X-ray objects within the Galaxy, particularly within the galactic center.

Other experiments included a plasma diagnostics package of fourteen instruments which measured space plasma and electromagnetic fields; it was jettisoned and later recovered by means of the Canadian-built remote manipulator arm. A vehicle-charging experiment shot a weak electron beam into space and measured electrical charge and voltage changes on the orbiter. Three solar telescopes detected fine details of violent processes in several different regions of the Sun's atmosphere and identified the elements involved in them. One solar experiment accurately measured the total energy output of the Sun. A physics experiment measured some of the properties of superfluid liquid helium in low gravity. A plant growth experiment, conducted within the *Challenger*'s cabin, was designed to collect data on the effects of low gravity on the growth of plant seedlings. A medical experiment measured the degree to which low gravity causes calcium loss from crew members' bones by analysis of blood samples collected before, during, and after the flight.

The final experiment had no onboard hardware. It was performed from the ground by remotely observing the changes in Earth's ionosphere when the orbiter's main engines were fired, producing giant clouds of water vapor. The engines were to have been fired eight times over five ground stations in Massachusetts, Canada, Puerto Rico, Tasmania, and Kwajalein Atoll in the Pacific Ocean.

Knowledge Gained

The cosmic-ray experiment collected data on several hundred impacts of extremely high-energy cosmic-ray particles, as well as millions of lower-energy particles, and was able to extend scientists' knowledge of the cosmic-ray spectrum. The infrared telescope was partially blinded by an unforeseen, widely distributed cloud of infrared-emitting material around the shuttle. Nevertheless, the data from the telescope led to the creation of new maps of the infrared sky in short wavelengths and helped scientists determine that the so-called shuttle glow phenomenon, a faint emission detected near the surface of the shuttle as it flew through the ionosphere, was weak in the infrared part of the spectrum. The X-ray telescope produced many new images of clusters of X-ray galaxy sources and observed for the first time energetic X-ray sources very near the galactic center. The plasma diagnostic package was released overboard and continuously measured local fields and plasma densities as the *Challenger* made two complete "fly-around" maneuvers.

The most exciting results were the detection of the effects on the ionosphere of the electron beam generated by the vehicle-charging experiment and the direct observation of the electron beam itself when the *Challenger* was moved so that the beam could travel several hundred meters along Earth's magnetic field to the diagnostic package.

One of the solar experiments could not be activated until the last day of the mission because of an internal problem. Yet it produced some of the most important observations ever made of the Sun: long sequences of very steady white-light photographs of two small regions of the Sun's surface, including a sunspot, which resulted in films showing fine details of hot gas convection cells. Such details cannot be seen by observers using even the best ground-based solar telescopes because of distortions caused by Earth's atmosphere. A second solar telescope, which was sensitive to ultraviolet light produced by very energetic processes, photographed violent gas motions higher in the Sun's atmosphere and measured the most important chemical elements involved in these motions. The third experiment, an ultraviolet spectrograph, made a new, accurate determination of the relative amounts of helium, hydrogen, and several other elements in the outer atmosphere, or corona, of the Sun. This information is used to determine the temperature and densities of the extremely hot corona and helps scientists theorize about the evolution of the solar system. The solar irradiance experiment measured the ultraviolet energy output of the Sun with much more precision than is possible from the ground. It had been flown once before and would be flown again to provide a long-term history of changes in the Sun's total output.

The superfluid helium experiment proved somewhat problematic. Yet it did measure the motion of superfluid helium at a temperature of 1.5 Kelvins under different conditions: when the orbiter was very quiet and when the crew was deliberately very active. Several types of seedlings were grown in the plant experiment. Besides yielding photographs of their growth anomalies when gravity was absent, the experiment gave information on chemical processes in the plants as they grew— especially on the formation of the material lignin, which gives plants their structural strength. Analysis of blood samples confirmed earlier conclusions concerning bone decalcification in low gravity.

The ground-based ionospheric disturbance experiment was curtailed because of the reduced propellant available. Nevertheless, four major disturbances were produced by *Challenger*'s engines over ground stations: two over an observatory at Millstone Hill, Massachusetts; one over Arecibo, Puerto Rico; and one over Hobart, Tasmania. The ensuing chemical and ionic disruption and "healing" of the ionosphere were accurately measured. During the Hobart test, it was seen that radio waves from distant astronomical sources could more easily reach ground antennae when passing through the disturbed regions.

Context

Spacelab 2 was the third of an intended long series of Spacelab science missions. The Spacelab system is a modular set of support equipment designed and built by the European Space Agency (ESA). The equipment serves as a flying laboratory which interfaces with the shuttle system to provide a standard set of experiment mounting equipment (open pallets in the payload bay and laboratory racks in the manned module, which is also in the bay); standard electrical power, experiment control, thermal control, and data collection resources; and a habitable, shirtsleeve environment for experiments which require it.

Spacelabs 1 and 3, which flew before Spacelab 2, both included a manned module in the bay. Spacelab 1 had one exposed pallet, while Spacelab 3 had two experiments on a special exposed structure. Spacelab 2 had three exposed pallets: The ESA IPS with the four solar telescopes was on the first one, the X-ray telescope was on the second, and the infrared telescope, plasma package, and liquid helium experiment were on the third. The vehicle-charging experiment had equipment mounted on two of the pallets. The cosmic-ray experiment was mounted directly to the *Challenger*, and the remote manipulator arm was stowed along the left sill of the bay.

During the operation of experiments on Spacelab 2, it was crucial to ensure that it would always be possible to close the payload bay doors so the shuttle could land. Since the solar telescopes extended well out of the bay when the IPS was raised, provisions were made so that an astronaut could disconnect the cluster of telescopes from the IPS and eject the cluster overboard. It also would have been possible to jettison the entire IPS with the cluster attached. It was also necessary to make provisions—by scheduling, by use of mechanical restraints, and by computer software—to ensure that the X-ray telescope and the solar telescopes would not collide.

By the time Spacelab 2 had completed its scientific operations, not only had the experiments collected much important new data but also the Spacelab hardware had proved its value in the advancement of space science. After Spacelab 2, a manned module mission sponsored by West Germany (known as Spacelab D1) was flown. Additional Spacelab missions were later developed, including a series of astrophysics payloads and a Japanese-sponsored mission known as Spacelab J.

Bibliography

Froehlich, Walter. *Spacelab: An International Short-Stay Orbiting Laboratory.* NASA EP-165. Washington, D.C.: Government Printing Office, 1983. This resource discusses the role of Spacelab in the larger context of NASA's primary objectives. Contains many details about the Spacelab system. Illustrated with photographs and diagrams.

Lord, Douglas R. *Spacelab: An International Success Story*. NASA SP-487. Washington, D.C.: Government Printing Office, 1987. A complete history of the establishment of the international agreements and the design, construction, and flight testing of the Spacelab system, written by the first NASA Spacelab program director. Contains a step-by-step history, interspersed with personal observations, and a summary of the first three missions. With many sketches and color photographs.

National Aeronautics and Space Administration. *Spacelab 2*. NASA EP-217. Washington, D.C.: Government Printing Office, 1985. A well-illustrated guide to the design, crew members, objectives, and experimental equipment of the Spacelab 2 mission.

Shapland, David, and Michael Rycroft. *Spacelab: Research in Earth Orbit*. New York: Cambridge University Press, 1984. This useful book provides a broad overview of the goals of the Spacelab program and describes the various scientific fields which benefit from the data Spacelab gathers. Written for a general audience.

Urban, Eugene W. "First Results from Spacelab 2." *Nature* 319 (February 13, 1986): 540-542. A summary of the mission, this article also provides an early indication of the types of information acquired by the experiments.

Eugene W. Urban

Cross-References

Biological Effects of Space Travel on Humans, 188; The European Space Agency, 372; Marshall Space Flight Center, 908; The U.S. Space Shuttle, 1626; Space Shuttle Living Conditions, 1634; Space Shuttle Mission 19: *Challenger*, 1780; The Spacelab Program, 1884; Spacelab 1, 1891; Spacelab 3, 1904.

SPACELAB 3

Date: April 29 to May 6, 1985
Type of mission: Manned scientific mission
Country: The United States

Spacelab 3 conducted experiments in the growth of crystals and the behavior of fluids in conditions of weightlessness and provided experiment opportunities in other space science fields.

Principal personages

JOHN S. THEON, the program scientist
ROBERT NOBLITT, the program manager
GEORGE FICHTL, the project scientist
JOE CREMIN, the project manager
ROBERT F. OVERMYER, the mission commander
FREDERICK D. GREGORY, the mission pilot
WILLIAM E. THORNTON,
NORMAN E. THAGARD, and
DON L. LIND, mission specialists
TAYLOR G. WANG and
LODEWIJK VAN DEN BERG, payload specialists

Summary of the Mission

Spacelab 3 was the forerunner of dedicated discipline laboratories, which would cater to a handful of science disciplines rather than try to be something for everyone, as Spacelabs 1 and 2 had done. The Spacelab craft on this mission consisted of the 6.96-meter-long module and a 1-meter-thick multipurpose equipment support structure that supported two instruments outside the module.

Spacelab 3's crew conducted investigations in four major disciplines. Two, materials sciences and fluid mechanics, required that the space shuttle carrying Spacelab 3 curtail maneuvers for days at a time so that accelerations would be as low as possible. The materials sciences and fluid mechanics experiments were located within a meter or so of the spacecraft's center of gravity to reduce acceleration effects that would otherwise result. The other two disciplines were life sciences and atmospheric and astronomical observations. Experiment gear ranged from large multiuser facilities to single-purpose devices.

Space shuttle mission 51B (*Challenger*) was selected to carry Spacelab 3. The only problem of note during the countdown happened when the liquid hydrogen umbilical arm retracted with too much force, breaking the hydrogen vent arm and starting a small fire on the launchpad. Later, the countdown was held at T minus 4 minutes when a liquid oxygen replenish valve did not close as planned. The valves had to be closed by manual command and the count held another minute to allow enough time for oxygen to drain from the fill lines.

Spacelab 3 was launched at 11:02:18 A.M. eastern daylight time on April 29, 1985. All systems worked properly during ascent, and *Challenger* was inserted into an orbit 350 kilometers high, with an inclination of 57 degrees. As with other Spacelab missions, the crew was divided into two teams, each working twelve-hour shifts and for some time before and after in "handover" activities. Robert F. Overmyer, Don L. Lind, William E. Thornton, and Taylor G. Wang were the "silver" team; Frederick D. Gregory, Norman E. Thagard, and Lodewijk van den Berg were the "gold" team.

The first in-orbit activities involved not Spacelab, but a pair of secondary payloads added late in mission planning. These were Get-Away Special Experiment canisters modified to deploy small, inexpensive satellites. The first, Nusat (Northern Utah Satellite), was assembled by students from Weber State College in Ogden, Utah, to provide a calibration beacon for air traffic control radar. It was successfully deployed about four hours after launch. The second, GLOMR (Global Ocean Monitor Research), was designed by the Defense Advanced Research Projects Agency to assess the value of using small satellites to query remote data collection devices and relay that information to U.S. armed forces. Its canister lid apparently did not retract far enough to activate two microswitches that would trigger deployment. GLOMR was returned to Earth and deployed on a later mission.

Operation of Spacelab started about four hours after launch. The materials sciences project was made up of three experiments designed to grow crystals in space in a fluid experiment system (FES), a vapor crystal growth system (VCGS), and a single-purpose device. The FES housed a complex optical system for holographic, schlieren, and direct-imaging photography and observation of crystals growing in a solution within a 10-cubic centimeter test cell. Two crystals were grown, during 58- and 32.2-hour experiments, instead of the three originally planned, because there were problems with the preheating system and start-up was delayed. The VCGS placed a quartz ampoule inside heating coils to boil off a crystalline substance that was then condensed on a cooled string. One crystal was grown, at rates of 1 to 3 millimeters per hour, during a 118-hour period, and a second one was started. The mercury iodide crystal growth device vaporized crystals in closed ampoules and then recondensed them over a seventy-hour period to study nucleation effects. It had first been operated on Spacelab 1 in 1983, and it had yielded results warranting its inclusion on a second flight under different conditions.

The fluid mechanics category had two experiment facilities, a drop dynamics module and a geophysical fluid flow cell. In the drop dynamics module, scientists could manipulate 2- to 4-centimeter droplets of water or other fluids with three special loudspeakers. Such studies are vital to an understanding of the mechanics of atomic nuclei, of droplets in clouds, and of stars. Early in the mission, the drop dynamics module did not activate properly when a portion of its power supply apparently failed. Wang was the principal investigator and had been closely involved in assembling the drop dynamics facility; he was given permission to open the module and spend whatever time was necessary to repair it. Much of this time was spent in isolating the failed components and then rewiring the power supply so that it could operate on two of three units. This adjustment proved to be highly success-ful, and Wang was able to operate the module in two marathon shifts lasting sixteen hours each before one of the sound generators failed.

The geophysical fluid flow cell used a layer of oil between a sapphire hemisphere and a rotating brass ball to simulate the flow of stellar and large planetary atmo-spheres. An electric field across the fluid acted as "gravity," pulling the fluid toward the inner sphere, while the poles and equator were heated unevenly to induce circulation patterns as the sphere rotated. During the more than 103 hours of the experiment's operation, the crew was able to take about 46,000 images on 16-millimeter film. The experiment functioned for the planned eighty-four hours and for an additional eighteen hours when schedule adjustments freed some time near the end of the mission.

Life sciences investigations aboard Spacelab 3 were mostly intended to verify equipment designed for future dedicated discipline laboratories. A research animal holding facility carried sixteen rats and two squirrel monkeys plus analytical equip-ment to monitor their reactions to space. Although the facility itself worked much as planned, there were problems with containing waste and food particles when the crew changed food trays and collection devices. The crew had to improvise pro-cedures and use tape and plastic to seal off particulates. The monkeys reacted to space much as humans do. One adapted readily; the other suffered space adaptation syndrome for the first few days. Because of his illness, he learned that eating and drinking led to vomiting and thus was in danger of dehydration toward the end of the mission. On the fifth day of the mission, Thornton had to feed the monkey a few banana pellets by hand to revive his interest in food and water.

The urine monitoring system was attached to the waste management facility to provide daily samples of crew urine for studies of mineral and enzyme loss. All calibration tests with the monitoring system were performed as planned, but be-cause of airflow problems, only one of two crewmen scheduled to test it did so. An autogenic feedback training system investigated a possible means of helping astro-nauts combat spacesickness without drugs. Two crewmen served as test subjects, and another two served as controls.

The very wide-field camera was inserted through the air lock to photograph the skies at ultraviolet wavelengths. Its use was aborted early in the mission when the crew used incorrect procedures on the air lock and was unable to extend the camera. The atmospheric trace molecules observed by spectroscopy (ATMOS) device used a Michelson interferometer to observe how sunlight is filtered by the atmosphere at Earth's limb; by subtracting the filtered signal from unfiltered sunlight, the spectral signatures of chemicals in the atmosphere would be revealed. The auroral imaging experiment, conducted with television and still cameras, viewed the aurora australis during several orbits.

The original mission plan called for the ATMOS and wide-field cameras to be used at the start and end of the mission and for the shuttle to coast in a low-gravity attitude (with its tail pointed toward Earth) for several days in between to provide a long period of low acceleration for the materials and fluids experiments. It was quickly noted, however, that a power supply inside the ATMOS instrument was gradually leaking its helium pressurant into space. When the pressure became too low, there would be a short circuit in the power supply. ATMOS itself would continue to operate, but a laser that calibrated its optical path would be lost, rendering the instrument useless. As a result, the materials scientists agreed to defer their experiments for a day to allow ATMOS to gather as much data as possible before failing. It managed twenty occultation observations—out of fifty originally planned—each lasting three minutes. This failure indirectly helped Spacelab 3's cosmic-ray experiment, which used a small stack of plastics with rotating and fixed elements to provide a means of sampling cosmic rays and tagging their time of arrival and direction of flight. The rotation motor failed to start early in the mission. With instructions from the ground, on the fifth day the crew connected the cosmic-ray device to the now-defunct ATMOS's remote acquisition unit and was able to activate the motor.

A second rescheduling was necessary on the sixth day of the mission when the spacecraft had to be reoriented to place more sunlight on the aft thruster pods, which were becoming dangerously cool. This terminated some of the materials experiments, but there was no great loss of data.

Five hours before the end of the mission, Spacelab activities were halted as planned and preparations were begun for the return to Earth. The deorbit maneuver was performed at 11:04 A.M. eastern daylight time. Because two payload bay door latches failed to give "closed" indications (although they were seen to be closed), some entry maneuvers were avoided to reduce the chances of the doors' springing loose.

Knowledge Gained

The twenty observations by ATMOS recorded spectral signatures of a number of rare chemical compounds normally seen only at lower altitudes. These included chlorinated nitrite, dinitrogen pentoxide, nitrous oxide, and methyl chloride, a natural halocarbon.

The single crystal condensed from vapor in the vapor crystal growth system was mercury iodide, which can detect gamma rays at room temperature. (Other crystals must be refrigerated.) The crystal produced weighed 7.2 grams and was 1.2 by 1.2 by 0.8 centimeters in size. Mercury iodide has a gellike consistency and when grown on Earth typically is deformed by it own mass. The mercury iodide crystal grown on Spacelab 3, when subjected to gamma-ray diffraction tests, was shown to have a much cleaner crystalline structure than most crystals grown on Earth.

Similar results were obtained for the two triglycine sulfate crystals grown from an acid solution in the fluid experiment system. Preliminary indications are that this type of crystal, valued as a room-temperature infrared detector, performs better in space than does a similar crystal grown on Earth. The triglycine sulfate crystals on Spacelab 3 were crown-shaped rather than, as had been anticipated, disk-shaped.

Drop dynamics module experiments with rotating droplets confirmed a number of theoretical predictions, including the development of lobe shapes as a droplet spins. The point at which bifurcation (development of a lobe) occurs, however, came earlier than predicted. One unexpected result was the coupling of the inner and outer motions of a rotating droplet, causing it to increase or decrease speed without apparent outside influence.

The geophysical fluid flow cell, as seen through some 46,000 frames of 16-millimeter film, behaved in a manner much like that of stars and gas-giant planets. In one test run, the fluid developed a flow pattern mimicking the Great Red Spot of Jupiter. In another, it produced "banana cells" of pole-equator circulation that are believed to take place beneath the visible surface of the Sun.

The auroral imaging experiment provided three-dimensional images of the aurora australis by combining images taken as the shuttle moved across the edge of the auroral oval. (The aurora borealis was not visible, because the mission took place in the northern spring, or southern fall.) More than 274 photographs and five hours' worth of videotape were collected.

The cosmic-ray experiment recorded more than ten thousand hits, many of which were heavy-mass, high-energy "anomolous" cosmic rays.

The animal studies on Spacelab 3 provided the largest amount of data for post-flight analysis. The monkeys ate less food than is normal on the ground and were less active. Both adapted well to their return to Earth and continued as test subjects for NASA and other experiment programs.

The rats were killed within a day of their return to Earth; they were to have been killed immediately after flight, but earlier problems in landings at Kennedy Space Center had forced a rerouting to Edwards Air Force Base. Heart rate and body temperature measured during the flight were similar to ground measurements; growth of the small rats was normal, but the large rats grew more slowly. Both sizes lost mass in their hind leg muscles; the loss in the small rats was especially pronounced compared with that in control rats kept in identical cages on the ground. The loss apparently was caused by cell shrinkage rather than cell death. A number of other factors, such as growth hormone release, metabolism (as determined by liver content), bone growth, and kidney receptors were found to have undergone changes as a result of weightlessness. Curiously, indications of psychological stress were absent.

The feedback training experiment predicted that one crewman (identified only as crewman A) would have greater success than crewman B in controlling his space adaptation syndrome symptoms. This, indeed, was the case: B had a "severe symptom episode" and A had none. Two control crewmen had several episodes despite taking standard medication.

Finally, the urine monitoring system appeared to work largely as planned, despite some collection problems.

Context

Spacelab 3 was designed to provide more information about operations in weightlessness, and in that respect, it was highly successful. Unfortunately, many of the results were unanticipated and even undesirable.

The fluid experiment system provided an important lesson in low-gravity fluid behavior when the sample chambers were being preheated. At first, their circuit breakers would activate after a few minutes, indicating that the whole unit was overheating. The preheat cycle was meant to melt any unwanted crystals in the solution. The system designers, however, had overlooked the fact that in space, a body of fluid will not have the convective currents normally caused by temperature differences. Without circulation, the fluid in the FES acted like a solid block and was warmed by conduction rather than convection. Ironically, one of the reasons scientists want to do experiments in space is to avoid those convective currents. Fortunately, holographic and schlieren images taken with FES showed that these techniques can indeed be used to visualize solute concentrations in a fluid.

Once the experiment was under way, the crystals did not grow in the manner anticipated. Rather than growing as enlargements of the disklike seed crystals, they grew in the shapes of crowns. Postflight studies revealed a very simple answer: Since there is slightly more surface area exposed at a crystal's edge than at its face, the solute will condense faster there, causing more solute to diffuse inward and increase the growth rate. Future experimenters will have to polish seeds in a curve to eliminate this effect. The crystals that were grown, however, appeared to be more uniform than those grown on the ground.

The mercury iodide crystals grown in the vapor crystal growth system also showed extremely high quality in initial analyses, even though the sample was only 15 millimeters wide by 10 millimeters high, a fraction of the size of the 500-millimeter crystals grown on Earth. The crystals also provided clearer gamma spectra than calibration crystals when exposed to isotope radiation, thus validating this technique for growing strain-free crystals.

Experiments with the drop dynamics module provided quantitative measurements of fluid behavior that had been theorized for more than one hundred years but had gone untested because large, free droplets are impossible to manipulate on Earth. In one test, a rotating droplet deformed into a dog-bone shape and stabilized at a lower rotation speed than expected. Another test showed, when a droplet suddenly stopped and restarted rotation after sound was cut off, that there was more friction than expected between a droplet's inner and outer layers.

The auroral images confirmed the presence of thin, horizontal layers that had been theorized but unconfirmed in ground-based observations. Thin, vertical layers also were observed for the first time. Passage through the auroral arc, and thus through the downward-streaming particles, showed that low-energy events, at least, do not pose a serious radiation or electrical charging hazard to the crew.

Another of the low-gravity mechanics lessons was from the animal facilities. Postflight studies of the eating habits of rats show that a rat will break off a piece of a food bar and chew on the crumbs, thus creating more crumbs. The monkeys were more active than expected. The animal facilities will be redesigned to provide better ventilation control and to prevent food and waste from leaving the pens. The problem's visibility on nationwide television and the crew's comments proved embarrassing to NASA.

Data from ATMOS carried the greatest long-term implications for space science. Two chemical compounds in particular, dinitrogen pentoxide and chlorinated nitrite, were detected in the upper atmosphere for the first time and must now be included in studies of halogen and other cycles in atmospheric chemistry. More than thirty other species were measured at a level of detail never reached before. The instrument's sensitivity also ruled out the presence of other chemicals by placing an upper limit on their concentrations and provided a comprehensive spectral atlas of the Sun in the near- to mid-infrared spectrum. It was expected that ATMOS would be deployed several more times in the 1980's and 1990's to provide a comprehensive inventory of the chemistry of the upper atmosphere.

The feedback experiment showed that noninvasive, drug-free means of combating spacesickness merit further research.

Overall, the Spacelab 3 results were so promising that virtually all the experiments were to be repeated on later flights.

Bibliography

Covault, Craig. "NASA Distributes Spacelab Payload for Analysis Following Landing." *Aviation Week and Space Technology* 122 (May 13, 1985): 18-21. This article provides an overview of the Spacelab 3 mission and its difficulties, including how experiments were rescheduled to accommodate one another's problems. Also includes a discussion of sanitation problems with animals.

_____. "Spacelab Flight to Test Commercial Processing Hardware, Operations." *Aviation Week and Space Technology* 122 (April 22, 1985): 85-89. This illustrated article provides an overview of the mission plans and experiments that were to be conducted during Spacelab 3. Suitable for readers with some technical background.

_____. "Spacelab 3 Demonstrates Crystal Growth, Animal Care." *Aviation Week and Space Technology* 122 (May 6, 1985): 18-20. This article summarizes the operation of the mission at its midpoint, including difficulties encountered during flight. Understandable by general audiences with an interest in space.

National Aeronautics and Space Administration. *Spacelab 3*. NASA EP-203. Washington, D.C.: Author, 1985. This NASA educational publication provides a preflight overview of the experiments. Written for the lay audience and reporters, it provides clear prose and illustrations depicting the experiment plans.

_____ . *Spacelab 3 Mission Science Review*. NASA CP-2429. Washington,

D.C.: Author, 1985. Proceedings of a conference held by the Spacelab 3 investigators' working group to report preliminary results of experiments.

Office of Space Science and Applications. Microgravity Science and Applications Division. *Microgravity: A New Tool for Basic and Applied Research in Space.* NASA EP-212. Washington, D.C.: Government Printing Office, 1984. An introductory text on materials sciences in space and how the low-gravity environment can benefit research on materials formation processes.

Pentecost, Elizabeth, comp. *Microgravity Science and Applications Bibliography.* NASA technical memorandum TM-86651. Rev. ed. Springfield, Va.: National Technical Information Service, 1984. This semitechnical booklet provides a description of materials science facilities, including those flown on Spacelab 3, and how they may be used by researchers. The text also describes low-gravity simulation techniques used on Earth.

Rockwell International. "51-I Press Information." Downey, Calif.: Author, 1985. This is a press kit written to describe the Spacelab 3 mission; it contains a list of major mission activities.

Dave Dooling

Cross-References

Biological Effects of Space Travel on Humans, 188; The Get-Away Special Experiments, 550; Materials Processing in Space, 933; The New Astronomy and the Study of Cosmic Rays, 1059; Space Shuttle Living Conditions, 1634; The Spacelab Program, 1884; Spacelab 1, 1891; Spacelab 2, 1898.

SPACEPLANES

Date: Beginning April, 1986
Type of technology: Aeronautics
Country: The United States

Horizontal takeoff, single-stage-to-orbit vehicles would provide routine access to space and reduce the costs of delivering payloads to orbit. Hypersonic cruise airplanes may evolve from the same technology and make it possible to travel halfway around the globe in less than three hours.

Principal personages

ROBERT R. BARTHELEMY, Program Manager, National Aero-Space Plane Joint Program Office

KENNETH E. STATEN, former Program Manager, National Aero-Space Plane Joint Program Office

RAYMOND S. COLLADAY, Director, Defense Advanced Research Projects Agency

ROBERT M. WILLIAMS, former X-30 Program Manager, Defense Advanced Research Projects Agency

LAWRENCE A. SKANTZE, former Commander, Air Force Systems Command

WILLIAM R. GRAHAM, Director, Office of Science and Technology Policy

ROBERT S. COOPER, former Director, Defense Advanced Research Projects Agency

GEORGE A. KEYWORTH, former Science Advisor to the president

EDWARD C. ALDRIDGE, Under Secretary, U.S. Air Force

BERNARD P. RANDOLPH, Commander, Air Force Systems Command

WILLIAM F. BALLHAUS, JR., Associate Administrator, Office of Aeronautics and Space Technology, NASA

ROBERT A. JONES, chief of the High-Speed Aerodynamics Division, Langley Research Center

ANTHONY A. DUPONT, duPont Aerospace Company

Summary of the Technology

The goal of the United States' National Aero-Space Plane Program is the development of the technology for a new generation of spacecraft: single-stage-to-orbit launch vehicles and hypersonic cruise vehicles. One of the most challenging aerospace projects ever attempted, the spaceplane program is expected to be under way by the beginning of the twenty-first century.

A spaceplane is an airplane that can take off from a conventional runway, fly through the atmosphere—reaching a speed twenty-four times that of sound at 61,000 meters above Earth—and, with minimal rocket power, enter a low Earth orbit. It can then circle Earth several times, reenter the atmosphere, and land, again on a conventional runway. After being serviced, it can repeat the whole procedure. Such a plane would make access to space cheaper, safer, and more reliable. It would not be as big as the U.S. space shuttle's launch system and would not be launched by booster rockets, because its air-breathing propulsion system would render liquid oxygen tanks unnecessary.

An air-breathing, liquid hydrogen-fueled propulsion system is more efficient than a solid- or liquid-fueled rocket. Its specific impulse, or amount of thrust per kilogram of propellant used per second, is three to seven times that of a rocket fueled by liquid hydrogen and liquid oxygen. A spaceplane functions like a jet airplane for the primary acceleration phase; indeed, the main engine used for this phase is a supersonic combustion ramjet, or "scramjet." Because the air-breathing propulsion system is so efficient, even at low thrust levels, and because it can be throttled, an air-breathing vehicle can cruise at subsonic, supersonic, and hypersonic speeds. (Hypersonic speeds exceed five times the speed of sound.)

The National Aero-Space Plane Program, a joint Department of Defense-National Aeronautics and Space Administration (NASA) undertaking, officially began in 1986; President Ronald Reagan mentioned it in his State of the Union address on February 4 of that year. Technology development was scheduled to continue through mid-1990, when a decision would be made on whether to build an "X-airplane," the X-30, to demonstrate the feasibility of a spaceplane. The cost of the program, including the X-airplane, was initially estimated to be a little more than three billion dollars. The program is managed by a joint program office at Wright-Patterson Air Force Base, Ohio.

Three airframe contractors—General Dynamics, McDonnell Douglas, and Rockwell International—and two propulsion contractors—the Pratt and Whitney corporation and the Rocketdyne Division of Rockwell International—were early participants in the program. These corporations agreed to provide considerable support at their own expense, perceiving that the spaceplane program would involve important new technology.

The X-30's ancestors were early supersonic and hypersonic research aircraft. Charles (Chuck) Yeager broke the sound barrier in the X-1 in 1947. Almost twenty years later, the rocket-powered X-15 reached a speed of 2,305 meters per second and an altitude of 107 kilometers. A spaceplane would fly through the atmosphere at speeds of more than 6,880 meters per second, demonstrating a tremendous jump in speed capability and thus in technology. In the late 1980's, the fastest air-breathing airplane was the SR71, which had a maximum speed of about 1,032 meters per second.

One source of the spaceplane's performance potential is liquid hydrogen fuel, with its high energy content, fast burn rate, and large heat sink capacity. Liquid hydrogen has three times the combustion heat and five times the burn rate of jet fuel. Stable at -253.6 degrees Celsius, it can be used to cool the plane's engine and portions of the airframe.

There are three critical areas of spaceplane technology: propulsion, structures and materials, and computational fluid dynamics. Some interdisciplinary areas are also extremely important: engine-airframe integration, thermal management, and integrated controls. Most of the disciplines are linked to others, yielding fields of study such as thermal management's effect on propulsion performance. Synthesizing and optimizing the vehicle design is an enormous undertaking in itself.

The propulsion system represents the greatest technological challenge. The basic principles of scramjet technology, however, are simple. The housing for the engine's inlet, diffusor, and combustor is mounted on the underside of the vehicle slightly downstream of the midsection. Neither a ramjet nor a scramjet has any rotating machinery for compression of the incoming air; they use the forebody of the airframe for precompression and the afterbody as a high-expansion ratio nozzle.

The inlet is a narrowing duct that compresses the air and at the same time reduces the air's velocity. It feeds into the engine's diffusor section, which in turn opens into a gently expanding combustor section. The injection and burning of the hydrogen fuel occurs in the combustor; the burn results in a substantial pressure rise and is the source of the engine thrust.

Scramjets and ramjets differ in the speed at which the air moves through the engine. In a ramjet, the air inside the engine is moving subsonically; combustion therefore occurs at subsonic speeds, even though the craft is traveling supersonically. In a scramjet, the airstream is slowed but maintains supersonic speed within the engine, allowing the aircraft to reach hypersonic speeds. At velocities greater than six times the speed of sound, the supersonic combustion process is the more efficient means of propulsion; it also transmits less heat to the combustor walls than does its subsonic counterpart.

The rapid burn rate characteristic of hydrogen fuel is very important to the supersonic combustion process. When hydrogen is injected into the engine, it mixes with the oxygen in the supersonic airstream and automatically ignites.

Unfortunately, to create enough air pressure for a ramjet or scramjet to produce thrust, the vehicle must already be traveling at supersonic speeds; therefore, conventional engine technology is needed. Conventional, turbojet engine technology can be incorporated into a ramjet/scramjet to produce a propulsion system that can operate at slow speeds and also accelerate to supersonic and then hypersonic speeds. Thus, the spaceplane propulsion system consists of a turbojet, a ramjet, and a scramjet. Once the plane is moving twenty times faster than sound, a rocket is used for further acceleration and transition to orbit.

The "air-breathing flight corridor" represents a compromise between two opposing constraints on a spaceplane. Aerodynamics and propulsion needs require the spaceplane to fly in the lower atmosphere, with its higher air density, for best performance. Airframe structures and materials, however, function best at a higher altitude, in thinner air, where they can remain relatively cool. The flight corridor is a region that is neither too high for the engine nor too low for the airframe.

For a single-stage-to-orbit mission, minimal structural weight is very important. Moreover, the spaceplane must be designed to cope with wind gusts and runway bumps at takeoff; large thermal gradients, resulting from hot external surfaces at hypersonic speeds and the extremely cold interior of the liquid hydrogen tank; and the need for weight to be distributed evenly throughout the vehicle. The spaceplane's materials are also important, since they will be affected by the intense heat encountered during both ascent and reentry. Temperatures of several thousand degrees are possible at the nose, at the wings' leading edges, and in the engine. These areas will be actively cooled with cryogenic hydrogen or shielded with carbon and carbon composites. Uncooled surfaces, which could reach temperatures as high as 800 degrees Celsius, may be made of titanium.

It is impossible to simulate the flight environment of the X-30 perfectly. The program is therefore highly dependent on the use of advanced computational methods for predicting performance at speeds greater than those simulated by ground-based wind tunnels. Advances in computational algorithms and high-speed computers have permitted detailed analysis of the plane's aerodynamic performance over a range of flight conditions. Computers are also used to predict how various thermal loads and thermal management systems would affect temperature distributions, cooling loads, and hydrogen flow.

Finally, the spaceplane will require an integrated control system that will couple the aerodynamic, propulsion, and thermal controls with sophisticated flight sensors.

Knowledge Gained

The National Aero-Space Plane Program promises to lead to new technology and new knowledge. The development of strong, rigid, light materials able to withstand very high temperatures will affect many industries. The development and application of scramjet technology will give rise to hypersonic passenger planes that will cut travel times dramatically. Integration of spaceplane engines and airframes will tax the capabilities of computers and algorithms and no doubt provide impetus for advances in both areas. Because of the spaceplane's complex instrumentation, intricate couplings, and highly sensitive controls, its designers will need to develop a new synthesis technology, which in turn may influence the design of existing systems and systems not yet envisioned.

The spaceplane itself is expected to provide routine access to space at considerably less expense than the space shuttle. Journeys to and from space platforms will become practical ventures, encouraging pharmaceutical and metallurgical companies to undertake zero-gravity research and development programs that could spawn new industries. Scientists will study the biological production of regenerative atmospheres, and colonization of the Moon and other planets may become feasible.

Context

The spaceplane endeavor is a technological revolution. To develop a machine capable of air-breathing propulsion to near orbital velocities requires wholly new materials and engine technology and an unprecedented degree of technology integration across discipline lines. Because the spaceplane's design eradicates the distinction between the engine and the airframe, engine companies and airframe builders must work as a team and develop new management approaches. The need for new materials has caused the spaceplane contractors to form a materials consortium, which is coordinating the development of the required materials.

The spaceplane program is not without risk, nor should it be; leaps forward require bold visions. The spaceplane is a great technological challenge, but the challenge can and will be met.

Bibliography

Becker, John V. *The High-Speed Frontier: Case Histories of Four NACA Programs, 1920-1950*. NASA SP-445. Washington, D.C.: Scientific and Technical Information Branch, National Aeronautics and Space Administration, 1980. Becker provides a history of the high-speed airfoil program, transonic wind tunnel development, the high-speed propeller program, and high-speed cowling, air inlets and outlets, and internal flow systems. Recommended for undergraduate-level readers.

Bergman, Jules. *Ninety Seconds to Space: The X-15 Story*. Garden City, N.Y.: Hanover House, 1960. A history of the rocket-powered X-15 airplane which flew in the 1960's; it recorded the fastest speeds (Mach 6.7) and highest altitudes (107,000 meters) any airplane has ever flown. Accessible to general readers.

Hansen, James R. *Engineer in Charge: A History of the Langley Aeronautical Laboratory, 1917-1958*. Washington, D.C.: Scientific and Technical Information Office, National Aeronautics and Space Administration, 1987. A history of NASA Langley during its four decades as the flagship research facility of the National Advisory Committee for Aeronautics.

Miller, Jay. *The X-Planes: X-1 to X-31*. New York: Orion Books, 1988. The author presents a history of the X-airplane programs from the 1940's to the late 1980's, including Chuck Yeager's faster-than-sound flight of October, 1947. Essential reading for an understanding of how X-airplane technology has grown. For high school readers and above.

Smith, Melvyn. *Space Shuttle*. Newbury Park, Calif.: Haynes Publications, 1985. An easy-to-read history of the evolution and design of the U.S. space shuttle.

James L. Hunt

Cross-References

The Apollo Program, 28; The Commercial Use of Space Program Innovations, 253; The Gemini Program, 487; The Jet Propulsion Laboratory, 662; U.S. Launch Vehicles, 749; The Development of the Mercury Project, 947; The U.S. Space Shuttle, 1626.

ALPHABETICAL LIST

CATEGORY LIST

PROBES

EARTH RESOURCES SATELLITES

METEOROLOGICAL SATELLITES

SPACE EXPLORATION